Handbook of Institutional Advancement

*A Modern Guide to Executive Management,
Institutional Relations, Fund-Raising,
Alumni Administration, Government
Relations, Publications, Periodicals,
and Enrollment Management*

SECOND EDITION

A. Westley Rowland
General Editor

Foreword by James L. Fisher

Handbook of Institutional Advancement

SECOND EDITION

Jossey-Bass Publishers

San Francisco   •   London   •   1986

HANDBOOK OF INSTITUTIONAL ADVANCEMENT
*A Modern Guide to Executive Management, Institutional Relations,
Fund-Raising, Alumni Administration, Government Relations,
Publications, Periodicals, and Enrollment Management*
  by A. Westley Rowland, General Editor

Copyright © 1986 by: Jossey-Bass Inc., Publishers
433 California Street
San Francisco, California 94104

&

Jossey-Bass Limited
28 Banner Street
London EC1Y 8QE

Library of Congress Cataloging-in-Publication Data

Handbook of institutional advancement.

  (The Jossey-Bass higher education series)
  "A modern guide to executive management, institutional relations, fund-raising, alumni administration,
government relations, publications, periodicals, and
enrollment management."
  Includes bibliographies and index.
  1. Public relations—Universities and colleges—
United States—Addresses, essays, lectures. 2. College
publicity—United States—Addresses, essays, lectures.
3. Educational fund raising—United States—Addresses,
essays, lectures. 4. College publications—United
States—Addresses, essays, lectures. 5. Universities
and colleges—United States—Admission—Addresses, essays,
lectures. I. Rowland, A. Westley (date). II. Series.
LB2342.8.H36   1986   659.2'937873   85-45912
ISBN 0-87589-689-8 (alk. paper)

Manufactured in the United States of America

JACKET DESIGN BY WILLI BAUM

SECOND EDITION

Code 8618

The Jossey-Bass
Higher Education Series

Foreword

Since its first publication in 1977, the *Handbook of Institutional Advancement* has become the basic reference work for professionals in the field. Other books, monographs, and articles fill in important parts of the picture, but only this handbook provides a comprehensive overview of the complex process of presenting an educational institution to its constituencies so as to garner their support for its security and well-being.

In the past decade, institutional advancement has grown much more important to colleges, universities, and independent schools. And because the next decade may well be the most trying period in the history of American higher education, advancement's role will become even more critical.

Despite the leveling off of inflation, costs in labor-intensive education are rising faster than resources. Enrollments are a major issue as the number of eighteen- to twenty-two-year-old students declines. With federal and state support wavering and the competition for students growing, tensions between private and public institutions mount. Although some areas of private support—chiefly corporate—have shown gratifying increases, the overall growth rate of private support has slowed. And today we worry about the health of that most basic underpinning of education—America's tradition of private philanthropy.

In this climate, our colleges, universities, and independent schools need public understanding and support as never before. The communications professionals' skill in mapping strategies to build understanding and the alumni administrators' ability to strengthen alumni loyalty will be crucial. The work of these professionals undergirds the equally vital activities of those in fund-raising, government relations, and student recruitment as they strive to convert understanding and goodwill into dollars and students.

To be equal to the challenge, fund raisers, communicators, alumni administrators, government relations officers, and others in advancement must increase their professionalism. One way to do this is by taking advantage of advancement leaders' best thinking— the thinking presented in this new edition of the *Handbook of Institutional Advancement*.

When the time came to develop this new edition, the Council for Advancement and Support of Education (CASE) had no doubt about who should lead the effort. As with the first edition, the natural choice was A. Westley Rowland, former vice-president of university relations and now professor of higher education at the State University of New York at Buffalo. We were delighted when he agreed to undertake this formidable task. The project has been a collaboration between CASE and A. Westley Rowland: CASE vice-presidents have worked closely with him in identifying section editors and chapter authors, and CASE has underwritten the expenses involved in preparing the manuscript.

Instead of merely updating the existing book, Rowland enlisted a new team of section editors, who then recruited chapter authors. In addition, Rowland commissioned chapters on important and timely topics not covered in the earlier work. The resulting volume is truly a new book, not a revision. Reading this volume and comparing it with the first edition gives an interesting perspective on how advancement has matured in the past decade.

As advancement professionals confront the challenges of the next ten years, they will benefit from the insights and information in this book. CASE is grateful to A. Westley Rowland, to the section editors, and to the chapter authors for making it possible.

Washington, D.C.   James L. Fisher
April 1986   *President, Council for*
                           Advancement and Support
                           of Education

Preface

For those new to the field or those contemplating entering it, it is important to define *institutional advancement*. Broadly, this term encompasses all activities and programs undertaken by an institution to develop understanding and support from all its constituencies in order to achieve its goals in securing such resources as students, faculty, and dollars.

In 1977, when Jossey-Bass published the first edition of the *Handbook of Institutional Advancement*, it was the first book to deal thoroughly and systematically with the entire advancement field. Since then, there have been a number of important changes not only in the maturing and expansion of the advancement function but also in the way professionals carry out their responsibilities. There have also been changes in the law as it affects advancement. Hence, the need for the second edition of the handbook.

More than 80 percent of the material in this second edition is new. In addition to revisions and expanded viewpoints developed in each chapter, we have added the following *new* topics: technology in advancement; speech writing; periodicals; enrollment management; the chief executive and advancement; advancement for two-year colleges, independent schools, and small and developing institutions; law and advancement; and market research.

This book is a valuable tool for all who work in institutional advancement—from newcomers in the field to experienced professionals. It is designed as a practical, functional resource for the wide variety of professionals who write and edit news releases, design and prepare publications, edit periodicals, raise funds, work with alumni, coordinate relationships with government, recruit students, work with community groups, write and give speeches, arrange special events, prepare radio and television programs, direct special events, take photographs, do research, or manage the advancement function. The thousands of volunteers who work for their institutions will also be able to rely on the solid, practical guidance this book offers.

In addition to advancement professionals, this book is important to chief executives of colleges, universities, and independent schools. Also, members of administrative staffs—provosts, vice-presidents, deans, department chairs, and program heads—will find many parts of this publication of value to them as they interrelate with both the internal and external constituencies of their institutions. Members of boards of trustees, too, will gain a firm understanding of the importance and nature of the advancement function from this publication, and it will assist them in interpreting their institutions to the various external publics as well as in fund-raising and government relations.

Members of the faculty and professionals involved in intercollegiate competitions of all kinds work with students, alumni, foundations, corporations, advisory groups, and government agencies. These educators play an important part in the public relations programs of their institutions through their writing, speaking, teaching, and coaching efforts. This book will assist them and enhance that public relations role. Administrative staff involved in admissions, student recruitment, and financial aid to students will also find this book useful as it applies to enrollment management.

This handbook is designed to serve such a broad audience because, truly, advancement is a matter of total institutional commitment.

One of the chief goals in the development of this book has been to present in one volume the most comprehensive and up-to-date information available. Work on this volume has been a collaborative effort on the part of the Council for Advancement and Support of Education (CASE), the general editor, and the publisher. Preparation of the manuscript involved months of careful planning and work with experts in all areas of this important field. Editors of the sections and chapter contributors were selected because of their extensive experience; they represent current thinking, practices, and trends in institutional advancement at colleges, universities, and independent schools of all sizes and in all parts of the country. In short, the authors are professionals, from institutions of varying sizes and geographic locations, whose wide-ranging perspectives have yielded the wealth of material that forms the basis of this valuable compendium.

We are deeply indebted to the Council for Advancement and Support of Education, under whose aegis this book has been developed. CASE president James L. Fisher and his staff have made important contributions to generating the concept of the handbook, to its editing, and to its completion. In particular, Virginia Carter Smith, CASE vice-president, played a vital and essential role as coordinator and was also especially helpful in editing the manuscript.

Special appreciation goes to Steven Muller, president of Johns Hopkins University, whom we were fortunate to enlist as the author of the first chapter, and to the section editors, who carried a heavy responsibility for the major contents of the handbook: Harvey K. Jacobson (executive management); Howard Ray Rowland (institutional relations); William L. Pickett (educational fund-raising); Gary A. Ransdell (alumni administration); Richard L. Kennedy (government relations); Ann Bennett (publications); Maralyn Orbison Gillespie (periodicals); and John Maguire (enrollment management).

For their important contributions to the special topics section, we are indebted to G. T. Smith (the chief executive and advancement); Jane A. Johnson (two-year colleges); Wesley K. Willmer (small and developing institutions); Edes Gilbert (independent schools); Walter C. Hobbs (legal issues in institutional advancement); and Cletis Pride and Joseph S. Fowler (market research).

Although they are as old as some of the oldest of our educational institutions, advancement programs and activities were not organized into formal structures until the early 1900s. Since that time, those structures have changed, not only in their names but also in the nature and scope of their functions and in the diversity and professionalism of their programs and activities. It is my hope, shared by all the chapter authors, that this second edition will be a contributing element in the maturing of the institutional advancement function as it seeks to interpret, support, and develop understanding for education.

Buffalo, New York   A. Westley Rowland
April 1986

Contents

Contents

Contents

Part Nine: Special Topics
A. Westley Rowland, Editor

The Authors

 A. Westley Rowland is professor emeritus of higher education in the Department of Educational Organization, Administration, and Policy at the State University of New York at Buffalo. Formerly, he served as coordinator of the Higher Education Program in that department. For fourteen years he was vice-president for university relations at SUNY-Buffalo and for one year was executive director of the University at Buffalo Foundation, Inc. For ten years previous to his association with SUNY, Rowland served at Michigan State University as university editor, associate professor, executive news editor, editor of the news service, and director of the centennial. Prior to his service at Michigan State, he was for eleven years professor and head of the speech department and director of publicity at Alma College, Alma, Michigan.

A native of Kalamazoo, Michigan, Rowland received his B.A. degree in social sciences in 1938 from Western Michigan University, his M.A. degree in speech from the University of Michigan in 1941, and his Ed.D. degree from Michigan State University in 1955, with higher education being his major field.

Active in the field of institutional advancement for almost

forty years, Rowland was president of the American Public Relations Association (ACPRA), now the Council for Advancement and Support of Education (CASE), in 1966–67, president of the Niagara Frontier Chapter of the Public Relations Society of America (PRSA), and president of the State University of New York Public Relations Council in 1968–69.

Rowland was chairman of the CASE Summer Institute in Communications in 1976. Previously, he served three years on the faculty of ACPRA's Summer Academy.

For four years, Rowland was executive editor of *New Directions for Institutional Advancement,* a series of sixteen books published by Jossey-Bass. He is also the author of *Research in Institutional Advancement,* published by CASE in 1983. His latest publication is an annotated bibliography of the literature of institutional advancement (Jossey-Bass, 1986).

Among the awards Rowland has received are the Distinguished Service citation for his professional contributions to the field of institutional advancement by the State University of New York Public Relations Council (1972); the Daemen College President's Award for Distinguished Service to Daemen College, higher education and the community (1978); the first Alice Beeman Award by the Council for Advancement and Support of Education (CASE) for significant editorial contributions to the field of institutional advancement (1981); the Community Advisory Council's Babbidge Award for "helping to initiate, maintain, and promote harmonious relations between the Western New York area and the University" (1983); and recognition as a Season Sage of ACPRA for more than twenty-five years of leadership in institutional advancement activities. Rowland is also an accredited member of the Public Relations Society of America and is listed in *Who's Who in America.*

Stephen L. Barrett is executive director of Brigham Young University Alumni Association, Provo, Utah.

John S. Bartolomeo is executive vice-president of Clark, Martire and Bartolomeo, Inc., New York City.

Ann Granning Bennett is a consultant with Publications and Communications Management in Portland, Oregon.

Michael A. Berger is director of the Corporate Learning Institute at Vanderbilt University, Nashville, Tennessee.

Steven L. Calvert is associate director of Alumni Programs and director of Alumni Continuing Education at Dartmouth College, Hanover, New Hampshire.

Linda Carl is director of Alumni Programs, University of North Carolina, Chapel Hill.

Arthur V. Ciervo is president of Arthur Ciervo and Associates, State College, Pennsylvania.

Ross Cornwell was formerly executive assistant to the president of Clemson University, Clemson, South Carolina, and is now president of Cornwell Associates.

Norman A. Darais is director of University Publications, Brigham Young University, Provo, Utah.

Kent E. Dove is counsel to the Capital Campaign, University of California, Berkeley, and vice-president of the University of California, Berkeley Foundation.

David R. Dunlop is director of Capital Projects, Cornell University, Ithaca, New York.

Richard Emerson is executive director of the University of Colorado at Boulder Alumni Association.

Gary A. Evans is vice-chancellor for development and university relations, University of North Carolina at Chapel Hill.

John Forasté is photographer in the Office of University Relations, Brown University, Providence, Rhode Island.

Joseph S. Fowler is assistant director of promotion and educational services, National Geographic Society, Washington, D.C.

William Freeland is director of communications, LaGuardia Community College, City University of New York.

James W. Frick is assistant to the president, University of Notre Dame, South Bend, Indiana.

Ann D. Gee is director of the Office of Alumni and Special Programs, Texas Christian University, Fort Worth, Texas.

Edes P. Gilbert is the head of Spence School, New York City.

Maralyn Orbison Gillespie is associate vice-president of Swarthmore College, Swarthmore, Pennsylvania.

Elise Hancock is editor of *Johns Hopkins Magazine,* Baltimore, Maryland.

Brice W. Harris is assistant to the chancellor for the Metropolitan Community Colleges of Kansas City, Missouri.

Daniel L. Heinlen is director of alumni affairs, Ohio State University Alumni Association, Columbus.

Walter C. Hobbs is associate professor of higher education, State University of New York at Buffalo.

David R. Hoover is director of university publications, Ohio State University, Columbus.

Theodore P. Hurwitz is vice-president for institute relations, California Institute of Technology.

Harvey K. Jacobson is associate professor of journalism, University of Wisconsin at Oshkosh, and former administrative officer for development and university relations, University of Michigan, Ann Arbor.

Jane A. Johnson is director of communications and development, Community Colleges of Spokane, Washington.

Richard L. Kennedy is vice-president for government relations and secretary of the university, University of Michigan, Ann Arbor.

Deirdre A. Ling is vice-chancellor for university relations and development, University of Massachusetts, Amherst.

McRay Magleby is art director, Brigham Young University, Provo, Utah.

John Maguire is president of Enrollment Management Consultants, Concord, Massachusetts.

David May is director of communications programs, Syracuse University, New York.

Gladys McConkey is director of publications, College of Engineering, Cornell University, Ithaca, New York.

Jack H. Miller is executive vice-president of the University of Nebraska Alumni Association, Lincoln.

R. Keith Moore is vice-president of university relations, Carnegie-Mellon University, Pittsburgh, Pennsylvania.

Steven Muller is president of Johns Hopkins University, Baltimore, Maryland.

Mary Kay Murphy is director for development/foundation relations at Georgia Institute of Technology, Atlanta.

Mary Ellen Myrene is editor of *Connections* magazine, Community Colleges of Spokane, Washington.

Jeffrey B. Nelson is director of planned giving and corporate/foundation support, South Dakota State University Foundation, Brookings, South Dakota.

Terry D. Newfarmer is editor of *Communicator* magazine, University of Utah Public Relations, Salt Lake City.

Scott G. Nichols is director of development, DePaul University, Chicago, Illinois.

Donald R. Perkins is director of the Office of Public Information, Wittenberg University, Springfield, Ohio.

William L. Pickett is vice-president for university relations, University of San Diego, California.

Richard J. Pokrass is director of public information and alumni affairs, Burlington County College, Pemberton, New Jersey.

Cletis Pride is vice-president of the National Geographic Society, Washington, D.C.

Gary A. Ransdell is director of alumni relations and executive director of the Alumni Association, Southern Methodist University, Dallas, Texas.

James F. Ridenour is vice-president for development, Berry College, Mount Berry, Georgia.

Stephen W. Roszell is executive director of the University of Minnesota Alumni Association, Minneapolis.

Howard Ray Rowland is director of information services, Saint Cloud State University, Minnesota.

Kathleen L. Rydar is director of development, San Francisco Museum of Modern Art.

James J. Scannell is vice-president for enrollments, placement, and alumni affairs, University of Rochester, New York.

John J. Schwartz is president of the American Association of Fund-Raising Counsel, New York City.

James M. Shea is professor of communication in the School of Communications and Theater, Temple University, Philadelphia, Pennsylvania.

Carole Rolnick Shlipak is director of development, Dallas County Community College District, and executive director of the Dallas County Community College District Foundation, Inc., Dallas, Texas.

Jeffery R. Shy is president of Jeffery R. Shy Associates, Williamsburg, Virginia.

G. T. Smith is president of Chapman College, Orange, California.

Barbara W. Snelling is president of Snelling, Kolb and Kuhnle, Inc., Washington, D.C.

J. Arthur Stober is head of the radio and television section of the Department of Public Information and Relations, Pennsylvania State University, University Park.

Bobbie J. Strand is senior associate of Bentz, Whaley, Flessner, and Associates, Inc., Kalamazoo, Michigan.

M. Fredric Volkmann is associate vice-chancellor and director of public relations, Washington University, St. Louis, Missouri.

Patricia S. Wager is assistant director of alumni relations and annual giving, Loyola University Medical Center, Chicago, Illinois.

Robert G. Wark is administrative assistant for communication, Washington State Board for Community College Education, Olympia.

Bud Weidenthal is vice-president for public affairs and information, Cuyahoga Community College, Cleveland, Ohio.

Wesley K. Willmer is director of development, Wheaton College, Wheaton, Illinois.

D. Chris Withers is associate vice-president, University of Richmond, Richmond, Virginia.

Handbook of
Institutional
Advancement

*A Modern Guide to Executive Management,
Institutional Relations, Fund-Raising,
Alumni Administration, Government
Relations, Publications, Periodicals,
and Enrollment Management*

SECOND EDITION

Steven Muller

The Definition and Philosophy of Institutional Advancement

The task of colleges and universities to pursue and transmit advanced knowledge requires faculty, students, and teaching facilities. This basic academic community requires some obvious supporting services: records must be kept, buildings and equipment must be serviced, library collections must be staffed, revenues must be received and expenditures disbursed, and so forth. These needs result in numerous nonacademic personnel and in the presence of the administrative management. In addition to the people who perform these services, American colleges and universities also employ people full-time in the area of institutional advancement.

The institutional advancement staff is responsible for external and internal communications, government and public relations, fund-raising, and alumni relations. These activities, regarded as necessary on every American campus, are not generally found in colleges and universities of other countries. Institutions of higher education in other countries have faculties, students, and support personnel, but they rarely use employees in the functions collectively known as institutional advancement. Institutional advancement is a uniquely American component of higher education. Perhaps the best way to understand this fact is to examine the differences between the colleges and universities of the United States and those of other countries.

Most foreign institutions of higher education are agencies of the central government. Although they have varying degrees of academic autonomy, they are not merely owned but also managed by government. Their operating and capital budgets, derived either exclusively or primarily from government funds, are assigned and often substantially managed by government. Also, most of these institutions receive no tuition income because no tuition is charged. Almost universally, higher education in other countries is an activity sponsored, and to varying degrees controlled, by government. Most countries have national university laws that govern this situation. A student's opportunity to enter higher education in other countries is a benefit conferred by government, restricted to a minority, and very much sought after.

In the United States, state colleges and universities resemble our independent colleges and universities more than they do the government-owned universities of other nations. The reasons for this, derived from the distinctive character of American society and history, largely explain why institutional advancement is so vital a part of American, and only American, higher education.

From its beginning, higher education in the United States has been regarded (as it is abroad) as an activity in the public interest. Accordingly, it is viewed as a public responsibility. However, in the United States, at least until the present day, a public responsibility has not necessarily meant a responsibility of government. The public responsibility for higher education in this country was initially expressed by a fundamental act of public policy that exists today: Colleges and universities were exempted from the payment of taxes because their activities were viewed as having high priority in the public interest; similarly, private gifts to them were, and are, tax deductible. Equally significant is the fact that in the Constitution of the United States no responsibility for education was assigned to the federal government.

For most of our history, the role government has played in higher education has been carried on primarily by the state governments. This role has been substantially different from the practice in most of the rest of the world. In this country, state and sometimes local governments have chartered and supported colleges and universities, but they have not directly operated or governed them. This fact is rooted in several historic traditions. First, many of our colleges and universities were initially founded by religious denominations, primarily to educate men for the ministry; the emphatic separation of church and state in the United States created a legal barrier between these institutions and government. Second, the commercial character of American society produces a view of higher education as a commodity to be purchased rather than a benefit to be conferred by society through its government—a viewpoint in which the principle of tuition payments is solidly rooted. Third, Americans tend to rely on private contributions to sustain public causes. This tradition was reinforced in early history, when colleges and universities catered primarily to the sons of the wealthy; this, in turn, created additional incentives for benefactors. Fourth, and most fundamental of all, American emphasis on individual initiative and enterprise has limited government to being a regulator, rather than principal executor, of the public interest.

However one may assess the reasons, higher education in the United States first developed primarily in the private sector. Some of the older and larger states, such as New York and New Jersey, had no state universities until the mid 1900s. The state colleges and universities that were established in the nineteenth and twentieth centuries were modeled largely on the independent institutions that already existed. State institutions were governed by publicly appointed or elected boards of regents that were counterparts of the boards of trustees of independent institutions. They were not governed by state departments of education directly.

A major consequence of this unique pattern of higher education with minimum government control is that American colleges and universities are competitive enterprises. Even those that are government-owned compete for public resources with others. In the absence of government control over higher education, this competition varies throughout the states, with each state commanding highly varied resources and demonstrating highly varied priorities for higher education. In the international context, American colleges and universities are unique in that they compete with each other, not only for resources but also for students and to some degree for faculty members. This is not so in other countries: a student abroad does not compare the advantages or disadvantages of the colleges and universities of a country. In the United States, however, reputation is an important factor in the availability of resources; for institutions that live on very thin financial margins, not only their well-being but also their very existence may be at stake. Support is usually more generous for colleges perceived to be growing rather than declining.

In this context, we can see that the function of institutional advancement in American institutions of higher education is to enable each individual college or university to do well in a competitive environment and to assist the whole sector of higher education to compete effectively for available resources. In a nation that contains such an enormous variety of institutions, each college and university needs to develop and pursue its own distinctive strategy for the acquisition of resources. It does so within a society where no effective national policy governs the matter and in which the public policies of the different states, regions, or localities vary significantly. It is primarily the individual institution, rather than the government, that is responsible for its own well-being and even survival. Those college and university employees who work in institutional advancement are not directly concerned with the academic quality or performance of their institutions. Instead, their task is to devise and achieve the means that will provide the academic enterprise with needed resources. Unless their efforts succeed, the entire campus enterprise will suffer.

This sounds as though the single function of institutional advancement is fund-raising. This is true only if fund-raising is used in the most broadly descriptive, and largely unspecific, sense. The sources of support for colleges and universities are so varied and complex that *fund-raising* as a specific term is inadequate. The term *fund-raising* is commonly used to describe the solicitation of gifts from private sources. Central as such an activity is to institutional advancement, it falls far short of being comprehensively descriptive. It is true, however, that virtually all American colleges and universities engage in fund-raising from private sources, the only difference between independent and government-owned institutions in this respect being one of degree. Independent institutions derive a much higher proportion of resources from private sources than government-owned institutions.

It is also true that virtually all colleges and universities derive support from government sources—federal, state, and local. The effort to secure this support, also part of institutional advancement, is not usually referred to as fund-raising. The business of dealing with various levels of government and the clusters of political power and sentiment that influence government policy is a vital part of institutional advancement for both independent and government-owned institutions. The state colleges and universities are, of course, heavily dependent on their states for support, and they must maintain constant liaison not only with state legislators and executives but also with others in the state who may play influential roles. Many states now provide funding of some kind for which independent colleges and universities are eligible. Pursuit of public policy to make such funding available, as well as the effort to secure some of it for the individual institution, requires independent institutions to also maintain liaison with key government and business figures.

Even at the state level, however, this is only part of the picture. Federal law now requires states to maintain commissions to coordinate higher education activities within their borders. Each college and university in every state must relate to such an agency. States also have departments of education that address higher education, or they have agencies specifically oriented toward higher education. Although these concentrate primarily on the government-owned institutions, they cannot be entirely ignored by independent colleges and universities. In virtually all government relations by institutions of higher education, only part of the effort is positive in the sense of renewing or increasing resources. The other part is defensive, attempting to prevent the withdrawal of benefits, the narrowing of revenue sources, or an allocation more to the advantage of other institutions than one's own.

This is a point of particular importance with respect to the relations of colleges and universities with the federal government. Until the mid 1900s, federal relations played a rather minor role in the life of American colleges and universities. Then came a vast expansion of federally sponsored research, not only in traditional areas such as agriculture and health but also, as part of the aftermath of World War II, in the sciences. Although most of the older federal programs had essentially affected only major research universities, funding for science research became available to a far greater spectrum of institutions, either directly or because members of their faculties were able to solicit and receive grants. In recent years, federal funding has also become available for the arts and humanities. In addition, the federal government has evolved huge programs of assistance to students, who constitute a source of revenue to colleges and universities. This evolution began on a large scale with scholarships to veterans after World War II, was reinforced by a series of programs aimed at encouraging students in certain fields that had high national priority, and culminated in today's multi-billion-dollar programs designed to underwrite basic educational opportunity through a complex mixture of scholarships, loans, work-study grants, and other devices. As a result, almost every college and university in the United States now benefits in significant ways from federal funding—a far cry from the situation forty or fifty years ago, when only a few major research universities received a few small grants and the federal impact was represented on most campuses primarily by the presence of a Reserve Officer Training Corps (ROTC) program. The high levels of funding that occurred in the 1960s and 1970s, however, are now being curtailed, and the possibility of returning to the concept of funding for selected research institutions is very real indeed.

Another result is even more striking: Federal regulation of higher education now exists through the channels established by federal funding. Under the Constitution, the federal government still has no authority over higher education; however, insofar as colleges and universities are contractors with the federal government, administer federally funded student aid programs, receive federal tax exemptions and administer federal tax policy as employers, use federal funds for facilities or equipment, and offer equal opportunities as corporate citizens, they are comprehensively subject to federal regulation.

Inevitably, therefore, government relations has become the biggest growth area within the field of institutional advancement in American higher education during the past few years. It is still necessary to deal with complex programs of assistance and regulation; however, for those engaged in institutional advancement, the biggest challenge is to try to shape newly emerging legislation and regulation into the most favorable form possible. The greatest achievement is often the legislative proposal that fails or the regulation that does not take effect. For instance, colleges and universities labored extensively (and, to date, mostly successfully) to protect from being abolished as part of successive efforts at tax reform those aspects of federal tax policy that permit and encourage gifts to them by individuals and foundations.

Another important source of revenues for colleges and universities is the student population. Institutional advancement is therefore concerned directly with students. Students, or their families, pay tuition. They must, therefore, find a college or university attractive enough to attend, and they must accept tuition charges as fair and reasonable.

More important, students graduate into alumni. Every effort is made by colleges and universities in the United States to cultivate and retain the loyalty and support of their alumni, the most fertile and readily identifiable source of continuing assistance. This effort is often assisted by the fact that alumni are identified with the college or university they have chosen. Whatever the chemistry may be between a college or university and its alumni, the fact is that in the competitive climate of American society, institutions of higher education need allies and supporters; and they rely on their own alumni to play this role. Therefore, a central part of institutional advancement is *alumni relations:* the continuous effort to maintain and strengthen that uniquely American sense of community between a college or university and its graduates.

It follows that even small colleges must communicate with large and varied audiences that are geographically dispersed. A publications program is the indispensable means for this communication and a vital part of institutional advancement. Larger or more affluent institutions may add film, television, and other media to their communications programs. Clearly, reputation counts in a highly varied and competitive environment, and so one part of institutional advancement relates to the media. A growing number of colleges and universities buy occasional advertising. Other facets of institutional advancement include special events to bring alumni and others to the campus; cooperative efforts to generate improved understanding and support for all of higher education, or major sectors of it; and the special treatment of trustees and regents, who are as often as not governors, alumni, and donors all at once.

It also follows that there is some degree of built-in tension between the faculty of an academic institution and the staff engaged in institutional advancement. Neither can do without the other, but neither is ever quite satisfied with the other. Part of the problem may be due to a misunderstanding of the nature of the role each plays in the institution. The tension might be resolved by increasing the degree and quality of communication between the faculty and the institutional advancement staff.

The attitude of the college or university president toward institutional advancement is important to consider. His or her success will depend partly on the efforts of the professionals in institutional advancement. Lack of success will be largely because of lack of appreciation of and attention to the tasks of institutional advancement. A distinguished faculty, fine students, and good management are essential ingredients of a good college or university, but they depend on the availability of adequate resources. The task of institutional advancement is to make their virtues familiar to the sources supporting the entire academic enterprise.

An experienced college or university president will also appreciate at least four basic ground rules that govern successful institutional advancement efforts on American campuses. The first is that, although the specific components of institutional advancement are individually highly professional and technical, they are also interdependent. It makes good sense to treat all those employed in institutional advancement as a single staff under the direction of a single executive who reports directly to the president. Uncoordinated separate staffs or competing staffs would be less effective than a coherent team.

A second ground rule is that the staff in institutional advancement cannot function as an adjunct to the rest of the campus enterprise but only as an integral part of it. The pursuit of resources must fully interact with the use of resources. It is useless to develop an academic plan without consultations with those who must develop the resources to implement it. They cannot respond to unrealistic or arbitrary targets. Often, they will encounter suggestions for academic development that they themselves cannot pursue, but that they can relay to academic management.

The staff in institutional advancement has no monopoly on contact with the external constituencies of colleges and universities. On the contrary, much of the world outside the campus will communicate directly with a student, a faculty member, or an administrator. Therefore, the third ground rule is that the morale of a campus is probably the greatest single factor affecting its outside reputation, and it is a vital task of institutional advancement to achieve effective internal campus communications and to make whatever contributions it can to high internal morale.

The fourth, and final, ground rule, as the experienced president knows, is that there is a continuous need for institutional advancement. Even a brief interruption or loss of momentum will have damaging consequences. A single encounter, action, or conversation rarely generates support by itself. Results usually come only from continuous effort that stays tuned to every development and constantly fosters new loyalties while nurturing the old. The job of institutional advancement is to do all the things necessary to maintain an adequate supply of resources to a college or university. In the unique world of American higher education, this is a crucial task, as diverse as our colleges and universities themselves, as urgent as next year's budget, and as complex as the host of people whose responses spell out failure or success.

Part One

Management
Challenges
and Strategies

Harvey K. Jacobson, Editor

1   *Harvey K. Jacobson*

Skills and Criteria
for Managerial Effectiveness

Management plays a significant role in the successful operation of the modern college and university. Every educational organization requires the making of decisions, integration of activities, planning of programs, coordination of people, and evaluation of performance directed toward institutional objectives.

Nature of Management

What is management, and what does it do? In general usage, the word *management* identifies a group of people selected to direct effort toward achieving a shared purpose. Commonly stated, *management* is getting things done through other people. For the purpose of this book, *management* is defined as the process by which a cooperative group directs actions toward common goals. The treatment of management in this and the next seven chapters is based on the following six assumptions:

The practice of management can be improved. "Retrenchment, constricting finances, new competition, marketing, and rapid changes in the academic and demographic areas all spell the end of the traditional, unobtrusive style of organizational leadership on campuses. . . . American higher education needs . . . to take its own management more seriously, and to create new forms of institutional decision making if it is to cope with and help shape the new environment in which it finds itself" (Keller, 1983, p. 39). Institutions of higher learning require "better planning, strategic

13

decision-making, and more directed change. To accomplish this, colleges and universities need new procedures, structures and attitudes" (p. 27).

Interdisciplinary study facilitates improvement. The development of effective managers can best be achieved by coupling experience with directed study of the subject of management. It is therefore advantageous to integrate and apply the knowledge developed by numerous disciplines. Valuable insights into effective management are provided by sociology, psychology, political science, history, and economics, as well as by the more eclectic fields of management science, organizational theory and behavior, communication processes and effects, marketing, forecasting and futures study, decision theory, computer science, social and organizational change, financial management, planning, and comparative higher education.

Managers should be sensitive to the nature of nonprofit organizations. Managers can learn from practices in businesses, but they should be wary of wholesale adoption of those practices. Twelve differences in the operating elements in profit and nonprofit environments have been suggested by Ryan (1980); they are presented in Table 1-1.

Management possesses elements of art and science, practice and profession. Management is a subtle blend of art and science. Managing is doing—applying skills to achieve a desired result; people often use the word *knack* or *craft* in this regard. When thoughtfully exercised, the management process is also based on knowledge. Thus management also has its scientific side. Science involves seeking new knowledge through the use of a rigorous method of collecting, classifying, and measuring data and testing hypotheses. In recent decades, management literature has been increasingly focusing on scientific dimensions. Art and science are complementary concepts for managers. Likewise, practice and profession can proceed hand in hand. The day-to-day pragmatics of problem solving are highly important. Indeed, it is primarily on this basis that many managers are judged. At the same time, however, the need for professionalism cannot be slighted. The codification, study, and sharing of principles of institutional advancement contribute to the field as a whole and benefit

Table 1-1. Operating Elements in Profit and Nonprofit Environments.

Operational Characteristics	Operational Environment in Profit Organization	Operational Environment in Nonprofit Organization
1. Organizational objective	Generate profits	Provide service
2. Organizational accountability	Stockholders	Appointed or elected board
3. Size relative to economy	Approximately 80 percent	Approximately 20 percent
4. Marketplace impact	Responds readily	Responds more slowly
5. Revenues relative to costs	Maximize revenues	Balance revenues to costs
6. Marketplace contact	Indirect contact	Direct contact
7. Social awareness	Emerging	Inherent
8. Resource utilization	Capital intensive	Labor intensive
9. Ratio of professional personnel	Low to total	High to total
10. Personnel advancement	Function of achievement	Function of time
11. Performance measurements	Clear, measured by profitability	Vague, measured by quality of service
12. Management controls	Historically financial	Historically absent

Source: Ryan, 1980, p. 7.

participants, whether they view institutional advancement as a profession or as an occupation. The question of the degree to which institutional advancement has achieved the level of a profession is not merely an academic matter. It raises the serious question of how institutional advancement managers of the future can best prepare for the assignment.

The manager should develop strategies for dealing with change. The manager lives in a dynamic, changing world and works in an organization that is filled with fluctuations and uncertainties. Managers should anticipate, welcome, and introduce change in the organizations of which they are a part. What models are available to help cope with change? Scholars have spent considerable time and effort studying and writing about organizational life, both as it is and as it should be. They offer models addressing the manager's attitude toward using the information from the academic disciplines, the manager's processes in dealing with human and nonhuman factors, and the manager's priorities for action. Approaches cover a broad territory, ranging from muddling through (Lindblom, 1959) to planned change (Bennis, Benne, and Chin, 1961) to organized anarchy (Cohen and March, 1975). The manager can be a change agent, helping to resolve conflict, diagnose problems, and implement strategies for accommodating change.

The most accomplished managers are both movers and shapers. The mover emphasizes the short term, recognizes deadlines and resource constraints, and obtains satisfaction from being a button-pusher who is realistic, practical, and concrete. The shaper examines the long term, monitors social and economic trends, and takes pride in being an analyst who is objective, curious, and relativistic. The mover is a pragmatist with an ability to reject perfectionism and take action without delay. The payoff is results and resolution of the problem, at least for the time being. The shaper has a sense of proportion and profession that acknowledges a need to learn and modify the knowledge of others. It is useful to apply the modification model, which blends empirical evidence with experience and common sense. "The manager is not forced to have his head in the clouds or his hands in the grease" (Massie, 1971, p. 237).

It has long been said that the institutional advancement manager must avoid being an errand person and functionary and must be a policy maker. This same thought applies in the role to be played in serving institution and/or profession; the manager should contribute to both.

Understanding the Process

The successful manager must develop three categories of skills—the technical, the human, and the conceptual (Katz, 1955). It is the third category that is especially difficult to describe and challenging to attain, yet it is the most significant component of management at the higher levels of the organization. One of the most severe tests of the ability to conceptualize comes in answering the all-important question: What business are we in? Or more precisely, What business should we be in?

Mary Parker Follett, a pioneer management consultant, had a window shade company as a client and persuaded its owners they were really in the light control business. That realization expanded their opportunities enormously. The great lesson, of course, is that when the environment changes, an organization must reconceptualize its purpose in regard to the changing world or face the consequences. We all know the railroads should have known long ago that they were in the transportation business and not just railroading (Naisbitt, 1982).

The Process of Management. A helpful way to view the process of management is to identify the basic functions that together make up that process. Various authorities suggest various names for the key functions of management. However, there is general agreement on most of the actual duties of a manager. In this book, the following eight functions (adapted from Massie, 1971) are used to examine the management process: (1) *decision making*, the process by which a course of action is consciously chosen from available alternatives for the purpose of achieving a desired result; (2) *organizing*, the process by which the structure and allocation of jobs is determined; (3) *staffing*, the process by which managers select, train, promote, and retire personnel; (4) *planning*, the process by which a manager anticipates the future and discovers alternative courses of action; (5) *evaluating*, the process of assessing programs, people, and products; (6) *controlling*, the process of guiding performance toward a predetermined goal; (7) *communicating*, the process by which ideas are transmitted to others for the purpose of effecting a desired result; and (8) *directing*, the process by which performance of personnel is guided toward common goals.

All these closely interrelated functions are built on a foundation of mission, goals, and objectives. Thus the subject of planning and priorities receives attention in Chapter Three. To accomplish something, a group of people must know the structure and process by which a cooperative group of human beings works toward common objectives. Organization and structure are treated in Chapter Two. The allocation of resources and responsibilities is also a significant undertaking. The management of financial resources is covered in Chapter Six, and the management of human resources is discussed in Chapter Four. It is necessary to assess the overall effectiveness of operating programs and to consider trends and needs in order to help develop new programs. Chapter Eight addresses the topic of research and evaluation. Because of the changing emphases of institutional advancement managers, this revised edition includes two chapters on subjects that will continue to be of increased importance in the coming years: the management of volunteers (Chapter Five) and the management of technological applications (Chapter Seven).

Adopting a philosophy that there is no one correct way to approach management and that it is productive to nurture a critical attitude toward all management thought, the authors of these chapters encourage readers to develop syntheses of their own based on the particular needs of their organizations. References are provided in each chapter, and bibliographic essays are offered to stimulate further study.

The Process of Institutional Advancement. Institutional advancement is the management process "primarily responsible for maintaining and improving the relationship of an institution of higher education with society and selected publics in a way that most effectively contributes to the achievement of the institution's purposes" (Jacobson, 1978, p. 2). To the words *maintaining* and *improving* could be added *structuring, creating* and *enhancing,* but an even more significant word is *relationship.* It is the relationships between the educational institution and society and between the educational institution and its various publics that are of critical importance to the institutional advancement function. Marketing experts refer to this relationship as seeking an *exchange of values.* Communication specialists refer to an *exchange of meaning.* Institutional advancement measures, evaluates, and interprets the attitudes of various relevant publics. It also helps the institution and the public accommodate one another, comparing institutional objectives with the interests, needs, and goals of various publics

(Robinson, 1969). Responsible managers facilitate exchange relationships by applying experience and knowledge to bring about the highest possible degree of adjustment between the publics and the organization. Thus the institutional advancement manager seeks to develop relationships that lead to mutual adaptation.

This approach has evolved from a narrower view of the business we are in. Earlier conceptualizations pictured the job of institutional advancement as (1) mastering the publics or (2) blocking and parrying. The mastering viewpoint placed advancement practitioners in the role of technicians accepting directions for carrying out one-way communications with constituencies, serving the desires of the college or university involved; the publics were regarded as targets of the institution's self-interests. The blocking-and-parrying viewpoint saw advancement officers as reactors to developments and problems, responding to events or the actions of others by blunting them; the organization was considered to be fairly independent, responsible largely to its management and members.

Now the predominant view is interdependence, giving institutional advancement managers an opportunity to play a major role in resolving conflicts and arbitrating between environmental demands and organizational needs. The longer that advancement managers wait to adopt this comprehensive view, the greater their chances of inhibiting institutional adaptivity or abdicating responsibilities to other segments of the organization. Institutional advancement offices that through the years have been sluggish in adopting a consumer-orientation or user-responsive mode of operation now find themselves uncertain about how to relate to marketing initiatives that have blossomed in admissions or other departments. The integration of marketing activities is further discussed in Chapter Two.

What business are we in? In institutional advancement, we build relationships. The bottom lines are understanding and support. One of the most constructive ways to conceptualize the institutional advancement process is to look at it as a progression of stages from "uncontacted" to "taking action." This perspective sees the process from the standpoint of social psychology, looking at attitudes and behavior of human beings as the key ingredients.

The stages of progression are these, which may be thought of as steps on a ladder, moving upward from 1 to 8:

8. Action
7. Conviction
6. Involvement
5. Interest
4. Comprehension
3. Awareness
2. Attention
1. Contact

Institutional advancement programs are designed to affect attitudes and behavior of selected audiences. Sometimes activities are carried out to inform, sometimes to persuade, sometimes to elicit action. The manager designs strategies based on the type of effect desired.

Let us examine a variety of effects you may wish to achieve. When your goal is informing people, you might be content to attain attention, awareness, and comprehension effects. When you seek to persuade people, you might desire to achieve creative effects (creating attitudes among persons who previously held none on the topic concerned), or you might desire to achieve reinforcement (intensifying attitudes that already exist), conversion (converting persons to a point of view opposite the one they held), or neutralization (reducing partisanship or diminishing the intensity of existing attitudes without accomplishing conversion) effects. Sometimes, your principal desire is to elicit some overt act, such as casting a vote in a given direction in the legislature, contributing money to a campaign, writing a letter of support, or purchasing tickets, memberships, or memorabilia. In these cases, your chief intent is activation effects. When you shift from an interest in responses of individuals to a consideration of changes in social patterns, your goal is mobilization.

The vocabulary of institutional advancement effects will expand as managers share various practical experiences and as researchers in a variety of disciplines add their refinements. One of the most widely applied process models is that espoused by Dunlop

(1978), whose typology has been widely applied by fund-raisers. Steps in the commitment process are identification, information, awareness, interest, involvement, and commitment. A popular model for communication officers is that advanced by Barton (1980, p. 39), who diagrams "where to invest communication efforts" in terms of awareness, comprehension, motivation, and commitment. Some of the most successful applications of process models have occurred in the field of advertising. The Defining Advertising Goals for Measuring Advertising Results (DAGMAR) model and other models help managers visualize and gauge results according to a prospect's progress along a series of mental steps leading to a final sale (Runyon, 1984).

Issues in an Emerging Profession

The field of institutional advancement continues to progress toward maturity and professionalism. Today, many leaders of higher education consider institutional advancement to be one of the top four functional areas of college and university management, the other three being academic, financial, and student affairs (National Association of College and University Business Officers, 1974). This configuration reflects the recognition accorded institutional advancement on the modern campus in the United States. However, a number of issues and trends pose challenges that must be addressed if institutional advancement is to continue to evolve to its fullest potential. Leading factors that deserve attention are discussed here.

Quest for Professionalism. There is considerable agreement on criteria that must be satisfied for an occupation to become a profession. The field in question must (1) perform a unique and essential service, (2) develop a comprehensive self-governing organization, (3) place greater emphasis on service than on private economic gain, (4) receive a broad range of autonomy, (5) demonstrate that its practitioners accept broad personal responsibility for judgments and actions, (6) emphasize intellectual techniques, (7) be characterized by a long period of specialized training for acquiring a systematic body of knowledge based on research, and (8) possess a code of ethics that has been clarified and interpreted by concrete cases (Lieberman, 1956).

The seventh criterion will prove to be a severe test of our mettle. Institutional advancement managers must have comparative figures—benchmarks or gauges that can replace ballpark figures with sounder empirical evidence. Carefully collected data instruct participants about costs and experiences in their own and other organizations, providing a basis for comparative judgments. Sharing of reliable findings is to be encouraged because it reduces reinvention of the wheel and contributes to the body of organized knowledge upon which managers can act.

The Challenge of Renewal. Changing demand, increasingly scarce funding, and increased competition are forcing educational institutions to wrestle with retrenchment (Richards and Sherratt, 1981). Resistance to change cheats an organization of an opportunity to engage in healthy self-examination, strengthen its sense of community, and achieve the rewards of renewal. Uncertainty and inaction in revitalizing institutional advancement offices can become more disheartening than retrenchment itself. By taking initiatives, managers can explain why institutional advancement budgets deserve to be viewed as a legitimate investment essential to serving the central mission of the institution (H. Jacobson, 1984). One of the most delicate dimensions of the revitalization process is the effect on the morale of members of the academic family. Participative planning can build hope and excitement. Poorly handled cutback management can breed anxiety and anomie, eroding the quality of life and exerting a negative influence on the intellectual impact of academic institutions (R. Jacobson, 1984). Institutions that fail to practice civility in their internal deliberations and actions set a poor example for all their members. "A university is not merely a knowledge factory; it is one of the great humanizing influences of civilization. . . . Surely, our academic communities and the students who go out from these communities must apply on a world scale those same values of tolerance, compassion, and humanity which are needed in our nation if we are to deserve the adjective 'civilized' " (Fleming, 1968, pp. 12, 14).

Propensity for Factionalism. The idea of consolidated direction of advancement functions was advanced as a goal more than twenty-five years ago at the Greenbrier Conference. Yet a number of practitioners fail to transcend functional specialties, leading a distinguished leader in the field to lament "our continuing tendency to regard ourselves as fund raisers, or publications editors, or alumni directors . . . with little or no interest in all the others" (Beeman, 1976, p. 7). A corollary barrier to progress is the tendency of some institutions to elevate one function to a domineering role above its sister functions. Citing the danger in this practice, one national official (Jackson, 1980, pp. 28–29) warned, "If in your institution development is the be-all and end-all, and the public-relations . . . activity reports to development, . . . you're setting up an unnatural relationship and leaving your president relatively defenseless, because the question always is going to be, well, will they give money? Many of your publics will never give you a nickel, and yet you need their support."

High Turnover. A national survey of institutional advancement personnel found that half of the respondents (49.2 percent) had been employed in the field of institutional advancement for five or fewer years, and 12.2 percent had been in the field only one year (VanSlyke, 1982). Managing in an environment of high turnover demands care to preserve organizational continuity and quality control.

Orientation to the Short Term. The author of *Megatrends* has chronicled the short-term orientation of American managers and their willingness to "make the current quarter look better at the expense of the future" (Naisbitt, 1982, p. 79). The critical restructuring of American society, he maintains, means moving from a society run by short-term considerations and rewards in favor of dealing with matters in much longer time frames. Busily putting out fires and knocking on doors of potential donors, many institutional advancement officers find themselves more involved with concerns of immediate constituencies than with accountability to future generations. Managers tied to traditional techniques need to find ways to avoid preoccupation with tactical operations to the detriment of strategic planning.

Ethical Concerns. Historically, American colleges and universities have performed with comparatively high ethics. However, the Carnegie Council on Policy Studies in Higher Education reported evidence of student cheating, misuse of public financial aid, inflated advertising in student recruitment, and other threats to academic integrity. Indeed, one foundation official declared there to be an "Ethical Crisis in Education" (Martin, 1974). The commendable reach for professionalism among institutional advancement officers is intricately laced with moral and ethical considerations. Claims of tax avoidance in deferred giving, corporate strings on gifts, and ill-advised stock divestiture illustrate the array of sensitive areas subject to attack. The president of Harvard University issued an open letter on "Reflections on the Ethical Problems of Accepting Gifts" (Bok, 1979). Others have offered advice on when to say no (Kemeny, 1978; Martin, 1980). Guidelines for conduct may be found in codes of ethics issued by the Council for Advancement and Support and other national associations, such as the American Association of Fund-Raising Counsel and the Public Relations Society of America. Managers must continue to consider intended and unintended effects of public relations and fund-raising campaigns and programs.

Qualities of Successful Managers

Successful managers possess polished communication skills, a willingness to take risks, a wide range of interests, plentiful energy, tolerance for stress, and rich dimensions of leadership, knowledgeability, and resilience. The tenor of the times and the nature of the challenge for institutional advancement managers in the coming years cause the following qualities to emerge as characteristics of special importance.

> *Conceptual pluralism.* Managers who formerly embraced a single approach to the tasks of management will be more successful if they develop an eclectic view. Ritualistic patterns may have sufficed in a more stable environment, but the dynamics of the modern workplace require flexible thinking that nurtures flexible action. This view of

management has been best articulated by Bolman and Deal (1984), who advocate the use of diverse outlooks to obtain a more comprehensive understanding of organizations and a broader range of options for managerial action. They identify four theoretical frames: (1) structural frames, characterized by goal direction and task accomplishment; (2) human resources frames, which emphasize human needs, skills, and roles; (3) political frames, incorporating power relationships, coalitions, conflicts, and problems of resource allocation; and (4) symbolic frames, which refer to shared values and cohesion. Viewing the four domains as mutually supporting, the manager can use the various vantage points to order the world and decide what action to take.

Flair for cutting through the fog. In an era that is data rich and information poor, the decision makers who excel will quickly reduce complex situations to their essentials, make their way through dense detail and obfuscation, and go straight to what seems the obvious course of action.

Respect for the long term. The manager will weigh potential long-term consequences against immediate gains. Society's short-term solutions in dealing with the dumping of toxic wastes and the dissipation of nonrenewable natural resources serve as reminders of the consequences of shortsightedness.

Judgment. Expanding applications of the computer dramatically expand horizons for operational data bases, management control, and strategic planning. These developments place a premium on quantitative analyses that assimilate large volumes of data for meaningful decision making. The ability to assemble and analyze data is a fine talent, but even more important is the ability to interpret the facts, assign proper weight, and come to sound conclusions.

Imagination. One longtime observer of the campus scene maintains that "we have seen fewer creative academic administrators since the early 1970's than in any equivalent period before" (Glazer, 1984, p. 32). Needed are executive managers who dare to dream. New ideas involve risk, and conservative institutions will avoid the new for the sake of the safe. "The greatest danger in modern technology isn't that machines will begin to think like men, but that men will begin to think like machines" (Runyon, 1984, p. 317).

Optimistic attitude. The student is not likely to be attracted to a campus drowning in self-doubt. No one is more easily depressed than a potential donor. The superior manager will be a positive thinker who casts new ideas in terms of potential and opportunity.

Sensitivity to academe. Institutional advancement managers must be highly sensitive to the values of the academic institution. They must have respect for the worth of the individual and faith in the power of human intelligence. When Borst and Montana (1977) studied service organizations they concluded that what academic institutions need is not to be more businesslike but to be more university-like.

Character. Successful management assumes high standards of institutional integrity and personal conduct. Practice what you preach. If your standards are no higher than those of your colleagues, you are not likely to emerge as a leader.

Compatibility with the chief executive officer. Perhaps the most critical factor in managerial success in the academic institution is the compatibility of the chief advancement officer and the chief executive officer. No matter what qualifications show up on paper credentials, the advancement officer will find it difficult to achieve teamwork without being on the same psychological and ideological wavelength as the chief executive officer.

Sense of legacy. One of the highest rewards managers can experience is the satisfaction of passing the legacy of stewardship to others, repayment for the heritage their predecessors presented to them.

Bibliographical Essay

The contemporary literature dealing with institutional advancement practice focuses on descriptive and prescriptive statements frequently presented as case studies, how-to articles, and definitions. Sources that give greater attention to process and/or more systematic conceptualizations of institutional advancement include Leslie (1969, 1971), Dunlop (1978), and Jacobson (1978). Theory-building in a more formal sense has been done in such specialized fields as marketing—for example, in *Theory of Marketing* (Cox and others, 1964)—and personnel relations—for example, in *Personnel Management: A Situational Approach* (Crane, 1974). Ehling (1984) has made progress toward a theory of public relations management.

Classics that remain extremely helpful for institutional advancement managers include the theory of human needs developed by Maslow (1970), Theory X and Theory Y (McGregor, 1960), and studies of personality and organization by Argyris (1957, 1964). These and other major contributions to management literature are reviewed by Bolman and Deal (1984).

A bibliography rich with references on higher education management is available in Keller (1983). Readers seeking information on time management should consult Mackenzie (1972).

References

Argyris, C. *Personality and Organization.* New York: Harper & Row, 1957.

Argyris, C. *Integrating the Individual and the Organization.* New York: Wiley, 1964.

Barton, D. W., Jr. "Events by Objectives." *CASE Currents,* June 1980, pp. 38-39.

Beeman, A. L. "No Future Without Risk." *CASE Currents,* Dec. 1976, pp. 4-7.

Bennis, W. G., Benne, K. D., and Chin, R. (eds.). *The Planning of Change.* New York: Holt, Rinehart & Winston, 1961.

Bok, D. C. "Reflections on the Ethical Problems of Accepting Gifts: An Open Letter to the Harvard Community." Cambridge, Mass.: Office of the President, Harvard University, May 4, 1979.

Bolman, L. G., and Deal, T. E. *Modern Approaches to Understanding and Managing Organizations.* San Francisco: Jossey-Bass, 1984.

Borst, D., and Montana, P. J. (eds.). *Managing Nonprofit Organizations.* New York: American Management Associations, 1977.

Cohen, M., and March, J. G. *Leadership and Ambiguity: The American College President.* New York: McGraw-Hill, 1975.

Cox, R., and others. *Theory of Marketing.* Homewood, Ill.: Irwin, 1964.

Crane, D. P. *Personnel Management: A Situational Approach.* Belmont, Calif.: Wadsworth, 1974.

Dunlop, D. R. "Major Gifts Fund Raising." Paper presented at CASE Summer Institute in Educational Fund Raising, Dartmouth College, Hanover, N.H., July 30–Aug. 5, 1978.

Ehling, W. P. "Application of Design Theory in the Construction of A Theory of Public Relations Management I." *Public Relations Research and Education,* 1984, *1* (2), 25–38.

Fleming, R. W. "Inauguration Address: The University and the Humane Citizen." Address prepared for inauguration ceremony, Mar. 11, 1968. Ann Arbor: Michigan Historical Collections, University of Michigan.

Glazer, N. "Pondering the Aftermath of the Student Revolt of 1964–72." *Chronicle of Higher Education,* July 11, 1984, p. 32.

Jackson, P. "The Media." *AGB Reports,* July–Aug. 1980, pp. 28–30.

Jacobson, H. K. (ed.). *Evaluating Advancement Programs.* New Directions for Institutional Advancement, no. 1. San Francisco: Jossey-Bass, 1978.

Jacobson, H. K. "Communicating About Cutbacks; Straightforward Strategies for the Retrenchment Era." *CASE Currents,* Apr. 1984, pp. 40–42.

Jacobson, R. L. "AAUP's Leader Assays Decline in Faculty Morale, Governance." *Chronicle of Higher Education,* June 27, 1984, pp. 17, 19.

Katz, R. L. "Skills of An Effective Administrator." *Harvard Business Review,* Jan.-Feb. 1955, pp. 32-42.

Keller, G. *Academic Strategy: The Management Revolution in American Higher Education.* Baltimore, Md.: Johns Hopkins University Press, 1983.

Kemeny, J. G. "Why A President Might Refuse a Million-Dollar Gift." *CASE Currents,* Jan. 1978, pp. 26-28.

Leslie, J. W. *Focus on Understanding and Support: A Study in College Management.* Washington, D.C.: American College Public Relations Association, 1969.

Leslie, J. W. *Seeking the Competitive Dollar: College Management in the Seventies.* Washington, D.C.: American College Public Relations Association, 1971.

Lieberman, M. *Education as a Profession.* Englewood Cliffs, N.J.: Prentice-Hall, 1956.

Lindblom, C. E. "The Science of 'Muddling Through.' " *American Society for Public Administration,* Spring 1959, pp. 79-88.

McGregor, D. *The Human Side of Enterprise.* New York: McGraw-Hill, 1960.

Mackenzie, R. A. *The Time Trap.* New York: American Management Associations, 1972.

Martin, J. B. "When to Say No, Thank You." *CASE Currents,* Dec. 1980, p. 9.

Martin, W. B. "The Ethical Crisis in Education." *Change,* June 1974, pp. 28-33.

Maslow, A. H. *Motivation and Personality.* (2nd ed.) New York: Harper & Row, 1970.

Massie, J. L. *Essentials of Management.* (2nd ed.) Englewood Cliffs, N.J.: Prentice-Hall, 1971.

Naisbitt, J. *Megatrends: Ten New Directions Transforming Our Lives.* New York: Warner Books, 1982.

National Association of College and University Business Officers. *College and University Business Administration.* (3rd ed.) Washington, D.C.: National Association of College and University Business Officers, 1974.

Richards, M. D., and Sherratt, G. R. *Institutional Advancement Strategies in Hard Times.* American Association for Higher Education/Educational Resources Information Center Higher

Education Research Report No. 2. Washington, D.C.: American Association for Higher Education, 1981.

Robinson, E. J. *Public Relations and Survey Research.* New York: Appleton-Century-Crofts, 1969.

Runyon, K. E. *Advertising.* (2nd ed.) Westerville, Ohio: Merrill, 1984.

Ryan, J. E. "Profitability in the Nonprofit Environment." *Journal of Systems Management,* Aug. 1980, *30* (8), 6-14.

VanSlyke, J. K. "We the People of CASE." *CASE Currents,* July-Aug. 1982, pp. 27-31.

2

James M. Shea

Organizational Issues in Designing Advancement Programs

&❦The environment for higher education has changed significantly during the past decade. Altered values, new life-styles, and dramatically shifting demographics have produced a buyer's market. Admissions offices scramble to attract students from a dwindling supply of high school seniors at ever-increasing tuition rates. To keep a competitive edge, more and more educational institutions are turning to marketing techniques traditionally identified with for-profit organizations. Colleges and universities are doing this to the extent that "many observers are now predicting that academic marketing will eventually turn from an option into a necessity, even for the most prestigious institution" (Denison, 1983).

Integrating a marketing orientation into more commonly practiced institutional advancement functions seems to be a logical organizational step to improve outreach efficiencies and organization effectiveness. This new emphasis serves to underscore the roles institutional advancement staffs have always played in marketing their institutions to their various constituencies.

When given the assignment to organize or reorganize, look first to existing institutional advancement organizations to understand their evolution and present role. Four reference works are good instructors. They are Persons's *Public Relations for*

Colleges and Universities: A Manual of Practical Procedure (1946); the American College Public Relations Association's *Advancement of Understanding and Support of Higher Education* (1958); Leslie's *Focus on Understanding and Support: A Study in College Management* (1969), and the Council for Advancement and Support of Education and National Association of College and University Business Officers's *Management Reporting Standards for Educational Institutions: Fund Raising and Related Activities* (1982).

These sources cover the changes in organizational patterns from the period of the enrollment explosion after World War II to the early 1970s. Organizational patterns for institutional advancement programs have changed little between then and now. In the 1980s, titles shifted somewhat, drifting from university relations more to institutional advancement and development and reflecting the leaner economic times and the resultant pressures on presidents to balance the budget. The new technologies also came into use in institutional advancement offices during this time.

The 1958 Greenbrier Conference report (American College Public Relations Association, 1958) provides the most lucid description of how this area of management developed in higher education. Cosponsored by the American Alumni Council and the American College Public Relations Association (ACPRA), the Greenbrier Conference examined existing organizational principles and patterns of college and university relations. The conference strongly endorsed the principle of "administrative co-ordination of the functions" and concluded that "this usually implies the supervision of these activities by a single executive office" (p. 7). Functions have grown markedly in the last three decades, making the case for coordination stronger than ever.

The span of control now assigned to organization and structure is substantial and will grow with the inclusion of activities commonly called marketing (Barry and Allen, 1977; Fowler, 1983; Kotler, 1977; Snyder, 1978). Keep in mind this range of activities as we discuss organization and how to chart it.

Each college or university has its own nervous system and must develop the organization it needs. The variety of configurations found in higher education emphasizes that fact.

Universities and colleges are different from most commercial enterprises. A university is not "just another organization," said Harold Enarson, former president of Ohio State University. "It is a very special kind of place. It is more like the Metropolitan Opera than the Metropolitan Life Insurance Company. It is more like a church than a factory, more like a research lab than the highway department. The university is an intensely human enterprise. And it is not so much managed as it is led" (Enarson, 1973, p. 16).

The organization chart begins with the president. The original intent in gathering together the separate functions of institutional relations (including public relations, publications, and periodicals), fund-raising, alumni work, and service management was to help the president as general manager of the enterprise. Theoretically, the aid provided to the president in these specialized operational areas makes more time for educational leadership.

The vice-president, director, or dean (whatever the title) serves as an extension of the president in management. Whether an institutional advancement officer actually helps the president as a manager depends largely on the relationship between them. It must be special, differing from those of other department heads and other specialists. In principle at least, the president is the chief institutional relations and development officer. This tenet seems cut in stone. Persons (1946, p. 3) stated it forty years ago: "The public relations [Persons used *public relations* for all the functions we today call advancement] of any organization are the rightful responsibilities of its chief administrative officer. However he may arrange and delegate, as to operations, the responsibility remains his because he, and he alone, represents the institution as a whole."

Unless the president believes in institutional advancement activities, even the best-formed organization will fail. Not lip service, but firm conviction is necessary. In describing the president's outlook, Persons said, "If he elects to look upon his public relations responsibility as a nuisance, he will not be disappointed. If he seeks to find in them new sources of influence and help, he will get them" (p. 4). That truth is unchanged.

Analysis is the first step in restructuring or organizing from scratch. It includes a thorough view of goals, present structure, sources of support, and financial potential. The goal is to organize a team of specialists that meshes together efficiently and communicates regularly, even when housed in different locations. The exact composition of the team will vary from institution to institution but includes those in charge of institutional relations, fund-raising, alumni relations, the service-management areas, and potentially, government relations and marketing. Resist the temptation to shape your model after another institution's simply because it appears to have worked there. The mix of people, the setting, and the history of the institution are different; and transplants, unless perfectly typed, do not usually succeed.

There are really only two basic organizational models: centralized, in which the functions come together under one officer who reports directly to the president, and noncentralized, in which the functions are loosely coordinated, and one, two, or as many as four individuals report to the president. This second model has many variations.

Although it is not necessarily the best model, a centralized model, with the institutional advancement officer responsible for all the functions, is the most common. The idea is not new. Persons built a centralized model in 1946. There has been a trend toward togetherness ever since. In 1957, just before Greenbrier, 20 percent of the institutions responding to an ACPRA questionnaire had a centralized model, and at Greenbrier, 86.4 percent of the conference delegates favored the arrangement (Leslie, 1969). Between Greenbrier and the 1970s, centralization gained popularity, reaching about 50 percent. At the same time, the activities of institutional advancement also increased.

Others felt no need to change, or else they had problems with the budget, a reluctant administration, a tenacious old-timer blocking the reorganization, or resistance from the faculty or from other administrators suspicious of new power figures "particularly if they are interposed between themselves and the top level" (American College Public Relations Association, 1958, p. 18). The practitioner must give serious consideration to both the practical difficulties and the intangible ones when planning for change. Although it does not show on the charts, campus politics are always at play. Faculty groups, other administrators, students, trustees, and, in some instances, alumni must be consulted and sold on the idea.

In the most common model, the president delegates to the institutional advancement officer the full responsibility for a wide range of activities (see Figure 2-1). In Leslie's (1969) study, the centralized model was the favorite model for state and private universities and colleges. Small institutions with enough staff for the separate functions can use this model. (The smaller the institution, the less likely you are to find a list of activities under service-management.) In Leslie's analysis, "Four persons—maybe three in certain cases—constitute the minimum professional staff for an effective advancement program. Otherwise, the staff would be spread so thin that effective impact would be jeopardized" (p. 66). This model helps communication and puts accountability and responsibility directly under the president.

One variation on the centralized model is worthy of note. It is found frequently in insurance companies and large banks. This model can apply in states with higher education systems that include central offices with administrative responsibilities for their institutions. The addition of an executive or senior vice-president between the president and the advancement officer and staff moves them one step away from the president. This model may develop because of the large size of the institution, but more likely, it reflects the president's deepest feelings about advancement's priorities and the time they take.

In the noncentralized model, no single officer directs the entire program. Figures 2-2 and 2-3 present some variations of this model. The dotted lines show further variations and suggest the possibility of outside help. External counsel sometimes offers objectivity. Under certain conditions, it costs less than maintaining a full-time staff.

Private foundations are not uncommon on the advancement chart. Some states have regulations prohibiting state institutions from soliciting and distributing private gifts. Institutions in these states have turned to foundations to avoid state restraints. Sometimes, alumni set up a foundation to raise money for special purposes, such as football. No matter how it starts, the "fund-raising or development foundation is a matter of organizational

Figure 2-1. Centralized Model.

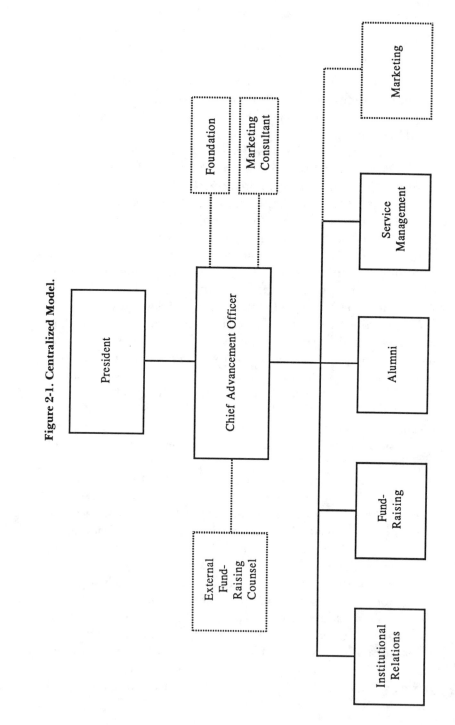

Figure 2-2. Noncentralized Model, Type A.

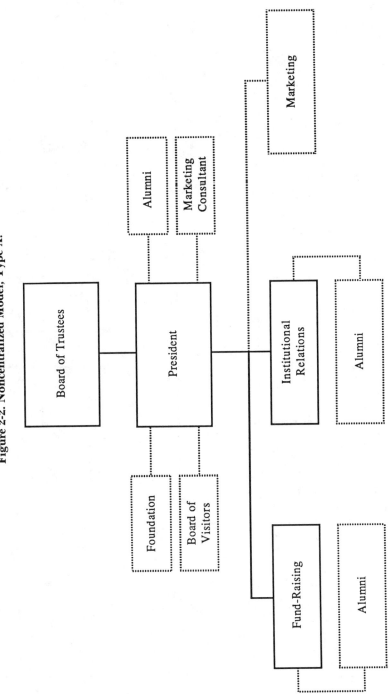

Figure 2-3. Noncentralized Model, Type B.

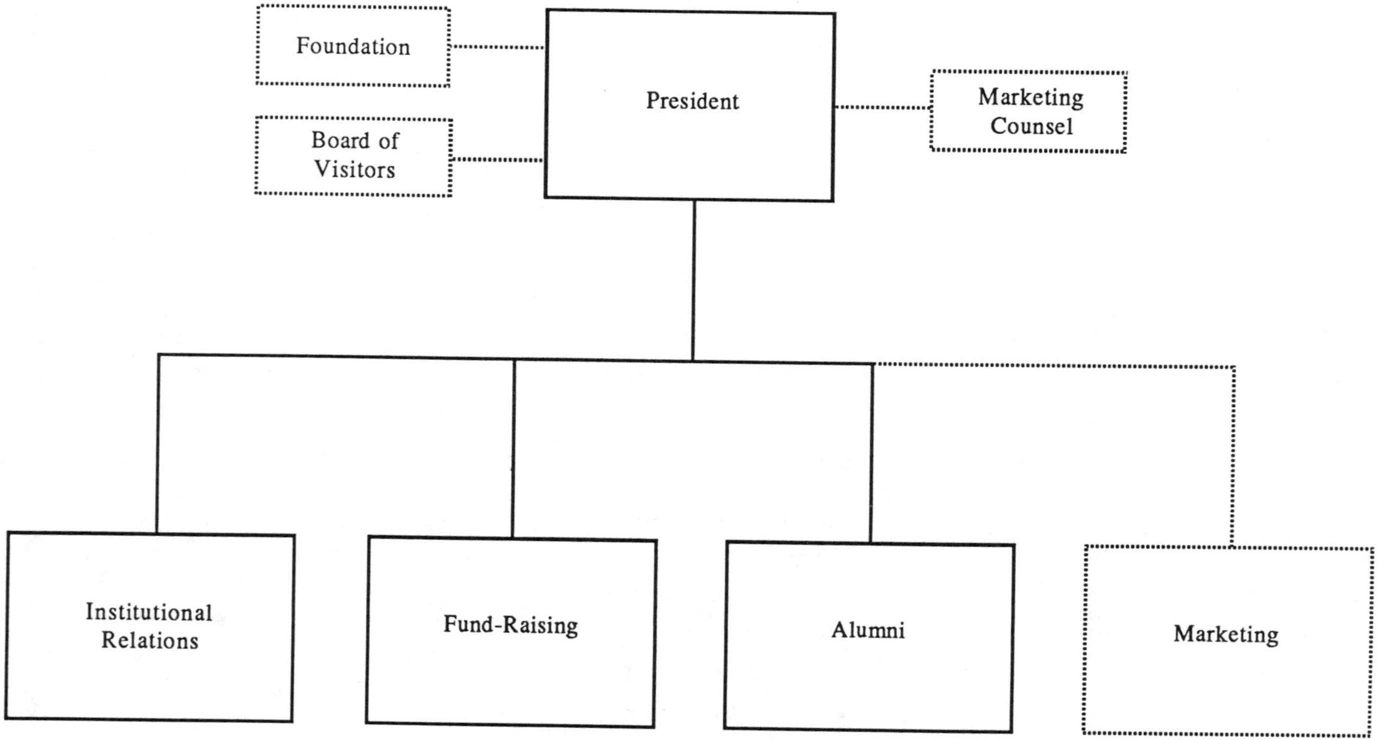

concern for the president and the advancement program managers"
(p. 69).

Finally, the charts suggest coordination. Many marketing
activities, especially setting the criteria for admissions, traditionally
have been part of the academic side of the house. A good leader can
develop the required close coordination, but only when a
compelling need has been demonstrated.

Organizing visiting committees or volunteer specialists is
another way to expand the staff at little or no cost. Visiting
committees are not new. Persons (1946), who worked with them
forty years ago, called them "prestige" committees (p. 49). Today,
visiting committees go by several different titles—advisory councils,
associate committees, university councils, advisory committees, and
boards of visitors. They are outsiders "whose principal function is
to counsel the respective administrative units on implementation of
their objectives. A secondary objective is to raise friends and funds
for the institution" (Greenfield, 1970, pp. 1-4).

The committee members are volunteers selected for their
professional competence and also, perhaps, for their philanthropical potential. Their handling is a delicate matter. The rule is to
involve them in something important so they understand the reason
for their membership. Do not set up a committee unless you can
keep the members interested and busy. They must feel that they are
accomplishing something worthwhile and their efforts are
appreciated. More information on volunteer groups appears in
Chapter Five.

When trustees or regents are slow to include women and
other minorities on the governing boards, the visiting committee is
an excellent medium for bringing them into the institution in
important advisory positions. To be complete, the organization
chart should include the visiting committee in a lateral position
with a line to the president or the institutional advancement officer.

Titles are important and should both reflect status and
responsibility and describe the job. It is impossible to tell the weight
of a title. The director of development in one institution may have
more power than a vice-president for university relations somewhere
else.

Figure 2-4. Comprehensive Organizational Model.

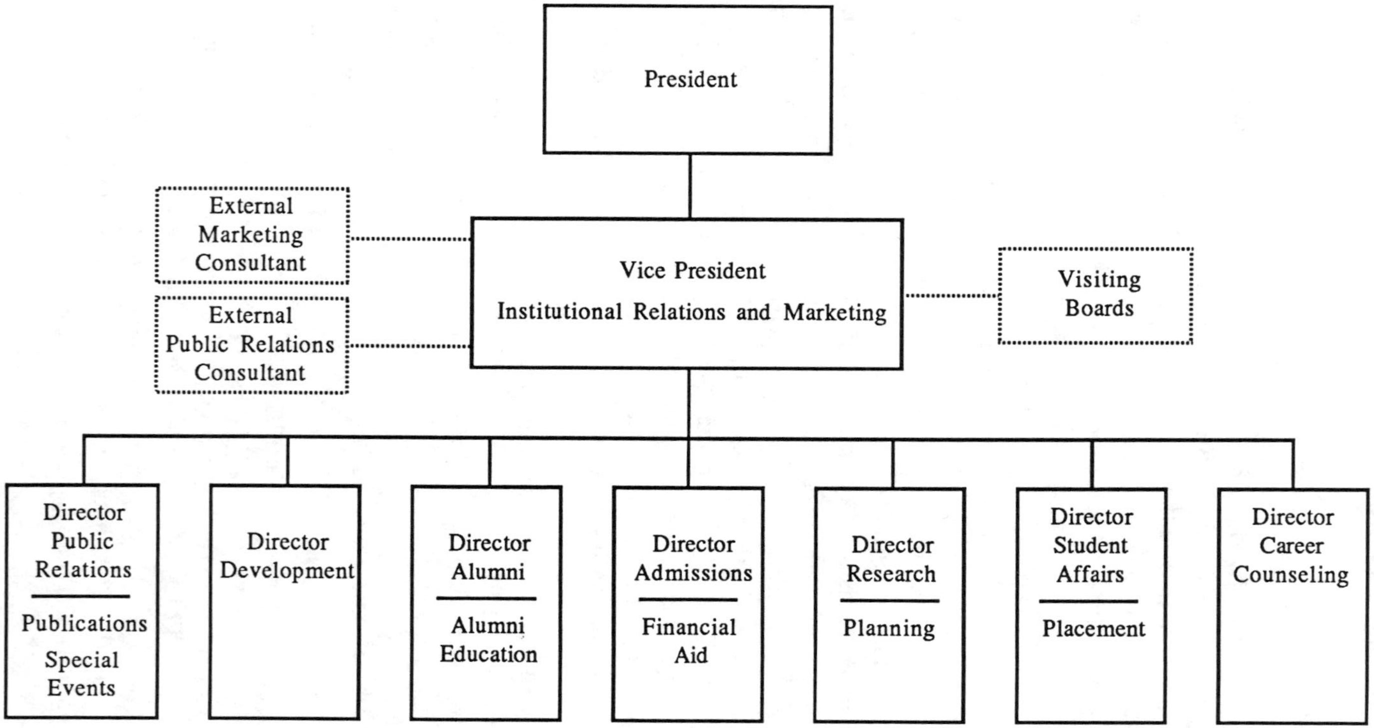

Titles have changed little since the Greenbrier Conference. In the mid 1970s, vice-president for institutional advancement was added to the lexicon that still lists vice-president for development, vice-president for planning and development, vice-president for public affairs, vice-president for university relations, vice-president for communication and development, and vice-president for university relations and development. Assistant to the president, dean, and director are other titles.

Marketing is becoming more accepted and will show up on more charts. The term *institutional advancement* is the vogue now, but its replacement may be just around the corner.

The signs suggest the formal practice of marketing has arrived. If integrated with institutional advancement, the span of control alone suggests a single supervisor working with the president "to help create a marketing orientation in the organization" (Kotler, 1982, p. 136). It suggests other things as well: the critical need for institutional advancement professionals to understand and apply marketing principles (Grunig and Hunt, 1984) and to consider comprehensive organization models with marketing more prominently recognized as a component function (Figure 2-4).

Bibliographical Essay

The organizing function of the management process is discussed by Pfiffner and Sherwood in *Administrative Organization* (1960) and in Chapter 6, "Organizing and Staffing," of Massie's *Essentials of Management* (1971).

Marketing applications in institutional advancement are reviewed in two special issues of *CASE Currents*. They are the Council for Advancement and Support of Education's "Special Issue: Marketing" (May 1977) and "Special Issue: Marketing and Student Recruitment" (Nov.-Dec. 1983).

References

American College Public Relations Association. *The Advancement of Understanding and Support of Higher Education.* Washington, D.C.: American College Public Relations Association, 1958.

Barry, L. L., and Allen, B. H. "Marketing's Crucial Role for Institutions of Higher Education." *Atlanta Economic Review,* 1977, *27* (4), 24–31.

Council for Advancement and Support of Education. "Special Issue: Marketing." *CASE Currents,* May 1977, pp. 7–9.

Council for Advancement and Support of Education. "Special Issue: Marketing and Student Recruitment." *CASE Currents,* Nov.–Dec. 1983, pp. 20–23.

Council for Advancement and Support of Education and National Association of College and University Business Officers. *Management Reporting Standards for Educational Institutions: Fund Raising and Related Activities.* Washington, D.C.: Council for Advancement and Support of Education and National Association of College and University Business Officers, 1982.

Denison, C. D. "Selling Colleges in a Buyer's Market." *New York Times Magazine,* Apr. 10, 1983, pp. 48–50.

Enarson, H. L. "University or Knowledge Factory?" *Chronicle of Higher Education,* June 19, 1973, p. 16.

Fowler, C. R. "Making Marketing Work: How a Coordinated Approach Improved a College's Enrollment, Retention, and Public Image." *CASE Currents,* Nov.–Dec. 1983, pp. 20–23.

Greenfield, J. M. "Why Have Visiting Committees?" *Techniques,* Mar.–Apr. 1970, pp. 1–4.

Grunig, E. J., and Hunt, T. *Managing Public Relations.* New York: Holt, Rinehart & Winston, 1984.

Kotler, P. "Why We Need Marketing." *CASE Currents,* May 1977, p. 4.

Kotler, P. *Marketing for Non-Profit Organizations.* (2nd ed.) Englewood Cliffs, N.J.: Prentice-Hall, 1982.

Leslie, J. W. *Focus on Understanding and Support: A Study in College Management.* Washington, D.C.: American College Public Relations Association, 1969.

Massie, J. L. *Essentials of Management.* Englewood Cliffs, N.J.: Prentice-Hall, 1971.

Persons, C. E. *Public Relations for Colleges and Universities: A Manual of Practical Procedure.* Stanford, Calif.: Stanford University Press, 1946.

Pfiffner, J. M., and Sherwood, F. P. *Administrative Organization.* Englewood Cliffs, N.J.: Prentice-Hall, 1960.

Snyder, R. P. "College Staff and Outside Counsel Strengthen Admissions Program." In H. K. Jacobson (ed.), *Evaluating Advancement Programs.* New Directions for Institutional Advancement, no. 1. San Francisco: Jossey-Bass, 1978.

3

Jeffrey B. Nelson

Planning: Establishing Program Goals and Strategies

ᗡ᠑ Planning is an essential component of the management process. Despite its fundamental importance, managers are by no means unanimous in assessing its role and scope. Detractors claim that planning is a waste of time. Proponents maintain that "planning is an integral and central function of every manager's task. If you don't plan, you become a crisis manager, responding to rather than driving the environment of your job" (Slevin, 1979, p. 15).

Nature of Planning

This author, who recently returned to institutional advancement after a few years in the industrial world, can state without reservation that a major difference between management in profit organizations and nonprofit organizations is the great attention given to planning by business people. Nonprofit managers could learn from and, if you will pardon the word, profit from their example.

There is no question that the environment for planning is much less structured on a college campus than in an industrial concern. Our chain of command is more diffuse, our bottom line less clear-cut, our product line more vaguely defined. Planning, for us, is more challenging, but certainly no less necessary. Institutional advancement programs are generally considered to be analogous to the marketing, advertising, sales, and public relations

44

functions in the business or industrial environment. Those operations lay strategic plans to support company goals. Institutional advancement units must likewise plan in order to support the organizational mission.

Much of the criticism of planning stems from naiveté about its nature and purpose. One major misinterpretation is the depiction of planning as an executive straitjacket. It is not. At least it need not be. True, a formal plan put together yearly might be overtaken by events, but having made a plan does not mean that one cannot adjust. To take some liberty with Tennyson, it is better to have planned and modified than never to have planned at all. Another distracting assertion is the assumption that there is a choice of planning or not planning. Any person with authority over resources "makes decisions that affect the organization in the future and, therefore, plans" (Grindlay, 1978, p. 8). People and organizations are differentiated, not on whether or not they plan, but on the degree of formality of their planning. Both formal and informal planning have their merits (Grindlay, 1978; Stengrevics, 1983). The challenge is to find the degree of formality that is appropriate for your office and your organization.

Need and Purpose. Planning is nothing more than determining how to get from here to there; the need for it is universal. Assuming general agreement by decision makers on where "here" is and where "there" ought to be, we can use the following questions to instigate the planning dialogue:

Where are we now?
How did we get here?
Where are we going?
Where should we be going?
How will we get there?

A solid institutional plan has many useful effects within and outside an organization. Thurston E. Manning (1980) of the North Central Association of Colleges and Schools notes these benefits of a plan:

1. It helps build confidence in the organization and its leadership because it demonstrates that the organization knows what it needs to do and wants to do.

2. It helps build informed commitment to the institution on the part of persons both within and outside the organization.

3. Reporting of the goals as they are realized provides accountability to the institution's supporters and clients.

4. As an aid to fund-raising, it provides a guide to the kinds of gifts needed and the ways they will be used to further the work of the institution.

Planning is essential in colleges and universities, according to Keller (1983, p. 70), "because it brings decision making out of the closet; it replaces muddling through with purpose. What academic leaders [who engage in planning] are doing," he said, "is turning their private plans based on general aims and prejudices, into ones that are public and based on data, explicit objectives and rational strategies."

For those who are motivated by financial gain, it might be pointed out that researchers who study management maintain that "the more planning a manager does, the more he is paid. . . . Chairmen of the board and presidents are constantly dealing with five- and ten-year time horizons, while blue-collar workers on the production floor may be dealing with time horizons of only a few minutes. The longer the time frame, the more responsible the job, and the higher the pay" (Slevin, 1979, p. 15).

Types of Plans. What constitutes a reasonable and workable plan? To determine this, it helps to focus on just what type of planning is being considered. Rhyne (1984) has cited at least five types of plans and identified their characteristics (see Table 3-1).

The Planning Process

Basic Elements. There are divergent opinions on the mechanics of planning and the framework of the planning process. By common agreement, however, any plan will contain these three elements: mission, the most general level; goals, the next; and objectives, the most specific.

Table 3-1. Characteristics of Five Types of Plans.

Type of Plan	Objective	Time horizon
Short-term forecasting	Identify near-term operating results	Less than 1 year
Budgeting	Financial control of operating results	Normally 1 year
Annual planning	Identify problems, opportunities, and turning points on an annual basis	1 year
Long-range planning	Identify problems, opportunities, and turning points to maximize results of current or closely related operations over a longer period	5, 10, or 15 years
Strategic planning	Identify both new areas in which skills may be applied and threats to current operations	5, 10, or 15 years

Source: Rhyne, 1984.

Mission refers to the reason for the existence of an organization or an entity within it. "The mission gives meaning and direction to programs and activities. The mission, therefore, is usually stated in broad, philosophical, and sometimes inspirational terms" (Jacobson, 1978, p. 20). The college or university "mission statement sums up the academic identity of the institution" and covers "the kind of educational philosophy it espouses and the specific educational aims and purposes it seeks to fulfill" (Guardo, 1982, p. 25). Institutional advancement responsibilities derive from the institutional mission.

What do we need to accomplish, and by when, to achieve the mission? *Goals* are the desired end results to be achieved over long periods of time. They are expressed in a series of statements that break down the mission into a set of intentions. Testifying to the importance of knowing and following institutional priorities, Smith (1982, p. 30) stated, "Sometimes the institutional agenda will tell us we need to refuse a proffered gift. That is difficult. But as I look back on twenty years of fund-raising in American colleges and universities, I see far too many gifts that ended up costing too much. Gifts should not be costly. Gifts should help accomplish the goals we have set for our institutions."

Objectives separate each goal into a set of more specific intentions or behaviors. Objectives are shorter in range than goals, quantifiable, and set within a time frame. Sources helpful for implementation of management by objectives (MBO) are listed in the bibliographical essay at the end of this chapter.

Many planning practitioners—particularly those in the business world—believe that this framework is incomplete, that it tends to ignore the elements that truly give the planning process wings. These missing elements are, first, tactical action and, second, evaluation and adjustment. We shall discuss them shortly.

Long-Range Planning. A six-step method for planning in nonprofit organizations has been postulated by Brady (1984):

1. *Define concepts and terms.* Brady regards *goals* as long-term outcomes, usually two years or longer, that are somewhat generally stated. *Objectives* are regarded as short-term, one-year performance tasks, stated in more specific terms and indicating what will happen, by when, and with what service or program. *Action plans* are defined as the who and how of objective and goal attainment, the day-to-day work details, specific tasks and dates of completion.

2. *Gather data that help determine the course of planning.* Surveys and audits of internal and external publics can be used to answer such questions as how people perceive the organization and its work, what they feel the organization should be doing, and the level of community or constituent support.

3. *Use simple, concise terms.* When writing goals, objectives, and action plans, remember that an organization can accomplish perhaps only two major goals in each year of a plan. A five-year plan, then, would have no more than ten goals at a maximum, with each goal having two or three objectives. "One important fact to remember in basic planning for nonprofits is to establish plans based on a 40 percent work effort. This is not because nonprofits are that inefficient, but the workload and

reactive nature of most nonprofits is such that staff and volunteers spend about 35 percent of their time performing operational tasks and 25 percent reacting to daily crises historically part of the organization" (p. 49).

4. *Obtain feedback on the planning effort.* Avoid planning in a vacuum behind closed doors. Feedback may be obtained by use of a questionnaire that covers three basic points. First, what will be the outcome if this objective is achieved? This outcome should be visible and measurable. Second, what will be the effect on the long-range goals and other objectives if this objective is not accomplished? These effects should be specific and suggest possible alternative actions or goal modifications. Third, what changes should be made if the objective is only partly achieved? How can it or the action plans be modified to complete the objective if it is viable? Good feedback and information exchange encourage flexibility and a capacity for change.

5. *Consider contingency planning as the technique for making changes in the process.* Because we develop plans by using historical data and assumptions about the future, we must make them flexible enough so that, if our prognostications about the future do not come true, we can change our goals and objectives to meet those changes. Changes are not necessarily cutbacks; established targets can be increased.

6. *Choose the planning committee carefully.* An effective planning committee should meet quarterly to review, analyze, and discuss goal, program, and organizational accomplishments. Because long-range planning is not a static effort, it is important to monitor, discuss, and modify plans regularly. The makeup of the committee should include key board and staff members and either the head of the organization or unit or an appointee who has the authority to speak for that individual.

One of the main advantages of planning is the communication the process requires among the people involved, a healthy and beneficial result in itself. This is the view expressed by Copeland (1975), who has proposed these planning steps for departmental project planning: (1) determine departmental objectives, (2) coordinate these with previous objectives and programs, (3) research all available facts about the project, (4) determine alternative courses of action and their consequences, (5) select a course of action, (6) implement the plan with proper control to ensure that it can be carried through to completion, and (7) evaluate the degree to which the objective has been attained.

Strategic Planning. In addition to the familiar mission/ goals/objectives structure, there is another element often inserted into the planning process—again particularly by business planners. That is the term *strategy*. Strategies are not to be confused with *tactics*, which describe the specific steps to be taken. A *strategy* merely outlines how an objective is to be accomplished. An example, using an institutional advancement problem, helps to clarify the macro-to-micro flow of the planning process:

> *Goal:* To create a preference for the alumni travel program of ABC College, rather than commercially available tour packages.
>
> *Objective:* To gain a 20 percent increase in alumni travelers, ages forty years and older, during the next fiscal year.
>
> *Strategy:* Communicate the cost savings and the "you're among friends" advantages of the alumni tour program, using testimonial advertising to the target audience.
>
> *Tactics:* Direct mailings in October, February, and May. Accompany space advertising in the alumni magazine with human interest feature stories about the most recent alumni tours.

For some institutional advancement units, such as development offices, return on investment is a growing concern numbered in dollars spent versus dollars gained. Those units may also wish to consider the business-oriented planning model known as the strategic marketing plan.

Marketing's expanding role in institutional advancement has been outlined by Richards and Sherratt (1981) and Topor (1983). In *Marketing for Non-Profit Organizations,* Rados (1981) reminds us that the gap between business-style customer marketing and nonprofit-style marketing is becoming narrower all the time. He draws these parallels:

> Identifying target markets versus finding potential donors
> Determining how customers behave versus assessing donor motives
> Planning the marketing effort versus planning the fundraising campaign
> Implementation and control versus implementation and control

Here is a representative outline for a strategic marketing plan:

I. Situation Analysis
    A. Government, economic, social and other influences
    B. Marketplace characteristics
        1. Size and trends
        2. Customer (donor) characteristics
        3. Competition and competitive reaction
    C. Internal resources
        1. Our own capabilities and restraints
        2. Current and expected resource allocation
        3. Sales (outreach) and marketing capabilities

II. Generic Strategies (for example, percentage of desired increase in new donors this year)

III. Performance Goals and Objectives
    A. Do our objectives meet overall institutional objectives?
    B. What are current and desired sales (contribution revenues), share of market, percentage return of investment, necessary promotional expense?

IV. Specific Strategies
    A. Product or service (campaign)
    B. Price (contribution level sought)
    C. Place (mailings, visits, events)
    D. Promotion (communication strategies)

V.   Evaluation and Feedback
   A.   Mechanisms for collection
   B.   Mechanisms for evaluation

VI. Tactical Action Calendar
   A.   What needs to be done?
   B.   When?
   C.   By whom?

A strategic market planning process, according to Kotler (1976), consists of analyzing opportunities, choosing objectives, developing strategy, formulating plans, and carrying out implementation and control. He cites four major factors that can affect an organization's goals and objectives for the coming year: (1) long-run goals, such as target enrollment growth, target fund-raising growth, or target return on investment, (2) recent results, such as enrollment, fund-raising, or return on investment growth, (3) current outlook, such as the economic, higher education, public policy, or competitive outlook, and (4) interest group expectations, such as students, trustees, faculty and staff, or administration.

Auditing the Planning Process. Many organizations are still in the stage of designing and implementing planning systems. However, those that have ongoing systems in place are exploring ways to monitor, or audit, the planning process itself. Where actual results do not match plan objectives, or where a planning system has been unsuccessful in increasing performance level, a planning process audit (PPA) can be used to uncover people-oriented dissatisfactions with current planning systems (Kelley, 1984). "The purpose of the process audit should be to provide a means for participating managers to communicate problems they have encountered in the process of accomplishing their planning responsibilities, as well as their individual perspective on inconsistencies that may hamper future planning efforts" (p. 14).

Guidelines for Planning

Massie (1971) has identified several general guidelines for planning that may be useful to the manager:

1. A plan should be directed toward well-defined objectives. Unless plans help lead toward well-understood goals, performance in the future cannot result in purposeful effort.
2. Plans made by different specialists should be coordinated through adequate communication among specialists.
3. Planning is a prerequisite of other functions of management. The concept of control is meaningless without planning.
4. Adaptation of plans to current actions demands continual redrafting of plans. Plans must be reviewed periodically, and changes warranted by new developments made.
5. Planning pervades the hierarchy of an organization. At lower levels, planning is more detailed and for shorter periods; planning at higher levels tends to be more general and for longer periods of time.
6. Plans should retain flexibility. Planning tends to preset a rigid course of action unless opportunity for change is incorporated in plans.

Manning (1980) offers these worthwhile principles:

1. Be sure the mission and the purposes of the institution (and its institutional advancement operation) are clear and known to all. Otherwise there is a constant temptation to make decisions catering to personal preferences or narrow interests.
2. Start small. Project the schedule over a limited time frame. Do not try to deal with the whole of a complex organization at once. Experience, fortified by past success, is essential.
3. Make the planning process as public as possible. Involve as many persons, both within and outside the organization, as is feasible. Participation can build commitment to the institution and its goals.
4. The leadership of the organization must participate fully and obviously in the planning process.
5. All planning will confront controversial issues, and not everyone will agree on goals or the resources needed. Begin with the mission and purpose and explicitly relate resources and organization to the accomplishment of those purposes.

6.   Do not express goals and objectives in grandiose terms. If the plan is to be a guide to action, it must be concrete and specific.
7.   Do not set unattainable goals. The plan should not be a wish list. However, do not set goals so modest that the organization will not have to stretch some to attain them.

Educational institutions and other nonprofit enterprises have not historically been strong in defining priorities and tacking into the winds of the future confident of their course. However, institutional advancement officers should understand as well as, or better than, anyone the demands of accountability and the imperatives of a competitive environment. Those who grasp the techniques—and the necessity—of strategic planning can serve as models for their organizations. Their efforts will bring increased efficiency and solid results.

Bibliographical Essay

Assistance in employing approaches in college and university management is provided in books by Deegan and Fritz (1976) and Harvey (1976). The use of MBO on the campus has included applications in fund-raising programs (Elam, 1978a, 1978b) and in public relations programs (Thies, 1978).

Policies and procedures for planning are described by Kerzner (1979). He provides suggestions and checklists and reviews techniques such as Program Evaluation and Review Techniques (PERT) and the Critical Path Method (CPM). A management tool that is helpful in assessing a unit's readiness to plan, the Programming Status Test, is presented by Miller and Thompson (1984).

Increased attention is being given to issues management—that is, a program an organization uses to increase its knowledge of the public policy process and enhance the sophistication and effectiveness of its involvement in that process. According to Seitel (1984), who discusses how to organize such a program, more than 200 American companies have created executive positions for issues managers.

The American Cancer Society is among the nonprofit fund-raising organizations to use the strategic marketing plan model. Major elements of the society's plan are situation analysis, the strategic plan, the operational market plan, the communication plan, the tactical plan, and the budget. The organization's planning experience is detailed by Hansler (1984).

References

Brady, T. S. "Six Step Method of Long Range Planning for Non-Profit Organizations." *Managerial Planning,* Jan.-Feb. 1984, pp. 47-50.

Copeland, J. L. "Planning—A Principal Principle." *CASE Currents,* Mar. 1975, pp. 10-11.

Deegan, A. X., and Fritz, R. J. *MBO Goes to College.* (2nd ed.) Boulder: Regents of the University of Colorado, 1976.

Elam, D. "MBO Brings Results." *CASE Currents,* Jan. 1978a, pp. 21-22.

Elam, D. "Use of Management by Objectives for Evaluation." In H. K. Jacobson (ed.), *Evaluating Advancement Programs.* New Directions for Institutional Advancement, no. 1. San Francisco: Jossey-Bass, 1978b.

Grindlay, A. "First Plan—Then Play." *CASE Currents,* Jan. 1978, pp. 8-11.

Guardo, C. J. "Defining the Mission of a University." *CASE Currents,* Sept. 1982, pp. 24-27.

Hansler, D. F. "American Cancer Society's Market Planning Process." *Fund Raising Management,* June 1984, pp. 32-38.

Harvey, L. J. *Managing Colleges and Universities by Objectives: A Concise Guide to Understanding and Implementing MBO in Higher Education.* Wheaton, Ill.: Ireland Educational Corporation, 1976.

Jacobson, H. K. (ed.). *Evaluating Advancement Programs.* New Directions for Institutional Advancement, no. 1. San Francisco: Jossey-Bass, 1978.

Keller, G. *Academic Strategy: The Management Revolution in American Higher Education.* Baltimore, Md.: Johns Hopkins University Press, 1983.

Kelley, C. A. "Auditing the Planning Process." *Managerial Planning*, Jan.-Feb. 1984, pp. 12-14.

Kerzner, H. *Project Management: A Systems Approach to Planning, Scheduling and Controlling.* New York: Van Nostrand Reinhold, 1979.

Kotler, P. *Marketing Management: Analysis, Planning and Control.* (3rd ed.) Englewood Cliffs, N.J.: Prentice-Hall, 1976.

Manning, T. E. "Institutional Planning for Development." *Bulletin on Public Relations and Development* (Gonser, Gerber, Tinker, and Stuhr), Mar. 1980, pp. 1-4.

Massie, J. L. *Essentials of Management.* (2nd ed.) Englewood Cliffs, N.J.: Prentice-Hall, 1971.

Miller, J. E., and Thompson, H. L. "23 Management Guidelines to Improve Fund Raising." *Fund Raising Management*, July 1984, pp. 32-42.

Rados, D. L. *Marketing for Non-Profit Organizations.* Boston: Auburn House, 1981.

Rhyne, L. C. "Strategic Information: The Key to Effective Planning." *Managerial Planning*, Jan.-Feb. 1984, pp. 4-10.

Richards, M. D., and Sherratt, G. R. *Institutional Advancement Strategies in Hard Times.* Higher Education Research Report, No. 2. Washington, D.C.: Clearinghouse on Higher Education, George Washington University, and American Association for Higher Education, 1981.

Seitel, F. P. *The Practice of Public Relations.* Westerville, Ohio: Merrill, 1984.

Slevin, D. P. "Management Functions: What to Do and When." In G. Zaltman (ed.), *Management Principles for Nonprofit Agencies and Organizations.* New York: American Management Associations, 1979.

Smith, J. P. "Setting Fund-Raising Priorities." *CASE Currents*, Sept. 1982, pp. 28-31.

Stengrevics, J. M. "Manager's Journal: Corporate Planning Needn't Be an Executive Straitjacket." *Wall Street Journal*, Sept. 26, 1983.

Thies, A. H. "Practicing PR by Objectives." *CASE Currents*, Jan. 1978, pp. 23-25.

Topor, R. *Marketing Higher Education.* Washington, D.C.: Council for Advancement and Support of Education, 1983.

4

Michael A. Berger

Maximizing Staff Performance

၌Imagine that you have just been asked to coach the U.S. basketball team in the next Olympics. What would you do? The general process you would follow to coach the basketball team could very well be the same process you would follow to get the most and the best from your institutional advancement employees.

The purpose of this chapter is to discuss the principles described in the management literature for getting the most and the best from our employees. The analogy between an institutional advancement executive and a coach may be useful in helping us to understand these principles. To be successful, both roles involve at least eight major skills: (1) selecting the right person, (2) clarifying what is expected, (3) training the person to perform, (4) motivating for excellence, (5) appraising performance, (6) coaching for improvement, (7) creating a special culture, and (8) practicing self-improvement.

Select the Right Person for the Job

As an Olympic basketball coach, you would select the best players you could possibly find. You would expand your search beyond your particular area to uncover the most talented players to help you achieve your objective, the gold medal.

It is true that institutional advancement executives rarely have the time, energy, or inclination to recruit on an extensive basis or to search at length for the most qualified candidate. It is easier to rely on trusted recruiting channels and select the first person who seems good enough for the position.

However, excellence does not flow from such practices. If institutional advancement executives settle for a near match, hoping that a little training and/or experience will close the gap, they may set the stage for poor performance that requires correction later on.

After searching as extensively as possible, executives should interview the candidates carefully, being on the lookout for the following danger signals. First, does the interviewee state that the reason for application is that it is time for a change or that the previous employer was incompetent? Second, does the person focus on salary and benefits too early or talk exclusively about himself or herself, instead of exploring the nature of the job? Third, does the applicant have the enthusiasm, poise, and presentation skills necessary for institutional advancement work? It is possible to get a good idea by observing carefully the person's energy level, knowledge about the job, and attire. Finally, is the applicant technically suited for the position? Attitude and appearance are important, but technical expertise and/or experience in the job are excellent predictors of high-quality performance in the future.

Clarify What Is Expected

Many frustrations and problems occur because employees do not know what is expected. In basketball, if players do not know where to go, when to go there, or what to do once they get there, the team's ability to score will be hampered considerably. When it comes to institutional advancement, the outcomes are no different.

To deal with this problem, employers can often refer to a job analysis form or role description that has been used in the past. In addition, executives can generally assume that the new hire will know, in broad terms, what the job should be and will be able to learn the ropes from other employees.

However, such assumptions may leave too much to chance. Many advancement positions do not have job descriptions, new hires do not always know their jobs, and people vary in their ability to learn the ropes.

The problem is that, in many educational organizations, the work of institutional advancement cannot be compartmentalized into neat and discrete roles. Everybody must pitch in to get out a mailing, prepare properly for calls on potential donors, or complete a capital campaign. Under these circumstances, role descriptions are at best unrealistic and at worst downright dysfunctional.

In these types of situations, the executive is left with the unenviable task of clarifying every role. This is a tall order, but an essential one. Research has shown that people perform better when there is a minimum of role ambiguity (Kahn, Wolfe, Quinn, and Snoek, 1964). The manager must make sure that all employees know both the functions of the institutional advancement office and what is expected of them. If these expectations can be formalized, it is helpful. If they cannot, the executive must sit down periodically with each employee to clarify what that individual must do to achieve excellence.

Train the Person

A good coach knows that, no matter how skilled players are when they join the team, some training will be necessary. Training involves teaching the knowledge, skills, and attitudes that will help an individual perform at the highest possible level. In effect, new, better ways must be learned and old, inappropriate habits (for the situation) must be unlearned.

The problem for institutional advancement executives is that there are limited opportunities for formal training. With the exception of Council for Advancement and Support of Education (CASE) conferences, workshops, and institutes, there are few classes; internships are impractical; and the time that is needed for training takes away from the time available for getting the institutional advancement job done. In spite of these hindrances, education for the job should be viewed as an investment rather than a cost (Nadler, 1980) and will yield dividends in the form of improved performance. Some executives like to do their own training; others prefer to provide opportunities for new employees to learn their jobs from others (Nelson, 1979). Whatever the choice, it is essential that the executives identify what each employee should know, feel, and do to be effective on the job.

Motivate for Excellence

Effective coaches know that getting the right person on the team, clarifying roles, and training are necessary, but that they alone are not enough to produce peak performance. The player must be motivated to do what is expected. All the talent in the world will be useless unless it is channeled in the right direction.

Institutional advancement executives are in a difficult position where motivation is concerned. The manager's ability to provide financial rewards and promotions is often limited, and although it is nice to think that members of the staff will be internally motivated, this is often not the case. The executive must develop creative ways to motivate employees.

A great deal of research has been done on the topic of motivation. Despite the academic debates and language differences, it is possible to discern four principles that can guide the formulation of a motivation strategy (Stoney, 1983).

1. *Integrate employee needs and organizational goals.* Motivation depends directly on what people obtain in exchange for their efforts. Because each person is different, executives must be sensitive to what the various members of the staff want out of their particular jobs. Jobs should be designed so that institutional and individual goals are advanced simultaneously.

2. *Create conditions that facilitate performance.* The challenge here is to develop a climate that will enable all employees to perform to their fullest. Institutional advancement employees are professionals with strong needs for autonomy, involvement, and status. Executives who supervise too closely, fail to include their staff in decisions that affect them, and neglect to confer status on the institutional advancement function will find their employees unwilling to make the effort to achieve the goals of their institution.

3. *Develop a fair management style.* Employees are sensitive to issues of equity. They constantly observe and assess who gets what. Managers who say, "We are all in this together" and "We

all have an equally important job to do," must exhibit behavior that reflects these principles.

4. *Recognize both good and bad performance.* There is a tendency at job appraisal time to dwell on employees' strengths. It is difficult to tell someone bad news or give negative feedback, but individuals need to hear about both the good things they are doing and the behavior that needs correction. If good performance is not recognized and poor performance is ignored, employees will get the message that it does not matter what they do as long as they are doing something. This puts emphasis on effort rather than results.

Appraise Performance

The preceding discussion has touched on the topic of performance appraisal. Effective coaches constantly tell their players how they are doing. Some coaches are more vocal in this area than others, but the successful ones continually appraise performance both formally and informally, so their players always know where they stand.

The norm in academia, however, does not often allow for frequent and timely performance appraisal. More often than not, performance is appraised only once a year and in a less-than-satisfying manner. Preparation time for the appraisal is often short or nonexistent, the goals for the appraisal are not always explicit, and in the end, appraisal becomes an unpleasant event that everyone does, but with no real effect.

This should not be the case. Appraisal should occur every day of the year. The executive must develop a systematic procedure to let all employees know how they are doing. When it is time for the appraisal interview, the executive should put the employee at ease, explain the purpose of the interview, listen to what the employee has to say, avoid arguments, focus on performance, point out both strengths and areas for improvement, and develop a plan for employee development.

Common pitfalls in performance appraisal ratings have been reviewed by Creviston and Freed (1983, p. 86), who warn against the "recency effect" (over-attention to a contribution or mistake made just prior to the review) and the "central tendency" (rating all employees average by choosing mostly middle ratings).

Coach for Improvement

The coaching analogy in this chapter has not been accidental. The coaching concept applies to executives in general and institutional advancement executives more specifically. To be sure, the roles of boss and supervisor are still essential for effective operation of the institutional advancement office. Increasingly, however, the literature of management adds to the executive's job description the role of mentor or coach (Kirkpatrick, 1982).

Coaching, like any other skill, can be learned, although some managers are more effective in the process than others. Coaching is largely a matter of attitude. To be a successful coach, one must endorse with enthusiasm the responsibility for employee development.

The following are some principles that can guide successful coaching within the institutional advancement office. First, the executive should initiate contact with the employee to discuss development. Second, mentoring should be done on a regular, on-going basis (with good and poor performers alike). Third, executives should offer advice on both what to do and how to do a job more effectively. Finally, if there are problems in the employee's performance, the executive should help the employee determine the causes of those problems and plan strategies to overcome the performance barriers.

Create a Special Culture

One of the fundamental lessons coming out of the management literature in the past several years is the importance of shared values as a performance factor (Peters and Waterman, 1982). Japanese managers sensitized us to the significance of culture, and American authors have observed that the most successful organizations—public and private—seem to have strong, cohesive cultures that bind members together in a familylike way (Deal and Kennedy, 1982).

The concept of culture is not difficult to understand. Put simply, *culture* means "the way things are done around here." All organizations have their own special culture. Although most cultures develop in a haphazard way, modern management thinking assigns the executive the responsibility to create a special culture (Deal and Kennedy, 1982).

How can this be done? First, the executive must become aware of the impact of symbols in the organization. Advocates of culture argue that rituals, ceremonies, heroes, stories, and networks communicate the organization's critical values and have an important effect on the way the employee behaves on the job. Where such symbols are congruent with the essential values of the institution, a strong culture will result. Where they are not, or where there is a conflict in values, a fragmented culture will be evident, and people will feel less attached to the organization.

Second, if it is true that symbolic representations are significant in the management of human resources, then it follows that the organization's critical values must be made explicit. This process usually occurs through the development of slogans, logos, and philosophical statements as to what the organization stands for. If this has not occurred, institutional advancement executives should create ways to communicate what their school is all about.

Third, advocates of culture recognize the importance of rituals and ceremonies in reinforcing and transmitting the organization's culture to its constituencies. Graduation falls into this category; the prescription here is to look for and create a whole host of other rituals that (1) recognize excellence, (2) communicate the importance of students, (3) celebrate the institution's founders, (4) allow employees to play and relax together, (5) dramatize the institution's mission, and (6) affirm everyone's contribution to the organization as a whole.

Fourth, stories that underscore the key values of the institution should be told and retold. Stories transmit the institution's history, heroes, and heroines. Stories are important, not only because they are interesting to hear and share but also because they communicate the ingredients of the culture and the values that should guide behavior.

Fifth, the heroes and heroines of the organization should be recognized. At many colleges and universities, there is a founder's-day type of celebration, but advocates of culture go much farther. They argue that heroes and heroines of the present should be anointed and acknowledged. Achievements that are noteworthy should be rewarded, and effort that has failed to produce results should be recognized for its innovative, risk-taking value.

Finally, executives should become more sensitive to the importance of cultural networks. Networks do not always mean formal relationships and the organizational chart. To the contrary, the concept of network includes all the informal systems that make the organization run. The principle is that it is important for executives to identify and use the natural linkages that hold people together, for these networks transmit information, get the tough jobs done, and enable people to come together in times of adversity.

Practice Self-Improvement

No coach retains a leadership position without self-development. Likewise, human resources managers must not stop learning, growing, and changing. They must attend seminars, read widely, expand their areas of expertise, and share their knowledge with others. They must consider sociological, economic, political, and technological trends that determine the institutional advancement environment so that they detect trends and resolve problems as they develop. Managers must be prepared to confront the following sorts of major issues:

1. *Scope of training programs.* Training and development programs must be broadened to enable personnel to adjust to the rapidly changing nature and mix of functional responsibilities and the skills needed to perform them. The assignment grows more complex in accommodating with fairness minority groups, women, the handicapped, and older persons seeking employment.

2. *Retrenchment decisions.* Pressures faced by colleges and universities in adapting to limited resources and financial constraints require managers to learn and enforce proper

termination procedures for insufficient performance and required cutbacks and/or redirections. They must also appreciate and understand grievance and complaint procedures and must work sensitively with other areas of the institution on maintaining and enhancing organizational morale.

3. *Employee involvement programs.* Many nonprofit organizations are expanding employee involvement programs that stress the importance of clear, two-way communication. Academic institutions have long prided themselves on the principles of shared governance and a free exchange of information and ideas. Within the organization, the institutional advancement office can be looked to as a place that believes in and practices team spirit and quality-of-worklife programs.

4. *Entitlement Expectations.* To what degree are personnel entitled to complete medical care, high wages, long vacations, sick pay, regular wage increases, and training? "Entitlements will increasingly be viewed as taxes—a necessary cost of doing business. . . . Failure to meet this growing expectation will assure an employer of a substandard workforce" (Search, 1983, p. 154).

Bibliographical Essay

Information on the selection process is discussed authoritatively in Middlemist, Hitt, and Greer's (1983) book *Personnel Management: Jobs, People, and Logic.* The Kahn, Wolfe, Quinn, and Snoek (1964) volume *Organizational Stress: Studies in Role Conflict and Ambiguity* is the classic empirical work on the deleterious effects of role ambiguity.

Leonard Nadler's (1980) book *Corporate Human Resources Development* makes the education-as-an-investment argument. Nelson (1979) underscores the importance of training new employees.

Stoney (1983) examines the topic of motivation. Performance appraisal and the notion of coaching appear in Kirkpatrick's (1982) book *How to Improve Performance Through Appraisal and Coaching.*

Shared values and culture as determinants of high performance appear in two recent management best sellers. The first is by Peters and Waterman (1982), *In Search of Excellence*; the second is Deal and Kennedy's (1982) *Corporate Cultures*. Another helpful source is Sayles's (1981) *Managing Human Resources*.

References

Creviston, R. L., and Freed, J. W. "Performance Appraisal." In W. K. Fallon (ed.), *AMA Management Handbook*. (2nd ed.) New York: American Management Associations, 1983.

Deal, T., and Kennedy, A. *Corporate Cultures*. Reading, Mass.: Addison-Wesley, 1982.

Kahn, R., Wolfe, D., Quinn, R., and Snoek, J. *Organizational Stress: Studies in Role Conflict and Ambiguity*. New York: Wiley, 1964.

Kirkpatrick, D. *How to Improve Performance Through Appraisal and Coaching*. New York: American Management Associations, 1982.

Middlemist, R., Hitt, M., and Greer, C. *Personnel Management: Jobs, People, and Logic*. Englewood Cliffs, N.J.: Prentice-Hall, 1983.

Nadler, L. *Corporate Human Resources Development*. New York: Van Nostrand Reinhold, 1980.

Nelson, D. "Sandpapering, Polishing, and Buffing Your Clones." *CASE Currents*, June 1979, pp. 20–23.

Peters, T. J., and Waterman, R. H. *In Search of Excellence*. New York: Harper & Row, 1982.

Sayles, L. *Managing Human Resources*. (2nd ed.) Englewood Cliffs, N.J.: Prentice-Hall, 1981.

Search, R. M. "Human Resources Management—Looking Ahead." In W. K. Fallon (ed.), *AMA Management Handbook*. (2nd ed.) New York: American Management Associations, 1983.

Stoney, C. "40 Carrots: To Motivate Employees, Try Listening to Their Needs." *CASE Currents*, May 1983, pp. 22–27.

5

Barbara W. Snelling

Recruiting, Training, and Managing Volunteers

❧ The volunteer is central to the effectiveness of institutional advancement, an irreplaceable member of the team. Each new recruit inherits a tradition for volunteering that is as old as the United States itself. As Alexis de Tocqueville observed more than 150 years ago, nothing is more typical of democracy in this country than the eagerness of its citizens to "give each other mutual support when needed" ([1835, 1840], 1966, p. 546).

Significance of Volunteers

Today, more than 84 million Americans over age twelve perform some sort of voluntary service. The estimated monetary value of such work is $64.5 million a year (Independent Sector, 1984). More important than the monetary value, volunteering adds value to the individual or group helped, to the individual who volunteers, and to society.

Volunteering in all its various forms—from board member to phonathon worker—is essentially the process of giving freely of one's time, energies, and endorsement to a worthy cause. It is a philanthropic act, representing a gift that can be as valuable to an institution as the contribution of money or property. Thus the volunteer deserves the careful attention that is usually reserved for donors and donor prospects. Indeed, the giving of time and talent seems to correlate with the giving of dollars. *Giving USA* (American Association of Fund-Raising Counsel, 1984) points out that volunteer workers are much more apt to be financial donors to their own cause, and even to unrelated causes, than those who do not work as volunteers.

Volunteers, however, are essential to the institutional advancement effort for what they do, quite separately from their potential as financial contributors. A key ingredient in the institutional advancement process is involvement, and the volunteer personifies involvement, through personal actions and through interaction with others. The successful institutional advancement manager understands and values the irreplaceable role of volunteers and recognizes that building strong volunteer relationships is the underpinning of an effective program.

Motivation for Volunteering

A survey by the U.S. Bureau of the Census (1974) found that individuals listed "Wanted to help others" as the leading reason for volunteering. "Enjoy volunteer work itself" and "Had a sense of duty" were also high on the list.

The source of the motivation for volunteering may be argued, but whether it is a desire for self-satisfaction or a genetic concern for the survival of the human race, the motivation is the same for both forms of philanthropy—a desire to improve the quality of human life. Volunteering might well be considered the primary form of philanthropy because, without the gift of talent and work, there would be little use for the gift of money. Certainly our society will only be able to preserve the tradition of voluntary financial contributions if our institutions recognize that the value of the gift of self is at least equal to the gift of wealth.

Role of Volunteers

Volunteers provide to an institution strength that is available from no other source. The testimony of volunteers concerning their beliefs builds trust in others. Through their dedication, they visibly demonstrate their personal endorsement of the institution's mission and objectives, lending their own reputations as validation of that mission. Because they act without direct self-interest, volunteers provide a depth of credibility that no one else can offer. Their message in support of the institution carries a compelling sincerity and conviction that employees of the institution, because of their presumed self-interest, cannot manage.

Volunteers bring enthusiasm, energy, advice, new ideas, and a fresh perspective. They serve as effort multipliers, extending programs in ways that the institution could not otherwise afford. They provide a personal communication link with the constituencies they represent. This means they serve as an interface in interpreting the institution's goals and in asking for support. Of equal importance, as they report the reactions and feelings of their colleagues, they provide the institution with an external perspective on its performance.

Relationship to Professionals

The volunteer and the professional are partners in a cause. In order to make the partnership function effectively, the professional must accept certain principles, which are essentially the professional's part of an unspoken contract given in exchange for the volunteer's gift of time and endorsement. These inherent principles were recognized officially in this country when philanthropy was institutionalized and the role of volunteers, in the form of trustees for not-for-profit corporations, was written into law. Volunteer and staff relationships are derived from these same underlying principles.

The professional must endorse a concept of volunteers that affirms their role as disinterested, objective guardians of the institution's mission. This means acceptance of a belief that ultimately the best policy, decisions, and actions will come from the education, participation, and responsibility of a volunteer group that is given full exposure to the problems and challenges of the organization. It also means giving the volunteers full authority and opportunity to work out solutions and new directions. Clearly, the professional and the volunteer must share a dedication to the leadership, mission, and future of the institution.

The professional should inform, educate, guide, and inspire without directing in an authoritarian fashion. This leadership is more in the sphere of art than science and will never be reduced to technique. It is, nevertheless, the essence of the process of a successful relationship and is the distinguishing characteristic of the best institutional advancement professionals. "A professional sets his or her sights high and doesn't settle for anything but the larger dream" (Kendrick, 1978, p. 25).

The art of leadership is made more difficult by the fact that not all volunteers serve at the level of the board of trustees, where practice is usually defined clearly in bylaws and precedents. However, the principles remain the same, no matter what the volunteer assignment. Volunteers should have the opportunity to participate in setting goals, in deciding on the implementation plan, and in the outcome of any project. Skillful professionals willingly engage in the goal-sharing process, because they recognize that enfranchising the volunteer is crucial to motivation and continuing interest.

Volunteers can function productively at every level of an institution's organizational structure. The range of opportunity is wide: boards of trustees, foundation boards, visiting committees, advisory councils, institutional relations committees, alumni boards, alumni program committees, development councils, and annual, capital, and planned giving committees, among other functions. Although the most effective and significant use of volunteers is in providing an interface with the constituencies they represent, there is also a multitude of specific services that they can perform.

No matter what the role of the volunteer, the volunteer's gift of time should be respected by the professional. There is a responsibility to see that this gift is cherished, not wasted or abused. The stewardship of the volunteer's time is analogous to, and should be taken as seriously as, the stewardship of a voluntary gift of money in which considerable care is given to ensure that the money is managed well and used only for specified purposes.

Organization and Planning

The volunteer/staff partnership is productive only if the institution invests adequate staff time and budget. Careful guidance and logistical support provide the framework for a sense of purpose and achievement.

Each level of the volunteer structure necessitates corresponding levels of administrative staff providing support. The president, with appropriate assistance, is the prime staff for the board of trustees. Vice-presidents, deans, and institutional advancement officers serve as staff to other groups of volunteers. All staff members serving in this role should understand the implications of the volunteer/staff relationship. Orientation sessions for academic and administrative staff increase understanding of the value of volunteers and how to work effectively with them.

Thoughtful advance planning is the best guarantee that volunteer involvement will fulfill expectations. Well before recruitment begins, the professional staff should analyze the reasons for using volunteers. It is wise to define in writing the purpose of the group, their responsibilities, the extent of their governance role (if any), the range of their decision powers, the restrictions on their role, their reporting lines, and the way in which their activities will be staffed.

It is also useful to decide in advance whether there will be an established termination for the volunteer group, terms of office, or some kind of automatic review of the need to continue the activity. There should also be an estimated timetable for various accomplishments in order to clarify the scope of the project. It is also necessary in a large institution to identify those other volunteer groups and professional staff with whom they will interact. There should be a clear mandate for their actions. If there will be any overlapping responsibilities, or even competing groups, guidelines should be included that define the way in which potential conflicts will be clarified and resolved, or managed and coordinated.

Although not all volunteer activity will fit neatly into a hierarchical structure, most will. In each case it should be possible to designate the appropriate administrative officer responsible for working with the volunteers. This type of organizational structure provides a visible career ladder for volunteers that allows them to progress to more responsible positions.

Advance preparation is followed by informing appropriate parts of the institution of the plan so that groups who might not otherwise appreciate the program will not only tolerate but also support the volunteer effort.

Selection of Volunteers

Job descriptions for individual volunteer positions or roles should be prepared, based on written analyses and definition of purpose. Descriptions should specify the tasks to be performed, activities to be undertaken, and required talents and skills. A decision should be made as to whether the volunteer group will need to be representative of a variety of constituencies, age groups, or geographic areas. If the committee will serve as a communication link, the membership must have an effective relationship with the larger membership of the constituency with which they will be working. They must not only know the territory in terms of being familiar with the formal and informal structural systems but also should know and be known by the decision makers and should be considered peers by those with whom they will work. Whatever it is they will ask of others, they must have demonstrated their own willingness to perform. To determine the optimum number of volunteers required, consider the scope of the assignment and the need for representation. Identifying a pool of prospects, including first, second, and third choices for each position, is useful whenever possible. The objective is to create a team that will function well together and will enjoy and benefit from each other's company.

Highly important is the selection of the chair of the volunteer endeavor. The most important characteristics are dedication and commitment of the individual to the institution and knowledge and understanding of its purpose and direction. The individual should be articulate and effective as a public spokesperson for the group. If the chair has experience and skill as a leader, the group will function more effectively. The chair should be the most appropriate person for the specific assignment, time, and circumstance.

When selecting volunteers for any position, the following traits should be paramount: "commitment and loyalty to the institution; influence, clout, respect in community; knowledge about institution; history of financial support to institution; persistence; commitment of time; ability to communicate; enthusiasm; leadership ability; and ability to work with others" (Chambers, 1978, p. 25).

Recruiting

Recruiting all volunteers, including the chair, should be done face-to-face by the highest-level volunteer and staff member commensurate with the importance of the group to be recruited. Sometimes only the chair of the board and the president will do. In other cases, the activities of the group will be so far removed from these individuals that this approach may be inappropriate. The most influential and effective volunteers should be recruited first. They can assist in attracting others. Recruiters should give personal assurance that the request is for a task that is genuinely important to the institution and that all necessary assistance and support will be guaranteed from the top for the project's success.

Recruiting is a kind of selling. However, twisting the arms of those who are not really willing to commit themselves is a serious mistake. Too many names listed on volunteer committees represent inactive members who never wanted to be on the committee but acquiesced under pressure. This is a debilitating handicap to any volunteer project. The positive aspects should be stressed, but there should be total honesty in assessing the work that is necessary for successful accomplishment. If volunteers do not understand from the beginning what is expected of them, they will be annoyed and frustrated as the project progresses.

Good public relations enhances recruitment. Everyone prefers to join a successful venture. It is valuable to have the success story known by as many people as possible. Effective media coverage and stimulating publications are critical. Skillful press relations place the accomplishments of the volunteers before others.

Training and Education

Many volunteers will be familiar with the institution. However, they will possess varying degrees of knowledge.

Orientation sessions should be organized carefully. They should be pleasant, sociable, and genuinely educational. They should inform the volunteer about problems as well as assets of the institution. The objectives of the specific project should be clearly set forth. Above all, sessions should emphasize the importance of the volunteer to the success of the overall project. These sessions are a time for goal-sharing and team-building, generating motivation and enthusiasm that translate into momentum for action.

The educational effort should not be limited to the initial orientation. A continuing flow of information and concern is essential. Letters, newsletters, meetings, and phone calls help reassure, reinforce, and motivate.

Evaluation

As with good management in any organization, evaluation of the performance of volunteers starts with their participation in planning the work assignment. If the program is carefully planned by the volunteer/staff team, with agreed-upon goals and implementation plans, there will be little doubt whether the objective has been achieved. The professionals are responsible for intervention with alternative strategies if plans get off track or prove to be faulty, but the key person in regrouping the volunteers—chiding, remonstrating, or encouraging as needed—is the chair of the committee. This is one more reason why the selection of the chair is crucial to the outcome.

Appreciation and Recognition

Representatives of the institution must express appreciation at all stages of the project—at the beginning, while in process, and at the conclusion. Volunteers deserve the reward of recognition and tribute appropriate to the task. Usually this will be public, but sometimes a volunteer genuinely wants anonymity. In such cases, personal phone calls and private dinners are useful. Persons who have enjoyed a rewarding experience will volunteer again for tougher assignments. They will supply an experienced and reliable source of continuing help. Those who have been outstanding should be recruited promptly for higher responsibilities with broader scope and increased visibility. This will encourage others and demonstrate that volunteer work well done brings both gratitude and an opportunity for greater service.

Recognition programs are conducted at many levels. National programs include the Volunteer Recognition Program of the Council for Advancement and Support of Education. Independent Sector and the Advertising Council used television, radio and print media for publicizing its "Lend a Hand" campaign to encourage gifts of time and money to nonprofit organizations. At the local level, campuses have developed a wide assortment of plaques, awards, recognition walls in buildings, dinners, publications, and communication programs.

The Volunteer's Perspective

Day in and day out, institutional advancement professionals should work at increasing their understanding of the staff/ volunteer partnership from the volunteer's point of view. One of the most effective ways to gain this perspective is to serve as a volunteer for another organization. Institutional advancement officers should place themselves in the shoes of volunteers by championing the "Bill of Rights for Volunteers" developed by the American Red Cross:

> (1) The right to be treated as a co-worker, not just as free help, not as a prima donna. (2) The right to a suitable assignment, with consideration for personal preference, temperament, life experience, education, and employment background. (3) The right to know as much about the organization as possible—its policies, its people, its programs. (4) The right to training for the job, thoughtfully planned and effectively presented training. (5) The right to continuing education on the job, as a follow-up to initial training, including information about new

developments and training for greater responsibility. (6) The right to sound guidance and direction by someone who is experienced, well-informed, patient, and thoughtful and who has the time to invest in giving guidance. (7) The right to a place to work—an orderly, designated place, conducive to work and worthy of the job to be done. (8) The right to promotion and a variety of experiences—through advancement to assignments of more responsibility, through transfer from one activity to another, through special assignments. (9) The right to be heard—to have a part in planning, to feel free to make suggestions, to have respect shown for an honest opinion. (10) The right to recognition, in the form of promotion and awards, through day-to-day expressions of appreciation and by being treated as a bona fide co-worker [American Red Cross, 1982].

Bibliographical Essay

Edited by Maddalena (1980), *Encouraging Voluntarism and Volunteers* discusses the growth of volunteer involvement in higher education, the role of volunteers in fund-raising and alumni programs, and the value of communication and training programs. A valuable bibliography is also presented.

O'Connell's (1983) book of readings, *America's Voluntary Spirit*, collects speeches, articles, chapters, and papers about giving and volunteering over the past 300 years. The bibliography includes 500 titles.

Volunteers, by Lauffer and Gorodezky (1983), outlines step-by-step procedures for successfully recruiting volunteers, assigning tasks, handling orientation, training volunteers, and supervising their work.

A special issue titled "Here's to Volunteers!" was published by *CASE Currents* (Council for Advancement and Support of Education, 1978). Another special issue focused on students (Council for Advancement and Support of Education, 1977).

References

American Association of Fund-Raising Counsel. *Giving USA: 1983 Annual Report.* New York: American Association of Fund-Raising Counsel, 1984.

American Red Cross. "The Bill of Rights for Volunteers." *Fund Raising Management,* Aug. 1982, p. 26.

Chambers, O. W. "Recruiting: Don't Just Guess." *CASE Currents,* Mar. 1978, pp. 25–26.

Council for Advancement and Support of Education. "Special Issue: Students—How to Attract, Assist and Involve Them." *CASE Currents,* Mar. 1977.

Council for Advancement and Support of Education. "Special Issue: Here's to Volunteers!" *CASE Currents,* Mar. 1978.

Independent Sector. *A Four-Year Review.* Washington, D.C.: Independent Sector, 1984.

Kendrick, M. "Eight Faults to Avoid." *CASE Currents,* Mar. 1978, pp. 22–25.

Lauffer, A., and Gorodezky, S. *Volunteers.* Beverly Hills, Calif.: Sage, 1983.

Maddalena, L. A. (ed.). *Encouraging Voluntarism and Volunteers.* New Directions for Institutional Advancement, no. 9. San Francisco: Jossey-Bass, 1980.

O'Connell, B. (ed.). *America's Voluntary Spirit: A Book of Readings.* New York: Foundation Center, 1983.

Pray, F. C. (gen. ed.). *Handbook for Educational Fund Raising: A Guide to Successful Principles and Practices for Colleges, Universities, and Schools.* San Francisco: Jossey-Bass, 1981.

Tocqueville, A. de. *Democracy in America.* (J. P. Mayer and M. Lerner, eds.) New York: Harper & Row, 1966. (Originally published 1835, 1840.)

U.S. Bureau of the Census. *American Volunteer,* 1974, pp. 12–13.

6

James F. Ridenour

Analyzing Costs
and Allocating Finances

❧ Common measures of the success of an institutional advancement office are staying within the budget, managing to avoid any major public relations faux pas, raising the dollars to achieve the established financial goal, and keeping the alumni and legislators happy. These may be familiar approaches to assessing performance, but they may all fall short when it comes to resource management. Perhaps the institution should be attaining higher levels of moral and financial support by spending additional resources wisely. The lost opportunity is a cost that needs to be considered in institutional advancement.

Therefore, raising more money with less is not the central interest of this chapter. Rather, we shall examine how we can allocate our resources to attain the best results. We should place our resources of people and dollars where they will be the most effective for the mission and goals of the institution.

Institutional advancement involves all the activities undertaken to improve the resources needed to achieve these goals. "It is one of the functions of planning and management to define each of the advancement activities for the institution, so that each of them furthers the total institutional purpose. This coordination also prevents resources from being wasted on duplication" (Jenny, 1977, pp. 499-500).

The management of financial resources can be termed the cost-effectiveness side of the enterprise. Although this bottom-line approach carries with it the measure of our institutional advancement programs, it also carries the opportunity to do a more effective job for our institution. In short, the manager assures that the advancement program builds a logical, orderly, and sound process for securing and allocating resources to get meaningful results.

Cost of Raising a Dollar

Solid information on how much it costs to raise a dollar is unfortunately a scarce commodity. The studies by John Leslie (1971, 1978) and G. T. Smith (1974, pp. 37–47) are excellent. Many other persons have collected data here and there in an attempt to obtain a new staff member or justify a new expenditure. The common problem of definitions remains—just how much do we count gifts and expenditures? Unless some common measures are agreed on, the collected data will be of limited value. Mixing apples and oranges in a balance sheet provides nice fruit salad, but it is not helpful in measuring performance, even between similar institutions. For the first time, these definitions have been made by a Council for the Advancement and Support of Education and National Association of College and University Business Officers committee and published in *Management Reporting Standards for Educational Institutions: Fund Raising and Related Activities* (Council for the Advancement and Support of Education and National Association of College and University Business Officers, 1982). When an institution can put its records into this standard format and an effective data collection process can be implemented, the ideal of being able to compare results with others can be achieved. The standards and management report formats provide sound tools for monitoring not only fund-raising but also the relationship between fund-raising efforts and associated program activities in public relations and alumni affairs. A helpful background paper on the standards has been published by Heemann (1981).

The Initial Steps

The first step in resource management is to determine, with administration and trustees, the mission of the institution and the long-range goals that will fulfill that purpose. It is sad, but true, that many institutions have lost sight of their mission, or their mission statement is not clear or distinctive enough to warrant support. The National Center for Education Statistics lists 3,331 institutions of higher education for 1984–85 (Jacobson, 1985, p. 2). Therefore, there should be 3,331 definable and salable cases for support. Without a strong case, specific objectives are difficult to define, and effective resource allocation is not possible.

The second step is to develop the specific objectives for the next twelve to eighteen months. If a capital campaign is a part of these specific objectives, the campaign should be outlined separately, covering the length of time involved. Although the campaign should be coordinated with the regular objectives, it should have its own budget and resource allocation.

Break-Even Point Analysis

Before you begin to put together a budget for these specific objectives, it would be helpful to establish the break-even point for each of the major objectives. Determine the fixed and variable costs for both the programs you have and the ones you wish to have. "The process of classifying costs is a necessary first step in a break-even analysis. At times, this process is complicated by the fact that the types of costs being classified may be partly fixed and partly variable" (Massie, 1971, p. 109). By developing a break-even point for each program, it is possible to see how much money must be raised and how spending more or less on the variable costs will affect the bottom line.

Take a deferred-giving program as an example. Fixed costs could be the salary and benefits for a deferred-gift director and basic secretarial support. Variable costs are the costs of travel, entertainment, publications, and mailings.

Some programs may be judged to be successful below the break-even point, with other measurements used to determine effectiveness. Many public relations functions fall within this category—but it is clear that a total advancement program in which public relations and fund-raising are out of balance will have difficulty justifying itself. An institution cannot argue convincingly that it is doing things just for some abstract public relations value. On the other hand, public relations programs that inform, cultivate, and reinforce are an essential part of the total institutional advancement process and contribute to bottom-line results in fund-raising, government relations, and student recruitment. Fortunately, progress is being made in evaluating public relations effectiveness (Jacobson, 1978; Tirone, 1977). The Public Relations Measurement Project in one organization developed procedures to assess six functions, leading the project director to conclude, "I think we have proved factually and decisively, that it is possible to measure some aspects of public relations performance" ("How the Bell System Measures Public Relations," 1978–79, p. 5).

Some fund-raising programs, particularly ones that seek to attract new donors, may be deemed successful if they merely break even. If the trustees and administration wish to broaden public awareness of the institution and its case of support, a program may well be launched with success measured merely by paying the fixed and variable costs.

Hence, the specific costs to raise a dollar may vary significantly by program and by institution. Institutions with mature deferred-giving and capital-giving track records find these costs below 10 percent of revenue. Overall advancement costs vary tremendously by institution, but a fair goal to shoot for seems to be between twenty and twenty-five cents on each dollar raised. Cost studies show personnel and fringe benefit costs to be an increasingly large part of the advancement budget. The percentage figure has risen steadily, from 30–35 percent, salary only (Leslie, 1971), to 60–65 percent, salary and fringe benefits (Leslie, 1978), and 65–70 percent, salary and fringe benefits (Ridenour, 1983). As CASE-NACUBO standards are increasingly applied, benchmarks will become more widely based and more reliable.

Program Priorities

Before starting on the budget, it is wise to look at your present resources for allocation or reallocation. Then you can select priorities. In response to immediate demands, most operations tend to grow year by year by adding personnel, paperwork, and programs. Are all of them necessary? Remember, at least 50 percent of your money should come from 1 percent of your donors, and 40 percent more from the next 10 percent of your donors—90 percent of the dollars from 11 percent of your constituency. Are you allocating resources to take advantage of this fundamental fund-raising principle? Are you planning for the replacement of those key donors in the future? Sometimes the temptation is strong to let the program be dictated by the noisy majority of "what we have always done" and, as a result, to neglect the importance of the key donor, present and future.

How well is your organization staffed to implement the three basic areas of fund-raising—the annual fund, capital and endowment projects, and deferred giving? How well are you staffed to fulfill your goals and objectives in alumni, governmental, and public relations? Are there special characteristics of your mission, such as church relations, that require special attention in staffing and resources?

With the information in place from the above exercises, you are now in a position to recommend and defend a budget requesting the resources needed to accomplish the objectives. Accountants and financial officers should coordinate the budget system for the institution but not prepare budgets for other departments. You have a responsibility to prepare your own budget. If you can demonstrate a bottom-line return, both present and future, your chance of a satisfactory experience through the budget processes is enhanced. Without a reasonable, well-conceived resource management program, there is little opportunity for success, either for the budget or the total advancement program.

CASE-NACUBO Management Study

The CASE-NACUBO study, *Management Reporting Standards for Educational Institutions: Fund Raising and Related Activities* (Council for the Advancement and Support of Education and National Association of College and University Business Officers, 1982) can help by analyzing the past, forecasting the future, planning programs, and managing resources. As with a number of CASE programs, the study encourages professionalism in the advancement field.

First of all, the booklet defines how to count gifts, both by source and by purpose. The variety of ways this has been done in the past is endless, but with the definitions provided, each institution will be able to establish a uniform pattern. The advantages in this are obvious—the comparability of data from year to year within the institution as well as from one institution to another. The annual survey of the Council for Financial Aid to Education has adopted these same definitions and format to further encourage uniformity in the profession (Council for Financial Aid to Education, 1985).

Second, the study outlines a suggested method for listing costs by major area and by program. With these data, a manager can measure costs against revenue received from year to year and soon will be able to check costs against groups of similar institutions. The importance of this practice in setting priority and reallocating resources can hardly be overstated.

Reporting Financial Data

Because financial matters have taken center stage in higher education, a word should be said about the presentation and interpretation of financial statements. "There remains not a single academic institution in this country where the debates over money are not at least as central as those over study content and student life" (*Change* Panel on Academic Economics, 1976, p. 13).

First, the language of finance is a special language. It takes some getting used to. The layperson may find the shorthand of financial reporting quite perplexing. This suggests that persons on the advancement staff can play a significant role in making financial reports comprehensible to readers.

Second, keep in mind the concept of reporting in absolute and relative terms. Basic financial statements and many supporting schedules set forth economic data in absolute terms. For example, the balance at year-end in the balance sheet and the totals of revenues, expenditures, and other changes for the year are expressed as so many dollars for each category, source, function, or fund.

However, economic values can also be expressed in relative terms by comparing figures with a standard, norm, guideline, budget, forecast, prior year, or other point of reference (Robinson, 1975, p. 2).

Third, financial data constitute a one-dimensional expression in a multidimensional environment. "Money is only one of three major resources employed by institutions of higher education; the others are people and facilities. All three resources have meaning not as ends in themselves, but only in relation to the primary functions of the institutions: instruction, research, and public service" (p. 2).

The Mixture of Art and Science

I have stressed the importance of cost-effectiveness. It is equally necessary to state the importance of ethical human relationships. "You shall love your neighbor as yourself" (Matt. 19:19) is a sound base for ethical relationships. It is often the little things we do that make a big difference in fund-raising. As Harold J. "Sy" Seymour noted in his classic *Designs for Fund Raising* (1966, p. 183), "The first of my operating suggestions to newcomers, and perhaps the best, is to quickly acquire the habit of being ever watchful for the tremendous trifles."

This idea is reinforced by the authors of *In Search of Excellence* (Peters and Waterman, 1982), who warn that we are in danger of losing staff productivity if we overemphasize bottom-line accounting. John Naisbitt (1982) in *Megatrends* refers to the need for "high touch" to go along with the element of "high tech." It is just as important to be a teacher and a leader as to be a manager in finding the best role for the staff. These ideas are further developed in Chapter One, "Skills and Criteria for Managerial Effectiveness," and Chapter Four, "Maximizing Staff Performance."

Most people attracted to institutional advancement want to be successful and to know how well they are doing. They welcome the benchmarks provided by measuring progress toward clearly stated objectives. They appreciate a chance to find a place where they can excel. The secret to a successful office remains in the proper mixture of art and science.

Keep in mind the advice of James Binns, then sales manager, later president and chairman of Armstrong World Industries, given to me as a fledgling salesman thirty years ago. He said, "There may be three or four ways of doing a job, but be sure to select one—and then make it work." Too often in education, it seems, we spend too long talking about the alternatives, forgetting that nothing is going to happen until we do something.

Now is the time to do something about the generation and allocation of resources at your institution.

Bibliographical Essay

Colleges and universities now have available four publications that advance the cause of presenting uniform standards for financial accounting and reporting in higher education. These references are the AICPA guide *Audits of Colleges and Universities* (American Institute of Certified Public Accountants, 1973), Part 5 of NACUBO's Administrative Service and of the third edition of *College and University Business Administration* (National Association of College and University Business Officers, 1984), the NCHEMS *Higher Education Finance Manual* (National Center for Higher Education Management Systems, 1977), and the CASE-NACUBO *Management Reporting Standards for Educational Institutions: Fund Raising and Related Activities* (1982).

Other suggested references are Heemann (1979), Leslie (1969, 1971, 1978), Munger and Ridenour (1983), Ridenour and Munger (1983), and Ridenour (1983). Also recommended is *Financial Responsibilities of Governing Boards of Colleges and Universities* (Association of Governing Boards of Universities and Colleges and National Association of College and University Business Officers, 1979).

References

American Institute of Certified Public Accountants. *Audits of Colleges and Universities.* New York: American Institute of Certified Public Accountants, 1973.

Association of Governing Boards of Universities and Colleges and National Association of College and University Business Officers. *Financial Responsibilities of Governing Boards of Colleges and Universities.* Washington, D.C.: Association of Governing Boards of Universities and Colleges and National Association of College and University Business Officers, 1979.

Change Panel on Academic Economics. *Colleges and Money: A Faculty Guide to Academic Economics.* New Rochelle, N.Y.: *Change Magazine* and Educational Change, 1976.

Council for the Advancement and Support of Education and National Association of College and University Business Officers. *Management Reporting Standards for Educational Institutions: Fund Raising and Related Activities.* Washington, D.C.: Council for Advancement and Support of Education and National Association of College and University Business Officers, 1982.

Council for Financial Aid to Education. *Voluntary Support of Education, 1983–84.* New York: Division of Research, Council for Financial Aid to Education, 1985.

Heemann, W. (ed.). *Analyzing the Cost Effectiveness of Fund Raising.* New Directions for Institutional Advancement, no. 3. San Francisco: Jossey-Bass, 1979.

Heemann, W. "Reporting the Results—A New Tool for Fund Raisers." *CASE Currents,* Sept. 1981, pp. 46–48.

"How the Bell System Measures Public Relations." *Utilities Section F.Y.I.* (Public Relations Society of America, New York), Winter 1978–79.

Jacobson, H. K. (ed.). *Evaluating Advancement Programs.* New Directions for Institutional Advancement, no. 1. San Francisco: Jossey-Bass, 1978.

Jacobson, R. L. "The New Academic Year: Signs of Uneasiness amid Calm and Stability on Many Campuses." *Chronicle of Higher Education,* Sept. 4, 1985, pp. 1–3.

Jenny, H. H. "The Management of Resources." In A. W. Rowland (ed.), *Handbook of Institutional Advancement: A Practical Guide to College and University Relations, Fund Raising, Alumni Relations, Government Relations, Publications, and*

Executive Management for Continued Advancement. San Francisco: Jossey-Bass, 1977.

Leslie, J. W. *Focus on Understanding and Support.* Washington, D.C.: American College Public Relations Association, 1969.

Leslie, J. W. *Seeking the Competitive Dollar: College Management in the Seventies.* Washington, D.C.: American College Public Relations Association, 1971.

Leslie, J. W. "Analyzing Resource Allocation in Institutional Advancement Programs." Paper presented at District 1 Conference, Council for Advancement and Support of Education, Hyannis, Mass., Jan. 31, 1978.

Massie, J. L. *Essentials of Management.* Englewood Cliffs, N.J.: Prentice-Hall, 1971.

Munger, P. L., and Ridenour, J. F. "Deferred Gift Reporting." *Business Officer,* Feb. 1983, pp. 16–17.

Naisbitt, J. *Megatrends.* New York: Warner Books, 1982.

National Association of College and University Business Officers. *College and University Business Administration.* (3d ed.) Washington, D.C.: Administrative Service, National Association of College and University Business Officers, 1984, updated annually.

National Center for Higher Education Management Systems. *Higher Education Finance Manual.* Boulder, Colo.: National Center for Higher Education Management Systems, 1977.

Peters, T. J., and Waterman, R. H., Jr. *In Search of Excellence.* New York: Harper & Row, 1982.

Ridenour, J. F. "Annual Giving and the Capital Campaign." *Counsel* (Marts and Luncy, Inc., New York City), Spring 1979, pp. 2–3.

Ridenour, J. F. "Comparative Data on Fifteen Coeducation Colleges." Technical report, Development Office, Western Maryland College, Westminster, Md., 1983.

Ridenour, J. F., and Munger, P. L. "Reporting Deferred Gifts: CASE-NACUBO Guidelines Ensure Consistency." *CASE Currents,* Apr. 1983, pp. 34–36.

Robinson, D. D. "Analysis and Interpretation of Financial Data." *NACUBO Professional File,* June 1975, pp. 1–4.

Seymour, H. J. *Designs for Fund Raising.* New York: McGraw-Hill, 1966.

Smith, G. T. "Developing Private Support: Three Issues." Paper presented at seminar on the president's role in development, American Alumni Council, Washington, D.C., 1974.

Tirone, J. F. "Measuring the Bell System's Public Relations." *Public Relations Review,* Winter 1977, pp. 21-38.

7 *Jeffery R. Shy*

Applying New Technologies

ᑲᑯ High technology has arrived. It affects my office. It affects your office. And it is here to stay.

In the 1950s, two major revolutions burst upon the American scene: television and the electronic computer. These two advances have fundamentally altered the communication system of the United States. They continue to exert an irrevocable impact on the nation's colleges and universities, including the advancement function.

When the first Eniac was built, more than thirty-five years ago, it weighed 30 tons, occupied 15,000 square feet, contained 4,000 vacuum tubes, and used 150,000 watts of electricity. A computer eighteen times faster than the first Eniac can now be purchased for less than $400, carried in a briefcase, and operated on four batteries. We find computers in videogames, microwave ovens, and even the shock absorbers of cars. The new Boeing 767 has more than a hundred computers on board. It is said to be able to fly without the aid of a pilot.

New technologies assist us in our offices as well. On-line computer systems bring increased accuracy and productivity to our offices. We now have the benefits of automated acknowledgment letters, mass-produced letters of solicitation, laser printing, and other word processing features. Computers keep track of our alumni and friends, track their association with the institution, and record their gifts. Electronic mail allows us to send messages to one another in a matter of moments. Digital voice technologies allow us to record phone messages and answer those messages without ever speaking to the other party. Systems can now keep track of our

89

calendars, automatically schedule meetings, and alert staff members to meet with us. Computer graphics give us new insight into both the esthetics of presentation and the realities of cash flow. Teleconferencing allows us to "meet long-distance" while having the resources of the home office at hand. Electronic spreadsheets allow us to project what-if situations quickly and accurately. International satellite communication challenges us to find new ways to communicate with alumni scattered around the globe.

It is inevitable that automation has come—or will come—to your office. The only question is when and how. Will you control it? Or will it control you?

The Politics of Computing at Educational Institutions

To seize control of this issue, the professional must first understand the politics of computing at the educational institution.

First, although there is a lack of resources for capital investment at most institutions, substantial investments are required to acquire computer systems. Consequently, most educational institutions have inadequate, insufficient, or inappropriate hardware to serve the computing needs of the institution.

Second, the relative lack of financial resources at the educational institution adversely impacts the quality and quantity of personnel available to program and operate the computers. In a field growing as fast as the computer industry, there is a great demand for personnel. This drives up the salaries for these positions. In general, our institutions have been unable to respond quickly to such salary demands, and as a result, educational computer centers tend to be training grounds for new computer programmers. Our institutions train these people; then industry hires them away. Those who stay may be required to work on equipment that is not state-of-the-art, and if this is the case, they become less competitive in the industry and, within a short time, are unqualified for new jobs; they have become stuck in their jobs. The institution ends up either with trainees or with people lacking training or motivation to keep abreast of the advances in their field.

Third, the new trends in computer technology toward

decentralization are frequently treated by personnel at the computer center as a threat to its existence. As machines become more easily managed, and more and more programs become available to serve our needs, the computer center staff as we know it today will become obsolete, and the computer center will no longer produce software or run the hardware. Instead, we expect to see technology czars who will assist the user in the selection and application of software and hardware. In the end, the user will make the final selection and become the manager-user of the system.

Fourth, most centralized computer centers also have centralized budgets. In this scheme, the computer center is budgeted for the computing needs of all users on the campus. As a department makes use of computer resources, its account at the computer center is debited for an amount computed by the center. Unfortunately, this transfers control of these funds from the user to the center. For example, a user who wanted to deduct $3,000 from a computer center account for something such as travel for the capital campaign would be unable to do so. However, that same user would have been allowed to make the decision to transfer the funds from virtually any other account under his or her control. The institutional advancement officer is detached from the entire process and thus cannot evaluate the effectiveness of any particular request for information; thus, the officer has no control over this account and takes no responsibility for it. Without responsibility, there is no accountability and no guarantee of responsible use of resources.

Finally, it is difficult to configure a computer system to serve the needs of all users. There are three basic uses for computer resources at an educational institution: (1) academic computing, which includes instruction and research, (2) data processing, which is primarily for large data bases, such as student records and alumni records, and (3) the new tasks of office automation, including word processing. Unfortunately, it is difficult to reconcile the differences between these users and configure a computer system that can meet all of these needs while maintaining peak efficiency. Although some machines are designed to address the data processing needs, or even data processing and word processing needs, it is very difficult, if not impossible, to configure a truly responsive large machine for the varying needs of all users. On the contrary, the smaller the machine, the less expensive and less complex will be its operation. Therefore, the trend in the industry continues to move toward smaller machines, each specialized for its individual tasks.

The Concept of the Integrated Data Base

An important consideration in the review, selection, and use of a system is its ability to integrate with other data systems on the campus. Three main areas of integration for the institutional advancement data base must be considered: student records systems, business office systems, and word processing systems.

Before looking at each of these systems individually, consider the concept of total integration. The theory behind an integrated data base is that a record—for example, a prospective student record—is entered as the individual becomes an applicant for admission, is automatically passed to the student records system on matriculation, and finally is passed to the alumni system on graduation. During this entire period, all this information is available to each office in the institution.

Unfortunately, two factors inevitably prevent this total integration from occurring. First, different offices have different standards for the collection and maintenance of data. Unless all offices can agree on a procedure for implementing these standards, the system cannot succeed. Even though all of the administrative offices have the same general objective of enhancing the well-being of the institution, this agreement is difficult to obtain because each office has its own goals and objectives. Second, the implementation of such a system is expensive, and most institutions simply do not have the resources or the expertise to implement the complete system.

The most critical area of integration is that of the alumni and student records systems. At the end of each semester, the names of those students who do not reenroll need to be incorporated into the alumni system. (We say those who do not reenroll rather than those who receive degrees because it is important for all former students to be included in the alumni files, not just those who have received degrees.)

The names from the student records system can be brought forward in one of two ways. First, the registrar can furnish a list that contains the names and addresses of all applicable students. A computer operator would then type these names into the alumni files. Second, the names and addresses could be electronically forwarded from the registrar's files to the alumni files, either by tape or telecommunications.

It would seem that the second method is preferable, but this is not always the case. First, the registrar's files do not always utilize the types of procedures and standards that must be followed in the alumni files. For example, student records are typically recorded in uppercase only, whereas alumni files must be stored in both uppercase and lowercase to conform with word processing standards. It is impossible to write a computer program that will correctly and completely make this conversion. The only way to properly translate this information is to manually review and update appropriate records. Although up to a point, it is actually less expensive and less difficult to enter the data manually than to execute an electronic transfer followed by manual corrections, it is sometimes more appropriate to implement an electronic transfer. Translation of a few hundred records can be most easily accomplished by hand; translation of a few thousand records can be most easily accomplished electronically. Each institution will have to decide which approach to take.

The second type of data integration that is important to the institutional advancement office is the transfer of data from the development system to the business office system. Each day, the individual gift transactions should be recorded in detail for each donor. At the end of the day, the totals for each account must be transmitted to the business office records. It is not necessary—in fact, it is undesirable—to transmit the complete details of each transaction to the business office. This would represent not only a duplication of work but also a potential breach of security. Only summary information should be compiled and transmitted daily. This transmittal can be accomplished via an electronic transfer. However, most business offices will not be able to receive these data without greatly altering their computer systems and their auditing systems. In the end, the most frequently chosen method of transmitting these data is a written transmittal, which details the amount of cash for each account. The key points to remember are that the information must be transmitted daily, that the information should be detailed by account, and that ability periodically to reconcile business office records with development records must be maintained.

The third important interface is with word processing systems. Names and addresses must be passed to word processing software, which is capable of mass-producing letters to any number of constituents as well as automating acknowledgment letters. To accomplish this, both data and equipment factors must be considered. Data factors include the following: The data must be in uppercase and lowercase letters; salutations must be included as part of the data base; and all address changes must be entered with correspondence standards in effect (for example, spelling out *Road* in an address rather than entering *Rd.*). It must be possible to easily merge these data with the word processing software to produce typewritten-quality correspondence.

Finally, it is important to remember that whether the various administrative data bases reside on a single computer or on several computers, the issues regarding the integration of the various data bases and the transfer of information from one to another are the same.

Sharing Information

Whether you decide to share a computer with others on campus or to acquire your own computer system, every effort should be made to share as much information as possible with others. This not only allows you to provide a service to other offices on campus but also creates the attitude among others that they should assist you in collecting and correcting information. All too often, we find ourselves acting as referees between offices (even alumni and development offices) over questions of who should be able to see and update data. These debates do little to serve the organization's interests in information gathering and dissemination.

The Minicomputer/Mainframe Dilemma

One of the questions that arise as you look at computing alternatives is how to assess the differences between mainframe software systems and those that operate on a minicomputer.

The mainframe has the advantage of having more resources available to the user during peak periods of use. For example, if a large amount of data entry were to be entered as a result of the mailing of a questionnaire, data entry personnel at the center might assist the alumni office. However, this same condition of sharing resources leads to a potential problem. Because you are sharing the mainframe with other users, you may not always be able to control the priorities of system use. When registration time comes, system resources may be taken up by the student records office. When programming is required, your priorities are analyzed by a committee that has the responsibility of allocating programmer time but lacks the knowledge of how your priorities impact your effectiveness. Finally, in most instances, the larger the system, the more expensive it is to run. Although many of the costs associated with the computer center may be in internal allocations only, these allocations represent actual costs to your institution—and often to your budget, even though you will have no real control over these costs.

Costs are less of a problem with a minicomputer. Not only will they generally be lower than with the mainframe, they will also be more clearly allocated directly to computer usage. That is, you will normally be charged for the exact expenses that are incurred. This will give you control over these expenses. On the other hand, these expenses will most likely be included in your budget, and because many of your computer expenses were formerly buried in the computer center budget, this may actually appear to increase your expenses. You will be responsible for operating your system and for maintenance, backup, supplies, and other items the computer center may have handled for you previously.

Perhaps the most significant advantage to you will be that you will set and adjust your own priorities. If you are the only user of your system, you can determine when and how you use it. You are in control, and you assume the responsibility for that control.

The Review Process

If you have made the decision to change your records system, it is best to follow a predefined series of steps to assist in the selection and implementation of a new system. These steps should be undertaken whether you intend to develop a system internally, to overhaul the existing system, or to purchase a system commercially.

1. Define your objectives. What do you want from the system? More word processing? Better gift accounting? List the items you are missing in your current system that cause you to be looking for a new system at this time. What items might you need in the future?

2. Decide on the types of output you want from the system. Design each anticipated printout format. In essence, you are beginning at the end of the system and working backward toward the beginning.

3. List all the data elements that will be required to prepare the reports that you have just specified.

4. Describe how each data element is collected and entered into the computer. If a data element seems important to you, but you cannot determine an efficient and accurate way of collecting or inputting the data, discard that data element. Incomplete or inaccurate information is worse than no information at all.

5. Define all operational concerns that impact on the system. Where will gifts be received? Who opens the mail? Will all addresses be changed in one office?

6. Decide which procedures will not be computerized. Some things are better done by hand. Determine those items before you begin the process of implementing a new system.

7. Plan for the interface of your system to others on the campus. Whether this will be done manually or electronically, establish the plan in advance.

8. Specify your needs for terminals, printers, and other hardware. In particular, you should set out the volume of various functions that you will perform. For example, how many

mailings do you send to the entire alumni body? How many letters do you expect to write? How many records will you maintain on the system? Are you going to include parents and friends as well as alumni?

Pitfalls to Avoid

It might be useful at this point to review some critical, but frequently overlooked, elements of an alumni-development data base. Generally, the following must be considered when we decide whether to limit our expectations for a system and how we may use it.

Each record may require multiple preferred addresses. Alumni mailings may be directed to the home address while athletic mailings may go to a business address. Each type of mailing may require its own preferred mailing address. The only way to handle this type of problem is to accommodate an unlimited number of preferences.

To make most effective use of word processing, the system must be capable of storing an unlimited number of salutations. A single nickname is simply not sufficient. The system must be able to accommodate and incorporate a salutation for each individual to whom a letter may be addressed from each author who may write to that individual. This capability is particularly important for acknowledgment letters, which must be selected automatically by the system on the basis of gift information.

Generally, development officers overlook the need for complete, detailed gift information. Each gift must include a number of data elements, not the least of which is the account number. By including the account number used by the business office, the development office will be able to fully reconcile its records with business office gift records. Moreover, a complete history of all gift transactions is critically important. This becomes most useful during a capital campaign, when such a gift history can show all the giving interests of a potential top prospect.

Once a capital campaign begins, pledge billing can be critical in tracking the realization of the top gifts. A system should be capable of tracking multiple pledges to multiple restrictions with varying payment schedules.

The capital campaign will also require a fairly extensive prospect-tracking system that can track proposals, volunteer assignments, contact results, and follow-up appointments.

In the end, it is never advisable to limit a system. That is, it should accommodate an unlimited number of entries of most types of data elements.

The Review Process

If you elect to request bids from software suppliers, be careful that your search effort is consistent with the scope of your purchase. A recent example is that of a state purchasing office that submitted a "Request for Proposal" to software vendors, asking for certain information about system operation. The document was reasonably well prepared and served to highlight differences between the various competing systems. Unfortunately, the scope of the responses required vendors to spend from $1,500 to $3,500 preparing responses. The state review process required approximately $25,000 of state personnel time. Additionally, during the time frame of the review (an excessive six months), the cost of the selected software increased by $10,000. Thus the state, in an effort to save money and ensure an appropriate review of all alternatives, spent $35,000 reviewing proposals for a $130,000 contract. Clearly this effort was not in line with the type of system being purchased and served neither the interests of the state nor those of the user.

It is also important to look at the priorities of the various groups assisting you in your review. In the preceding example, the state purchasing office was not necessarily looking for the most economical system or the most functional system. Their interest was protection of the state from suits by unhappy losing vendors. This purpose may have been well served, but the interests of the alumni-development office were not.

Classic Mistakes in System Selection

One of the most common mistakes in the selection of a new office automation system is the selection of the hardware before software. You may have heard the advice of the real estate agent who said that the three most important items in a real estate purchase are location, location, and location; well, the three most important considerations in the purchase of a computer system are software, software, and software. Although certain types of hardware are better suited to certain kinds of applications, the software will be much more critical in the final performance of the system. The software vendor will most likely select hardware that will be suitable for the type of application that is being made. Therefore you should select the software before the hardware.

Another common mistake in the selection of a new system is the use of existing hardware because it is there. It may appear on the surface that the use of existing hardware is the most economical course, but the use of such hardware often so confines the purchase of software that an appropriate software selection is difficult if not impossible. And without software, there can be no system. Therefore, do not constrain the selection of the system by requiring the use of preexisting hardware.

For most institutions, development of in-house software is not a realistic alternative. Development of a complete alumni-development software system could cost from $100,000 to $450,000 or more (not including word processing). Most computer centers are simply not able to devote the kind of effort required to put such a system together; nor are they able to allocate the staff needed for such system development. But most important, the institutional advancement office must realize that if it decides to develop its own software, it, too, must allocate substantial personnel resources to the specification and design of the system and to the installation and training of personnel.

User satisfaction of technological applications will be enhanced if you sincerely seek and attend to ideas of potential users during the design of the system (Andolsen and Andolsen, 1983; Kitsmiller, 1983).

You should avoid simple-minded solutions to technological problems. Justification of new applications of technology is usually attributed to cost savings, intangible benefits, cost avoidance, improving services, or improving decision making (Roche, 1983). Computer applications in alumni records can save dollars by automating repetitive manual and clerical tasks. Intangible benefits that defy economic quantification are simplicity, proven reliability, good will, and moral responsibility. Cost avoidance means that a cost of one alternative is not treated as such but rather as a benefit of another alternative. Reducing turnaround time on gift acknowledgment improves service. Adopting a management information system that provides reliable data for quality analysis contributes to better decision making.

One final common error: Do not expect perfection. No matter how good the system you purchase is, no matter how carefully you have planned, there will be problems. No system is perfect. You can minimize the difficulties by anticipating, isolating, and methodically correcting problems. Likewise, do not expect a good computer system to solve all problems within your office. A computer system cannot design an effective fund-raising campaign, set policies for the handling of hometown news stories, or solve personnel difficulties, but it can provide you with the tools to use to do so.

Mathematician/philosopher John G. Kemeny, former president of Dartmouth College, has summarized well the promise and the pitfalls of technological applications (Kirch, 1978). He notes that, if the computer is understood and used properly, it serves as a simplifying agent against the threat of complexity and cost— as an aid in decision making. At the same time, he warns that overreliance on computers snuffs out common sense. The message: You should not subordinate your mind to the computer; only the human mind can make value judgments.

Bibliographical Essay

Two numbers of *CASE Currents* provide information on technology management specific to institutional advancement offices. System requirements, automated typesetting, computerized news, and an alumni tracing system are among the topics in "Special Issue: Computers" (1978). "Special Issue: Computers in Alumni and Development" (1983) includes articles on computer-phobia, software selection, and user requirements.

Fallon's *AMA Management Handbook* (1983) includes a section on "Information Systems and Technology." Edited by Martinson (1983), the section examines information systems planning, equipment, operating software, data base management systems, purchased services, the electronic office, and sources of information, such as trade associations, consultants, academia, data banks, and journals.

Readers interested in obtaining helpful periodicals should consult an annotated list of magazines and journals published by the *Chronicle of Higher Education* ("What College Computer Professionals Read," 1984). The list includes names and addresses of two dozen publications read regularly by many persons involved with computers on American campuses.

References

Andolsen, A. A., and Andolsen, B. H. "Office Systems Management." In W. K. Fallon (ed.), *AMA Management Handbook.* (2nd ed.) New York: American Management Associations, 1983.

Fallon, W. K. (ed.). *AMA Management Handbook.* (2nd ed.) New York: American Management Associations, 1983.

Kirch, P. C. "A Computer Philosopher Shares His Time." *CASE Currents,* Sept. 1978, pp. 4-6.

Kitsmiller, G. "You Are What You Program: Invite Users to Develop Your Computer System." *CASE Currents,* Mar. 1983, pp. 24-27.

Martinson, S. A. "Information Systems Technology." In W. K. Fallon (ed.), *AMA Management Handbook.* (2nd ed.) New York: American Management Associations, 1983.

Roche, R. B. "Applications." In W. K. Fallon (ed.), *AMA Management Handbook.* (2nd ed.) New York: American Management Associations, 1983.

"Special Issue: Computers." *CASE Currents,* Sept. 1978.

"Special Issue: Computers in Alumni and Development." *CASE Currents,* Mar. 1983.

"What College Computer Professionals Read." *Chronicle of Higher Education,* Oct. 10, 1984, p. 27.

8

Harvey K. Jacobson

Research and Evaluation: Tools for Successful Management

꧁ Peter Drucker places at the top of the list of requirements of the modern manager the ability to innovate. "Managing innovation will increasingly become a challenge to management, and especially top management, and a touchstone of its competence" (1974, p. 786). The manager who wants to be a policy maker rather than an administrative functionary must know how to select, introduce, and implement change. Thus research and evaluation come to the fore more than ever before.

Major factors in the higher education marketplace underscore the growing need for research and evaluation. They are:

1. *Accountability.* Institutional advancement officers can no longer depend on time-honored homilies to justify their existence. Information as quantitative and reliable as possible is imperative for effective management. Research and evaluation are needed in good times and in bad, but financial stringencies heighten the pressure for successful adjustment strategies. Can you deliver more bang for the buck? Prove it.

2. *Professionalism.* Research and evaluation provide an index that shows how far a field has progressed toward professional stature. No field of endeavor can claim to be a profession if it fails to have a systematic body of knowledge as its base. Research and evaluation can help build that needed body of reliable knowledge.

102

3. *Pragmatics.* The late Angus Campbell, social scientist, observed that it is the measurable problems that attract society's primary attention: "Nothing seems to make a problem come alive to people in positions of decision like a finite count, whether it is number of people unemployed, crimes committed, highway accidents, [or] illegitimate births" (1971, p. 100). Decision makers want solutions to problems. The longer we wait to find reliable ways of assessing the factors that underlie our problems, the longer those problems will be with us. In other words, we need a measurement-oriented data base for practical operational control.

Definitions of some basic terms will help us relate these concerns to the practice of institutional advancement. The word *research* sums up the methods used to obtain reliable knowledge. In carefully conducted research, the scientist undertakes a systematic effort to learn something new and to make sure that this information is not spurious. Thus research is really a process; the person who obtains knowledge scientifically follows certain rules and introduces controls that help in analyzing the information. Basic (pure or fundamental) research seeks to extend the boundary of knowledge, whereas applied research is concerned with assisting managers in making better decisions.

To *evaluate* means to place a value on something—to determine its significance or worth. Sometimes the manager will make such judgments on quick notice, with minimal reflection. At other times, it will be appropriate to make a judgment based on careful appraisal and study. In such cases, evaluation becomes a type of research activity conducted in a serious and systematic manner.

A term that is gaining increased usage among both scholars and managers is *evaluation research* (Agarwala-Rogers and Alexander, 1979, p. 537). *Evaluation research* refers to studies conducted on a systematic basis to measure various aspects of programs in order to provide a scientific basis for decision by program officials. The degree to which evaluation research is carried out in a systematic and scientific manner will depend on the individual manager, usually depending upon organizational need and personal competence, inclination, and choice.

The manager asks, What can evaluation do for me? Evaluation must have a purpose; it is not an end in itself. The need for evaluation derives from the decision-making process, which is a prelude to action. The principal reason for evaluation is to assist with future decision making.

Managers need to understand and appreciate evaluation as a technique for determining the value of various elements of their domain—programs, projects, people, activities, products. Evaluation is hardly a new phenomenon for managers. Within the organization, there are many information streams directed toward a variety of decision areas. Take the budget review, for example. Monthly or quarterly reports compare actual expenses with projected expenses. The initial allocation of funds is predicated upon some kind of assessment of competing requests for funds; priorities are set and then balanced within the overall budget.

The degree to which the manager formalizes the commitment to evaluation depends upon that manager's "commitment to rational decision making—the desire to bring objective evidence to bear on organizational decisions whenever possible rather than to rely only on prior experience, subjective judgments, and ad hoc data. Common sense and experience are important to a manager; evaluation can add another string to his bow" (Agarwala-Rogers and Alexander, 1979, p. 539).

Evaluation can help you to:

- Demonstrate stewardship—that is, document the wise use of resources for the purposes intended
- Help personnel within your operation better understand their roles in relation to the mission of the total organization
- Reduce uncertainty by providing greater organizational stability through a planned program that incorporates change and improvement in a systematic manner
- Enhance your personal reputation by expanding and sharpening the collection of wares in your management tool kit
- Decrease your reliance on crisis management by providing information on which to base long-range operational plans
- Contribute to the professionalism of institutional advancement by the exchange of data, analyses, and conclusions

Guidelines for Evaluation

1. *Take a position on your philosophy concerning evaluation.* Your attitude toward evaluation is the single most important factor in its success or failure in your operation. Are you evaluating because you are forced into it or because you believe in it? Do you consider systematic measurement to be poppycock? Or is it an essential component of your programs?

Perhaps we can agree that, at present, many elements of institutional advancement programs seem to defy precise measurement. However, we need not succumb to the absurdity of not measuring at all. Rather, the issues are as follows: What should be measured? Which measures are appropriate? How precise can they be? A wealth of measurement literature and instruments is available to draw upon. It is the desire to do so that is too often lacking.

2. *Acquaint yourself with the 'why' of evaluation—with what it can do for you.* We have already said that evaluation helps you in the decision-making process. The feedback you obtain helps you conduct daily operations, control current performance, and plan strategically for the future.

3. *Acquaint yourself with the nature of evaluation.* This is a sophisticated area, and you should not expect to become an instant expert. Appreciate and respect the complexities of evaluation.

Research is a tool for answering questions, much as a watch is a tool for telling time. "And, like a watch, it is very intricate. Research is full of statistics and strict scientific method the way a Swiss-movement watch is full of wheels and springs, all working together in harmony to produce the correct information. A watch is used to tell time because it is presumed that there is some order in the world. . . . Social research . . . assumes likewise: there is order and purpose to the way people behave" (Mohn, 1981, p. 8).

All research, whether physical or social, moves through a basic four-step process that begins with a substantive question, moves on to a statistical/methodological question, obtains statistical results, and then interprets these results into answers to the initial question. Researchers express these results in terms of *sample error* and *confidence levels* because they want to let you know, with as little of a shadow of doubt as possible, that the results from the research are answering your question.

Measurement is the assignment of numerical values to observations. This subsequently allows a more efficient expression of observations through statistical reduction of numerical values in the data analyzed.

Research designs can range from *qualitative* studies, such as questioning a few knowledgeable individuals in an exploratory way, to *quantitative* studies, which are designed to explain what is happening and the frequency of its occurrence and which employ formal and structured procedures aimed at controlling bias in the data collected.

Evaluation experts speak in terms of formative evaluation and summative evaluation. These two types of approaches differ in the functions they perform, the methods they employ, and the way organizations carry them out. *Formative evaluation* focuses on tentative and in-process measures of a program or activity. A diagnostic tool used for immediate decisions, it gives provisional information to managers. *Summative evaluation* studies the demonstrated effects of programs. Managers use the findings to make decisions about a program's continuation, discontinuation, modification, expansion, or curtailment.

4. *Develop a model or plan of the type of evaluation program to be employed.* The evaluation framework presented in Figure 8-1 will help you organize your thoughts and review your options when selecting the emphasis you want when you assign or commission a study. This model is useful in answering the question: What do you measure?

The model presents three categories of indicators that help you determine the effectiveness of your institutional advancement programs. The categories are effort, performance, and effects.

Effort examines the extent of commitment to the programs. Indicators are articulation of mission, goals and objectives; financial support; resource deployment; organization and structure; and provision for policy input.

Performance refers to progress in program implementation—the degree to which some goal or objective is being achieved.

Figure 8-1. Framework for evaluating institutional advancement programs.

Category	*Indicators*
I. Effort (institutional commitment)	A. Articulation of mission, goals, and objectives *(What is the role of institutional advancement programs in the life of the institution?)* B. Financial support *(Is funding appropriate to the institution's financial resources and institutional advancement objectives?)* C. Resource deployment *(Is there an appropriate balance of personnel, facilities, equipment, supplies, and services?)* D. Organization and structure *(Does design serve functions?)* E. Provision for policy input *(What role does/should institutional advancement have in institution policy-level formation?)*
II. Performance (progress in program implementation)	A. Personnel *(Does performance meet expectations?)* 1. managers 2. staff 3. other (for example, volunteers and consultants) B. Activities *(Are desired activities being implemented as planned?)* C. Products *(Are desired outputs being produced?)* D. Financial performance *(Are funds being acquired and used as planned?)*

III. Effects (user impact)	A. Contact (exposure, attention)
	 (Did program reach people it set out to reach?)
	 B. Response (attitudes and behavior)
	 (Did program get its message across? Did users understand? Did users support? Did users benefit?)
	 1. information
	 2. persuasion
	 3. reinforcement
	 4. activation
	 C. Relationship (between institution and user)
	 (Did program alter relationship?)
	 1. nature and status of relationship
	    a. institutional image
	    b. user satisfaction
	    c. goal discrepancy
	    d. barriers to information flow
	    e. university-community compatibility
	    f. provision for feedback
	 2. change in relationship
	    a. attitudes (for example, confidence level)
	    b. behavior (for example, financial support)

Source: Jacobson, 1978.

Indicators include personnel (Does performance meet expectations?), activities (Are desired activities being implemented as planned?), products (Are desired outputs being produced?), and financial performance (Are funds being acquired and used as planned?)

Effects refers to the impact of programs—the consequence that output has on affected individuals. Indicators are contact (Did the program reach the people it set out to reach?); response, in terms of attitudes and behavior (Did the program get its message across? Did users understand? Did users benefit?); and relationship (Did the program alter the relationship between the initiator and the user?).

Space limitations prevent additional discussion of the indicators here. However, explanations of each indicator and examples of applications in studies at colleges and universities around the nation are presented in *Evaluating Advancement Programs* (Jacobson, 1978).

5. *Zero in on the specifics you intend to pursue.* You should play a pivotal role in formulating questions to be investigated.

Choose a focus. Do not try to measure everything at once. Perhaps you should begin by concentrating on one or two functional components—for example, media relations, annual giving, internal publications, or government relations. State your written goals for the specific area. State your written goals for measurement. Choose your variables.

Refrain from running to a researcher to do your thinking for you before you have first examined what you want to be doing and why. Ask yourself what it is you want the research to do for you and how the results are to be applied.

What types of studies are most useful to managers of institutional advancement programs? The following is a checklist of studies to consider:

- *Feasibility study.* Usually involves assessing potential for conducting a capital campaign: Will it work? Can also apply to other functional program areas.
- *Communication audit.* Measures effectiveness of an organization's communication programs and techniques for internal

and external groups. Sometimes reviews networks, channels, barriers, satisfaction levels.

- *Public relations audit.* Assesses effectiveness of an organization's public relations programs. Seeks ways to improve programming.
- *Public opinion survey.* Measures opinions of general public or selected target publics. Specialists distinguish between opinion research and attitude research, the latter being more complex. Objectives of a study will determine which type of research to employ.
- *Impact study.* Measures impact of a given program or component of a program. Also known as *effects study.*
- *Future trends study.* Projects direction and speed of existent and emergent trends into the future.
- *Key issues survey.* Presents thoughts and attitudes of leaders in business, government, and/or other key groups on selected issues.
- *Needs analysis.* Surveys needs as expressed by a given group.
- *New program opportunities.* Identifies issues, audiences, and activities as targets for new program initiatives.
- *Environmental monitoring.* Observes and monitors trends in selected environments (sociopolitical, economic, technological, legal, and others).
- *Readability study.* Tests reading ease of printed materials, helping communicator to gear the message for the reading ability of the intended audience.
- *Readership/listenership/viewership studies.* Audience studies probe degree of attention to the medium and/or matters of content, balance of presentation, style, usefulness, and demographics.
- *Content analysis.* Study of content of messages by word, theme, space, time, or other units.
- *Cost studies.* Includes cost-accounting techniques and cost-benefit, cost-outcome, and cost-effectiveness analyses.
- *Marketing research.* Uses market orientation to determine market characteristics, potentials, share, competition, forecasts, new-service acceptance and potential, pricing, and other factors.

- *Economic impact study.* Assesses economic impacts of an institution or program on its community.

6. *Choose the people who will do the evaluation.* Once you have narrowed down what it is you want to measure, you have less difficulty knowing what kind of expertise to assemble. You may want to employ an external evaluation expert, or you may want to look for expertise right in your own organization.

Figure out a way to assure technical competence. The expert should watch for reliability, validity, and other technical aspects. Your organization should know what kind of analysis it wants to buy and be able to judge the competence of the analysts. These two requirements are inseparable.

The researcher can play an active and supportive role in the decision-making process, but the responsibility for making decisions rests with management.

Before retaining an outside consultant, ask for a list of clients, particularly institutions similar to yours that have posed problems similar to yours. Call selected references to help judge professional competency. Also ask for copies of the final study reports the firm prepared for other institutions to determine whether the data are well presented and, most important, easily understood. Avoid the firm that bows out immediately after the computer run. You want meaningful findings that translate into action plans. The most professional firms will supply interpretations, recommendations, and options.

7. *Formalize the evaluation commitment.* We could paraphrase Mark Twain and say everyone always talks about evaluation, but no one ever does anything about it. Most institutional advancement offices are busily engaged in the routine of daily responsibility. You need to build measurement into the routine, which you can do by adopting an evaluation plan that includes orderly implementation through a purposefully administered system. Assign overall implementation and coordination responsibility to an appropriate staff member. Consider appointing committees or task forces to assist in evaluation, and spell out evaluation responsibilities in job descriptions. Make

assignments. Adopt timetables. Specify data base needs. Budget the financial support.

    8. *Acquaint yourself with the literature of evaluation.* You can educate yourself by using a variety of helpful sources. The three most comprehensive works on evaluation in institutional advancement are books by Leslie (1969), Heemann (1979), and Jacobson (1978). Leslie's *Focus on Understanding and Support: A Study of College Management* reports on his detailed survey of costs and revenues at 700 institutions of higher learning. Heemann's *New Directions for Institutional Advancement: Analyzing the Cost-Effectiveness of Fund Raising* includes findings from "the most thorough analysis of fund-raising costs to date" (p. xi), the study undertaken under the auspices of the Consortium on Financing Higher Education, which examined costs of fund-raising and university relations at twenty-five private colleges and universities. The Jacobson volume, *New Directions for Institutional Advancement: Evaluating Advancement Programs,* describes evaluation concepts and techniques, presents case studies from six colleges and universities, and illustrates techniques and findings with examples from alumni affairs, fund-raising, public relations, publications, and government relations.

    Both the Heemann and Jacobson books provide extensive bibliographies of articles, books, manuals, guides, and reports. Additional sources for study and assistance are noted in the bibliographical essay at the end of this chapter.

Conclusions

    Challenge to Individual Managers. Contrary to commonly expressed opinion, even among many present-day practitioners, programs of institutional advancement can be evaluated on a sound basis (Robinson, 1969; Grunig, 1977; Heemann, 1979; Jacobson, 1978). More often than not, the problem is that no systematic effort has been made to obtain measurement.

    To move ahead in evaluation and research, follow these tips:

1.   *Do* make a decision about evaluation. Take the offensive. If you hesitate, outsiders will come in and impose their criteria and standards on you.

2. *Do not* try to do everything at once. Take the first step. A series of small steps can help you make great strides. Begin a project. Talk to an expert. Assign a task. Zero in on a single problem, and tackle it as an experiment, trial, or learning experience.

3. *Do* remember that an evaluation program is destined for failure if it does not have approval from the top.

4. *Do not* conduct evaluation in isolation. Relate your studies and your findings to your organization, the world around you, and the world of scholarship.

5. *Do* build up a bookshelf or a file of evaluation materials. Look at kits, tools, and examples from other organizations. Take a market researcher to lunch.

6. *Do not* go overboard. Recognize both the potential and the limitations of evaluation programs. Do not assume that only numbers are required for ultimate judgments. Keep things in perspective by remembering that a wine taster, after all, can evaluate a wine without knowing its exact chemical composition.

7. *Do* consider the possibility of joint ventures, such as shared-cost surveys. Shirttail or piggyback studies can save you money.

8. *Do not* misuse the results of measurement. Figures can lie and liars can figure. You bear the responsibility for intelligent and ethical use of findings.

Pursuit of Professionalism. Pressures are increasing for institutional advancement officers to be more exact in setting goals and measuring progress in reaching them. Effective deployment of resources requires tracking, documenting, and analyzing current operations and detecting emerging issues and trends.

Needed increasingly are systematic studies whose findings can be used to build reliable and comparable information banks. The assembled information will contribute to a body of knowledge that helps the institutional advancement field in its quest for professionalism.

Data are much more valuable if they are compatible. Therefore standard definitions and procedures should be established. Efforts by various organizations to standardize the reporting of revenues and expenditures for private gift programs are encouraging. Examples are the projects organized by the Council for Advancement and Support of Education and the National Association of College and University Business Officers (CASE-NACUBO) and the National Society of Fund Raisers and Institute of Continuing Education (NSFR-ICE). These efforts have been reported by Heemann (1981) and Smallwood and Levis (1977). Another promising development is the emergence of doctoral dissertations that are contributing to a more sophisticated body of knowledge in institutional advancement. Leading examples are the studies by Pickett (1981), who contrasted successful and relatively unsuccessful fund-raising programs at 94 private colleges; Willmer (1980), who developed norms for justifying and comparing institutional advancement programs by surveying 191 small, independent colleges; Swanson (1981), who studied factors influencing the development of university foundation programs, and Mack (1983), who analyzed foundation relations in private colleges.

What can be done to strengthen the application of research and evaluation? Professional associations should adopt the following goals and work toward them through systematic plans and action programs:

1. Conduct advance research and analysis leading to the improved understanding, planning, management, and operation of institutional advancement offices.
2. Encourage the development and application of appropriate methodologies and techniques from many disciplines to further such research, evaluation, and planning.
3. Encourage the collection, interpretation, exchange, and dissemination of information with respect to institutional advancement processes and effects.
4. Further the professional development and training of individuals engaged in research, evaluation, and planning.
5. Develop financial support that facilitates progress toward these goals.

Bibliographical Essay

Robinson (1969) presents an excellent introduction to the research process as applied to public relations. Barcus (1968) analyzes organization and financial support in alumni affairs. Lindenmann (1977) offers helpful suggestions for attitude and opinion research. Rowland (1979) explains assessment techniques useful to managers of news services and public information offices. Francis (1979) examines the use of surveys in institutional advancement offices.

Suchman (1967) gives a scholarly review of conceptual, methodological, and administrative aspects of evaluation. Tripodi, Fellin, and Epstein (1971) outline the process and techniques of evaluation. The Tripodi team reviews monitoring techniques (accountability audit, administrative audit, time and motion studies), social research techniques (experiments, surveys), and cost-analytic techniques.

Indicators that can be used for gauging performance in institutional advancement programs are advanced by Leslie (1969), Heemann (1979), and Jacobson (1975, 1978, 1982).

Pertinent journals include *Public Opinion Quarterly, Journalism Quarterly, Journal of Advertising Research, Journal of Marketing Research,* and *Evaluation Quarterly.*

References

Agarwala-Rogers, R., and Alexander, J. K. "Evaluation of Organizational Activities." In G. Zaltman (ed.), *Management Principles for Nonprofit Agencies and Organizations.* New York: American Management Associations, 1979.

Barcus, F. E. *Alumni Administration.* Washington, D.C.: American Alumni Council, 1968.

Campbell, A. "Measuring the Quality of Life." Remarks to the National Council of Editorial Writers, Pittsburgh, Pa., Oct. 4, 1971.

Drucker, P. F. *Management: Tasks, Responsibilities, Practices.* New York: Harper & Row, 1974.

Francis, J. B. (ed.). *Surveying Institutional Constituencies.* New Directions for Institutional Advancement, no. 6. San Francisco: Jossey-Bass, 1979.

Grunig, J. (ed.). "Measuring the Effectiveness of Public Relations." *Public Relations Review,* 1977, special issue, *3* (4).

Heemann, W. (ed.). *Analyzing the Cost-Effectiveness of Fund-Raising.* New Directions for Institutional Advancement, no. 3. San Francisco: Jossey-Bass, 1979.

Heemann, W. "Reporting Your Results: A New Tool for Fund Raisers." *CASE Currents,* Sept. 1981, pp. 46–48.

Jacobson, H. K. "Know Thyself: Program Evaluation in University Relations and Development." *CASE Currents,* Nov. 1975, pp. 7–9.

Jacobson, H. K. (ed.). *Evaluating Advancement Programs.* New Directions for Institutional Advancement, no. 1. San Francisco: Jossey-Bass, 1978.

Jacobson, H. K. "15 Ways to Measure Fund Raising Program Effectiveness." *Fund Raising Management,* Dec. 1982, pp. 24–28.

Leslie, J. W. *Focus on Understanding and Support: A Study in College Management.* Washington, D.C.: American College Public Relations Association, 1969.

Lindenmann, W. K. *Attitude and Opinion Research: Why You Need It? How To Do It.* Washington, D.C.: Council for Advancement and Support of Education, 1977.

Mack, B. A. "Foundation Fund-Raising by Private Liberal Arts Colleges." Unpublished doctoral dissertation, School of Education, University of Michigan, Ann Arbor, 1983.

Mohn, E. "Understanding the Research Process." *ANPA Research Report* (American Newspaper Publishers Association, Washington, D.C.), Sept. 3, 1981, pp. 8–11.

Pickett, W. L. "Prerequisites for Successful Fund Raising." In F. C. Pray (gen. ed.), *Handbook for Educational Fund Raising: A Guide to Successful Principles and Practices for Colleges, Universities, and Schools.* San Francisco: Jossey-Bass, 1981.

Robinson, E. J. *Public Relations and Survey Research.* New York: Appleton-Century-Crofts, 1969.

Rowland, H. R. "Evaluating the Use of Mass Media." In A. V. Ciervo (ed.), *Using the Mass Media*. New Directions for Institutional Advancement, no. 5. San Francisco: Jossey-Bass, 1979.

Smallwood, S. J., and Levis, W. C. "First Draft: Model for Financial Reporting of Fundraising Activities." *Philanthropy Monthly*, 1977, *10* (10), 8–28.

Suchman, E. A. *Evaluative Research*. New York: Russell Sage Foundation, 1967.

Swanson, J. W. "University Foundations: Environmental Factors That Influence Their Establishment and Development." Unpublished doctoral dissertation, School of Education, University of Michigan, Ann Arbor, 1981.

Tripodi, T., Fellin, P., and Epstein, I. *Social Program Evaluation: Guidelines for Health, Education and Welfare Administrators*. Itasca, Ill.: Peacock, 1971.

Willmer, W. K. *The Small College Advancement Program: Managing for Results*. Washington, D.C.: Council for Advancement and Support of Education, 1980.

Part Two

Strengthening Institutional Relations

Howard Ray Rowland, Editor

9

Arthur V. Ciervo

Emphasizing Professionalism, Performance, and Productivity

&❧ A reporter for the now defunct *Washington Star* once asked me to tell him something about institutional relations because, as he put it, "When I get tired of working on this newspaper, I'd like to settle down into a nice, quiet job on campus." Obviously, this journalist, about forty-five years old, remembers another day, when worn-out reporters, tired of the hustle and bustle of newsrooms, sought refuge in the low-key publicity operations of college campuses.

What that reporter didn't realize is that seeking solace in institutional relations today is rather like going to a rock concert to get away from the noise. The heavy work load in most all institutional relations offices was highlighted several years ago by representatives from university workshops in Washington, D.C. Asked to list their public relations duties, they came up with an overwhelming thirty-four different ones, including acting as a ticket agent, coaching the basketball team, teaching journalism classes, and serving as the campus Perle Mesta.

In addition to such extracurricular activities, colleges are small cities that generate a voluminous amount of publicity. Such demands on small staffs forced many public relations offices to focus their efforts on responding to requests for help. There was little time to think about goals and objectives. But, thank goodness, this is changing.

Promotional campaigns, public opinion research, marketing strategies, communication audits, and issues management are

119

rapidly becoming a part of the college public relations person's vocabulary.

Many factors brought about the transformation of publicity offices into full-fledged institutional relations operations. These include the decline in enrollments in the 1980s, the financial squeeze on campus budgets, the general public's questioning of the value of higher education, equal opportunity objectives, and a growing awareness of how institutional relations can effectively support university-wide goals. Almost any college striving for academic excellence, for example, will depend on the development office to bring in monies for endowed chairs, faculty fellowships, and student scholarships.

Consequently, today's institutional relations people face rapidly increasing demands on their time and talents. They are expected to assist the admissions office when enrollment is a problem, to help with fund-raising where there is a financial crunch (and this is just about everywhere), to be mediators in town-gown relations, to monitor evolving issues, and to support a variety of lobbying efforts in Washington or the state capital. Yesterday's institutional relations operation, to be sure, is no longer adequate for today's tasks.

George Keller (1975, p. 3) indicated that to meet new challenges a new conception of the institutional relations job is needed: "[Institutional relations] men and women now come from business, political posts, or alumni work. They bring new and novel public needs and objectives in, as well as sending stuff out. They are less the dutiful servant and more the professional broker. Like some sort of ombudsman, they facilitate the flow of ideas, information, and opinion both ways. They advise the president and faculty of new data, legislation, and trends and act as professional counselors. They help the college reform itself to meet new public needs, and they, more than anyone else, alert the campus to the new needs and realities of the public."

The game is changing dramatically, but the players aren't keeping pace. In November 1980, the Public Relations Society of America Task Force on the Stature and Role of Public Relations noted in its report that public relations "has lagged behind in the evolution of the society in which it functions and has allowed itself to grow without intelligently assessing the role it can fill and defining the means to fill it. It has allowed prejudices against it to persist, misconceptions to entrench themselves and weaknesses within the field to be perceived as endeavors."

Another study done that year, by Group Attitudes Corporations, found that top executives, including some in education, feel that many public relations practitioners are less competent in their chosen field than financial analysts, chief engineers, and attorneys arc in their respective fields.

Some clues to why public relations practitioners are not held in high esteem come from Professor Robert Miller, formerly of American University. In a survey of presidents of business and industrial firms in the "Fortune 500," he found that presidents felt that the public relations person's background and training were often not broad enough. "The main criticism," Miller (1974) reported, "is that the public relations man is skilled in writing and in publicity-getting techniques and mechanics but that he is not as useful to the firm as he should be, because he lacks an understanding of the overall economic picture and of the total corporate situation."

If this is the case for colleges and universities as well, then what type of person is needed to improve performance in institutional relations? According to Richard M. Schrader and Earl C. Bolton (1972), the ideal institutional relations professional would incorporate the following seven characteristics:

1. A deep dedication to higher education and an understanding of its many facets
2. A dedication to the institution, working continually at understanding it better
3. Acceptance, as a member of the administrative team; acceptable to the governing board, the chief executive, fellow administrators, the faculty, students, and alumni
4. Knowledge of the principles of good management and sound administration, clearly demonstrating this knowledge in difficult situations

5. An expert communicator in the written and the spoken word, who constantly tries to improve techniques in the use of language and the transmission of ideas
6. Possession of the endurance of the extrovert and the patience and analytical skills of the introvert, belief in the worth of the effort, and the ability to ask for help and for money
7. The professional enthusiasm to stay current with the relevant literature in the field—including that which deals with government affairs and tax information; new techniques for institutional relations, development, and communications; the best thinking and writing by practitioners in other institutions; and the writings and speeches of educational leaders on campus and in government

Everyone has a list of favorite characteristics, and this one is by no means comprehensive. But possessing good characteristics is not enough. What really counts is how well the characteristics are applied to performance and productivity. In the final analysis, practitioners are judged not only by what they know but, more important, by what they accomplish. The following suggestions are offered to help you increase your professionalism, performance, and productivity.

Set High Ethical Standards

Credibility is to an institution what morality is to the individual. Without it, acceptance from the public is difficult, if not impossible, to attain. The credibility of an institution can be established and maintained by an insistence upon the utmost candor and honesty in dealing with various publics (such as alumni, legislators, trustees, donors, students, and local citizens) and the press.

Unfortunately, not all campus administrators subscribe to the principle that a frank and free flow of information is vital. Such administrators claim that the public would not be able to interpret facts properly or judge the institution accurately on the basis of limited information, or that bad news would hurt the institution's image in the community. Such an obsession with *positivism,* the need to put one's best foot forward at all times, destroys credibility. As Tom Wicker (1971) of *The New York Times* once wrote about President Johnson, "He so consistently sought to put a good face on everything that he no longer has much ability to put a good face on anything."

David Finn, chair of the board of Ruder and Finn, Inc., also stressed this point: "Finally, I think it's time to reconsider the wisdom of that age-old adage to always 'try to put our best foot forward.' This has long been considered one of the axioms of public relations, but it is quickly becoming discredited in this era of sweeping reappraisal. If we do have a bad foot, there's no sense of trying to hide it. In a time of crisis, we will surely be subjected to a thoroughgoing inspection, and our faults will be exposed. If we have made an effort to cover up our shortcomings, our critics will discover what we are trying to hide. Then our shortcomings will be blown out of proportion. If we try to give an honest picture of who and what we are, the bad as well as the good, our critics—and the public—will respect us. And this respect can be our greatest asset when the values of our policies are being debated" (1974, p. 36).

One of the most valuable assets of the institutional relations person is the confidence of representatives of the media. Without this confidence, the person's value to the institution is limited, and the credibility of the entire institution is undermined. One way of preserving credibility is to always follow policies and procedures that will gain the respect and confidence of both the media and the general public. Essentially, this is accomplished by being candid and cooperative. In this, the support of the president is crucial, and it should be put in writing.

In 1972, R. J. Henle, then president of Georgetown University, issued such a press policy. It stated that the director of public relations (or designated members of the staff) was responsible for releasing information pertaining to emergencies, crimes, controversies, and other events to which the press has a reasonable claim. All administrators were directed to give the director and staff the facts as quickly as possible so that a decision could be made, sometimes in consultation with others, about what information was to be released. The press policy permitted the office of public relations to follow the precept that the best publicity is always honest publicity, and to quickly obtain information from the faculty and administration without argument over what could or could not be released, thus gaining the trust of the media and other important publics.

In 1976, John W. Oswald, then president of the Pennsylvania State University, expanded this policy to encourage staff officers receiving press queries "to respond directly if the request pertains to a matter for which he or she has responsibility." It also included guidelines for faculty and administrators' handling of queries.

Set Goals and Stick to Them

Inundated with requests to publicize every activity, institutional relations persons are often tempted to direct their energies toward less important activities. Publicity is a vital part of any institutional relations program, but it should be directed toward attaining certain goals.

These goals are determined primarily by the president and the board of trustees, in consultation with faculty, alumni, administrators, and other constituents. Only they can define the institution and what it will become, and they must consider, among other things, its traditions, operations, assets, liabilities, purposes, and commitments. Will the institution need to expand recruitment efforts? to raise more funds from private donors? to increase opportunities for continuing education? Some goals will be short-range (six months to a year); others will be long-range (five years and beyond).

Once the institution's goals have been defined (and they should be in writing), the institutional relations person can take the master plan and design institutional relations policies and programs to implement them. These goals should be consistent with the institution's goals, in line with the president's thinking, designed with the institution's financial resources in mind, and realistic enough to be attained.

People in institutional relations have certain goals in common. These include:

1. Conveying a positive public image of the institution to engender public confidence in its objectives
2. Fostering public interest and participation in activities of the institution
3. Recruiting students, in conjunction with the office of admissions
4. Generating financial support from government, business, industrial, and private sources, in conjunction with the development office and government relations office
5. Assisting in attracting top-level faculty, staff, and students
6. Promoting the image of the college or university as an institution worthy of private and public support

Goals must be tailored to the institution's resources and requirements. Does the administration, faced with a financial crunch, want institutional relations to concentrate on raising $100 million for the capital campaign? to work with the admissions office to increase dwindling enrollments? Or should institutional relations work to overcome the institution's reputation of being isolated and provincial by obtaining coverage in the national media?

Whatever the circumstances, it is important to focus your efforts on helping the institution solve its problems and promote its programs. In addition, you must also set specific objectives in your operations in support of university goals. For example, the short-term objectives of one institutional relations office included the following:

1. Improve personal contacts with key elements of the university community by hosting lunches for key members of the faculty and administration, sponsoring seminars for the student press, and sending staff members to a variety of meetings and events.
2. Increase coverage of women's athletics through more hometown releases and initiation of stories with local media.
3. Improve the quality of radio programs.
4. Make the university magazine one of the best in the country by improving both content and design.

Once you have established goals and objectives, establish priorities and develop programs that will help you achieve them. For example, one institution listed increasing its contribution to the United Way as an immediate goal. To achieve this, the institutional relations office helped formulate a program that included enlisting volunteers, organizing staff, planning solicitations, reporting results, publicizing the effort, and structuring the campaign timetable.

Another university, under federal court order to double the enrollment of black students over a five-year period, enlisted the help of its public information office. Working with the admissions and alumni offices, a marketing plan was drafted to include advertisements in newspapers and on radio stations; luncheons with representatives from the black media in two major cities in the state; a publicity campaign featuring black faculty, staff, and students; and dinners for black alumni hosted by the president. As a result of these and other efforts, black enrollment at the university increased significantly.

Agree with the people involved on a reasonable timetable for achieving the objective. Once you have a commitment that the objective can be accomplished within the time allotted, be sure, if something goes wrong, to take a close look at how employees are handling the program. Establish review procedures, including periodic reports of what is being done to meet objectives. In this way, adjustments can be made to meet changing situations.

Keep Abreast of Emerging Trends

In 1974, Samuel Irvin, presiding over the Senate's investigation of Watergate, introduced the television audience to his lightning bug theory. Responding to testimony by Nixon aide Robert Haldeman, Irvin said the lightning bug lights up in back and therefore has a lot of hindsight. The bug sees more of where it has been than of where it is going.

Looking ahead in institutional relations comes under the rubric of *issues management,* a growing and important function of institutional relations. This means that the practitioner should scan the political, social, and economic landscape for emerging trends and call them to the attention of the administration for use in strategic planning. The purpose is not to manage the issues. Not even President Nixon could do that effectively during Watergate. It is an effort to manage the institution's position vis-à-vis the emerging trend. An example is the early warning—and subsequent planning to deal with the problem—when statistics showed in the 1970s that the baby boom was over and, as a result, college enrollment would decline the following decade.

E. W. Brody, president of The Resource Group, said it well:

> The impact of Alvin Toffler's *The Third Wave* and John Naisbitt's *Megatrends* on every component of society is creating both challenge and opportunity for public relations practitioners. In the area of public relations, it means focusing more on becoming a proactive rather than a reactive profession.
>
> . . . Logically, issues management can become a major part of the public relations function provided that practitioners:
>
> 1. Maintain adequate levels of knowledge concerning the emerging issues. At minimum, they must acquire and assimilate considerably more information than heretofore has been essential to professional practice. . . .
> 2. Become skilled in 'what if' analysis and planning; able to anticipate the scope and magnitude of issue impact; and adequately delineate the organizational alternative which may arise as a result. Membership in the World Future Society and regular reading of that organization's publications will be most helpful in this context.
> 3. Regularly prepare for management analytical assessments of emerging issues, corporate options and action recommendations to facilitate decision-making on a timely basis and thus enhance subsequent activities which traditionally have been a part of public relations practice [Brody, 1984, p. 15].

Issues management, now focused on the corporate world, is moving onto campus, along with strategic planning, advertising, telecommunications, computer networks, and marketing plans. Institutional relations directors who do not keep pace will find the future does not belong to them.

Serve as an Ombudsman

Increasingly, the institutional relations person is being called on to receive complaints and to investigate their legitimacy and recommend suitable action. The complaints may be relatively minor: An alumnus is unhappy with the appearance of the campus grounds, or a student's request for financial aid has been mishandled. Or it can be of more major consequence. For example, a donor may be offended because the development officer failed to acknowledge a gift, or the president of the alumni association may be outraged because his or her child was denied admission to the college.

An ombudsman must view policies and practices with multiple vision to a degree not done by any other staff officer. Honesty and objectivity are essential and must take precedence over loyalty to the president or the institution. An ombudsman attempts to get problems solved before they explode into a front-page story. This requires that rarest of talents—the ability to listen. Abraham Lincoln once advised a friend: "Keep close to the people—they are always right and will mislead no one." Twice a week he set aside some time for conversations with ordinary folk. He called the conversations his "public opinion baths." The sessions probably provided Lincoln with more complaints and requests than he wanted to hear, but they worked. He always seemed to know what the people were thinking.

There are many informal ways of obtaining feedback in a college or community environment. You can listen anywhere—at social functions (relaxing over cocktails encourages people to talk more freely), on reporting assignments, walking across campus, reading the campus publications, hosting coffees with students, and in a multitude of other ways. Structured feedback, such as the opinion survey, is even more effective.

Pennsylvania State University uses suggestion forms for feedback. The forms are kept in public contact points, such as the student center and information centers. Anyone who has a suggestion fills out a form, describing the nature of the complaint or suggestion. Suggestions are forwarded to the director of public information, who returns the original to various department heads for action. The director keeps one copy. The director follows up to make certain that some action has been taken on the suggestion and that the person submitting it has received a response. The university has received complaints about a discourteous teller at the campus bank, inadequate parking spaces for visitors, the untidiness of the campus, and suggestions for installing an express-line copy machine in the student center and for keeping the campus bookstore open on alumni reunion weekends, among many others.

The role of ombudsman is a highly sensitive one. No administrator likes to be told that something is wrong in the operation and that it should be corrected. To perform the ombudsman's function in a diplomatic manner requires following two simple rules.

First, be certain your president understands what you want to accomplish, feels that it is essential to good management of the institution, and is willing to support your efforts. Once this approval has been obtained, it should be discussed, with you present, at a cabinet meeting so that the role can be properly explained and questions can be answered.

Second, always work through channels. When complaints or suggestion forms are used, the channel for processing them has already been established. It is more difficult when a problem arises through other means. When this happens, discuss the problem first with the supervisor in charge of the area. That individual will appreciate being contacted first, and as a result, will most probably be more open-minded about the issue. But if the problem needs corrective action, and the action is not taken, then it might be necessary to go through channels all the way to the president's office. Occasionally, time may be important, and you may have to bypass some of the channels to bring about quick action. Be certain later to explain this to all affected people. As a general rule, avoid all unnecessary pressures; they only create ill will and make it more difficult to obtain the cooperation needed to implement an institutional relations program.

Use Research in Your Work

In the 1920s, while defending Loeb and Leopold in the famous murder trial in Chicago, Clarence Darrow used a simple form of research to quiet the public outcry against his two clients (Stone, 1958). He sent men to mingle with the crowds in the Loop to ask people whether they thought Loeb and Leopold should hang. Sixty percent of those questioned said yes. He then had the fathers of Loeb and Leopold issue a letter to the press in which they said Darrow would not attempt to get an acquittal but only to prove the boys insane and that Darrow's fee (rumored to be a sell-out figure of a million dollars) would be set by the bar association. The letter received good play in the newspapers. Afterward, Darrow's men went back to the Loop to ask the same questions. They found that 60 percent of the people were now willing to accept life imprisonment for the two boys.

Darrow's quick, informal survey demonstrated that even the simplest research can be used to gain an understanding about public opinion and to make a communications effort to change it. Whether simple or complex, research is very much a part of institutional relations; to operate without it is to operate under a handicap.

The three functions of public relations research, as listed by Robert D. Carlson, public affairs adviser of Standard Oil Company, New Jersey, are to conform, to clarify, and to reorient thinking about matters with public relations implications. Too many institutional relations people shy away from research, either because they do not understand it or because they feel that it costs too much. This is unfortunate, for practical, project-oriented research ought to be a part of every practitioner's tool kit, regardless of the size of the institution. We can have greater confidence in our decisions (and so can the president) when they are supported by solid information, acquired systematically.

A good example of research applied in support of an institutional program is a survey described by Curtis L. Barnes (1971), former director of publications at Syracuse University. The survey was conducted to assist the admissions office in determining the effectiveness of materials made available to prospective students and guidance counselors. Barnes writes:

> The survey form asked secondary school guidance counselors to indicate all of the resources (for example, catalogues, profile books, admissions office visits, college nights, and so forth) they currently use to provide information about higher education to their students. They were then asked to indicate the three best resources that they as counselors used and the three resources most used by students. Finally, they were asked to indicate which of the currently available items could, or should, be eliminated.
>
> The survey was mailed to a selected sample of 124 secondary schools in the eastern United States area, from which Syracuse draws the majority of its students. A 60 percent return on the sample (72-125) was received in ten days.
>
> As one might expect, college catalogues are still a basic source of information for both students and counselors, supplemented by school visits by admissions office personnel. Two surprises that did turn up, however, were that the Barron's college profile series and the Admissions Search Kit (ASK) rated second and third among the student use items.
>
> Since Syracuse currently does not have an individual Barron's profile available, the immediate response to this information was to arrange to have one produced this spring in time for use during the summer and fall recruiting seasons. At the same time, arrangements were made to update the Syracuse information in the ASK kit.

The total time elapsed from the original decision to initiate the survey and the decision to develop the new program (Barron's) suggested by the research data was three weeks. In addition, the strong negative response to college nights and the use of alumni-admissions representatives for recruiting indicates that both of these programs will have to be carefully reconsidered [pp. 1–4].

In my experiences with research, I have learned, as did the people at Syracuse, the following three facts. First, a doctorate is not necessary to conduct usable research for public relations operations. A magazine readership survey can be conducted, for example, by simply following guidelines listed in the literature. One of the best articles on this subject was prepared by Cletis Pride (1973).

Second, it is not necessary for research to be costly. Many professional organizations, such as the Council for Advancement and Support of Education (CASE) and the Public Relations Society of America (PRSA), have qualified people on their staffs who will consult with members, at no cost, in a variety of areas related to public relations. Also, researchers on the campus should not be overlooked, particularly those in planning, communications, sociology, and psychology departments.

Third, and most important, the institutional relations person cannot afford not to do research. Even when research services must be paid for, the cost is offset by savings. One institution, for instance, paid $3,000 for listener surveys to gauge interest in its thirty-minute radio program. On the basis of this study and other research, the program was dropped and a highly successful two-minute program was instituted in its place, at a savings of about $60,000 a year. Such results are well worth the effort.

Emphasize the Role of Counseling

The administration has begun to realize that institutional relations people can serve as a seismograph predicting public reaction to management decisions. Growing pressures in many areas (from governments, alumni, faculty, students, competitors, and others) have forced key administrators to turn to institutional relations people for advice as well as for communications. This is one of the greatest challenges for institutional relations personnel. Each should be prepared to offer campus leaders guidance on matters relating to the institution's fundamental posture, areas of vulnerability, promotional opportunities, and relations with various publics. To do so, it is necessary to work from a broader base of knowledge. This can be accomplished by keeping the following suggestions in mind:

1. *Study your organization.* Learn everything about the institution and where it fits in the spectrum of higher education: its goals, strengths and weaknesses, policies, priorities, academic and nonacademic plans, history and tradition, and faculty-student-staff relationships. This will help you view things from the same perspectives as the president and other key officers and to understand overall interests and the contributions made by each component. This kind of knowledge can provide the insight necessary to formulate balanced judgments. Much of the information needed can be found in past records, campus publications, policy reports and manuals, press releases, and newspaper files; it can be supplemented with information from faculty, administrators, students, and other persons related to the school. George Bernard Shaw said, "You get to a man through his religion, not through yours." It is important that our thinking be consistent with what the president is trying to accomplish, not what we think the president wants done.

2. *Keep your objectivity.* To best serve the president, and the institution, objectivity is essential. Admittedly, this is most difficult to do, especially when many presidents tend to surround themselves with staff people who tell them what they want to hear. In such situations, the institutional relations officer who expresses an objective opinion may be looked upon as a maverick who is not a team player. But let nothing dissuade you from expressing honest, even unpopular, views to the administration. This is both a personal and a professional obligation.

3. *Keep confidences.* Develop the same type of trust with key administrators that physicians have with patients, lawyers with clients, and priests with parishioners. Failure to maintain

confidentiality eventually leads to the lockjaw syndrome, a strange silence that afflicts those who have lost faith in an institutional relations director who is unable to keep secrets.

4. *Advance your education.* American statesman Newton Baker said it well: "The man who graduates today and stops learning tomorrow is uneducated the day after." Like physicians, teachers, and lawyers, institutional relations people need to continually upgrade their skills and expertise, and this can be done in various ways: reading professional publications such as *Currents, Public Relations Journal, Public Relations Review, PR Reporter, Practical Public Relations, Marketing Communications, Advertising Age,* and *Fund Raising Management* and such books as *Voice of the People* (Christenson and McWilliams, 1962), *Megatrends* (Naisbitt, 1983), *Effective Public Relations* (Cutlip and Center, 1971), and *Lesly's Public Relations Handbook* (Lesly, 1971); attending meetings and seminars of the professional organizations, such as CASE, PRSA, and the International Association of Business Communicators; working on advanced degrees, whether in public relations or related fields; and writing professional articles for publication. (Publishing scholarly work will help gain acceptance from the faculty.)

5. *Learn all you can about public opinion.* A major part of your job is to interpret and influence public opinion. Poet James Russell Lowell compared public opinion to the atmosphere: "You can't see it," he observed, "but all the same, it is sixteen pounds to the square inch." Volumes have been written on public opinion, and you should understand how it is formed and how it affects the institution and its publics.

Do you know what community leaders are thinking? Or what students, parents, and alumni are thinking? Do they listen when you tell them about great improvements in education on your campus? If not, why not? Do they appreciate the educational and cultural roles your institution plays? Do not assume that everybody reads and absorbs the messages in your press releases. Maybe everybody does, but you should find out through opinion research.

Public relations counselor Earl Newsom listed four principles of public opinion in Cutlip and Center's *Effective Public Relations* (1971):

(1) *Identification principle.* People will ignore an idea, an opinion, or a point of view unless they see that it affects their fears, desires, or hopes. Your message must be stated in terms of the interest of your audience.

(2) *Action principle.* People do not buy ideas separated from action. Unless a means of action is provided, people tend to shrug off appeals to do things.

(3) *Principle of familiarity and trust.* People buy ideas only from those they trust; they are influenced only by opinions or points of view put forward by individuals, corporations, or institutions in whom they have confidence. Unless the listener has confidence in the speaker, he or she is not likely to listen or to believe.

(4) *Clarity principle.* The situations must be clear, not confusing. The thing read, seen, or heard, the thing that produces the impressions, must be clear. To communicate, it is necessary to employ words, symbols, or stereotypes that the receiver comprehends.

Work on Productivity

In any operation, says Odiorne (1971), there are three ingredients: input, activity, and output. Too much time is usually spent on the first two and not enough on the third, which can also be called results of productivity. In the competition for students and funds, all of us are expected to do more with less.

Most people do not work beyond 60 percent of their capacity. Therefore, there is a lot of unused capacity in all of us, including harassed people in institutional relations. If managers challenge individuals to do more, give them the responsibility and hold them accountable, their unused capacity can be unlocked. Not surprisingly, most people can learn how to increase their productivity, and as a result, end up being happier with themselves. To increase your productivity, learn to:

1. *Utilize time.* William Penn once observed that "Time is what we want most, but what, alas, we use worst." According to some management consultants, only about 10 percent of American workers have learned how to use time well. The trouble is that everyone feels he or she is part of the 10 percent. Beware of the time

wasters: telephone talk, indecision, interruptions, meetings, and mistakes. An excellent book that covers this subject is *Managing Your Time* by Ted W. Engstrom and R. Alec Mackenzie (1968).

2. *Organize the work.* Charles Poors was right when he said, "There is nothing so complicated as simplicity. Infinitudes of distractions or irrelevancies must be forced into perspective to achieve it." Organization helps us simplify our lives. This can be done in many ways. Some people like to draw up a plan of action—a list of duties to be performed during the day, in order of priority—and then work systematically at getting them done. Resist the temptation to go off in too many directions at one time.

3. *Delegate properly.* All of us have the tendency to want to do everything when we could delegate some responsibilities to another employee and thereby increase productivity. For example, some of us like to deliver copy to the printer or to attend all meetings and top-level social functions. We would probably be able to use that time and our talents more effectively by delegating certain of these responsibilities. It is best to list all duties in your operation and then decide what should be done personally and what can be assigned to others. Supervisors are often reluctant to pass on to subordinates responsibilities that they do well themselves. The result is that supervisors are trying to cram sixty hours of work into a forty-hour week, while their employees are trying to stretch thirty hours of work into a forty-hour week.

4. *Insist on deadlines.* Once someone is assigned a responsibility, agree on a deadline for completion. People given deadlines tend to meet them. It is easier to fit the assignment into the work routine than to wait, like students rushing to complete their term papers, until the last minute. It is also important to outline interim steps to meet this deadline with the person responsible for the assignment.

Evaluate Performance Regularly

Self-evaluation is good for the operation. It can be done extensively through an elaborate committee or by bringing in outside consultants who can appraise an operation more objectively. In the interest of saving time and money, you can evaluate your performance by asking yourself:

1. Am I anticipating problems? Or am I waiting for the story to break on the front page of the newspaper or for my boss to arouse me from complacency?
2. Am I spending too much time on petty problems and not enough on the major issues?
3. Am I managing efficiently and effectively?
4. Am I checking up on myself—using systematical technique to measure if, and to what degree, the message is getting through?
5. Are members of my staff more interested in a meal ticket than a mission?
6. Have I done anything lately to advance my professionalism? attended a seminar? read a book or professional publication? enrolled in a course to learn more about telecommunications?
7. Are my sights set high enough? Am I willing to reach for the stars and make the sacrifices, both personally and professionally, to get there?

In educational institutional relations, practitioners are constantly faced with new challenges. One of these is to keep pace with the knowledge in a rapidly growing field. If you can see the light at the end of the tunnel, goes an old adage, turn around. You are facing the wrong direction.

References

Barnes, C. L. "Mini-Research Can Improve PR." *Techniques,* Dec. 1971, pp. 1–4.

Brody, E. W. "Look to the Issues." *PR Casebook,* Jan. 1984, p. 15.

Christenson, R. M., and McWilliams, R. O. *Voice of the People.* New York: McGraw-Hill, 1962.

Cutlip, S. M., and Center, A. H. *Effective Public Relations.* (4th ed.) Englewood Cliffs, N.J.: Prentice-Hall, 1971.

Engstrom, T. W., and Mackenzie, R. A. *Managing Your Time.* Grand Rapids, Mich.: Zondervan, 1968.

Finn, D. "What to Do when the Next Crisis Strikes Your Association." *Association Management,* Nov. 1974, pp. 36-39.

Henle, R. J. "Press Policy for Georgetown University." Georgetown University, Sept. 28, 1972.

Keller, G. "Is College Public Relations Obsolete? It May Be . . ." *Techniques,* Apr. 1975, pp. 2-4.

Lesly, P. *Lesly's Public Relations Handbook.* Englewood Cliffs, N.J.: Prentice-Hall, 1971.

Miller, R. I. *Developing Programs for Faculty Evaluation: A Sourcebook for Higher Education.* San Francisco: Jossey-Bass, 1974.

Naisbitt, J. *Megatrends: Ten New Directions Transforming Our Lives.* New York: Warner Books, 1983.

Odiorne, G. S. *Personnel Administration by Objectives.* Homewood, Ill.: Richard D. Irwin, 1971.

Oswald, J. W. "Press Policy for Penn State." Pennsylvania State University, May 17, 1976.

Pride, C. "Let's Take a Survey." *Techniques,* June 1973, pp. 17-20.

Schrader, R. M., and Bolton, E. "Professionalism in Campus Public Relations and Development." *Techniques,* June 1972, pp. 14-19.

Stone, I. *Clarence Darrow for the Defense.* New York: Bantam Books, 1958.

Toffler, A. *The Third Wave.* New York: William Morrow, 1980.

Wicker, T. "America and Its Colleges: End of an Affair." *Change,* Sept. 1971, pp. 22-25.

10

Howard Ray Rowland

Building Effective Internal Relations

❦ A college or university that neglects its internal relations cannot maintain an effective external relations program. Institutional advancement professionals know that cultivation of broad understanding and support begins on the campus and in the surrounding community. The institution must be understood, trusted, and appreciated in its own home and neighborhood, so to speak, before it can gain credibility and acceptance beyond its borders.

As it does in all social institutions, communication occurs constantly within a college or university. But unless there is a reliable and authoritative communication system, members are often confused and misguided. As observed by Etzioni (1964), problems created by incorrect information and by lack of information can be eliminated, or at least greatly reduced, by an increase in authentic communication. Although psychological barriers often inhibit the communication process, they can be overcome by a communication program that provides interpretation as well as facts (Shook, 1969). It is in management's best interests to operate a comprehensive internal relations program and a communication network that serves everyone within the organization, from custodian to professor. Credibility is the key. A program of internal relations cannot be effective unless it functions in a climate of trust (Cutlip and Center, 1978).

If people in and around a college or university are uninformed or misinformed, if they have little opportunity to respond to messages received, if they are not persuaded to identify with institutional objectives, then the institution is in deep trouble with all of its publics, internal and external. Even minor misapprehensions are greatly magnified when faculty and staff members communicate with outsiders—and they communicate often and are accorded great credibility (Pullman, 1970).

Advancement officers in higher education recognize that private industry is now placing greater emphasis on internal communication. When a national poll of chief executive officers asked them to list their major concerns, employee communication was second only to productivity improvement (Newfarmer, 1984). Ironically, other surveys indicate that chief executive officers generally view communication within the organization more positively than managers and employees. Members of an organization usually want more information than they get. They also want more opportunities to respond to downward communication. But feedback channels are generally deficient (Cutlip and Center, 1978).

The formal organizational structure, which prescribes lines of authority, may be appropriate for many of the institution's needs. But it is not necessarily conducive to clear and easy communication involving all members of the organization (Shook, 1969). The most common failing in employee communication is in selling a management view downward without stimulating an equivalent upward flow of employee views (Cutlip and Center, 1978). Management must support a system that enables employees to communicate upward—to call attention to issues important to them—in a manner that poses no threat to them. The open channels can be as simple as easy access to supervisors, suggestion boxes, a mail-in form, or a column in the employee publication for asking questions or making comments. Each inquiry must be acknowledged and answered. Suggestions that are adopted should be widely publicized. Such a system demonstrates the organization's ability and willingness to respond to the individual employee with sincerity and respect (Cartier, 1984). Even though only a few employees are likely to participate, management's response will favorably impress all employees.

In their illuminating analysis of the best-run U.S. companies, Peters and Waterman (1982) found that the excellent firms put a great deal of emphasis on open communication, creating in all employees an understanding of the company's goals, an awareness that their best efforts are essential, and an assurance that they will share in the rewards of the company's success. The members of those organizations are never in doubt about what the company is doing, why it is being done, and how it affects them. It is this constant flow of information, ideas, and inspiration that separates the outstanding companies from the mediocre.

College and university presidents should make frequent appearances on the campus to learn first-hand what is happening and to show interest in what employees are doing. This kind of personal involvement, which Peters and Waterman call management by wandering around, is practiced by executives of this country's most successful companies. "There is no reason acceptable to employees for the boss's itinerary to be confined to a private parking place, private office, executive dining area, and top-staff meetings," warn Cutlip and Center (1978, p. 300). "There is no reason acceptable to employees for his or her internal communications to be confined to memos and bulletins."

Like any organization, the college or university that relies heavily on indirect, one-way communication methods is not meeting the needs of its members and is working against its own best interests. "We have learned from innumerable studies in communication that face-to-face communication is the most effective means," reports Thaddeus Bonus (1984, p. 2). "We've learned from opinion and attitude surveys that the subordinate looks to the immediate supervisor as the preferred information source, not just about job problems but about the organization."

An internal communication survey of 100 corporations and nonprofit organizations ranked four types of face-to-face communication as more preferred sources of information than all forms of mass media. More than 90 percent cited "my immediate supervisor" as a preferred source, whereas about half wanted small group meetings, top executives, and an orientation program as sources (Newfarmer, 1984). In fifth place among the preferred information sources was the communication vehicle considered to be the prime information source by many college and university administrators: the organization-wide employee publication. Employee preference for personal attention and involvement explains why there has been a shift of emphasis in employee communication from printed and visual media to work-group and study-group meetings (Cutlip and Center, 1978). It seems clear that an internal communication program supported entirely by a backbone of publications will collapse (Blake, 1983).

Why so much demand for face-to-face communication in an age of sophisticated communication technology? There are several reasons: first-hand information on current developments, the highest possible credibility, and the opportunity for instant feedback. But from the management perspective, there are obvious disadvantages: scheduling meetings, lost work time, the logistics of involving a large portion of employees, and the difficulty of finding appropriate leadership for meetings. Another potential disadvantage is that holding meetings to discuss problems creates the expectation that actions will follow (Newfarmer, 1984).

To be effective and productive, meetings require purpose, careful planning and arranging, and skillful direction. Exchanging views openly can benefit everyone if comments are kept on track. That will happen only if the moderator is an experienced, articulate discussion leader (Cutlip and Center, 1978).

Although face-to-face communication is preferred by employees, even audiovisual presentations, such as videotapes, films, and multimedia slide shows, are considered more personal and more credible than the printed word. This is probably because of the one-to-one relationship between presenter and viewer (Newfarmer, 1984). Thousands of corporations, schools, and nonprofit organizations now use videotapes for internal communication. Regular in-house newscasts have high viewership and high credibility. Administrators and other news sources seem more personal on the screen than in print. But videotape presentations are difficult for many colleges and universities because of both the time and expense involved and the problem of finding enough locations at which to show the newscasts to a large segment of the faculty and staff (Newfarmer, 1984). Nevertheless, this is the direction of internal communication in the years ahead.

In its ability to appeal to the emotions, film is unsurpassed by any medium. Film commands undivided attention by combining voices and music with colorful, moving images on a large screen in a darkened room. It is the superior medium for messages that need emotional impact. However, films are relatively slow and expensive to produce and difficult to change (Newfarmer, 1984). They will continue to be used for internal communication by colleges and universities, but sparingly. Multimedia slide shows serve a wide variety of purposes at comparatively low cost and short production time. Also, they are easily revised.

Telephone hotlines are becoming increasingly popular and useful. They provide the campus and the community with current information on events, job openings, volunteer opportunities, and special services. They are also used to spike rumors and give instructions in crisis situations, such as storms, fires, and strikes. Operating a full-service hotline is like running a small radio station, but at far less expense. Two disadvantages are the need for continuous updating of information and continuous publicizing of the hotline number (Newfarmer, 1984).

Perhaps the fastest-moving development in campus communication is sending messages through computer networks. As more offices are linked by computer terminals, electronic mail lessens the volume of conventional mail and telephone calls. The system also extends into the community as college and university employees connect their home computers to the campus network. Businesses and government agencies in the community can be included if it benefits the institution. Although an electronic mailbox reduces human contact and the pleasantries that accompany phone calls, users extol the convenience and efficiency of the system. As the technology continues to improve, electronic mail will supplant many of today's printed messages and small group meetings. Computer networks will be used to conduct conferences as well as to schedule them. The office with the primary responsibility for campus and community relations cannot ignore this new communication system. Sending expensive and time-consuming printed messages by conventional mail is no longer viable when the information can be delivered instantly and personally by electronic mail.

Electronic message boards, with ever-changing information displayed on a screen, are used on many campuses to supplement controlled bulletin boards, which continue to be an effective way to attract attention. For making announcements in campus buildings, closed-circuit television is preferable to public address systems, which should be used sparingly because frequent interruptions are irritating.

Regardless of size, nearly all colleges and universities use newsletters and newspapers or magazines to communicate regularly with members of the campus and the community. Although employees would rather receive information important to them through face-to-face contacts, no internal relations program can succeed without publications. Through print media, management conveys to employees in an official, systematic, organized manner, information that may confirm, reinforce, interpret, and, at times, counter what they have learned in other ways. In addition to regular publications, management also provides reference materials, such as an employee handbook, a policies manual, and the annual report. Included among special publications that serve both campus and community members are a campus map, services and resources guide, speakers directory, and telephone directory. A periodic report summarizing the economic impact of the institution on the community serves a worthwhile purpose. Community residents are reminded that the college or university bolsters the local economy to such an extent that costs attributed to the presence of the institution are relatively insignificant.

Yoder (1984) lists fifty communication ideas for improving internal relations; they range from the conventional (orientation programs for new employees) to the unconventional (rap sessions with governing board members). Among her ideas: letters from the president, displays and exhibits, public relations training programs, service and merit awards, reduced rates for campus events, and a president's reception or dinner. Some of her suggestions could be difficult to implement at an institution where employee contracts are negotiated through collective bargaining.

Collective bargaining is primarily a political process—a power struggle with both sides trying to prove the rightness of their interpretation of the facts (Stephenson, 1971). The longer negotiations drag on, the more difficult it becomes to maintain credible communication. Nevertheless, the administration must make every effort to keep avenues of information open during negotiations, within legal limitations. No worthwhile purpose is served by curtailing internal communication until a contract is signed. On a unionized campus, an important communication channel is the regularly scheduled meet-and-confer session between management and bargaining unit representatives.

Institutional communicators tend to disregard the pervasive influence that the student-run newspaper and radio station have on campus and community relations. They should make every effort to cultivate good working relationships with those media and to keep them supplied with information. If they respect student press freedom and treat the student newspaper as they do other newspapers, they generally will receive fair treatment. However, administrators should not be unduly alarmed when the student newspaper errs or attacks. Most people on the campus and in the community make allowances for the excesses of the student press. But inexperience and enthusiasm should not excuse student journalists from observing the ethical standards of conduct practiced by professional journalists.

As with the student-run newspaper, the primary audience for the student-run radio station is on the campus and in the community. Although much of its programming is music, the station may broadcast a variety of campus news, features, interviews, and activities if it gets assistance and encouragement. A college or university with its own television station or access to a television channel can improve campus and community relations through selective programming. Many opportunities exist for communicating with local audiences through news programs, interviews, forums, call-in shows, and coverage of campus activities. The integration of computers and television to provide interactive information systems will lead to profound changes in communication, commerce, education, and life-styles in general. Customary ways of becoming informed and responding to that information are being supplanted by the new technology. Recognizing the implications of these developments, professional communicators must program information and services into these systems to benefit their institutions. For further information on internal relations, see Chapter Forty-Eight.

The proliferation of information hinders internal communication efforts on any campus. Bombarded by messages from many sources, faculty and staff members tend to ignore most of them and skim the rest. Thus they often claim that they were not informed about something when, in fact, the message was sent but not received. There is no simple solution to this problem, although it is obvious that, to command attention, internal communicators must make their messages brief and compelling. And they must remember the axiom for communicators: If you want a message to get through, send it more than one way (Newfarmer, 1984). No matter how excellent a single medium of communication, the information in it will reach only a portion of the audience.

Emergencies that occur on campuses around the nation each year underscore the need to develop strategies for internal communication under adverse conditions. Although the exact nature of a possible crisis cannot be anticipated, a broad plan of action should be prepared and practiced so that individuals and offices will know what to do in stressful or life-threatening circumstances. For example, it should be known in advance that when a crisis comes, official announcements will come from only one office—a command post staffed by preassigned personnel. Internal communication channels must be cleared and reserved for immediate and sustained use. To allow the operations center to initiate calls to obtain current information, telephone lines must not be tied up by incoming calls. Provision must be made for rapid dissemination of information to the campus and community through radio, television, the computer network, the telephone system, and print media. Every institution should periodically conduct crisis preparedness sessions to review and revise its plan.

A number of colleges and universities have systematically improved their internal relations in recent years. Shippensburg State College, concerned about a nettlesome attitude problem in the late 1970s, adopted a comprehensive plan to enhance management/employee relationships. It included more frequent meetings between managers and employees, a telephone hotline to provide and receive messages, and a program to recognize employees who make money-saving suggestions (Cartier, 1984). In 1981, Portland State University administrators learned through a readership survey that the support staff needed more attention in the institution's internal publication. Consequently, the publication carried a series of feature articles on individual employees providing university services, which helped the university reinforce a sense of community, one of its internal relations goals (Cartier, 1984). In 1975, Eastern Michigan University propped up employees' sagging morale by publicizing their achievements in a new publication and producing a daily events calendar, distributed both on the campus and in the community (Fountain, 1977). In 1977, the University of Wisconsin-Stout minimized the adverse effects of an employee strike by clearly defining administrative objectives and maintaining an open communication system (Enger, 1977).

As these examples suggest, internal relations will be deficient unless the primary responsibility for planning, coordinating, and evaluating those programs is assigned by the chief executive to a highly qualified communicator or to an office staffed with trained and experienced professionals, supported by adequate resources to achieve institutional objectives.

To foster a favorable climate for two-way communication, an internal communication policy must be adopted and disseminated. The policy should obligate the administration to provide employees with timely and useful information on the institution's objectives, plans, and operations. A survey of employees at the University of Utah revealed that the topic of greatest general interest for them was the institution's future plans, even though they were also very interested in such concerns as job advancement opportunities and personnel policies (Newfarmer, 1984). Employees need to be informed through internal channels about important matters that affect them before the information reaches them through external channels. Employees should be persuaded that their ideas and suggestions for improvements are important and will be considered by management. Achievements of employees should be recognized and commended through both internal and external media. The bottom line in assessing the effectiveness of an internal communication policy is how this question is answered: Are the employee's interests being considered, or is management sending only one-way messages?

What are the essentials of an internal relations plan? A variety of communication channels must be established and maintained, with emphasis on upward communication. In communicating, it is better to err by repetition than by omission. Opinion and attitude surveys should be conducted periodically for both faculty and staff members. The findings will reveal what they do not know, what misinformation they have, and what troubles them about the institution. Instead of guessing, the professional communicator learns what needs to be done to improve internal relations. Exit interviews provide another useful source of information. Why are people leaving? What should be done to retain employees? Orientation programs for new employees usually can be improved. The benefits program of the institution should be promoted because it is probably better than most employees realize (Bonus, 1984).

A good example of a productive employee survey is the one conducted in 1976 at the University of Oregon Health Sciences Center. Sponsored by the university relations office and supported by the president's office, the poll gave every employee an opportunity to participate in the institution's planning process and communication network. Most of the recommendations resulting from the study were implemented as part of the center's internal relations program. Improvements included adoption of internal communication objectives, regular meetings of the president with faculty members, addition of a president's newsletter, implementation of an employee suggestion program, and publication of a faculty handbook (Lockwood, 1977).

The communication office and the personnel office must plan and work together to enhance internal relations. Each has resources the other needs to accomplish common objectives. The communication office can publicize and promote activities for employees conducted by the personnel office, such as service or performance recognition programs, recreation and fitness programs, training sessions, orientation programs, and counseling services. The personnel office can support activities for employees conducted by the communication office, such as public relations workshops and employee surveys. The communication office also can help the personnel office improve its employee publications.

Built into every internal relations program should be ways to measure the effectiveness of various activities toward achieving specific objectives. The tendency to get caught up in the mechanics of doing something often results in neglecting the more difficult job of determining what is being accomplished. There will never be sufficient time, staff, or budget to do everything that could be done under the rubric of internal relations. Priorities must be determined and choices made. An annual program review, matching results with objectives, is a good approach to assessment and accountability.

Professional communicators charged with internal relations responsibilities must ask themselves key questions in evaluating their performance:

1. Are you helping supervisors at all levels get information of importance to those who report to them? Are you helping them find ways to communicate?
2. Are you planning ways to help top administrators reach more directly into the campus community?
3. Are you finding persons with expertise in developing small group meetings and working them into the campus communication programs? (Reuss, 1984).

Although conducting an internal relations program is a complex operation, the guidelines are simple. To expect support and loyalty from employees, management must demonstrate interest in employees, respond to information from employees, and participate with employees in activities (Cutlip and Center, 1978).

Despite the changing nature of many institutions of higher education, the need to maintain good campus relations remains paramount. Management must strive to keep everyone in and around the institution informed and involved through communication channels and support systems. Internal harmony facilitates external achievement. Had colleges and universities been more sensitive to campus relations during the quarter of a century after World War II, they might have avoided many external problems.

Administrators now realize that effective institutional relations are built from the inside out (Winkler, 1984).

The institution's chief executive and its designated advancement officer have the primary responsibility for improving understanding and relationships among faculty, students, staff, and administrators in order to attain shared objectives. Their ability to meet the challenge can contribute substantially to institutional well-being.

References

Blake, J. P. "Creative Approaches to Institutional Internal Relations." *Public Relations Journal,* 1983, *39* (3), 22–24.

Bonus, T. "Work for an Open Internal Communication Policy." In *Improving Internal Communication.* Washington, D.C.: Council for Advancement and Support of Education, 1984.

Cartier, L. "The Internal Communicator's Prominent Role in PR." In *Improving Internal Communication.* Washington, D.C.: Council for Advancement and Support of Education, 1984.

Cutlip, S. M., and Center, A. H. *Effective Public Relations.* (5th ed.) Englewood Cliffs, N.J.: Prentice-Hall, 1978.

Enger, J. K. "Strategy During a Strike." *CASE Currents,* Nov. 1977, pp. 20–21.

Etzioni, A. *Modern Organizations.* Englewood Cliffs, N.J.: Prentice-Hall, 1964.

Fountain, J. C. "A New Image Begins at Home." *CASE Currents,* Nov. 1977, pp. 24–25.

Lockwood, M. A. "Employee Survey Raises the Campus Consciousness." *CASE Currents,* Nov. 1977, pp. 13–16.

Newfarmer, T. D. "How to Communicate Internally Through Multiple Media." In *Improving Internal Communication.* Washington, D.C.: Council for Advancement and Support of Education, 1984.

Peters, T. J., and Waterman, R. H., Jr. *In Search of Excellence: Lessons from America's Best-Run Companies.* New York: Warner Books, 1982.

Pullman, D. "Planning the Internal Role." *College and University Journal,* 1970, *9* (1), 39–41.

Reuss, C. "Writing for the Internal Audience." In *Improving Internal Communication.* Washington, D.C.: Council for Advancement and Support of Education, 1984.

Shook, D. D. "A Plan for Internal Communication." *Techniques,* Nov.-Dec. 1969, pp. 18-20.

Stephenson, H. (ed.). *Handbook of Public Relations.* (2nd ed.) New York: McGraw-Hill, 1971.

Winkler, H. D. "Backyard Diplomacy." *Currents,* Sept. 1984, pp. 34-38.

Yoder, S. L. "Five Steps to Developing an Internal Communication Plan." In *Improving Internal Communication.* Washington, D.C.: Council for Advancement and Support of Education, 1984.

11   *Donald R. Perkins*

Interpreting the Institution to External Constituencies

❧ Each fall, colleges and universities in the United States enroll about 12 million students, or approximately 5 percent of the nation's population. Some 78 percent of those students are admitted to public institutions; 22 percent matriculate at private schools. During an academic year, American higher education awards approximately 1 million bachelor's degrees, 295,000 master's degrees, and more than 30,000 doctorates. Full-time and part-time professors employed in colleges and universities number about 700,000. Each year, higher education spends about $95 billion, making it one of the leading industries in the United States.

An enterprise of this magnitude, if it is to achieve maximum success, must enjoy the confidence of the many publics on which it depends for understanding and support. It must also fully accept and support the thesis that an informed public is most often a supporting public. Although the task of interpreting a college or university to its many constituencies belongs to a wide range of persons connected with the institution, leadership for external relations rests primarily with external relations professionals.

External relations in a college or university can be defined as the broad, conscious effort of an institution to foster in the public eye: first, its identity; then, understanding of its mission and priorities; and ultimately, support in dollars, enrollment, and awareness of acceptable image. College external relations professionals must know well the institution's history, mission and priorities, board of trustees, president, faculty, students, alumni, and friends. Also required is an understanding of the particular setting in which the institution is located, with strategies to maximize strengths and minimize weaknesses.

External relations programs that make maximum contributions to their institutions are those demonstrating an understanding that the many factors affecting the lifelines of higher education are increasingly important and ever-shifting. Moreover, the status of external relations programs in an institution, and the support given them, often depends on the degree to which they exert an influence on those factors.

The ancient Greek motto "We never step twice in the same river" aptly describes higher education today. Only a cursory examination of the climate in which higher education operates is required to set the agenda for a dynamic, comprehensive external relations program that adapts to changing times.

When applied to college enrollments, demographics are less than promising. As one authority has noted, "The babies have already not been born." He meant that as fewer children enter elementary school fewer will eventually graduate and achieve the first requirement for college matriculation. One stark witness to lower enrollments is the number of elementary school buildings standing empty or for sale. High school consolidations are further evidence that fewer pupils are progressing through the school systems. Projections that show an increase in college enrollments by 1997 offer hope for the future, but meanwhile, colleges and universities face more than a decade of declining enrollments. A shrinking high school graduate pool has, in recent years, generated increased efforts and adoption of new recruiting techniques by college admission officers, including appeals for more help from the institution's external relations professionals.

The number of potential college freshmen is being further eroded by private enterprise, which in recent years has established schools offering courses from cosmetology to computer programming. The armed forces spend millions of dollars advertising that they can help fund a college education that is deferred until after active duty. The battle for enrollment has also been joined over rising costs, especially in private higher education, but with costs rapidly accelerating for both private and public college educations.

Add to these factors the erosion of the U.S. dollar by inflation, and the problem of finding sufficient numbers of qualified students to fill college classrooms becomes more than mildly alarming.

For the state-assisted institutions, the pressure is no less severe to secure funding based on head-count enrollment. The economies of many states have been sinking, with consequent lowering of per capita funding to state colleges and universities. In a number of states, tuition at state schools has been raised to help cover the gaps.

Moreover, federal regulations (which make it less attractive for the wealthy to make contributions) and reduced giving by donors to unrestricted purposes are eroding dollars raised by both private and state colleges and universities.

Against this background, the highest degree of validity is to be found in external relations strategies that interpret the institution's mission and priorities to its constituents in ways that win support in dollars, enrollment, and acceptable image.

Success in contributing to the first two forms of support—dollars and enrollment—is not difficult to assess. Did the institution meet its fund-raising goals, including annual support goals and the goals of any special or restricted fund drives? And was the student population, especially the freshman class, of a caliber and number consistent with expectations? The question must then be asked: What significant, documentable contributions did external relations make in the effort to secure dollars and students?

Measurement of the impact of external relations programs on the third form of support—acceptable image—is often more inexact. Numerous research tools are available to determine what perceptions of an institution are held by constituencies or target audiences. Some college alumni offices enlist the aid of their psychology or sociology departments in devising questionnaires aimed at discovering graduates' attitudes about their alma mater. Many colleges and universities try to keep abreast of constituent opinions by constantly testing the waters; this informal method calls for all external relations professionals having contact with constituent groups to report what was heard about the institution—positive and negative.

An external relations program aimed at making significant contributions to dollars, enrollment, and acceptable image must be based on careful planning and wide consensus.

The most effective external relations planning results from the free exchange of ideas by professionals of similar training, ingenuity, and creativity. Equally essential is the endorsement of plans by higher-level administrators (including boards of directors, presidents, and vice-presidents) and the adoption and enthusiastic support of program-level persons who must implement them.

By now, most higher education institutions have subjected themselves to the rigor of determining their mission and priorities. It is an inestimable asset for external relations professionals to have the institution's mission and priorities spelled out in writing, for it is on these that all external relations planning should rest. The best external relations plan will adhere unchangingly to the guidelines of the institution's mission while changing priorities when the institution's priorities change.

An institution's priorities are intended to span a definite time frame, with five years often considered the optimum length. Priorities generally center on preserving what has been judged excellent, improving what exists but may be subpar, and on acquiring what is not already available. If codified statements of institutional mission and priorities are not available, the resourceful external relations professional can, by close attention to statements, decisions, and actions of the president and the board of trustees, discern major directions and primary concerns and projects. From whatever source, then, external relations persons should secure an understanding of the institution's mission and priorities. Such understandings are seminal to planning; they are the taproots for strategy, for it is from the institution's mission and priorities that all external relations programs flow. Perhaps one of the most readily discernible institutional priorities is the capital campaign. A decision to launch a major fund drive gives external relations persons marching orders for the duration of the effort.

From a statement of mission and priorities for the institution, effective external relations professionals construct the mission and priorities of the external relations program. A statement of mission for an external relations program describes what is going to be done, and why. A statement of priorities defines those tasks within the mission that are being chosen because (1) they are the most important things to be done at a specific time or (2) they are the things that are the most accomplishable at a specific time.

A typical statement of mission for an external relations program might conclude: "External relations programs seek to inform all of the institution's constituencies of the past achievements of the institution, which have contributed to its current high stature; to describe its achievements as it keeps abreast of modern higher education; and to portray its future hopes and aspirations as it seeks to maintain and enhance its position as a leading institution of higher education. The purpose of this effort is to gain constituency support in the form of gifts, student enrollment, and good will toward the institution."

It is important that an external relations statement of mission clearly define the ways in which programs and activities fit into and help advance the overall mission of the institution. Like the statement of mission of the institution, the statement delineating the role of external relations programs may not change.

If an institution's five-year set of priorities focuses on a capital campaign, the statement of priorities for external relations might be as follows: "To further position the institution as one on the rise academically and fully capable of being compared with its peer prestige colleges nationally. The primary motivation behind this effort is the planned capital campaign. Intense efforts will be made to heighten the institution's visibility in areas where fund drives will be conducted. These efforts will coincide with fundraising strategies."

Priorities are most useful when they are set for specified periods of time and are flexible and able to change as demands change. However, all priorities ever established should further the mission and priorities of the institution.

The benefits of constructing a statement of mission and priorities for external relations are many, but prime among them is its usefulness in helping keep in focus the aims and objectives of programs while aiding significantly in assessing progress toward goals and in evaluating individual and group performance. It is also useful in explaining what external relations does and does not do and the reasons for decisions on what is to be done.

A statement of mission and priorities is, in addition, an important sign of professional competence, which can be of significant aid in justifying staffing and budgeting.

With the guiding philosophy of external relations in place in the statement of mission, and the pragmatic objectives delineated in the statement of priorities, attention can be turned to planning for effective outreach.

Four steps, carefully thought out, will greatly enhance chances for success. They are

1. Defining target audiences
2. Defining themes
3. Defining methods
4. Evaluating results

When defining target audiences, it is important to ask:

1. Who must be reached with news and information, publications, alumni programs, and other outreach efforts? In short, what people must know (that is, your institution), what you do, and the significance of it because their understanding and support are vital to the continued well-being of your institution. Who are the most important individuals and groups?
2. Why should those particular persons, groups, or organizations be reached? What is the significance of their relationship to the institution? Is it for dollars, students, or acceptable image?
3. What action or actions do you want those particular persons, groups, or organizations to take?
4. What response will indicate that the desired action has been achieved?

A college or university will have multiple target audiences, but seldom will efforts be pointed at reaching all of them with the same message. A list of typical external audiences might include:

1. The community where the institution is located
2. Alumni
3. Current and past parents of students
4. Potential students
5. Parents of potential students
6. Foundations and corporations
7. Current and potential donors
8. State (and possibly national) legislators
9. Citizens of the state in which the institution is located
10. The region in which the institution is located
11. The nation

If the institution is church-affiliated, another important target audience is obvious: members of the sponsoring denomination.

When defining themes, the important questions to ask are

1. What messages are important to transmit to the target audience?
2. What are the most important facts in the messages; that is, what facts need constant repetition so as to make a lasting impact?

Themes are the concepts or ideas about an institution that define what it is, what it does, and why it does it. For example, one institution might list as its themes:

1. Ours is a small, independent college concentrating on the liberal arts.
2. The academic program is rigorous but is balanced by a rewarding life outside the classroom.
3. The college is a caring place where individuals receive personal attention.
4. Academic standards are high.
5. The college is well-managed, with stable enrollments and sound financial resources.
6. The college accepts people as part of the family.
7. The professors are master teachers who care about their students and give them a great deal of personal attention.

8. The students are bright, imaginative, and a challenge to their professors.
9. Persons who graduate from our college are successful.
10. The college and the community in which it is located have a cooperative and productive interaction.
11. The president is a confident, hard-working higher education leader widely respected for his (or her) knowledge and ability.

Best results are most often obtained when external relations efforts reflect one or more themes. This includes such outreach techniques as news releases, photographs, admissions literature, alumni magazine, alumni programs, and fund appeals. The most effective use of themes is made by matching information about the institution, or programs that represent it, with the interests or need to know of the target audience or audiences. Moreover, some themes or combinations of themes may be more effective than others in eliciting target audience response in support of dollars, enrollment, or acceptable image. Knowledge of target audiences, the ranges of their interests in the institution, and the ways in which interests can be matched with information becomes paramount.

The themes or messages selected for communication to the target audience or audiences must be delivered by the vehicle that offers the greatest degree of assurance that the message will be received and that the desired response will be made. For example, if popular media are the chosen vehicle, a determination of the reading, listening, and viewing habits of the target audience or audiences will provide guidelines for communications strategies. Depending on the target audience, other vehicles might include alumni magazine articles, alumni meetings, brochures, special appeal mailings, or invitations to campus—all the communication methods that can be drawn from the external relations professional's wide range of knowledge and experience.

The answers to four basic questions can play a major role in helping evaluate the success of an external relations program:

1. Based on the desired response, was the correct target audience or audiences selected?

2. Did the delivery system, or vehicle, effectively reach the target audience or audiences?
3. Did the themes, messages, programs, or other methodology suit the target audience?
4. Did the target audience or audiences make the desired response?

The technique of determining target audiences, themes, and methods and evaluating results can be used not only for an overall external relations program but also, in miniature, to guide a single external relations effort.

One of the most important ways in which overall external relations planning can be miniaturized is in community relations. Regardless of how widespread a college or university's constituencies may become, the institution must first live successfully in its own backyard. Many different strategies have yielded success in developing and enhancing relationships with the college's closest target audience. One institution helped persons from the local community form a Community Advisory Council that meets periodically with campus administrators and representatives from student groups, fraternities, and sororities. Another college invites members of the city and county administration and police and fire departments to an annual fall meeting on campus with administrators. Discussion centers on past, current, and foreseen problems and how to cooperate in solving them.

A speakers' bureau, made up of faculty, administrators, and students, can be a conduit for exchanges of information between campus and community, especially if time is left for questions at the end of presentations. A Midwestern university claims outstanding success after constructing a new all-purpose building in a campus location that provides ready access for use by community groups at little or no cost. Discovery that it had not for many years invited local persons to a campus open house was a spur for a successful fall event at one college.

Tours of campus should not be limited to prospective students and special visitors. Making campus maps available in a central location and clearly marking routes will encourage local persons to engage in self-conducted campus visits. For examples of other programs for communicating with the external public, see

Chapters Thirty-Five, Thirty-Nine, Forty-One, Forty-Seven, and Forty-Nine.

Many colleges and universities try to ensure local understanding and support by electing to the board of trustees persons of means and stature from their immediate areas. If they are kept fully informed, such persons can be valuable emissaries, heading off rumor, spreading good will, and by personal example, lending validity to the institution's mission and priorities.

Some academic departments have benefited by forming advisory committees of leading local persons who offer advice on such things as updating curriculum, programs, and job placement activities.

All higher education institutions exert a significant economic impact on their local areas, and periodically, a reminder of this fact can reap positive results. Some colleges print an economic impact brochure that details how many dollars are added to the area by faculty and staff salaries, goods purchased, construction projects, events surrounding opening and closing the academic year, homecoming, and alumni and parents' weekends.

Since Harvard, the first higher education institution in the United States, opened its doors in 1636, external relations has been important to the survival and success of the nation's colleges and universities. Facing the 1990s and beyond, higher education will be no less reliant on strategies that promote public understanding and support.

12

R. Keith Moore

Expressing the Institution in the Print Media

In the 1960s, an unpopular war aroused skeptical youths, from the University of California's Sather Gate in Berkeley across the nation to Colby College atop the grassy Maine slopes of Mayflower Hill. Vietnam, Woodstock, pot, and student protests forced the best academic news services to mature as they endured their most divisive campus crises since the first academic news bureau was set up at the University of Michigan in 1897.

During this historic period, while the effective news services assured their reputations, many sleepy operations destroyed their credibility with the media for years to come. When surveys during that period proved that the respect of Americans for educational institutions had hit an all-time low, colleges everywhere revamped their news services to rebuild that lost respect.

One person who worked those sixties demonstrations from the news bureau side is Robert Beyers, head of Stanford University's news service.* He says the secret to sustaining media trust is amazingly simple. "Think like a journalist and you'll serve your campus well; write like a journalist and you'll serve it better," he advises. Jerrold Footlick, a senior editor at *Newsweek*, recollects finding an excellent news operation during that period when news services everywhere matured. "Cornell's news bureau set up every interview, pro or con, that we requested," he remembers.

*Unless otherwise indicated, the quoted material in this chapter was obtained through personal conversations or other communications between the author and the party cited.

Editor Footlick, in hindsight, is convinced that Cornell's cooperation should be emulated by other institutions that wish to "put their own spin on controversial stories, potential scandals, rapes, assaults, or robberies." Institutions usually depend on their news services to portray their programs positively in order to help recruit students and court donors. With these expectations and habits, the campus that can digest only life's vanilla experiences soon chokes on controversies. Institutions, through their news services, should make hay, according to Beyers, by promoting ideas, even controversial ones that have a potential to alter our lives. "Give me an Apple Macintosh and the freedom to cover any campus in the country as a journalist, and we'll succeed," he promises.

Beyers's advice to search and publicize ideas is not uniformly practiced. For one reason, the personalities on campus, on any campus, normally confound most inexperienced campus news professionals, who may become intimidated by the constraints that academics put upon them. Newcomers often are unprepared to deal with the personality contradictions they discover.

Another confusing aspect of an academic news service is the way the main activities of education (imparting knowledge and developing within a young person that precious ability to think for oneself) can be obscured by the greater news impact of a research breakthrough, a firing of a high-level administrator, a student protest, or a winning sports team. Did the cheating scandals that made news at the U.S. Air Force Academy more than a decade ago mean that all the academy's students cheated? Of course not. Then, too, why do so few people recognize the stars from among 7,000 faculty of the University of Southern California while millions recall, instead, many of the 7,000 athletes, coaches, and officials who spent two weeks in 1984 residing there in one of the two Los Angeles Olympic villages?

A third contradiction facing newcomers is that few people can answer the question: Is the news operation benefiting the institution? Surveys, for instance, showed that 125,000 daily visitors and 2.5 billion viewers familiarized themselves with the USC campus during the Olympics, but almost no direct correlation has been documented between this exposure and increases in student enrollment or in financial or legislative support. One might conclude incorrectly that, although some modern news services are finding ways to measure the results of their work, no validation exists for the raison d'être of a news service.

Finally, a fourth quirk recognizes the deluge of the broadcast and television media, but news services still focus almost total energies on attracting space in the print media. Why? Well, there are several reasons, including expense, convenience, and comfort. At least one, and perhaps several, of the almost 2,000 daily and 8,000 weekly periodicals in the United States are at the institution's own doorstep. In addition, magazines have expanded rapidly during the past three decades, with 4,000 new periodicals reaching the stands since 1950. These provide attractive new markets directed to women, health and exercise buffs, computer and science advocates, and many others.

Lee Mitgang, New York–based Associated Press education writer, observes another clue to academia's bias toward print. He says, "Comparatively speaking, the reporters find the relationships with education are far healthier and more open than those with government or business." Sustaining those healthy relationships resembles, for both parties, a small-risk operation, like an appendectomy, not a heart bypass.

Setting Up Shop

Where do you start? Whether you anticipate running a news service for a small institution with limited resources or a large shop with an unlimited budget, your most prized possessions will be the same everywhere—your telephone, typewriter (or word processor), copier, campus telephone directory, and a set of good resource guides.

The set must include one of the many media contacts directories published by *Editor and Publisher*, Gebbie, IMS Ayer, and other firms. In addition to a thesaurus and a dictionary, you will need a stylebook (by, for example, the University of Chicago Press, *The New York Times*, Associated Press, or United Press International) for producing professional copy. The media guides will tell you the addresses and telephone numbers of periodicals, describe deadlines and operating methods, and give you the names of the people you will contact. The other tools will assure that your materials are prepared professionally, as long as you apply the standards religiously.

Methods of each news office, as you might expect, reflect its institution's coverage opportunities as well as the emphasis the college or university desires. Many large offices at colleges with good sports programs oversee the sports information function. These offices will invest in a set of valuable sports guides, such as the directory of staff members of the National Collegiate Athletic Association (NCAA) member institutions, NCAA record books, and sets of statistical forms for major sports. Any service with a medical center will probably secure a copy of a medical dictionary (for example, those by Dorland, Stedman, and Taber) and a textbook or two from the freshman internal medicine or surgical nursing course. Whatever the related specialties are, reliable sourcebooks are musts.

Your filing system must be comprehensive enough to put every essential at your fingertips and limited enough to permit quick use. You will start by setting up biography files for key professors and administrators (perhaps, at a small institution, for students and trustees, too). Each file should include a recent photo, pertinent biographical information, copies of releases and articles previously published, and clippings from past news coverage mentioning that individual. You cannot exist for long without other files:

1. A clippings file to record chronologically what has been published already
2. A file of photo contact sheets of shots taken by the staff photographer(s) or free-lancers
3. A file of the institution's most important documents, including annual reports, long-range plans, presidential speeches, enrollment projections, and fund-raising summaries
4. A general file on special projects, such as commencements, convocations, homecomings, and lectures
5. A file of ongoing faculty research projects, proposals, and grant applications to use for some of your most interesting stories

6. A media information file for notes on personnel changes, correspondence, and records of contacts with the news media

Directing a News Service

If you have assembled all these necessities and assume you have mastered the job of directing a news service, think again. As any newcomer quickly discovers, this job varies greatly from institution to institution. Three San Francisco Bay Area examples illustrate this diversity.

If any shop is typical, it is probably the small shop with limited resources. At Mills College, for example, a campus of almost 1,000 women students in Oakland, California, directing the news office demands a generalist. The staff there includes Susan Shea (a director of college relations), an associate director (who handles seventy-five publications with a publishing budget of approximately a quarter of a million dollars), and an assistant. The office's equipment inventory reveals push-button telephones, a self-correcting typewriter, a radio, and a television set (to monitor the electronic coverage) but no dedicated copier. That is down the hall.

Here, the director's job description holds her "responsible for planning and implementing a comprehensive, coordinated communications effort in support of college goals." According to the office's annual summary of activities, priority projects for the year were "preparation for the upcoming (capital) campaign and development of budgets and plans for expanding publication management." To achieve its news aims, "the office distributed 90 press releases, 15 radio and television announcements, and 190 student 'hometown' news releases."

Although Mills's staff contains more professionals than many others, Mills typically expects the director to perform numerous duties beyond relating to reporters. A study of similar operations conducted in the mid 1980s for the College and University Public Relations Association of Pennsylvania revealed communicators who performed darkroom work, solicited donations, produced TV tapes, and taught undergraduate courses. It is not unusual, for example, to see the small college equivalent of a Ms. Shea with an Olympus OM-10 camera in hand, photographing a check presentation. This director of college relations also represents Mills in activities relating to the state legislature and supervises convocation details.

Flexibility is the rule for the generalist who runs a small shop, but as the news operations get larger, more specialization appears, and operating philosophies may differ immensely.

At Stanford University, in Palo Alto, where the staff sends out around 1,800 news releases annually, Beyers has a backup copier in the office in case trouble develops with the primary machine. Always focusing on those ideas mentioned earlier, the prolific Beyers and his colleagues work in offices located in both a central headquarters facility (six writers) and college buildings throughout the campus (eight to twelve more). They are rich in resources with a faculty that has included 9 Nobel prize winners, more than 115 members of the American Academy of Arts and Sciences, and more than 70 members of the National Academy of Science. Every idea they can handle, they publicize in a news release and in articles in the *Stanford Observer* (mailed to 150,000 readers seven times per year) and *The Stanford University Campus Report* (which reaches 16,000 supporters close at hand). The TRS-100 typewriter on Beyers's desk accounts for two features per day, if possible. But the real workhorses are the copiers and a word processing system that can set publication galleys directly from the writers' original keystrokes.

Some news services target their efforts with a rifle; some use a shotgun approach. Stanford salutes major ideas as if they were war heroes—by exploding a row of cannons. The news service has sent a single release to up to 1,000 people, a total so large it shocks many news professionals. For important releases, in addition to exhausting media lists, Stanford may use one of several business newswires available to educational institutions. "We spend millions of dollars on research, and it is unwise to have a $30 decision about whether or not to use a PR newswire drive the system," Beyers believes. So he advocates a supplemental newswire when appropriate. Because he revises his mailing lists annually, he insists that everyone on the list wants to be there.

To him, success results from spreading an idea as broadly as possible. "When an idea is totally ignored and gets no debate, it really galls me," he says. One idea he published widely a few years ago revealed inadequacies in the school's library, hardly a popular gambit at many educational institutions trying to recruit students. Beyers suggests that his release was partly responsible for Stanford's subsequently upgrading its library facilities. On another occasion, the university received a $21 million gift from a private corporation when two of the company's trustees discovered an idea they liked in the *Observer*.

Similar news principles are practiced nearby in a prestigious public institution, the University of California. Public information offices of varying sizes are on each of the nine campuses, at major contract laboratories, in the medical centers at Davis, Los Angeles, and San Diego, in the extension divisions and cooperative extension service, and in the system headquarters. These offices, particularly the one on the renowned Berkeley campus, exhibit how a public system runs its news service. Some normal competitiveness exists among the news services, accountability is to the state legislature, and information energies are directed in part to 750,000 alumni of the UC system.

"There aren't many differences between news services in private and public institutions," says Ray Colvig, long-time manager of UC Berkeley's Office of Public Information. "The taxpayers pay good money for the educational programs, and they should know how their money is being spent. We are necessary because the news media can't possibly cover all that's going on here."

Colvig's staff cannot always cover all the news either. To cover the 9 professional schools, 75 to 80 teaching departments, 25 to 30 research units, and about 2,000 researchers and teachers, as well as the campus administration, Colvig assigns his small staff expansive beats. They break down this way. As manager, he covers the campus administration and does troubleshooting. An assistant manager oversees news in education, social sciences, health services, and the women's center. A senior information representative covers physical and biological sciences, engineering, natural resources, space sciences, seismology, the campus environment, libraries, and enrollment matters. A veteran writer covers the business school, environmental design, law, governmental studies, most humanities departments, and international studies. A newer writer handles public health, nutrition, and other health-related fields. An administrative assistant and two full-time clerical workers complete the staff. For photography, Colvig hires free-lancers or calls on the publications office for help.

The University of California at Berkeley, like Stanford, erupts regularly with stories that need no promotion. In 1984, when archeologists discovered in Ethiopia bones of a female form that apparently pushed back the date of the earliest known recording of mankind's existence, *Science* magazine summarized the controversial find in a story entitled "The Problems of Dating an Older Woman." The staff's output in recent years has exceeded 400 releases annually (including calendar shorts, memos announcing photo opportunities, and so forth). Berkeley is one of the few campuses existing today that equip a full-time press room for off-campus media personnel who visit the campus. The staff may receive as many as 100 media requests in a single day. Basic science stories, such as those on astronomy, archeology, and paleontology, draw the most attention; social science stories about controversies that impinge on personal life-styles place second. "We don't go out looking for lecture announcements because we simply don't have time to do them," Colvig says. "We try to help offices do their own announcements if they need publicity. We're busy trying to keep up with reporting the major news each day."

Attracting Local News Coverage

So, which methods will help you get maximum exposure for your institution? Whether you saturate the country with an idea, as Stanford advocates, or focus your resources on particular specialties, as UC Berkeley does, relationships with the local media are crucial. Local media usually must first publish the story if you expect to extend your institution's coverage beyond the valley where your recital hall sits. Barriers, however, may inhibit local coverage. One senior member of the Education Writers of America, Jim Bencivenga of *The Christian Science Monitor*, regrets that local newspapers often put junior reporters in the position where campus news services should have their strongest ties—that of education editor. "Education is a parking spot until some better position at the paper opens up," Bencivenga observes. Occasionally, an inexperienced reporter will misunderstand an expert's comment, jeopardizing the mutual trust that must be built on both fronts to avoid your professor's research appearing as a candidate for a "golden fleece" award.

After establishing ties with the education writers, you must make personal contacts with the reporters covering science, business, arts, entertainment, society and life-style, community events, sports, real estate, features, and, if the school is affiliated with a religious order, religion. The good news officer knows when reporters face a deadline and avoids suggesting story ideas during these busy times. You need to read the stories each reporter writes to gain an appreciation for his or her writing habits—brief news pieces versus longer human interest features, or personality profiles rather than trend stories. The professionals will read national papers for articles on topics that may offer one of their faculty experts an opportunity to be interviewed in a follow-up on the teacher's specialty, whether it be heart disease or pop music. Newspapers, of course, often have different tastes and requirements for how to submit copy and photos, and the news director learns these immediately (from the media guides or by asking the editors).

You will have at your disposal an almost infinite repertoire of techniques for attracting news media coverage. First, however, you must master that ubiquitous communications tool—the news release.

News Releases. Everyone, of course, knows about starting releases in the inverted pyramid style with the five important *W*'s at the top. By answering the most pressing questions (Who? What? Where? When? and Why?) at the opening, you allow editors to slice off the least essential elements you have placed at the bottom while retaining the essence of the message. This method has been accepted for scores of years.

Releases are often useful to report dean's list designees, award honorees, faculty promotions, varsity letter–winners, and similar achievements of individuals to small local papers that print hometown news. *Hometowners,* as they are known, still saturate city rooms at small papers and the desks of regional supplements at the large metropolitan papers. However, *Los Angeles Times* education editor Anne Roark speaks for a majority of news writers when she says, "I don't know why I get 99 percent of my releases." Roark faithfully opens each release envelope and expects to find the release folded so that she needs only to slide it up an inch or so to read the headline and first sentence. "They've got a headline and one sentence to get my attention," she says. "If that lead isn't interesting or doesn't describe something that will interest my readers, I toss it without pulling out the contents."

One release she probably would have read, if the University of Pittsburgh had sent it to her, heralded "New Evolution Theory Links Humans and Orangutans." It was written in the proper style, with a contact's name, address, and telephone number printed near the top of Pitt's news release stationery. The words "FOR IMMEDIATE RELEASE" boldly advised reporters when they could use the following news:

> "PITTSBURGH, April 4—The orangutan— not the chimpanzee—is man's closest relative, according to a University of Pittsburgh anthropolo- gist in an article published today."

This enthralling lead practically propels the copy from the envelope.

Unfortunately for the news service profession, if you know *when* to send a release, this separates you from the majority of news services, which react too readily to prompting from their bosses. They mail releases without good news reasons. Beyers sends out tons of releases, but he mails no story that even remotely resembles promotion or institutional puffery. Roark finds that she receives an amazing number of releases publicizing faculty awards, even though she writes stories about new research or what is happening in the classroom. She also gets releases announcing conferences that have already ended by the time the release arrives at her desk.

Better ways of attracting media attention today are replacing the release. We describe several of these here.

Editorials. Written by the paper's editor or an editorial board, editorials are often overlooked by campus news officers as vehicles for institutional news. However, each anniversary or major milestone and every national recognition or research breakthrough at your institution gives you an excellent opportunity for a laudatory editorial. During the week after the Grenada invasion in 1983, the *San Francisco Chronicle* published editorials on thirteen subjects. Two were education related. As the news officer, you can prepare a short one- or two-page information sheet on why the institution's feat deserves an editorial and then make an appointment with the editor to discuss it. If you time your approach properly, say a week or ten days prior to the time you want the material to appear, you may convince the editor to publish the editorial on the preferred date.

Special Events. Commemorations, anniversaries, homecomings, commencements, and lectures present you with abundant possibilities. Consider the ways in which the University of Southern California's news service prepared for the media representatives who attended the 1984 Summer Olympics. Staff members produced 32 separate fact sheets on USC's academic and administrative units. They developed a list of 101 story ideas on the university and the Olympics and turned their weekly faculty-staff newspaper into a daily. The staff also passed out a trio of quarter-inch-thick media guidebooks. One was a university factbook. Two others were entitled "USC and the Olympics"—one written for broadcasters and the second filled with story tips and summaries of news releases pertaining to the preparation for the Olympics. Staff members conceived, researched, wrote, designed, printed, and distributed an eighty-page, soft-cover, full-color book honoring the more than 200 past USC Olympians. They made information easily accessible to more than 8,000 reporters—a magnitude greater than most campuses see in a decade.

Backgrounders. Few institutions host Olympic games, of course, but all colleges and universities hold major events, plan town-gown cooperative ventures, and have faculty experts who are available to comment on public issues. These situations offer opportunities to pull together an on-the-record (all comments are for attribution) or an off-the-record (not for publication) backgrounder. Many institutions, like Wittenberg College, have built strong rapport by inviting town media representatives to talk candidly with their president about the college's plans. Another productive backgrounding technique gets media representatives together with respected faculty experts in an informal analysis of a topic of intense interest, such as an upcoming election, the economy, crime and violence, nuclear war, old age, student mores, and so on. Relationships formed here frequently result in interviews later.

Media Resource Guides. Another common practice helpful to both the media and the news service director is publishing a list of institutional interview resources. News directors categorize faculty experts by their specialties, from "Abortion" to "Zymurgy," so that the press can refer quickly to the list and call for an authority's comments. The news service professionals, along with the faculty experts, are listed with their correct titles and telephone numbers (both work and home, if the professors agree) for quick access. Media representatives will place the directory on their reference shelf and reach for it when they need a quote. (These guides assist local reporters but engender disdain from national journalists, who may receive up to a hundred of them regularly.) Preparing this directory is a first-rate way to get yourself in touch with your faculty's strengths, but take care that the experts are genuine authorities in their field. Otherwise, such a guide will undermine your credibility with the media.

Opinion Articles. News services also prepare opinion articles, called op-eds, on public issues for the local press. Op-eds are printed in the paper opposite the editorials. They will contain 500 to 1,500 words on topics ranging from "Why Johnny Believes in TV More Than Books" to "How Psychohistory Explains the Present." Op-eds may originate from a professor's address to the Modern Language Association or the American Chemical Society. You, with the professor's blessing, can translate the material into lay terms and ultimately submit it under the professor's signature. A strong op-ed will appear in print a couple of days to six weeks later, reflecting positively on your institution in the readers' eyes. These readers possibly include a large number of the community's most influential opinion shapers.

Moving Beyond the Local Media

The number of newspapers being tossed onto the porches of 62 million Americans is roughly the same today as it was decades ago, but only one of every three magazines on the market today is older than the students we attempt to publicize. Most magazines are special interest periodicals for a distinctive reader. *Forbes Magazine* appeals to readers with six-figure incomes. *Stamp Monthly, Lapidary Journal, Opera News, Arts of Asia,* and *North American Whitetail* cater to clusters of stamp collectors, gem cutters, opera and arts buffs, and deer hunters. Hundreds of other magazines segment the population into audiences based on age, income, and buying habits. An increasing number of magazines, wire services, and syndicate feature services are beckoning for the best educational stories. If you expect to compete on the media fast track, you need to construct query letters, tipsheets, and features. These approaches work locally, of course, but have appeal regionally and nationally as well.

Query Letters. Contacting *New York Times* education editor Edward Fiske may be the toughest job anywhere, because almost everyone tries it. But if you cannot wangle a game of squash with him, the next best approach is through a well-written query letter. He looks for ideas to fill about 250 slots per year for his weekly columns, articles in the *Times* education supplements, and special assignments in other sections of the paper. "I cannot possibly return all the phone calls I get," he complains. *Parade* articles editor Frances Carpentier agrees, and adds that few of the 500 envelopes she receives each week contain well-written letters. Those letters that she accepts—and about one of every four stories eventually published is health-related—get passed along to free-lancers for subsequent research.

The huge potential for queries cannot be summarized completely here. However, *Writers Market,* published annually by Writer's Digest Books in Cincinnati, Ohio, lists periodicals and explains their requirements. Your best regional targets will include Associated Press and United Press International bureaus; flight magazines that seek stories on executive productivity, time management, travel, culture, arts, and other subjects of interest to airline travelers; and city magazines, which provide outstanding opportunities for features with a fresh angle on the community.

It is easier to get stories into many semiprofessional publications than into the *New York Times, Parade, U.S. News & World Report, Newsweek,* or *Time.* Wray Herbert, writing in October 1980 for *Humanities Report,* states, "Reporters depend, for example, on such 'gatekeeper' publications as *Nature, Science,* and *The New England Journal of Medicine* to guide them to the most important news in a broad range of science and health fields." You will not want to ignore one such gatekeeper periodical that is often overlooked: *The Chronicle of Higher Education.* It goes to more than 70,000 college faculty members and administrators and covers trends in the field of higher education. The *Chronicle's* well-trained reporters will give your idea thorough, thoughtful consideration and a clear rationale for the action they recommend. Be warned, though. A news director, we suspect, is more likely to win the lottery than to be granted a profile of his or her president or institution, unless it fits neatly into a national trend.

A good query letter has a strong lead and is targeted and timed perfectly to get an editor's attention. The letter must be no longer than a page or two, and you must explain clearly the angle and next step expected. Don Hale, Carnegie-Mellon University's public relations director, grabbed the attention of one national media producer with a lead saying, "Japan will become the world's dominant economic power by the end of this century, according to a new book by [our] public policy expert." When his letter misfired, he reloaded and on this effort aimed specifically for *Times* economics writer Leonard Silk. This letter, however, he sent over the president's signature. Silk eventually quoted from the book in one brief mention and followed up with a second column devoted to the professor's opinions.

If Fiske likes your letter, he will call you for more information and either pursue the story himself or assign another reporter to it. There is no need for a follow-up call asking, "Did you receive my letter?" In fact, *Monitor* reporter Bencivenga has stopped taking calls from public relations agencies because, he insists, they are the worst offenders. Fiske considers these calls a red flag. "I learn quickly who will waste my time," he says.

Tipsheets and Features. Generally, queries are customized to an individual reporter or editor. One practice, the tipsheet, teases these reporters with brief capsules and another, the features service, provides entire articles for reporters to use. The highly successful features service to science writers begun by Ohio State University in the 1970s is still being copied widely. A tipsheet, with five or six short, enticing capsules, may be sent every month or two to a selected group of human interest, life-style, cultural, arts, and trends reporters who are directed to call or write for the complete story or to set up their own interview.

It is possible to use more specific mailing lists, like the one comprising science and technology writers who receive a long, monthly, multipage packet of stories from Ohio State University's research service. OSU sent one typical item on how timberland researchers were using plastic trees to lure the spruce budworm's enemy, the woodpecker. It sent another on a researcher's opinions on Santa Claus as a sex symbol. From Brown University, the following tip appeared on a list of "Story Ideas" sent to selected writers at national periodicals and newspapers: "If you 'ankle a show' you walk out early, but if you 'heel a joint' you leave without paying. These are two examples of the colorful language of American popular entertainment . . . collected by a Brown University professor. . . ." From St. Louis, Missouri, where the Washington University feature service mailing list is pruned, cleansed, added to, and guarded more closely than the contents of Anthony's famous wine cellar, came an effort that needed to be precisely timed to be effective: "Are all those watery, itchy eyes, sneezy noses and stuffed-up heads really caused by the dusty mass of microspores called pollen? . . . In the midst of the sneezing season, a Washington University plant biologist explains how much the field of allergy treatment has advanced. . . ." The topics range from the ludicrous to the sublime, but each feature service and tipsheet is tailored specifically for a particular type of reporter and publication with those interests.

Equipping the Office

Years ago, administrators argued about whether the news service needed electric typewriters, a clippings service, more than one telephone line per person, or an office copier. In today's highly competitive media relations arena, the news service telephone must connect the caller on the first try or the reporter will call the competition across town. The number of lines matters little, as long as you do not inhibit the calls coming to you. The clippings service is essential, too, if you wish to evaluate whether your release was used or which programs are gaining more public visibility. Most professionals insist that clippings services are worth a modest monthly charge, plus a per-clipping fee, to study and report on your accomplishments. Your copier must reproduce, reduce, enlarge, and collate quickly. It must be available weekends or evenings when a large portion of the news occurs.

Some telephone expenses may be more than you desire, but you may actually save by furnishing your telephones with call forwarding, selective call forwarding, call waiting, conference calling, and automatic dialing for your most frequently called numbers. Push-button telephones decrease dialing time by three-fourths, and speed-dialing features may reduce your effort to a single touch. For an extra charge, you can add a feature that displays the number of the caller before you answer the ring or automatically redials the number you were trying when you got the busy signal. You will save time and money if you pay close attention to changes in telecommunications and speed mailing in the next few years.

Typewriters are being replaced by personal computers and word processors of all shapes and sizes that not only type but accomplish other tasks as well. At Kenyon College, computerized operations have been sorting hometowners by zip codes for years. At other institutions, they have been distributing them automatically to papers that circulate in those hometown zip codes. At Mississippi University for Women, the professionals learned long ago how to send releases directly into newspaper composing rooms over telephone lines. On a word processor, unlike a typewriter, you never need to retype information. Once you enter the keystrokes, the word processor edits, deletes, revises, and merges information at your command until it is ready for distribution.

Research universities, such as Brown, Carnegie-Mellon, Emory, Washington (in St. Louis), Dartmouth, Southern California, Texas A&M, and Oregon State, are pioneering the computerization of news services. Tom Hennessy, an academic news veteran and head of Boston College's communications office, is a professional who praises the link that, in the early 1980s, married his word-processing and typesetting activities. Four Wang System 25 terminals and two peripherals—a letter-quality printer and a Compugraphic 7700 typesetter—"reduced typesetting costs by at least 50 percent," he says. He predicts it will increase productivity four times.

At California Institute of Technology, News Director Dennis Meredith is convinced that his computer technology increases his ability to cover a "relatively small education institution wrapped in a very large research institution." He praises the multiuser word processing system that got him started. It can accommodate several simultaneous users who share common word processing software, including a Wordstar word processing package, a 100,000-word dictionary to check spelling, a punctuation and style guide checker, and a thesaurus. He plans to add other software advancements as they become available. Meredith runs a small news shop, so the multiuser system is ample for his needs and still gives him access without waiting in a campuswide queue. Meredith, Hennessy, and the others revise their systems regularly as technology improves.

Future Possibilities

Office systems experts predict that the news service of the 1990s will consist of a decentralized computer word processing system tied to a central data base, interacting with all advancement areas. In their projections, the futurists envision a personal computer (PC) on the desk of each clerical and professional worker. These PCs, through local area networks, provide immediate access, improve privacy, and reach higher levels of reliability (because a single user, not many, runs the machine) than terminals tied to a campus mainframe computer. This network of PCs, they predict, will feature sophisticated office software to drive the hardware. In addition to normal word processing of releases and articles, PCs will accomplish, routinely, the following news office activities:

1. Scheduling photo assignments and other appointments for the entire staff
2. Announcing events campuswide on an electronic bulletin board
3. Producing and sending news releases
4. Distributing hometown releases
5. Filing clippings and data
6. Updating sports rosters and statistics
7. Shipping reports across the country in minutes (on such national computer networks as ARPANET, TELENET, and BITNET)
8. Producing artwork for charts, pies, and graphs
9. Setting camera-ready art for publications
10. Tabulating the circulation and exposure totals of periodical publicity

For tasks requiring hard copy, you will need a letter-quality printer that prints at the rate of at least two to four pages per minute. These printers will produce mailing list printouts, address labels, prepare letters on department stationery, and accomplish a variety of other specialized tasks now done over and over by hand. Not too far into the future, offices will rely upon low-sound, high-speed jet laser printers with extensive graphics capabilities.

If this seems amazing, consider that telephone, television, and computer technology have merged to form an integrated information system that permits instantaneous interactions among people who are oceans apart. The global information revolution, which began with Sputnik in 1957, is finally confronting people on the street. It also threatens to bypass those educational news services that fail to adapt readily to the capabilities and demands of modern communications.

13

J. Arthur Stober

Broadcasting Opportunities and Techniques

☙ At a seminar of college public relations executives, sponsored by *Newsweek* magazine, an audiotape was played to dramatize the emotional impact of broadcasting. On the tape, Arch Obeler, one of this country's outstanding radio writers, described a radio drama he had written many years before.

The story was of a fifteen-year-old girl being buried while her family grieved at graveside. Obeler explored the subconscious of each of the girl's friends and relatives as the clods of dirt were being thrown in. Then he went into the grave, into the mind of the young girl, who wasn't dead, but only in a cataleptic fit.

"She was screaming in her mind, 'Mother, help me, I'm not dead, I can hear you. Please, I'm not dead. Mother, don't you remember . . .' She was appealing from every viewpoint in her experience against the family's reaction as they mourned for her, and then finally you hear the screams die out as the dirt falls into the grave."

When it was broadcast, public reaction was extreme. Obeler recalls it "produced an immediate response of 50,000 letters. It almost took me out of the profession permanently because, you know, nowadays if a television sponsor gets three letters, he gets worried. Fifty thousand letters, and then one letter. This letter was from a woman somewhere in the Midwest, and she said, 'Dear Mr. Obeler, we buried our sixteen-year-old daughter yesterday. Remember the rest of your life what you've done to us.' And I have remembered."

The script had been read by a number of executives and approved for broadcast without concern. But when the drama unfolded through the spoken word to radio listeners, the impact was devastating. The first lesson to learn about broadcasting is that the airwaves do not have the same impact as the printed page, and that a listener is often more involved than a reader. Television has carried this involvement even further. By adding sight to sound, television assaults the senses to an extent unequaled in other media.

Research documents this public involvement and acceptance. The Roper Organization has studied the public's attitude toward television and other mass media for more than twenty-five years. Their studies show television moving steadily upward from a secondary position in 1959 to become the dominant medium in people's lives. The public now regards television as the number one source of news and the most believable medium. It leads newspapers by a two-to-one margin on this score.

What does this electronic dominance mean to a public information program? Traditionally, a college or university has a print orientation, but can print releases alone reach the mass audience that needs to be influenced in favor of higher education? Hardly.

You may "know" that everyone reads *The New York Times,* but a study done by CBS Radio reveals a different story. CBS's research shows that in the New York marketing area, 88.9 percent of the households do not receive the daily *Times.* In Chicago, 74.7 percent of households do not receive the *Chicago Tribune,* and in Los Angeles, 75.7 percent of the homes in that marketing area do not receive the *Los Angeles Times.* In fact, in most U.S. markets, anywhere from one-half to nine-tenths of the households do not receive the leading newspapers. Knowing this, college public information offices cannot ignore broadcasting or merely regard it as an occasional supplement to print.

A public information office that is not experienced in broadcasting techniques can begin its education by getting to know local broadcasters. Radio and television program managers are usually readily accessible because, by tradition, broadcasting is public-service oriented. Broadcasters actively seek public reaction to, and input for, their programming. Every station has someone assigned the responsibility of doing public services. In larger stations, this is a full-time job; in smaller stations, it is usually handled by the program manager. Public information personnel need good working relationships with these public service directors.

Another key person in the broadcast operation is the news director. One member of the public information operation should be appointed as the institution's contact with the news director. Some broadcast news departments also have assignment editors, whose responsibility it is to assign specific stories to reporters. Because assignment editors largely determine what stories are used on a news program each day, they are important persons to know. On slow news days, assignment editors like to have quick news-feature possibilities available. If you can set up a story on short notice and the assignment editor knows this, your institution can get valuable additional news exposure.

Because news departments rarely have secretaries, written correspondence seldom gets prompt attention, so it is best to contact stations in person or by telephone. The best time to call is usually in the middle of the day. In the morning, the staff is involved in setting up the day's assignments, and the late afternoon is filled with frantic preparations for the early evening newscast.

Radio News

The United States wakes up with radio. A survey conducted for CBS Radio by Opinion Research Corporation of Princeton, New Jersey, found that 52 percent of all Americans get their first news in the morning from their radios. Only 21 percent turn to a morning newspaper for news, and among those with higher family incomes, the figures are even more in favor of radio. Working habits in the United States have created radio's prime time. The largest audiences are attracted during morning hours, six to nine o'clock, as workers get up, dress, and drive to their jobs. Another peak listening period is the "drive time," from four to six o'clock in the afternoon, when commuters are going home. Some stations have added noon-hour newscasts, which attract large numbers of listeners during their lunch breaks.

Because radio is everywhere, all the time, no public information program can have maximum efficiency without using it regularly. For a public information office with no experience in broadcast news and a budget that does not permit hiring a full-time broadcaster, radio is the place to start.

Print Releases. Only print releases of interest to a large general audience should be sent to local radio stations. If the stations have the time and staff available, they will occasionally rewrite the releases and put them on the air. But because even a small broadcast newsroom gets hundreds of releases each day, the chances are remote that the reporter will have the time to select a particular story and rewrite it for broadcast. As a result, most print releases end up in the station's wastepaper baskets, unread. Try shortening the story and rewriting it in broadcast style. The Associated Press *Broadcast News Handbook* (1982) offers valuable advice. Every written release sent to a station should include the telephone number of the news maker as well as that of the public information office. Large stations often prefer to call the news maker directly to record an actuality. Actualities are much preferable to a paraphrased statement from a spokesperson for the news maker.

Beeper Reports. Another method is to call a station and read a report directly into the phone. The station records the message for later broadcast. Such efforts are more likely to be aired than written releases, but news directors still prefer stories built around the actual voice of the news maker.

Actualities. To provide stations with actualities, a public information office must produce and distribute its news stories on tape. Begin with a cassette recorder of reasonable quality. Simple to operate, this machine can produce airworthy tapes. Because recorders are portable, it is possible to record newstapes on location. The natural sounds associated with locations frequently add a dimension that makes tapes more interesting than those recorded in a studio. For example, the natural sounds in a gym add authenticity to an interview with a basketball coach. But be wary of noises that distract. Even low-level distractions, such as the hum of fluorescent lights, can reduce the air quality of a tape.

The simplest method of getting a tape to a radio newsroom is to send it by telephone. This can be done by connecting the recorder to the telephone mouthpiece with alligator clips, which are sold in electronics stores. Any radio news director can demonstrate the method. It is easy, but because the telephone's mouthpiece must be dismantled, it is inconvenient for regular use. If you plan to send tapes regularly, ask the telephone company to install a recorder-coupler to the telephone. Such a device is inexpensive, easy to operate, and ensures high-quality transmission.

Radio actualities frequently need careful editing, and this is difficult with tape cassettes. Therefore, for editing, material on cassettes must be transferred to open-reel tape. (The material can, of course, be recorded initially on reels.) With an open-reel recorder, an editing block, a razor blade, and a reel of splicing tape, it is possible to produce finished radio news stories.

The usual maximum length for these stories is sixty seconds. This commonly consists of a twenty-second introduction by a reporter, a thirty-second actuality, and a ten-second tag by the reporter. Making any or all of these elements shorter improves the chances of the story being aired. This sixty-second format can be used by most stations, but it is also long enough to allow more ambitious news operations to edit the tape to fit their own needs.

A Radio News Network. Expanding news coverage beyond a local area requires planning a news network via the telephone. Each year, *Broadcasting* magazine publishes the *Broadcasting/ Cablecasting Yearbook,* which lists every radio and television station in the country and includes pertinent information about it. This information can be used to select stations that cover an institution's marketing area. Once this area has been defined, the network can begin to operate. Such an operation at Pennsylvania State University is delivering between 500 and 800 telephone tape feeds each month, serving about 180 stations throughout Pennsylvania.

One of the advantages of this system is instant feedback. News directors often respond to a story as soon as they receive it. These reactions usually show that nothing can compete with a hometown story or a story tailored to a specific geographical area.

Virtually all radio stations strive to serve their local audiences by tailoring news to the hometown area. Statewide and national news are left to networks and wire services.

For example, a story about a dean or college president announcing a new curriculum on the environment would be of little interest to a radio station a hundred, or even twenty-five, miles from the campus. But a story about a student from the station's coverage area who is majoring in this new curriculum would be readily used.

Television News

There are several methods for placing stories about educational institutions into television news. But before you try to get a story on television, make certain it meets the demands of television news. The primary interest of television is people, interesting people. The topic of the story should have local appeal. It need not be a hometown story, but it should be a topic in which hometown people have an interest. Moreover, it should be visually interesting and, if possible, action-oriented.

A Philadelphia news director explained his news-gathering philosophy openly: He would not cover a campus news conference because he felt the public was not interested in the pronouncements of academic figures using an unfamiliar vocabulary. He explained that if the academic story were of a doctor announcing a cure for cancer, he would cover it by interviewing cancer victims about what this cure would mean to them. The broadcaster felt that whereas the general public could not relate to a doctor's scientific terminology, it would be emotionally involved with a person who had just been given another chance for life because of the cure.

Television news directors, especially those with small staffs, generally consider press conferences and speeches difficult to cover, time-consuming, and visually uninteresting. Pictures and charts may help a conference, but by its very structure and length, a general press conference presents problems for the television reporter who needs only a thirty- to sixty-second statement for the story.

Technical problems include uncertain lighting and difficult microphone placement, especially if there are several participants in a conference and several stations covering the event.

To some degree, the same problems are true for speeches. A reporter needs an advance transcript of a speech to plan the segments to be taped for the story. Without a transcript, the entire speech must be taped, an effort that is too time-consuming for some stations. Given a choice, most television reporters would prefer to take a news maker aside, before or after an event, and ask one or two questions in front of their own cameras. Providing this opportunity may mean the difference between good, bad, or no coverage of an event.

When the principal part of a story comes from a statement or interview, cutaways will also have to be shot. *Cutaways* are action shots that are inserted into the interview to illustrate the story and make it more interesting. A person speaking directly into the camera is known as a *talking head,* something television editors try to avoid. Therefore, when an interview is arranged, make sure that cutaways are included. As a professor talks about research, for example, laboratory shots can show the work being performed. Tell the assignment editor about these picture opportunities; it will help sell the story.

Coverage by Stations. Of the several ways to get a story on television news, this is the most direct. A college or university located in an area that a station covers directly with its own news staff can call the assignment editor and hope to make the story sound worthy of consideration. The advantage of this method is that it costs nothing and a station that tapes a story itself probably will air it. A disadvantage is that the story is being covered by only a single station. If the campus is located outside the area that a station generally covers, usually a maximum of fifty to seventy miles from the studios, the story will receive limited, if any, attention from the assignment editor.

Copy and Slide Releases. An institution can mail print releases to television stations. If the story is of sufficient interest, it will be used. But because such a story has no pictures and therefore can only be read on camera, it will most likely be reported in the briefest manner, if at all. If you include 35 mm slides with written copy, you will improve the chances of having the story aired.

Producing Your Own Television Newstapes. The story produced on videotape has the best chance of getting air time. Although a number of stations in major markets have a policy against using handouts, most stations will consider airing a well-produced newstape offered by a college or university. The growth of news on cable and local, as well as network, stations is also opening up new and important markets. If a college or university has the budget and the facilities, producing television newstapes should be a priority of the public information operation.

Broadcast Copy. "I have discovered that properly done, and I cannot emphasize it too strongly, *properly done,* TV newswriting is indeed the clearest and most economical way of telling people what is happening and why." The quote is from Gilbert Millstein, writer for NBC news, formerly of *The New York Times.* In an article in *The Quill* (Long, 1975, p. 22), Millstein comments that the *Times* wastes thousands of words: "Words are wasted with an extravagance I find unbelievable. That was not driven home to me until I came to television."

When writing for broadcast, condense your news releases. Fifteen-second stories are common on newscasts. Radio newstapes rarely run over sixty seconds, and unless they are visually outstanding, television stories frequently adhere to similar standards of brevity. Use simple declarative sentences and a conversational style in writing broadcast copy. Cramming who, what, when, where, and why into the first sentence seldom works. The ideas need to flow from one to the next. Both sentences and stories must be short.

Public Service Announcements (PSAs). The spot announcement aired on free time is an important vehicle for public service organizations, but in recent years, two major changes have occurred that have altered this traditional market. First, spots have become shorter. The sixty-second PSA has virtually disappeared. Currently, more than 85 percent of the spots on the air are thirty seconds long, and experts say the trend is to even shorter spots. Communications executive Ted Hearne expects the ten-second PSA to be common in a few years. Second, deregulation has removed the legal need for stations to run PSAs. But because stations generally consider it excellent public relations and good business to serve community groups, it is highly unlikely that stations will totally discontinue free public service time. Colleges and universities should continue to consider PSAs as a viable and important marketing tool.

These changes are making the market for free broadcast time very competitive. In order to appeal to stations, many PSA producers are tackling problems and tough issues, such as drug and alcohol addiction, minority conflicts, and child abuse. Negative is out; positive is in. No longer do spots for the American Cancer Society try to scare you. They express hope by showing people who have been cured. No longer do cerebral palsy PSAs dwell on pictures of handicapped children; they show adults who have cerebral palsy competing and winning. Public service organizations are also improving their marketing techniques. For example, the Anti-Defamation League is stressing personal contact and follow-up calls for their campaigns. The Leukemia Society and the Campfire Girls have their spots personally delivered to stations by local representatives.

The Detroit zoo effectively used many of these techniques in its 1982 PSA campaign. The zoo was plagued by reduced budgets and declining attendance, problems not unlike those faced by institutions of higher education. Zoo officials took their problem to N. B. Donner and Company, a local advertising agency. The agency recommended a television PSA campaign and volunteered to produce it as a public service.

The zoo's concessionaire donated $10,000 to get the project rolling. This paid for the actors' voices, music rights, and videotape editing. The costs of the crew, studio recording, film and processing, dubs, publicity, air time, and the agency's time and personnel were all donated. In the normal commercial market, this production would have cost around $70,000. Both a thirty-second and a sixty-second spot were produced, but the agency's work did not stop there. Now the important job of marketing the campaign began. The agency producer hand-delivered the spots to the public service director of each Detroit station, explaining the details of the campaign. He visited local newspapers with still photos of the PSA being produced, and he did interviews on radio stations. The Detroit media gave the zoo a lot of publicity before the spot even went on the air.

When the spot aired, mail poured in from delighted viewers, including a letter from Isabella Fiesselmann, a ninety-three-year-old resident of Southfield, Michigan. She was so impressed by the spot that she wrote: "I long to visit the zoo once more, but I'm in a walker and it's hard for me to get around." Moved by the letter, the zoo director sent it to the agency for some kind of action, and he got it. September 2, 1982, was declared Isabella Fiesselmann Day at the Detroit zoo, with free admission to people over sixty-two years of age. Area Boy Scouts participated by helping the senior citizens get around. It was such a success that Isabella Fiesselmann Day is now an annual event at the Detroit zoo.

And that's not all. This campaign started during a pro football strike, so all the spots ran on the air with this tag: "This Sunday come see the Lions play at the Detroit zoo. It's the only game in town." Attendance was up 20 percent at the Detroit zoo after the PSA campaign. In a city with a severely depressed economy, that is nothing short of sensational. The success of the PSAs led to a national version that was produced and distributed through the American Association of Zoological Parks and Aquariums.

The Detroit zoo's use of television public service time and imaginative marketing are techniques that colleges and universities should emulate.

A large budget is not always necessary to mount a successful television PSA campaign. Penn State, using the simplest production techniques and a budget under $1,000, produced a PSA that has reached audiences in all fifty states and continues to be aired by stations after two years. The spot offers a free brochure, produced by the university, explaining student aid. It consists of a series of talking heads shot by a camera crew from the institution's public television station. The students ad libbed their comments, and the remarks were cut and edited together to make two thirty-second spots. This is the script of one of the spots:

SLIDE:
"YOU CAN AFFORD   *ANNO:* You can still afford
COLLEGE"   college!

GIRL 1   *GIRL 1:* College is the best
                                     thing that ever happened to me.

BOY 1   *BOY 1:* Your college education
                                     is an asset that you will never
                                     lose.

GIRL 2   *GIRL 2:* And there is still fi-
                                     nancial aid available to help.

BOY 2   *BOY 2:* Without financial aid, I
                                     wouldn't be here.

GIRL 3   *GIRL 3:* If you are interested, it
                                     would be well worth your time
                                     to get more information.

SLIDE: ADDRESS   *ANNO:* Send for this free bro-
                                     chure on how to finance your
                                     college education. Write Stu-
                                     dent Aid, Department 1000,
                                     University Park, Pennsylvania
                                     16802. Write today.

These student-aid PSAs were aired by most of the stations in Pennsylvania, but more important, the spots were also accepted and played on WTBS, the Ted Turner superstation in Atlanta, and by WNEW-TV, a powerful regional station in New York City. The spots were on the air for two years and pulled more than 10,000 requests for the brochure from every state in the union, including Alaska and Hawaii, plus the Virgin Islands and Puerto Rico. Although the PSAs are officially retired, several stations continue to air them from time to time, so Penn State is still receiving about a dozen letters a week generated by these spots.

These modest spots produced such outstanding results because they performed a genuine public service. They presented a problem: paying for college; and they offered a solution: an informational brochure. Stations accepted and aired the spots because they believed that this was a concern of a great number of their viewers. An elaborate, expensive production was not necessary to deliver that message.

Radio Talk Shows

In recent years, the audience for radio music has moved to FM stations with their high-fidelity and stereo sound. To fill the void and to attract their own audience, many AM stations have increased their news and information programming and have discovered talk shows. Talk radio offers colleges and universities an excellent vehicle for their promotional efforts.

The *Broadcasting/Cablecasting Yearbook* (1985) lists all the stations across the country that have talk formats. Contact the talk stations in the geographical areas that you are interested in reaching, and make them aware of the faculty members on your staff who would make good interviews. This is an excellent method of promoting your university for several reasons. First, the price is right. It costs the barest minimum to get a faculty member on a major station. There are no production costs, and no electronic hardware is needed. Most stations even pay the cost of telephone calls. Second, it takes little of your time and little of the time of your faculty members. There is no travel time or travel expense involved. Faculty members do the interviews over the telephone from their offices or from their homes. Third, faculty members have more time to talk. One of the complaints often heard is that the broadcast media don't give people enough time to express their thoughts. We know that quotes on the news are severely edited and often run thirty seconds or less. On radio talk programs, interviews often run for an hour, sometimes for two hours or more. The shows are most often done live, so there is no editing. Fourth, talk shows are good for the nonvisual guest. We know that television usually avoids talking heads. On radio, this is not a problem, so liberal arts professors, who don't have laboratories filled with exotic equipment to occupy the television camera, are welcome. And fifth, you can get coverage from coast to coast. There are major talk shows in every metropolitan area in every section of the country, and most will call interesting guests anywhere.

Trends

In the average American home, someone is watching television nearly seven hours a day. Surveys indicate that time spent in front of the television set is increasing each year. A decade ago, the average American family might have had three channels to watch. Today a cable-equipped home could have as many as a hundred channels to choose from. And the American family is making choices, often at the expense of the three traditional networks.

For the first time in broadcast history, the average size of the network audience is decreasing—a small amount, to be sure, but a definite decrease. To combat this new competition, the networks are producing more specials and running more promotional announcements in prime time than ever before. Much of this is at the expense of public service announcements. Some national organizations are reporting decreases of 10 to 15 percent in the amount of public service time they normally receive from the networks.

That is the bad news. Now the good news: As free public service time is decreasing on the traditional networks, the new technologies—cable, low-power stations, and the like—are providing institutions with new forums for their messages. Yesterday there may have been only ABC, CBS, and NBC, but today there are also some forty-two operating cable networks, and there are more than a dozen others in the planning stage. About ten of these cable networks are pay channels and do not accept advertising or PSAs, but the others are advertiser-supported and make free time available to public service organizations.

In addition to the cable networks, there are also powerful local stations that distribute their signals by microwave relays to cable systems far and wide—stations such as KSHB-TV in Kansas

City, Missouri; KSTW in Tacoma, Washington; KTVT in Fort Worth, Texas; and WNEW-TV in New York City. These stations are reaching millions of viewers in hundreds of communities in states beyond their normal coverage areas. For example, WSBK in Boston covers all of New England, and WNEW-TV, New York, covers millions of homes in New York State, New Jersey, Connecticut, and Pennsylvania.

One of the most interesting developments in broadcasting during the past decade has been the advent of the superstation. This phenomenon began in 1976, when entrepreneur Ted Turner put the signal of his Atlanta UHF station, WTBS, on an RCA satellite. Initially, four cable systems received WTBS's programs. Today, superstation WTBS is carried by nearly 6,000 cable systems, with a subscriber base that approaches 30 million homes. In 1978, two years after WTBS went national, WGN-TV also went on the satellite. As Chicago's super channel, WGN-TV is carried by some 4,300 cable companies with a universe of about 10 million homes. In 1979, WOR-TV in New York became the third station to use a communications satellite to spread its signal. Over the air, WOR reaches some 8 million homes in the New York market. Via the satellite and 675 cable systems, WOR adds another 5 million homes across the country to its audience. In 1984, WPIX-TV in New York City became the fourth station to go on the satellite. These four superstations use PSAs. A single play on one of these channels can give you an audience of millions, covering the entire country.

In broadcasting, as in many aspects of modern society, the past is prologue. The medium described here exists today, but only temporarily. Continuing technological developments and changes in federal regulations are altering the relationship between public service organizations and broadcasters. The demands are tougher and the standards are higher, but never have the opportunities for colleges and universities in the electronic media been greater.

References

Broadcasting/Cablecasting Yearbook. Washington, D.C.: Broadcasting Publications, 1985. (Published annually)
Broadcast News Handbook. New York: Associated Press, 1982.
Long, C. "TV Network News Writing." *The Quill,* March 1975, pp. 20–25.

14

Kathleen L. Rydar

Planning and Conducting Special Events

∞ A talented and energetic young woman recently remarked that she wanted to change her career focus, to move out of the area of special events and into real development work. Her message and motivation were clear. To prepare for the leadership of a total advancement effort, it would be wise to master as many facets of our profession as possible and to learn to integrate them effectively for the accomplishment of institutional goals. However, my experience up the professional ladder has been that special events never seem to get left on the bottom rung. They climb up with you.

When managed well, special events are at the heart of the institutional advancement process, assimilating every aspect of the university relations and development effort to enhance the educational program. The role of development is to involve people in the life of the campus, knowing that involvement fosters commitment. Rarely does the million-dollar gift arrive from a total stranger, however much we sometimes wish it would. Special events define the area of university advancement that brings people together, increases their understanding, and enables them to share in the community of friends also participating in their investment. Real development work depends on special events.

Events are planned for a variety of reasons: to persuade, honor, dedicate, reward, announce, educate, initiate, investigate, commemorate, and celebrate. As institutions seek to build closer relationships with individuals, corporations, and foundations capable of providing the necessary financial support, special events become vehicles for personal involvement, through which an awareness and enjoyment can lead to benefits on all sides. Attending events appeals to our human need for collectivity and to our deeper sense of shared ritual.

Making special events count in the total university relations and development program starts with planning. Some events celebrate special occasions within the calendar year, following the seasons: new student orientation, alumni homecoming, pregame and postgame gatherings for institutions with sports programs, retirement dinners, open houses, parents' weekend, and commencement. Other events are more singular in their timing and particular drama: building dedications, ground breakings, inaugurations of new presidents, special anniversaries. Sprinkled among these milestone events, on campuses of every size and complexity, meetings bring people together in the regular regimen of campus activity: luncheon meetings to introduce heads of major corporations to presidents of universities, meetings of community leaders with campus planners, programs to enlist alumni in helping with admissions and fund-raising efforts, or a campus tour to interest a potential donor in the restoration of an aging building. All of these events bring people together to make unfamiliar information more familiar and with the hope of accomplishing positive results.

Although the heart of an educational institution will always be the academic program, the manner in which others are brought into the family reveals its soul. We know this best as the spirit of the place. Some campuses are known as lively, interactive places, responsive to the wider community; others seem dull or stuffy (the unapproachable ivory tower!). The campuses with dynamic energy are those with a sense of pride in their past accomplishments and traditions as they seek to explore new relationships and interactions, the possibilities for building an abundant future.

A special event has the potential to focus the creative energies of the total advancement area. A large-scale event pulls together all aspects of institutional relations, appealing to the print and electronic media and utilizing various publications (brochures, posters, commemorative booklets) as well as films and slide presentations to communicate a certain message. A college or university has a tremendous opportunity to make a collective impact on a significant group of people, with results that can be measured in terms of dollars and decisions in favor of the institution's goals.

The special event focuses attention on the institution in a dramatic way. Whether the event is the inauguration of a new president or an all-university open house, the occasion gives the public the opportunity to know the people and the traditions that make that particular institution different from any other place in the country. Capturing the flavor of an institution is perhaps the key to the success of a strong public relations or development program because people want to know what sets you apart from all the rest. Finding the uniqueness of your college or university and knowing why people want to become involved with your program will help you determine the kinds of events to plan for various constituencies.

Often, special events can defuse and help solve problems that emerge at times of change within the institution or in the lives of its people. Springfield College in Massachusetts targeted an alumni effort to attract the young graduate by organizing a series of Cape Cod clambakes and alumni-in-residence programs designed to involve the recent graduate. At the other end of the age spectrum, Purdue University in Indiana developed an association for retirees. Its goal was to provide special benefits and educational and social programs, as well as a forum for exchanging information among retired faculty and staff, most of whom lived in areas adjacent to the campus but with no organized way to remain in contact. What began as a gripe session, filled with concern and fear, concluded in a positive program that included a newsletter and special events benefitting the retiree as well as the total university.

Holiday seasons provide opportunities to showcase the campus and student talent in dramatic and meaningful special events. Music concerts and theatrical events are natural opportunities to involve special donors in the life of the campus. Some campuses combine a seasonal holiday with an ecological solution. For example, at the State University of New York at Buffalo, the public relations office has coordinated a Christmas tree recycling program, with students and community service groups joining forces for a festive event that meets environmental objectives.

These events, and others like them, are all ways to incorporate volunteers into the life of the campus. No office ever has a large enough staff to be able to accomplish all of the excellent programs possible to achieve. A well-organized office will incorporate volunteer alumni, students, and faculty, who often enjoy being asked to take part in campus activity outside of their fields of study. As corporate-giving programs increasingly reflect the interests of the employees of particular firms, the involvement of corporate staff as university volunteers can also lead to increased contributions. The Atlantic Richfield Foundation recently developed a program of grants to nonprofit institutions at which their employees volunteer their time and talent. Where better to engage a bright volunteer than in the planning of outreach efforts through special events!

All events begin with the same strategy and planning process. Some events take longer to plan because they are more complex, determined by their purpose and audience. The more significant the event to the institution, the more elaborate the planning process and the longer lead time needed. The University of Michigan spent four years in preparation for its 150th anniversary celebration. This was a major campus event, a landmark community occasion, and a focus of international attention. From throughout the world came nearly seventy distinguished speakers, including President Zakir Husain of India, Gerald Ford, and numerous university presidents. More than 2,000 volunteers participated in as many as 600 separate events, with a total of 200,000 people in attendance.

Occasionally, the world will beat a path to your doorstep via an internationally televised event, such as the opportunity the 1984 Olympic Games provided for several campuses in southern California. The University of Southern California used the focus of attention as one of the main Olympic Villages to welcome alumni, parents, donors, and friends to an "Olympicnic" a few weeks prior to opening ceremonies. The festive atmosphere anticipated the village the athletes would experience once the games began and the campus site would be off-limits to visitors. During the games, an estimated 125,000 people walked through the USC campus daily.

Events such as these, when integrated with the overall objectives of the institution, can provide launching points for university-wide campaigns or special programs to accomplish departmental objectives. The University of Michigan anniversary celebration set the stage for the largest fund drive ever mounted in the history of the institution. For the University of Southern California, the Olympics provided the catalyst for special art exhibitions and brought to fruition a plan to build two new exhibition galleries for the schools of Architecture and Fine Arts. The generous donor saw that the completion of the galleries was essential to maximizing attention to the arts on campus during this dramatic time in the history of Los Angeles. In addition, an exhibition of California sculpture was installed in the main exhibition gallery and a larger-than-life-size bronze by internationally recognized artist Francisco Zuniga loaned from a private collection in New York. Each of these creative activities provided opportunities for special events to celebrate donors and artists during an exciting period in the cultural expansion of the community.

It takes an organized staff to be able to respond to such opportunities as they arise. By employing systems to manage the details and the communication process involved, even a small staff can handle a variety of special activities in addition to the traditional university events.

The basic steps to organizing special events include: determining the goal, establishing a time line, documenting information in a written format, rewarding those involved with the process, and evaluating the results. Simple as these steps might sound, it is amazing how many institutions skip one or all of these when attempting to involve individuals and groups in campus activity.

In order to determine the goals of an overall program of special events or a specific event, a committee must be established, composed of key persons who will be capable of assuring the success of the event. The program director should determine who these people will be. For example, if the special event involves a large number of guests and the necessity to park an equal number of cars, then the head of parking operations could be an important individual in determining the success of the event. There is nothing more troublesome to a guest than not being able to find parking in the vicinity of an event. If the event involves alumni, a representative of the alumni staff and at least one volunteer from the alumni body should be on the committee. The same is true of events involving parents, students, legislators, corporate executives, and so forth. Too often, we second-guess the desires of a particular audience or the dates when members are available to attend an event. Consequently, we plan programs that neither meet their needs nor match their time schedules. Even though they might not have time to participate fully on a committee, representatives of the audience for the event at least should be consulted about the goals and elements of the program.

A time line will help all of the players stay on schedule prior to the event. Sharing the time plan with others will help related departments know the work load of the program director and staff. Time is the least tangible of the elements we deal with in the process of living and accomplishing goals, so it is essential to make the time structure as real as possible by committing it to paper. Include in this time plan all activities to be completed by a certain date: mailing of invitations, ordering of plaques, selection of menu, printing of brochures and programs, and so on. For the date of the event itself, construct another time plan for the structure of the day: arrival of guests, time points for moving crowds from one location to another, times for program to begin and conclude, as well as any time elements in between.

The documentation of detail is a necessary part of managing special events. The checklist can save time as well as allow the program director to sleep at night, knowing that the details have been organized and checked through the simple process of list-keeping. For those offices managing large numbers of events, a master checklist can be helpful for specifying all of the details that must be arranged for a successful program. Incorporate in the checklist such items as room setups, audiovisual needs, menu selection, parking arrangements, invitations, programs, musical accompaniment, telephone numbers for members of the committee, and budget information. Because small pieces of paper are easily lost or misplaced, try to arrange as much of this detail information as possible on a single page or a stapled series of sheets. To avoid misunderstanding and miscommunication, share the information you have documented with all others involved in the preparation of your event. As soon as possible prior to the event, document all expected costs and income on the budget sheet, and share this information with those responsible for signing off on expenditures as well as those on whom you must rely for spending to acquire the items. Nothing dampens the enthusiasm of a successful event more than learning too late to make adjustments in your total budget allocation that an element of the program has doubled in cost.

Because people make events happen, be sure to reward those who were involved in the success of the event. Respond to those who made you look good in whatever manner is appropriate for the occasion. Expressing your sincere appreciation for a job well done will make others feel good about being a member of your team.

Finally, evaluation of the program will help you plan better events by determining weak points and methods of improvement. One of the most difficult tasks is to achieve perfection in program planning. Even the most organized effort will have its surprises— elements that are sometimes beyond your control, such as weather and power failures. Careful evaluation will help you determine backup systems and better methods of communication. In order to evaluate objectively, ask some of the guests (or all, if appropriate) to suggest ways to improve your program. Point of view very often determines the opinion of the success or failure of a particular event. The worst mistake is to feel confident that you have successfully engaged a group of people in understanding your institution, when in reality, they went home grumbling about the arrangements, the acoustics, the menu, and their misspelled names. Through systematic evaluation you will be able to strive for perfection, plan events that meet your goals, and showcase the excellence of your institution in ways that will reverberate beyond the event itself.

Exhibits 14-1 through 14-3 offer a suggested time line and a planning guide for special events as well as a sample checklist for organizing details. Once you have mastered the systems that provide the settings for each program, you will be free to concentrate on what makes an event truly special—the people honored, celebrated, educated, commemorated, and involved.

Exhibit 14-1. Time Line for Special Event.

Advance Planning—Six months ahead
    Select committee and arrange to meet
    Set date (for major events, sometimes a year's advance planning is required) and put hold on facilities
    Determine purpose
    Plan general format
    Establish method for volunteer involvement and communication
Advance Planning—Four months ahead
    Check supplies and order materials needed
    Prepare invitation list
    Determine format for design of invitation
Advance Planning—Two months ahead
    Assess audiovisual needs
    Recruit volunteers for mailing invitations
    Plan checklist for all bases to be covered on day of event
Advance Planning—One month ahead
    Mail invitations
    Brief staff for responses
    Share information with related departments and field inquiries
    Plan menu
    Order flowers
    Hire photographer
    Alert security
    Send final draft of day's program to printer
Day Before Event
    Type final guest roster
    Check all arrangements with staff and volunteers
    Review materials and handouts
    Brief senior administration on event progress, and detail notes for their participation
Day of Event
    Recheck all room setups
    Test audiovisuals
    Hold final staff briefing

Exhibit 14-2. Special Events Planning Guide.

Purpose/goal of program: _____

_____

_____

Date: _____

Location: _____

Size of audience expected: _____

Number to be invited: _____

Form of invitation: _____

_____

Staff coordinator: _____

Volunteer coordinator: _____

Committee representatives: _____

_____

_____

Required arrangements

Room setup: _____

_____

_____

_____

Audiovisual needs: _____

_____

Name badges: _____

Place cards: _____

Musicians: _____

    Physical arrangements for musicians: _____

_____

Coat check: _____

Menu: _____

_____

_____

Exhibit 14-2. Special Events Planning Guide, Cont'd.

Flowers/table decorations: _____

_____

Security: _____

_____

Printed program, materials, or handouts: _____

_____

Follow-up

Letters to guests: _____

_____

Letters and calls to volunteers:_____

_____

Evaluation/comments: _____

_____

_____

_____

_____

Budget projection attached: _____

Exhibit 14-3. Sample Special Events Checklist.

(Because every event requires its own kind of arrangements, a checklist should be designed for each one)

____ Invitations ordered

____ Invitations mailed

____ System established for responses

____ Rooms requested

____ Program details finalized

____ Menu arranged

____ Setups requested

____ Coat check ordered

____ Place cards and name badges ordered

____ Flowers/table decorations ordered

____ Musicians requested

____ Sound system ordered

____ Staff/volunteers briefed on responsibilities

____ Budget written

____ Parking arrangements requested

____ Checks requested to pay _____

____ Security arranged

____ Seating finalized

____ Access for caterer, florist, etc., checked

____ Publicity handled

____ Plaques/certificates ordered

____ First aid arranged

15

Ross Cornwell

Writing Creative and Persuasive Speeches

᭥ Speech writing, once relegated to the smallest of bit parts on the institutional advancement stage, has moved into a major supporting role. Advancement programs that are adroit at cashing in on the box office appeal of their star players—their president and other top officials—usually do so because they understand the value of creative speech writing, creative speech giving, and creative speech exploiting. We have discovered anew that the good speech can be a magnificent tool for moving people and advancing an institution's objectives.

This chapter focuses on five steps involved in speech writing. Its principles apply equally to the one-person shop or the million-dollar-budget operation. They also apply whether you are writing for the president, a dean, or yourself. Before moving into a recipe for the speech writer, let's put speech writing into its larger context.

Think of the entire speech process as a continuum. The process moves from (a) selecting a suitable platform for a speaker to (b) selecting a message that will help advance institutional objectives, (c) gathering information to construct the speech, (d) writing the speech, (e) coaching the speaker, and (f) exploiting the speech in terms of news value and publicity. Points (b), (c), and (d) are properly the concern of the speech writer and of this chapter.

The other points should, however, also be the concern of the advancement officer and will get some attention in these pages, beginning with this comment about point (a): Potential speaking engagements for the chief executive officer (CEO) of the institution should be screened, selected, or finagled with the utmost care. Your CEO should seek or accept few ritual speaking engagements and should in no event make speeches that do not help further the objectives of your institution. If your president does not already have someone on staff to handle speech assignments and if the president cannot bear to say no to invitations, you could do worse than to get yourself assigned to help make those decisions and to serve as "no person" when the time comes. Assuming that an appropriate speaking invitation is accepted, however, what's next?

Step 1 in speech writing: Sit down and talk with the speaker to cook up a good, hot topic. The topic has to be something in which your speaker has a burning interest. If not, the speech that results is likely to end up tasteless, zestless, and cold. That seems obvious, but frequently during this kind of discussion, you may find that your speaker really does not have a definite topic in mind. You may have to probe around, send up some trial balloons, and pry away at your speaker until you hit something that really turns the speaker on, turns you on, and most important, will turn on an audience.

Most people in top positions on campus have a whole set of strong values and strong opinions about all sorts of public issues. The speech writer must learn to get the lid off those things and use them to get at a speech topic, which is why the speech writer should always discuss the speech face-to-face with the speaker, not through an intermediary. The more frequently a writer works with the speaker, the easier this whole process becomes. Incidentally, it is a good idea to tape-record this planning session with the speaker. It will free you from taking notes and will also give you a ready reference of the speaker's speech patterns.

The topic must not only be exciting to your speaker, it must also be timely and relevant for an audience. That usually means controversial. And that is desirable because elements of controversy, skillfully employed in a speech, can help keep the audience hanging in there with your speaker. Cole (1981) suggests a number of questions to ask at this point to help you generate relevant topics. Examples: What is government doing that makes our work easier or harder? What is technology doing to our field now and what will it do in the future? What problems of society are we helping solve?

What is likely to happen in our field in the future, and have we any predictions worth sharing? What are our biggest external problems, and what internal problems are we dealing with that an audience could learn something from? Do we need to clear up any public misconceptions about us? If such questions do nothing more than get you and your speaker thinking out loud together, they will serve you well.

Now make sure you have a final, clear understanding of what specifically this speech should accomplish. There are four reasons to give a speech: to inform people, to inspire or entertain them, to change their minds, or to motivate them to do something. Which should your speech do? Do you know what you want to get across? what action you want people to take? what you want them to remember? Answer these questions and you are ready to press onward.

Step 2: Do some meaty research on your audience and your topic. Many speech writers do a beautiful job researching their topic and writing a speech only to see it fail to connect because research on the audience was insufficient. Talk to the person in charge of the event. Get in touch with the person handling public relations. Find out who will be in the audience, why they are there, how many will be there, what they know about your speaker, who else will speak, the names of some local people who could be mentioned by the speaker, what the natural or logical connections are between this organization and your institution, and so forth. Information like this is crucial in helping you help your speaker establish quick rapport with listeners and communicate effectively with them.

Thinking again about the entire speech process as a continuum, remember that there are four potential audiences for every speech: the people who will actually hear it; their acquaintances, to whom they might just pass along some idea from the speech; the audience reached by the news media who covered the speech; and any other people you can reach through such devices as printing the speech, converting it into a magazine article, or simply sending copies of the speech with a brief note attached to key individuals. Always remember this key question: How can we use this speech assignment to further our objectives?

It is said that a great speech is 90 percent great content and 10 percent great delivery. The exact ratio may be questioned, but what is unquestionable is that solid research of the topic is the sine qua non of successful speech writing. Facts must be lined up to support positions and contentions. What others have had to say about the topic must be timely as well as accurate. Your library and reference librarian are good places to start. If you can get access to them, however, do as Karanjia (1980) suggests and first consult the *New York Times* Information Bank or similar services offered by Dow Jones or other organizations. Plug in key words and phrases and find out what is being said throughout the country about your topic. Also check with your experts on campus, both faculty and administrative.

There is another kind of research process that ought to be an ongoing project for the speech writer. Call it the "Pack-Rat Research Technique." It means reading a lot, listening a lot, and collecting a lot—from daily newspapers, books, good magazines, television news specials, speeches by other opinion leaders, seminar and conference speakers, after-dinner speakers, bumper stickers, letters that come to your attention, junk mail, talks over coffee, opinion surveys, and everything else you can think of where you might find useful scraps of information. It is a good idea to enhance your collection by subscribing to such publications as *Vital Speeches* and *Representative American Speeches,* and to such newsletters as *Speechwriter's Newsletter* and *The Executive Speaker.* They offer a wealth of ideas.

You should have three-by-five card files, three-ring notebooks, or manila folders full of indexed anecdotes, impressive facts and statistics, zippy quotations, bright anecdotes, bons mots, one-liners that may have been jotted down on cocktail napkins, sparkling turns of phrase, newspaper and magazine clippings, examples of clever analogies, speech excerpts—in short, anything you have come across that could conceivably be used in a future speech. When researching your speech topic, you should also be able to sift through an impressive pack-rat collection to come up with ten to fifteen nuggets that can be adapted and used to adorn the particular speech you are writing. With your research completed, you are ready for the next step.

Step 3: Boil your ideas down to a bare-bones central point, and then outline the speech. A short speech should have a single main idea you want to get across and can state in one clear sentence. State it. There should never be more than four or five (two or three are ideal) major supporting points. List them. Then gather all your research on the audience, on the topic, and from your pack-rat collection and systematically set about outlining how the speech will develop.

There are a number of good techniques. You can simply do a traditional outline as if you were writing a formal paper. You can try a more ingenious method called mapping the writing journey (Boyle and Buckley, 1981). With this you get to integrate functions of both hemispheres of your brain by drawing a geometric shape to enclose your main speech topic, with lines extended for major supporting points and branches of smaller lines for supporting details. This is a delightful and effective way to structure ideas and get a comprehensive grasp of the total speech. Still a third, and extremely effective, method is to get one of those small Post-it notepads made by 3M and jot down on separate sheets the key words for each of your research items, for your main topic and supporting points, for your anecdotes and jokes, and for your quotations. Take these sheets, which are the greatest invention since the paper clip, overlap them slightly on a sheet of paper, and rearrange them until you have the flow of points exactly as you want them.

In approaching the next step in the speech writing process, recall the admonition by Billhymer (1984, p. 3) that "a speech is a communication event fraught with danger. It offers potential for intense, immediate impact. However, it is always on the verge of spinning out of a speaker's control. A writer unaware of the inherently different character of the written and spoken word, the inherently different capacities of listeners and readers, can eliminate the possibility of control before an equally unwary speaker has uttered a word."

Step 4, then, is take all your ingredients and write the speech, but season it for the ear, not for the eye. Some tips about achieving a fluent oral style will be covered shortly, but first some comments about getting started writing, time, and the three parts of every speech.

Getting started. By this point in the process, you should be able to come up with a good headline-grabbing title for the speech, something that will be provocative and sound juicy to news editors and look enticing in publicity materials. Speaking of headlines, Karanjia (1980) actually recommends that the first thing you ought to do after your research is completed is not to begin composing the speech, but to write a news release about it, complete with substantive quotes, that you would like to see appear in the daily newspaper. He maintains that news coverage is the only legitimate reason to give a speech in the first place. This sort of exercise can certainly help you get into a frame of mind to keep the speech on target and your words sharply focused. It might also suggest some quotable comments to work into the text.

Whether you choose to start the writing process by writing a title or a news release, the important thing is to get started. Flesh out your outline. It is a good idea to get a first draft down quickly. It can help keep your speech conversational. Another effective approach is to assemble all your notes and then compose the speech on the run, using a tape recorder. Imagine that you are the speaker, and then just talk out the speech. Transcribed, this can give you an excellent rough draft that will likely be significantly longer than you need, so you can spend the remainder of your time rewriting, pruning, polishing, and adding those clever turns of phrase.

Time. Busy people who have grown accustomed to ten-second television commercials and to magazines and newspapers with a TV "look" offering brief chunks of boxed information for reader consumption simply are not inclined to listen to extended oratory. In general, as speeches venture past twenty minutes, they get into hostile territory. A speaker who goes way past twenty minutes gets into hot water. James Roosevelt put it best: "My father gave me these hints on speech-making. 'Be sincere. Be brief. Be seated.'" That is good advice for the speaker and the speech writer. Also, because of the pressure of time and because audiences grow impatient with long explanations, avoid getting bogged down with too much data or too many supporting details. Commit to memory what Voltaire said: "The secret of boring people lies in telling them everything" (Voltaire, 1785, p. 51). In the world of the speech writer, brevity is the soul of wit, and the measure of a good talk is its depth, not its length.

Three parts of every speech. When you sit down at the keyboard and write the speech, you have to try to conceptualize the speech in real time. In a twenty-minute speech, your speaker will need two or three minutes (10 to 15 percent) for the introduction or warm-up period. About one minute (5 percent) will do nicely for the conclusion. The sixteen minutes (80 percent) that remain constitute the main body of the talk, the real meat-and-potatoes you want to dish out to the audience.

That first two or three minutes are crucial to establishing the rapport necessary to get the listeners with and behind the speaker and make them receptive to the message. First impressions are all-important. Although most of that is out of the speech writer's hands—the one up there in the spotlight is the one actually creating the impression—the writer can at least make sure that all the guns are loaded when the time comes. Writing tightly and with every bit of wit and cleverness and economy you can muster, put into the script the obligatory acknowledgments and formalities (audiences expect them), and then give your speaker something that will link the audience with the speaker. It might be a joke relevant to the occasion or a suitable reference to the location of the event or to some of the people in the audience. It may be an anecdote about the host organization or the host city, or it may be a simple statement or two about a current problem that puts everyone in the room, including the speaker, in the same boat. Now here is the wet blanket: After you have written all this down, you should encourage your speaker, with every bit of persuasive power you can summon, not to read any of this stuff. More about talking versus reading a speech will come later, but it is particularly critical that the speaker not read these introductory comments.

The main body of the talk should begin on a provocative note. Give your speaker something startling or controversial to say. Have the speaker do something dramatic, such as ask for a show of hands or make a promise to do something during the speech. Whatever you write for the speaker to say or do, it should have the effect of galvanizing the audience into full attention and should introduce that single main idea of the speech (remember Step 3?).

And the old backwoods preacher's saw about sermonizing—advising his young colleague of the cloth to "Tell 'em what you're gonna tell 'em. Then tell 'em. Then tell 'em what you told 'em agin"—is something no speaker or speech writer should ever forget. In writing the speech, spell out early what the main point and supporting points are, elaborate on them, and when it comes to time to wrap up, summarize them.

Throughout the remainder of the talk, embellish the main point and major supporting points. The techniques are many. Discuss things from a chronological point of view. Quote other authorities to compare and contrast viewpoints of the topic. Offer personal testimony. Deliver some of the facts uncovered in your research, the statistics and other data that support your argument. Tell anecdotes, including humorous anecdotes, that make sharp points in support of your position. Ask pointed questions and then provide the answers. Discuss examples of the points you want to make. Above all, make a compelling argument, and write it with sparkle.

When the point comes for the one-minute conclusion or resolution of the speech, summarize the main idea. If the objective of the speech is to sell people on the idea of taking some action, remember to close the sale by telling them what you want them to do. No matter whether the last words of the speech are a restatement of the main idea, a choice quotation, or a call to action, wrap things up with good speed. Nothing can blunt the effectiveness of a good speech more than lingering too long at its ending.

Throughout the writing, aim for a fluent oral style and one that is adapted to the style of the speaker. (The latter is where your tape of the planning session with the speaker will come in handy, as will any other tapes of previous talks given by that speaker.) Tarver (1983a, 1983b) and Perlman (1984) offer some excellent tips for writing for the ear. Prefer the active over the passive voice. Don't say, "The drop-out phenomenon is not yet understood." Say, "We don't really understand the drop-out problem." Use strong, active verbs. Not "In 1984, we received a budget reduction," but "In 1984, they chopped our budget." Use simpler, more direct vocabulary than you would in writing for the eye. Take Winston Churchill's advice: "Short words are best and old words, when short, are best of all" (McGowan, 1958, p. 164). Aim for specific, concrete details that paint verbal pictures, and employ apt metaphors. You could say "I was hot and tired and thirsty," but an audience will get the picture better if they hear "The sweat fell off me. I didn't have the strength to wring out a T-shirt. It was so dry I couldn't spit." Vary sentence length to avoid monotonous rhythm. And use talking words and phrases: "He pulled himself back into that boxing ring. What courage!"

Repetition for emphasis can be an excellent device if used appropriately. Go back and read or listen to a tape of Martin Luther King's "I have a dream" speech (King, 1963) to get a feeling for the power of repetition. Use structural devices to make smooth transitions between points—the simple "First, . . . Second, . . . Third." Avoid the "Lee" family of adverbs: *firstly, importantly, alternatively,* and others that a speaker just about has to twist out of the mouth. Use vivid illustrations. For example, do not just talk about "parts per million" or "parts per billion," tell the audience that one part per million is the equivalent of one drop of vermouth per 500 barrels of gin. Be conscious of the subtle distinctions between written and oral speech. "We didn't go, as the car wasn't ready" reads fine, but try saying it out loud and see how unnatural it sounds. Use *because,* not *for* or *as,* in such cases.

Use good, short quotations and do not shy away from appropriate humor, but do not overdo either. Make sure the quotation makes a point more clearly and with greater impact than you can some other way, and as Perret (1984) demonstrates, make humor one of your strongest allies by localizing it, using it to add spice and flavor to the presentation.

When your first full draft of the speech is done, put it on the shelf to cool off overnight. The next time you come back to it, it will be blood-on-the-floor time. Read it aloud. If you have trouble saying parts of it, if there are rough spots that trip you up, chances are your speaker will have trouble, too. Cut everything that can be cut without being missed—words, phrases, whole paragraphs if necessary. Make it tight and lean. You have to be able to hear in your mind that speech being delivered, the applause being given. When you get it in that shape, you are ready to run the draft by your speaker, make any necessary adjustments, and then prepare for the final step in the speech-writing process.

Step 5: Serve the speech in a manuscript format that is appealing to the eye. Some speakers like their script typed in all caps, but it is easier to read in regular uppercase and lowercase orator-size type. Type the script in a narrow column—fifty-character width is fine—in the middle of the page. Leave the bottom third of the page blank. It will help keep a speaker's chin from dropping too low. Number pages in the upper right corner; put "MORE" at the bottom of each page and "END" at the bottom of the last page. Indent the first line of each paragraph, and hold paragraphs to about ten lines maximum. It can be effective to leave five or six spaces between sentences within a paragraph. It is a good idea to add extra spacing between paragraphs. Some speech writers use subheads on each page. Use eight-and-a-half- by eleven-inch paper, preferably dull-finish and buff-colored to minimize glare. Provide the speaker with three copies of the script—one to mark up and use, one to file, and an extra to carry along in case the first is lost. Give the speaker a simple businesslike black folder in which to carry the speech up to the lectern.

Now that you have delivered copies of the speech into the hands of the speaker, the actual speech-writing job is over. However, it is highly appropriate for you to sit in on a rehearsal session or two with the speaker to critique the delivery and evaluate the overall impact of the speech. Whether you do that or not, do try to convince your speaker, if convincing is necessary, to practice, practice, practice the speech. Mastery of the material is the only way that the speech you have so carefully and creatively put together will ever do to an audience what it is intended to do.

With all the foregoing now said, here is the speech writer's paradox: The best speeches, as a general rule, are never read. There are occasions where reading a text or large parts of a text verbatim is recommended; for example, in announcing policy, testifying before committees, or covering highly technical information. Most speeches, however, are vastly more effective if the speaker focuses on communicating with the audience, rather than speaking at the audience. That means using your speech manuscript as, at best, an outline, or actually converting the speech into note concepts, an outline of key words that will trigger the speaker's thoughts and enable the speaker to talk for thirty seconds to five minutes for each key word or phrase. This would be a Step 6 in the speech process if your speaker prefers to talk from this kind of material. A Step 6 does not mean that all the speech writer's time and effort are wasted. But it can mean that the speech draft you come up with will not have to be so highly refined and polished because it will now serve more as a reference piece that the speaker can read and reread to get the full flow of the ideas in mind. A great speech is still 90 percent great material and only 10 percent great delivery, and the great material can come from the speech writer's development of a topic, the research, the thinking through the issues, and the articulating on paper of the main point, the major supporting points, and the supporting details.

The speech writer's role has been an emerging one in institutional advancement. Once handled in the most ad hoc fashion or just dropped into the lap of staffers who would get the job done with a minimum of overt complaining, the speech writing assignment is recognized increasingly as one of the most important, and one of the most intellectually and creatively demanding, functions that advancement offices can offer. The speech writer, like the news writer, can help people across the campus tell an institution's story.

References

Billhymer, C. "A Speechwriter Speaks Out: It's No Job for the Meek." *Headlines* (publication of the St. Louis Chapter, International Association of Business Communicators), Feb. 1984, p. 3.

Boyle, O., and Buckley, M. H. *Mapping the Writing Journey.* Berkeley: University of California, Berkeley/Bay Area Writing Project, 1981.

Cole, R. S. *The Practical Handbook of Public Relations.* Englewood Cliffs, N.J.: Prentice-Hall, 1981.

Karanjia, N. N. "The Nitty-Gritty of Speechwriting." *Public Relations Journal,* May 1980, pp. 17–19.

King, M. L. "I Have a Dream." *Freedom March on Washington.* (Phonodisc) 20th Century-Fox Records, TFM 3110. 1963. (Also, TFS 3201, 1968.)

McGowan, N. *My Years with Churchill.* New York: British Book Center, 1958.

Perlman, A. M. "Writing for the Tongue." Special insert in *Speechwriter's Newsletter,* Aug. 31, 1984.

Perret, G. *How to Hold Your Audience with Humor: A Guide to More Effective Speaking.* Cincinnati, Ohio: Writer's Digest Books, 1984.

Tarver, J. "Putting Words into Their Mouths." *CASE Currents,* Feb. 1983a, pp. 20–23.

Tarver, J. *Your Next Speech: 66 Ways to Improve It.* Chicago: Lawrence Ragan Communications, 1983b.

Voltaire. "Sixième Discours de la Nature de l'Homme." In *Oeuvres Completes de Voltaire.* Vol. 12. Kehl, France: Imprimerie de la Société Littéraire-Typographique, 1785.

16

John Forasté

A Photographer's View on Communicating Through Photography

ॐ We use photography in our business of advancing higher education because of its special ability to communicate information and feelings in a manner simply not available to words. It is a visual medium that, although by no means objective, presents the world in a largely familiar way. It effectively blends documentation and interpretation and thereby relates to the real world in a manner that distinguishes it from other forms of communication.

Ways of Seeing

Seeing the world and forming what we see into a photographic image are not one and the same. Seeing is a continuous process in which our eyes and mind work together to scan, select, and assimilate things in the real world to form our perception of it. Making a photograph is a process that goes beyond seeing. The photographer uses seeing to experience and understand what is to be photographed and then makes a decision—given the strengths and limitations of the medium—on how to form that mind's-eye perception onto a two-dimensional plane of gray tones or colors that communicates. He or she must decide on one moment, one point of view, one composition, one set of relationships between people and objects. A still photograph is the result of this process—nothing more, nothing less.

217

The photographer must see as a person, a journalist, and an artist—and then work as an artisan. An assignment can, and indeed should, begin with infinite possibilities but must, by definition, end in a specific image. The execution of that image can range from quick and simple to extremely time-consuming—a logistical challenge. The photographer's perception, creativity, initiative, and time, as well as understanding of its projected use, have a lot to do with the photograph that results.

Photojournalism

A photograph that is assigned, made, and used for purposes of communicating must work on two levels: the photographic and the journalistic. Photographically, it must be visually effective; journalistically, it must contain sufficient and accurate information. Although the relative importance of the form and content can vary widely according to its purpose and use, a photograph should never be devoid of either. In fact, it is often the superb orchestration of these that makes a photograph great.

Photographs and snapshots should never be confused. A snapshot is a picture concerned principally with content; it is made to help us remember someone or something. It can have tremendous personal values because of who or what is in it. A photograph, however, may or may not have inherent significance to the viewer; its value may be determined not merely by what is in the picture, but also (or even principally) by how it is photographed.

Types of Photographs

The photographs we make and use tend to fall into certain areas:

People: The Simplest Portrait. Despite its simplicity, this type of photography should be done skillfully. It can be tight or medium, on location or in a studio, formal or informal, by available light or by photographic lights. A head shot need not be a mug shot. It can be relaxed, natural, engaging, and nicely lit.

People: Controlled Environmental Portrait. Although the

person remains undoubtedly the primary subject, the environment adds information and interest. Given control of the environment and the cooperation of the subject, the photographer can organize and simplify the image to heighten its impact. Control need not be synonymous with stiffness. Even though you may wish a stylized look, this type of portrait can also be done in a natural way. This is achieved mainly by good interaction between the photographer and the subject, which translates in the photograph into interaction between the viewer and the subject. In this type of situation, a tripod can be useful to maintain camera position and allow the photographer to engage and relax the subject. The environment can be real or symbolic. A real environment can be the subject's everyday work space or, instead, a place that best communicates that subject's field of work. There are no limits to the creation of a symbolic environment or the use of symbols.

People: Documentary Environmental Portrait. The subject may or may not be aware of the camera but is clearly not affected by its presence. Indeed, the strength of this type of portrait lies in its strong sense of reality. It can act like a window, allowing the viewer to witness a person—for a moment—in an actual situation. Although it is pretentious and ridiculous to think that a photograph can capture the essence of a person (or thing), a good portrait can communicate a sense of character and personality.

Documentation of an Event. Producing a single still image of an event for purposes of communicating that event to an audience in absentia is a tall order. There is no right or wrong type of photograph; an all-encompassing, wide-angle picture may be the best in one situation but may show (tell) nothing in another. It is quite possible that a medium-wide shot with something significant in the foreground and a good sense of the environment to fill out the picture may work most effectively to tell the story; or maybe a relationship (established by the camera) between a person and something in the environment; or perhaps even a detail of a person or object. It is fine, even helpful, for the photographer and the user to have ideas before an assignment, but a good photographer must have the freedom, sensitivity, and journalistic instinct to respond to what he or she actually encounters on the assignment.

Editorial Illustration: Documentary. The purpose here is to give a feeling for a type of activity that, unlike an event, happens often. It shows something specific only insomuch as a photograph is, by definition, always specific, but it is intended to go well beyond the particulars to permit the viewer to experience the nature of the activity. Its original purpose and use are generic. Because the viewer draws no particular meaning from who or what is in the picture, the way it is formed determines its success. A skilled photojournalist, forever the participant/observer, can translate an ordinary, uneventful situation, such as a class, into a strong and informative photograph. A photograph conceived as a documentary environmental portrait might later serve well as an editorial illustration, and vice versa. (Think of a professor or student in class, an athlete competing, or an alumnus volunteer in a meeting.)

Editorial Illustration: Created. Objects, details, or graphic images can, at times, illustrate a story most clearly. Do not fight the obvious for fear that it may appear trite; the photograph's effectiveness will be a direct result of its execution. A story on medicine, for example, might lead off with a simple, but visually strong, photograph of a stethoscope.

Color. Because color can be exciting, rich, and beautiful, it is definitely growing in use. However, a color photograph is not just a colored black and white picture. A bright red sweater, unnoticed in a black and white photograph, might dominate in a color one. That can be good or bad. The photographer must be both knowledgeable and deliberate in the use of color. Color also projects itself as less journalistic. It always faces the danger of putting more emphasis on the color than what is colored. The viewer is presented with a picture that may seem designed more to please than to inform.

Sequential. Sequential photographs are usually made and used for audiovisual shows. Each picture considered individually should be capable of standing on its own; however, primary consideration must be given to the development, rhythm, and cohesion of each segment and the entire show. For this reason, although photographic files are a great resource, putting a slide show together from existing material, no matter how good, may not work.

Fund-raising. Photographs made for fund-raising purposes are surely of the types above, but there is one critical difference: Who is in the picture is all-important to the fund-raiser. The demands of the fund-raiser often lead to photographs that are artistically limited. Nonetheless, the photographer must work with the stated need and always try, often against great technical odds, to make the best possible pictures.

Communication between the photographer and the user of the pictures before an assignment can sometimes help generate ideas about the shooting situation or the use of the pictures that will have a positive influence on the type of photograph that is made. One example of this is the grip-and-grin, or check-passing, photograph. Short of outlawing it (not a bad idea), a pleasing and effective picture can be made by photographing the donor with either the gift itself or a symbol of it (building, room, symbolic environment). Always remember that words and photographs are two different media. An important gift of money is not best communicated by a picture of the donor and the president standing together, ill at ease, as they shake hands and pass a white envelope between them. It does not make them or the institution look good.

Elements in a Good Photograph

The following elements may be closely interrelated in a photograph. Their successful orchestration makes a photograph good, perhaps even great. Even though a picture is worth a thousand words, we will try our best to consider these elements without the benefit of illustrations.

Content and Form. A photograph contains information and presents it in a certain way. The content and form are inextricably connected and must be understood as such by both the photographer and the user. The photographer is responsible for producing visual images that meet editorial needs; the user, for selecting and using these images based on both criteria.

Composition. One of the photographer's most important and demanding jobs is to organize, place together, compose things in the seemingly chaotic real world to create an image that hangs together in an intelligible and effective manner. The photographer must decide what is in (and, consequently, what is out) and how it is in. The camera establishes relationships within a photograph that, although certainly there in the prephotographed world, are fixed and heightened in the still image. The photographer must be schooled in this fundamental phenomenon: The camera records everything it finds in its viewfinder.

Simplicity. A logical extension of the photographer's job of composition is a responsibility to define and simplify. Simplifying means either carefully minimizing the number of elements or organizing them in a coherent fashion. A simple photograph can actually contain a lot of information. The purpose is to focus the viewer's attention.

Involvement. A viewer's involvement with a photograph will result from the photographer's involvement with the subject. The photographer is forever both participant and observer and needs to get into the situation enough to feel what is going on yet remain outside of it enough to see it clearly.

Documentation. The camera faithfully records what it sees, but what it sees is determined by the photographer. A photograph, then, is never objective, but is an interesting and often effective mix of documentation and interpretation—much the same as the story in journalistic writing. Because the photograph communicates a special sense of reality that other visual forms do not, the photographer and the user must understand the power that this carries with the viewer and accept the responsibility that goes with it. The best that the photojournalist can do in this regard is to strive for honest photographs that are neither affected nor contrived.

The photographer's best method of operation in any situation is to ask (1) What is going on? and (2) How can it be visually communicated? Then, all that remains to be done is to record it on film.

The Moment. The still photograph is, by definition, an image of a moment in time—a moment that is often critical. Indeed, much of a photographer's time and energy are spent searching for just that decisive moment. A person's expression and body language, the relationships of people and objects, and the quality and play of light are elements that often distinguish a particular moment.

Light and Lighting. Obviously, light is needed to make a photograph. Although the quantity of light is always relevant, it is the quality that gives a photograph its character and mood. A photographer most often tries to work with the light that is available. It makes the job easier and often makes the image more natural as well. However, because film needs a certain amount of light and cannot begin to record the range of light that the eye sees, a photographer must be prepared to use photographic lights. The usual reason for using other than available light, then, is to permit the film to make pictures that appear natural. If this is done well, the viewer will be unaware that the resulting photograph was lit.

Image Quality and Reproduction. Photography relies on technical tools that require constant and detailed attention. Because a photograph is, in a technical sense, merely a series of gray tones or a collection of colors, the photographer must render them sharply, cleanly, and at their fullest. The printer must, in turn, take care that the tones and colors are reproduced as faithfully as possible.

The Assignment

Every assignment requires a progression of decisions and actions.

Discussion. The photographer and user discuss all available information. The user presents the nature of the story, personality of the subject (if relevant), space and format options, photographic ideas (if any), logistical information, and deadline. The photographer has an opportunity to respond with ideas or to point out potential problems. Because the photographer is producing pictures for a specific purpose and because photographs cannot be reworked after an assignment the way words can, a full exchange of information and ideas before the assignment is critical. If the person using the photographs (editor or designer) and the person presenting the assignment (writer or program director, for example) are not the same, the photographer and the user should communicate in some way to make sure that editorial and design needs are fully understood.

Making the Appointment. The photographer should make his or her own appointments, despite the time involved. This not only permits logistical items to be dealt with directly (for example, agreeing on a time and location for purely photographic reasons, explaining and receiving the time required to produce a certain type of photograph) but also allows valuable interaction between the photographer and subject before the assignment.

Checking the Location. It is sometimes useful to visit a location before the shooting to check for such things as special lighting requirements or, in the case of an event, good camera positions that require preplanning.

Making the Photograph. On the assignment, having assimilated all the requirements, the photographer must respond to the situation or person to be photographed. In addition to never losing sight of what is expected by the user, the photographer must have and accept both the responsibility and the freedom to respond to whatever is going on.

Processing and Contacting. This is the most purely technical, but no less critical, stage. Film must be processed cleanly and consistently.

Selecting the Photograph. The photographer, who knows what he or she was trying to do on the assignment, should indicate the images that seem preferable—those with all the elements that make for a good photograph. Grease-pencil checks on the contact sheets or pencil checks on the slide mounts can identify these preferences to the user. At this point, the user is no longer dealing with ideas and possibilities, but with specific images. It is now the user's role to respond to these images.

Printing (Black and White). Although technical in nature, printing demands innumerable judgments that significantly affect the finished print. Because a black-and-white photograph is merely a series of gray tones, their interpretation is critical.

Reproduction. Even the best-reproduced print loses something in tone and sharpness. Optimal reproduction is important and is attainable with reliable printers.

Critiquing. The photographer should engage in constant

critical self-analysis of all completed work. It is also useful for the user and photographer to share feedback on how each felt the finished image worked.

Use of the Photograph

The first step is to select what photograph to use. Then decide how to use it most effectively. A single photograph can be used well in large size. A vertical can be bled off the page, and a horizontal can utilize an entire spread by jumping the gutter. Size alone, however, does not determine the effectiveness of a photograph. The overall design of a spread or page can actually contribute more to the photograph's effectiveness than can size alone. For example, imagine a double-page spread containing all type except for a simple but strong one-column photograph. Often, two photographs together can have greater impact than either one can have alone. Presenting two photographs, not just as two individual images but as a special relationship between the combination, helps the viewer experience the sensation of the whole being greater than the sum of its parts. Similar things can happen when headlines and photographs are carefully blended. Good reproduction faithfully transmits the tones or colors of the original print or transparency so that the viewer can enjoy it fully.

Selection is, of course, all-important. It is difficult to use a bad photograph well. Size is a negative factor when a good but complex photograph is used too small for all the information it contains or when a poor or average photograph is used large. Poor reproduction can destroy the impact, enjoyment, and even the information of the original print or transparency. Cropping is a very sensitive issue. A photograph that is made specifically for a cover, opening page, or design is conceived and executed for that format. It should not be cropped. Most photographs are made fully utilizing the given format of the camera, usually 35 mm. A good photograph has an integrity that may not allow it to be manipulated. However, at the risk of opening a Pandora's box, it needs to be said that certain good photographs can be cropped sensitively.

Technical Considerations

Equipment. There is no ideal arrangement; you work with the best tools available to suit your needs. Because the photography business entails mostly location work where portable, versatile, and quality equipment is required, the 35 mm, single lens reflex (SLR) camera serves us well.

Although the choice of lenses is very much a personal thing, there are some commonly accepted uses for various lenses. The 24 mm, f2.8 lens is not only superb for its ability to show a lot when in a tight space but also for emphasizing a person or object in the foreground while maintaining a sense of the environment (as in the environmental portrait); it also accentuates the perspective in interesting and exciting ways. The 35 mm, f2 lens is excellent for medium portraits; some photographers use it as a normal lens. The 55 mm, f2.8 macro is a sharp, flat-field lens designed for close-up and copy work. The 105 mm, f2.5 lens is renowned as a portrait lens. The 135 mm, f2.8 lens, while also useful for portraits, is versatile and effective as a medium/long lens. The 180mm, f2.8 lens is an amazingly versatile, longer lens because of its speed and size.

The tripod did not go out with the advent of 35 mm hand-held cameras. It is a must for long exposures and a great help in certain portrait situations. The motor drive is used to quickly advance the film so the photographer is always ready to pursue the next decisive moment. It should not be used in continuous blind bursts.

Lighting equipment is necessary when the available light is too little or too uneven for the film's relatively small contrast range to handle (as, for instance, when the subject is against a strongly lit window). It is also essential for most studio work. A number of small, independent, variable-power, slaved strobes with small, powerful, rechargeable gel cell batteries; small tripod screwed C clamps; and a totally reliable strobe meter can fit into one portable case. These can be arranged rather quickly (clamped to things or rested on shelves) to make interior work with Tri-X at ASA 400 easy and beautiful and Ektachrome 64 not only doable but gorgeous. Regrettably, a single bounced strobe is often the only viable option.

Direct flash, however, should be used only when the photograph is absolutely necessary and there is virtually no other way to make it. A CC50M (magenta) filter with daylight film can actually make most photographs taken under fluorescent lights look good.

Film. Tri-X is versatile and a standard for black-and-white work. Exposed at 400, and developed properly with a fine-grain developer, it can produce handsome, full-bodied prints. Exposed at 800, and pushed carefully, it permits strong, sharp, tight-grained prints—although they require patient printing. Ektachrome 64 for reproduction and audiovisual work yields rich, smooth images, though its excessive contrast is unfortunate. Unlike Kodachrome, it can be processed locally in as little as three hours. Limit use of high-speed color films to the option of last resort; they are disturbingly grainy and unable to hold fine highlight detail.

Printing. Polycontrast, F-surface, fiber-based paper, dried matte produces a sharp, full bodied, semimatte print, which is excellent for quality reproduction and good for handling. Double weight is durable and easy to work with. Resin-coated (RC) paper is practical and acceptable for contact prints, but inferior for finished prints; it is noticeably less sharp and never as rich.

On Assignment. Technical considerations directly affect a photographer's options. Consider such things as the amount and nature of the light available, the ability to light in only certain ways, or the disturbance factor (never is the photograph more important than the subject to be photographed!). These technical constraints are often frustrating, but they are important to understand and work with.

Filing. Negatives, original transparencies, prints, and contact sheets are a tremendous resource. They require cool, dry, clean, and safe storage. Negatives should be individually sleeved in acetate; transparencies, in plastic pages; contacts and prints, by subject. Physical protection is critical; organizing is tedious but important.

Time. Although time alone yields nothing, a photographer needs a certain amount of it in order to be able to "see" well and pursue what is seen.

Working Relationships

In institutional relations, editors, writers, designers, audiovisual directors, program directors, and photographers are all members of a team working together to achieve institutional objectives. The photographer, as a professional, should be expected to produce quality work and should be given the time, assignments, and support (equipment and staff) to deliver.

Part Three

Educational
Fund-Raising

William L. Pickett, Editor

17

William L. Pickett

Fund-Raising Effectiveness and Donor Motivation

◈ Educational fund-raising has long held a position of preeminence among the various disciplines of institutional advancement. The financial challenges facing educational institutions in the last two decades of the twentieth century mean that this preeminence will continue. Nonetheless, educational fund-raising takes place within the total framework of a comprehensive advancement strategy. No matter how well done technically, fund-raising will not be effective without imaginative and assertive public and constituent relations.

The chapters in this section present the best and most current thinking on the significant components of educational fund-raising. This chapter, however, addresses two major, general issues that have direct impact on the success of individual fund-raising efforts but that are often not considered by the fund-raising practitioner. The first of these deals with fund-raising effectiveness. What are the institutional and policy variables that determine the achievement of fund-raising potential? The second issue runs throughout all discussions of fund-raising activity but is often not directly addressed. It seems to answer the question, Why do people make gifts? What are their major activating motivations?

Fund-Raising Effectiveness

All institutions raise differing amounts of gift income. Some raise hundreds of millions a year; others seem to scrape by with a few hundred thousand or less. Even institutions that appear to be quite similar rarely raise the same amounts of gift income. It is important for fund-raising practitioners to understand the basic dynamics that determine ultimate fund-raising success or failure. This understanding rests on two notions. First, total dollars raised is not the best measure of fund-raising success or failure. Second, important institutional and non-fund-raising policies have substantial impacts on ultimate fund-raising effectiveness.

Consider the difficulty of using total dollars raised as the criterion of effectiveness. Suppose college A raises $1 million and college B raises $3 million. An obvious conclusion might be that college B is clearly the more effective. However, if another important and realistic factor is added, the conclusion might be reversed. Say that it was possible to determine the potential fund-raising achievement of each college and that college A had a potential of $2 million whereas college B had a potential of $9 million. It then appears that college A achieves 50 percent of its potential and college B achieves only 33 percent of its potential. From this point of view, college A is the more effective college and is the one worthy of further study to determine the variables underlying fund-raising effectiveness.

Fund-Raising Potential

Quantitative, rigorous research has demonstrated the possibility of establishing measures of fund-raising potential, which, in turn, permits the type of analysis suggested above. Researchers have tested a variety of internal and external variables in the attempt to identify those that explain variation in gift income. This research, focused on various types and sizes of colleges and universities, has shown that it is possible to identify variables that help explain why some colleges seem to have higher potential for fund-raising than others. The results obtained by this author appear to have the most interpretive significance.

This author analyzed a total of fifteen environmental factors and institutional characteristics in terms of their individual and group relationship to a three-year average of gift income. Four of the variables were significantly and importantly related to gift income. These four were market value of endowment, percent of graduates attending graduate or professional school, number of alumni, and cost of attendance (which included room and board costs in a weighted average). These four variables could account for almost 70 percent of the variation in gift income. Each of the following factors interprets the four variables.

Wealth. Endowment is clearly a measure of institutional wealth. It represents resources that the institution does not need to consume in its current operations. Endowment results from operating surpluses generated in prior years, from appreciation of endowment principals, from bequests, or from direct gifts often restricted for use as endowment. In any event, endowment is the result of past fund-raising or operating success.

Endowment permits an institution to achieve a successful pattern of current operation. A college with a larger endowment than another is better able to withstand short-term financial or enrollment shortfalls without sending crisis signals to its external environment. Endowment provides the financial flexibility to achieve and maintain a successful pattern of operation.

In short, the wealthier institutions simply have a greater potential for fund-raising than institutions of more modest means. This is not to say that the wealthier institutions are the more deserving of financial support or indeed that they necessarily receive more gift income, only that they have a greater potential.

Quality. The perceived quality of a college or university is an important factor in determining a college's potential for fund-raising. Educational quality is one of the most elusive terms in use today. The issue here, however, has to do with perceived quality. The percentage of the graduating class attending graduate or professional school and the average Scholastic Aptitude Test (SAT) score of the entering class are typical measures of quality that are used by those outside the academy.

This single notion of quality stands for much more, however. It has to do with an organization that is accomplishing its proclaimed mission at a high level of effectiveness. Organizations that are good at what they do appear to have a greater potential for fund-raising than organizations that are mediocre.

Size. The research clearly demonstrated that colleges that were larger in terms of number of alumni as well as current enrollment were more likely to raise larger amounts of money regardless of the fund-raising policies implemented. The larger a college is, the bigger the impact it has on its community and the more families are touched directly or indirectly by its educational, research, and public service programs. As a result, there are more potential advocates for the college or university in the larger community.

Whatever may be said to the contrary, contemporary American culture appears to value bigness. Larger size is a prima facie statement of success quite apart from whatever negative aspects may accompany large size. Even in the comparison of small organizations, the larger ones will tend to have the advantage in terms of potential for fund-raising.

Socioeconomic Level of Clientele. Price is an effective measure of the socioeconomic level of consumers. A college that is more expensive than another will tend to serve a higher socioeconomic clientele. This is crucially important in the search for gift income. American culture prizes upward social mobility; it has no taste for downward mobility. The result is that the children of those who have made it tend to keep making it. A college that serves these families will have easier entrée to individuals who have or control wealth.

To some, these results may be depressing. A new organization with little wealth that aspires to serve low-income families will find it much more difficult to raise money than an organization that is large, serves wealthy families, and has a sizable endowment. This is the hard reality of doing business in contemporary American culture. It appears that the organizations that need money the most are the ones least likely to get it. The research tends to support this conclusion.

These statements are true. It is better to deal with reality than illusion and fantasy. However, the fact that an organization has greater potential does not mean it will necessarily achieve or overachieve that potential. Conversely, the fact that an organization has a very low potential for fund-raising does not mean that it will be unable to raise money or that it will necessarily raise very little.

The specific policies used and the effectiveness of their implementation will determine the final outcome. Those who seek funds for low-potential organizations should be realistic about their chances and should particularly avoid unrealistic comparisons with high-potential organizations.

Fund-Raising Policies

Given that each college or university has a potential for fund-raising, that potential does not completely explain the variation in gift income. That final explanation has to do with the way a college goes about its task. The author's research included this final step. Fund-raising potential was computed for each college and compared with the actual three-year results. The colleges were ranked based on the percent of potential actually achieved. The top 25 percent were identified as overachievers and the bottom 25 percent as underachievers. Both groups were then surveyed with regard to their institutional and fund-raising policies, and significant differences between the two groups were identified. There were clear differences in institutional direction, trustee leadership, and fund-raising effort.

Institutional Direction. The most significant difference between overachievers and underachievers was that significantly more of the overachievers had a clear sense of institutional direction, as evidenced by a written case statement. The existence and use of a written case statement was an important indication that the college had gone through the process of long-range planning. It had reviewed its past and present, assessed its environment and the demands likely to be faced in the future, and focused its efforts through the lens of institutional mission. This process had been formal enough so that the resulting product was written.

The impact of institutional direction is significant on the entire institution, but especially in fund-raising. Volunteers and donors are motivated by clearly articulated institutional goals and mission. A sense of institutional direction enlivens the members of an organization in the pursuit of common goals.

Trustee Leadership. A second characteristic of an overachieving institution is the presence of trustee involvement and leadership. Trustees are representatives of the larger community served by the college. Their command of affluence and influence means they can speak for the college in ways not available to the paid staff. Trustee financial commitment sends a message to the college's constituencies that those who know the college best are wholeheartedly in support of the college and its goals. Trustee leadership is signified by the active work of trustee committees, especially the committee on institutional advancement.

Fund-Raising Effort. Overachieving colleges spent more money and employed more staff than underachieving colleges. Remember that the overachieving colleges were not those that raised more money than the underachieving ones but rather those that significantly exceeded their potential. These colleges put their money where their mouths were. They were serious about fund-raising and made the investments of money and personnel required for success.

In addition to more effort, the overachieving colleges deployed their resources in a certain fashion. As a group, they invested professional staff time in the four basic fund-raising programs: annual giving, planned giving, capital giving, and prospect research. It is clear that a major reason for overachievement is the combination of these four basic programs.

Educational fund-raisers need to keep these results in mind. All colleges and universities are not created equal. Organizations that are larger, wealthier, of higher quality, and serving a higher socioeconomic clientele have a greater potential for fund-raising than other organizations. Whether an organization achieves its potential depends on its ability to create and communicate a sense of institutional direction, the leadership and involvement of its trustees, and the quantity and character of its fund-raising effort. Whatever resources are made available for fund-raising should be used to provide professional staff attention to annual giving, planned giving, capital giving, and prospect research.

Donor Motivation

The aim of institutional advancement is to build voluntary, long-term relationships between persons and organizations. During the course of each relationship, there will be calls to action, which will be invitations for the person to take supportive action toward the organization. In educational fund-raising, these calls to action will be gift solicitations. To be successful, these solicitations and the cultivations that precede them must focus on the motivations of the potential donors.

This critical area of human motivation is difficult to define, and fund-raisers must come to their own conclusions in this matter. To assist in this process, the rest of this chapter presents six important motivations of gift giving: belief in values of organizations, obligation, community position, ego needs, self-interest, and self-actualization.

Belief in Values of Organization

People give money to organizations because they believe in the mission and goals of the organization. Although this is true of all donors, it is especially relevant for major gift donors. An individual who is considering a gift of capital magnitude is concerned about the long-run implications of the gift. It is a concern that goes beyond institutional success and survival and runs to the core problem or need addressed by the organization. Beyond this, the donor will be motivated by the character of the organization and the values that enliven and activate it as an organization of human beings.

Obligation

People are also motivated out of a sense of obligation. With the achievement of certain social standing goes the expectation of philanthropic activity. Many approach their gift giving out of a sense of religious or spiritual obligation. This may be self-imposed, or it may be legislated by a community of religious believers. Political relationships within a community may dictate charitable giving directed toward specific organizations. Gift giving may be a part of the countervailing power relationships in a community. Finally, certain communities may have long-standing traditions of charitable giving by certain individuals, families, and organizations. These traditions can become so strong as to be effectively coercive. However, although individuals strongly motivated to give by obligation are highly likely to donate, they are unlikely to achieve extraordinary giving levels unless other motivations become important as well.

Community Position

Gift giving can be an important variable in achieving, maintaining, or improving social or community position. Very often an affluent individual who is new to the community will seek to establish community standing by making significant gifts to the established educational, social, medical, and cultural organizations. Persons of long standing in a community who have significantly improved their financial position will seek to provide evidence of this by making larger-than-expected gifts to the highly visible philanthropic organizations.

Ego Needs

The most powerful set of motivators are those related to the needs of the human ego, the self-identity of each person. This constellation of needs is in constant flux; the interrelationships change over time. The fundamental ego needs are for power, success, affection, and security. Each of these can be important in specific gift giving decisions. The person strongly motivated by need for affection will approach gift giving much differently than someone using a gift to acquire power. The fund-raiser involved in major gift work must become adept at understanding these ego motivations and understanding which needs are operative for each prospect.

Self-Interest

Many individuals give gifts because of what they receive in return. The most recognizable and acceptable of these motivations is the income tax deduction. Very often gift premiums and recognition groups and activities provide objects and services deemed to be of value by the donor. In corporate giving, the motivation of self-interest is not only widespread but also legally required. The only justification for corporate giving is that it somehow, either directly or indirectly, benefits the corporation and its shareholders. Fortunately, only rarely does a prospective donor seek such a return for a gift that the proposed transaction becomes an economic exchange rather than a philanthropic gift.

Self-Actualization

Finally, there are those donors who see their gift giving as part of living a full human life. Their motivations are altruistic in the best sense of that word. They seek to experience the joy of sharing their substance with others rather than any psychological, economic, or social benefit.

In reality, the motivation for gift giving is the same as the motivation for any human behavior: mixed and changing. All of the six motivations discussed here are operative in each human being. The potency of any particular motivation will vary over time for any individual. The fund-raiser must remain aware of the complexity of human behavior and the changing formulations of motivations. Cultivation and solicitation activities must reflect these complexities.

Conclusion

Those involved in educational fund-raising serve education in an important and fundamental way. This will be even more true through the end of the twentieth century. The ability to fulfill these important demands depends upon the recognition of the determinants of fund-raising effectiveness and the complex human motivations that lead to charitable gifts.

18

Gary A. Evans

Organizing and Staffing the Development Office

Organizing the Office

❧ When organizing for any task, it is good to consider the cliché "Form follows function." The function or purpose of the development office is clear—to raise money. At the most basic level, there are three things a development office must do if it is to achieve that purpose: identify who can, should, or might give support; take the necessary steps to obtain the gift; and record the gift and thank the donor. The development office should be organized to cover these major responsibilities.

Each of these functions can be further divided into other activities that must occur if fund-raising is to be successful. Whether a development office is large, with a number of development professionals specializing in different activities, or small, with many activities shared by a few, the staff, budget, time, and effort should be organized around the three basic functions: finding a potential donor, obtaining a gift, and recording the results.

Identifying the Donors

Because it is clear that there must be a donor if there is to be a donation, every development office should have some portion of staff and budget devoted to identifying potential donors and maintaining files with their names, addresses, telephone numbers, job titles, professional positions, and other demographic data. The full potential donor file should include all alumni, parents of current and former students, interested neighbors, previous donors, and any others with whom some connection of interest can be established. In addition to including individuals, the potential donor file should also include the names of foundations, corporations, and other organizations that might have interest in giving support. But a basic name-and-address file for all constituents is only a beginning. Among the potential donors to any organization are the 10 to 20 percent who can make the sizable gifts that assure the success of the institution. In addition to maintaining demographic records on all constituents, the office should conduct research on those prospects who have the greatest gift potential. For these individuals, the files should include their philanthropic interests, hobbies, signs of affluence, life-style, family connections, and other information that suggests giving potential. Corporate and foundation files should indicate a reason for interest in the institution, possible connections, past giving, primary philanthropic interests, and other information that might show a logical relationship between the organization and the institution.

In a small office, the same person may maintain the records and conduct the research. Larger organizations may have several people whose primary responsibility is maintaining the accuracy of demographic information while others research the resources and interests of potential major donors in order to define the logical link for solicitation. Whatever the office size, it must be organized to maintain basic name-and-address records of everyone who is solicited and to research more extensively the prospects of greatest gift potential.

Obtaining the Gift

Records and research have little value unless they lead to the desired result—a gift. The solicitation program of the development office should be organized around the major programs of fund-raising.

Annual giving is the foundation of a solid development program. Every office should commit some portion of time, budget, and staff to seeking annual contributions, which meet the basic expenses of the institution—heat, light, salaries, books, student aid, and so on. A development office must organize itself to solicit for annual giving, whether by letters or brochures put out by a part-time staff member or by phonathons, personal solicitation, reunion gift programs, and a variety of other techniques carried on by a large professional staff.

Special gifts are the contributions from individuals, foundations, or corporations above the level of annual giving. Because special gifts provide 80 percent or more of gift income, the development office should be organized to devote a comparable portion of its human and financial resources to special gift solicitation. In many institutions, those responsible for special gift solicitation conceive, plan, and implement cultivation steps that precede solicitation. Larger offices may have staff members who plan the strategies while others handle the logistics for special events, VIP dinners, and other cultivation moves. What is important is that the sequence of cultivation, involvement, and solicitation be managed as a continuum and that the responsibility for planning these steps should not be divided but should rest with one person or team, even though different persons may assist in implementing different stages.

Because individuals are the major source of gift support, the deployment of staff to handle special gifts should favor the tracking, cultivating, and soliciting of individuals over corporations and foundations. An institution may wish to have one or more persons devoted to corporations and foundations, but the number devoted to these organizations will usually be less than the number devoted to individual special gifts prospects.

The degree of organization necessary to attract deferred gifts is a matter of common sense. If an institution is relatively young, with few senior citizens among its constituents, there may be limited potential for deferred gifts, and the organization of the office should reflect those limits. In that event, a special gifts professional might be trained to work with the few deferred gift possibilities that arise. However, if the institution has a reasonable pool of older alumni who enjoy some affluence, then a full-time person (or persons) should seek deferred gifts. In either event, deferred giving prospects normally come from those who have been identified, cultivated, and involved through the special gifts activity. Therefore, a deferred gifts program should normally come after annual giving and special gifts.

Recording and Acknowledging Gifts

Because the third basic function of the development office is to receive, record, and acknowledge gifts, the office must be organized to accomplish those tasks. At the most basic level, there should be three important types of records. First, there should be a separate record for each contributor—individual, corporation, foundation, or association—showing the history of giving to the institution. Second, there should be records that show giving according to constituent groups. Decision makers need cumulative gift results for such groups as alumni, parents, friends, foundations, corporations, and others. And third, there should be records to show the purpose of gifts: unrestricted, restricted (current and capital), gifts-in-kind, and so forth.

Exhibit 18-1 is a relatively simple matrix for recording gifts by both source and purpose.

In addition, properly maintained records provide ease of information retrieval. A good records system not only tells who gave how much and to what purpose but also provides information in a way that assists management decisions. Development officers should be able to use gift records to make projections of future fund-raising based on historic data. The records should also support prospect research by providing a growing data base of information about donors. Simply stated, the organization of giving information must not only be accurate but must also help development officers make management decisions and plan intelligently for the further solicitation of donors.

Because each gift received is preparation for the next, acknowledgments and stewardship reports should be timely, accurate, and a recognized part of the continuing cultivation process. The responsibility for acknowledging gifts and sending stewardship reports may rest with those who receive and record

Exhibit 18-1. Gift Income Report.

Part I: CURRENT OPERATIONS

DONOR PURPOSES	INDIVIDUALS			ORGANIZATIONS					TOTAL
SOURCE	ALUMNI A	PARENTS B	OTHER C	FOUNDATIONS D	CORPORATIONS, BUSINESSES E	RELIGIOUS ORGANIZATIONS F	FUND-RAISING CONSORTIA G	OTHER H	
1. Unrestricted									
2. Academic Divisions									
3. Faculty and Staff Compensation									
4. Research									
5. Public Service and Extension									
6. Library									
7. Operation and Maintenance of Physical Plant									
8. Student Financial Aid									
9. Other Restricted Purposes									
10. Restricted (lines 2-9)									
11. Total--Current Operations									

Part II: CAPITAL

DONOR PURPOSES

12. Property, Buildings, and Equipment									
13. Endowment and Similar Funds: Unrestricted Income									
14. Endowment and Similar Funds: Restricted Income									
15. Loan Funds									
16. Total--Capital									
17. Grand Total (lines 11 + 16)									

gifts, or it may fall to the development staff responsible for the various program elements, such as annual giving and special gifts. Wherever the responsibility lies, these activities should not be so routinized and mechanized that the human ingredient is lost. Whether gifts come from corporations, foundations, or individuals, people make the decision to give. The acknowledgment and stewardship process should be as personal as the gift.

Figures 18-1 and 18-2 show typical organization charts for small and large offices. The common element in each is the coverage given to the three basic functions: finding the potential donor, obtaining the gift, and recording the results.

Figure 18-1. Typical Organization of a Small Development Office.

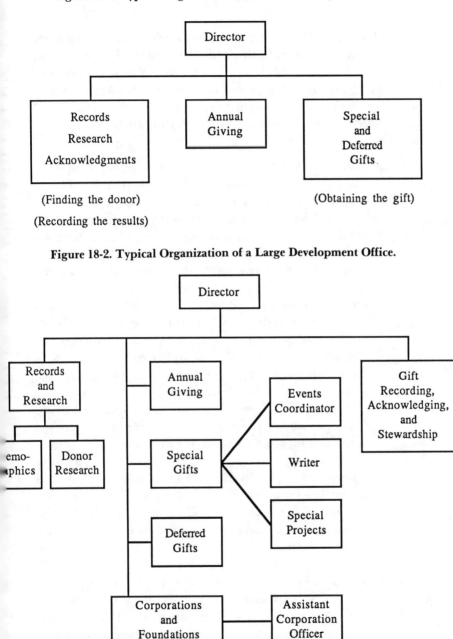

(Finding the donor)   (Obtaining the gift)

(Recording the results)

Figure 18-2. Typical Organization of a Large Development Office.

'inding the donor)   (Obtaining the gift)   (Recording the results)

Staffing the Office

If form follows function in organizing the development office, then staffing must fit the form that is established. Assuming that different persons will be selected for the separate functions of researching, soliciting, and recording, different characteristics will be needed by people in the separate functions.

Successful researchers have the following characteristics:

Attentiveness to Details. Researchers should enjoy digging. They should be both interested in gathering the obvious information, such as the wealth and major interests of potential donors, and attentive to the little things such as habits, subtle likes and dislikes, and other details that offer insight into people and why they behave as they do.

Curiosity. There are two levels of research. Almost anyone can compile a profile of an individual based on information that is readily accessible, such as address, job title, clubs or activities while in college, and stockholdings, if publicly reported. A good researcher takes the search to a different level. The truly curious person looks for information not publicly reported, such as friends, leisure activities, vacation patterns, charitable interests, and signs of affluence that not only indicate giving potential but also suggest possible approaches to the donor and involvements with the institution.

Recognition of Relationships. The ability to identify linkages among individuals or between individuals and corporations or foundations is important. A research assignment that begins as a routine attempt to find useful contacts with a corporation may become an extensive piece of research on an individual uncovered in the process.

Orderliness. Research information will come from a variety of sources and will probably reflect a variety of perceptions and images of a potential donor. The researcher must take this variety and put it together in an orderly fashion to create a coherent and useful body of information to support the cultivation and solicitation effort.

Successful solicitors have the following characteristics:

Bottom-line orientation. A good fund-raiser knows that, sooner or later, success is measured by gifts received. This in no way suggests that a development officer puts the gift ahead of ethical behavior and a fair consideration of both the donor and the institution. However, development officers never move their sights far from the ultimate goal.

Eagerness to be measured. Fund-raising results are measurable. They cannot be disguised or hidden. Persons who resist being evaluated by visible results or are intimidated by performance appraisals will probably not be successful or happy as development officers. A professional in development welcomes specific goals and expects—even wants—to be measured by the success of achieving them.

Cause orientation. Many professions call for persons who are oriented to the bottom line and welcome the measurement of their performance. However, development officers should also believe in grand causes. A development officer is representing education and often serves as the means through which the generosity of individuals satisfies important educational objectives. Development officers are more than fund-raisers. They are educators, and they should believe strongly in the intrinsic values that education brings to individuals and to society.

Inner drive. Defining an intangible is difficult, and identifying it in potential staff is even more so. However, every effort should be made to draw into the development profession people who ultimately set for themselves goals greater than those required by bosses or budgets. A successful development officer is one whose desire is always to do something better than it was done the time before and who knows that even a successful proposal or event can be improved through careful thought and creative effort. The inner drive to succeed, to rise above past experience and performance, to derive fulfillment from hard work for a lofty purpose are the traits that characterize the best development professionals.

Stamina. Only after one has worked all day in the office and then driven two hours to a phonathon, inspired the volunteers and led the cheering, driven two hours back home arriving after midnight, and risen early to repeat the process the next day is one aware of the importance of stamina to the development professional.

Capacity to absorb rejection. No one likes rejection. Some people have such difficulty with it that they resist circumstances in which it might occur. A good development officer does everything possible to avoid a negative response, but if it comes, the professional rises above it and even accepts it as a challenge to work harder for future success. The development officer who can absorb rejection as yesterday's experience and move on to tomorrow's success is better able to meet the demands and expectations of the job.

Integrity. The issue of integrity in a development officer goes beyond the honest handling of gifts. Integrity in the profession means a genuine concern for the interests of the donor, even to the point of counseling against a gift that would be unwise for a donor to make. It also means representing the institution honestly and openly and not sacrificing institutional values in order to obtain support.

Many of the characteristics required by researchers are also needed by the staff who receive, record, and acknowledge gifts; these include attentiveness to detail and orderliness. (For this reason, research and records may be organizationally combined.) Other important characteristics include:

Orientation to numbers. Those who receive, record, and acknowledge gifts must be comfortable working with accounts, ledgers, and numbers.

Accuracy. Comfort with numbers is not sufficient. Ability to deal with them precisely and accurately is essential.

Attitude of appreciation. A gift processor must be precise and accurate but must also be aware that a gift is an extension of a fellow human being. (Even in corporations and foundations, people make the decisions.) Gift clerks and managers should approach their work with an appreciation of the donor that leads them to acknowledge gifts promptly and with sensitivity and to write stewardship reports that give donors a real understanding of and joy in what their generosity has helped to accomplish.

Screening and Selection of Staff

The personal résumé is an interesting piece of creative writing. It may often disguise more than it reveals. A cleverly written résumé can make superficial job-hopping look like desirable breadth of experience. The reader must look beneath the surface. Does the résumé cite specific accomplishments in each previous assignment, or does it only give generalized job descriptions? Does it indicate whether the writer had responsibility for specific results in previous assignments, or was the writer staffing and supporting the work of others? Has the applicant remained in other positions long enough to have made a contribution? What is it?

Interviews are equally abused. Often the interviewer uses the meeting as an occasion to sell the applicant on the job rather than using it to learn about the applicant's qualifications for the position. Something of the applicant's motivation and drive can be learned by asking such questions as What kind of work do you like to do? What do you dislike doing? Of what accomplishments are you most proud? What are your hobbies, interests, and volunteer activities? At what have you failed? How did you handle it? What will you do if you don't get this job? How do you feel about being objectively evaluated by your results? What contribution or contributions do you believe you have made in your current and previous positions?

An absolutely critical step in selecting staff is reference checking, but it is amazing—even appalling—how many people are offered responsible positions with no check of their references or no conversation with previous employers.

Reference checks should definitely include conversations with current and previous employers. Specific questions should be framed to learn what the applicant actually did and accomplished and not merely what the previous job description called for. After describing the position you have open and asking questions about the applicant, it is good to ask, "Now that you understand the position I am filling and knowing what you do about the applicant, would you hire the applicant for this job?"

Training

Once staff have been hired, the important process of training begins. Too often, new employees receive only a basic orientation to the specific job they will do without putting that job in context. Training begins by orienting the employee to the role of the institution in education and the mission it has defined for itself. The training includes an explanation of how the institution is organized and how it functions. The development office should be explained in the same way. After establishing the setting (education, institution, office), the training moves to the specific details of the job. At first, the supervisor should describe the job conceptually— that is, describe its role in the context of the development office and the specific way in which the job aids the office in achieving its objectives. Then, the supervisor should track the specific details of the job and how to perform it.

Training should also include a planned sequence of readings, beginning with what the institution says about itself, then proceeding to the professional literature of development such as *Designs for Fund Raising* (Seymour, 1978), *The Art of Asking* (Schneiter, 1978), *Fund Raising: The Guide to Raising Money from Private Sources* (Broce, 1979) and *CASE Currents*. Development professionals should also be familiar with the Jossey-Bass sourcebooks on institutional advancement and some of the how-to manuals that pertain to various activities within the development profession.

The training program should extend beyond a few weeks so it includes a plan for long-term professional development. Additional readings, visits to colleagues at other institutions, and attendance at professional meetings, conferences, and institutes should all be part of a program of training and development for employees.

Motivating Staff

If the qualities needed for the position are identified, and if good people have been screened, hired, and given adequate training (including opportunities for professional development), the manager's final responsibility is motivating them. In reality, good people who possess inner drive do not need much external stimulation to motivate them. But the manager can create an environment in which capable people motivate themselves by setting clear job descriptions, establishing clear goals that are both realistic and ambitious, giving recognition—even praise—for success and prompt feedback when mistakes are made, and providing adequate compensation. When motivation falters, it is occasionally due to the fact that the individual lacks enthusiasm and drive to be successful. More often, the absence of motivation is not the result of inherent weakness in the individual but the result of a vague understanding of the job, poor feedback (positive or negative), unrealistic goals, or inadequate compensation that fails to recognize outstanding performance.

Professional development work may be more of an art than a science. Almost every major development campaign has received a miracle gift, which appeared without apparent effort from or knowledge of the development office. As long as a decision to give is made by human beings, the process will be subject to human whim or inspiration. However, whims and pure inspiration are rare. Gifts are more often the result of the development office's having done the right things at the right time in the right way. Therefore, organizing properly to accomplish what must be done, and staffing with good people carefully selected and properly trained, can help assure success in educational fund-raising by creating those miracles that are rarely the result of whim but usually the result of good solid professional work.

References

Broce, T. E. *Fund Raising: The Guide to Raising Money from Private Sources.* Norman: University of Oklahoma Press, 1979.

Schneiter, P. H. *The Art of Asking.* New York: Walker, 1978.

Seymour, H. J. *Designs for Fund Raising.* (Rev. ed.) New York: McGraw-Hill, 1978.

19 *Scott G. Nichols*

Annual Giving Programs: Responding to New Trends and Realities

❦ Annual giving had its origins at Yale University, where the first Annual Fund Office was organized in 1890. Almost a century later, annual giving still has the three characteristics initially outlined at Yale. First, annual giving provides operating support for the institution. Pomona College has used *funds to live by* as the phrase that best describes what annual giving dollars are meant to do. This provides a useful distinction from capital funds, or *funds to grow by*. Second, annual giving seeks funds on a yearly basis. Successful annual giving programs are based on developing a habit of giving annually. There must be an explicit, or at least an implicit, commitment to produce support yearly. Finally, annual giving is an organized effort. It is not the sum total of gifts received in a twelve-month time frame. Rather, it is a formal, active program for which there are clear guidelines and patterns for maximizing gifts of crucially needed annual budget dollars.

Nationally, there is good news and bad news with regard to annual giving. The best available measures of effectiveness in annual giving solicitation reveal that the majority of educational donors are responding in greater numbers with larger gifts. Counterbalancing the positive trend upward is the sobering fact that, on the average, fewer than one in five alumni give (19.4 percent in 1982–83). Clearly, there is much to be done.

Annual Giving in a Total Development Program

A popular myth is that annual giving programs are less vital to an overall development effort than programs seeking the big gifts. Such thinking is misguided and shortsighted. The reasons are simple.

First, annual giving dollars are real and significant. There are few alternative sources of income for an institution. These dollars cover costs that are not passed on to students in the form of higher tuition. They are also the institution's living endowment, equalling the income of fifteen to twenty times the endowment total required to replace them.

Second, annual giving provides an institution with a base of supporters. Few institutions survive or flourish without a substantial number of advocates. Such a constituency helps stimulate enrollment, promote a strong reputation, and identify leadership donors. Without a broad base of support, institutions have difficulty convincing major philanthropists and corporate, foundation, and political leaders that they are worthy of substantial support.

Third, annual giving solicitations are important cultivation events in the life cycle of major donors. Large gifts, particularly bequests, rarely come from those who have not had long and positive histories of annually supporting an institution. Good annual solicitation is an indispensable part of major gift identification and cultivation programs.

Fourth, annual giving programs are important staff training grounds. The experiences gathered by those managing volunteers for a specific job within a specific time are exceptionally valuable. Frontline experience has been shown repeatedly to be more valuable than superior intellect or management expertise in development executives. Those who know what works do better than those who rely on logic alone. Annual giving programs offer a wealth of such pragmatic lessons.

Annual and capital giving programs require close coordination. Strong annual and capital giving programs are, and must be, intertwined. The designation of prospects as either exclusively annual or exclusively capital often has negative consequences for both efforts. An integrated approach is necessary.

Before the first letter is mailed or the first call made, plans must be focused and specific. The eternal goals of getting more and doing better are not enough. Dollar and donor goals must be quantified. Equally important, they must be segmented to reflect the constituencies involved. There are some excellent planning models to support segmentation.

1. Trend analysis. An analysis of national trends can help determine dollar and donor goals. Both *Giving U.S.A.* (American Association of Fund-Raising Counsel, 1984) and *Voluntary Support of Education* furnish data on annual fund results. For example, when either national or peer institutions statistics reveal increases of 8 percent, projections much above or below 8 percent should be carefully scrutinized. These two key sources not only give important planning guideposts but also present data to educate administration and staff as to realistic expectations for improvement.

In addition to dollar and donor goals, the annual fund-raiser must project other variables and must do this for more than a twelve-month period. Harry Gotwals, director of development, Duke University, has developed an effective model. Using results from the previous two years as a guide, he projects several key variables as illustrated in Table 19-1.

There are many other areas that can be reviewed in this systematic way. These include giving clubs, recognition books, computer resources, associates programs, all volunteer leadership positions, prospect research, and annual cultivation events. Such analysis becomes a useful, ongoing tool for measuring progress.

2. Frame-of-reference analyses. All institutions can identify colleges and universities with which they share important similarities, such as size, heritage, applicant pools, curricula, or faculty composition. These peer institutions offer approximate norms to help evaluate programs. Only the foolhardy will avoid snatching ideas and plans that have been implemented successfully at other places. Almost every program has a few ideas worth stealing. In fact, simple comparisons of size, volunteer structure, budget, special interest groups, staff, and growth can provide

Table 19-1. Planning Model by Year.

			Year			
	-2	-1	Current	+1	+2	+3
Dollar goal	$650,000	$650,000	$700,000	$770,000	$860,000	$946,000
Percentage increase		+0	+7.7	+10	+12	+10
Dollars received (actual)	628,432	641,869				
Percentage increase		+2				
Average gift	108	106	108	103	101	100
Percentage increase		-2	+2			
Donor goal	6,000	6,000	6,500	7,500	8,500	9,500
Donor count	5,783	6,029				
National chair	J. Jones	B. Smith	M. Brown C. White	H. Gray	R. Black	L. Green
Trustee giving	$32,400	$51,700	$70,000	$85,000	$70,000	$100,000
Leadership gifts ($1,000+)	221,300	278,900	300,000	330,000	375,000	435,000
Amount/number	68	79	100	115	130	150
Alumni gifts	584,360	586,691	650,000	715,000	800,000	880,000
Amount/number	5,694	5,891	6,300	7,100	8,000	9,000
Parents	14,118	21,090	40,000	45,000	50,000	55,000
Matching	37,090	39,320	50,000	70,000	85,000	95,000
Athletics	16,290	14,161	18,000	22,000	25,000	28,000
Library	1,035	1,411	1,500	1,600	1,600	2,000
Arts association	3,842	4,296	5,000	6,000	7,000	8,000
Staff giving	854	1,312	2,000	3,000	4,000	5,000
Friends	4,940	5,390	8,000	10,000	13,000	16,000
Special strategy			Launch $1,000 Club	Alumni Directory	Challenge I	Challenge II
Phonathon	42,000	112,453	150,000	175,000	200,000	225,000
Budget	78,000	84,000	102,000	125,000	140,000	170,000
Professional staff	1	1	2	2	2	3
Support staff	1	1	1.5	2	2	2.5

benchmarks for past performance and future objectives. Comparative data are available from public sources (Council for Financial Aid to Education) or can be obtained by contacting colleagues at sister institutions.

3. *Scale of gifts.* Like those of capital campaigns, annual giving results tend to follow certain patterns. Rubrics like "80 percent of the money comes from 20 percent of the donors" are based in fact and are important for planning and measurement of performance.

The scale of gifts as exemplified in Table 19-2 is an important tool for pinpointing needed gifts. Historical analysis of each preceding year of a program can show the appropriate pattern. Commensurately, analyzing the scale of gifts from frame-of-reference schools can reveal where institutional giving ranges are strong or weak. The scale of gifts can be used with subsets or market segments within annual giving programs. The decimal point may move significantly, but it is valuable to use this same analysis with individual constituencies, such as parents, classes, regional clubs, friends, special interest groups (athletics, library), or matching gifts.

Segmenting constituencies is the most common form of planning and programming found in annual giving operations. Three particular ways of dividing the prospect universe are most

Table 19-2. Annual Giving: Scale of Gifts Needed to Raise $1,500,000.

Number of Gifts	Range	Amount
1	$ 50,000	$ 50,000
2	30,000	60,000
4	25,000	100,000
10	10,000	100,000
40	5,000	200,000
290	1,000	290,000
200	500	100,000
400	250	100,000
2,000	100	200,000
9,000	Below 100	300,000
Total 11,947		$1,500,000

successful. The first is by level of support. Strategies and tactics for upper-level prospects differ considerably from those for general or low-level prospects. Accordingly, segmenting the prospect pool by gift level permits targeting that reflects the dollar impact of each group. Second, segmenting by class has proven exceptionally effective. Venerable and traditional institutions have long capitalized on class loyalty. Easily structured, the plan for one class can be repeated with all classes. Coupling annual giving with reunions has been dramatically successful in the Ivy League and at smaller, residential colleges. The third form of segmenting the prospect pool is geographical. Satellite alumni clubs offer an existing structure around which solicitation can happen. Costs are often high, but many schools find that improved results warrant the expense. Like classes, individual alumni clubs are manageable, easily defined, and contain personal solicitation workers.

Other forms of segmentation—by college, by profession, by special interest—exist but are not as effective or prevalent. Highly developed programs often segment using several dimensions, such as by giving level for each class within a specific region. Regardless of the approach, the prospect pool must be segmented into distinct units for which plans can be tailored.

No planning process is complete without a budget. How much is needed, and what is an acceptable cost factor? In previous years, the formulas were simple and relied on direct costs compared with direct dollars raised. Better programming now precludes a simple cost-benefit analysis for budgeting purposes. There is general agreement that annual giving dollars are the most expensive ones to raise, that program costs are not neatly divided among development programs, and that budget judgments must be made over several years. Most annual giving operations spend between twelve and twenty cents to obtain each dollar. Costs under the median range are suspect. Keeping costs low is all too often a matter of borrowing against the future. Costs running as high as thirty cents on the dollar are frequently well warranted when starting a program or preparing for a capital campaign. The immutable law of annual giving budgets should be engraved on the desk of every chief development officer—dramatic improvement in annual giving totals requires dramatic improvements in annual giving budgets. Normal, healthy growth of a strong annual fund dollar total should be between 5 and 12 percent. Planned increases beyond that are extraordinary and require extraordinary budgets.

Being worthy is not a sufficient criterion for attracting support. The case for support must be more than assumed. There must be a clear, concise statement that answers the initial reaction to any appeal for support: Why should I give? As annual and capital campaign strategy have grown closer, the need for, and effectiveness of, a strong case statement has been established. Unlike the capital campaign case statement, the annual campaign requires brevity and variety. The attention span for annual solicitation, whether personal, by telephone, or by mail, is generally short. Additionally, annual appeals recur with much greater frequency than capital ones. Thus a creative case must be new and fresh each year.

Designing a case statement is one of the few things that should not be done by theft. A case should reflect the uniqueness of one's own institution. A good case statement answers the following questions: (1) What is annual giving? (2) Why should I give? (3) How will my gift be used? (4) Why does this particular institution deserve support? and (5) Why now?

Strategies for Success

There are three ways to ask for support—face-to-face (personal), by telephone, or by mail. Elaborate phonathon efforts and sophisticated direct-mail pieces have achieved important successes. But the history of fund-raising teaches one lesson over and over. Personal solicitation is the strategy for success.

Personal Solicitation. In the perfect university, Nirvana U., the only proper market segment will be the individual. One-fifth of the constituents—the best fifth, of course—will be active, committed, generous volunteers, who will each solicit four fellow constituents face-to-face, asking for a significant increase over last year's sacrificial gift. Hence all prospects will be personally solicited, abolishing the need for phonathons and direct-mail solicitation.

Unrealistic? Yes, but the goal is one all should adopt. The most successful programs are simply the ones that do the most, and best, personal solicitation. Experience shows that soliciting a gift personally has a success factor several times greater than a telephone request. Equally important, the gifts are larger. The harsh reality is that there are limited volunteer and staff resources for approaching large numbers of prospects. Nonetheless, each year should witness more personal solicitation than the preceding one.

Rationing scant volunteer and staff resources should be done in descending order according to the scale of gifts. Who does the soliciting? Preferably a peer solicitor. A $5,000 donor should ask a $5,000 prospect. Few can be as effective as the person who has made the commitment. Top priority for an annual giving director is identifying leadership prospects and organizing leadership volunteers to solicit them. Most duties pale in importance when compared with the identification, recruitment, training, staffing, and stewarding of leadership solicitors. This effort is manifest most often in the form of a trustee annual giving committee, a national chair, a national committee, a class chair, and a board of directors for upper-level giving societies.

Because of the crucial value of personal solicitation, most programs should establish giving clubs or societies. Once again, the scale of gifts provides the blueprint as to what levels are most appropriate. The upper ranges, generally $1,000 and up, indicate where precious staff and volunteer hours can and should be spent implementing face-to-face solicitation. Caution must be exercised in erecting and supporting these upper-level giving clubs. Many an institution has been lured into providing extensive benefits and elaborate events for membership in a giving club. Programming for these clubs must be focused on solicitation activities and not cultivation ones. Leadership gifts are seldom, if ever, motivated by plaques, certificates, ties, and the like. As a general guide, it is wise to provide a few, but first-rate, benefits and to be sparing in activities for giving clubs.

The fundamental reason for success in personal solicitation is that people respond to people, not proposals, pieces of paper, or telephone machines. It is difficult to overemphasize the importance of directing annual giving efforts toward personal solicitation. The only place that conducts enough personal solicitation is Nirvana U.

Telephone Solicitation. The next best thing to being there is truly telephone solicitation. Because few have ever had enough of the right kind of volunteer solicitors, annual fund raisers rely on the next most effective method—the telephone. The first recorded phonathons began in the 1950s and quickly showed that the telephone request was most effective as a mass solicitation tool. Current results indicate that, on the average, telephone solicitation will be ten to twenty times more effective than a good direct-mail appeal. It is personal and permits all-important two-way communication. And for the cost-conscious, it offers a reasonable cost-benefit ratio.

Models for good phonathons abound, and there is even some good literature on the techniques most favored (Cover, 1984). Organizing and planning a good telephone program require good segmentation and staff homework. Matching callers with the right prospects and arming them with information relevant to the solicitation rely heavily on good records and trainable callers. Having the right information—telephone number, address, gift history, targeted amount—is a matter of creating a proper data base on the prospect pool. Having good callers often raises important and contested issues.

Who are the best callers? In the early 1970s, Yale fund-raisers committed heresy. They hired people to call. Breaking the staunch tradition of using only volunteers to solicit for the alma mater, they blazed a new trail. Today, one of the upshots of that experiment is the proliferation of fund-raising firms specializing in using paid callers. Commonly referred to as *phone-mail,* the technique enjoyed marvelous success at Yale and a wide variety of other institutions, including the University of Pennsylvania, the University of California at Berkeley, Columbia University, the University of Chicago, the University of Minnesota, Boston University, and De Paul University. Commonly misperceived as antivolunteer, these phone-mail programs supplement existing volunteer structures and have shown dramatic results in rapid order. The debate over paid student callers versus volunteer students or alumni volunteers is artificial. The appropriate strategy is to use all available resources that can provide the most personal and effective solicitation. If there were sufficient volunteer workers to call all prospects who are not seen personally, there would be no need to find additional solicitors. This is not the case. Paid callers are effective, exceptionally cost-efficient, and in no way injurious to any volunteer programs.

How much is the right amount to ask for over the telephone? The same amount for which one would ask face-to-face. Capacity or willingness to give does not change substantially when the telephone is used. Responses are seldom as generous as when a personal visit is made, but a person's ability and potential should determine the target.

Direct Mail. Sending a letter or direct-mail appeal is the solicitation of last resort. Acceptable response rates generally fall within .5 to 2 percent, and gift amounts tend to be low. There are always the delightful surprises found in return envelopes, but big gifts coming in direct-mail responses indicate a less thorough effect for personal and telephone solicitation efforts. More disturbing, direct mail is generally decreasing in effectiveness while increasing in cost.

Direct mail has a variety of values. Mail solicitations should be considered donor acquisition appeals. Dollar totals are better influenced by telephone and personal solicitation. Reaping in a large number of donors is a more realistic goal of direct mail. Additionally, harvesting information should be a crucial goal of a direct-mail program. Every mailing piece response device, the business reply envelope, should request key information that will allow the prospect's graduation to a phonathon or personal strategy. A reply envelope that does not ask for a home telephone number is a waste.

Perhaps the greatest single impact of direct-mail pieces lies in their educational value. The message and style of our appeals make the case and establish the climate for effective solicitation. Even the best appeal, however, is an inert, nonresponsive piece of paper. Deliver the message and stimulate a response; the strategy remains—the more personal direct-mail pieces are, the better the response. This provides the basis for deciding whether to use stamps or a postage meter, whether to mail first class or third class, and whether to word-process or print letters. Personalization reflects concern and quality. The more quality and individual attention reflected in the letter, the better the results.

The subtleties of designing effective mail are infinite. The multibillion-dollar direct-mail industry furnishes a limitless array of sophisticated analyses on how to do effective mail solicitation. The Direct Mail Marketing Association is the best source for these. The most germane source of funds is an institution's constituency. The rule "Test, don't guess" is appropriate. Monitoring what pieces and styles have been most productive at home or at frame-of-reference schools can give the best information as to what works.

The ask, which is the heart of a direct-mail appeal, should be direct, compelling, and specific. Attention spans for virtually all mailings are exceedingly brief. A request must not be hidden or couched in educational verbiage. The appeal should have an urgency that answers the question, Why now? The ask should also specify an amount. The magic of data processing and word processing permits specification of targets for increasingly smaller segments of the prospect pool. Asking for a pinpointed gift amount prompts more, and generally larger, gifts.

Dramatic growth and rapid improvement should not depend on a direct-mail program. Yet it is important because it educates prospects, captures donors, and communicates information from our constituencies. Prudent allocation of staff time and budget must occur. Every time a gift arrives in a reply envelope, one wonders how much more the individual might have given if solicited more personally.

Priorities of Dramatic Upgrading

A few lucky development operations enjoy the luxury of having reasonable goals. The pressure to produce badly needed operating funds seems to grow every year. Annual giving offices are being asked to regularly achieve growth rates of 20 percent or more. Such dramatic increases require dramatic budget increases, and there are four basic program strategies that offer the best chances for rapid expansion.

Challenge Giving. The capacity to establish challenge funds is universal. The premise is simple. A sum of money, preferably large, is offered by a donor or group of donors; it will be given to the institution if certain increases are obtained in annual giving totals. Most common is matching new and increased gift dollars. Another popular variation is establishing a donor total that must be achieved to fulfill the challenge. Whatever the psychological reasons, people respond to challenges. Several prominent institutions have found such challenges so successful that they have repeated them for three consecutive years with good results each time. And it can be a most effective stimulus for a major gift prospect, individual, corporation, or foundation to make a meaningful and special contribution. If no major prospect is available, an alternative strategy is simply to ask a small group of top annual donors to pool their donations into a challenge fund. The cardinal rule of challenge programs is "Keep it simple." If a challenge fund cannot be explained to a prospect in one or two sentences, chances for success are greatly diminished.

Leadership Gift Clubs. People like to be with those who share their interests and values. They also feel more comfortable being part of prestigious organizations. Out of these human traits have emerged leadership gift clubs. Whatever the reasons, individuals respond better when asked to join the president's or headmaster's club than when asked to give to a budget account. Segmenting leadership donors and prospects is a top priority, and quick progress is almost always seen after the introduction of upper-level gift clubs. What level is considered leadership? The scale of gifts should provide the answer by revealing the upper gift ranges. An almost universal cutoff is $1,000. The best guide is to find the highest level where under 5 percent (preferably fewer) of the top donors are found. The following are guidelines for establishing leadership gift clubs:

- Activities of the clubs must be weighted heavily to solicitation rather than cultivation.
- Never say forever. Annual giving clubs reward continuity and ongoing support.

- Benefits of membership should be few in number, high in quality.
- Policies of the club must be determined by the institution, not the volunteers within the club.
- Aim ever upward. Long-range plans should always be mindful of establishing the next, higher gift club.
- Always be flexible. Ability to alter membership and benefits must be maintained for our successors.

Extensive Telephone Solicitation. Stories of dramatic improvement following the introduction of large-scale telephone efforts abound. Programs that are lean on leadership volunteers or leadership prospects can use mass calling efforts for short-term gain while pursuing the rather lengthy matter of building a strong volunteer structure. Programs that rely heavily on direct mail can see quick improvement by shifting their requests to the telephone. Whether with volunteers or paid callers, phonathons permit a small staff to erect a solicitation program that works quickly. For the more efficient and aggressive minded, the many phone-mail models using paid callers provide a path to quick, exceptional growth.

Alumni Directory Incentive. Many institutions have experienced great increases when linking ·a published alumni directory with annual giving. Making such a volume available only to supporters has, in many instances, brought forth a horde of new dollars and donors. At DePaul, alumni donors tripled in the year that the directory was offered to those who made a new or increased gift of $25 or more. Although the real work came the next year in the efforts to retain all the new donors, the directory incentive began the all-important annual giving habit for many. It is important to stress that annual giving, even when promising a directory or other tangible incentive, is philanthropy and not selling.

Special Concerns. The philosophy and fundamental strategies of annual giving are simple. The variables to manipulate in a good program are not. Special dimensions, such as parent funds, reunion giving, matching gifts, senior class programs, and gift acknowledgment, are important but require more space to discuss than is available here. Internal concerns of staffing levels, data management, research and records, and educating faculty and staff are real and deserve attention. The reader is encouraged to use the bibliography to find appropriate sources for further discussion. Particular attention should be paid to *CASE Currents,* in which articles have appeared on every one of the subjects just mentioned. Keeping yourself and your annual fund alive and well is a matter of continuing education. Unfortunately, relatively little literature exists that is germane to all. A big part of determining what works can be obtained only in home laboratories or in conference settings. Using institutional programs as a constant testing ground is not only necessary, given the paucity of research available; it is also clearly the most pertinent and the most reliable source of information. The profession of fund-raising encourages collegiality or, phrased less delicately, fund-raisers' mimicry. Some have made careers of adapting everyone else's tested ideas, thereby negating the need for original thought. Colleagues and sister institutions are vital sources of information. Finally, it is a terribly enlightening research experiment to become an annual giving volunteer (for another institution, of course). The perspective gained by living the life one preaches has drastically altered many a development officer's approach.

Annual giving is vital, a habit to be cultivated, and an indispensable part of the effort to advance institutions. Major gifts depend on it. Planning and implementing personal solicitation efforts are the top priorities for annual giving officers. This is most effectively done through segmenting constituencies, adopting proven methods for success, and focusing efforts on the top prospects in strategy similar to capital campaigns. With sufficient planning and homework, dramatic upgrading can not only be achieved, it can be assured.

Selected Bibliography

American Association of Fund-Raising Counsel, Inc. *Giving U.S.A.—Annual Report, 1984.* Annual publication. New York: American Association of Fund-Raising Counsel, 1984.

Andrews, F. E. *Philanthropic Giving.* New York: Russell Sage Foundation, 1960.

Carlson, M. E. *Why People Give.* New York: Council Press for Stewardship and Benevolence, National Council of Churches of Christ in the U.S.A., 1968.

Council for Advancement and Support of Education. "Annual Fund." *CASE Currents,* Nov. 1976, special issue.

Cover, N. (ed.). *A Guide to Successful Phonathons.* Washington, D.C.: Council for Advancement and Support of Education, 1984.

Curti, M., and Nash, R. *Philanthropy in the Shaping of American Higher Education.* New Brunswick, N.J.: Rutgers University Press, 1965.

Cutlip, S. M. *Fund Raising in the United States: Its Role in America's Philanthropy.* New Brunswick, N.J.: Rutgers University Press, 1965.

Fund Raising Institute. *Annual Giving Idea Book.* Plymouth Meeting, Pa.: Fund Raising Institute, 1981.

Hodgson, R. S. *Direct Mail and Mail Order Handbook.* Chicago: Dartnell Corporation, 1974.

Seymour, H. J. *Fund Raising: Principles, Patterns and Techniques.* New York: McGraw-Hill, 1966.

Sheppard, W. E. *Fund Raising Letter Collection.* Plymouth Meeting, Pa.: Fund Raising Institute, 1969.

Sutterlin, R. *Matching Gifts Detail.* Washington, D. C.: Council for Advancement and Support of Education, 1977.

Welch, P. A. (ed.). *Increasing Annual Giving.* New Directions for Institutional Advancement, no. 7. San Francisco: Jossey-Bass, 1980.

20

D. Chris Withers

Generating
Corporate Support

❧ This chapter on corporate giving contains a "broad-brush" review of the history of corporate giving, a discussion of the motivations and priorities of corporate contributions, a description of some particular sources for prospecting, and a presentation of some specific cultivation processes to bring corporate prospects closer to a gift. A brief review of the actual solicitation process and various recognition methods, a description of a matching gift emphasis, and a summary follow.

History

Although Thomas Hollis is credited with making one of the first individual gifts to higher education through his gift of the first endowed professorship to Harvard in 1721, corporate giving as a defined entity did not occur until two centuries later. Some of the earliest examples of corporate giving to higher education date back to the first twenty years of the 1900s, even though deductibility for such contributions was not allowed until 1935, and the legality of these gifts was not established until the 1950s. Tax incentives and determination of the legality of corporate gifts stimulated the growth of corporate support.

In 1935, after considerable political wrangling, deductibility of charitable contributions by corporations was allowed by legislation. At the time, President Roosevelt opposed the proposal on the grounds that it allowed corporate executives to make contributions of money actually belonging to the stockholders. Nonetheless, the legislation was signed. Finally, in 1953, some eighteen years later, the courts upheld the legality of a contested corporate gift to Princeton University.

The court found that such contributions were in the national interest because elimination of corporate support to private colleges and universities would seriously threaten the survival of those institutions. This court decision not only confirmed the legality of these contributions but also affirmed the importance of private higher education to the national interest. The findings of the court were generally interpreted more broadly to include all charitable organizations in addition to colleges and universities. The key to the court's decision was the notion that socially beneficial contributions indirectly benefit corporate stockholders along with the rest of the nation (Paton, 1978).

Sources of Prospects

Clearly there are differences in the way in which gifts are sought from individuals and foundations. A proposal to a local family-owned bank, for example, is quite different from a proposal to a major national corporation. Fund-raising on the local level requires a far more personal approach. Whether on a national, regional, or local level, there is a concentric-circle method of list building, beginning with those corporations or businesses most closely associated with the institution and then working outward, category by category. Such a list might include:

1. Those already supporting the institution
2. Those operating in the local or regional area
3. Distantly owned companies having heavy installation and large numbers of personnel employed in the area
4. Those standing to benefit, directly or indirectly, from current or projected research, teaching seminars, and institutes at the institution
5. Those having large and profitable sales volume in the area
6. Those successfully recruiting graduates and having large numbers of alumni in leadership positions

7. Those selling a large volume of goods to the institutions on a regular basis and who have thus become loyal vendors
8. Those having alumni, parents, or friends as directors, chief executive officers, or other officers
9. Those vulnerable to "undeniable" requests by prominently placed friends of alumni of the institutions
10. Those having mutual relationships with members of the faculty where they may serve as consultants

Corporations give in two ways, through separately established foundations and through corporate contributions programs operated within their company. Some companies use both methods. The same information is available on company-sponsored foundations as on any other private foundation. Therefore, when doing research, be certain to consider both areas. Several specific reference works of significant interest in seeking corporate gifts are *Standard & Poor's Register of Corporations, Directors and Executives, Million Dollar Directory, Taft Corporate Giving Directory,* "The 500: The *Fortune* Directory of the Largest U.S. Industrial Corporations," "The *Fortune* Service 500: The *Fortune* Directory of the Largest U.S. Non-Industrial Corporations," "The *Forbes* 500s: The Nation's Largest Companies Ranked Four Ways," chamber of commerce directories, corporate annual reports (including their specific guidelines), and the Yellow Pages of your local telephone directory.

Motivations and Priorities of Corporate Contributors

Enlightened self-interest—such as supporting nonprofit organizations that have the most impact, directly or indirectly, on the corporation or the employees—is a prime motivator in corporate support. For example, Amway supplied the underwriting of a national symphony tour of Europe, a market that Amway wants to enter. Mobil Oil Company provided the funds to construct at Marietta College a mud lab from whose research could come important impact in the oil industry. Dennis J. Murphy, whose corporate support program research project contacted more than one thousand of the largest corporations in the United States, feels that "corporations look for cost efficiency, local service delivery and the ability to fill an unmet need." His project suggests that almost 90 percent of responding companies rated "potential benefits to the employees" as very important in determining the amount of charitable contributions (Murphy, 1982, p. 4). In any given day, a manager of corporate contributions may receive between twenty-five and forty requests for contributions. More and more nonprofit organizations are seeking corporate support in trying to make up the amount that has been trimmed from the federal government social-spending budget in recent years. Because accountability seems to be an important emphasis, it becomes incumbent upon the nonprofit sector to seek out relationships that capitalize on this enlightened self-interest. As one corporate chair put it, "If you are not supporting higher education, you are not minding your business."

Thomas E. Broce (1979, p. 124) has noted that these considerations include "direct benefit to the business, improvement of the local area, improvement of society, public relations, personnel recruitment, and preservation of the free private enterprise system." "In addition," he continues, "there are also many business people who just plain care and are attracted to worthy causes." Conversely, not all agree.

The criticism of corporate giving does not come from just one side. Some people argue that companies should not be giving away their shareholders' profits in the first place. Sam Sternberg (1984, p. E-8), who edited the recently published *National Directory of Corporate Charity,* concludes that "there is a large group of companies that give plenty but only in areas that get them some tangible return." Anne Klepper, senior research associate at the Conference Board in New York, a business-financed research group that, among other things, monitors corporate giving, said, "There is no overwhelming set of facts on one side or the other. Executives of many companies believe that companies have no responsibility to donate to charity and think stockholders should make those kinds of decisions with investment profits." She quickly added, however, "that no corporate executive with any sense of public relations is going to say that" (1984, p. E-8).

**Six Steps to a Grant, Including Cultivation, Solicitation,
and Recognition**

In the December 1980 issue of *Foundation News,* an article
written by the community affairs director for Syntex, Frank Koch,
made three predictions: (1) Corporate gifts will continue to rise
to the 2 percent pretax earnings level that the Filer Commission
recommended. (2) Corporations will require more clearly defined
guidelines from educational institutions about how the gifts will be
spent. (3) There will be an increase in cooperation between
nonprofit organizations all seeking resources within the same city
(Koch, 1980).

One would hope Mr. Koch is correct; the 5 percent limit on
charitable deductions for corporations has not been a hotly debated
issue, because aggregate figures show that corporate charity
amounts to only about 1.5 percent of corporate net income. A few
corporations give amounts approaching the limit, but most give
considerably less; thus the emphasis to continue to rise to the 2
percent level is an important goal.

As the plans are developed for either the annual or capital
campaign emphasis among corporations, a number of the
following items should be considered:

1. *Developing your case.* Be sure to answer the question, Why
should we give to you? Do extensive research, and document your
institution's impact upon the community and the state. The case
should focus on economic impact, payroll of the institution, the
number of employees, and how that number ranks the institution
as an employer in the community. What kind of expenditures, both
operating and capital, are made in the community? What kinds of
expenditures do students and visitors make for special functions
that they attend?

Be certain to document the trustee, director, and/or alumni
impact. How many alumni live within the institution's community? How many are attorneys, physicians, or other professional
people? How many alumni serve as officials in the legislature or
other government positions? How many major business concerns
are chaired by alumni? How many are educators, clergy, teachers,
accountants, and so forth?

Be certain to research the organization's cultural and athletic impact. List, for example, the number of cultural or athletic presentations—concerts, plays, art exhibits, football games, basketball games. What kind of attendance does the organization draw from its own geographical area?

What about educational and social impact? How many people are enrolled in a continuing education or special program? What about library usage by nonstudents in the community adjacent to the campus? Are there guest books for those who visit the campus, particularly for visitors to the museums, hospitals, and so forth?

2. *Identifying the impact.* Identify the impact of your institution upon the particular corporation being solicited. Be certain to document the number of alumni employed by that corporation, their business, and the number of corporate employees enrolled in particular courses. If the corporation interviews regularly on campus, compile a list of faculty who serve as consultants to the corporation. What business does the university do with that corporation each year? Try to interpret this into dollars expended for goods and services. Is the business a past donor? Does it support a consortium or statewide independent foundation from which the school, college, or university could benefit?

3. *Cultivation.* Consider a regular routine of clipping the newspaper and sending congratulatory notices; visit those corporations in your city and regularly review with them your organization's latest plans; send copies of annual reports and other pertinent information. Consider scheduling a regular corporate day on campus. Many universities have had special days featuring interaction of individual corporate representatives with students majoring in the discipline tied to that particular company. The day might involve faculty members who teach subjects that tie into the corporation. For example, duPont de Nemours day might focus on chemistry or physics. The program need not be lengthy: a light lunch, perhaps, and a special exhibit in the library. Some have had one a month, or even more often, at the height of a major campaign. That would provide the groundwork for seeking repeat gifts later.

Some universities have brought together business executives who represent cross sections of business enterprise. Issues to be discussed could include portfolio management, lease purchase, or year-end tax strategy. Finally, consider developing a specific corporate newsletter to be sent out on a regular basis illustrating and documenting the particular ties between the institution and the corporation.

4. *Soliciting gifts.* As your strategy develops, try to determine where the target corporation ranks in the pecking order of the similar corporations in the community. Many nonprofit organizations have had success in securing a very large commitment from those ranked third or fourth and then levering that with the corporate prospects ranked higher.

A number of institutions have been able to secure major corporate gifts by combining the efforts of volunteers and staff (president, trustees, and development). This takes people with cash, class, and clout. The old adage of having the right person calling on the right person for the right amount is indeed axiomatic to success. Too many development offices leave their corporate programs to chance. Instead, take regular initiatives. Suggest that three or four people make the calls, particularly when seeking the major gift. The overview of the campaign can be given by the general chair, the president can provide the university perspective, the proposal can be reviewed by the staff person, and the closing and presentation of the proposal can be made by the campaign chair. Once the actual presentation has been completed, follow-up words of appreciation on behalf of the group are important. Encourage all members of the solicitation team and advisory boards to write letters of appreciation. Corporations require prompt, accurate reports on how their funds were used and what results were achieved. They often request special additional documentation. This might be presented in brochure format or in the form of a "shareholders" report. Some institutions have had success sending a weekly campaign flash listing the names and chief executive officers of the corporations that have made gifts to the institution. Those who receive the newsletter were asked to send follow-up words of gratitude to other company officers and directors. Keep cultivating even after a gift is received. Repeat gifts are much easier to obtain than new ones.

5. *Recognizing gifts.* Prompt acknowledgment of the gift is vital. Many consider that a thank-you letter and receipt should be mailed to the donor immediately, noting any billing instructions suggested by the donor.

Many organizations provide named gift opportunities. This could take the form of a scholarship, a professorship, a chair, a specific project, a research laboratory, or other brick and mortar projects. In terms of the latter, general rules of thumb require a contribution of 50 percent of the actual cost in order to carry a particular name. That may not be true for endowed professorships or scholarships; generally the naming amounts for those vehicles start at $100,000 and go up.

6. *Matching gifts.* The Council for Advancement and Support of Education (CASE) serves as a national clearing house for corporate matching gifts programs. CASE now produces four separate brochures listing the names of those companies that match gifts to (1) higher education, (2) two-year colleges, (3) cultural organizations, and (4) health and welfare agencies. Many of these corporations have multiple matches, such as two-for-one or three-for-one. The matching gift is initiated by the individual donor to the institution by attracting a corporate matching gift form that is then completed by the nonprofit organization and sent to the individual corporate personnel office for processing. Many consider this to be free money and work hard at developing campaign strategy to increase the flow of corporate matching gifts. Few disagree that this money is well intended. Yet, there are some who have objections because (1) corporate matching-gifts programs seem to abdicate responsibility of judgment (that is, they are open-ended in terms of who can qualify); an organization is not forced to document and justify its case; (2) there is little control of the matching-gift money in the budget; and (3) it skews the money in favor of prestige institutions and/or the public sector, while emerging institutions generally have fewer people in prestige corporate positions and therefore are unavailable to take advantage of the major money that is distributed.

Summary

It is true that corporate contributions have increased tenfold during the last three decades and now exceed $3.1 billion. Likewise, the percent of pretax net income contributed has topped 1.5 percent only twice since 1950. Still, several questions linger. Will contributions from corporations resume their lock step with profits, or is a new pattern emerging? Unquestionably, according to the Conference Board's *Corporate Contributions Outlook,* "the corporate contributions function has become of age. No longer is it viewed as an odd semi-peripheral corporate activity. They have grown in value and effectiveness and are seen as addressing complex issues that impinge directly on the business environment. The function is being institutionalized in the corporate structure and increasingly is being integrated into corporate strategic plan. Multi-million-dollar contributions programs require detailed planning focusing on programs stated and agreed upon priorities and sound budgeting" (Klepper and others, 1984, p. 3).

Most corporate contributions officers still feel that accountability will be the most important word in generating corporate support throughout the 1980s. It is important for the nonprofit sector to constantly remind corporate boards, stockholders, and contribution committees what is in it for them. Why should they support this school, college, or university versus this hospital or art museum? The case must be solid and justifiable. Corporations are no longer responsive to emotional appeals. They are not into swapping war stories, worn out jokes, football tickets, or parking privileges. Corporate cultivation and solicitation programs must be sophisticated; therefore, do your homework! Sell. Be accountable. One might even be viewed as an "insistent voice of doom." One must constantly involve corporate people through advisory committees, campus visitations, corporate board presentations, lists of corporate donors, and other rosters. Although the state of the economy will continue to be a dominant factor in corporate giving, how well one institution does its homework versus another will, quite literally, determine the level of success.

References

Broce, T. E. *Fund Raising: The Guide to Raising Money from Private Sources.* Norman: University of Oklahoma Press, 1979.

Klepper, A. "Corporate Giving Grows." *Richmond Times Dispatch,* Oct. 1984, p. E-8.

Klepper, A., and others. *Corporate Contributions Outlook.* New York: Conference Board, 1984.

Koch, F. "Corporate Philanthropy in the 1980's." *Foundation News,* 1980, *21* (6), 17–21.

Murphy, D. J. *Corporate Giving Watch.* Washington, D.C.: Taft Corporation, 1982.

Paton, G. J. "Federal Income Tax Incentives for Encouraging Private Philanthropic Support to Higher Education." Unpublished doctoral dissertation, Department of Education, Stanford University, 1978.

Sternberg, S. "Corporate Giving Grows." *Richmond Times Dispatch,* Oct. 1984, p. E-8.

21

Mary Kay Murphy

Raising Funds
from Foundations

❧ As is true of other members of the development team, foundation relations officers do not raise funds singlehandedly. The measure of success is their ability to achieve fund-raising goals through the efforts of others. Foundation fund-raisers must set up a process to involve faculty, volunteers, foundation officers, and other staff in securing funds from general purpose, family, community, and corporate foundations.

Three Critical Skills: Leadership, Craftsmanship, and Grantsmanship

Foundation fund-raisers achieve their goals by applying three necessary skills: leadership, craftsmanship, and grantsmanship. Leadership results in the right person making the best request of the key person in the foundation. Foundation fund-raisers use leadership in setting this sequence in motion and following it through.

To manage and monitor the fund-raising process, foundation fund-raisers must have craftsmanship skills. Success requires judicious collection and evaluation of research data on foundations, careful identification of ways to influence and leverage foundation requests, and artful matches between campus priorities and foundation programs.

Grantsmanship skills properly applied can do much to

increase the number and percent of foundation projects successfully funded. It is generally estimated that only about 7 percent of the nearly one million foundation proposals submitted each year are subsequently funded. It is the purpose of this chapter to help foundation fund-raisers improve these odds.

The most successful foundation fund-raisers develop a proactive approach to organizing and carrying out their responsibilities. They set goals and develop record and tracking systems. They involve prospect researchers and volunteers. They work with faculty and administrators to identify priorities and projects. They deploy key volunteers to call on foundation officers. They work with foundation staff, officers, and trustees to initiate, monitor, and follow up on proposals.

The Process of Raising Funds from Foundations

There are seven basic steps in foundation fund-raising. These include determining project needs on campus, identifying prospect foundations, coordinating campus contact, writing the proposal, submitting the proposal, responding if turned down, and assuming responsibilities if successful.

Determining Project Needs. Diverse as the nation's 22,000 active grant-making private foundations are, they share the common characteristics of making awards to projects that have priority with foundation officers and trustees. The first step for a foundation fund-raiser to take is to become familiar with campus programs, goals, and priorities. These can later be matched with project interests among foundations.

Faculty hold the key to knowledge of campus projects that are the priorities of the institution. Foundation fund-raisers rely heavily on faculty and key administrators to identify and rank the top campus needs. Academic programs, building priorities, student scholarship and fellowship needs, and faculty development and research areas provide information on campus projects. A coordinating and approval system should be set up to ensure that faculty projects proposed for foundation funding have the endorsement of top academic administrators on campus.

After identifying the top campus projects, the foundation fund-raiser's next step is to ask key questions of faculty to determine how these projects might relate to academic or research priorities of foundation prospects. What other sources of funding are available for this project? Where will this project be located? How long will the project last? When will the funds be needed? What is the project budget? Who will be the project directors? What are their professional credentials? Is this the first time a project of this type has been proposed? If not, how does it relate to other projects of its kind? Is this an award to be made to an individual or to the institution? Is this a project for operating funds, endowment, or capital needs? Will indirect costs be requested? If so, at what percentage of total costs? Answers to these questions will guide the foundation fund-raiser in matching campus projects with foundation priorities.

Not every project merits a written communication with a foundation. In fact, writing a proposal for project support is generally the last step to take in the process of raising funds from foundations. If any written communication is considered at this time, the most appropriate is a letter requesting the annual report. Not all foundations are large enough to produce annual reports. If these are not available, other research techniques should be used to identify foundation priorities.

If a match appears to be possible between the campus project and the foundation priority, the next written communication would be to request a meeting with the foundation officer. An abstract of the proposal should be prepared for use in this meeting. If a full proposal is invited, then, and only then, should the complete document be prepared.

Many foundations have a strict policy against meeting with grant seekers until after a preliminary proposal has been submitted and reviewed. When this policy prevails, the foundation fund-raiser should write a two-page letter that succinctly describes the background, need, plan, and budget of the project. Favorable review of this preliminary letter will prompt an invitation for a meeting, a proposal, or both.

Long distances, tight budgets, and foundation policies often limit or restrict meetings between foundation officers and foundation fund-raisers. When such conditions prevail, the telephone is a useful communications tool for filling this gap. The telephone has many uses for the foundation fund-raiser, including finding out about current programs and priorities, identifying interest on the part of the foundation in the campus project, and paving the way for receipt of the proposal by the appropriate foundation officer.

The telephone is also useful in confirming, verifying, and updating information on foundation officers and trustees, addresses, telephone numbers, and assets and gifts from previous fiscal years. Successful foundation fund-raisers use the telephone as an important research tool for identifying foundation prospects and following through on the process of raising funds from foundations.

College deans and key academic administrators serve as important links in the foundation fund-raising process. They can suggest faculty for foundation fund-raisers to contact about campus programs. Also, they are necessary in approving projects for foundation funding. Deans and academic administrators sign off on proposals before they are submitted for funding consideration.

Further, college deans and top administrators, especially vice-presidents of academic affairs or provosts, often make effective solicitors on foundation calls. These administrators play important roles in assuring institutional accountability of foundation awards.

Identification of Prospect Foundations. A second step to take in the process of foundation fund-raising is to identify the top grant-making foundations from which the college or university might solicit funds. Although there are more than 22,000 active grant-making private foundations, generally fewer than one hundred will be serious prospects for most colleges or universities at any given time.

How are these foundations identified? By applying a circle-of-influence screening tool, foundation fund-raisers can identify top prospects. Which families closely involved with the college or university have private foundations? Which small foundations within the community or state are likely prospects to support the institution? Which corporations with company-sponsored foundations are located near the college or within the state? Which national corporate interests might relate to the institution's curriculum, to its research, or to students who will be available for employment after graduation? Which national foundations have previously supported programs at the college or university? Can such past support be extended to future college or university endeavors? Which foundation officers or trustees are close to the college or university?

The rationale behind these questions is to identify foundations that have the closest ties to the institution and to solicit these first before extending the circle of influence beyond them to those whose connections are less direct. After answering such questions as these, the foundation fund-raiser rank-orders the top fifty to one hundred foundation prospects for intensive research, cultivation, and solicitation.

The successful foundation fund-raiser uses a variety of sources to identify foundations and to plan a funding search. Directories, indexes, annual reports, IRS 990 forms and other documents in the public record, and computerized data base searches are important sources of information on foundation funding.

A sophisticated foundation research industry has grown steadily since 1969, when foundations were required by law to disclose information on grants, trustees, and assets. The Foundation Center and other publishers of information on foundation and corporate philanthropy use data from the IRS 990 reports, among other sources, to compile their annual directories, grant indexes, data books, foundation profiles, and computerized searches.

The successful foundation fund-raiser will organize an office library containing current sources of information on foundation giving. Directories such as *The Foundation Directory* and the *Taft Foundation Directory* describe awards made by the largest foundations in the country. Smaller foundation awards are included in the Foundation Center's *National Data Book*. A bimonthly grants index, later compiled into an annual index of foundation awards, is published by the Foundation Center. Profiles of foundations are updated quarterly in the Foundation Center's *Sourcebook Profiles.*

After screening out those foundations that are not likely prospects, the foundation fund-raiser carefully collects materials on the top fifty to one hundred prospects. These materials include annual reports published by the largest national and state foundations. To identify information on foundation prospects that do not publish an annual report, the foundation fund-raiser collects IRS 990 forms on smaller key foundation prospects. These forms will provide information on officers, size of gifts, recipients, and market value of assets usually included in a foundation's annual reports.

Another important source of funding information is provided by computerized data base searches. These are indexed by foundation location, project purpose, and amount and type of award. Computerized searches are available through the Foundation Center, the Lockheed Dialog Service, NEXIS, and others. A low-cost computerized list of awards by category is published for ninety-one subject and geographic listings by the Foundation Center in its *COMSEARCH* series.

Between printings of annual directories, grant seekers can keep updated on foundation gifts and recipients in monthly newsletters such as Brakeley, John Price Jones, Inc.'s *Philanthropic Digest* and Taft's *Foundation Giving Watch* and *Corporate Giving Watch.* Some foundations such as the Ford Foundation and the Carnegie Corporation publish their own newsletters. Many foundations issue special news releases, often of interest to grant seekers. Research on trustees and officers of foundations is aided by use of Standard and Poor's *Register of Corporations, Directors, and Executives,* Marquis's *Who's Who in America,* and Taft's *People in Philanthropy.*

A final source of information on foundations is verbal information gained from a personal visit with a foundation officer or from a telephone conversation. Frequently, this type of information—if reliable—is the most up-to-date and important source of information on a foundation. Its importance comes from its immediacy.

Unlike the federal government, foundations generally do not issue a list of programs that will be funded in the future. Nor do foundations generally invite competitive proposals. On occasion, foundations will solicit proposals by special invitation to a select group of colleges or universities. Most usually, foundations select, from among proposals submitted during a specific time period, those that most directly match their current philanthropic interests.

The foundation fund-raiser must carefully analyze the profile of an institution and compare it with the giving patterns of target foundations in their awards to colleges and universities. Are awards to the institution increasing in the areas of science, social science, or environmental programs? Are awards to liberal arts programs declining? What can the foundation fund-raiser do to take advantage of these institutional trends?

Watchful foundation fund-raisers will use statements in annual reports and newsletters and compare them with IRS 990 forms or grants indexes and directories to analyze giving patterns. Did past awards support the stated priorities of the foundation? If not, what type of projects received support? Are there clear giving patterns or trends in amount of support?

Foundations, especially the larger ones, print guidelines for the purpose of informing the public of current funding priorities. A prudent early step in funding research is to review the guidelines of a foundation's awards program. These may be included in the annual report or printed as a separate publication. Smaller foundations do not publish annual reports or guidelines. The IRS 990 form is a useful means of identifying and analyzing a foundation's past funding patterns. Cross-referencing of grants information in *Sourcebook Profiles* (Foundation Center, 1985) or directories and grants indexes will verify information on types of priorities funded by foundations.

Analyzing programs funded over a three- to five-year period will provide information about actual funding priorities and giving levels. These can be compared with stated priorities in annual reports or inferred priorities gleaned from review of IRS 990 reports.

Foundation grants follow patterns common to other types of philanthropic giving. People give money to people they know and trust. The successful foundation fund-raiser identifies links between college or university people who know foundation trustees and staff.

Earlier reference was made to the circle-of-influence screening tool. This device is beneficial in determining linkages between the college or university and the foundation trustees and staff. Which alumni or parents affiliated with the institution are trustees or staff members of foundations? Which faculty members or trustees of the college or university know foundation trustees and staff?

The purpose of using personal contact is to find an advocate for a proposal among foundation trustees and staff. If foundation trustees and staff are not known by those involved in foundation fund-raising, it is important that they become known. Office visits, telephone calls, and letters of inquiry can be used to establish this identity and acquaintance. However, use of institutional influence with foundation trustees and staff must be judicious. There is a fine, delicate line between being known and recognized by foundation trustees and staff and bringing unwanted and inappropriate pressure to bear on support or funding for a proposal.

The foundation fund-raiser identifies individuals of influence and discretion who can gain the attention and support of foundation trustees and staff for a project. When staff are employed, the foundation fund-raiser works through them, never around them. Staff are useful as advocates of a proposal. It is their professional responsibility to serve as the link between the grant seeker and the grant maker.

Foundation trustees who are known by college and university leaders also have a role to play as proposal advocates. Their peers, primarily college or university trustees, can legitimately and ethically solicit their support of a proposal. Successful foundation fund-raisers set these networks of influence in motion and use them to their advantage in the most ethical and judicious ways possible.

Foundation guidelines, annual reports, and yearly directories become outdated rapidly. The prudent foundation fund-raiser makes a practice of always calling a foundation representative to verify guidelines, to inquire about current priorities, and to discuss range of gifts and awards. Other items to confirm are the names of current foundation trustees and staff, the address and telephone number of the foundation, and the format in which to prepare the request.

Coordination of Campus Contact. A third step to take in the process of foundation fund-raising is identification of one campus office for contact with foundations. This office, generally the development office, is responsible for initiating all contacts with foundation staff and coordinating all requests for foundation funding.

Foundation staff prefer that requests from colleges and universities be made for projects that have the highest institutional priority. They also prefer to receive one request at a time. They leave the identification of that request to the college or university. As foundations move, more and more, to professional staffing, the trend requires one central campus office to coordinate requests made of foundations.

The Proposal. One of the major benefits of having one campus office to coordinate foundation activities is that a smooth process of proposal production can be established. Proposal development is a major component of a successful foundation fund-raising program. Few awards are made without a written document to request funds. The content and format of foundation proposals is markedly different from those requested by federal funding sources.

Foundation proposals are shorter, sharper, clearer, and more direct than their federal equivalent. There are two types of foundation proposals: the preliminary proposal and the final proposal. Their uses are as follows.

Many foundations require that the first contact from a grant seeker be in the form of a preliminary proposal, or a letter of intent. Generally two pages, this document presents in clear, concise prose the background of the college or university, the project proposed (most usually a new or innovative program), the costs of the project, the links between the college or university and the foundation, the institution's ability to address the problem, methods of evaluating the project's success, and future funding sources.

Successful letters of intent directly or indirectly identify a match between the college or university's institutional readiness and strengths and the stated or implied priorities of the foundation. Based on information provided in the preliminary proposal, foundation staff will review the plan and either request a full proposal or reject the letter of intent.

Complete proposals to foundations differ markedly from their counterparts for federal funding. Full foundation proposals average five pages. They are written in clear, concise, sharp prose. Ideally, the full proposal adheres to the guidelines and basic format requested by the foundation.

If no specific format is required, the following components of a foundation proposal should be included:

> *Proposal summary* covering the scope of the project and its costs
>
> *Introduction* providing background on the college or university and the framework and context in which the project will operate
>
> *Problem statement* documenting the problem, defining its components, and linking it to the institution's ability to address it
>
> *Project objectives* that are specific and measurable
>
> *Project methodology* identifying activities and personnel
>
> *Project evaluation* regarding measurement of results against objectives
>
> *Budget* including personnel and nonpersonnel costs
>
> *Supporting materials,* especially tax-exempt letters, audited financial statements, and lists of governing boards or trustees

Submission of the Proposal. Foundation staffs are becoming more organized, structured, and professional. Personal calls or telephone contact will be useful in identifying the deadlines for proposal submission, format and content of the proposal, and enclosures and attachments of supporting documents.

A cover letter summarizing the request, purpose, and budget of the project should be signed by the college or university president and should accompany the proposal for formal submission. The letter and proposal should be sent to the key contact designated to receive the proposal.

Protocol of foundation-staffing relationships should be of great importance to the foundation fund-raiser. If the letter and proposal are sent to the president of the foundation, copies with personal notes should be sent to staff members who assisted in proposal development.

When college or university board members or trustees know the foundation's trustees, it is appropriate to have them send a copy of the submitted proposal to the trustee's office address with a note requesting support of the proposal. If a corporate foundation is involved, it is important both to find an influential corporate employee who will act as an advocate for the proposal within the company ranks and to identify support for the proposal at the board level. Corporate philanthropy is driven by the quid pro quo equation. It is necessary for the foundation fund-raiser to find a corporate link and a corporate purpose to be served when seeking support from a corporate foundation.

Contacts and linkages are important to the successful funding of foundation proposals. Those who are closest to the institution and who have the most influence with foundation decision makers must be brought into the process of foundation fund-raising. The most successful foundation fund-raisers are those who are most adroit at setting these contacts and linkages in motion.

What to Do if Turned Down. Only 7 percent of all foundation proposals submitted are funded. Foundation fund-raisers expect proposals to be rejected. When this happens, the first response is to send to the foundation a thank-you letter for considering the request. If possible, the foundation fund-raiser must determine why the proposal was turned down. A telephone call, letter, or personal visit should be used to make this determination.

If there is interest on the part of the foundation, the foundation fund-raiser should explore the possibilities of correcting deficiencies in the project or proposal and in resubmitting it for future funding. If no such opportunity is possible, parts of the program should be researched and directed toward other foundation funding sources.

What to Do if Successful. The first step to take in accepting a foundation award is to review the conditions of the grant and accept, alter, or reject them. If all conditions of the grant are acceptable, the foundation fund-raiser, in the name of the college or university president, must write a letter of thanks for the award.

Good stewardship requires that the foundation fund-raiser send periodic progress reports to the foundation on use and results of the foundation grant. An invitation for a site visit should also be extended to a foundation representative during the period of the award. Continued updating of the foundation officer on use of the grant and results of the foundation's investment should take place after the award. Once a foundation has funded a program at a college or university, it forges close ties with the institution. Such ties are the basis for solicitation of the foundation for a future award. And so the cycle moves.

Conclusion

Foundation fund-raising is best accomplished when a team of faculty, professional staff, and volunteers work together toward priorities of mutual benefit to the college or university and to the foundation.

Successful foundation fund-raisers set up a process whereby campus needs are determined, top foundation prospects are identified, contact with foundations is coordinated through one campus office, the proposal is written and submitted, appropriate response is made if turned down, and specific responsibilities are assumed if the proposal is funded.

As in other forms of private philanthropy, people in foundations give money to people they know and trust. The successful foundation fund-raiser utilizes close ties between the college or university and the foundation, including the ties of personal relationships, history of affiliation, and geographical and philosophical proximity. The major objective in setting up this process and maintaining it is to improve the odds and increase the opportunities for colleges and universities to receive foundation funding.

From the beginning of the process to the end, the successful foundation fund-raiser will remember the importance of personal contact and knowledge about the motivation of foundation trustees and staff.

The Reverend Pierce Harris, a Methodist minister in the inner city of Atlanta, Georgia, after World War II, knew the importance of understanding the motivation of congregations and foundations when he said, "The nerve that controls the pocketbook is the tenderest nerve in the human body."

References

Brakeley, John Price Jones, Inc. *Philanthropic Digest.* Washington, D.C.: Brakeley, 1985.

The Foundation Center. *The Foundation Center COMSEARCH Printouts.* New York: Foundation Center, 1985.

The Foundation Center. *The Foundation Directory.* (9th ed.) New York: Foundation Center, 1983.

The Foundation Center. *National Data Book.* (9th ed.) New York: Foundation Center, 1985.

The Foundation Center. *Sourcebook Profiles.* New York: Foundation Center, 1985.

Marquis—Who's Who, Inc. *Who's Who in America.* (43rd ed.) Chicago: Marquis—Who's Who, 1984.

Standard & Poor's Corporation. *Standard & Poor's Register of Corporations, Directors and Executives.* New York: Standard & Poor's, 1984.

Taft Corporation. *People in Philanthropy: A Guide to Philanthropic Leaders, Major Donors, and Funding Connections.* Washington, D. C.: Taft, 1984.

Taft Corporation. *Taft Corporate Giving Directory.* Washington, D.C.: Taft, 1985.

Taft Corporation. *Taft Corporate Giving Watch*. Washington, D.C.: Taft, 1985.

Taft Corporation. *Taft Foundation Giving Watch*. Washington, D.C.: Taft, 1985.

Taft Corporation. *Taft Foundation Reporter*. Washington, D.C.: Taft, 1985.

22

Kent E. Dove

Changing Strategies for
Meeting Campaign Goals

જ્જિ A capital campaign is an organized fund-raising effort on the part of an institution to secure extraordinary gifts and pledges for a specific purpose or purposes during a specified period of time. To define today's capital campaign more precisely than this is difficult. The nature of campaigns, like much of higher education itself, is in fundamental transition.

Fund-raising campaigns to support higher education began nearly three hundred and fifty years ago. The first deliberate fund-raising effort was organized in 1641 to assist financially troubled Harvard College. Thomas Weld, Hugh Peter, and William Hibbens represented the college on a trip to England and returned a year later with several hundred pounds.

Colleges and universities began to organize their alumni for financial support in the 1820s, but it was not until after the Civil War that alumni and other individuals became centrally important to fund-raising. The Civil War produced a number of new millionaires who had benefitted from the conflict; by its conclusion, the concept of stewardship had become secularized. During the late nineteenth and early twentieth centuries, capitalists, among them Andrew Carnegie and John D. Rockefeller, began underwriting libraries, museums, research, and even entire universities.

As a result of both the rise of industrialization and the attitudes of major donors toward colleges and universities, major gift fund-raising became a twentieth-century phenomenon. Fund-raising and public relations firms, such as the John Price Jones

Corporation, were established to assist not only colleges and universities but also other nonprofit organizations that lacked the staff or expertise to conduct these efforts.

One of the first successful major campaigns was directed early in this century by Charles Sumner Ward for the Young Men's Christian Association. During three decades, his fund-raising techniques raised more than a half billion dollars for this organization. Because of his efforts, Ward became known as the "master campaigner," and his strategies were copied by many other successful fund-raisers. They became the foundation on which today's campaigns are still built.

The importance of a capital campaign to an institution at critical moments in its history has always been great. Throughout this century, it has been the one public undertaking that exposes the hopes and aspirations of an institution to critical and discerning market segments that are ultimately asked to make positive judgments regarding the imperative investments of time, energy, and financial support critical to its quality and, at times, its survival. Today, as budgets tighten, enrollments level or decline, resources become more scarce, and fixed operating costs escalate more rapidly than the rate of inflation, the role of campaigns and their impact on the future of institutions is becoming ever more important. More and more, campaigns are becoming a necessary part of a development program. Their increasing frequency and ever-larger fund-raising goals are weaving them into the basic fabric of the advancement cloth.

Preliminary to the Major Campaign Program

Before a campaign is undertaken, precampaign work and sometimes even pre-precampaign work is necessary. First and foremost in any capital campaign effort is the need for commitment on the part of the board, administration, and volunteer leadership. Teamwork is essential. A campaign cannot be successfully undertaken by staff alone, nor can it be done by outside professionals alone. Any successful campaign must have support and time commitments from all key groups. An institution must have a clear image of itself and put forth a plan for growth and improvement. The program must be based upon important and legitimate institutional planning, goals, budget, and needs. Before a campaign is publicly launched, the case must be developed, a market survey conducted, and leadership enlisted and educated and substantial lead gifts must be in hand.

Four rather distinctive campaign forms or models can be found today: the traditional capital campaign, the comprehensive campaign, the single-purpose campaign, and the continuing major gifts program.

Traditional Capital Campaign. The traditional capital campaign is a fund-raising effort designed to secure gifts of capital assets from donors to be used to address capital needs of an institution, to build buildings, and in some instances, to build the endowment. Its characteristic features include a significantly motivated volunteer group striving in a highly organized and tightly managed manner to meet a specific overall capital goal consisting of one or more objectives during a specific time period, usually three years or less. Volunteers make every reasonable effort to see all alumni and special friends face to face because the campaign is a once-in-a-lifetime program. As a result, traditional capital campaigns typically are spaced many years—indeed, decades—apart and are often superimposed on the ongoing development effort. In some instances, fund-raising efforts, especially annual campaigns, are suspended or suppressed during the traditional capital campaign. It is common to have a separate campaign office, budget, and staff created for the sole purpose of supporting the effort.

At least four important developments in campaigning methods have made the traditional method less fashionable today and have led to increasing use of two additional methods, the comprehensive campaign and the single-purpose campaign. First, traditional capital campaigns seek gifts of capital assets from donors for capital needs of the institution. Today's capital campaigns often have goals that include needs other than capital ones, and more and more today, gifts are being made in many forms, including capital, by the donors. Second, the traditional capital campaign typically is a once-in-a-lifetime effort for an institution and is marketed that way to prospects. This is no longer as true as it once was. Many institutions hardly complete one campaign before announcing the next. The third factor is sheer economics—the cost of fund-raising. The traditional capital campaign attempts to reach all the alumni and friends of the institution on a one-to-one, face-to-face basis. The number and geographical distribution of alumni and frequency of campaign efforts today simply preclude financially, not to mention logistically, this kind of activity for most schools, colleges, and universities. Finally, the institution using the traditional capital campaign operational methodology runs the risk of restricting or damaging established, ongoing giving programs. This is a risk fewer and fewer institutions are willing or able to take.

Comprehensive Campaign. More popular today is the comprehensive campaign, a major development program with specific goals and timetables. It almost always includes under one umbrella current operations, one-time goals, and endowment objectives. The comprehensive campaign generally lasts three to five years, although some campaigns are longer and some are conducted in phases. Gifts and pledges of all kinds, including annual and deferred gifts, are often sought and counted in the campaign dollar total. In many instances, the dependence on volunteers is lessening, as is, coincidentally, the involvement of campus administrators and staff. And on a selected basis, involvement of faculty as both cultivators and solicitors is increasing. This type of campaign concentrates on maximizing, through intense personal solicitation, the gifts of its major donor prospects ($100,000 plus) and special donor prospects ($10,000 to $100,000). The general prospects (less than $10,000) are often solicited by telephone or direct mail. It also often encompasses in a mutually beneficial way all ongoing giving programs.

Single-Purpose Campaign. Also currently popular is the single-purpose campaign, a campaign for a single building, for an endowment fund for the library, or for any other single purpose. It is not a comprehensive campaign. It often does not reach beyond the special-interest constituency group to which it is directly pointed, and it generally is not undertaken as part of the entire development effort, although it is related to it. This form of campaign activity is leading many institutions to employ a professional fund-raiser, sometimes with a staff, whose responsibility is major and special gifts and whose title denotes this kind of responsibility. Many institutions today are continually into and out of single-purpose campaigns and, occasionally, into two or three more at the same time.

Continuing Major Gifts Program. The fourth campaign model is the use of the continuing major gifts program as an integrated part of a planned, ongoing development program. Realizing there is a limit to the number of times extraordinary fund-raising efforts can produce quick and effective solutions to today's problems, campus leaders are accepting two premises: (1) strategic academic planning will become an accepted (even required) practice and (2) this type of planning will eventually lead to better management practices and better managers at educational institutions and for institutional development programs.

When an institution uses strategic academic planning, development programs become multiyear, planned efforts designed in concert with institutional strategies. This results in perpetual campaigning to satisfy capital and other needs through fund-raising. Thus major campaigns are harmoniously integrated into the ongoing fund-raising program and are less obvious as extraordinary fund-raising efforts than they would be with the other models. A major gifts program is designed to be more proactive in gaining financial support for a planned future. Professional staffs (such as those currently running annual giving programs) exist, and the major gifts program functions continually in much the same way as other ongoing program elements.

This should not suggest that institutions utilizing strategic planning will not from time to time continue to engage in intensive, time-specific campaigns that have defined goals. They will. Beyond the sheer volume of dollars that can be raised this way, institutions occasionally will simply want to bring to themselves the special attention such a campaign provides. Formal campaigns, as they have been known, will probably become less frequent, but when undertaken, they will, curiously, have many of the traditional characteristics of the campaigns Mr. Ward organized seventy years ago.

The selection of a campaign model to be used in a particular situation will be influenced by a number of factors. These include (1) the commitment to and quality of strategic institutional planning, (2) the current level of maturity and sophistication of the development program, (3) the development staff's experience and ability, (4) the availability of campaign leadership, (5) the impressiveness of the case, and (6) the range and scope of the anticipated campaign effort. There is no one correct model for all institutions or all situations. In fact, there may be opportunities to incorporate features of more than one of the models into a unique model designed to best serve a particular situation.

Case Statement. The single definitive written piece in any campaign is the case statement. One of the best definitions of the fund-raising case statement is that of Harold J. Seymour: "This is the one definitive piece of the whole campaign. It tells all that needs to be told, answers all the important questions, reviews the arguments for support, explains the proposed plan for raising the money and shows how gifts may be made and who the people are who vouch for the project and who will give it leadership and direction" (Seymour, 1966, pp. 42–43).

A case statement should be logical and concise, even though it may, in fact, be lengthy. It presents a substantial plan for the future, not a burdensome revisiting of the past, no matter how honored and glorious. In a real sense, it is a prospectus; it invites investment.

The organization of case statements takes many forms. However, a good case must include messages of endorsement and commitment from top leadership, a detailed plan for using the resources sought and a compelling rationale for providing them, a budget detailing the gift opportunities, and a listing of those who will lead the campaign as well as those who have management responsibility for the institution. Case statements may be typewritten pages contained in three-ring binders, or they may be elaborate printed pieces. Where good planning is present, the case significantly mirrors the planning document. Effectively, these documents are companion pieces.

Experienced campaign directors know that the case preparation is often the first, and can be the most formidable, hurdle in any campaign effort. Absence of an effective case, or someone capable of formulating it promptly, can consume precious time when time is at a premium at the beginning of a campaign effort.

The case communicates the importance of the institution and its financial goals and programs. It also is very often used by those doing the market survey as they measure the potential of the constituency. The case also can be helpful in educating and, eventually, enlisting leadership.

Determining Goals for the Program

To determine goals for a successful campaign, an inventory of needs and a determination of priorities is essential. There is a great deal of difference between an institutional wants list and a needs list. It is absolutely essential that the wants list be carefully pared to a substantiated and documented needs list. The needs list is initially generated in-house. It evolves from a planning process to determine all important needs that might be met with private funding. Then the needs must be ranked in priority order. Institutional planners should always be cognizant of identifying goals that appeal to the constituencies. Legitimate institutional needs should not be dramatically altered or abandoned because of lack of constituency appeal, but items of little or no interest to the constituency generally should not appear as a major component of a campaign goal. In cases where it is possible, goals should be brought under one umbrella to make the campaign a unified one. This makes sense both in terms of organizing the fund-raising volunteers and in terms of ensuring institutional cohesion.

The final determination of how much constituency appeal a particular campaign component has can best be determined by selectively surveying key constituents.

Market Survey

The major purpose of the market survey is to provide an accurate assessment of the factors that might impact on the campaign. An essential objective is to determine, based on reaction to the case statement, attitudes toward the institutional priorities and the campaign goal and, if warranted, to suggest changes in either or both. Other objectives are to educate potential major donors and campaign leadership, to identify and evaluate those thought best suited to give leadership as workers and/or lead donors to the campaign, and to provide to the institution an analysis of all information gathered.

Market surveys are conducted through personal interviews with a carefully selected cross-section of board members, community leaders, alumni, friends, and other key constituents. The interview population is selected on the basis of its close relationship to the institution, familiarity with persons and situations pertinent to fund-raising, potential as donors, and ability to influence others to work and give. Focus groups and direct-mail questionnaires are increasingly being used to supplement and further validate surveys.

Does the institution conduct the market survey itself? Ordinarily not. Generally, it hires an outsider to do it. Why? Even though there are advantages to doing it in-house (insiders know the institution best, they have in-house expertise to assist in the effort, and they can usually do it less expensively), there are also disadvantages. Insiders may not view the institution with detachment, in-house surveys often lack credibility, and insiders may lack experience in conducting surveys. On balance, outsiders bring credibility, expertise, experience, and objectivity to a campaign. Today, in many situations, a compromise arrangement is possible. The outsiders select the sample, develop the questionnaire, and conduct the survey, providing analysis and reporting. The institution can provide the managerial, logistical, and clerical support services.

Campaign Leadership

The selection of leadership is of utmost importance in a campaign. Leadership should be excited and exciting. It should come primarily from within. Any institution should be able to find within its board, alumni organization, foundation board, development council, advisory groups, and so on the bulk of the leadership for any campaign. An absence of leadership at this level is an early warning sign that the institution is not adequately prepared to undertake a campaign. Top leadership should consist of respected individuals who have immediate name recognition with the institution's many publics, who are strongly identified with the institution and have a history of active involvement with it, who have established a substantial record of major gift support to the institution, and who will be forceful, dynamic leaders with influential colleagues and friends.

The power structure of a community may also provide supplemental leadership. It divides into four main groups: those who have inherited both wealth and its tradition of public service; the newly rich and powerful, Horatio Algers of the modern world; the top professional managers of key corporations; and those whom John Kenneth Galbraith describes as "men and women of standing."

For a campaign to be successful, it is necessary for top leadership to make a commitment of time, effort, and giving. The following plan should be followed in recruiting volunteer campaign leadership. An organizational chart and job descriptions should be prepared that clearly describe the specific responsibilities of the job and the amount of time that will be required and the number of meetings that will be necessary to complete the tasks. Recruitment should begin at the top and work down so volunteers recruit the people who will work for them.

After volunteers have been recruited, institutional staff must educate and train them. It should never be assumed that a volunteer knows as much about a particular campaign and/or institution as the professional staff. The individual may be a successful volunteer fund-raiser, but the assumption that the individual knows enough about a particular campaign and institution to represent it forcefully should never go unchallenged. Education is absolutely necessary for even the most experienced volunteers, including members of the board. Never leave to chance the education of top volunteer leadership.

Major Campaign Personnel

Higher education's most influential public is that group of citizens who have taken upon themselves the primary responsibility for seeing that colleges and universities are maintained and perpetuated: governing board members. How far a campaign can go depends on how far the board will carry it. Between 20 and 40 percent of the goal of most successful campaigns is subscribed by the board itself. There are a very few instances in which boards have done less than 20 percent, but there are records of more than 40 percent. If there is not the capacity or the willingness within the boardroom to make this kind of commitment, the institution probably is not ready to undertake the effort. There are, of course, special situations and circumstances that can invalidate this axiom. For instance, many independent schools find this generality does not accurately predict success or failure. And many tax-assisted institutions must look for alternatives because of the limited size and political nature of their governing boards.

The board sets policy for the program. Each board member should take a place in the volunteer organization and be a worker and a giver as well. Board gifts should come early, and all members should participate with gifts that are generous within their means and the overall scope of the campaign. Each member should be informed and enthusiastic about the campaign and should work to bring other workers into the program. Each should be an effective communicator in the community and set examples for others.

The institution's chief executive officer must be the principal spokesperson for the fund-raising program. This individual will have to provide inspiration and leadership to volunteers, to leadership, and to donor prospects. Because the chief executive will be the key solicitor of major gifts, this officer's time should be used wisely. The chief executive should work only with major prospects but should be involved in all the thinking and planning of the campaign.

The chief development officer is an educator, manager, researcher, communicator, facilitator, leader, guide, and stimulator and should rank equally with others just below the chief executive. A principal role is to lead and obtain understanding in support of the total program. This individual must provide support for the chief executive, governing board, and key volunteers in the fund-raising campaign and must see that calls are made on prospects, not just planned and talked about.

The chief development officer often works in the background. This individual must coordinate the public relations effort and see the long-term view while actively working on the short-term campaign. In addition, the chief development officer must be an effective manager of staff and must inspire confidence in all co-workers. In modern campaigns, chief development officers are doing some soliciting themselves. There are pros and cons to such a role. Suffice it to say that increasingly, and debatably, development officers will be frontline solicitors, too.

How to select outside professional counsel properly and use it wisely is discussed in another chapter, but it is generally concluded by almost every institution that undertakes an ambitious campaign that counsel can be of value. In fact, almost all the major institutions, both public and private, that have conducted successful capital campaigns over the last twenty years have used counsel in one way or another.

Campaign Organization

Any campaign structure requires a number of committees, or at least a committee functioning in a number of ways. A typical list of committees includes policy committee, steering committee, prospect evaluation committee, major gifts committee, special gifts committee, general gifts committee, and public relations committee.

The development committee of the board generally functions as the policy committee. It determines the general policies of the program and sets the goals. It approves the organizational pattern, staffing and budget requirements, and proposed timetable. It also sets guidelines under which memorial gifts or named-gift opportunities may be established and determines guidelines for gift acknowledgment and donor recognition. The top development officer staffs this committee.

The steering committee provides general direction and active management of the program. It coordinates activities of volunteers and sets the operating schedule. The steering committee generally includes the chairs of the several campaign operating committees, advisory groups, and top administrators. The chief executive of the institution and the chair of the board should be ex-officio members. This committee, too, is served administratively by the top development officer.

The prospect evaluation committee should be active early in the program, measuring both interest and financial capability. It evaluates what prospects can give (not what they will give) in terms of both effort and contributions. Confidentiality and anonymity are absolutely essential to this committee. The research staff of the development office staffs this committee.

The major gifts committee (generally concerned with donors of more than $100,000) has the critical tasks of evaluating, cultivating, and soliciting the institution's most important prospects. Because 90 percent or more of the campaign goal will probably come from 10 percent of the donors or fewer, it is important that the most affluent and influential group possible be enlisted to serve on this committee. The use of figureheads should be avoided. The members of this committee must be the best volunteers who can call on the best prospects at the appropriate times to secure maximum investments. Often, committee members are assigned only one or two prospects at a time.

The special gifts committee ($10,000 to $100,000 prospects) deals with substantial gifts just below the major level. The duties of committee members are similar to those of members of the major gifts committee. The ratio of one worker to three or four prospects is commonly used. Liaison may be provided by development staff other than the top development officer.

General gifts solicitation is generally the clean-up phase and, in most modern campaigns, is targeted to the general alumni body. Personal solicitation is encouraged, but telephone solicitation and direct-mail solicitations are often used. In personal solicitation, one worker to five prospects is the generally accepted ratio. Telephone techniques are second in effectiveness to direct solicitation and are growing increasingly more popular; mail techniques are the least effective of the three techniques. Some significant successes have been recorded recently using phone-mail programs.

The Gift Table

An essential component of any campaign is a gift table. It indicates the number and size of various gifts that will be needed if the institution is to reach its goal successfully. It also serves as a reality test, especially with the board and the major donors from whom leadership gifts are expected. It can have a sobering influence.

Certain mathematical assumptions are followed in arranging a gift table. The 80/20 rule says 80 percent of the money will come from 20 percent of the donors. This is a common rule of thumb, although in very recent years, many campaigns have seen 90 percent of the money come from 10 percent of the donors, and in at least one case, 99 percent of the money came from 1 percent of the donors. In his book on fund-raising principles, Seymour (1966, p. 32) stated his rule of thirds. Succinctly put, this theory says that the top 10 gifts in any campaign will represent 33 percent of the goal; the next 100 will represent another third of the goal; and all the rest of the gifts will represent the final third of the campaign goal (Seymour, 1966). When plotted on a gift table, all these equations generally work out mathematically to about the same kind of representation—except, of course, a situation in which 99 percent of the dollars come from 1 percent of the donors (a rare situation, although it may become more common in future years). A typical gift table for a $25 million campaign can be seen in Table 22-1.

Public Relations/Marketing/Publications. Another essential committee is the public relations committee. This advisory group is of great importance in any well-planned and professionally administered campaign. Committee members should be expert—public relations executives, marketing experts, and senior members of advertising firms. This group should review and recommend program materials, media coverage, and special events.

The campaign should be named. Whatever name is used, it should have dramatic impact and have meaning for both the institution and its constituency. Symbols, logos, titles, themes, and other identifying and identifiable marks should be developed for and used throughout the campaign. The committee can often be extremely helpful here.

There may need to be a packaging or marketing strategy determining the length of the campaign and whether it should be conducted in phases. The packaging and marketing of the program will also be affected by its relationship to the rest of the de-

Table 22-1. Standard Gift Table. Goal: $25,000,000.

Phase	Gift Level	Number of Donors	Total
Major gifts	$2,500,000	1	$2,500,000
	1,000,000	4	4,000,000
	500,000	4	2,000,000
	250,000	6	1,500,000
	150,000	10	1,500,000
	100,000	23	2,300,000
Special gifts	50,000	42	2,100,000
	25,000	54	1,350,000
	10,000	135	1,350,000
General campaign	5,000	420	2,100,000
	1,000	2,100	2,100,000
	under 1,000	33,000	2,200,000
Total		35,799	$25,000,000

velopment efforts. How will the campaign interface with the annual fund? How does planned giving fit into the campaign picture? Which prospects, individuals, foundations, and corporations will be protected for cultivation and solicitation by the campaign alone?

The importance of the case statement has already been stated. Seen more frequently today is a program brochure. Many institutions consider this a case statement. Unfortunately, it is not; rather, it is often a shortcut taken because the institution has neither the will nor the ability to prepare a proper case document. Even with a well-stated case, a program brochure is a necessity, but such a brochure cannot and does not replace the case. The principal differences between the case statement and the program brochure are length, quality of design and printing, and scope of distribution. The brochure should be attractive, but not too elaborate, and should not be overwhelmingly expensive. This type of document is often best hand-delivered. When mailed, it should be accompanied by a personal note. The format should be flexible to allow for inclusion of companion pieces for specific programs or projects, particularly in a comprehensive campaign encompassing several objectives.

In addition to the case statement and the program brochure, there are several other written pieces for which the committee can provide counsel, guidance, and technical expertise. They include:

A brochure on tax information and estate planning in making major gifts

Instructions to workers

A question-and-answer folder

A fact book on the institution

A pledge or contribution card or form

An impact of institution brochure—financial impact study

A campaign or program newsletter

Campaign reports

Typescript materials (major gift presentations and foundation and corporate proposals)

In addition to these kinds of documents, a number of audiovisual materials should be prepared, including a synchronized sound–slide film show, a motion picture, cassette and portable presentations, and flip charts, graphs, posters, and so forth.

After the campaign has been thoroughly planned, it should be formally announced through a major media event, such as a formal dinner or a major press conference or both. A significant portion of the campaign goal should have been achieved before the formal announcement, and the media should be used to keep the campaign's progress before the public. In addition to cultivating newspaper and broadcast media coverage, the institution should use its publications to provide continuing publicity for the campaign. Printed materials, such as the president's report, alumni and other external magazines and bulletins, and athletic programs and newsletters, all should be used to keep the campaign before the institution's publics.

After the campaign has been completed, a victory dinner should be conducted, and a final report should be written and issued to everyone involved in the campaign.

Campaign Management

Management of the campaign is the primary responsibility of the chief development officer and the development staff. To be able to provide organized, timely, and accurate information as required, it is necessary to have in place management and reporting systems covering prospect status, volunteer assignments and activity, financial reports covering gifts and pledges as well as the campaign operating budget, and staff responsibility and activity.

Internally, the campus community must be made aware of the campaign and must feel it has an active part to play. Key administrators should be consulted or informed on all proposals and fund-raising activities that relate to their specific areas. At the same time, key institutional personnel should be actively involved in the cultivation and solicitation process.

The chief development officer should insist that the external fund-raising effort not be undertaken before a comprehensive campaign plan, organizational chart, and campaign schedule are developed and accepted. There should be a leadership/recruitment system and schedule and a public information plan and schedule covering media, printed materials, typescript materials, and audiovisual materials. The development staff should see that provisions are made for production of a prospect list as well as an evaluation system for all campaign prospects; this system should include evaluation committees for larger-gift prospects and formulas of giving for smaller-gift prospects. There must also be a campaign budget and expense control system, a system for recruiting volunteer workers, informational meetings for those recruited, and training workshops for volunteers and leaders.

It is important that the development staff establish a progress reporting and control system for prospects. This should include a prospect pledge card assignment system, a worker assignment system, a report meeting schedule, progress report mailings, a worker activity review system, and a prospect reassignment system with a pledge card redistribution system. A gift tabulation system and a campaign audit system should be well thought out and planned for in advance, including the section list posting, master list posting, and auditing of all cash and pledges. Additionally, steps should be set forth to address organization, volunteer recruitment and training, the public kickoff, subsequent report meetings, and follow-up and clean-up necessary to the success of area campaigns. There should also be a gift acknowledgment system, a collection system, and a final follow-up system.

Budget

Campaign budgets can vary significantly. However, the operating budget will generally be 6 to 9 percent of the campaign goal. The important thing to remember when preparing a budget is to consider all the campaign's needs and to budget accordingly at the outset. Most campaign budgets have lines for the following items: salaries and benefits for professional, administrative, clerical, and part-time personnel; fees for consultants; office supplies and printing; telephone and other communications networks; leased equipment; computer services; outside mailing service; clipping service; travel; publications; advertising; public announcement event (kick-off); entertainment; leadership workshops; area campaigns; special events; office furnishings; unclassified; campaign victory celebration; and an undistributed amount, usually 3 to 5 percent of the total budget, to meet inflationary and other unforeseen factors.

Conclusion

No fund-raising program is more exciting, complex, demanding, or critically necessary periodically in higher education today than the capital or major gifts campaign. With good institutional planning and careful advance preparation, most will enjoy success, given an institutional commitment to the program, a compelling case, influential and active volunteer leaders, major gift prospects who are willing and able to give, a commitment to personal solicitation, qualified fund-raising staff (and counsel), and an adequate budget.

Given the budgetary constraints limiting most institutions today, the successful campaign will be as cost-effective as possible. The campaign that maximizes its effectiveness will raise the largest amount of gifts and pledges, especially when not only the overall goal but also each of the component objectives is satisfactorily addressed, in the shortest period of time while expending the least amount of institutional resources reasonably required to complete the campaign.

Reference

Seymour, H. J. *Designs for Fund Raising*. New York: McGraw-Hill, 1966.

23

Theodore P. Hurwitz

Designing and Managing
Planned Giving Programs

৩৯৩ The title of this chapter may be confusing to the novice fund-raiser because all gifts should be properly planned. For the most part, donors contribute to charitable organizations because they believe in their philanthropical goal or mission. However, tax considerations can play an important role in the final determination of the amount of the gift, the timing of the gift, and the method by which the gift will be made. These considerations enable donors to plan properly their programs of philanthropy.

A properly planned gift will enable a donor to take advantage of the tax incentives included in tax laws and help resolve some of the complexities of a financial portfolio by taking into consideration financial needs and charitable goals. Any donor contemplating a gift that might significantly affect taxes should review that gift plan with legal, financial, and tax advisers to ensure that the gift will take maximum advantage of available tax benefits. Because tax laws are continually changing and because this chapter is intended to provide a broad overview of planned giving techniques, there is no detailed discussion of the tax implications of planned gifts even though planned giving does involve federal income, gift, and estate tax issues as well as state and other local tax questions.

This chapter provides a broad review of the substance of a planned giving program, discussing the various methods of giving that are identified with these programs, such as bequests, life income plans, gifts subject to a retained life estate, gifts of life insurance, and charitable lead trusts. In addition, the internal requirements of administering a program, the various options available in marketing planned gifts, and the characteristics that might be found in a successful planned giving officer are discussed. All these items should be given thoughtful consideration before any planned giving program is initiated.

Among professional fund-raisers, the term *planned giving* has historically come to mean more than well thought-out giving. Planned giving has been used to describe that area of a development office that has responsibility for raising funds through bequests, life income trusts and annuities, life insurance, and gifts of real property with retained life estates. These gifts are known as deferred gifts, and *planned giving* is often synonymous with *deferred giving*. A deferred gift is a gift that is made now but does not take effect until sometime in the future. As development programs have become more sophisticated, planned giving has come to include much more than deferred gifts. It includes lead trusts and often any other type of gift that requires some tax or legal planning before it can be made. However, deferred gifts usually constitute the major component of a planned giving program.

Bequests

Bequests, the most common type of deferred gifts, are the easiest to incorporate into any fund-raising program. No technical or legal expertise is required of the fund-raising staff, nor is any great expense needed to market bequests. Donors make their gifts now by including a charitable organization in their wills. The bequest will not take effect until sometime in the future when the donor dies. It is important to remember that bequests are revocable and subject to amendment or modification if the donor's circumstances change or if that donor becomes unhappy with the institution. This is especially important if a bequest secures or completes a pledge or other commitment.

Bequests can be marketed in various ways: a face-to-face ask, direct mail, or an advertisement in an institutional or other publication. The method used will relate to the personality and style of the institution. Although it may take different forms, the substance of the message is basically the same and reads essentially as follows: "Bequests are an important source of our institution's total support. . . . All individuals should have a will. . . . Because personal circumstances change, you should periodically review your will with your attorney. . . . When you meet with your attorney, we hope you will include our institution in your estate planning."

Life Income

Life income plans are a popular way of giving for many donors who are not able to make an outright gift. Donors use these plans to obtain an immediate tax deduction, to ensure gift and estate tax savings, to avoid capital gains taxes on gifts of appreciated securities and real estate, to diversify stock and bond portfolios, to increase spendable income, to avoid the delays and cost of probate, and to make a meaningful gift to a favorite college or university during their lifetime. All life income plans must be irrevocable and can be established directly with a tax-exempt organization or other entity (trust company) authorized so to act. Without going into an in-depth discussion, the following are the highlights of life income plans:

Gift Annuity. In consideration of a gift, the institution agrees to pay a fixed dollar amount to a designated beneficiary for life. This is a simple contract guaranteed by all the assets of the institution. Because an annuity is part gift and part sale, a substantial portion of the payments to the beneficiary may be treated as a tax-free return of principal.

Deferred Gift Annuity. Same as the gift annuity, except that annuity payments are not paid until some mutually agreeable future date—for example, the first annuity payment will be made two years from the date of the gift and further payments quarterly thereafter.

Pooled Income Fund. This arrangement merges the gifts of many donors into a common fund, much like a mutual fund, and all of the fund's income is distributed to the beneficiaries on a pro rata basis. Other assets of the organization and gifts under other plans are not involved. The commingling enables the organization to take advantage of size and diversity in its investment policy.

Pure Unitrust. This trust will pay a specified percentage of the market value of the trust's assets, as valued annually. The income will fluctuate from year to year in relation to the changing values of the trust assets. If the income earned by the trust is less than the amount required to be paid to the beneficiary, the difference is taken from the trust principal. If the income earned is greater than the required payout, the difference is added to the trust principal.

Net Income Unitrust. All the net income earned will be paid to the beneficiary up to a maximum percentage of the trust's market value. The income paid out will fluctuate in relation to the increase or decrease of interest, dividends, and fair market value of the trust's assets. When the income exceeds the stated percentage, the excess is used to make up deficiencies of previous years; if there were no deficiencies, the additional income is added to the trust principal.

Annuity Trust. The trust will pay a fixed dollar amount annually of at least 5 percent of the initial fair market value of the trust assets. This plan differs from a gift annuity in that the payments are not guaranteed by the organization but solely by the trust itself.

Life Estate

Another type of deferred gift is a gift of a personal residence or farm subject to a life estate. Donors can make gifts of residences and continue to reside there for their lifetimes. The donor obtains an immediate income tax deduction based on the fair market value of the residence less the present value of the donor's life interest in the property. The latter is based on actuarial tables in effect at the time the gift is made. The donor will usually assume all costs of maintenance while living on the property. This type of gift is ideal for a donor who intends to live on the property and has already bequeathed the residence to a charitable institution. Possession of the property is delivered at death, but now the donor has generated a current income tax deduction as well and has ensured a prompt transfer to the institution without delays and expense of probate.

Life Insurance

A gift of life insurance is a popular way to make a gift to a charitable organization. As an individual grows older, the need for life insurance diminishes and the original reasons for acquiring insurance protection are no longer compelling. The children have grown and are self-supporting. The mortgage has been paid. If the policy has value (as a whole life policy would), then an amount close to the actual cash value of the policy is deductible as a charitable contribution for income tax purposes in the year of the gift. Insurance proceeds can also be used to establish life income plans or can pour over into an existing unitrust or pooled income fund.

Lead Trust

For individuals with high personal income, a charitable lead trust may be helpful. A lead trust is the "mirror image" of a unitrust or annuity trust. In the lead trust, the charitable organization receives an annual income for a fixed number of years, and then the trust assets revert back to the donor or to a designated beneficiary, such as a child or grandchild. Such a trust will qualify the donor for tax benefits if it pays the charitable organization either a guaranteed annuity or a fixed percentage of the fair market value of the trust each year. The income tax benefit to the donor is either exclusion of the income paid to the charitable organization or a deduction for a charitable gift, but not both. To qualify for a charitable income tax deduction, the transfer of interest in the trust, though temporary, must be irrevocable. If the trust is for a period of ten years or more, the donor does not have to pay income tax on the income paid to the charity, but no charitable deduction is allowed. If the trust is for a period of less than ten years, the income paid to the charity is taxable as income to the donor, but the donor is entitled to an immediate charitable deduction for income tax purposes for the present value of the total interest to be paid to the charitable organization.

The greatest advantage of a charitable lead trust may be to provide a tax-efficient way to fulfill charitable obligations and to pass on wealth to children or grandchildren. This plan can minimize gift or estate taxes and avoid such taxes on future appreciation of the donated property. These gift and estate tax savings are often the primary motivation for using a charitable lead trust. Lead trusts qualify for charitable deductions for gift and estate tax purposes. The deductions are based on the present value of the annual payments that will pass to the charitable organization, and any appreciation of the trust assets during the course of the trust term is free from gift or estate taxation. Therefore, donors are often able to pass on to their heirs a much larger estate than they might have done without a charitable lead trust.

Real Estate

A planned giving officer will usually be responsible for negotiating gifts of real estate and other hard-to-value gifts. Whenever a gift of real estate is offered, a charitable organization should ask three questions. First, can the organization use the property for its own charitable purposes? Second, does the organization want to hold the property for its own investment purposes? (The charity will have to pay taxes and other maintenance costs.) Third, if the organization accepts the property, can the property be promptly sold? In the latter case, the sale should not be so low that the donor's charitable deduction will be in jeopardy.

In addition to gifts of real estate, the office of planned giving will usually be involved with hard-to-value gifts, such as partnership interests, stamp and coin collections, art, antiques, and other items of tangible personal property. The tax laws make a distinction between gifts of tangible personal property that the charitable organization accepts and intends to use for its own charitable purposes and gifts that the charity accepts with the intention to sell. In the latter case, the tax laws limit the charitable deduction and impose stringent guidelines on both the donor and the charity.

Administration of a Planned Giving Program

An active planned giving program involves four administrative functions. Large institutions may be organized in four separate offices, and each administrative function may have its own vice-president or other administrative officer. Smaller institutions may administer all four functions out of one or more offices. These four functions are development, legal, accounting, and investment.

The development office provides the sales force for the institution's life income program. It is responsible for publications, advertising, seminars, mailings, and all other marketing devices. It also has the technical experts needed to negotiate trust, annuity, and other planned gifts. The planned giving specialist, whether a lawyer, accountant, estate planner, or simply a seasoned development professional, is a fund-raiser whose principal motivation is raising funds for a particular charitable organization.

The legal office should have responsibility for the drafting of all documents, especially the various trust and annuity agreements. In addition, this office should ensure that, if the institution is acting as a trustee, it has the authority so to act and is acting responsibly. Planned giving is the one development area where legal questions constantly arise, and the development office should work closely with the legal office.

The business office must assume responsibility for ensuring that the trust and annuity beneficiaries receive correct checks in a timely manner. In addition, it must provide each income beneficiary with proper income tax information. The business office must file the proper tax returns for each trust.

The investment office must ensure that each trust is properly invested, diversified, and generating an income adequate to meet the payout requirements of each trust. Oftentimes, the treasurer or chief investment officer will advise the development officer on the payout limitations of a particular gift.

All four administrative functions relate to each other, and all have the common goal of properly servicing donors and beneficiaries. When accepting responsibility for the administration of trust and annuity gifts, a charitable organization must be willing to organize itself in such a way as to provide full service to the donor.

Therefore, a department similar to a bank trust department though on a smaller scale is warranted, and the full cooperation and coordination of these four administrative functions are imperative.

Marketing Planned Giving

There is no one way to market planned giving; each institution must determine what works best for it. Cultivation and patience are paramount. A planned giving mailing is used to provide leads for the development officer to follow up and is not intended to bring in cash immediately. Planned gifts usually require an educational process for the donors. This includes an explanation of the various plans, an understanding of their differences, and an opportunity to consider the various tax implications of each plan. All of this takes time, and it often takes three or more years for a particular gift to be consummated. Consequently, sales techniques develop leads that give the development officer an opportunity to educate the prospect over a period of time. Once that process has been completed, the economic climate will often dictate when the gift is actually made. It often happens that a trust prospect will investigate the possibilities of a trust or annuity gift and, after a full review, will decide that an outright gift is the best alternative.

The best prospects for a trust or annuity gift are those individuals who have already made such gifts. If they are pleased with the benefits provided them from their first gift and are pleased with the professional manner in which their first gift has been administered, they are more than likely to make additional gifts. It is, therefore, important to build into a planned giving program a strategy that will provide for professional servicing of prior donors.

At least once a year, the development officer who assisted in the gift should personally visit each donor. Additionally, all donors should receive an analysis of their trust portfolios at least once a year. Naturally, there are those donors who ought to be visited more often, and some donors ought to be advised as portfolio changes are made. The development officer must know the donors and respond to their interests and needs. Income payments and tax information must be sent to a beneficiary in a timely manner, and this must be coordinated by the development office, even though another office actually prepares the checks and tax statements. Delays will only work against the institution. If possible, all communications to donors and beneficiaries should be sent from the development office, and it is best to try to include a personal note. The development officer should communicate with each donor at least once a month by forwarding trust data or general information of interest on the institution. Continuous visits and mailings will ensure that the donor does not ever feel forgotten. The more personal the communication, the more the donor will feel that the institution cares.

Individuals who have told an institution that it has been included in their wills are excellent prospects for life income gifts. The ultimate benefit to the institution will be the same. However, a life income plan will enable a donor to obtain an income tax deduction, which is not available from a bequest. A life income plan may also be a way for donors to increase income during their lifetime. In other words, there is available to bequest prospects a tax incentive that can work for the mutual benefit of the prospect and institution.

Mailings are often used to advertise the merits of planned gifts. They can be used for educational purposes or to elicit a response seeking more information. An educational mailing can be a newsletter or brochure mailed regularly to a broad mailing list. The purpose will be to familiarize the readers with the various methods of giving. The mailing may prompt a response when an example relates to a donor's specific situation. In the other mailing approach, the development office sends a brochure that highlights the advantages of life income plans to an older audience. The brochure might be accompanied by a letter from some well-recognized trustee or other individual in the financial, banking, or estate-planning community. The letter, which tells of the benefits and popularity of the life income program, the importance of estate planning, and the tax advantages of life income gifts, urges the reader to return a confidential reply card requesting additional information. Those who respond should then receive a personal letter from the planned giving officer and a booklet that fully describes the various life income plans. The development officer who sends the booklet should call the prospect within ten days to discuss the program and answer any questions. The objective should be to obtain an appointment for a personal visit to talk about the institution and how the life income program is administered.

Many of the best prospects for trust and annuity gifts are those over sixty-five years of age. The older the donor, the greater the donor's charitable income tax deduction. Moreover, planned giving can be related to an overall estate plan, and most people over sixty-five are more concerned about their estate planning than younger individuals.

Estate planning seminars that include a discussion of methods of giving are often effective marketing devices. Institutions that have an older constituency can often find that such a seminar provides a real service. The seminars can be strictly technical in nature, or they can include some discussion and a slide show or film about the institution. If done on a campus, they can be combined with tours and lectures on other topics not related to estate planning. Whether such seminars are broad in scope, on campus or at a downtown hotel, or combined with a lunch or dinner all depends on the personality of the institution and the interests of the audience.

The conventional rules of fund-raising suggest that development professionals recruit the volunteers who do the soliciting. Planned giving is an exception. A planned giving professional must be available to discuss directly with the prospect the various methods of giving and their tax consequences. Volunteers can open the door so that the planned giving expert can meet with the prospect, and volunteers can follow up afterward. Certainly, some volunteers who are lawyers or accountants can do the job in some cases, but as a general rule, a planned giving professional is best qualified to negotiate with a donor. Volunteers can also provide advice on proposed deferred giving publications and mailings and can host receptions that include estate planning discussions.

Many uninformed volunteers will suggest that trust officers are a tremendous resource for new trust and annuity business. They believe such individuals can direct to an institution donors who will eventually establish a charitable remainder trust or include the institution in their estate planning. There are some isolated cases where a trust officer, lawyer, or accountant was able to direct a donor to an institution, but those situations are not common. Most lawyers never have an opportunity to suggest an institution to a client. Clients usually know quite well which charities they want to support, and it is the lawyer's job to develop a plan that will accommodate a client's wishes. Accountants can often suggest to a client that it makes sense to make some charitable gifts, but the client usually knows which charities will be the recipients of such gifts. Trust officers usually must adhere to the terms of an existing trust that already identifies the charities to be supported.

It is always helpful for a development officer to cultivate, educate, and befriend various professionals, such as lawyers, accountants, real estate agents, life insurance agents, financial advisers, trust officers, and stockbrokers. One never knows when one of them will have an opportunity to direct a major grant to an institution. However, this type of cultivation has low priority.

There is one professional who can be a much likelier resource than the others, and that is the stockbroker. A stockbroker knows which clients are locked into certain holdings because of substantial capital gains. Brokers are in a position to counsel their clients about charitable remainder trusts that will enable them to avoid the capital gains tax, diversify their stock portfolios, and generate some brokerage commission for the stockbroker. The donor/client makes a gift of appreciated stock to fund such a trust, and the donor's stockbroker is given the business to sell the stock and possibly even to reinvest the proceeds. This can be a great incentive for the stockbroker to seek such gifts for an institution.

Planned Giving Officer

What kind of a person will make a good planned giving professional? A lawyer who recognizes that he or she is a fund-raiser and not an attorney can make an excellent planned giving officer. This person will have most of the technical background that is required or will be a "quick study." Further, the law degree gives the person credibility with prospects and donors. However, many lawyers who go into the development field are unable to leave the legal responsibilities to the legal office, or they tend to draft letters or make other presentations too technical for the average donor. The best planned giving professional will have a good command of the technical requirements, be able to relate easily to older people, and have the ability to explain technical material in a simple, easily understood manner. A background in life insurance, financial planning, accounting, or tax law can all be helpful to a qualified planned giving officer. Any person who can learn the technical aspects of planned giving, likes to work with people, can obtain the confidence of older people, and understands or has a flair for fund-raising can be very successful in planned giving.

The successful planned giving officer will have a good understanding of tax laws and how charitable giving can provide tax benefits to a donor. Tax laws are forever changing, and it is imperative that a planned giving officer keep up-to-date on the law and have opportunities for continuing education. A successful planned giving office will have, as part of its budget, funds that will enable its professionals to keep current on the law and to have reference material readily available.

There is no one way to organize, administer, and develop solicitations in a planned giving program. What works well for one institution may not work for another. However, individual donors relate to a charitable organization in a unique way, and because the relationship is a very special one, we must ensure that the program is managed as professionally as possible.

24

David R. Dunlop

Special Concerns
of Major Gift Fund-Raising

༄ The dramatic difference between the present and what the future might hold for most private secondary schools, colleges, and universities rests in the hands of a few individuals. For some institutions, the number is less than 10. For many, it is just a few dozen. Rarely does the number exceed 200.

Twenty-five years ago the late Harold J. (Sy) Seymour used to tell his clients, "In any substantial capital campaign you have to get about a third of the money from the top ten gifts, another third from the next 100 largest gifts, and the last third from everybody else" (Seymour, 1966, pp. 32–33). That rule of thumb still applies. The experience at countless colleges and universities, both in and out of campaigns, has shown that the gifts of a few top donors account for the largest share of the total given. This chapter is devoted to fund-raising among those few individuals who have the capacity to give large gifts. It focuses on the essential principles and concepts that distinguish major gift fund-raising from the fund-raising designed for smaller gifts. The chapter concludes with observations about the development of prospect tracking systems and their relevance to the essential concepts that distinguish major gift fund-raising from other forms of fund-raising.

Short-Term Versus Long-Term Fund-Raising

There are many kinds of fund-raising that seek to gain the support of prospective large-gift givers. One type of fund-raising is little more than skillful collection. It emphasizes getting the right solicitor, at the right time, to ask the right prospect, for the right gift, for the right purpose with the right cultivation and the right follow-up. This type of fund-raising, with its focus on the solicitation, is based on the fact that giving is usually a reactive process. Although there may be some recognition of the need for cultivation and follow-up, this approach is based primarily on assignments oriented toward asking for the gift. Instead of making long-term investments, such as building relationships with prospects and emphasizing their involvement in the life of the institution, this kind of fund-raising focuses on short-term cultivation.

However efficient, short-term fund-raising alone seldom yields the largest gifts that major gift prospects are ultimately capable of giving. These ultimate gifts are reserved for causes and institutions with which the prospects' lives are closely entwined. Though acknowledging the value and necessity of short-term fund-raising in dealing with larger numbers of prospects, this author advocates a long-term view of major gift fund-raising oriented toward obtaining the top prospects' ultimate, as well as intermediate, gifts.

What Leads a Person to Make a Major Gift

The specific experiences of each major gift giver are bound to differ. However, an examination of these individuals' histories will reveal some stages that are common to all. Major gift givers are likely to have had experiences that caused them to become aware of the institution, to develop knowledge of it, and through increasing concern and caring involvement, to become committed to it. Understanding these common stages provides insight into how one can offer potential givers the opportunity to experience the same steps and thus increase the likelihood of their making major gifts. Consider the following:

Awareness must come first. If one had a perfect view of each giver's experience, perhaps one could spot the moment at which an individual first became aware of the school and the project he or she eventually supported. These moments of beginning awareness spring from a wide range of stimuli: the printed word, comments by a friend, a speech, a broadcast, a public event, a chance visit. Think about the ways important causes that you now support were first impressed on your own consciousness. The variety of experience is unlimited; as many are accidental as are planned.

Knowledge and understanding do not necessarily follow awareness. The fund-raiser must make sure that information is available to the major gift prospects that will help build their knowledge and understanding of the institution and of the projects and purposes for which major gifts are sought. Without knowledge and understanding, there is little hope of gaining commitment.

Caring for an institution or a project does not necessarily follow knowledge. What makes one person care about a school or project and others not? Personality, values, experience, interests, proximity, relevance, timing, and friendships are some of the factors that affect caring. There are certainly more. There is no science that explains how to develop a prospect's sense of caring. The fund-raiser's attention to insights from those who are closest to the prospect, the fund-raiser's own relationship with the prospect, and the sensitivity of the fund-raiser all can help.

Involvement develops naturally from caring if opportunities are provided. Although smaller gifts are made by people who simply care and are not involved, substantial giving is usually based on involvement. Involvement shifts a person's perspective from the third person to the first person, from a view of the institution and its people as "they, them, and those" to the view of "I, we, and us." When this occurs, the process of giving is no longer a matter of giving resources away, but rather of giving to a purpose of which the giver is a part.

Commitment is often used synonymously with gift or pledge, and for good reason. When the elements of the relationship between a person and an institution create a feeling of being committed, the prospective giver will seek out the means by which to effectively express that commitment. Once engendered, the major gift prospect's sense of commitment can yield important moral, political, social, personal, and financial support.

These steps—awareness, knowledge and understanding, caring, involvement, and commitment—through which prospective givers move are central to major gift fund-raising. For the fund-raiser, however, there are steps that must precede them.

Concepts of Major Gift Fund-Raising

The Process of Major Gift Fund-Raising. A few years ago, one of our country's outstanding college fund-raisers, G. T. (Buck) Smith, expanded and adjusted Sy Seymour's concept of fund-raising into a continuum of initiatives designed to create prospect awareness, interest, involvement, and commitment (Smith, 1977). Smith recognized that one must first identify a major gift prospect and gather information to build awareness, interest, involvement, and commitment. His continuum, which he called the "Five I's of Fund-Raising," can be seen in Figure 24-1.

Figure 24-1. Smith's Five I's of Fund-Raising.

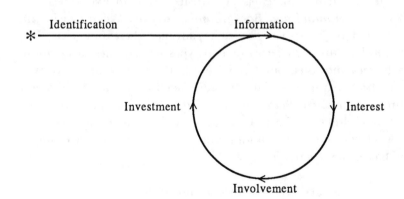

My own view of the process of major gift fund-raising evolved from both Seymour's and Smith's and can be seen in Figure 24-2.

Figure 24-2. The Process of Major-Gift Fund-Raising.

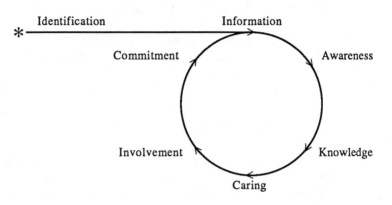

Regardless of how the process is viewed, the business of major gift fund-raising should be concerned with human values, the purposes the gifts will serve, and the development of relationships based on those values and purposes more than it should be concerned with the means of giving and dollar goals.

Major gift fund-raising requires the active cooperation and participation of people both on and off campus and in a variety of positions: faculty, students, staff, trustees, and other volunteers.

Foreground and Background Activities. When considering the kind of initiatives needed to advance these functions, it is helpful to think in terms of two types of activities: background activities and foreground activities. Both are absolutely essential, and both require carefully coordinated investments in thought, time, and budget. *Background activities* are those initiatives that, although they do have an impact on individual prospects, are conceived and carried out for groups. Following are some examples of background activities:

Visiting committees for academic units
Advisory councils
Alumni magazines

Newsletters
Alumni class activities and organizations
Alumni club activities
Special events on and off campus
Annual reports
Student recruitment and interviewing
Brochures and promotional materials
Films and slide shows
Club receptions and dinners
Campus tours
Sports events
Class reunions

Foreground activities—initiatives that are conceived, planned, and carried out for specific individual major gift prospects—include such things as:

Meeting with the dean
Borrowing art for showing on campus
Private dinner with faculty
Report on the impact a gift has had
Visit from the president or provost
Use of home for college reception
Testimonial dinner
Message of congratulations over promotion or other business
  success
Asking for advice in area of special competence
Telephone call from faculty member to express thanks for
  gift
Borrowing private plane to bring VIPs to campus
Presentation of award for distinguished service
A student's letter or visit to express thanks for scholarship
Special seating at institutional functions
Naming a garden on campus in recognition of service and
  generosity

Who Does the Work. Successful, efficient major gift fund-raising requires frequent and regular review, planning, coordination, execution, and evaluation of initiatives. Some institutions assign staff or volunteers to the cultivation of major gift prospects on a class, geographical, or giving program basis rather than in recognition of the existing personal relationships. When the stakes are high, it is better to recognize that there are persons—for example, a friend, classmate, student, business associate, or former professor—who provide a natural link between the prospect and the institution. For some prospects, there may be just one or two such persons; for others, there may be a dozen or more of these key individuals. It is most effective to identify those individuals who form an existing and natural link to the institution than to artificially impose one.

Not all of the prospect's friends associated with the institution will be willing and able to help manage initiatives. Some may be too close to the prospect to perform this role. Careful investigation is required to determine whom to ask. Those who are willing and able to help with the prospect become the key players.

Fixing Responsibility. From among the key players for each major gift prospect, the fund-raiser must identify those in the best position to help decide on the most appropriate and constructive initiatives. To do this, a few colleges are using what has become known as a *system of primes and secondaries.* This refers to assigning responsibility for initiatives to staff, administrators, trustees, or other volunteers. The ground rules require that the person designated as prime will, with a member of the development staff, have the primary responsibility for developing, coordinating, executing, recording, and evaluating fund-raising initiatives toward a given prospect. Those designated as secondaries will be consulted about these initiatives and will be kept informed of developments affecting the prospect's relationship with the institution. Only one person should be designated as prime; any number of people may be designated as secondaries. Input from the secondaries should be invited as new strategies are developed, although final word in determining the strategy should rest with the prime.

Using a system of primes and secondaries allows the major gift staff to receive input from many quarters and to distribute responsibility for fund-raising strategy and initiatives to those most knowledgeable of the prospect and of the prospect's relationship to the institution and in the best position to carry out these responsibilities. However, the active involvement and participation of the development staff is essential to make sure that sufficient, timely, and appropriate initiatives are being taken with each prospect by the primes and secondaries and to provide impartial judgment to offset the mirror syndrome described next.

Mirror Syndrome. There is a phenomenon that occurs among primes and secondaries that convinces them that their own personal interest is the prospect's priority interest at the institution. The term *mirror syndrome* describes the natural tendency of a person to reflect the interests of those with whom he or she speaks or meets. For example, when a major gift prospect, Mr. Jones, and the director of athletics meet, they will likely talk more about athletics than anything else. The director of athletics leaves the encounter honestly convinced that Mr. Jones's foremost interest at the college is the athletics program. When the chair of the art department meets with Mr. Jones, they speak almost entirely of matters relating to art. The art department chair goes away equally convinced that art is Mr. Jones's greatest interest at the college. The truth may be that Mr. Jones's greatest interest is in neither of these areas. The system devised for major gift fund-raising must provide for an honest broker whose function is to help the primes and secondaries determine accurately where their prospect's interests really lie. This is one of the roles of the staff person(s) assisting primes and secondaries: to serve as an honest broker in gauging competing prospect interests at the institution.

The Requirements of Major Gift Fund-Raising

Quantity, Frequency, and Continuity of Initiative. Major gift prospects give their largest gifts to institutions with which they are closely and frequently involved. An institution seeking a major share of a person's resources must hold up its end of the friendship with that person. It must invest enough regular initiatives, thoughtfully planned, with a continuity that builds the prospect's awareness, knowledge, caring, and involvement toward the making of major commitments. Many fund-raisers fail to achieve this because they spread their efforts too thinly over too many prospects.

The Moves Concept to Measure Fund-Raising Progress. The measure of dollars and donors has long been the standard of fund-raising success. Major gifts, however, are often not realized until long after the initiatives that spawned them—sometimes years or even decades later. The timing of a truly major gift is more often tied to the life cycle of the giver and to the cumulative effect of initiatives than to a specific fund-raising initiative or even to the institution's need. For these reasons, counting dollars and donors in a given year is a very poor indicator of fund-raising effectiveness. Several years ago G. T. (Buck) Smith came up with the idea of keeping track of initiatives as a measure of the progress of major gift fund-raising. He called these initiatives *moves* (Smith, personal communication). To fully understand the moves concept, one must recognize that a move involves six steps:

1. Review of the prospect's relationship with the institution
2. Planning the appropriate initiative to advance the prospect's awareness, knowledge, interest, caring, involvement, or commitment
3. Coordination of the planned initiative with the appropriate prime, secondaries, and staff
4. Execution of the initiative
5. Evaluation of the initiative
6. Reporting and recording the results of the initiative

With each move requiring these six steps, and with each prospect requiring at least one move a month, one can appreciate the amount of communication, coordination, and record keeping needed to plan and carry out a sufficient stream of initiatives for each prospect. For example:

> 100 major gift prospects
> × 12 moves per year per prospect
> 1,200 moves

Just how many prospects and how many moves can a development staff person manage? A staff member assigned responsibility to manage and support moves will typically have less than twenty-six weeks to devote to managing moves if normal distractions are taken into account:

       52 weeks per year
      −26 weeks deducted as follows:
              − 3 vacation
              − 1 sick leave
              − 7 office time for personnel, budget, special
                 projects, reports, acknowledgments, admis-
                 sion matters, and other indirect fund-
                 raising work
             −14 special events, dedications, testimonials,
                 VIP visits, ground breakings, and the like
              − 1 training and professional development
        26 weeks net per year available for moves manage-
           ment and support

During each of those twenty-six weeks available for the management of moves, at least one full day will be spent on various kinds of meetings. This leaves us with

        26 weeks per year
       × 4 days per week
       104 days net available per year per staff member
           assigned to moves management and support
       × 4 moves per day (3 may be more realistic)
       416 number of moves supported per staff member per
           year

Although calculations such as these are not precise, experience at institutions employing the moves concept in managing major gift fund-raising supports the conclusion that a major gift staff person can manage and support something on the order of 400 individual moves per year. However, another important factor comes into play before one can calculate the number of moves and the number of prospects for which an individual staff person can reasonably be considered responsible. Earlier in this chapter, background and foreground activities of fund-raising were described. The estimate of 400 per staff person pertains to moves individually planned and executed for specific prospects (foreground moves); however, major gifts prospects are also the beneficiaries of background moves (moves that stem from activities planned for groups of people). These moves are created from the type of activities listed as background activities earlier in this chapter. Such moves are likely to equal or perhaps exceed the foreground moves in number. Although they may be less tailored to the individual prospect, they are often more effective because they so frequently include the prospect's peers. They are also less demanding on the move manager's time because of the involvement of others responsible for the move-generating activity. Taking both background and foreground moves into account, the number of moves per staff member can reasonably be doubled to something on the order of 800 to 1,000. Based on a minimum of 12 moves per year per prospect, each major gift staff member can be responsible for approximately seventy to eighty prospects.

Whereas the short-term major gift fund-raising referred to at the beginning of this chapter—with its focus on solicitation with minimum cultivation—typically requires a prospect-to-staff ratio of 250 to 1, long-term major gift fund-raising—with its greater emphasis on the prospect's relationship and involvement with the institutions—will require much higher staff-to-prospect ratios. To dilute the prospect-to-staff ratio much beyond the 70 or 80 to 1 will erode the critical mass of fund-raising initiatives upon which the very largest gifts depend.

Selective Focus. Major gift fund-raising is costly, not only in the time it requires for management and support but also in the demands it makes on the time of key people: the president, trustees, volunteers, faculty, and administrators. Initiatives are also expensive—dinners, travel, special events, even chartered planes. In light of these costs, some choices have to be made. When making these choices, it is better to allocate resources to support adequate initiatives with a smaller number of prospects than to spread the same resources too thin.

Relationship to Other Fund-Raising. Major gift fund-raising takes place within the context of an institution's other fund-raising, organized along class, geographical, or project lines. Major gift fund-raising need not be separate from these other efforts; it can be coordinated with programs, such as reunion campaigns, to take advantage of their special strengths and appeal. This coordination, however, requires substantial communication in what is often a complex matrix organization. With the advance of computer-assisted prospect tracking systems, this coordination is now more feasible.

Prospect Tracking Systems

For many years, colleges and universities have been using computers to keep track of information about givers and prospective givers. However, it is only in recent years that institutions have developed what have become known as *prospect tracking systems,* as opposed to the more common prospect information systems. Because of their special relevance to the basic concepts of major gift fund-raising, prospect tracking systems deserve attention.

To understand prospect tracking systems, one must recognize that fund-raisers need two types of information about prospective givers: (1) biographical information and (2) a record of developments in the prospect's relationship with the institution. These two types of information are needed in different circumstances and with different frequency. As a result, the needed information is prepared in separate formats. The biographical data in a prospect information system typically include:

Name of prospect
Address(es)
Family
Business
Directorships and professional associations
Undergraduate activities

Campus interests
Other interests
Campus visits
Financial information
Bequest and trust information
Gifts to the institution
Significant gifts elsewhere
Primes and secondaries

In contrast, prospect tracking systems typically include:

Name of prospect
Who is assigned (prime, secondaries, staff)
Gift objective
Strategy
Recent history of initiatives
Next initiative

In 1978, John Hanselman, working with Bill Boardman and members of the Harvard University major gifts staff, developed the first computer-based system for keeping track of initiatives directed toward individual major gifts prospects. The Harvard staff created a significant breakthrough with their prospect tracking system. The advantages of this system include: a quick turn-around from input to output, a capability to sort information once recorded, and a facility for generating reports keyed to each user's need to know. Other institutions quickly recognized that the tracking system could be used to reorganize and facilitate major gift fund-raising along lines that took advantage of the potential of both the moves concept and the concept of primes and secondaries that G. T. Smith had developed years earlier. They recognized the potential a tracking system affords for conducting coordinated initiatives toward prospects who are at once involved with up to a dozen or more key individuals and several different departments or programs. They enable higher levels of coordination by keeping more key players (primes and secondaries) informed of plans and initiatives directed toward prospects in whom they have a common interest.

Whether tracking-system information is recorded manually or on computer, there is a need to accumulate the recent-history portion of that record to create a chronological history of the prospect's relationship with the institution. That history becomes a helpful resource in planning appropriate moves.

The distribution of tracking-system reports to primes and secondaries does more than help manage prospect initiatives. It raises in the consciousness of faculty, staff, and trustees a greater awareness of their role in fund-raising. An effective teaching device, the report serves as a dynamic record of the steps that lead to each major gift. Of course, discretion is required in the distribution of tracking-system reports. The information contained in them is often sensitive and confidential.

However they are used, tracking-system reports are becoming a basic tool for managing the quality, frequency, and coordination of the initiatives major gift fund-raising requires.

Summary

This chapter has focused on fund-raising geared toward top prospects from whom the institution hopes to receive its largest gifts. Emphasis is given to building a genuine relationship with them and to involving them in the life of the institution. This can be done best by the people who are naturally involved with the prospect regardless of their position—the primes and secondaries. A prospect tracking system functions as a basic tool to assist primes, secondaries, and staff in working together to develop the prospect's awareness, knowledge, caring, involvement, and sense of commitment that are essential steps toward major gift giving. Major gift fund-raising derives benefits from initiatives directed toward individual prospects as well as initiatives directed toward groups; in other words, in major gift fund-raising, background activities are as important as foreground activities.

Whatever the method of fund-raising, this is a business based on human values and relationships that require frequent, thoughtful, and caring attention.

References

Seymour, H. J. *Designs for Fund Raising.* New York: McGraw-Hill, 1966.

Smith, G. T. "The Development Program." In A. W. Rowland (gen. ed.), *Handbook of Institutional Advancement: A Practical Guide to College and University Relations, Fund Raising, Alumni Relations, Government Relations, Publications, and Executive Management for Continued Advancement.* (1st ed.) San Francisco: Jossey-Bass, 1977.

25

Bobbie J. Strand

Building a Donor Information Base

ை "Finders, keepers; losers, weepers" is a childish taunt that all too often describes the approach to prospect research and information storage in the institutional development operation. A fundamental need is to get the "finders" to share their information and the "losers" to commit themselves to an information system designed to store live data that effectively support the prospect cultivation and solicitation processes. The program of research and records must provide for the gathering, storing, retrieving, analyzing, and utilizing of information without being so overcome with the mechanics that the processing of facts becomes more important than using them. The goal of this program is to support the evaluation of individuals or organizations as prospective donors and to aid in the development of cultivation and solicitation strategies.

Prospect Research

Create a Prospect Pool. When organizing prospect records, the first move should be to survey existing constituencies. Trustees or directors, previous donors, alumni, former patients, ticket subscribers (in education, health care, and the arts), and staff are basic constituents. Others are family members of the basic constituents (including parents of students); prominent families or leaders in the community, state, or region; relatives, descendants, or friends of families or individuals prominent in the life of the institution; and known philanthropists in the area.

For foundation prospects, fund-raisers should survey those geographically nearby and identify those with philosophies and interests compatible with those of the institution. Foundations that carry the name of, employ, or have on their board of directors individuals directly or indirectly affiliated with the institution are prospects. A systematic perusal of all sources, printed and otherwise, for foundations that might have matching interests should contribute to the prospect pool.

Major corporations headquartered nearby or with local subsidiaries or auxiliaries are the most approachable. Vendors or companies that do business with the institution are possible prospects. Entrepreneurial and privately held companies are a major force in the economy. Although acquiring the needed information about them is more difficult than it is for public companies, they should be included.

Development staff members alert to the names of possible individual, business, and foundation prospects can assist greatly in the maintenance of a "fresh water" pool of prospects.

Early Prospect Screening. Early in the process, it is necessary to refine the enormous numbers in the prospect pool into more and less likely prospects. This refinement might be called the halving principle. The goal is to identify the prospects with the greatest financial capacity. To develop usable information, the numbers have to be small enough for the researcher or research staff to handle. In varying degrees, the halving principle applies regardless of the size of the constituency.

Those most likely to have potential to make a major gift should be researched first. It is necessary to determine what constitutes a major gift for the institution. Depending on the size of the fund-raising goal and the development of the giving process among constituents, it might be $25,000, less, or more. For purposes of this chapter, $50,000 is considered a major gift. The early screening process applies some general criteria to the prospect pool to assist in halving it or dividing it into smaller groups.

1. For individuals, 2.5 percent of liquid wealth, including salary, investments and holdings easily converted to cash, and short-term investments, is a possible outright gift (usually payable over three years). Major donor prospects (based on a major gift of $50,000) would have $2,000,000 in liquid assets. In this early evaluation of financial worth, the obvious criteria are business, family names that suggest inherited wealth, zip code of residence, known holdings, and life-style. The knowledge that staff and other advisers among volunteers and in the financial community have of the prospect should also be considered, even though it will need to be tested later in the process.

2. For corporations, one-tenth of 1 percent of annual gross sales should be a reasonable gift. By this standard, a corporation would need to report annual gross sales of $50 million to generate a $50,000 gift. Obviously, in every category, the level of interest and involvement can raise or lower the percentages rather dramatically.

3. Foundations are one of the easiest types of prospects to screen because giving activity, interests, and persons involved are public information. Early screening may be accomplished by dividing the foundations into groups according to size of gifts they make, interests of the organization, and persons involved in operating them.

Because the prospect pool is always being fed, the early screening process is never-ending. However, once staff has screened the basic constituency of the institution, the research task becomes more manageable. If enough information is available at this time, a preliminary capability rating is possible. This rating will become more precise as the prospect moves through research.

Development of Prospect Information. One of the major problems in major donor research is that most files contain too much of the wrong kind of information and too few vital data. Quality of information, rather than quantity, should always be the emphasis. Prospect research should deal with these issues:

1. What is this prospect's financial giving capacity?
2. How interested in this institution, or similar institutions, is the prospect?

3. What particular project important to the institution is the prospect most likely to care about?
4. Who can influence the prospect to give to this institution for this purpose at this time?

    The sources of information are the lifeblood of a research operation, but here again, the quality is more important than the quantity. A volume should be used often to earn a place on the researcher's shelves. A reasonable, orderly progression when doing research will save time and enhance the quality of the data.

1. Determine what is known. The researcher should examine in-house files exhaustively and interview persons within the institution who may have memory-held information.
2. Check printed sources. It is not necessary to own everything possibly needed at some time. Survey nearby libraries, professional offices, city and county buildings, and neighboring similar institutions for resources. An attorney might agree to share his Martindale and Hubbell directories on occasion. Resource and business libraries or divisions can be especially helpful. Printed sources cannot be current because of the time lapse in preparation; check by telephone, if necessary, to ascertain current data.
3. Magazines and newspapers give more current information than other printed sources, but often it is not as carefully documented. File 411 on the "Dialog System" is helpful in finding sources of current information. "Dialog" is an electronic data base system available from Dialog Information Services, Inc., whose address is listed with other information sources at the end of this chapter.
4. Staff review and interview with individuals who know the prospect will contribute specific information and will also often provide clues that will help the researcher uncover key sources of pertinent data.

    Creative use of information available to the public in local, state, and government offices will often add the ingredient most necessary to the success of the solicitation. Some useful public records are wills (available to the public while in probate), which can be used to help determine inherited wealth, and property records in the tax assessor's office. A list of publishers and corporations that provide material important to research is included at the end of this chapter.

The researcher cannot be successful without a careful pacing and balancing of the work load. One great help in this is the identification of the kind of research needed. The goal should always be to produce enough information—neither too many unnecessary facts nor too few facts to answer the important questions. The following levels can be used as guidelines:

Level 1: Basic information. Name, address, telephone, minimal family and business information, institutional affiliation.

Level 2: Biographical sketch. Basic information plus career track, major interests, more family information, giving patterns, relationships with institution, and estimate of financial worth, all from in-house files and printed sources.

Level 3: Complete summary of all available data. All of the above, with the addition of information from sources outside the institution, government records, interviews, and the like. An analysis of the information that will assist the development of a cultivation and solicitation strategy may also be included.

In summary, the goal is never merely to know about a prospect, but as far as is possible, to know the prospect as a whole person and to relate that prospect to the advancement goals. This complete picture will be source- and date-documented and will include:

1. Accurate, current, basic information
2. An accurate as possible estimate of the financial worth, adjusted as new information is received
3. Ways in which the prospect uses his or her wealth
4. Suggestions for strategy for leading the prospect in developing a positive relationship with the institution

5. Giving capacity, considering other obligations and liquidity of assets
6. Interests about which the prospect demonstrates care
7. Particular projects important to the institution that match the interests of the prospect
8. Persons who can influence the prospect to give to this institution for this purpose at this time

If the prospect is well known by members of the institutional advancement staff, level 1 research might be enough to assist them in completing the picture of the prospect. If not, add level 2 or portions of it. Once a prospect has been established as one with major capacity, level 3 might be needed to assist in the development of strategy.

It is important to assign a clear, concise financial capability rating. This may change several times as more becomes known about the prospect. Some institutions use rather complicated point systems to assign a gift propensity rating. An easier method is to organize prospects into levels of solicitation readiness. This will be a major tool in setting the priority for cultivation strategy.

Prospect Management Systems

The prospect management system is designed to help organize major gift prospects and provide the senior development officer with a tool with which to monitor and influence prospect contacts. The system should:

1. Track and coordinate cultivation and solicitation progress of every major donor prospect
2. Identify at any given time the prospects who are the most ready to make a major gift
3. Provide an active file with tickler and review systems, for new major donor prospect names

A priority system based on solicitation readiness will assist in identifying the most important prospects at the moment. These should be reviewed by the staff and assigned for the appropriate level of cultivation and solicitation. The following numbers of major donor prospects are based on a constituent base of approximately 20,000.

Priority 1 (Goal: about 50 prospects)

1. Assigned for immediate intense cultivation
2. Reviewed by staff every two weeks
3. Solicitation expected within six months
4. Interest and financial capability reasonably certain
5. No major problems in the relationship

Priority 2 (Goal: about 100 prospects)

1. Assigned for immediate moderate cultivation and reviewed every month
2. Solicitation expected within six to eighteen months
3. Interest and financial capability may need refining
4. Relationship probably needs strengthening

Priority 3 (Goal: at least 200 prospects)

1. Assigned for beginning serious cultivation
2. Reviewed every two months
3. Solicitation expected within nineteen to thirty-six months
4. Major interests probably unknown, and capability estimated
5. Relationship is probably weak, or there are other problems

Priority 4 (Goal: at least 100 prospects)

1. Not yet specifically assigned; may need further research or may have recently made major gift
2. Reviewed every three to six months
3. Time for further solicitation not yet set
4. Areas of interest and capability probably need serious research
5. As more specific solicitation goals are set, prospects will be moved to other priorities

Two calendars helpful in the tracking process and most effective on the word processor are

1. *The cultivation calendar,* which is used in coordinating planned institutional activities with the known interests of prospects
2. *The foundation/corporate calendar,* which provides a reminder of foundation and corporate proposal review dates, dates of expected contacts, and reporting schedules

New prospect names should always be introduced at priority 1 review meetings unless enough is known about the prospect to set a solicitation date. Names will be placed in lower priority unless staff can defend the readiness for priority 1.

A report document should be produced following the staff review sessions. It gives each staff member a record of all assignments made at the review meeting. An effective procedure is to put the document on a word processor and simply update changes. Suggested report headings are as follows:

Date   Prospect   Assigned to   Contact   Date   Result   Next Step

The first date (the date of the assignment) never changes until the staff person reports the result in the review session. This becomes a meaningful tool in measuring which members of the staff are making contacts and also which individual prospects have been without contact. It is a tool of self-discipline that automatically calls attention to staff assignments not fulfilled without any person having to bring it to the attention of the group. If assignments are made to volunteers, they should always be made through a staff person, with staff having responsibility for setting appointments and reporting results. The next step becomes another line item as it is developed.

Data elements needed for prospect management tracking, whether computerized or in hard copy, can be diversified according to the specific style and needs of the operation. However, the following are some of the basic elements:

1. *Status.* This is the step in the cultivation process at which the prospect is at a given time. Codes should reflect personal and institutional style, but here are some suggestions:
   - Possible prospect—needs research and screening
   - In cultivation process
   - Assignment made for solicitation (amount and purpose of gift have been determined)
   - Solicited, no decision made
   - Solicited, decision made (gift amount will illustrate whether successful or not)
2. *Priority rating.* This is solicitation readiness, explained in detail earlier.
3. *Capability rating.* This is the prospect's financial capability and should have as its bottom level the lowest amount the institution considers to be a major gift.
   - $2,500,000 and above
   - 1,000,000–2,500,000
   - 500,000–1,000,000
   - 250,000–500,000
   - 100,000–250,000
   - 50,000–100,000
4. *Date of last contract*
5. *Solicitor assigned*
6. *Action code.* This list should be tailored to fit the needs of the institution, and can be shortened or lengthened.
   - HV—Home visit
   - OV—Office visit
   - LU—Lunch
   - DI—Dinner
   - LE—Letter
   - PH—Phone call
7. *New status*
8. *Date of next action*
9. *Next solicitor assigned*
10. *Next action code*
11. *Comment field.* Narrative for particular discussion. If the information is computerized, this should be a minimum of sixty-three characters.
12. *Update.* This is the date this information was added to the record.

If this information is on computer, there should be room to add a limitless number of entries for these twelve items in the contact report.

Three major reports that should be maintained by research for the development officers are

1. *Prospect profile.* This is a report of level 1, 2, or 3 research in a consistent format that is acceptable to and usable by all of the development officers.
2. *Prospect tracking.* This is a report of all contacts with the prospect, the data elements for which are outlined above.
3. *Staff prospect review report.* This is the document that is produced following review sessions; it includes assignments for the next period of time.

To be able to get a complete picture of a prospect and that prospect's status, the development office should be able to access the prospect profile and tracking reports together.

Records and Reporting

Good storage of information is vital to the research process. In-house data are the most easily accessed, the most personalized to the institution, and the only source that can document the relationship of the prospect to the institution. Guidelines for information storage:

1. Centralize files as much as possible.
2. Avoid creating duplicate files, except one set, which should be stored for security. Duplicate files will never be updated consistently, and this will create confusion about the prospect status.
3. Establish firm guidelines for the use of the files; guidelines should include security measures and check-out procedures.
4. If development officers need working files, make copies of documents and label them *do not file* so the master file will not be cluttered with duplicates.

5. Insist that every document filed have a date and source documentation. This should include newspaper clippings, photographs, and other special items in the file.
6. Set up document filing procedures. Usually in an alphabetical file, material in the folders should be in chronological order, with the most recent addition at the front of the file.
7. Designate someone in the office as file manager to make sure guidelines are followed.
8. Insist that all development officers keep filing up to date. A Friday filing rule might be established, stipulating that no one leaves on Friday until that week's filing is finished.
9. Routing procedures for material that needs to be reviewed by various staff members before filing should be monitored to make sure the information is added to the file in a timely fashion.
10. Create a schedule for file cleaning and maintenance.

If the development office is using a combination of information storage mediums, such as hard copy and computer, one must become the official source document. Usually, this will be the computer. This simply means that basic information, names, addresses, telephone numbers, and other pertinent elements will be added to, or changed first on, the computer. The computer information, in this case, will be the most current and should be used over all other sources.

Summary

It is important that information flow in both directions between the researcher and the development officers. Sophisticated record keeping and data management cannot keep their promises unless all viable information is available. When development officers request research on any prospect, an indication of how much they already know, or specific information if it is available, may save the researcher many hours of searching.

The following are helpful guidelines for successful relationships between the researcher and the development officer:

1. Communicate clearly to the researcher the kind of information needed about the prospect and the purpose of the report.
2. Share any information already available.
3. Give clear datelines indicating when the finished report is needed.
4. Provide enough lead time for the researcher to have the satisfaction of doing quality work.
5. Report the results of contacts to the researcher so the information can continue to build.

Keep research in perspective! It is intended to lead to solicitation of funds and success in converting major donor prospects into major donors.

Sources of Information

American Council on
   Education
One Dupont Circle, Suite 30
Washington, D.C. 20036
(206) 833-4700

Boyd's City Dispatch (donor
   and other lists)
Upper Main Street, Box 1087
Sharon, Conn. 96960
(203) 364-0614

Council for Financial Aid to
   Education
680 Fifth Avenue
New York, N.Y. 10019
(212) 541-4050

Council for Advancement and
   Support of Education
11 Dupont Circle, Suite 400
Washington, D.C. 20036
(202) 328-5900

Dialog Information Services,
   Inc.
3460 Hillview Avenue
Palo Alto, Calif. 94304
1-800-982-5838 (California)
1-800-227-1927 (Outside
   California)

Disclosure, Inc.
5161 River Road
Washington, D.C. 20016
(301) 951-1350

Donors Forum
208 South LaSalle Street
Chicago, Ill. 60604
(312) 726-4877

Dun and Bradstreet
99 Church Street
New York, N.Y. 10007
(212) 285-7000

Fund-Raising Institute
Box 365
Ambler, Pa. 19002
(215) 975-1120

Gale Research Company
Book Tower
Detroit, Mich. 48226
(313) 961-2242

The Grantsmanship Center
1031 South Grand Avenue
Los Angeles, Calif. 90015
(213) 749-4721

Public Services Materials Center
111 North Central Avenue
Hartsdale, N.Y. 10530
(914) 949-2242

Resource Development, Inc.
   (research for planned giving)
Three Corporate Square, Suite
   3-100
Springfield, Mo. 65804
(417) 882-7777

Standard & Poor's Corporation
25 Broadway, P.O. Box 992
New York, N.Y. 10004
(800) 221-5277

Taft Corporation
5125 MacArthur Boulevard
Washington, D.C. 20016
(202) 966-7086

26

John J. Schwartz

Role and Selection
of Professional Counsel

◆ Fund-raising is not a science but an art. It deals with a field in which the methods and problems are increasingly complex. To be effective, a fund-raising manager must have access to many different skills. Effective professional counsel has grown with these developments and includes staff who can deal with many specialties. In addition to the thirty member firms of the American Association of Fund-Raising Counsel (AAFRC), there are a number of reliable, reputable, and experienced counseling firms that are not members. Most of them, however, follow the AAFRC's Fair Practice Code (American Association of Fund-Raising Counsel, 1984). Developed from many years of experience and designed to give maximum protection to client institutions, the code is useful as a guide in the selection of professional fund-raising counsel:

Fair Practice Code of the American Association of Fund-Raising Counsel

1. Members of the Association are firms whose primary business is providing consulting and management service and raising funds for philanthropic organizations. They will not knowingly be used by an organization to induce philanthropically inclined persons to give their money to unworthy causes.

2. While the association does not prescribe any particular method of calculating fees for its members, the organization should base its fees on services provided and avoid contracts providing for contingency, commissions, or a percentage of funds raised for the client.

The organization should base its fees on high standards of service, and should not profit, directly or indirectly, from materials or services billed to the client by a third party. Member firms will not offer or provide the services of professional solicitors.

3. The executive head of a member organization must demonstrate at least a six-year record of continuous experience as a professional in the fundraising field. This helps to protect the public from those who enter the profession without sufficient competence, experience, or devotion to ideals of public service.

4. The association looks with disfavor upon firms which use methods harmful to the public, such as making exaggerated claims of past achievements, guaranteeing results, and promising to raise unobtainable sums.

5. No payment in cash or kind shall be made by a member to an officer, director, trustee, or adviser of a philanthropic agency or institution as compensation for using his or her influence for the engaging of a member for fund-raising counsel.

6. In fairness to all clients, member firms should charge equitable fees for all services with the exception that initial meetings with prospective clients are not usually construed as services.

When a college or university is ready to consider a major development program for capital improvements, professional counsel will almost always recommend a precampaign study (often called a development planning study or a feasibility study) to minimize guesswork and maximize the chances of a program's success. This study is an examination of the institution's fund-raising capital potential, which must be sufficient if the program is to prove feasible. As Harold J. Seymour (1966, p. 173) said, "The function of the professional firm is not to raise the money, but to help you raise it."

An institution can reach its potential if it has the five essentials of case, leadership, volunteers, cultivated constituency, and campaign dynamics; but their strength must be tested in an objective study to determine whether a projected campaign goal is feasible. The study is important at this stage because it helps set priorities and determines the most important needs, it delineates program responsibilities for leadership, and it motivates the administrative staff and all others concerned with the institution before the campaign is launched.

Because a counseling firm does not guarantee results or promise to achieve unattainable goals, the feasibility study sets the pattern for both counsel and the client institution. A firm brings an objective point of view and its accumulated experience to bear on the problems that usually occur, sometimes unpredictably, in any major program. The firm's knowledge is gained from a variety of campaigns, and it does not attempt to solve major problems on a solo basis. Usually, the assigned director will consult with a supervisor and a group of officers in the firm to obtain a solution based on their collective experience.

In some cases, the precampaign study process, which usually includes personal interviews, may be combined with specific actions essential to a successful campaign. Such actions include identification of matching grants. In any case, the client should rely on the firm's judgment as to the type of study and elements to be included. The extent of the possible philanthropic market for an institution must be assessed, and the capabilities of the volunteers and the leadership who will be advancing the campaign must be equal to the task.

The study begins with interviews of key individuals who represent areas of philanthropic support or who can objectively assess the relationship of the institution to its peer groups. From 25 to 100 or more individuals are interviewed in person and on a confidential basis. They include trustees, parents, alumni, executives of foundations who have a record of interest in programs of similar institutions, business leaders, leaders of the community in which the campus is located, and individuals in leadership roles with related and competitive institutions.

Interviewers normally ask questions like the following: What is the general setting against which a case for this particular college or university must be formulated? (This is a review of the field represented by the institution—whether it be private or state supported, small or large.) How well is the institution serving its constituencies? What do the leaders really feel and think about the institution? What do leaders, representative alumni, or staff have to say under the protective cloak of confidentiality? When such people are given the opportunity to speak frankly, what do they see as the real strengths and weaknesses of the institution? What past efforts have been made to assess the case? Are the problems recognized? In the past, have key individuals supported the institution to the extent they should? What is the fund-raising track record of the institution? What is the state of the development office? Will it be an asset in a major campaign or a liability?

Relationships of the college or university to the community are examined. Troublesome areas must be clearly defined. Leadership that will commit itself to the program must be identified. The principal sources of funds must be examined, and the potential leadership gifts have to be identified. Without pace-setting contributions, no major effort has a chance. Also assessed are any specific qualifications that should be made known before a major campaign is presented to public view. This study process can take between three and six months, but it establishes the feasibility of the institution's goals and needs.

The key officers of the professional fund-raising counseling firm then plan the development program, including the goal, the time needed to raise the money, the phases of the campaign (often set up for a one-, two-, or three-year period), the type of staff needed within the institution, the budget (professional counsel is experienced at estimating the cost of such an effort and staying with an agreed-upon budget), the role of the trustees (very important because if the trustees accept the findings and the recommendations of the feasibility study, they also agree to do their share in implementing the plan), the role of the key administrators, and finally, the role of professional counsel.

Conducting a feasibility study is a separate assignment that does not imply a future obligation to or relationship with a client. Most counseling firms offer these services as a separate counseling function, with no obligation on the part of the institution to retain the firm for further counsel or campaign direction.

After a study has been performed, the trustees often decide either not to proceed with the plan as it has evolved or not to use the professional counseling firm that performed the study. Sometimes they hire another firm to implement the findings, although in such a case, the second firm will usually choose to do further review on its own. Sometimes the feasibility study shows that the institution is not ready to go into a major program until certain improvements have been made within the institution and in its activities, and the trustees do not always accept this professional judgment. But when an established professional counsel makes a recommendation not to go into a development program, the client should listen attentively. Firms that are not really professional may say that the institution can raise the kind of money it wishes to raise, just to obtain a client.

Implementing the development plan advocated by the feasibility study requires a high quality of professional activity on the part of both counsel and development staff. Together, they need to avoid or solve such problems as:

1. A too-rigid, military-type table of organization
2. A preoccupation with trivia, which can cause them to lose sight of the important objectives
3. An incomplete research program—for example, a file of names and addresses of alumni without data on current interests, career achievements, or directorships of corporations and foundations
4. Not enough field trips planned; too many important prospects not called on
5. Too heavy a staff orientation, especially in solicitations (although staff specialists can often provide invaluable

assistance, informed, motivated volunteers are the certain way to get maximum gifts)

6. Not enough volunteer input and participation (staff must encourage volunteers to be active)

7. Lack of recognition of the many other priorities of volunteers

8. Lack of organized staff work, which results in wasted volunteer time

9. Donors not given adequate recognition

10. Enlisting persons for key positions who are not representative of top leadership

11. Approaches for gifts that fall short of carefully screened leadership levels

12. Neglecting to keep key people—the president, board chair and members, and deans—fully informed of the fund-raising progress and needs

13. Taking for granted the constituency's knowledge of an institution's program and objectives. Remember, efforts to improve communications must be continual.

There are some things a professional fund-raising counseling firm cannot do and thus must expect the institution to do for itself. For example, a program must be designed to fulfill proven needs. The firm will not accept an institution as a client unless it has committed leaders who are both influential and affluent. The institution must have a developed constituency, volunteers to work on a development program, and an audience aware of the importance of its programs and needs. The institution's goals and objectives must be realistic.

Professional counsel will not relieve top leadership or key administrators of responsibilities for the success of the program, nor, in fact, will counsel make their jobs any easier. Good professional counsel will make top people work harder than they would otherwise. Except in the rarest circumstances, professional counsel will not solicit gifts directly. Moreover, if a program is not proceeding at the proper pace and too many problems are unsolved, counsel will be the first to suggest that a contract be canceled or postponed or that the firm's services be reduced both in scope and in fee. Finally, although professional counsel cannot provide any magic formulas, they can show how everyone involved can work to obtain maximum results.

Effective counsel will help appraise potential and sharpen priorities. If they advise that a college can raise only a certain number of dollars, leadership can then decide how the money can be spent most profitably for the institution. Counsel will identify strengths and weaknesses and, wherever possible, will help build a program to convert weaknesses into strengths. They will set up the conditions for action. Their efforts will be focused both on getting the board of trustees to support a program and commit themselves to soliciting major gifts and on enlisting leadership to give the program the proper launching pad. Counsel will provide their collective and broad experience with similar programs. Problems that arise will be tackled by a group of the firm's officers who, in the aggregate, have many times the experience of any individual on staff.

Counsel project costs and maintain rigid budget controls. They also provide the plan for the program (schedules, quotas, goals, deadlines, and the structure of the development organization). They help the leadership organize top volunteers into the most effective committees for important solicitation. They work carefully with the institution's staff to support the efforts of volunteers. Members of the counseling firm backstop staff and strengthen their position and their ability to work effectively after counsel has left the scene. Finally, an effective, professional counseling firm has its own reputation at stake each time it engages in a major program. What former clients say about its professionalism can be one of the firm's most important assets. This leads to further business.

The firm wants to keep costs low and clients not only satisfied but also pleased with the services rendered. One college president who was served well by a firm commented that the firm wanted to see that the institution got "money without regrets." The institution not only needs the funds it has set out to raise but also wants to enhance its reputation with its constituency as much as possible.

What are the costs of engaging fund-raising counsel? The second item in the AAFRC's Fair Practice Code states, "While the association does not prescribe any particular method of calculating fees for its members, the organization should base its fees on services provided and avoid contracts providing for contingency, commissions, or a percentage of funds raised for the client." There are good reasons for this. A standard percentage fee on an especially large campaign might be too much compensation for the services provided. A percentage fee might lead to some reports of unconfirmed commitments or might encourage a counselor to settle for a small, immediate gift from a prospect who, if carefully cultivated over a long time, might have donated many times the gift in hand.

For these reasons, the fees are based primarily on the number of hours the counseling firm's personnel apply to the client's program. The development planning study gives a professional judgment on just how extensive (and therefore how much) these services should be. The fee, therefore, is specified in advance and agreed on by both parties. Because most of the programs conducted by professional counseling firms are for major goals, the costs are remarkably small. An example: Since 1980, twenty-one colleges and universities served by AAFRC member companies raised $303,129,000 for an average fee that equaled .06 percent of the total raised.

Basic services provided vary with client needs. Professional counsel provides many services, but these three are typical:

1. A resident director for the major portion of the campaign (this service always includes the part-time supervision by an officer of the firm)
2. Per diem counseling by an officer of the firm who works with an experienced development officer and staff
3. On-call counseling by an officer of the firm, a service most used during the early build-up phase of planning a major program or as a follow-up when tying up loose ends

Well-established, effective firms offer further appropriate and useful services. One of these is to conduct an advancement audit, which differs from the traditional feasibility planning development study in two distinctive ways: (1) it focuses more on the internal management of development management affairs, and (2) it does not include interviewing many donors and potential donors as is done in a feasibility study. The advancement audit seeks to review the institution's written plan for each year; its long-range plan, if there is one; exactly how development staff members manage their office and programs; how they screen and evaluate major gifts prospects; their systems relationships between the administration, the board of trustees, and the development office; and how they market their case.

Another service is to develop a prospect management system by evaluating how the institution screens and evaluates major prospects. With the use of a computer, prospects are tracked to answer such vital questions as: When was any previous solicitation effort made? When is the next action planned, and by whom? Which staff member is assigned to track each major prospect? How is that prospect rated, not only in dollar potential but also in degree of interest and readiness? In the case of a large institution, which school or college has priority on what prospect at that point in time?

Consulting firms often assist in strengthening the annual fund. The base of the annual fund is inevitably broadened during the well-planned capital program. This has a positive effect on increasing the yield of the annual fund, not only during the time of the capital program but also after its completion. As with a capital program, counsel can provide objectivity and broad experience in planning and stimulating more effective organized solicitation for the annual fund.

A number of consulting firms provide specific services for executive search in hiring and are prepared to help in this important area. Through relationships with a number of institutions, counsel has access to potential candidates and can measure the professional potential of candidates against the background of broad experience in development programs.

Effective counseling firms fully recognize the critical importance of assigning residence staff that will be compatible with the institution, its administrators, and its leadership. Counsel, therefore, gives careful attention to this selection and makes a potential staff member available for visits and interviews before the final assignment is confirmed. Remember, consultants desire good results as much as the institution and therefore will conscientiously draw upon the best and most appropriate staff available.

Most counseling firms provide ancillary and support services, such as publications, use of computer technology, writing special presentations and campaign brochures, foundation and prospect research, management services to help set up the campaign office, prospect files, and gift acknowledgments. Most professional firms also refuse to set up a long-term contract with a client even if the client wants one. Thirty to sixty days is the average span in which either party can cancel the arrangement. Counsel is usually the first to say that the campaign is not going as planned and that it will be far better for the client to be disengaged at this point or that the services should be cut to a level that keeps costs within reason.

Reputable firms serve only worthy projects that offer the prospect of fund-raising success, and the client should make sure a firm can offer this success by examining its track record. How does an institution select the best fund-raising counsel for its program?

To verify the qualifications of any firm, fund-raising managers should follow the same good business practices used in choosing a legal or tax counsel, an architect, or any other professional service. The best method is to ask each of the firms being considered to provide a list of its clients and then speak directly to the clients. Some questions one might ask the former clients include: What is your evaluation of the firm's services? Did the firm provide a reasonable estimate of fund-raising costs? Would you engage the firm again for a similar program?

For a number of reasons, an institution should consider three or four counseling firms. Discussing program and plans with them helps bring into focus both the needs and the feasibility of the projected program. These interviews will in no way obligate a potential client. This is a personal business, and there are many reasons one might prefer one company over another.

Finally, everyone—both employees of a college or university development staff and development managers of professional counseling firms—should always remember that this is really a people business. The most precious commodity is volunteers' and leaders' time. Professionals must assume a positive stance and motivate these people for action. Sometimes this can be an uphill battle. A volunteer does not have the incentive of a paycheck and is often discouraged because things are moving too slowly or intimidated by outside factors. But if an institution observes the essentials, it can raise money even under adverse circumstances.

References

American Association of Fund-Raising Counsel, Inc. "By-Laws of the American Association of Fund-Raising Counsel, Inc." May 1984.

Seymour, H. J. *Designs for Fund Raising.* New York: McGraw-Hill, 1966.

27

James W. Frick

Educational Philanthropy:
A Perspective of
Three Decades

During my more than three decades of experience in the field of advancement for higher education, our country, higher education, and educational philanthropy have all changed greatly. Even greater changes are on the horizon.

Our population continues to grow. The percentage of older Americans is greater than in earlier years. They have more wealth, but affluence is no longer confined to middle age and beyond. Entrepreneurs in the computer industry are only one example of younger citizens who have attained substantial wealth at an early age because of technological advances. The computer companies collectively have already surpassed the automobile industry in sales, and it is predicted that, before the turn of the century, computer sales volume will be greater than that of the oil industry. And even while this is happening, the years immediately ahead will bring additional technological developments and discoveries that will even eclipse the computer era in which we live. It remains true, however, that even with the same resources, an older person is more likely to support eleemosynary institutions to a larger degree than a younger person on the way up. This would seem to argue for different educational and cultivation processes for those people of affluence who are in their early forties or less.

Whether young or old, just about everyone with substantial resources is affected by the tax consequences of a gift. There are perennial attempts to erode the deductibility of gifts on the federal income tax return. But in my estimation, the principle of gift deductibility will continue to survive at least until the year 2000. I do not believe that Congress can afford to shoot Santa Claus.

Just take a searching look around the country. It will become abundantly clear that those areas of our national life that are most reflective of our humanity, that are most illustrative of our religious and cultural heritage, that best exemplify our most important civilizing influences, that demonstrate our love and concern and compassion for our fellow human beings were made possible, to a very large degree, by philanthropy. These institutions include our private educational institutions from kindergarten through research universities, our libraries and symphony orchestras, our museums and hospitals, our operas and art centers, our churches and synagogues, our great service organizations and much of the medical research, the United Way, and on and on and on.

How much poorer we would be as a people without our generosity to one another! The federal tax form 1040-A recognizes this. Its contributions section, lines 17 through 20, acknowledges the intent of Congress that American citizens should be encouraged to make gifts to not-for-profit institutions that they freely choose to support. The taxpayer has no such latitude or control over any other section of the tax form. Having said that, I feel obliged to make one observation: I have never seen a person sacrifice to make a contribution. People contribute only that portion of their income that will not infringe in any way on their standards of living. In order to make a substantial gift, it is not likely that a donor is going to trade down from a Buick to a Chevrolet or give up a summer home or mount a garage sale.

The flat tax, or gross income tax, is an idea growing in popularity, whose time may arrive in the foreseeable future. I am inclined to think, however, that even if the flat tax were to become law there would be a provision for charitable contributions as a separate deduction in order to sustain and encourage philanthropy in our national life.

Earlier, I referred to computers and the way they are affecting our lives. They can also be expected to affect, to an even greater extent than at present, the way we development people work. For example, the computer is fast becoming the indispensable tool in identifying and researching prospects. When a college or university enlists four thousand volunteers for a capital campaign, using a computer to keep track of them beats using typed lists and three-by-five file cards by a mile. Your friendly campus mainframe can be like a private detective, tracking gifts and reminding you when it is time to give donors an account of your stewardship in administering their benefactions. The computer, by helping segment benefactors at various gift levels and degrees of involvement and association with the institution, can be helpful in devising a multifaceted cultivation program. In short, the development professional who does not comprehend the role of the computer in his or her work life will be akin to an old-fashioned icebox or a Model T—fit for a museum.

Another technological innovation bound to affect college and university advancement professionals and their work is the complex of communications devices epitomized by the satellite. In my judgment, electronic communications are going to change the way we work as much as the way television and satellite transmissions are changing politics and political campaigns. Today, we have mass fund-raising mailings, and we rush from city to city to present the case for our institutions and to generate gifts. And no matter how hard we try, we reach only a fraction of the institution's alumni and friends during any given year. Theoretically at least, a satellite overhead will make it possible to reach every member of our several constituencies; an alumni body of tens of thousands will become as easy to reach as the local alumni club. A campus satellite uplink may become as familiar as Old Main or the student union. The question is this: Are we elders in college development work able and willing to shift gears to take advantage of this new technology? Not many of us have any expertise in what amounts to television programming; the same could be said for faculty members. And the age of satellite transmission presents such a fantastic opportunity for continuing education of alumni. Can the professor, who is wedded to the fifty-minute lecture in the classroom, shift gears and operate effectively in a television studio before an unseen audience accustomed to sophisticated TV personalities? The potential of contemporary communications technology, then, presents challenges to the university's academic enterprise as well as to the public relations and development offices.

In this fast-moving world of computers and satellites, I am reminded that, in the case of two of the most important engagements of life, parenthood and philanthropy, there is at least one similarity: Both are activities for which there is little formal educational preparation. Although some colleges and universities have courses, programs, and even majors in communications, public relations, and advertising as well as marketing, psychology, and business administration, I am not aware of any undergraduate major to prepare men and women to become professional practitioners in the field of educational philanthropy. Among the fields or academic disciplines in which a professional development person should be well oriented are history of education, history of philanthropy, psychology and sociology, writing and speech, management, taxation, finance, computer science, economics, and investments. Clearly, the effective advancement person must draw on a considerable cluster of academic fields in order to be effective and successful in this work.

Along with that broad educational background and certain specific expertise, the successful development person of the twenty-first century will have to possess those individual characteristics commonly termed magnetic personal qualities—the ability to empathize and identify with others: "to walk in their shoes," to quote the old Indian phrase. All the academic preparation in the world will not change a retiring, shy introvert into a person who is really good at securing substantial gifts and commitments. The most effective advancement people I know have an absolute zest for fund-raising. To this individual, the prospective benefactor is like a battle to be won, a stream to be forded, a mountain to be climbed. What is called for, by and large, is an extrovert—a person comfortable with other people, whether in crowds or one at a time. The most effective persons in our field literally live fund-raising. The campaign never really ends. The challenge continues.

Work in the college and university advancement field can be exhilarating one day and depressing the next. I have witnessed great surprises—among them, an unsolicited $10 million gift for scholarships from an elderly, retired secretary in Rochester, New

York, who followed some good investment advice from her boss. And I have suffered through terrible disappointments from people who spent a lifetime accepting the university's hospitality and association but who never experienced the thrill of giving. Recently I asked a person for a commitment of $100 million for Notre Dame. After much conversation he agreed to try to work out such a gift. That evening we went to dinner with his wife. At just the proper moment, I said: "Jim, $100 million is a fantastic sum of money. What you and Mary are considering is unduplicated in the annals of Notre Dame and has happened only once to my memory in the history of higher education." (I was thinking of the Woodruff benefaction to Emory University.) "Why in the name of heaven," I continued, "would a person consider giving away $100 million?" After reflecting for a moment or two, he answered simply and slowly, "Because I need a touch of immortality!" Think of the power in that statement. Giving, particularly to a college with a religious affiliation, can have a dimension that is literally out of this world!

Along with the academic background and certain personality traits, the ideal development person is balanced. I have seen development staffers who may have brought back the gift or pledge but who left a bad taste in the mouth of the benefactor. Pressure should not be one of our tactics. The end does not justify the means. The seasoned professional knows when the time is right to ask for the big gift and when to back off and recognizes that the gift or pledge grudgingly made under pressure will likely foreclose the more substantial benefaction down the road. Solid academic preparation, an outgoing articulate personality, balance, initiative, integrity, and maturity, then, are among the components the successful development professionals of the future will bring to their work.

Although development professionals devote themselves entirely to institutional advancement, they will look increasingly to colleagues of the administration and faculty as well as volunteers for assistance. With development a notoriously mobile field in which many professionals spend only two or three years on any one campus, members of the institution's top administration can provide the thread of continuity and stability to benefactor-campus relationships. Associated as I am with a university whose founding religious community has been a presence of 142 years and whose president and executive vice-president have been in office for 32 years, I hope you will understand and accept my partisanship for continuity. In the case of my own institution, there are benefactors and prospects whose relationship with the campus had been entrusted to someone outside the development office. Of course, in multiyear capital campaigns, development contact at somewhat modest levels of giving must be assigned to volunteers. By and large, however, and particularly in the leadership gift areas, I contend that development work for a college or university is for those whose lives have been committed to the work of education and its advancement. I know that many universities, some of them among the most prestigious, have a different development philosophy. It works well for them, but whatever success I have enjoyed in advancement work has been based largely on large-gift solicitation by those people closest to the epicenter of the institution; this may be done, perhaps, in the company of volunteers, who may set the tone, but the case is articulated by the university representative.

I do not expect volunteers of themselves to bring big gifts and commitments back to the campus, but there are many ways in which nonprofessionals can contribute significantly to the general success of a campaign or an advancement program. Almost inevitably, the campaign chair is a volunteer whose work and professional background are far removed from the college development fund. Chances are, the same can be said of virtually all the key committee members with whom the chair is surrounded. So volunteers are important in the planning and execution of any important fund-raising endeavor. Another kind of volunteer is the couple who serve as hosts for a development-oriented function in their home or at their club. They may not personally raise money, but they provide the hospitable ambience in which others may do so. Volunteers also can pave the way for the big gifts by introducing a staff member to a prospect or by making an appointment to bring them together. If well trained, volunteers also can be effective telephone solicitors. They are, of course, indispensable in the identification, research, rating, and cultivation of prospects.

All in all, if I were a volunteer, I would expect the institution's professional development officer to assign me a task that I can do, about which I feel comfortable, that suits my talents, and that holds the promise of success for my effort. I would further expect to be told how the task is to be done and the time frame within which it is to be done and to be thanked when I had completed the task.

What about the magnitude of philanthropy as we move toward the year 2000? What may we expect from the various historic sources of philanthropy? I anticipate that the giving of individuals by the new millennium will be up 150 percent to 110 billion dollars. More people are acquiring more resources at an earlier age and are more willing to share those resources with those not-for-profit institutions with which they are associated. I predict that corporations will be increasingly generous, with contributions up 120 percent to almost 7 billion dollars. Corporation executives are demonstrating a greater social consciousness and are devoting time and corporate resources to those charitable organizations that are contributing meaningfully to the public welfare. This is particularly true in those areas where the quality of life of the corporations' employees is affected. Foundation grants, I believe, will experience a 100 percent increase to something in excess of 6 billion dollars. And although this will constitute a decreasing percentage of total philanthropy, it will remain a very crucial segment of it.

The greatest increase of support for higher education will come in the field of planned, or deferred, giving. With more people living longer, the United States will have an aging population. More elderly people will be consulting accountants and attorneys to determine the estate planning vehicles that best suit their situation, taking into account their heirs, the tax implications, and their philanthropic interests, among other considerations. With some colleges and universities garnering 40 percent or more of their support from bequests and other forms of planned giving, younger and less prestigious institutions will give greater attention to this fairly technical and sophisticated but increasingly important field. I foresee a 300 percent increase in planned giving to colleges and universities.

Sad to say, with all this predicted increase in philanthropy between now and the year 2000, it is a pronounced bittersweet situation. There will be more money for the support of our colleges and universities but fewer institutions to share it.

Will your institution receive its share of the philanthropic pie? That depends. It depends on these things, among others:

- The implementation of a comprehensive development program that embraces all the constituencies and all the programs of giving—annual, capital, ultimate, and deferred
- A continuous, careful, systematic planning process that provides an assessment of where you are, where you want to go, and the means by which you will get there
- An accurate determination of your constituency potential that permits the fashioning of a cultivation program for each leadership gift prospect appropriate to that prospect's relationship to the institution
- Your faithful adherence to the distinctive mission of the institution
- The continuity of programs and personal contact provided by the institutional advancement staff
- The intelligent use of volunteers in ways by which their talents are employed to advantage and from which they achieve a measure of satisfaction and fulfillment
- An annual forthright evaluation of the development operation, from people to programs
- Your accountability to benefactors for the effective use of the resources they have invested in the institution
- An ongoing educational program for all the constituencies that keeps them abreast of the reality of the institution today
- A willingness to employ the latest technologies that improve the effectiveness of the development program
- Fashioning a tripartite program of continuing education for all staff members aimed at improving their knowledge of higher education, their professionalism in the field of institutional advancement, and themselves as persons

- Establishing a reasonable set of expectations for each staff member and holding each responsible for the achievement thereof
- A small coterie of volunteers and administration/development people who find articulating the vision of the institution and inviting people to invest in it an ennobling experience for both themselves and the prospects

In any listing of a person's basic needs, the physiological requirements are generally of the lowest priority. Self-fulfillment is at the top of the ladder. So finally, your ability to generate funds for your institution as we look toward the twenty-first century will depend in some measure on your commitment to the field of institutional advancement, your commitment to your college or university, your need to serve a cause, and whether your primary reward for service is salary or self-fulfillment.

The vignette of Mark Hopkins sitting on one end of a log and his student on the other is a familiar one. Its counterpart in development would be the prospect on one side of the desk or lunch table or living room and the college representative on the other. Giving will continue to be primarily an emotional experience in the years to come, as it is now, but donors surely will be more sophisticated and more discriminating. They will want to know more about the institution and will certainly be more knowledge-able about the modes of giving. They will want to place their money where it will have the greatest impact for good as good is defined by their perceptions.

Major donors will know then, if they do not realize it already, that they belong to an elite group of the 5 percent of Americans who make fine institutions endure and good causes succeed. To identify such donors, to educate them about your institution, to involve them meaningfully in its affairs, and to commit them, first psychologically and eventually financially, to it calls for an elite development person—one who has the complete confidence of the president and who earns the complete confidence of the institution's benefactors. For the development person is the link, the liaison, the linchpin, the one who is crucial to the relationship between individual benefactors and the beneficiary institution. Such a role is a noble one in my judgment. It is worthy of dedicated men and women. It can, and should, be a vocation, even in a kind of religious sense. Not everyone is called to such work. Not everyone is suited for it. But for those who are called, it can lead to a very rewarding life. And remember, in this profession the best is not behind us. Indeed, it is yet to come.

Part Four

Alumni Administration: Building Institutional Support and Commitment

Gary A. Ransdell, Editor

28

Gary A. Ransdell

Understanding Professional Roles and Program Mission

alumni (a lum' ni) the plural of the term *alumnus,*
which describes a boy or man who has attended or
been graduated from a school, college, and so on.
Alumnae is the plural of the female counterpart,
alumna. Tradition has suggested common application of the word *alumni* in generic reference to an
institution's graduates and former students.

❧ The intent of the administration of activities relating to
alumni is distinctly twofold: to cultivate alumni to serve their
institution and to cultivate the institution to serve its alumni. The
ideal opportunity for service occurs when alumni and the
institution mutually agree that they are indebted to each other.

The profession of alumni administration predates almost all
the related professions described in this handbook. In fact, the
administration of matters relating to the alumni of U.S. colleges
and universities is clearly the forerunner and foundation of the
other components in the broader spectrum of institutional
advancement. Virtually every postsecondary institution in the
United States, beginning with its first graduation class, has
recognized the need to seek continued interaction with its former
students. This recognition has evolved into sophisticated forms of

communication, programming, and solicitation—the very essence of institutional advancement as we in American higher education uniquely administer it. Although most institutions include other constituencies in their advancement efforts, alumni have always been, and will continue to be, one of the primary audiences with whom positive relations must occur and from whom support must be obtained.

Historical Perspective

As early as 1643, former students of Harvard College began returning to commencement exercises to renew acquaintances with teachers and students. Yale, also established during the colonial period, recognized early in its history the importance of identification with one's class and of cultivation of spirit for the institution. The Yale custom for each class to appoint an alumni secretary began as early as 1792 (Brubacher and Rudy, 1976), but no formal alumni organization was established until much later. The first official, chartered alumni association was created at Williams College in 1821. It was called the Society of Alumni and was used to encourage alumni to return to campus for commencement.

The idea of an association of organized alumni immediately became popular with other colleges. It seemed logical that organized alumni could perpetuate the qualities and strengthen the weaknesses of an institution and, in so doing, add value to a degree earned at that institution. Some of the other early alumni organizations were established at Princeton University (1826), Miami University of Ohio (1832), University of Virginia (1837), Oberlin College (1839), Brown University (1842), Amherst College (1842), Columbia University (1854), and the University of Michigan (1860). By the late 1800s, more than 100 alumni organizations had been formed.

The purpose of these early alumni organizations was not unlike that of those in existence today. Their functions ranged from keeping undergraduate memories fresh to keeping intellectual interests alive, from enticing student patronage to soliciting support for alma mater. The initiative in forming the associations generally came from alumni themselves, but college administrators were not slow to appreciate the importance of keeping the association alive and strong (Brubacher and Rudy, 1976).

It was also quickly learned that the companion of support was a measure of control of the institution. Organized alumni would seek a voice in the determination of institutional policy. An 1865 legislative act completely separated Harvard University from the Commonwealth and shifted election of the board of overseers to the graduates. This device for pumping new blood into old institutions was soon recognized by other alumni groups as a means of freeing their alma maters from complete control (usually conservative) of the church and state. By the end of the century, the policy had become commonplace.

The proliferation of the land-grant university in the mid-nineteenth century and the firm entrenchment of the private institution (which simultaneously forged this country's unique dual system of higher learning) produced significant numbers of alumni who offered the potential to advance their respective alma maters. The rise of alumni to power after the Civil War suggested not only that alumni had the will to offer support but also that colleges and universities were in no financial position to frustrate that will. Postwar economic resurgence put alumni in a position of eminence and wealth and enabled them to join the faculty in the support of American colleges and universities (Rudolph, 1962). Therefore, whether welcomed or not, alumni became an essential and critical force in American higher education. President Porter of Yale admitted in 1870 that "alumni retain and somewhat liberally exercise the traditional privileges of all children, freely to criticize the ways of the household."

By the end of the nineteenth century, the relationships of alumni to colleges and universities began to take serious forms. Pride in one's alma mater became a measure of social significance. Alumni wrote many of the histories of American colleges and universities. In regional alumni associations and city alumni clubs, alumni found the means for propagating and sustaining the faith throughout the far-reaching territories where other alumni might be gathered. The appointment of a professional alumni secretary— the first one at the University of Michigan in 1897—brought formal institutional credence to the alumni movement. The function of the early alumni secretary was to keep records and to facilitate communication among alumni. By the early 1900s, traditional forms of alumni communication, such as alumni files, printed alumni bulletins, the reunions, clubs, and special events, were in place. Refinement in early alumni administration soon brought about annual fund drives, bequest plans, capital campaigns, and later, systematic forms of data storage and retrieval. Refinement also brought about the need for professionals to share common concerns and ideas. The American Alumni Council, organized in 1913, made this valuable interchange possible.

It was also at about the turn of the century that nongraduates were welcomed into the alumni fold. This elevation of the nongraduate gave the alumni societies individuals of wealth and prominence whose position as outsiders had been embarrassing to them and counterproductive to the institutions' efforts (Rudolph, 1962).

The alumni movement was of tremendous importance, but the participation of alumni in college and university affairs was not without compromise for both the institution and the profession of alumni administration. True, alumni, through their associations, did give generously of their time and resources to their alma maters. Alumni loyalty was a new and welcomed form of patriotism. It had its own rationale, its own purposes, its own life. And yet, these seemed remote from the purposes of the professors who nurtured the students who became the alumni. Some academicians (including many institutional decision makers) remained reluctant to offer alumni complete acceptance into the revered academic community. This became evident as intercollegiate athletics developed into a principal lever for stirring alumni loyalties. Unfortunately, the loyalty bred of this type of rivalry too frequently exaggerated the physical at the expense of the intellectual prowess of the university (Marks, 1926). Perhaps forgetting the primary mission of higher education, many alumni appeared to be more interested in coaches than professors, in stadia than libraries and laboratories. The alumni administrator was quick to capitalize on the drawing power of athletics, and this, combined with the social responsibilities of the job, perpetuated a less-than-serious professional posture. As with many postsecondary administrative positions, the credentials of the alumni administrator at times seemed less important than familiarities with the institution and the ability to reminisce with its alumni.

Alumni influence and institutional alumni directives were, however, in no means limited to social functions and athletics. At times, during the early twentieth century, alumni displayed an active interest in the educational programs of their alma maters. At Princeton, alumni pressure helped achieve a broader implementation of the elective principle (Schenkel, 1971), an important step in curriculum reform initiated by President Charles Eliot of Harvard at his inauguration in 1869. President Eliot, in his inaugural address, made another statement that has remained relevant over the years: "The University must accommodate itself promptly to the needs of those it has served and to the significant changes in the character of the people for whom it has existed" (Brubacher and Rudy, 1976, p. 365).

Although alumni administration is nearly as old as higher education in this country, its serious application is generally a development of the mid-twentieth century. As Robert Reichley of Brown University describes it, "the alumni movement has evolved from seminal beginnings to organization, maturation, sophistication, and in the post–World War II era, to professionalism" (Rowland, 1977, p. 277). In the last twenty-five years, a new kind of professional has begun to appear in the alumni office. Matched with counterparts in the development and institutional relations offices, the alumni professional was faced with new demands from both the constituency and the institution and often was expected to be accountable to both. Vast increases in enrollments following World War II and during the baby boom era brought impersonalization to what had been a highly personal business. Enter the computer and word processor and new tools with which the alumni professional must cope. Efficiency and cost-effectiveness (especially in the budget-conscious 1970s and 1980s) became a critical priority.

Currently, alumni associations in the public and private sectors face problems of adequate financing, but in different ways. In the public sector, alumni programs that traditionally were financed by the institutional budget are experiencing difficulty in acquiring increased funding and staff. A decreasing prospective student pool and high inflation have caused financial strains for most institutions. Consequently, alumni programs that have difficulty empirically measuring their value to the institution also have difficulty acquiring additional funds. This proves to be an unfortunate irony because institutional advancement generally begins with an emphasis on constituent relations, and few constituents are more important to an institution than its alumni.

The picture is different at public institutions with autonomous, independent alumni associations; these institutions have become more skilled in raising money from alumni (dues, annual gifts, and so on), primarily because of the need to respond to more difficult economic circumstances. As a result, independent alumni associations, especially at the large state institutions of the Midwest, have grown in stature and staff as they clearly demonstrated an increasing value to the institutions they serve.

The last decade has also been, in most cases, a growth period for alumni administration in the private sector. Private schools in the South, Southwest, and West began to catch up with the older private institutions in the East, where there was already a long and respected history of service to several generations of alumni. Private colleges and universities realized they must respond to difficult economic conditions by utilizing alumni as a base from which to gain greater support from the corporate sector, nonalumni parents of current students, and other friends. No longer could tuition, which had grown at astronomical rates, carry so much of the institution's budget load. As fund-raising in the private sector—by both public and private institutions—became more sophisticated, so too did the need for alumni administrators to create an atmosphere conducive to broad-based support.

The Professional and the Profession

The profession of alumni administration rises or falls with the competency levels of the people who administer the alumni programs for their respective institutions. During the past twenty years, more and more institutions have developed alumni programs. Meanwhile, the other advancement fields (fund-raising, institutional relations, and so on) have grown more sophisticated. In an effort to keep pace, institutional and alumni decision makers have recognized the need to encourage an increased professionalism among those who direct the alumni programs.

When staffing alumni programs, institutions have begun to look beyond the homegrown alumnus who knows everybody, loves the alma mater, and has a firm handshake. These qualities are still important, but relevant experience, proven productivity, advanced education, and a commitment to the educational process have become more relevant factors in the search for the alumni administrator at the progressive institution.

Education must be the central focus of the alumni professional who wishes to serve both the institution and the profession effectively. Alumni administrators must realize that they play a key role within higher education. Indeed, many institutions now seek alumni administrators who consider themselves to be educators, who are committed first and foremost to the values of the educational institution for which the alumni program is designed, and who are loyal to that institution. Those who are entering the alumni profession today should be encouraged to be professionals committed to the purposes and ideals of institutional advancement generally and dedicated specifically to the role of alumni relations as a primary segment of an institution's overall advancement effort.

Good alumni administrators possess a rich blend of skills and characteristics. They are highly organized, conscious of detail, and have the ability to plan and implement ideas. They are creative and visionary. They are conscious of the importance of quality and cost-effective productivity. They are enthusiastic people. Their personal integrity and credibility breed confidence and respect from peers and constituents. They are willing to work long hours to achieve the goals of the institution. They also understand the volunteer-staff partnership, and they are willing to allow others to take the credit for progress in reaching those goals.

The structure of the alumni program varies among institutions. Because of different traditions, the diversity in college management, the dual system of public and private higher education, and the historical evolution of the alumni movement, there is no one correct way to organize alumni associations or to structure an alumni program. Each is molded, as it should be, to comfortably fit the institution it serves. The structural spectrum of alumni programs is vast. The alumni program can be a department of the institution with a director who reports to an officer of the institution. It can be an autonomous organization with distinct articles of incorporation and an executive director who is hired and fired by a legally responsible board. Or it can be a hybrid of these two models, an association that receives some budgetary and supervisory support from the institution but also provides some of its own resources and governance.

There are cases in which each model works well, and there are examples of dismal failures. Dan Heinlen at Ohio State University suggests that the real test of success is whether there is genuine involvement of alumni and whether alumni have a voice in institution affairs. That does not mean alumni should run the institution. But it does mean there should be well-established channels through which alumni can express their views on issues of importance to the institution. Alumni provide five important things to their alma maters: money, new students, advice, service, and ambassadorial representation. How the alumni program is organized is perhaps less important than that it maximizes these contributions. Most admirable is the alumni program that structures itself to create effective support for the institution and to involve its constituents in the life of the institution.

Alumni and the alumni programs have great bearing on the institution. Alumni have often been called the absentee stockholders of the American colleges and universities. They might also be described as wise elders of our institutional families. It is their voice that rings loud in the decision-making process of most institutions—formally in trustee meetings and informally in alumni programs. The involvement of alumni in the life of an institution can best be witnessed by observing the cycle that occurs for students when they experience the collegiate milieu, leave the institution, serve and support it, and enjoy the satisfaction of helping the institution be more academically and administratively excellent than it was when they first enrolled. Quite simply, alumni have the collective power continually to enhance the value of their investment in a degree and in an institution.

Support

To invest is to support. An age-old axiom commonly used in discussions relating to alumni relations deals with this concept of investment. Using the letter i, the axiom suggests an equation: identify + inform + interest + involvement = investment. Clearly, the first four of these words describe the very essence of alumni administration. One important payoff of the alumni program comes when alumni invest in the institution.

The term *support* can, and should, be defined by the individual. Although the financial gift may be critically important to the vitality—if not survival—of the institution, other forms of support are also necessary. Support may mean recruitment assistance, career advice to current students or job placement for recent graduates, volunteer participation, attendance at institutionally sponsored events, and enthusiasm for alma mater. To provide the best service to both the institution and the alumni, the alumni program and the fund-raising program should be distinctive yet totally compatible functions in the institution's overall advancement effort.

Alumni administrators till the soil for the harvest of fundraising, but they also exist for more altruistic purposes. Robert A. Reichley states that "their altruism lies in the belief that an institution ought to retain a lifelong interest in its former students because they are the end result of its efforts and because the common experience they share is the unifying bond that helps make a college or university one of the most permanent of institutions throughout history. Virtually all alumni professionals, then, see their efforts as a blend of service and support in the creation of a lasting relationship" (Rowland, 1977, p. 282). J. Michael McGean of Dartmouth College views the relationship to fund-raising as follows: "There is no question that a strong alumni program is an invaluable contributor to successful development activities. Without a positive, well-balanced alumni effort, fund-raising would be infinitely more difficult. In the final analysis, however, the strength of an institution is measured not only in dollars, but in the degree to which people are willing to identify with it and share in its values. Alumni relations activities help further and deepen that commitment. It is a strong institution which can attract the valuable time and concern of capable alumni who freely give of their talents toward strengthening the institution" (Rowland, 1977, p. 283).

Mission

The mission of the total alumni program is only as effective as those who administer it, but it cannot be effective at all if it is not first thoughtfully planned and effectively monitored. The mission of a good alumni program should reflect the image of the mission of the institution. When one considers the mission of most institutions (teaching, research, and service), it becomes clear that the most effective alumni program is one that carries out these same functions. By inverting the emphasis of this triad—service, research, teaching—one can begin to shape a mission statement for the alumni program: service to alumni and from alumni, research to remain innovative and effective in light of desired goals, and teaching to continue the educational process for alumni.

The Committee on Alumni Administration of the Council for the Advancement and Support of Education (CASE) is the professional organization that facilitates the work of all alumni administrators and in which most hold membership. (The American Alumni Council was one of its two predecessors.) CASE has completed a long-range planning process (Ransdell, 1985, p. 28) for the profession of alumni administration and in so doing has adopted a statement of mission that can easily be modified to apply to any given institution or alumni association. It reads:

A.   Alumni Administration—A Mission Statement:
The alumni of a college or university represent a primary constituency which significantly affects the institution's present vitality and future strength. Therefore, the alumni relations program of a college or university is a major component in the institution's overall advancement effort. Given this, it should be administered by professional educators who possess a commitment to both the institution and the profession. The alumni program should also be

supported by key alumni volunteers who, together with the staff, offer the means through which the institution is advanced and positive relations with the alumni population are maintained.

B. Goals and Objectives:

1. Create an atmosphere which encourages a lifetime commitment among alumni and friends to offer financial support for and to participate in the life of the institution.

    a. Communicate the institution's qualities, strengths, concerns, and needs in accordance with the mission of the institution.

    b. Seek ways for alumni and friends to participate in alumni-related programs and become productive volunteers who facilitate the success of alumni-related programming.

    c. Involve alumni in the institution's effort to recruit and enroll quality students and create ways for alumni to advise current students with regard to career options.

    d. Design opportunities for alumni and friends to experience intellectual growth and to relate with faculty and gain access to educational activities.

    e. Conduct constituency research which seeks to solicit and properly channel alumni opinion, suggestions, concerns, needs, and trends.

    f. Encourage alumni awareness of and attendance at institutionally sponsored events.

    g. Sustain a historical perspective of the institution while constructively shaping its future.

    h. Educate current students as to their future responsibilities as responsive alumni.

2. Provide the structure necessary to plan, initiate, manage, and evaluate programs and services which stimulate interest, build loyalty, increase involvement, and generate support for the institution.

    a. Build a volunteer structure to the point where it fully maximizes lay participation and decision-making.

b. Ensure that the alumni population is represented by a governing board that is demographically composed of a cross-section of the alumni population.

c. Recruit and train talented, professional staff.

d. Stay abreast of contemporary technology and programming innovations.

Clearly, the effective alumni program is one that has successfully educated the institution concerning the need to serve the intrinsic needs of its alumni and has formulated meaningful ways in which to provide such service. In so doing, the institution establishes a continuing, genuine commitment on the part of its alumni to serve the institution.

The Future

The strategy of the alumni administrator will need to change as economic strains and other social conditions change the perspective of the alumni. There will be great competition among institutions and other nonprofit organizations for limited human and financial resources. A diversity of skills will be needed and tested. Success will be predicated on creativity, persistence, ability to take part in institution-wide decision making, and ability to facilitate learning among alumni and colleagues alike. The alumni administrator will need to work alongside others on the institution's advancement team to meet their common goals and facilitate the educational process.

The remainder of this section outlines the various areas that make up the contemporary alumni program and the repertoire of the growth-conscious alumni administrator. Managing the alumni program (the topic of Chapter Twenty-Nine) will require an eye for budgetary and financial administration, staffing, computerization and automation, data storage and retrieval, facilities management, and planning. The alumni board (discussed in Chapter Thirty) will require role definition, structure, effective staff relations, and proper recognition. Basic alumni programming (Chapter Thirty-One) will need to include emphasis on admissions, career assistance, student interaction, academics, athletics, numerous special events, and the programs for young and old alumni. Alumni continuing education (Chapter Thirty-Two) promises to be the cornerstone of the alumni movement in the future as it becomes more integrated with faculty activities and the broader academic community. Alumni chapter and constituent organizations (Chapter Thirty-Three) will continue to require consideration within the context of the total alumni program, but with emphasis on cost-effectiveness, reduced duplication, and maximum utilization of volunteers. Reunions (Chapter Thirty-Four) will take on a more serious posture as reunion programming and promotion begin to reflect the total institutional perspective. Alumni communications (Chapter Thirty-Five) will need to seek an even higher standard of journalistic excellence, maintain editorial freedom while reflecting the scope of the entire institution, design direct mail to compete well with noninstitutional mail, and remain technologically innovative. Auxiliary alumni programs (Chapter Thirty-Six) will need to produce greater revenue with fewer demands on staff time and institutional resources. Nontraditional institutions (Chapter Thirty-Seven) will need to structure programs to meet the needs of their respective institutions, yet learn from the successes of broader alumni programs at other institutions. Finally, alumni surveys and research (Chapter Thirty-Eight) will offer important information in the determination of proper programmatic goals, support capabilities, and alumni service for which empirical evidence has suggested a need.

References

Brubacher, J. S., and Rudy, W. *Higher Education in Transition: A History of American Colleges and Universities.* (Rev. ed.) New York: Harper & Row, 1976.

Marks, P. "The Pestiferous Alumni." *Harper's Weekly,* July 1926, pp. 144–149.

Porter, N. "The American College and the American Public." New Haven, Conn.: Yale University, 1870, p. 244.

Ransdell, G. A. *Long-Range Plan.* Washington, D.C.: Committee on Alumni Administration, Council for Advancement and Support of Education, 1985.

Rowland, A. W. (gen. ed.). *Handbook of Institutional Advancement: A Practical Guide to College and University Relations, Fund Raising, Alumni Relations, Government Relations, Publications, and Executive Management for Continued Advancement.* (1st ed.) San Francisco: Jossey-Bass, 1977.

Rudolph, F. *The American College and University.* New York: Random House, 1962.

Schenkel, W. "Who Has Been In Power?" In H. L. Hodgkinson and L. R. Meeth (eds.), *Power and Authority: Transformation of Campus Governance.* San Francisco: Jossey-Bass, 1971.

29

Daniel L. Heinlen

Managing the
Alumni Program

❧ The alumni profession has outgrown the time when flashy individual performance could substitute for productivity. The right person in the right job is a joy to behold, and it would be delightful if all alumni administrators were well suited to their tasks. But life is not that simple, and when a mismatch occurs in such a high-visibility position, the results can be ruinous for the individual and the institution.

How does one match the rightness of a talented personality to an institutional need when it comes to alumni administration? It has been said that "any enterprise is built by wise planning, becomes strong through common sense, and profits wonderfully by keeping abreast of the facts" (*The Living Bible,* Proverbs 24: 3, 4). The next few pages attempt to provide an overview of some alumni management characteristics and techniques that include wise planning, some common sense, and recognition of the value derived by keeping abreast of the facts. It is unfortunate that many of the benefits that result from an active and effective alumni program are difficult to quantify because they appear to be intangibles. But as relationships among involved alumni and their alma mater mature, the mystery of the effective alumni program is replaced by the reality of greater reward in the form of finances, new students, ambassadorial service, and advice to the institution.

Staffing

The single most important task of an alumni director is to pick the right people to work in the program.

Because we spend so much time working with volunteers, it is important that we provide quality staff and dependable management. Although it is tempting to select the most attractive and articulate individuals, who meet the public well, give a firm handshake, and engender instant confidence, it is crucial to look beneath the outer shell at integrity, ability, and readiness to follow through.

Where there is a choice, it is preferable to place professionals, that is to say paid staff, in positions of responsibility rather than volunteers, even volunteers who are highly talented, extremely capable, and deeply committed. Why? Because there can be only one boss, and it is the chief alumni executive who must unload Mr. or Mrs. Super Helper after they have disappeared at critical times in the program calendar or simply failed to give their volunteering a high enough priority. The administrator's leverage to manage volunteers is not strong enough often enough. However, in many programs there is no choice; either you use volunteers in your program or you have no program. When that is true, the best thing to do is again choose the very best people to populate the most responsible positions. Spend time with them, just as you would with paid staff. Do your best to inculcate a sense of responsibility, commitment, and professionalism. See that they clearly understand the nature of their task and how it impacts on the total institutional advancement effort. It helps if volunteers clearly understand both that the program is larger than just their part of it and how their work has impact on others.

The best way to organize the alumni office is to divide responsibility by functional area. Distribute the work load equitably through concise position descriptions. This forces the manager to clarify the distribution of tasks, helps to assess the human resource requirements, and clarifies the parameters of responsibility for each employee. For instance, the club director may have some responsibilities for mailing promotional materials and securing door prizes at the next alumni meeting. But who is responsible for the invoicing and accounting that must be done as the club makes repayment? Is it the club director or is it the bookkeeper? Well written job descriptions can resolve such dilemmas. (Wise planning!) Incidentally, it is often helpful to have a person who has been performing well in a position review and suggest modifications in that position's job description every two years or so. Indeed, the difference between the way many jobs are handled and the written description of how they are administered is often astounding. Job descriptions and the performance reality must be kept parallel or confusion will abound.

Training sessions for professional staff are a must. (Common sense!) Professional development through the Council for Advancement and Support of Education (CASE) or other organizations should be looked on as opportunities for growth and a cross-pollination of ideas. Almost invariably, thoughtful individuals will return from a professional conference with at least a half dozen workable ideas that can be modified to suit the organization's needs. And they should come back with their batteries recharged, full of new energy and enthusiasm for the challenge ahead.

There is also the problem of making the wrong choice in staff, whether paid or volunteer. When that happens, recognize it as early as possible (which you will be able to do if you keep abreast of the facts). Be kind and thoughtful, but counsel the person into a different position or line of work. Keeping the mismatched employee in the wrong place can be expensive in terms of both economics and the morale of the balance of your staff. However, dismissal is such a sensitive area that you should seek professional advice from the university's personnel officer or from legal counsel specializing in labor relations. Take precautions not to make mistakes when hiring. Take time to check references, probe into past job performance, and spend as much time as possible with the candidate.

Planning

Planning is difficult for many administrators. It is much more fun to implement. The simplest scenario for planning, which can be an extremely complex process, is to:

1. Examine your history and see where you and your organization have been

2. Evaluate where you are now
3. Determine where you want to go
4. Determine where you will end up at a given point in time (three, five, ten years from now) if you continue your present course
5. Decide how to alter your present course to get where you want to go

Dr. Robert E. Linson, vice-president of university relations at Ball State University, has provided helpful definitions of terms often used in the planning process in a talk he presented at the CASE Annual Assembly in July 1984:

> *Planning:* The ongoing process by which we reaffirm our mission and establish our goals and objectives
>
> *Goal:* A general statement of a desired outcome
>
> *Objective:* A statement growing out of a goal which has a specific outcome, is measurable and set within a time frame
>
> *Management:* Those processes, systems and techniques which are used by decision makers to achieve the objectives which were derived from the process
>
> *Evaluation:* The process of assessing the actual performance of programs, processes and procedures as weighed against the intended outcome and measurable objective

It is wise to involve all professional alumni staff early in the planning process. Basic guidelines should be charted before bringing the alumni board of directors and other volunteers into the process. In no way should you underestimate the authority or importance of a competent board, but you should know more about alumni administration and its impact on the institution than volunteers who, even when deeply committed, have only momentary contact with the mainstream of institutional decision making. A consultant in planning once suggested that a voluntary board, unguided by skilled professionals, could plot a course that would be clearly beyond the reach of the most talented staff and could lead to their (the staff's) demise.

In planning, as in anything, it is wise to break the process down into its simplest elements. Invite participants, both staff and board, to help develop goals and objectives, management strategy, and evaluation procedures. This is much easier to say than to do, and it requires great statesmanship on the part of the association's chief executive officer to effect a workable plan. The key is to maintain concise documentation of the entire planning process so that the plan can be followed and updated as needed.

Once completed, a well-conceived planning document provides clear guidelines that have been agreed to by all parties concerned and should fit comfortably into the association's and the institution's master plan for the future. An effective plan also provides a programmed response to off-the-wall proposals from the well-meaning but uninformed who propose the perfect program for your alumni association. ("Sorry, it is not in our long-range plan to enter into this kind of project.") Use your planning process to stay on track, keep the goal in sight, and do not be diverted by attractive but unrelated activity. Finally, full dissemination of the plan should be made to all the staff and board involved (and to key officers of the institution) so there can be no question about direction, priority, or resources that will be expended to achieve the goals outlined in the plan.

Financial Administration

The growth of alumni programs and the larger budgets born out of inflation and success put the alumni director heavily into the role of financial manager. That is particularly true of those associations that have resources separated from those of the institution. This most often occurs at large public institutions with alumni programs that are self-governing and include elements such as alumni camps, tours, investment income, and membership dues. Many colleagues with longevity in our profession suggest that fiscal conservatism is the best policy. It is the safest course of action where concern for organizational stability exists, particularly when the association has a strong life-membership program.

Controversy surrounds the life-membership concept in many associations that have dues programs. The life-member programs that continue to serve their organizations well have had set aside a portion of the fees in an endowment sufficient to cover the costs of servicing each member throughout that individual's actuarial lifetime. Alumni directors and boards who fail to do so, or who do not also reinforce their wisdom with actuarial reviews by competent professional counsel, risk devastating results down the road. Life-member funds that can easily grow into the several-million-dollar range call for astute financial management of an investment portfolio.

A word here about the investment portfolio. Some associations will accumulate liquid assets that can be managed for the benefit of the organization by skilled financial managers. With sizable investment portfolios, try to involve professional counsel. If this is not possible, then at least involve a primary financial officer at the institution. This may be required whether the association is independent or not. Professional counsel (if not an officer of the institution) should have recognized fiduciary license and should be paid a fee for the responsibility. Why? For one thing, it is difficult to fire volunteers when a change must be made. Further, it is wise to have an oversight committee of the alumni board, chaired by the treasurer or another competent officer, meeting regularly and monitoring performance. The investment counsel's job is to invest funds according to the directions given by the board (based on the mission and goals of the organization) so that the funds are safe, growing, and producing income (in some combination). Some further words of advice as you track performance of the portfolio managers are

1. Have a clear understanding with your board of directors as to what the association's investment goals and objectives are. Communicate this understanding to your investment counsel.
2. Hire competent investment counsel. Although there may be pressure to accept the work of an unpaid volunteer who has experience in this area, the better course of action is to resist. Interview prospects competitively, then pick the best (which may not be the cheapest!).

3. Insist on regular meetings involving the full investment committee of your board and counsel, with the latter reviewing detailed performance reports. Ask for performance comparisons with similar organizational portfolios.
4. Report audit results to your membership each year. Do so for your investments as well as current operations.

Overall financial management of the operations budget demands constant vigilance. If the association writes its own checks (as opposed to the university doing so in your behalf), you have an even greater responsibility for the implementation of sound business practices. These should be reviewed at least annually by outside auditors and reported to your membership. A monthly financial report to the board of directors is appreciated in many instances and is essential in most. Be candid in the explanation that accompanies the monthly financial statement. What most boards dislike more than anything is a surprise. If problems develop with cash flow, it is better to deal with them up front than to get into problems that cannot be resolved and to be forced to give the bad news to your board when you are unable to control the timing or the environment.

Budgets

Whether an alumni association is completely subsidized by the institution or has to generate its own resources, there is no question that the establishment and management of a credible and effective budget will go a long way toward ensuring survival, if not bell-ringing success. But budgets have a way of being friend and foe at the same time. Those who enjoy working with them are usually a step ahead of those who dread the thought of sorting out the monthly financial statement and surveying the damage. It is all the more helpful if the entire staff understands what responsibility each member has (and they all have some if they are either bringing in funds or helping to spend them through programs and events) and how each fits into the overall picture. There should be clear understanding by all staff members as to exactly what is expected, what portion of the budget they influence, and the depth of their authority to act for the association in financial matters.

The ability to control association costs by establishing cost centers and then assigning staff responsibility for the administration of those cost centers within budget guidelines provides a good way to monitor performance. It is an enormous help to use a computer and appropriate software to prepare reports that compare budget to actual activity and project performance at regular intervals during the year.

Budgets should be built using sound, realistic goals and expectations, with input from everyone who has income or expenditure responsibility. Once the parameters have been outlined, a draft budget should be prepared, based on present performance and future plans.

The first draft should be prepared six months, or more, in advance of the end of the fiscal year. It should show the budget figures for the current year, actual results for the year to date, projected year-end totals, and an estimation of the next fiscal year's figures based on the foregoing and future plans. Early on, projected expenses for the new fiscal year will almost certainly outstrip revenue. The ensuing staff discussions directed toward modifying the budget will help provide a better understanding of what makes the entire organization work financially. It enables the staff to enter budget justification with gusto. At the same time, the alumni director must maintain a tempering and harmonious environment so the management team continues to function smoothly.

Budgets, if well prepared, can provide marvelous illumination for an otherwise treacherous path and may also be used to blaze new trails where the footing is uncertain. In sustaining ongoing activities or beginning experimental efforts, the staff should put together a business plan that carefully outlines how much it will cost and where the money will come from. Any association that enters new activity without a clear understanding of the financial implications risks unhappy and surprising results.

Realistic expectations, clear goals, a fair budget, regular reporting, and helpful oversight are essential ingredients. As part of the annual financial review, your board of directors should establish an audit committee. This is often unsettling to the association's management, but it is good accounting practice and will provide a clean bill of health for the staff, assuming everything is in order. And, if all is not in order, that is all the more reason to have an audit committee.

Computerization and Automation

Without high-quality, reliable information on alumni, the effectiveness of even the most ambitious program will suffer terribly. In this, the information age, it will not be long before even the most modest budgets can afford quality data storage and retrieval capabilities. They are essential to the success of all alumni programs. Gary Kitsmiller, associate executive director of administration and information services for Ohio State University's communication and development office, suggests some basic components of records systems.

For many years, colleges and universities have been using the computer as a tool for fund-raising and alumni work. Alumni information systems are as diverse in size and complexity as the institutions they serve. Technological advances during the past few years have resulted in improved equipment at less cost. This, coupled with simpler programming languages and better software packages, has enabled even the smallest alumni shop to take advantage of the computer.

The following discussion will highlight some of the common elements in most alumni systems and look at some of the environments in which they operate.

File Contents. These days, it is hard to find anyone who refers to a "computerized alumni records file." It is now an "alumni data base" (even if it does not have the hierarchical or relational characteristics common to most current data base structures). Semantics aside, there are a number of data elements, or logical groupings of data, that are mandatory for good alumni records. Some of the typical data types are

> *Name and address data.* These are obvious. However, many
> alumni systems expand this to include preferred names
> (nicknames, and so on), specific salutations to appear on

automatically generated letters from different college officials (word processing interface), both home and business addresses (and specifying which one is preferred), plus the option for listing seasonal and former addresses. More and more, telephone numbers (both home and business) are becoming essential because of phonathons for membership or fund-raising campaigns.

Spouse data. This is absolutely necessary for effective alumni relations because of joint donor membership situations and because it is important to communicate the organization's message to both husband and wife.

Academic data. These data should include the year, level of degree (bachelor's, master's, and so on), college or school (if within a university), major area of study, and any honors received. For reunion purposes, many alumni systems include a preferred degree year. This is especially important for those alumni who attended but did not graduate and for those who have multiple degrees. Some alumni systems also include academic information relating to an individual's affiliation with other universities.

Business/occupational data. Listing the employer, title, and business address can provide valuable insights as to an alumnus's interest in and capacity for providing financial support and/or working as a volunteer. Some systems include occupation and industry coding schemes that allow for demographic statistics based on employment. Occupation coding can also be a powerful marketing tool for segmenting audiences (for example, alumni continuing education programs or student career counseling).

Activity/affiliation data. An individual's record of participation in the alumni organization's programs (tours, reunions, and so on) is vital to future communication with alumni. At many universities, there are a growing number of constituent alumni groups (special interest groups of the overall alumni organization) that must be identified. These data are also typically used to identify various types of volunteers, board members (past and present), and other important market segments. It is also helpful to know the extent to which the alumnus was involved during the campus experience in such activities as fraternity or sorority membership, student government, honorary societies, and athletic teams.

Any alumni data base should contain most, if not all, of the types of information just noted. Some systems contain far more. Beyond the scope of this discussion is the data necessary to support the development operation. Often for efficiency and to give the capability of using both for defining potential giving and membership markets, the fund-raising information is maintained on the same data base as alumni data. Generally, this centralization is an asset.

Storage, Maintenance, and Retrieval. Most alumni information systems use a magnetic disk (either hard or floppy disk) as the storage medium for data. Some systems are still magnetic tape-oriented, but with the advent of lower-priced hardware that uses magnetic disks, these are dwindling in number. The advantages of such use (especially the hard disk) as a storage medium are many, not the least of which are greater storage capacity and faster record access and processing than are possible with tape.

Maintenance of the data on an alumni system is handled by software (programs) designed to ensure that the new data are placed in the proper part of the record and that logical editing is achieved to preclude inputting improper codes or formats. The user of the system interacts with the maintenance functions through either a batch or an on-line process. In a batch-oriented system, maintenance changes (updated information) are all put together, or batched, in the form of keypunched cards, magnetic tapes, or magnetic disks. In an on-line environment, the user completes these transactions using a video display terminal. The latter method is the most efficient, most accurate, and most timely. It is also becoming the most widely used.

Because the ultimate users of the alumni data are basically concerned with the outputs the system can generate in the forms of lists, reports, statistics, and other general information that appears on video display screens and in other printed formats, data retrieval is of prime importance. Retrieval needs can generally be categorized into two groups: single-index and multiple-index.

Single-index retrieval is prevalent in on-line systems where the user can use one known index to retrieve a record or portions of a record. The most common index for record access is some type of identification number. Computers work well with numbers, so where this can be used, record retrieval is often faster. In addition to access by number, on-line alumni systems need access by name. Name indexing is usually slower because of the speed of alphabetic characters' recognition by the computer compared with numeric. However, to speed up the on-line response time, some systems have been developed with keyed indexes composed of numeric equivalents for alphabetic characters. This latter technique also affords the capability of easily building phonetic search routines that help those who cannot spell or do not know which spelling version of a name to use (for example, Shaffer or Schaeffer). Other types of single-indexing used by alumni organizations include such attributes as class year, geographic area, and membership category.

For more complicated data retrieval, a method of using multiple indexes is used. This usually takes the form of a variety of attributes that in some way help profile the individual. Such items as degree information (class year, degree, major), zip code or geographical area, membership categories, constituent affiliation, business codes, and so on are indexed in a way that allows the entire data base to be searched finding individuals meeting certain attribute criteria. Moreover, these can be searched in combination with each other to provide logical data sets (market segments) for further processing.

Sophisticated retrieval systems provide great flexibility, allowing the user to compose requests using simple statements that combine attributes to provide the needed group of records. For example, a user can enter into the terminal data that will provide a list of all alumni who live in California, who are lifetime members of the alumni organization, and who have graduated within the last ten years. As more and more alumni organizations find the need to segment their markets for effective communications, membership retention, gift prospecting, and other reasons, the appearance of highly sophisticated retrieval packages will become widespread.

Alumni systems typically operate in one of the following types of environments:

1. *A central university data processing center.* This is the norm for large colleges and universities where large numbers of records and processing volumes dictate the use of a large computer. The principal advantage is the shared technical expertise available from the professionals in the computer center. The primary disadvantage is the lack of total control by the alumni organization over its records processing. Alumni information usually is not the top priority with the central data processing center.

2. *A stand-alone computer at the alumni office.* This has become much more prevalent in recent years as technological improvements in miniprocessors, microprocessors, and word processors have been made more powerful and usable by non-data-processing professionals. Also, hardware costs have continually dropped over the past few years, making some of them affordable for the smallest alumni organization. The advantage here is the total control of the information. However, with control comes the responsibility of managing a data processing function. As the system grows in complexity, it usually becomes more expensive than relying on a central data processing organization.

3. *A contract with a data processing company.* Much more prevalent a few years ago, this method was used when many colleges did not have a computer or when a school's central computer was already overloaded. It still exists, often in the form of a time-sharing agreement with a computer service bureau, which is in the business to sell time on its computer. This is risky because the alumni organization must contend with priorities of other customers. The alumni organization, then, is totally dependent on the success of the service bureau for its information. If the service bureau fails as a company, the alumni organization is without an information system.

In recent years, some alumni systems have been operating in an environment that combines the methods noted in items 1 and 2 above. By installing a minicomputer at the alumni office and downloading certain data from the central computer via telecommunications or tape-to-disk transfer, alumni offices have gained the best of both worlds. They have retained the expertise of the data processing professionals and data management efficiencies gained from the central computing unit and they have total control over some of the more important data processing functions that can now be performed with their own computer.

In the not-too-distant future, most alumni organizations will find that state-of-the-art automation is well within their grasp. The continual decrease in hardware cost, coupled with a whole new generation of software (commonly called fourth-generation languages), will make the computer a very friendly device.

Those who do not take advantage of the marvels of automation will find themselves at a tremendous disadvantage as their organizations and their constituents grow in size and complexity.

Facilities Management

Having a place that alumni can call theirs on any campus provides enormous advantage to the affiliated organization that manages the property.

Many alumni centers across the nation have sprung up within the last generation. They provide office space, meeting rooms, entertainment facilities, and conference space with varying degrees of opulence.

It is important to consider how affluent such a facility should appear to the alumni population and to the users. Each campus will find its own answer, but keep in mind that the alumni need a place of which they can be proud and that reflects the greatness and the tradition of their institution. Anything less will not engender the enthusiasm so necessary for inspiring volunteers. Going overboard on luxury, however, could very well turn off a number of others. Most administrators seem to be opting on the side of tasteful distinction.

There may always be the question of sharing the facility with other university departments. Perhaps the surest way to avoid encroachment on your space is to have the entire facility wholly owned by the alumni association. There are obvious advantages when the alumni, development, and records offices are in close proximity; and when that combination works well, it greatly benefits the total institution. However, needs for space may become so critical that alumni facilities will be sacrificed in favor of other priorities. The point here is to try to preserve the alumni home away from home as the center of organized alumni activity and to maintain it as a viable property in which the alumni feel a sense of ownership.

Whatever the case, it is essential to have the proper backup in maintenance and service staff to keep the space attractive and assure that alumni guests receive hospitality of the highest order. This is not possible without quality maintenance and imaginative planning—and a public relations–minded service staff. An alumni administrator's leadership will make itself felt clearly in a physical facility as people form their own opinions about its appropriateness, cleanliness, and accessibility. It should be so reflective of the association and the institution that some enthusing of volunteer support occurs upon entering the alumni center door!

Perhaps you received some sense of the three items quoted from Proverbs at the beginning of the chapter—wise planning, common sense, and keeping abreast of facts. They are strikingly similar to the dictum of business schools everywhere: plan, organize, and control. (Solomon was more eloquent, however.) What has been related in this chapter is worthy of your implementation. Keep in mind, however, that none of it works without the alumni director's ability to manage. If you can say, "I've got the best job in the world," then perhaps you do. You can keep it that way and make it that way for those who work for you with planning, common sense, and good information.

30

Ann D. Gee

Working with
the Alumni Board

〜☞ The notion of an alumni board raises many questions: What is it? Why should we have one? How do we get one? What do we do with it once we've got it? How does it help us in our programs? Does my institution really want or need volunteers? Is there an opportunity for volunteers to participate meaningfully?

Answers to these and other questions are in this chapter. Remember to apply the general principles to your own particular situation and institutional need. Without a doubt, alumni boards vary from institution to institution in composition, type, purpose, organizational structure, and tradition.

All alumni boards, however, are made up of individuals who have attended your institution and who are organized to manage programs for other alumni. Beyond that distinction, the ways you identify board members, how you orient them to their work, and the methods that are used to select areas where they can be most effective may be different from the techniques used by the neighbor college down the street.

Board Purpose and Function

"A board can epitomize what your program is all about: people helping people and helping their alma mater in the process" (Wilson, 1978, p. 11). The alumni board exists to show the rest of the constituency that your institution has an alumni program, that there are alumni who are vitally interested in it, and that there is a sense of organization to it. According to Wilson, board members are at the center of all alumni who are informed and who understand the institution's mission.

The role of the alumni board in your program is manifested in two ways: by the responsibilities of the total board and by the duties of individual board members. The total board functions to organize and structure the ambiguous process of relating to that vast constituency called alumni. Board duties include deciding on goal and program priorities, identifying volunteer leaders, establishing a program of quality control for the kind of image projected, and representing other alumni to the institution.

Individual board members can open doors for staff members, provide a sense of history that professional staff have not had the luxury of obtaining, and impress and influence their peers when staff cannot. Even though they have been insiders at one time, alumni have a sense of detachment and can objectively offer advice and ideas.

What can a board do for your institution? It can, and should, be a place where future trustees are trained. Institutional goals can be internalized by the board as they seek solutions for the needs of their alma mater. The alumni board can be the repository of feedback from the alumni to the institution, and board members can disseminate vital information from the institution back to the alumni.

Most important, alumni have no career stake in your institution. Therefore an alumni board may establish policies less encumbered by politics or personalities. Such policies may have a broader and more far-reaching sweep than some conservative approaches inaugurated by staff.

Types of Boards

Because alumni associations operate both independent (separate from the institution) and dependent (a department of the institution) alumni boards, it is important to recognize the distinctions between them. Independent boards function outside the institution and have responsibility for managing and running the entire alumni association operation. Dependent boards, on the other hand, are recognized as groups of volunteers operating within the sphere of the institution.

The textbook definition of *board of directors* uses different terminology, but the qualities that represent independent and dependent are still the same:

1. *Advisory board*—does not make primary policy decisions about how the organization is going to run and has no legal authority for employing the executive staff member but does offer counsel about, and task-oriented behavior for, the activities of the alumni association. (This type is typical of dependent alumni associations.)

2. *Policy-making board*—makes decisions regarding the function, goals, and objectives of the organization and both hires the executive staff to implement the policy it establishes and evaluates their efforts. (This type is typical of independent alumni associations.)

Some institutions have an alumni board that is, in reality, a blend of both types.

If the alumni association is incorporated, members of its board of directors have the responsibility and authority to make certain the association is indeed managing itself as a corporation. That includes filing articles of incorporation with the state, having the name of the corporation approved by the state, writing by-laws, keeping minutes of all proceedings, and maintaining financial records on file at the principal office for three years. It is also considered wise to produce an annual report. (Even boards that function purely in an advisory capacity should initiate these practices in the name of sound business operations.)

For the policy-making board, sources of liability include failing to run the corporation properly (as just stated) and mismanaging the assets of the corporation. In keeping with their fiduciary responsibility, board members cannot loan monies from the corporation to individual board members or engage in activities that involve conflicts of interest. For example, board members who automatically receive contracts to provide catering or similar business services to the alumni association simply because of their relationship may be judged to have conflicting interests. To avoid potential liability, staff and the board should require competitive bidding on all projects that might employ alumni board members. Requiring bids provides protection for both the board of directors and the individual board members.

Members of a policy-making alumni board that violates its charter may be legally liable as individuals. However, these issues should not be a concern if the board is properly managed and is made aware of its responsibilities. The greatest concern arises when board members agree to serve without ever having been informed of their obligations.

Board Meetings: What They Should Accomplish

Board meetings are held for four reasons: to exchange information about the alumni association and the institution, to organize action and evaluate accomplishment of goals, to manage policy and procedural questions, and to permit socializing of board members. These processes should occur at each meeting, but their order of presentation may vary.

Information exchange is best when transmitted by a member of the board or by a volunteer invited to report on a particular program or project. Briefing may be in the form of committee reports, program summaries, or activity evaluations. Board members will often rely on the professional staff to facilitate the assembly and reporting of information.

Institutional updates are needed to keep the board current of the activities of their alma mater. Even though you may have been conscientious about communicating what has occurred on your campus since the last meeting, chances are board members need the perspective a staff member can offer. Ask other administrators, faculty representatives, and students to be guest speakers for a meeting.

Evaluation of goals should take place at each meeting. When scrutinizing the success of individual programs, board members often fail to relate the program to institutional or association goals. Programs must not be considered in a vacuum; the alumni board should see that program achievements represent progress toward the broader goals.

Social interaction is essential in keeping morale high, building team spirit, and creating a sense of common purpose. Whether meetings are held in the evening, over a weekend, or during the day, a portion of time should be allocated for informal visiting. A meal, coffee breaks, cocktail hour, or a football game can act as a needed intermission during which members can get to know one another better. Group effectiveness is enhanced as board members gain confidence in and appreciation for the individual members of the group.

Policy and procedural discussions are the nonroutine agenda items that represent the true function of the alumni board. It is these important discussions that make board member input important and volunteer service worth the sacrifice.

Board Organization

The board is organized to accommodate five basic tasks: (1) policy administration—providing leadership and planning, (2) finance—managing funds, (3) program evaluation—supervising the programs of the association and evaluating their success, (4) personnel management—identifying volunteers, and (5) public relations—publicizing the value and purpose of the organization. These five areas may be arranged so that staff and alumni board members each share portions of the responsibility. With a policy-making board structure, all five tasks are to be completed by the board; with an advisory board, alumni board members normally would manage the last three.

The more complex the work of the association, the more levels provided for in the board organization. A typical arrangement is a tiered organizational chart: president or chair at the top, officers next, and the board of directors at the bottom. The staff shares a dotted-line relationship with the president.

In addition to the president, officers should include a president-elect or vice-president, secretary, treasurer, and/or past president. Other positions can be added reflecting your areas of programming—for example, a vice-president for student relations.

Each officer should have an identifiable duty. Positions need not be created out of a reverence for history or an envy of a rival institution's complex structure.

Executive Committee. The president and officers may be organized into an executive, or steering, committee for the purpose of conducting business outside the board meeting. For discussions to be effective, executive committee membership should be small (eight to twelve people).

Generally, the executive committee meets more frequently than the board to discuss matters relating to the board agenda, policy issues that have not been resolved at board meetings, or particular subjects appropriate only for small-group discussion. A roll-up-the-sleeves meeting might be an apt description of the executive committee session.

Board of Directors. The directors' function is to deal with the discussion items handed down to them from the executive committee. Management of those matters includes delegating work to committees, suggesting future courses of action, and voting on issues that require approval by a representative body of the alumni association. The number of directors depends on the size of the alumni body, the number of special interest or geographical areas to be represented, and the amount of work to be done. An average size for a working board ranges from twenty-five to thirty-five people, counting members of the executive committee.

Meetings for boards of directors are held less frequently than those of the executive committee. Board meetings may occur two, four, or six times a year. The most typical schedule is a quarterly meeting that is held on the campus. (For institutions that are in remote locations, board meetings may be planned in cities where there is a heavy concentration of alumni board members.)

Standing Committees. Committees may be appointed to accomplish specific tasks. These committees would supervise programmatic functions, such as long-range planning, nominations and elections, program evaluation, and marketing. For effective involvement, each board member should be appointed to a board committee.

For recognition purposes, it may be necessary for individuals who hold other alumni association leadership positions to belong to some official organization other than the alumni board. An umbrella group could serve such a purpose well, with meetings held annually or semiannually to provide information about alumni association programs and the institution. Types of volunteers to be included could be past presidents of the association, homecoming and reunion chairs, class agents, constituent group representatives, and event chairs. Appropriate names for such an organization include Alumni Council, Directors' Club, and Leadership Circle.

Board Documents

To guide the board in its business operations, rules and regulations should be written. Although they may be flexible, they constitute the official process by which the board controls the activities of the alumni association.

Bylaws are rules adopted by the organization for the management of its affairs and the regulation of its programs. This document should describe the methods by which the organization is governed, the purposes for which it exists, and the means by which it is to continue. Component parts of bylaws include: a statement of purpose, description of staffing required, location of principal office, leadership positions needed, election procedures, a process by which constituent groups are ratified, an explanation of standing committees, meeting requirements, overview of programs, and explanation of auxiliary enterprises.

Job descriptions are a narrative explanation of the responsibilities of individual board members. Each volunteer who agrees to serve as a member of the alumni board should have a specific picture of the requisite duties for that position. According to a volunteer management expert, the job description should include several standard entries including the title of the position, its purpose, the general responsibilities associated with being a member of the board, the specific responsibilities for that job, the training required, the time obligation expected, the length of service needed, and the benefit of the position to the organization and to the individual. All of these are basic to a good job description (Carapetyan, 1983).

Neither bylaws nor job description need be complex. They should be written in a clear, straightforward language and should honestly reflect the nature of the work. And both should be able to be changed. If prepared correctly, these documents can act as an instruction manual on how to easily assemble the alumni association and keep it functioning smoothly.

Communication with Board Members

Our responsibility to alumni board members is to make sure they are informed enough to do the jobs we ask. That requires communication of two types. The first is job-related and involves materials that relate in particular to the board function. Examples of such items include board meeting minutes, notice of meetings, agenda for meetings (always sent in advance), committee reports, program reports, alumni association plans and goals, and job descriptions.

The second type is institutional and is designed to meet board members' need to know in a general way what is happening at their alma mater. Naturally, they receive your alumni or institutional publication, but beyond that, add other items of relevance including copies of important news releases, your internal newsletter, special event invitations, notification of general campus activities that are not alumni-related, institutional calendars, and copies of the minutes from your board of trustee meetings.

Be mindful that an overabundance of information can overwhelm, but a moderate, well-timed, well-chosen amount can, and will, impress.

Membership Selection

The best-laid plan for board programs to mesh with institutional goals, an impressive array of events, and a bulging file of past successes will be of absolutely no value if the wrong volunteers are chosen to provide the direction and carry the banner.

Problem board members are those who do not care, do not commit, have no influence or expertise, or are insincere in their motivations.

General Criteria. The right volunteers have something to lend your alumni program and your alumni board: They are workers, have been proven leaders, possess community influence, are previous donors, have a deep concern for their alma mater, and will give the time to help. Not every "right" volunteer lays claim to all these attributes, but your board members should have a majority.

Actual membership criteria are based on institutional needs. Basic requirements may include past alumni volunteer performance, a record of giving, other types of board service (for consideration at the officer position level), and an area of expertise (financial, management, communication). Factors such as class year, sex, race, geography, and special group association may also be important. Many institutions see their alumni boards as representing a general demographic cross section of the alumni population.

Selection Process. Once identified as possible candidates, names of potential board members should be reviewed and rated by a nominating committee. (Such a committee may be formed to function only at a designated time of year or may act as a standing committee requesting nominations and evaluating candidates throughout the year.) Some institutions ask the alumni constituency to respond with suggestions for nominations. Such a procedure may be democratic, but it is cumbersome because the general alumni population lacks knowledge of who or what is needed.

After screening has been completed, the nominating committee prepares a slate of proposed candidates. Slates sometimes contain more than one name for a position, but there is a danger in such a practice: one-half of your best and brightest are destined to lose. Evaluate carefully whether you want a system in which volunteers are competing with each other.

Elections may be real, or as is more common, there may be a ratification of the slate by some governing body. Many alumni boards, in effect, perpetuate themselves by affirming the slate. Other alumni associations prefer to mail the slate as a ballot to the alumni constituency. It is the role of the staff to determine which technique is most effective for your institution.

Once the slate has been approved, candidates for office should be asked to serve by the correct person. In most cases, that person is a peer and a current officer of the alumni board. The invitation to serve is most effective when issued by another volunteer who can offer unsolicited thoughts about what the job entails and why it is both rewarding and important.

Term of Office. Many alumni boards have adopted a rotation system for officers, allowing them to be elected in groups that retire after a given number of years. Average board service of directors is three years. If your board has twenty-one directors, elect them in groups of seven, so that each year one-third will be replaced.

Officers usually serve a shorter stint: one- or two-year terms. Sometimes, requirements that higher offices must be filled by those who have rotated up through the offices below may mean officers commit for a six- to eight-year track of service.

Board Service

Throughout the year, the alumni staff is responsible for continually teaching board members. But there are times when special attention is necessary.

Orientation for New Members. Even though it is safely assumed that those alumni who have newly agreed to join your board are enthusiastic, eager, and raring to go, it cannot be assumed that they know how to apply those energies. Two training tools are essential: a workshop for new members and a board manual.

The workshop is the opportunity to introduce new board members to each other and to the officers, to explain the work of the association and the alumni board, and to familiarize the neophytes with operations. All of these steps will ease the natural discomforts of being an outsider. An orientation session also provides the institution the chance to deliver its message rather than having the volunteers learn operations by osmosis.

A board manual or notebook presented on the day of orientation can serve as a ready reference on policies and procedures and a receptacle for all items pertaining to the association's work.

Schedules, a typical meeting agenda, organizational charts, bylaws, report forms, institutional telephone numbers, a board roster, budgets, short- and long-range goals, mission statement, and job descriptions may make up the manual. If it is a loose-leaf, periodic updates and reports are easily added.

As soon as a new member of the board has been oriented, that person should be assigned to a specific task and committee. Free floaters feel groundless, never knowing how or why they fit. The more specific a task can be, the greater success the individual is likely to have in achieving it.

Communication and Evaluation. Ask volunteers how they want to be supervised and evaluated. Their style may be to accumulate the necessary information, perform the task, and accept feedback at its conclusion. Others may desire constant communication and critique. If we fail to ask how they prefer to be treated, we run the risk of squelching their enthusiasm or abandoning them without enough structure.

Retiring the Board Member. Volunteers whose terms of office have expired represent a most neglected group. Frequently, they are shunted off with great fanfare to the heaven of alumni board retirees, where their knowledge and expertise are allowed to atrophy. These are the very people we have courted, counseled, cajoled, cared about, and called our leadership. We may have invested our time with them for as much as five to fifteen years.

Because there is an ever-changing board roster, staff interest shifts toward the new member; priorities naturally pull us in that direction. Understandable as this is, we should constantly remind ourselves that our previous leadership is still invaluable to us.

Retirees from the alumni board can be used effectively in a number of ways. They are a resource for nominating and recruiting future board members. With their sense of history, they are effective fund-raisers because of their long-term credibility with donors and prospects. In addition, retiring board members may be very willing to host events or represent the alumni association on selected occasions that require less of their time than full board service but still are significant programs or projects.

Board Planning/Evaluation

Without a sense of direction for the long term, the board may be able to successfully implement programs, but when pressed to explain their significance, be unable to do so. The lack of a plan is the most obvious pitfall for alumni programs, for a plan is the necessary link between present and future. Most important, it can be the key and the rationale for survival. Alumni staff and alumni boards unable to offer a future course of direction may become expendable weighed against more obvious and pressing needs of the institution.

To start planning for alumni association goals, first define the larger institutional problems and ask what the association can do to help. Programs are the outgrowth of goals; goals are not authored as the rationale for programs already on the books.

Goals for the association can relate to staffing, budget, programs, volunteers or membership, communications, and association functioning. Once the alumni board has recommended goals, staff must make decisions about their program priorities for each, based on staff time available, budget, and their institutional value.

Board Planning Retreat. To help board members shoulder the responsibility for creating a long-term plan and assessing current operations, a retreat is useful. A block of uncluttered time for honest reflection, often away from the campus, creates a sense of responsibility on the part of board members. They can see the plan as a document they've orchestrated and therefore they have an investment in its execution.

Program Evaluation. All programs of the association should be reviewed by the board. Evaluation may be conducted by committee, by written report and response, or as a discussion item at a meeting. Questions to be considered should include: Are our programs advancing the institution? Are they cost-effective? Do they make effective use of volunteer time? Do they project the image of our institution? Are they visible, well attended, and well run? Do they require too much staff time? and Are they providing the proper balance between service to the alumni and service to the institution?

By participating in program review, board members are made to feel accountable for the programs that are sponsored under the name of the alumni association.

Staff/Board Relations

The biggest problem between volunteers and staff results from unclear expectations about who is to do what. Staff is often frustrated when volunteers refuse to take the initiative; volunteers are uncomfortable when staff fails to supply enough information. Staff panics when volunteers run away with a program; volunteers try to exert leadership by doing the job they thought they were to perform.

In general, staff duties are to communicate opinions, to provide information, to train, to present needs to the administration, and to thank. Staff should not play favorites or bow to pressure for extraordinary favors.

Volunteer obligations are to attend, to offer opinions and creativity, to influence their peers, to provide leadership, to be loyal and dependable, to support the staff when volunteer manpower is needed, and to provide goodwill in the community. Volunteers should not agree to do a job that is distasteful to them or for which they have received inadequate information.

To clarify reporting lines for board members and staff, share a copy of the staff job descriptions with volunteers. A condensed description of staff duties can be included in the bylaws; however, it should be general enough not to restrict carrying out day-to-day activities.

Volunteers need a starting point. Staff must provide the reason for the race, the conditioning, the incentive to begin the race, the boundaries of the course, the refreshments stations along the way, and the reward at the finish.

Conclusion

To be most effective, your alumni board requires careful selection, diligent orientation, frequent communication, a plan, and goals for which to strive.

The sharp focus is provided by the staff. The energy and enthusiasm are provided by the alumni board. The products they produce together will create effective advancement opportunities for the institution.

References

Carapetyan, C. "The Management of Volunteers." Presentation to Texas Christian University Alumni Leadership Conference, Houston, April 1983.

Wilson, D. M. "Working with Alumni Boards." *CASE Currents,* Jan. 1978, pp. 11-13.

31

Stephen L. Barrett

Basic Alumni Programming

જી I discovered the genius of alumni programming in an excavation alongside the ruins of an ancient city on the Alto Plano Boliviano near Lake Titicaca in Bolivia. With me in that hole stood an eighty-two-year-old grandmother from Salt Lake City and a middle-aged auto dealer from Cleveland. Both had just discovered the truth of what their professor tour guide had been trying to tell them on the bus, that this city had once been on the shore of the lake now some miles away. The excitement in their eyes was a forerunner of what would become a long-term involvement with our university and its continuing education program. The grandmother enrolled in classes and encouraged her forty-seven grandchildren to attend college. The car dealer not only enrolled in a bachelor of independent studies course that eventually led him to a degree in anthropology but also became a substantial donor to the university.

Alumni programs provide, at the same time, service to the alumni and service to the institution. Both benefit because, while serving the alumni, such programs cement solid relations between these individuals who form the real foundation of the success of the institution and those from whom we generate many kinds of support for and in behalf of our educational efforts.

Alumni programs come in many types, sizes, and styles and are at their best when they invite a diverse audience to become highly involved with the institution. This chapter proposes a basic alumni activities program that is general enough to fit nearly every kind of institution yet specific enough to provide guidelines that can be followed by alumni or institutional administrators alike.

Purpose of Alumni Programs

Alumni programs are designed as a major institutional effort to involve former students with their alma mater. A primary goal is to create an understanding of the needs and goals of the institution so that, when support of any kind is solicited, the individual will respond positively.

Alumni programs should be designed to meet the specific needs of the alumni, the association, and the institution. Considerable cooperative effort by the institution and the volunteer alumni is required to design the philosophical priorities that will fit each individual institution and the leadership personalities and situations involved. A list of these priorities should be developed and updated by both the university administration and those who administer the alumni program to determine what those needs are and how the alumni may be mobilized to assist.

The Basic Alumni Program

In 1984, the Committee on Alumni Administration of the Council for the Advancement and Support of Education (CASE) developed a basic standard of alumni programs. Many established alumni programs have developed successful unique programs and procedures, and it is not intended that this standard should in any way supplant those programs. Nor is every institution expected to institute all of the programs outlined here. Many ongoing alumni programs will far exceed this basic standard—this is certainly the goal of all professionally operated alumni offices.

Alumni Activities. Every alumni association should be dedicated to serving its alumni and the institution through the cultivation of alumni, donors, friends, and perhaps parents of current students by offering an extensive selection of programs and activities for intellectual stimulation and social interchange. The following twelve points are offered as a sample of guidelines for good alumni programming:

1. Where it is economically feasible, conduct an alumni-sponsored activity or program within a one-hour driving time

for 80 percent of the alumni each year.

2. At least 5 to 10 percent of all invited alumni should attend these functions each year. For some events and programs, this percentage should be much higher; also, as alumni activities programs mature, this percentage should reach an overall total of at least 25 to 30 percent.

3. At least one opportunity per year should be made available for each alumnus to attend an on-campus event.

4. The alumni association should have an active program to involve the following groups with at least one activity per year sponsored (or cosponsored) by the association:
   a. Prematriculated students and recruitment
   b. Current students on-campus
   c. Young alumni (one to ten years out of school)
   d. General alumni
   e. Emeritus alumni (those forty years, and more, out of school)

5. Parents of current students should be invited to participate with alumni when appropriate (at least once each year).

6. Every alumnus and parent should be given at least two opportunities each year to make a financial contribution to the institution. This solicitation does not necessarily need to be done by the association but should come from some institution office that works closely with the alumni office.

7. A goal of 30 percent of the alumni contributing to the institution each year should be established.

8. At least one-half to one percent of the total alumni body should be involved in a volunteer capacity in alumni leadership at any given time.

9. Some form of off-campus volunteer organization (that is, clubs, regional councils, legislative networks) should be created and should meet at least annually.

10. The alumni association should be actively involved in providing some form of a lifelong educational experience to and for alumni at least once each year.

11. An awards/recognition program should be adopted to offer annual recognition of
    a. Distinguished alumni

    b.   Service by alumni and nonalumni to the institution

    c.   Donors to the institution

12.   When appropriate, a network of alumni should be developed to increase awareness of the institution on the part of the general public and the state legislature so that governmental support of the institution and higher education will be enhanced.

This basic alumni activities program is designed to provide an institution with what would be considered a rudimentary alumni cultivational support system.

Some Alumni Programs Currently in Use

In addition to the alumni programs outlined in Chapters Thirty-Two through Thirty-Six, the following basic programs are operated by many different institutions.

Admissions and Student Recruitment. Alumni have been used as a prime source for recruiting the best potential students for their alma mater. Alumni can be organized as advocates, admissions advisers, and recruiters. They can be asked to contact local high school counselors, the students themselves, and/or their parents to share information about the institution and encourage prospective students to attend. Some institutions require formal interaction (recommendation or interview) in their admissions process, and frequently the local alumni are asked to provide this service. Often, the recruiter is furnished information about prospective students who have listed the institution as a preferred educational possibility on their entrance test documents. If the student is a prime admissions prospect, the recruiter will be asked to make personal contact. The alumnus might offer assistance or invite the prospect to attend activities designed to encourage that student to enroll. Several institutions may be recruiting the same student simultaneously, and so the process can become competitive.

A similar program is used when alumni are asked to assist in recruiting prospective students who have special aptitudes, such as music, science, the arts, journalism, leadership, and athletic ability. It should be noted that the governing athletic conference and the NCAA have strict regulations on recruiting for athletes; those organizations should be contacted for more details.

Some institutions have employed the summertime services of current students to assist in contacting prospective students in their home areas to encourage enrollment in the institution.

Student Alumni Career Assistance/Alumni Placement. Some alumni associations have developed programs in which alumni are invited back to campus to counsel current students on career opportunities in their chosen occupations. In addition, these alumni often lecture selected classes and work with individual students. Day-long itineraries or brief assemblies are often employed to afford the chance for alumni and students to discuss potential career opportunities.

In most cases, reaction to this kind of program has been very positive for students and alumni alike. The alumni are flattered to be invited and to be given a legitimate voice in the student development process. The students like to gain practical insights about potential career choices.

Alumni placement programs designed to help former students make career changes have been implemented on a few campuses. These programs seem to work best at specialized institutions or colleges within universities where the faculty and/ or college placement service is qualified and willing to be involved.

Student Programming. At a number of institutions, programs involve students with the alumni association. These efforts bring the students, while still on-campus, into contact with the programs of the association and with individual alumni as they carry out selected activities. Often these contacts establish long-term relationships that prove valuable in future alumni programs.

Examples of student involvement include the following: Students help with fund-raising efforts through telefund campaigns aimed at alumni and, at times, even at fellow students. They conduct major campus events, such as intrasquad football games, bicycle races, and holiday festivities. And they can assist with alumni events, such as homecoming and reunion.

Frequently, alumni associations personnel are assigned to advise the senior class. This has proved useful in establishing good relations between students and the association before graduation.

Frequently, the senior class officers maintain their leadership roles until the class celebrates its first reunion.

At some institutions, organization of student groups has been formalized into student foundations and student alumni boards with specific tasks assigned to them by the association and/or institution. Staff members supervise such programs, and considerable service has been generated for the benefit of both the students and the institution.

Athletic Relations. Because of the general appeal to many alumni of the institution's athletic program, sports-related activities have long been a major interest of many alumni associations. Generally speaking, alumni associations plan major alumni activities in conjunction with athletic events to which alumni are invited. This has proved to be a good way to get alumni back on the campus, or at least to get them to attend events with large numbers of other alumni and friends of the institution.

Homecoming and Special Events. Homecoming, one of the longest running of any traditional alumni-sponsored events, has undergone some major changes in recent years. On many campuses, it is now more of a student activity with limited alumni involvement than an alumni event in and of itself. However, it still is the premier event that brings alumni back to the campus each year. For that reason, most alumni associations do major activity planning for that occasion. Often this is also the time of board meetings, reunions, parties, parades, and many other traditional events.

Working with the students in planning these events can be a valuable way to involve them with the alumni association. If students understand that homecoming is an important time for alumni to return to campus, then it provides a means for students to realize what the event can mean to them when they have left the institution and afterward "come home."

Special events in alumni relations usually refers to activities such as commencement, founders' day or perhaps to an even more unique event, such as a centennial celebration. A good alumni relations staff will plan such events to take advantage of these opportunities to provide special programs for alumni. This is often an opportunity to sponsor a special continuing education program, book offering, lecture, campus tour, reunion, or similar activity.

Alumni Recognition. Awards and recognition of alumni and others for voluntary services rendered have long been an important part of the good alumni relations program. The types of awards and recognition given vary greatly between institutions and associations, but they can be classified into the following basic categories:

> *Distinguished alumni.* These awards, usually the highest given by an association, are typically given annually to one or more alumni who have distinguished themselves in their occupations, in community or national service, or in some other way that has brought recognition to their alma mater. This award category is usually reserved for those who have reached an outstanding level of achievement.
>
> *Honorary alumni awards.* These awards, usually reserved for nonalumni who have performed considerable service to the institution, come in the form of special honorary service awards or honorary membership in the alumni association. They allow an institution to confer recognition short of an honorary degree and can be a useful tool in the total institution recognition package.
>
> *Miscellaneous service/achievement awards.* These are lesser awards, usually given annually in larger numbers to individuals, either on- or off-campus. Some examples would be a young alumni achievement award given to outstanding alumni under thirty-five years of age, an alumni community service award recognizing service rendered by an alumnus to his or her home community, or an award to a person who has helped in fund-raising, either as a donor or as a volunteer worker.
>
> *Hall-of-fame awards.* These awards, usually built around some specific program such as athletics, are a useful means of recognition. This program allows for the development of a historical tradition that can add significant meaning to the entire program as well as bring considerable publicity to the institution.

Other recognition. Another recommended form of recognition is to appoint alumni to boards and committees. Most alumni associations have a board of directors, or its equivalent, that serves as a primary group in planning and carrying out alumni activities. Being on the board is looked on by most alumni as a form of recognition, and if they are made officers, it becomes even more prestigious. There are many other ways that individuals can be similarly recognized on a campus—for example, nomination to visiting boards for specific schools within the university, to boards of trustees, to advisory councils, and to curriculum development committees.

Many institutions are also initiating a formal volunteer recognition program. These programs might include a Volunteer of the Year award for schools, colleges, or organizations within the institution and one eminent Volunteer of the Year award for the whole institution. The guest list for volunteer recognition banquet or gala is generally composed of past volunteer recipients and current volunteers.

Minority Alumni Programs. Many alumni associations have developed minority alumni programs to meet the special needs of these constituencies. Examples of such groups are black alumni associations, Hispanic alumni programs, Native American groups, and women's issues forums. These are organized to meet the needs of a specific group of alumni and thus develop in this group a greater loyalty to the institution. A natural consequence of this loyalty is the support of the institution or its component parts.

Young Alumni Programs. This recent development in alumni relations is rapidly growing as a means of meeting the needs of young alumni and of developing in them close ties to the institution. Colleges and universities can no longer afford to allow young alumni to become distant and thus make it necessary for the institution to undertake the difficult process of rekindling the flame. (Young alumni are generally considered to be those who have graduated, or withdrawn, from the institution within the last ten years.) At least one university with an extensive young alumni program has reported substantial increases in the participation percentage of the recent class giving to the institution as compared with older classes. They report, for example, that the percentage of class donors for the second-year class is now equal to the fifteenth-year percentage. Even though the dollar amounts are considerably less, projections indicate that the potential for the future is indeed positive if these younger alumni are cultivated properly.

Typical programming for young alumni includes a young alumni reunion, athletic-related activities, low-cost trips, professional self-development seminars, interclass competitions, and formal galas.

The creativity of the alumni staff or volunteers will determine the success of this type of activity. Perhaps the best way to organize such programs would be to turn the project over to a group of enthusiastic young alumni and let them suggest a proper structure and program.

Older Alumni Programs. Programming for older alumni usually takes the form of century clubs or emeritus organizations for alumni who have been out of the institution for forty or fifty years and more. In some instances, retired institutional staff members are also included. This is an important group of alumni to cultivate because they often possess the greatest feelings of loyalty toward the institution and at the same time enjoy a higher than average economic status—a very positive combination!

Many institutions have organized their older alumni into special clubs or societies that have a high degree of independence but are assisted by members of the alumni association staff. This seems to work well for both the alumni and the institution.

Activities include annual meetings, which serve the purpose of reunions for this group; luncheons with institution speakers; induction activities for the entering class each year; special awards; and many other programs.

Alumni Family Camps. This very specialized, yet successful, alumni program has been developed during the past few years. Such camps exist at only a few institutions (the University of Michigan, Indiana University, the University of California at Berkeley, and Brigham Young University are among them) and are not for the faint-hearted, but they do promote a high degree of loyalty for and involvement with the institution among those who participate.

Essentially these camps are family-oriented, recreational/educational programs that operate during summer, although some operate the year around. The camp provides the program and the basic facilities, usually on a weekly basis, for forty to eighty families per week who enjoy this special kind of association with one another and the institution. Sometimes these camps are conducted on-campus, but most often they are located in some prime recreational area. Some have even been developed in foreign countries.

Conclusion

This is not an exhaustive list. These alumni programs are but a few among thousands currently being carried out by creative and dedicated alumni professionals who are committed to leaving the exciting world of education a bit better than they found it.

32

Linda Carl

Strengthening Alumni Ties Through Continuing Education

❧ This chapter deals with several questions whose importance is magnified by the same demographic, economic, and social trends that are affecting all institutions of higher education: Should continuing education be provided to alumni; that is, what benefits can be expected to accrue to the alumni, the institution, and the alumni association as a result of such programs? Who should provide alumni with continuing education? Are the benefits commensurate with the cost? and Assuming that they are, how should the alumni association provide continuing education programs, and which types of programs might best meet the diverse needs of the alumni, the university, and the alumni association? To what extent are the answers to these questions peculiar to certain types of institutions—for example, public versus private, selective versus less selective?

Alumni associations exist for many reasons. One of these reasons is to encourage alumni to support the college or university politically and financially. The prospects for receiving this support are enhanced when alumni feel they are receiving tangible benefits from the institution. The most natural benefit and obvious market niche the college or university can provide is assistance with lifelong learning. Indeed, it is so logical an extension that Steve Calvert, director of alumni continuing education at Dartmouth,

426

asks, "Can anyone explain to me why, after paying little or no attention to undergraduates' social lives, we suddenly upon their graduation can think of little else for their reunions, alumni clubs, and the like?" (1982, p. 54).

Several recent studies support the notion that alumni desire continuing education. Duett (1975) and Morgal (1979) found that alumni generally have higher expectations for alumni continuing education than are realized in practice. Morgal also found that alumni want their alumni associations to provide them with continuing education opportunities more than they want the association to provide them with additional social activities. This is important because there is also evidence that the great majority of alumni who participate in alumni continuing education programs do not participate in chapter programs or reunions unless those programs themselves include some academic or continuing education component (Riggs, 1979; Nickles, 1976). Furthermore, even if alumni do not take advantage of these programs, they often wish they could. Often alumni staff hear such comments as "I love to read your brochures. I haven't taken a course yet, but I certainly hope to some day." Another impact is that alumni who participate in alumni continuing education programs may later participate in other alumni activities. In addition, reacquainting alumni with the raison d'être of the institution and the quality of the academic offerings may increase the probability that alumni will recruit their children and their friends' children as students.

Finally, some university and alumni leaders have argued that continuing education for alumni is a moral imperative, asserting that, once the educational process has begun, it is negligent to terminate the relationship after four years (McMahon, 1960). Few alumni associations have taken this charge seriously and asked, "What business are we really in? . . . What attractive and important set of services does our institution provide that people cannot obtain elsewhere better, faster, or cheaper?" (Keller, 1983, p. 121). And fewer still have answered "continuing education."

This is so in spite of the fact that alumni and university leaders have been talking about the significance of alumni continuing education since the early part of this century. As early as 1916, President Ernest Martin Hopkins called for it in his inaugural address at Dartmouth. However, although more alumni associations are bowing in the direction of continuing education by sponsoring occasional programs, relatively few have a serious commitment to continuing education as measured by number of programs, variety, length of programs, and content.

It is important to carefully distinguish between continuing education provided by alumni associations and that provided for alumni by other organizations. A major reason alumni associations are not sponsoring continuing education programs may be that other organizations on campus are developing programs that would be of educational and cultural interest to alumni. As a corollary, the most extensive continuing education programs seem to be offered by alumni associations that do not have to compete with another campus unit.

When an alumni association is confronted by competing units offering continuing education programs, what should be its response? Although it might seem inconsistent with the alumni association's self-interest to actively promote the continuing education program of other campus units, in the long run, it is not. If alumni feel that the institution is providing educational and cultural benefits for them, they may have a more favorable view of the institution and, therefore, become more active in alumni affairs and annual giving. For these reasons an enlightened policy might be to promote some of the following: (1) courses sponsored by other continuing education units, (2) on-campus programs sponsored by units, such as Friends of the University Library, the Society for the Art Museum, drama groups, or the university hospital, whose main function is not continuing education, and (3) special recurring events, such as a great decision series, named lectures, or special forums, that are sponsored by students.

This information can be disseminated in a variety of ways, including calendar inserts in publications, inserts in membership renewal notices, an 800 telephone number that alumni can call to find out about current programs, and perhaps on-line computer access. (Already Princeton alumni have computer access to their biweekly alumni magazine, which includes a calendar of activities.) Furthermore, the alumni association can regularly inform alumni about other educational resources, such as the procedures they can follow to audit courses or use the university library or the way to obtain the current titles offered by the university press. Alumni publications are already a major source of information. They can become even more self-consciously an agent of continuing education by providing mechanisms for carrying out activities. Many of these efforts capitalize on the resources already on-campus. Alumni associations might apply George Keller's advice on university planning to the planning of their continuing education: "Development depends not so much on finding optimal combinations for given resources . . . as calling forth and enlisting for development the purposes, resources and abilities that are hidden, scattered or are badly utilized" (Keller, 1983, p. 68).

Another strategy for expanding the alumni continuing education program is to cosponsor programs with an extension unit. This has the advantage of giving access to professional help without hiring extra staff. It has the potential disadvantage of causing the program to be more expensive than the alumni association would wish or, in some cases, giving the alumni association less visibility than it would want. Some continuing education units, for example, refuse to list the alumni association as a cosponsor in the continuing education catalog.

Because it is in the interest of the alumni association to see that continuing education is vital on its campus, it should do everything it can to promote the extension function. Furthermore, if the alumni association becomes a provider of continuing education, it should try to have a representative on the campus's continuing education council, so the association can both support continuing education in general and find allies for alumni continuing education.

In addition to being a conduit for continuing education, or a cosponsor with an extension unit, an alumni association may also decide to develop and administer its own programs if there are gaps in the variety and types of continuing education offered to alumni. Specifically, alumni associations should be prepared to go it alone if they do not get sufficient recognition from cosponsors. Additionally, they should recognize their unique strengths: (1) a natural entrée across the state and nation, through alumni chapters, to set up off-campus programs and (2) a greater rapport with the participants than other sponsors because of the multifaceted nature of alumni programs.

If, for any of the preceding reasons, the alumni association decides to cosponsor or sponsor continuing education programs, it must address the following areas: content, faculty, finances, planning, and administration.

Content

To what extent should alumni continuing education programs deal with subjects that cannot be taught by the institution's faculty or staff? If the alumni association wants to enhance the image of the university, it should probably avoid gourmet cooking if it does not have a hotel school and avoid gardening if it does not have a botanical garden. Even if they are financially successful, such programs may be discordant with the institutional image.

This becomes even more significant if the alumni continuing education offerings are few in number. Furthermore, if respect by the faculty is a concern, the alumni association must be cautious about the topics of the continuing education programs it sponsors. A program that includes bridge lessons might make university faculty reluctant to have themselves promoted in the same catalog.

Faculty

Who are appropriate faculty for alumni continuing education programs? The first caveat is that it is better to have a lesser-known teacher who is enthusiastic and an effective speaker than to have a famous scholar who is tedious. The latter may attract applicants, but it is the former who makes participants likely to return. However, enthusiasm among the faculty or the alumni association staff is insufficient for the design of serious and sustained continuing education programs. At some point, faculty or a content specialist should play a role in shaping the program's focus. Where should this faculty come from? First of all, from the institution's faculty. Second, from the alumni body and other outside sources. However, before combining an institution's faculty member with an outsider, it is prudent to check out your faculty's reaction to the outside expert.

Finances

What is the financial goal of these programs? Alumni associations generally try to keep costs low to attract as large a number of participants as possible. The sponsoring associations do not assume they will need to recover the salary costs devoted to staff time in continuing education. However, they often debate whether they should pay faculty members for their participation. Generally, faculty members who devote a significant amount of time (that is, as faculty coordinator for an alumni college) should be paid honoraria. However, faculty who do an isolated lecture may be paid nothing. Still, in the long run, the association will gain more respect from the faculty and enhance its own image as a serious provider of continuing education if it pays faculty.

One of the most troublesome aspects of alumni continuing education is keeping the program financially viable. If an institution initiates a continuing education program or quickly expands a smaller one, it should be prepared to lose money for three to five years. It takes time to build a new image and create a new business.

Audience

Is the audience for alumni-association-sponsored continuing education programs only alumni? Probably not, even though marketing efforts will be directed primarily at alumni. If the program is to be viable, it must attract a large number of participants and thus should also be marketed to friends of the university. Wider marketing also offers the association the opportunity to provide the benefit of a discount to alumni association members who enroll.

The acceptable ratio of nonalumni to alumni in a program is difficult to ascertain. High participation of nonalumni has caused some alumni associations to drop selected continuing education programs. However, some of the most successful alumni colleges in the country (Dartmouth College, University of North Carolina at Chapel Hill, Indiana University) may have as many as 40 percent of their participants who are not alumni or spouses of alumni. None of these institutions have received complaints from their alumni participants about the participation of nonalumni. Alumni who attend these programs come primarily because they are attracted by the intellectual stimulation and to a lesser extent because they are attracted to a program conducted at their alma mater (Carl, 1978).

Planning and Administration

Some alumni associations assign the responsibility of planning continuing education programs to an alumni continuing education committee. The disadvantage of this arrangement is the dependency on volunteers whose commitment and time cannot be controlled; this can be a problem even when there is backup support from association staff. More associations assign this function to the person who directs the program—usually this is a person who has other duties. Rarely does the association have a staff member with the title Director of Alumni Continuing Education.

After answering questions about such issues as faculty and finances, the alumni association can turn to the fun and work of deciding which specific programs it should sponsor. As the association makes these decisions, it has many models from which to choose among the successful programs already sponsored by alumni associations. Following are examples that describe the range of these offerings:

Alumni College on Campus. One program that many alumni associations have attempted is an alumni college. The term *alumni college* is used to refer to many types of programs. As used here, however, the term has a very specific definition: a five- to seven-day program in the liberal arts sponsored, or cosponsored, by an alumni association. Alumni colleges come in many shapes and sizes. Private institutions, such as Ohio Wesleyan University and particularly Ivy League schools (Dartmouth College, Brown University, Harvard University, Princeton University), have some of the oldest and best-established programs. Many of the large public institutions have attempted and dropped such programs (University of Michigan, University of Washington, University of Kansas, Ohio State University). However, a few persist at such institutions as the University of Illinois and the University of Colorado. Indeed, Indiana University has one of the largest and most successful alumni college programs.

Alumni continuing education is most successful and pervasive at prestigious private colleges and universities. The most likely reason for this can be summed up in one word—money. These schools have recognized for years that the success of their institutions has always depended on alumni support. Their reputations as academic institutions and their lack of prominence as major sport powers have attracted to them academically oriented students who graduate and become academically oriented alumni. A second reason that continuing education is dominated by private institutions is that their academic peers among the public institutions have, until recently, not felt the economic necessity of courting their alumni.

Alumni Colleges Off-Campus. Alumni colleges are occasionally held off-campus, sometimes because the home campus is not seen as attractive for a summer vacation. The University of Kansas, the University of Pennsylvania, and Johns Hopkins University, for example, moved to nearby states or to more scenic locations within their own state. However, only the Johns Hopkins program remained viable. In addition to negative reasons for moving off-campus, there are positive ones, such as the lure of a specific locale that relates to specific topics. For example, Southern Methodist University in Texas moved one alumni college to a historical fort in New Mexico to study the history, archeology, and geology of the Southwest. Similarly, Princeton and Amherst sponsor alumni colleges in Montana. The difference between these and other alumni colleges off-campus is their emphasis on nature and local history. There is little difference between these and shorter weekend programs off-campus. These programs are also close relatives of the alumni college programs abroad.

Conference Programs. There are numerous programs that try to bring large numbers of alumni back to campus for weekend programs. These are often cosponsored by the college of liberal arts and sciences and/or the graduate school. Participants are often able to choose between numerous topics. Alternatively, the alumni may focus on one topic, with all participants attending the same lectures. Topics by prominent alumni or nationally known figures are often featured as one aspect of these programs, which are from half a day to three days in length. The climax of the weekend is often a luncheon, dinner, or play or other performance.

The University of Minnesota's Spectrum, Stanford's Campus Conference, Indiana University's Alumni Day, the State University of New York at Albany's Homecoming Community University Day, and the University of Georgia's Alumni Seminar are a few examples of this popular type of program. The University of Georgia's Alumni Association has sponsored an alumni seminar for twenty-one years; it regularly attracts 400 participants.

Women's Day. These programs, which typically follow the alumni day format, may include issues of particular interest to women along with general issues. These continuing education programs have been especially popular in the Midwest (University of Illinois at Urbana–Champaign, University of Wisconsin, Ohio State University, University of Iowa). These programs, which had their origins in the sixties, were sometimes outgrowths of alumnae associations. Their audience has traditionally been the non-career-woman. As the separate alumnae associations have disappeared, and as women have gone back to work, the audience for some of these programs is diminishing. Therefore, some institutions have experimented with moving these traditionally weekday programs to Saturday or with trying to attract men and changing the name of the program in order to do so.

Special Audiences. Families—parents and children to-gether—may be invited to attend a lecture on-campus or to take part in one special program, such as a computer course, on-campus. Residential week-long computer courses have been popular for those alumni associations (Michigan State, Dartmouth, Bowling Green State University) that have sponsored them. The most typical continuing education programs for families on- and off-campus, however, include parents and children in distinctive learning experiences. Many of the alumni colleges include recreational and educational programs for children.

Another family setting, the off-campus family camp, includes faculty forums for adults along with its recreational programs. Faculty forums and/or coffees are offered by such institutions as Stanford, the University of California at Berkeley, Indiana University, the University of Illinois, and the University of Michigan. Another special audience for seminars is black alumni. The black alumni reunions at the University of North Carolina at Chapel Hill and Vanderbilt University incorporate seminars into the reunion weekend.

On-Campus Weekend Seminars. Week-long alumni colleges may be the most typical form of residential liberal arts continuing education programs, but they are not the only ones. Sometimes, alumni programs sponsor one or more weekend seminars during the academic year. The University of North Carolina at Chapel Hill's General Alumni Association, in cosponsorship with the Program in the Humanities, sponsors eighteen interdisciplinary humanities weekend seminars each academic year. Initiated in 1978, the seminar series has increased its participation each year. Programs on personal finance and career counseling are also sponsored by alumni associations, such as Rutgers and Stanford.

On-Campus Events. The opportunity to attend a lecture or seminar before a performance has also been used in a variety of formats: The University of Michigan has pretheater seminars on the afternoon of the performance, while the University of North Carolina at Chapel Hill incorporates a play in a weekend seminar each semester. Rutgers's Alumni Federation frequently invites alumni to a dinner before a performance by a campus or visiting group.

Sometimes a special historical event serves as the impetus for a continuing education program. Indiana University helped to organize and promote a symposium and workshop commemorating the signing of the Treaty of Paris.

Diverse Formats. Single lectures and daytime and evening seminars are offered by a variety of institutions. For example, the University of Michigan offers "Coffee with the Faculty," a morning series of informal faculty-alumni exchanges. These include visits to specific buildings as well as lectures by faculty.

Off-Campus Seminars. There are two types of off-campus seminars: Some are allied with chapters and are similar to those offered on-campus; others are off-campus because of their distinctive subject matter. The mountains, the ocean, or a wildlife refuge are often sites for successful programs. For example, the University of Georgia, Duke University, and the University of North Carolina at Chapel Hill all sponsor weekends on the coast in conjunction with their marine sciences program. In addition to nature programs, off-campus seminars or lectures have focused on special art exhibits at major museums or summer drama festivals.

Most of the Ivy League schools sponsor off-campus seminars in cooperation with alumni chapters or clubs. Indeed, some of these institutions cosponsor programs so that they can cut travel costs for their faculty. In 1984, Dartmouth, which has the most extensive of these programs, sponsored seventeen seminars, and with the addition of more staff in 1985, expansion was expected. Dartmouth's seminar program has several salient features: (1) The programs are subsidized, (2) the director of alumni continuing education at Dartmouth does as much work as can be done from the home campus (selection of faculty, guidance concerning topics of promotion, selection of topics, and background reading). The chapters, however, are responsible for their own local arrangements. These successful seminars frequently attract seventy-five to a hundred participants, and about half the clubs that sponsor seminars sponsor them each year. Volunteers who will be responsible for these seminars are invited to Dartmouth each year to be trained in a special workshop. Additionally, Dartmouth has prepared a complete handbook for alumni continuing education officers.

Humanities seminars on a single theme are not the only approach to off-campus programs. Harvard, for example, organizes the equivalent of an on-campus alumni day but takes the program to various centers for the alumni population. Between two and four such programs offered each year involve three to eight faculty members in a variety of disciplines.

Another type of off-campus chapter programming can be seen in the establishment of Continuum, a nonprofit organization set up to provide alumni continuing education for the Philadelphia clubs and chapters of almost thirty private institutions. Continuum is housed at, but separate from, Haverford College. The offerings are similar to the noncredit programs of many universities' extension units. Unlike most off-campus seminars, which take place over one weekend, Continuum's offerings may be spread over many weeks.

Continuing Professional Education. Few alumni associations plan continuing professional education programs; generally this is left to professional associations and professional schools. However, there are some interesting exceptions. Stanford University, which has no general extension unit, sponsors a spectrum of programs called the Stanford Continuing Education Executive Program. Some of these are conventional continuing education programs; others take a more unusual tactic of providing humanities programs for executives. The programs are expensive by the standards of conventional liberal arts programs, but they are competitive with programs offered by other elite business schools. At the other end of the spectrum, the University of Georgia has recently begun requesting each of its area committees to develop at least one semester of continuing education each year and to especially target such groups as principals, editors, and mayors. In 1983, the University of Georgia's alumni association took advantage of a teacher's work day to develop programs for public school teachers. Notwithstanding the success of a few institutions, it is unlikely that many general alumni associations will develop much in the way of professional programs unless the alumni association is incorporated with its constituent societies, which in turn sponsor these types of programs.

Travel. Almost every alumni association offers a travel program. Although all travel is educational, educational experiences are purposefully added to the tour program to enrich the traveler's experience beyond that of the conventional tour. At the outset, it must be recognized that this is a competitive field. The Smithsonian, the American Association of Retired Persons (AARP), local museums, and even travel agencies are among the competitors pursuing the educational travel market, but although there is no reason why alumni associations should not be successful in this market, few institutions orient their market around educationally enriched travel. And as with other continuing education programs, those that pursue this market are likely to be the more selective private institutions.

What are the types of educationally enriched tours that alumni associations currently offer or might offer? One type is that in which an institution's faculty member accompanies a packaged tour offered by a travel agency. Cruises, in particular, lend themselves to faculty involvement because the time on the water represents a real opportunity for faculty members to give a substantial lecture with discussion. Other than lectures, one of the most valuable ways faculty members can be utilized is by having them available at meals, on the bus, during cocktail hours, and at museums to answer individual questions of tour members.

Tour experiences can be enriched educationally in a variety of ways prior to or following the tour by means of alumni college area study seminars or weekend seminars, which may take place several months prior to the tour and may also be open to individuals who are not going on the tour, or predeparture seminars, which may be included as part of the tour price and be open only to tour members. These may take the form of a two-day seminar on-campus or a one-day seminar at the departure city. Additionally, the alumni association can send out bibliographies, newspaper and magazine articles, and paperback books on the places to be visited. A tour can also be educationally enriched by including guest experts from the host site (for example, having a briefing by the military or cultural attaché at the American embassy, lectures from specialists at a local university or museum, or talks by journalists or TV correspondents for American newspapers) or by actually holding the program at other universities and including formal lectures.

As we have seen in this chapter, the future of alumni continuing education is nebulous. On the one hand, there is a flurry of far-ranging activity including alumni colleges on- and off-campus, women's day, on- and off-campus weekend seminars, chapter and club seminars, conferences, programs for special audiences, and educational travel. On the other hand, the alumni continuing education enterprise is more fragile than we might expect after the rhetoric of the last fifty years. If one looks at the support given alumni continuing education by alumni and alumni leadership, it is apparent that alumni continuing education is still an idea that needs to be sold.

Thus, as alumni associations decide what course to follow in continuing education, it might be profitable to look back not to words of one of their colleagues but to those of a politician, Calvin Coolidge. Although President Coolidge is not often quoted in academic circles, he gave some excellent advice for those concerned with the issues in this chapter when he said, "The business of America is business." The business of educational institutions is education. Alumni leadership will do well to remember this.

References

Calvert, S. L. "Legitimizing the Bastard: The Natural Child of Higher Education—Alumni Continuing Education." In *National Issues in Higher Education.* Vol. 7: *Proceedings of the Role of Non-Credit Programs in Higher Education: Administrative Issues.* Manhattan: Kansas State University, 1982.

Carl, L. *The Alumni College Movement, 1977.* Washington, D.C.: Council for Advancement and Support of Education, 1978.

Duett, S. B. *American Higher Education Alumni Programs—A Goals Analysis.* Ann Arbor: Michigan University Microfilms International, 1975.

Keller, G. *Academic Strategy: The Management Revolution in American Higher Education.* Baltimore, Md.: Johns Hopkins University Press, 1983.

McMahon, E. *New Directions for Alumni Continuing Education for the College Graduate.* Chicago: Center for the Study of Liberal Education for Adults, 1960.

Morgal, R. "A Study of Four University Alumni Associations: Implications for Adult Lifelong Learning." Unpublished master's thesis, Interdisciplinary Studies, Hofstra University, 1979.

Nickles, F. P., Jr. "A Report on the Continuing Education Program of the Tufts Alumni Council." Unpublished report, Tufts University, March 1976.

Riggs, S. K. "Attracting 'New' Alumni Through Continuing Education." *CASE Currents,* May 1979, pp. 20-22.

33

Stephen W. Roszell

Alumni Chapter
and Constituent
Organization

◦§ There are two basic building blocks of any alumni relations program: geographically based organizations and college-based organizations. Geographical organizations of alumni may be called clubs or chapters. College-based organizations may be called college, divisional, or constituent groups.

Here, geographical organizations of alumni are referred to as *chapters*. Collegiate organizations of alumni are referred to as *constituent groups*. Chapters are normally organized in cities some distance from the campus where alumni are concentrated in significant enough numbers to warrant organization. Constituent groups are usually composed of alumni of one academic discipline (law, education, business) who organize to bond themselves to their particular academic program.

To better understand these two different organizational methods of alumni involvement, it is helpful to take a broader look at the process of alumni relations. Think of the process as a continuum that culminates in a commitment by alumni. The alumni relations continuum begins with *research* to discover what we know about our alumni. Following research is *identification*. Minimums of data maintained by most alumni relations programs to identify alumni include name, address, class year, college affiliation, degree, and date of graduation. Once identification is

440

complete, we have the *information stage,* during which alumni receive information from their institution. Newsletters, magazines, brochures, and direct-mail solicitations are typical of the written communication alumni usually receive. However, at this information stage, the chapter and constituent groups become vital because they enhance communication and produce opportunities for effective face-to-face communication. Chapters and constituent groups also are a conduit through which feedback can flow to those sending the written messages.

Finally, in the continuum you have involvement and closure, the *commitment stage.* Again, the role of chapter and constituent groups in these stages of alumni involvement is critical to a sound alumni relations program.

Alumni Chapters

The purpose of an alumni chapter is to organize the alumni of a certain geographic area into an advocacy group for their university or college. The history of the alumni movement reminds us that before the formal incorporation of general alumni associations, alumni in certain geographical regions gathered on their own to remember college days or renew acquaintances. Because alumni chapters preceded more formal organizations of alumni, some of these chapters feel autonomous, and this autonomy creates administrative challenges for alumni directors. A strong alumni chapter program that contributes to the goals and objectives of the alumni association is a careful balancing act of managing resources and volunteers to achieve certain alumni association goals while, at the same time, meeting the needs of the local alumni groups. The expectations of chapter volunteers often place enormous pressure on the alumni association to arrange programs, produce films, assign staff visits, and provide carte blanche service. Chapter volunteers often have the view that, rather than being in the office, alumni directors should be out visiting the chapters. But if they are out visiting chapters, those same volunteers may well feel that alumni directors are never in the office when they need them.

Chapters pose other challenges too. If they raise funds for scholarships or independently controlled programming, how is this integrated into the institution's fund-raising plans? If they recruit students, who trains them for this and grants them authority to do so? If they hold social events, who benefits—those attending or the institution? What is the measure of a successful chapter meeting—the number of people attending, the quality of the program, or the chapter's clout, either financially or as opinion leaders of the alumni audience?

To respond to these challenges, alumni associations must have a clear set of operating guidelines for management of a chapter program. Many of the difficulties chapter programs create are a result of neglect on the part of the alumni association, and a careful plan of chapter organization and development can eliminate many of these problems. Although most alumni directors do not have the luxury of starting a program from the beginning, there are several steps to be followed when determining the role your program will play. The first step is to determine the scope of your program. Do you want a state, national, or international network of alumni? The answer may be "ultimately, all of these," but consider limiting yourself to the national network, initially. Operating under the assumption that absence makes the heart grow fonder, look at major metropolitan areas outside a hundred-mile radius of your campus where there is a critical mass of alumni. (Critical mass may vary from 100 to 500 depending on the size of your institution; do not, however, view the numbers in abstract: consider donor and student potential and the demographic data on the alumni located in the areas.)

Typically, you can expect a 12 to 20 percent response from an uncultivated market. Once the organizational target areas have been identified, assign one staff person responsibility for managing your alumni chapter program. If you lack adequate staff, do not start the program. Lack of continuity and responsiveness kills chapter programs. If you cannot guarantee continuity and attention, you are better off not starting the program for the alumni association. This does not preclude identifying a group of alumni to work with admissions or development staff, but it does suggest that if you intend to establish a chapter, the staff and expense resources must be committed by the alumni organization.

Discuss with the administration of your institution those long-term institutional goals and objectives that would best be served by a geographical network of advocates. Commit your goals to paper, and use them as a purpose statement and a rationale for starting the program. Alumni chapters should not be organized for social reasons. A chapter program is an advocacy program, and alumni ultimately will be more committed and involved if they feel their participation in a local chapter is supporting the goals of their institution. Whatever socializing they receive as a result of their service is an important additional benefit, but it is not the basis for a program.

Start the program by identifying the best volunteers in the geographical area you intend to organize. Begin with ten, contact them, ask their help, and meet with them in their area. Review the purpose statement, and divide among these ten volunteers the responsibilities for assisting in accomplishing these goals. Holding a meeting should not be considered a goal. The meeting should be a mechanism to accomplish one or more of the goals, not an end in itself. As the group matures, it should elect officers and ultimately approve a constitution based on the model constitution your organization requires.

Duties of volunteers may vary according to your needs. Typical duties include annual fund chair, student recruitment chair, program chair, and publicity chair. Other duties, not as typical but still important, might include capital campaign chair, legislative contact, or chapter clipper (someone who sends local news on alumni back to your institution). Many alumni organizations have incorporated a welcome wagon function into their chapters; they provide information for transferred alumni or recent graduates moving into the area for the first time.

To maintain and motivate chapter volunteers, a clear description of duties and ongoing monitoring are necessary. A chapter handbook that describes the philosophy of your program, the duties of officers, and the operating procedures your alumni organization requires is essential. The handbook should be assembled in a manner that allows easy update and modification.

One of the biggest challenges of a chapter program is maintenance of the continuity of the program as you try to maintain activity that supports the mission of your institution simultaneously in a variety of geographical locations. Daily staff attention, an annual leadership day for chapter leaders held on your campus, and a monitoring system are all techniques that foster continuity.

The success of your chapter program depends on your ability to focus the geographical resources of the various chapters on projects that support your goals. The best way to maintain a focus is to centrally control the address lists and mailings. Before starting a chapter program, project the costs of lists, labels, and mail production two to three times per year in each of your target areas. Include personnel and travel costs for effective staffing, and be prepared to commit this total resource package for at least five years before measuring the cost-benefit ratio.

Alumni chapters give your program a national scope and, from project to project, can be extremely helpful in accomplishing your goal. But the key to a chapter's ultimate success will depend on the view your institution has of this valuable national resource. It is important that people who represent the institution as speakers or resources at chapter functions reinforce the stature of the chapter and, in their remarks and as part of their presentations, tie the chapter, the alumni, and the importance of their continuing support back to the institution.

As in other volunteer efforts, those volunteers who are asked to serve and who understand the importance of their service will stay involved. Those who are given nothing to do perceive their role as insignificant and will not stay involved. The true success of your program will be your ability to identify meaningful activities each year. The era has passed when socialization provided the bond; meaningful involvement is the key to chapter programs of the future.

Constituent Societies. Discussing the history of the first alumni association, Wilfred Shaw (1917), the alumni secretary at the University of Michigan, observed, "The desire to perpetuate college friendships and to revive memories of college days was undoubtedly the underlying cause which first brought alumni together to form alumni organizations" (p. 5). An analysis of this observation suggests that the primary motivation for the first alumni organizations was the opportunity for bonding—bonding with friends and bonding with your college. As alumni organizations have matured, an additional factor for alumni involvement is the opportunity for meaningful service.

If you accept these elements as essential for successful alumni organizations, it is easy to see how constituent groups have emerged as an important element of modern alumni organizations. The ability of an alumni organization to offer both bonding and meaningful service has been eroded as the size of modern educational institutions has increased. To be a member of the graduating class at the University of Minnesota means graduating with 12,000 students from a variety of academic disciplines. However, to be a member of the graduating class of the School of Journalism or Medicine reduces that group size significantly while ensuring commonality of experience. As a journalism graduate, one usually has experienced the same faculty and academic program, and many of the same facilities as fellow students. The same holds true for small institutions that have distinct degree programs or for professional schools that produce graduates whose identity is narrowly focused.

If we accept Shaw's conclusion that the lowest common denominator of friends and memories is vital, then alumni market segmentations by constituency interest group, either academic or special (such as marching band, ROTC alumni, or black alumni groups), makes profound sense. Within the past ten years, the market segmentation by constituency has been occurring at an ever-increasing pace at large colleges and universities. The way an alumni organization manages this change will have a significant impact on the future of alumni organizations as we know them today. Will segments of the market break off as independent alumni organizations, or will they operate under a central alumni association umbrella and contribute to the organization's central goal? The answer depends on the ability of alumni organizations to be responsive to constituencies.

The biggest challenge to most alumni organizations is management of growth. Scarcity of resources and the consensus-building required at most institutions make growth management difficult. The constituent program usually exacerbates this problem because effective constituency staffing usually encourages increased activity by the constituent group. This, in turn, creates the need for even more staffing. This vicious circle usually creates an environment where the alumni executive asks staff to stretch their service rather than adding staff to adequately meet staffing needs. Just as in the chapter program, adequate staff resources, control of the list and labels, mailing services, and financial services should be managed centrally. There are economies and efficiencies to be gained by centralizing these functions, but most important, centralization ensures coordination.

In institution-supported alumni organizations, all resources to support constituent alumni activities should generally be placed under the managerial control of the alumni director. In dues-based organizations, the financial arrangement for collegiate groups is more difficult to manage. Constituent groups often want to collect their own dues. If your general alumni organization collects dues, constituent dues are counterproductive. Typically, a dues-sharing arrangement is the most common model. Even if constituent groups charge their own dues, you should consider centrally managing the collection process. A straight pass-through of money collected is not most efficient; this encourages constituent groups to accumulate resources and feel ownership. A more effective model is an allocation based on head count supplemented by a pool of funds available for constituent groups to draw from for approved activities and projects. This incentive pool fosters the positive relationship between central alumni organizations and the constituent group, encourages a central programming review process, and vests financial management centrally.

The success of a constituent society program depends on the commitment of the head of the college unit. A dean or director who understands both institutional relations and the potential collegiate resource that organized alumni represent can move a constituent group forward quickly. Dean and department directors should be reminded of the ideal forum alumni activities provide to recognize and integrate faculty, alumni, and students into programs that support collegiate priorities. A properly orchestrated alumni gathering can provide an opportunity to recognize special faculty, students, or programs. This effort can both make faculty highly visible and personalize the important work of the college or department to alumni and can identify opportunity for alumni service.

Responsibility then moves to the alumni staff to translate the volunteer service into activities the collegiate administration views as meaningful. This staff service can be managed centrally if the dean or director views the staff member assigned to that constituent group as a facilitator of the constituent group's alumni program. This places a burden on the staff to meet regularly with the administration of the college to report the constituent group's progress. The dean may choose to delegate alumni responsibility to an associate dean or other staff member. This arrangement works, provided the dean continues to meet with the volunteers when necessary and provided the collegiate staff members clearly understand they represent the college and are not alumni relations professionals.

Decentralization of fund-raising has complicated constituent alumni management in recent years. Many institutions have assigned development officers to constituent units to raise funds. Often these officers are housed in the college and are given the assignment of working with constituent alumni of the college. This model can be successful if the players all understand their own individual roles in the institutional relations effort. The development officer in this situation should communicate the case for private support to the alumni and solicit alumni assistance in prospect identification and, in some cases, solicitation. The alumni group can also assist the development officer by incorporating donor recognition into alumni events and using alumni communication mechanisms to support the case for private support. The alumni group should not be viewed by the development officer as a gift resource only, for although alumni constituent volunteers should be the first to make gifts at a level commensurate with their means, the time in service and the valuable communication and networking tool alumni represent are the long-term resource for any constituent development effort. A partnership between alumni relations and development professional staff is the most successful model. In the partnership, the alumni staff should encourage alumni stewardship and involvement at all levels including (but not exclusively) giving to support the college. The development partners should view development in the broadest sense of the word and keep a long-term perspective on the value of a strong alumni relations effort.

As is the case with chapters, programming for constituent alumni should not be purely social. The emphasis should be on highlighting the academic strengths of the collegiate unit; involving students, faculty, and alumni in mentoring; and creating internships or other working relationships. Alumni programming for collegiate units should make the type of programs offered to all alumni "constituency specific." To do this requires the unique understanding the alumni professional staff should have regarding the market analysis of each specific collegiate group: Dentists require a marketing approach different from that for lawyers, for example. The alumni staff should undertake the necessary research to analyze each constituent market and then program accordingly.

Of all the alumni programs to emerge during the last twenty-five years, the constituent program represents the greatest challenge for alumni directors. As resources become scarce, and academic programs are threatened, a sincere interest in building a highly committed and informed constituency has become a priority for deans and collegiate units. The ability of a university or college alumni association to respond to this desire in a professional, service-oriented manner may ensure the future for alumni associations as we know them today. A confederation of strong constituent groups, working under the umbrella of the alumni association, is a far better choice than fifteen independent alumni constituencies, each working on its own agenda. Central alumni organizations will need to be innovative, responsive, and above all, highly professional if they hope to use the constituency movement as an opportunity to build rather than divide.

Reference

Shaw, W. *Handbook of Alumni Work*. Ann Arbor: Association of Alumni Secretaries, University of Michigan, 1917.

34 *Steven L. Calvert*

Planning
Meaningful Reunions

~&~ Reunions are probably the oldest and purest form of alumni relations. The first reunions took place deep in the history of higher education. The University of Pennsylvania has hazy recollections of class dinners all the way back to colonial times. Daniel N. White (1978) can place Princeton University's first reunions in the early nineteenth century. Members of Stanford University's Class of 1892 wasted no time organizing their first reunion, which took place five minutes after commencement. University of Notre Dame reunions date from 1869, when in the combined atmosphere of commencement and a general meeting of the alumni association, numerous toasts were offered "to alma mater, our nation, religion, education, alumni, the press, the Pope, old times, old friends, the flag, ad infinitum," or as one alumnus explained it, "They returned here to drink beer and lie."

Many other forms of alumni relations began as university relations; that is, universities initiated them primarily for their own benefit. Reunions, by contrast, seem more commonly to have begun when alumni yielded to their own urge to be reunited with each other in the university context where their relationships had begun.

Today, reunions remain the bread-and-butter form of alumni relations. They are the most common, best attended, and most successful form in terms of communication between alumni and the university, political advantage deriving from alumni support for public universities, and fund-raising from special reunion class gifts.

The apocrypha and the bona fide history of reunions make good storytelling. Princeton's P-rade, a gala reunion almost unbelievable to behold, sets a standard for sheer exuberant celebration of alma mater. Shirley Picardi and Joe Martori report that M.I.T.'s 1904 reunion provided substantial numbers of gathered alumni an opportunity to fight against being absorbed into Harvard, an idea then being proposed by M.I.T. President Henry Pritchett and Andrew Carnegie (Wylie, 1975).

No story, however, is nearly as interesting as the events, themselves, that we call *reunions*. In his gem of an essay on reunions, Princeton's Daniel N. White (1978) drew from Harvey Cox's *Feast of Fools* (1969) the elements of festivity and fantasy to explain the rich cultural and social atmosphere of Princeton reunions. White's assessment of the unique meaning that university reunions have for Americans led him to argue that these special events at their best provide for a balance of the social and the cultural. This conception of the university reunion "festival" as a complete cultural event is persuasive and raises interesting questions about the traditional shape of reunions at many of our universities, where they are almost entirely social.

It is worth asking, for example, why our university students live triple lives while in school—academic, recreational (that is, athletic, musical, or otherwise serious but extracurricular), and social—while so many reunion programs fail to recapture this rich balance and, indeed, typically neglect the academic or intellectual life altogether. A Martian, observing many college reunions, might think adolescents go to the university (as one wag has facetiously suggested) to carouse until they are old enough to come out and behave themselves. Certainly, our Martian would see little of the intellectual heart of the university, which brought alumni together as students in the first place. Of course, we may want to distinguish between the celebration and the thing being celebrated, but there is something esthetically inappropriate in the unrelieved raucous celebration of serious intellectual enterprise. What would be wrong with an intellectual celebration of an intellectual enterprise? More about that later.

For now, take a moment to consider how we use the word
reunion. We seem to mean reexperiencing a union of some kind.
Under the best of circumstances, three unions are celebrated at a
reunion.

First, a reunion probably ought to recapitulate the three-part
lives students lived as undergraduates—ought to recapture that
special union of the academic, the recreational, and the social.
Second, under favorable circumstances a reunion can celebrate a
previous union of individuals in a college class. (As any alumni
relations professional knows, for many classes this union is pure
fiction, because those classes were never united in the first place.)
Whether these classes were disrupted by a foreign war (such as
World War II or the Vietnam war) or just a war between deans and
students, students and faculty, or everybody and a president, they are
very hard to bring back for a fictional reunion. We might do better
to completely change our strategy for such classes and use special
communications, organization innovation, and programming to
build the first union they ever had. And third, after reunions have
reunited former students with their erstwhile integrated lives and
fellow students, they would ideally unite them with something they
have never known—the university of today. It is extremely helpful,
in this regard, not only to provide reunion alumni with intellectual
access to the faculty but also to have reunion classes hobnob with
the graduating class at commencement and with underclassmen,
who can serve as reunion workers. What is the university today if
not our current students and teachers? A complete reunion will
integrate all three of the goals suggested here, and with that kind
of integration, a reunion can hardly fail.

Such success is difficult to achieve, and we have developed a
great variety of reunion programs trying to succeed. There are
reunions in the spring (some tied to the commencement weekend,
but not if everyone cannot fit on campus at once) and reunions at
other times of year (often in the fall to coincide with major football
events). There are reunions to which every graduate is invited. More
often only quinquennial (every five years) or just major (twenty-
fifth, thirty-fifth, and fiftieth) classes hold reunions, but even under
this system, everybody receives several reunion invitations in the
long run. There are reunions for a university's colleges or graduate

and professional schools, and they are not always coincident with the BA and BS reunions. There are reunions that focus on classes, as well as reunions that focus on academic departments, graduates in a particular occupation, or minorities. There were once single-sex reunions; then a few children and spouses were allowed. Today, most reunions are family-oriented.

Still other types of reunions vary according to programming content. There are the stereotypical and almost entirely social events called reunions. There are professional refresher events called reunions. There are almost entirely athletic events called reunions. And (as we'll see later) a few universities are pushing their reunion programs in the direction of alumni colleges—alumni gatherings at which the intellectual atmosphere dominates the recreational and the social, as it presumably did in undergraduate days. There are reunions that are about the university, and there are reunions that are about the alumni themselves. In the former, fund-raising may dominate the program; the latter may be dominated by the alumni classes studying themselves at thirty, at midlife, or at retirement.

Reunions, Past and Present

With surprising frequency in older universities, we find that reunions predate serious alumni fund-raising. In many cases, the motivation seems to have sprung preternaturally from former students' urges to see one another again in the old setting, and the resulting reunions were mostly social. The enrichment of reunions to include recreational and intellectual content appears (if it appears) at each school in its own way. Sometimes, the university begins to see real usefulness in the reunion (not merely for fund-raising but also for the political education of alumni who can influence state budgets and for the development of alumni leadership in the classes, clubs, and other groups) and inspires recreational and academic enrichment in reunion programming. But clearly, the alumni themselves have demanded intellectual reunion content at some colleges and universities. Indeed at some institutions, the alumni have always kept a strong hand in shaping their own reunions. Perhaps we may be proudest of the education our universities provide in those cases where alumni demand a complete reunion experience decades after commencement.

Today, reunions may be as professionally organized—or as haphazard—as almost anything else the university does. The professional literature exhorts us all to do reunions right: to survey alumni for what they want, plan ahead, mobilize volunteers, promote long and often, program innovatively and thoroughly, and evaluate afterward; there is no need (or room) to discuss all that here because two complete versions of that exhortation appear in the February 1984 issue of *CASE Currents* (Bennett, 1984; Moore, 1984). Still, some discussion of the ways reunions have changed and how some of the more interesting reunion programs are run may be helpful.

Organization. At first, alumni planned them. Today the university typically contributes staff time, program planning, promotional expertise, facilities, and budget. Indeed, this may be the only area of university relations where the problem is not to get volunteer leadership involved, but rather to persuade volunteers to cede a reasonable amount of control to university officers.

Reunion Program Content. Although the best reunion programs take on the wonderfully idiosyncratic shapes of the universities and the classes that sponsor them, there is a typical reunion program. It is two or three days long. It is still primarily social but is shifting toward intellectual content. There are all-reunion luncheons or dinner dances, often featuring a presidential appearance; alumni parades or processions; and, of course, tents (more on this subject later). The annual alumni association meeting and individual class meetings, including election of officers and service awards, also feature heavily in most reunion programs.

But departures from this stereotype also abound. Notre Dame packs forty-two seminars and workshops into a mere two and one-half days; it also encourages miniseminars sponsored by reunion classes themselves; and religious events play a prominent role. Stanford's fall reunion format, Rediscovering Stanford, features six lectures by prominent faculty in addition to more traditional fare. At Brown University, where Sallie K. Riggs says reunions began in 1823 to raise money for medals to be won in declamation and other academic contests, the ubiquitous "Commencement Forums" dominate the landscape for an entire day of the reunion weekend. M.I.T., which for years invited only the fifty-year class back to campus (other classes held reunions elsewhere), now insists that major classes return to Cambridge for such events as M.I.T. Night at the (Boston) Pops and Technology Day, during which symposia (M.I.T. stresses alumni continuing education during reunions), a memorial service, a luncheon at which reunion gifts are presented, and the induction of honorary members of the Alumni Association make the reunion special to that institution. Because so many M.I.T. alumni are graduate school alumni only, a new M.I.T. program called a Management Reunion is attempting to include department-based as well as the usual class-based reunion activities. Probably the most significant and most recent changes in reunion programming may be found at Brown and Yale, where alumni directors Sallie Riggs and Eustace Theodore hold that reunions and all other alumni programs must have intellectual content and, ideally, faculty participation.

Reunion Scheduling. Reunions are generally held in the spring near commencement or on big fall weekends where football is king, but the availability of housing often determines their timing and location. According to Victor Koivumaki, director, classes and reunions, Harvard brings the major quinquennial reunion classes to campus but encourages the thirtieth, fortieth, and forty-fifth to avail themselves of Cape Cod. Lynn Carver, director of alumni relations, reports that Northwestern University saw a drastic drop in reunion attendance during the turbulent Vietnam era. Many schools did. But by 1973, Northwestern moved the major reunions (the tenth, twenty-fifth, fortieth, and fiftieth) to Homecoming weekend to play on the strength of its football programs, and this year, a massive experiment at Northwestern moved reunions to the spring for all quinquennial classes. In contrast, Stanford has always held its reunions in the fall to capitalize on football weekends and homecoming; there is no plan to compete with football by introducing seminars into that setting, even though Stanford has successful alumni college and educational alumni travel programs elsewhere and at other times of the year. For more than a quarter century, Dartmouth College's associate secretary of the alumni David Orr (recently with help from his colleague, associate secretary James Tonkovich) has run a large and complex reunion program that invites the oldest classes back for commencement weekend and the other quinquennial classes for one of the halves of the following week. Notre Dame separated reunions from commencement in the 1940s; they are held during their own week, later in the spring, when housing is more readily available.

Reunions and Fund-Raising. There is always the connection. Some universities are more overt about it than others. In general, universities treat reunions as their best form of alumni relations, and they either subsidize them or not, according to their fiscal ability, just as they would any other alumni program they know will eventually have a beneficial effect on the annual fund and capital gifts.

Future of Reunions

Reunions are so old, as alumni programs go, that many universities seem rather pleased with their current formats and anticipate few changes. Some do expect minor shifts; others plan striking alterations in the ways reunions bring alumni back in touch with alma mater. Although director of alumni relations Bryant O. ("Bo") Dunlap and director of programs Linda Carl at the University of North Carolina at Chapel Hill hesitate to impose academic programming onto a time-tested, and mostly social, reunion atmosphere, they will do more in the future to provide reunion alumni with a thorough understanding of the university's challenges and needs. This, of course, is alumni education of an important variety. Notre Dame, already providing one of the nation's most nicely balanced reunion programs (with lots of seminars, plenty of sports tourneys, and pleasant social events), will do more to support minireunions at which classes provide professional seminars for subgroups of classmates. The University of Pennsylvania will encourage more class activities outside traditional reunion periods. And Brown will encourage academic reunions based on departments' graduates in addition to whole graduating classes.

There is a small trend toward increasing the intellectual content of reunions. Brown and Yale lead the way, with Notre Dame close on their heels. In general, these leaders are both providing alumni continuing education experiences for reunion alumni and supporting the specific reunion seminar instincts of individual classes. This trend is by no means universal. Some universities still find seminars somewhat out of place in their wonderfully emotional, and more traditional, reunions; and some of these institutions have no plans to fight against that current. (Many of them provide alumni continuing education in other settings.) Still, the logic of Brown's belief that every alumni event should have intellectual content is inescapable. And Eustace Theodore, though not exactly fighting the current of emotion in more traditional reunions, wants to urge Yale's reunions gently toward academic programming—not suddenly, but as if he were carefully redirecting a gushing downhill stream.

It is all well and good to see the success of our very old reunion programs and feel little urge to fiddle, but there is something wrong with that inertia too. What is wrong in the 1980s and 1990s with fostering alumni reunions that are merely social is that our best universities must educate men and women capable of reeducating themselves several times during their lives. And if we succeed, we will have alumni who insist on programming their own reunions with some intellectual content to go with the social and recreational programs they now enjoy. We should do more than support that urge as time goes on; we should foster it, nurture it, and then provide for it in every way we can—at reunions and at other times and places alumni gather to share what they once did together. As Princeton's alumni office suggested during the research for this chapter, nurturing the intellectual life of our students and former students is, after all, what our universities do best. It is what our students come for in the first place, what they thirst for and cannot get as well anywhere else. If we remember who they are, and what the university is, our reunions will appear in their best form very naturally. As institutional advancement professionals, we may consider it our job to be sure nature takes its course.

Conclusion

There is no reunion unless there has been a union to relive. In this sense, some of our best alumni officers are the teachers and deans who make the university worth reliving at reunions decades later. Reunions, at their best, can celebrate the union of intellectual, recreational, and social lives that made up the undergraduates' overall educational experience; and there is absolutely no reason to shortchange any of these elements when that union is recreated in a reunion.

The social and recreational aspects of reunions have developed on their own from the instincts of alumni over the last hundred or even (for some of our colleges and universities) two hundred years. The place for universities to show new leadership is in finding appropriate ways for reunion alumni to relive the intellectual excitement that brought them to alma mater in the first place. In some cases, this will take time and patience. In others, the alumni will jump at the chance to participate in symposia, seminars, lectures on public issues, and serious discussions about who they are, and why.

We must not end this chapter, however, with a focus on improvements we can make in reunion programs. When all is said and done, perhaps the reunion tent—that symbol of pure human fellowship—still stands proudly at the very heart of alumni relations and at the very heart of our universities themselves. No one has made this point more memorably than J. Michael McGean (1974), who has been for nearly thirty years the driving force in alumni relations at Dartmouth. He deserves the last word to conclude this chapter:

> Reunions deserve a far greater understanding for what they mean to higher education than the all too stereotyped impression of a rollicking fun and games show that only alumni play. There is a simple but apparently overlooked fact about . . . higher education . . . which is that, by and large, those who build and preserve this remarkable system are those alumni who arrange and attend reunions. Think

about that for a minute. . . . higher education exists because there are those who believe in it . . . and it survives . . . because those same men and women in the reunion tents do not come back just to see each other. Far more importantly they return to check on an investment in what they consider a significant national asset. It is they who will meet a cross section of the undergraduate body, evaluate the quality of the physical facilities, and ask the important questions ranging from management performance to the ultimate fulfillment of purpose. It is they who check out the college and carry the word back. . . . Perhaps a reunion tent is the wrong symbol for the most important gathering of the college family each year. But the facts are clear, most of those on whom the future rests are tent people. There will be no pulling up stakes on them—unless to move their tents to heaven [p. 9].

References

Bennett, S. "A Touch of Class: 13 Ways to Make Your Reunions Sparkle." *CASE Currents,* Feb. 1984, pp. 10-12.

Cox, H. *Feast of Fools.* Cambridge, Mass.: Harvard University Press, 1969.

McGean, J. M. *Class of 1949 Yearbook.* (25th reunion.) Hanover, N.H.: Dartmouth College, 1974.

Moore, E. G. "Staging a Comeback: Ten Steps to a Successful Class Reunion." *CASE Currents,* Feb. 1984, pp. 20-22.

White, D. N. "The Festival and Fantasy of Princeton Reunions." *Princeton Alumni Weekly,* May 8, 1978, pp. 26-33.

Wylie, F. E. *M.I.T. in Perspective.* Boston: Little, Brown, 1975.

35

Jack H. Miller

Communicating with Alumni

❧ Not too many years ago, the role of alumni editor was added to the many responsibilities assumed by the alumni director. Alumni editors were not truly editors; they were part-time production managers. And although alumni periodicals enjoyed good readership, they were characterized by limited editorial freedom, meager budgets, and staid black-and-white reproduction.

The role and function of alumni communications matched the times. Then, only a select few in our society went to college, whereas today an unprecedented number of people can obtain postsecondary education. This means that we have a much larger, more diverse, and more widely scattered alumni body with which to communicate. And these readers are sophisticated and highly literate.

Alumni publications reach more alumni than any other single association program, and astute alumni directors, asked to list priorities for their associations, would likely place publications at or near the top of the list. No program or facet of alumni work costs more, has more potential, or can yield a greater return on investment. The administrator's ability to communicate effectively the association's concepts, programs, services, and needs to alumni will in large measure determine the success of the alumni program.

Colleges and universities now enjoy worldwide constituencies that can only be reached and influenced on a regular basis by effective alumni publications. Alumni will look increasingly to their institution's publications to tell them of their alma mater's success, prestige, ambition, and plans. They will also look to these publications to inform them of the accomplishments of faculty and fellow alumni.

Alumni Periodicals

Since the early days of alumni organizations, the chief channel of alumni communications for most institutions has been the alumni magazine, tabloid, or newsletter. Alumni audiences have witnessed a gradual change in format, from magazines to tabloids to today's commonly produced *magapaper,* a hybrid publication that combines the article approach of a magazine with the economies of a tabloid.

Today, it is critical to develop a consensus about the value and mission of the alumni periodical. Alumni directors, boards, and staff should ask, Why are we publishing an alumni periodical? To whom are we sending it—all alumni, paid members only, institutional donors, nonalumni, parents, corporate and community friends? What is the purpose of the periodical? Should it report all the news or only the good news? Or should it forgo news and offer primarily feature material? Should the periodical's content continue the educational process that first began when alumni were on the campus as students?

Editorial Control. Few topics in alumni administration have received more attention from the Council for Advancement and Support of Education (CASE) and its two predecessor organizations than the question, Who controls the alumni periodical? Is it the alumni association, the alumni editor, the alumni director, or some other component of the institution? If the chief alumni administrator controls the periodical, then what is the proper publisher/editor relationship? Over the years, some alumni editors have been forced to resign when the alumni administrator (or whoever controlled the periodical) objected to something they printed about the institution. And other editors have felt it necessary to resign as a matter of principle when they saw the periodical's editorial integrity threatened. The late 1960s and student unrest provided the greatest test to the question of freedom in alumni communications. But the debate goes on.

Today, the price of defining editorial freedom is a willingness to strive for common understanding. Most now believe that the alumni periodical has a responsibility to report accurately and responsively to alumni—the stockholders of the institution— the news, views, and featured programs of the institution. Alumni periodicals should not simply be used as a house organ on behalf of the institution. The modern alumni periodical has a responsibility to serve both the university and its alumni. To walk that tightrope successfully is the true test of the alumni editor.

CASE and its predecessors have provided a forum for discussing questions of editorial freedom in alumni periodicals. These periodicals are intended to help advance the institution, and it is not the role of the alumni editor to air the institution's dirty linen in the periodical. The editor has a dual responsibility, however, and when necessary, must have the freedom to report a view of importance to alumni that may not be in keeping with the administration's position. But in doing so, the alumni editor, director, and association must be willing to take responsibility for their actions.

Practical Considerations. Apart from philosophy, the alumni administrator and editor must consider practical questions of circulation, frequency, format, and content. Should the periodical be produced as a magazine or in a less expensive format— tabloid, magapaper, newsletter? Should it be sent to all alumni or only to the paid members of the alumni association? Should it be distributed to faculty? to parents? to donors? to major corporate leaders or state legislators? Should specially designed newsletters go to specifically targeted audiences? (For example, quarterly, semiannual, or annual newsletters might be sent to each class or to graduates of specific schools and colleges.) To what extent should volunteers be involved in the planning, editing, or evaluating of alumni publications?

Because changing times may require different approaches, alumni administrators and editors should ask these questions periodically. Individual institutions must develop their own answers within the context of their own philosophies, needs, budgets, and goals. One direction, however, is clear. In the future, it will become increasingly important to spend more time in targeting alumni publications because there will be no other single program in our alumni portfolio that so affects our alumni (or that costs so much!).

Periodicals of the Future. What will the alumni periodicals of the future be like? A closer look at the most successful alumni publications, as exemplified by the CASE Recognition Program winners, suggests that alumni periodicals will share a number of common attributes:

- They will be consistent in schedule and format.
- They will reflect continuity in their editorial content and, at the same time, in the administration of the alumni association they represent.
- They will present an image of a common understanding on the part of the alumni boards and the institution's administration, and they will convey the impression that the institution and association are committed to producing—and paying for—a quality periodical.
- The content will show that the association and institution respect alumni readers as serious, thoughtful individuals who are interested in much more than sports scores and club news.
- Finally, they will be on the cutting edge of publications design and layout. Their editors will recognize that their magazines, tabloids, and newsletters must be tasteful and eye-catching if they are to attract readers.

In the future, leading alumni periodicals will have to follow these basic rules to achieve distinction:

1. They will have to respond more effectively to alumni's needs and interests. Readership surveys are the best way to find out what is being read and what alumni wish their periodicals to contain. Armed with information from such a survey, plus information from more general research on alumni attitudes and opinions, editors and alumni administrators can map effective strategies for their periodicals.

2.　Instead of adding more pages and more content, alumni periodicals will probably have to manage within the limits of budgets that will grow no faster than inflation. We must improve the content and design while keeping costs low. We will have to be innovative in raising money through advertising and voluntary subscription campaigns, and we must use the new technology, especially word processing and typesetting technology, to keep costs low.

3.　We must recruit and employ the best possible people as our editors, writers, and photographers.

Today and in the future, our alumni magazines/tabloids will be forced to compete with an increasing number of specialized national and regional publications sold on newsstands, through memberships, and through subscriptions. An alumni periodical will be successful only if we maintain a capable staff, provide adequate financial resources, encourage responsible freedom in the reporting of news, and develop a policy that is respected by alumni, the administration, and our friends. We must learn to serve both the institution and its alumni. And most important, we must produce alumni periodicals that are believable and truthful in their presentation of information about the institution and its family.

The Supermagazine. Some institutions have begun producing supermagazines for alumni. These periodicals have more pages than our current magazines and are published monthly. A number of universities are seriously considering producing such a magazine for distribution not only to alumni but also to parents of students and to other interested constituencies. If carefully planned and executed, the supermagazine could reduce the number of direct-mail pieces now being used. On many campuses, there are far too many mailings going to alumni. Consolidation of some of these pieces would greatly enhance the image of the institution in the eyes of most alumni, and the cost savings in printing and postage are obvious.

The supermagazine, though expensive to produce and distribute, holds real promise for generating national advertising income if the alumni readership is sufficiently affluent. Most alumni magazines today have limited opportunity to sell national advertising because their circulation base is too small. But a supermagazine, with a greatly expanded, high-income reader base, offers interesting potential. The feasibility of such a publication depends on costs, availability of paper, and continued progress in technology. Future economies of scale and possible changes in federal regulations may also play a role.

Other Alumni Publications

In addition to periodicals, associations send many other printed pieces to alumni. It is vitally important that these create a positive image for the association and the institution it represents.

The Mission Statement. Although periodicals have a well-defined place in alumni communications, an association mission statement brochure is sadly missing from many alumni associations. It is imperative for an alumni association to have a brochure that explains why it exists and what its program is. Why belong? Why volunteer? What does the association do? How is it funded? All these points and more should be included in the mission statement brochure.

Direct Mail. Effective alumni communications programs devote careful attention to direct-mail pieces as well as to the major periodical. The association's image depends in large part on the entire spectrum of mailings from the alumni office to the alumni audience. Alumni club mailings, reunion announcements, brochures about alumni colleges and other specialized programs— all of these direct-mail pieces help create the image of the association and the institution.

Too often, the association spends money and time on the major periodical at the expense of developing similar quality for other direct-mail pieces. A well-managed association is concerned about its total image. Attractive, creative mailings can influence alumni positively. A carefully prepared announcement can boost attendance at alumni club meetings, and a lively sales piece can increase returns on a dues appeal. Therefore, associations must devote ample time, planning, and budget to direct-mail pieces.

Today most institutions recognize this, and the directors of communications in the most successful programs pay attention to every detail. For example, they know that the attractiveness of the carrier envelope can have a great bearing on whether alumni can open the mailing. These communicators also know that self-mailers must be attractive and exciting to stand out from the stack of promotional literature alumni receive every day.

Once the alumni communicator has mastered the basics of direct mail, it is important to stay abreast of the frequent changes in postal and other regulations that affect alumni periodicals and publications. Federal legislation and U.S. Postal Service policy have a major impact on alumni communications budgets.

The CASE Recognition Program, literature exchange, and conference sessions have done a great deal to improve the effectiveness of alumni direct mail. These forums have spread new ideas and rewarded excellence.

Staff and Resources

Historically, proper staffing and adequate budgets have been a major problem in alumni communications. Far too often, the alumni publications staff has been small—not more than one person at many institutions. (And even less than that—a part-time responsibility—at the smaller colleges.) In addition, not much attention has been paid to supporting alumni communications with adequate resources.

Today, however, most alumni administrators recognize the need to invest in excellence. They realize that staff members can exert superhuman effort only for short periods of time. Long-term quality requires adequate staff. Even the best-conceived alumni programs are only as good as the publications that convey their messages to potential participants.

A Marketing Approach

Today's top alumni directors, designers, and writers know that the alumni market is composed of many segments that respond in different ways to copy, graphics, type, and color. For example, a brochure for a young alumni ski trip certainly should look and read differently from a promotion of a fiftieth-year reunion.

In recent years, alumni administrators have begun to realize that they must look to marketing techniques to strengthen their alumni programs. They know that different markets require different approaches and different communications. They look to CASE as well as the American Society of Association Executives to help them acquire the techniques and skill so necessary to formulating successful marketing strategies.

The importance of the overall image of alumni communications cannot be overstated. It is extremely important that alumni administrators be aware of the image of their associations and their institutions. They must work hard to preserve and enhance positive images and must be willing to spend the effort necessary to change negative impressions.

A number of models of good communication exist across the country. Alumni administrators and editors seriously interested in improving their associations' direct mail, alumni periodicals, or other publications can study the CASE Recognition Program winners at the CASE headquarters in Washington, D.C., or they can visit the alumni offices of award-winners near them.

CASE has done much to set standards for quality and build a professional approach to alumni communications. Each year, CASE sponsors the top ten alumni magazine awards, awards for excellence in tabloid and newsletter publishing, and a program to recognize outstanding alumni direct mail. All of these efforts, plus CASE workshops and conferences, help upgrade alumni communications.

Technology and the Future

What will be the future of alumni communications? We are already witnessing experiments with satellites, Telstar, and microcomputers. In the next ten years, these new technologies may offer major new channels of communication with our alumni.

The idea of conducting fifty alumni meetings simultaneously is no longer merely a dream. It is a reality made possible through the use of satellites. This approach offers the potential for major cost savings in time and travel.

The future also will see increased use of dial-in computer systems using microcomputers. Although use of computer technology for communications will not serve our total alumni constituency for some time, it may soon become widely popular with the younger alumni who are comfortable with using microcomputers to access remote data banks.

Technology will not, however, be a panacea for communicating with alumni of the future. In my view, alumni periodicals will continue to be the keystone of the alumni communications program. Our alumni are slow to change. Just as colleges and universities are more traditional than secondary or elementary education, so, too, are our alumni. But change inevitably will arrive. And this will call for new expertise on the part of alumni communicators and administrators. They will need to innovate, while conserving precious resources. We will be called on to carefully review applications, implications, and costs for each new communication medium as it becomes available.

So what will the future bring? If increases in periodical costs stay in line with inflation, there will be a hesitation to adopt the new computer and satellite technologies. But if we experience significant increases in postal and paper prices, then we will see many colleges and universities rushing to embrace newer, more cost-effective technologies. Alumni administrators will join other advancement professionals in the search for new ways to tell their institution's stories and to describe the institution's alumni-related needs.

For additional information in this area, see Part Seven, "Periodicals: Formats, Uses, and Editorial Strategies" (p. 589).

36

Richard Emerson

Designing Auxiliary
Programs and Services

For scores of years, alumni organizations have offered a wide variety of auxiliary programs. This chapter focuses on those programs offered by most alumni organizations: alumni tours; alumni insurance programs; the sale of college, university, and school merchandise; and the publication of alumni directories. Contractual arrangements and unrelated business income are also discussed.

These programs can be an important part of a total alumni relations program, but they may be more productive cultivation mechanisms for some alumni organizations than others. Their success depends in large measure on the size of the alumni body and the advancement philosophy of the institution.

For alumni organizations with many alumni and an advancement philosophy advocating their use, there are four reasons to offer auxiliary programs. First, they offer service to alumni and friends. Second, they provide visibility for the alumni program and for the institution. Third, they generate additional income for the institution or for the alumni organization itself. Finally, they offer the prospect of greater support—financial and otherwise.

Alumni programs are, at least in part, service organizations. Much of the service they offer can be seen in the more traditional alumni programs: alumni chapters, class reunions, and alumni periodicals. Auxiliary programs offer other important service dimensions.

The benefit of these programs is not limited to alumni themselves. The institutions and the alumni organization benefit too. Whether participating in an alumni tour, displaying a new school clock or watch, purchasing additional insurance coverage through a trusted institution, or buying an alumni directory to keep track of one's former classmates, an alumnus is involved with alma mater. That involvement can strengthen the ties between the institution and the alumni.

The alumni organization benefits especially. For the alumni program, income from these endeavors provides funding for other alumni efforts that may not support themselves and that may not be supported financially by the institution. For the institution, auxiliary programs help form the foundation for much-needed support. Participants in auxiliary programs tend to be more supportive of their alma mater—financially, verbally, and actively.

The revenue produced by auxiliary programs is often the prime motive for having them. Alumni organizations also offer such programs for visibility, service, and as a means of engendering greater support from program participants. The best auxiliary activities are low-risk and high-quality and take limited staff time.

A number of alumni organizations throughout the country rely heavily on the revenue generated by auxiliary programs. However, there is a potential danger in spending so much time and effort in generating these funds that the organization loses sight of its real purpose, which is serving alumni and seeking alumni service for the institution.

Many alumni administrators think that alumni organizations should make a concerted effort to lessen the organization's need for institutional funding. A handful of alumni organizations have a history of financial and organizational separation from their respective institutions. Because of these histories, and the sheer numbers of alumni to whom such organizations have been able to appeal, auxiliary programs have been most successful. However, such economic self-sufficiency is not possible for most alumni organizations today.

It is laudable to lessen the alumni organization's financial dependence on the institution, but not at the expense of lessening the value of the organization to the institution. Most auxiliary programs should be handled by off-campus vendors, who should assume the day-to-day administration of the program, including financial liabilities.

Each auxiliary program should be low-risk; be high in visibility, image, and quality; and involve a limited amount of association staff time and resources. Most important, they should produce resources significant enough to benefit the alumni organization.

Alumni Travel

A popular auxiliary program for many larger programs— alumni travel tours—has many benefits. Gayle Langer, associate director of the Wisconsin Alumni Association, offers her observations on putting together such a program (personal communication, June 29, 1984).

A diversified alumni relations program gets people involved. That is the primary objective of a tour program, but there are others. Here are some to consider: (1) identification of key donor prospects, (2) potential for involvement in other programs and services, (3) increased service to alumni—travel with congenial companions at a competitive price, (4) enhancement of the educational program, (5) opportunities to bring faculty or administrators together with alumni in an informal setting, (6) meetings with foreign alumni, (7) alumni participating in special, off-campus events sponsored by the institutions (athletic activities), and (8) generation of revenue.

It is possible to achieve more than one of these objectives by establishing your objectives before designing the tour and selecting the agency. Specifically, a tour designed to attract young graduates could encompass the majority of the objectives but may not result immediately in increased contributions. It is obvious that the itinerary and cost of a tour would differ considerably depending on whether it is designed to attract young graduates or older alumni.

Consider appointing a voluntary group of alumni or encouraging an advisory committee to help plan and oversee the travel program. Try to use someone with travel agency experience. State primary objectives and invite proposals from travel agencies.

Conduct personal interviews with travel firms using a checklist of operational elements. Essentials of such a checklist include:

1. Itinerary: review schedule, carrier, accommodations, transportation and guides, meals, special events
2. Tour director: experience, responsibilities, procedures for emergencies
3. Promotion: brochures' printing and mailing costs, advertising policy, announcements to alumni, special promotional activities
4. Administration: inquiries, billing and receipting, information sheets, personalized items, itinerary, passenger lists, final instructions, ticketing
5. Financial arrangements: cancellation policy, complimentary passage for alumni representative, remuneration to alumni association for each tour passenger, liability coverage
6. References from the agency

In the final planning stages, an outline of special requirements should be discussed with the travel agency. These include possible seminars, alumni receptions, and a briefing session of tour participants with the agency representative.

One final step: Give a detailed briefing to the association's representative who will accompany the tour. Effective representatives know their responsibilities and will have obtained information on each passenger.

After the tour, additional communication with participants will add to the success of the program. This provides an opportunity for the completion of an evaluation form and the announcement of future tours or other programs. It also shows the association's continued interest in the individual alumnus.

Alumni Insurance

Quality is a necessity in auxiliary programs. It results in direct benefits to alumni through alumni insurance programs. Determining whether to have an insurance program can be done in several ways, as described by Kees van der Zee, associate director of the University of California at Berkeley Alumni Association (personal communication, July 8, 1984).

The use of surveys of members, an article or advertisement in the alumni publication, or a telephone survey will answer many questions. The answers can help you decide whether to launch or expand an insurance program.

Begin the first program modestly. As you prove its merits, expand the lines you offer. Ultimately, a wide range of programs from life to hospitalization and major medical to disability and dental can be made available. Expansion has its problems. Among them are (1) whether it will produce revenue or whether it should, (2) tax consequences, (3) how to promote it, and (4) which broker or company to use.

The program should be administered by a qualified insurance broker, not by the alumni staff. The broker knows the product, understands the laws, and can carry the administrative burden. Nationwide, there are several brokerage firms that specialize in not-for-profit organizations. The Council for the Advancement and Support of Education (CASE) lists many among its subscribers (see the back of the CASE membership directory).

When selecting a broker, get independent opinions; talk with several nonprofit clients of each firm. Claims offices should be near the area where there is a high concentration of members. Also compare the financial arrangements offered by the brokers you are considering, from both the alumni and the association point of view.

Supervise and approve all that goes out to your membership. As a program of the alumni association, it is necessary that all applications come to the alumni office. This is where control begins.

Payments and claims should be handled in the most efficient manner possible. If you require the insurance buyers to pay dues to your association, make sure that membership status is current. Annual verification of policy holders by your broker helps keep that part of your membership body. You may not be able to cancel insurance policies (state law) of non-dues-payers, but you could effectively discontinue billing, which in effect, would force cancellation due to nonpayment. As a side benefit, an address update could be based on annual verification.

You or your board may offer insurance as a benefit; this may allow some of the smaller schools to embark on such a program. Once proven, the program could be renegotiated. Some monetary benefit to the sponsoring organization is a must. This revenue can be obtained in the form of an administrative fee or, in the case of life insurance, as return of dividends.

Before embarking on this type of program, consult your accountant and attorney on tax matters, but the broker you select should also be able to advise you.

For years, comprehensive insurance programs were limited to a few alumni associations whose large alumni bodies made such a program financially feasible. However, now that alumni insurance has a proven track record, the insurance industry has scaled down its requirements. Some institutions with too few alumni have pooled their constituents or formed a cooperative on a regional or geographic basis.

An alumni insurance program, now easier to launch, can provide benefit to your members and your institution.

Merchandising

Merchandising, another specialty of Kees van der Zee, is one of the oldest ways of generating additional revenues for the alumni program, but it has changed in recent years. Although in the past it has been profitable to sell university scarves, T-shirts, pens, and so on, the present cost of labor and fulfillment has made these programs marginally successful. Small promotional items, often sports-related, still have a place in the alumni world but should be considered a service. The student bookstore is best able to handle that product line. There has been a shift to the singular, high-quality item that is promoted through and handled by professional companies. Institution-related merchandise of high quality has a great deal of appeal for alumni and a profit potential for the association. The continuing value of the quality product over the throw-away item also enhances the image of the organization.

Take care when selecting a vendor. CASE lists reputable firms (although, of course, there are others) in the back of its directory. You should establish with the vendor not only the quality of the product but also the turn-around time for orders (fulfillment) and the policy on money-back guarantees. Make it clear who is responsible for promotion, who pays for it, and what revenue your alumni association will receive. A contract should spell out the entire agreement.

Sales of items that generally have an institution reference make the activity a related one not subject to unrelated business income tax. Caution should be exercised, however, because interpretations may vary from one area to another.

Alumni Directories

From reaching a selected list of alumni through merchandising, it becomes apparent that it is a good idea to reach the entire alumni body in some way. Gayle Langer (personal communication, June 29, 1984) analyzes the desirability and benefits of publishing an alumni directory.

The crucial questions about an alumni directory are Why publish one? and How long will it be accurate? To determine why, we must ask another question: Who will benefit? A directory can provide incentive to stay in touch. Buying one lets the graduate contact classmates. Alumni like to see their names in print. About 10 to 30 percent of graduates will buy a copy if the price is right.

Benefits for the institution are expansive. It is an excellent way to get current information about alumni. Copies, with their extensive information on graduates, are important to development officers and administrators meeting alumni. The data gathered can be printed in myriad forms thanks to the use of computers.

Other benefits are that the directory helps administrators identify volunteers, it aids in pinpointing outstanding graduates for possible recognition or awards, and it lists alumni contacts for career networking and other contact with students.

Obviously, given how often alumni change addresses, the usefulness of a directory diminishes each year following publication. A new edition every four or five years is a normal pattern. This will maintain a high level of interest by alumni.

After deciding to publish a directory, you should examine what segment of alumni will be included. If the alumni total does not exceed 50,000, a directory of all graduates is feasible. Large institutions get good results by encouraging specific colleges to publish directories. Other forms include directories of donors or of association members.

The mechanics of publishing vary. The decision on how to go about publication will be based on the extent of involvement to which the institution or association is willing to commit itself. It will take personnel to collect, verify, and record current data from questionnaires, between 50 and 75 percent of which will be returned. To produce a directory that is current, the information must be processed promptly.

If the institution or association does not want to do the work, there are any number of directory publishing companies that can do it. Then the institution or association may assume certain production costs and promotional tasks and add a publishing markup to the cost of the volume to cover these. Some institutions or associations that choose not to sell the directory but to offer it as an incentive for new or increased gifts bear the costs of production.

The decision on the method for publishing should be made by program administrators in the alumni association in cooperation with the development office, alumni records, department and key administrators. Timing is important, and advance planning is essential. Set a date at least a year in advance. Advance notice about the directory in one of the alumni publications is essential to generate interest and increase response. The initial questionnaire is generally mailed about six months prior to publication; a follow-up to nonresponders should be sent two months later. This should lead to a high percentage of alumni reporting.

The successful completion of an alumni directory helps the association and institution in many ways and gives alumni the benefit of continued contact with classmates.

Contracts

Launching programs, such as publishing a directory or merchandising, requires the alumni administrator to deal with a variety of problems that require contracts. Tim Lemon, associate director of alumni affairs for Indiana University, offers specific suggestions to prevent time-consuming and costly contract disputes (personal communication, July 6, 1984).

Most states require that all contracts involving either the sale of goods for a price of $500 or more or the provision of services that require a period of one year or more to perform be put in writing. All such contracts should be put in writing to be legally enforceable. Most other contracts can be entered into orally, except contracts involving the sale of land.

However, even if a contract is not required, you should confirm all agreements in writing, and the agreements should be signed by all parties. With respect to telephone orders, a letter or memorandum detailing the goods or services and the price agreed on should be signed by all parties as soon as possible after the order is placed.

If you have any questions when you are negotiating a contract, or if you encounter any legal problems, be sure to confer with your legal counsel. Good legal counsel can save you substantial money—both in the short run and in the long run.

Taxes on Unrelated Business Income

Another area just as important as contracts involves situations in which the alumni association may be subject to federal income tax on revenue resulting from unrelated trade or business. Gayle Langer (personal communication, June 29, 1984) explores this issue.

The Internal Revenue Service (IRS) considers as income subject to tax income not generated through a program for which the association was granted its tax-exempt status. To determine whether a program represents unrelated business activity, consult IRS Publication 598. To summarize, IRS considers the following factors: (1) Is the activity a trade or business carried on with the prospect of profit, as compared with a program sponsored primarily as a service? (2) Is the activity regularly carried on by the association? Frequency and continuity are important considerations here. (3) Is the activity substantially related to the association's exempt purpose? Because income is devoted to educational purposes, it does not necessarily mean that the program contributes significantly to the organization's exempt purpose.

Interpretation of the three factors varies considerably. However, there are four alumni association activities—group tours, merchandise, insurance, and advertising—that are potentially subject to close scrutiny. Although it can be assumed the first three programs do provide a service for alumni, generally all four have the potential of generating a profit.

Structuring a program is an important consideration. For example, a tour program related to continuing education is viewed differently from one that is strictly social and revenue producing. Applying this principle to merchandise, the sale of products identified with the institution may be related to the tax-exempt purpose. On the other hand, income from sharing a list of alumni names and addresses with a merchandising firm to gain a commission or percentage on products sold is clearly unrelated activity and is subject to tax.

Similarly, insurance programs vary. An association that provides a list of its alumni to the insurance company in return for a predetermined fee would essentially be generating unrelated business income. A more acceptable program involves the sale of insurance offering the alumnus the opportunity to preassign the surplus dividend to the association or institution. When transferred to the association, this income is considered a charitable contribution deductible by the alumnus.

Paid advertising is clearly defined by IRS as unrelated business income. Consequently, to limit its tax liability from such activity if a profit is made, it is advisable for the association to file a 990-T federal form annually, in addition to the required 990 form, with the IRS.

Profit is the key. To facilitate annual filing requirements and minimize the amount of income tax, follow cost accounting procedures in which staff time as well as direct costs is assigned to each program. This ensures an accurate recording of costs. If the association provides funding for staff and fringe benefits, do a time study to provide detailed staff costs involved in administering the program. These all reduce, and often eliminate, any taxable profits.

An association that is organized and operated for educational purposes and engages in a significant amount of unrelated business activity may jeopardize its tax-exempt status. As a consequence, some associations have established a separate services corporation to handle unrelated business activities. Organized as a profit-making corporation, the subsidiary requires separate bylaws and elected officers and directors. The services corporation concept has been extremely effective for a number of large, independent alumni associations.

Programs that IRS may consider unrelated can be vital to the institution and the alumni association in terms of increased involvement and development and can provide essential funds to support other valuable programs. Close liaison with the administration and with legal counsel should enable the association to meet its programming objectives without jeopardizing its exempt status.

By following the concepts and suggestions proposed here, an alumni association can offer a wide range of auxiliary programs that serve the alumni and add strength to the organization.

37
Patricia S. Wager

Serving Alumni
of Nontraditional Institutions

◆❧Nontraditional institutions, such as two-year colleges, community colleges, professional schools, branch campuses, and independent schools, face unique challenges in establishing and maintaining an alumni relations program. These challenges, however, can be overcome if they are recognized and understood.

The definition of an alumnus for such nontraditional institutions as two-year colleges has been a widely debated issue. Should the term *alumni* be reserved for graduates only? According to *Webster's New Collegiate Dictionary*, an alumnus is defined as one who has attended or has graduated from a particular school, college, or university. This definition allows two-year and nontraditional institutions to foster alumni programs if they choose to set up guidelines for individuals who attend their institution.

Because the greatest percentage of community, two-year, and branch campus institutions serve a commuter and part-time enrolled student constituency, it becomes difficult to identify students who have completed a certain number of hours and bestow alumni status on them.

Additionally, if an institution considers any student who has ever attended to be an alumnus, the record-keeping expense, along with time and cost involved for a staff to maintain such information, would not be a worthwhile investment. Therefore, when organizing the institution's alumni program, it is extremely important to clearly define who is an alumnus and to be certain that staff can manage, serve, program for, and communicate with this group.

Professional and independent schools have an advantage over other nontraditional institutions because they can more readily identify their alumni. Class year identification and degree similarity tend to create a cohesive feeling. These are factors that professional, independent schools and four-year colleges can capitalize on in their alumni programs. Two-year and community colleges must look to their strengths to create a similar cohesive feeling. If class years are not meaningful to graduates, special-interest groups should be formed to enhance enthusiasm among alumni. Most two-year community and branch campus institutions offer a wide variety of curricula, such as nursing, horticulture, food service, and computer science, and the graduates of these special-interest groups should be the core of an alumni program.

Serving the needs of these small, identifiable groups becomes much more effective and productive than trying to serve the entire alumni population as one constituency. Within a two-year or nontraditional college setting, an alumni program should focus on involving identifiable groups, such as graduates.

When establishing or reevaluating the goals of an alumni organization at a nontraditional institution, several important factors must be considered. First, the mission and philosophy of the institution must be clearly reflected in the goals and objectives of the alumni association. The institution and the alumni association have a very special partnership of mutual support, and their goals and mission should not be in conflict or problems will occur. Priorities for fund-raising, public relations, communication, and programming must be established and understood by both the institution and the alumni association. In this way, specific and measurable goals can be established and evaluated.

A common pitfall experienced by alumni associations in nontraditional institutions is inability to adequately evaluate their performance or effectiveness. This evaluation cannot take place because specific goals or purposes were not developed for the alumni association. Certainly, to serve alumni is a worthy and desirable goal; however, such a general statement provides no basis for evaluation.

Guidelines are needed for measuring educational and social programs offered alumni. At the end of six months or one year, it is relatively simple to count the number of alumni programs and alumni participants and gauge a level of accomplishment and service. The right blend of quantity and quality in programming is essential for success.

It is difficult to operate an active alumni association without sufficient financial resources. Staff, office expenses, and initial program expenses are all items that require financial resources. Alumni associations that do not institute a dues program and have not established annual giving are totally dependent on money from the institution. It is a tough decision for presidents in nontraditional institutions to make to invest resources in an area that has an unsure payback. Traditional institutions have always depended heavily on alumni for financial support. However, the track record for community college alumni support is virtually nonexistent. The potential is there, but nontraditional institutions are not moving aggressively to identify and actively pursue their alumni for financial support.

To initiate any program or activity without careful planning is risky. Alumni association organizations are no exception. Knowing an institution—its strengths, challenges, demographics, constituency, and mission—is essential to good planning. The alumni administrator must realize the institution's strengths and capitalize on them while being knowledgeable of an institution's challenges and deemphasizing them. Nontraditional institutions should take advantage of the guidelines for alumni programs successfully established by traditional institutions.

However, they must tailor an alumni program that reflects the individuality and uniqueness of their own institution. In other words, if football games are a strong rallying point for students and alumni, good planning should incorporate football activities—but if a football team does not exist, try something else. As an example, homecoming at a traditional institution translates into pep rallies, football, and a dance. In a nontraditional institution, homecoming could involve alumni in seminars, continuing education, a banquet, or an open house. The diversity in programming is limited only by one's imagination. Devote time to planning a program that enhances your strengths.

An alumni program, especially in nontraditional institutions, must begin to involve students while they are enrolled. Students are an alumni association's future constituency and should be treated as such. Students who feel they belong to an institution will be most likely to want to stay involved through an alumni program.

Don't keep your alumni program a secret at your institution. Instead, actively involve students by awarding scholarships, appointing students to serve on alumni social and educational event committees, cosponsoring campus activities, and becoming involved in orientation sessions. It is difficult to try to instill loyalty and a desire for involvement in individuals after they have left school. A common retort among two-year college graduates is "I was never involved as a student, why should I be involved now?"

What can a nontraditional institution reasonably expect to receive in return from its investment of time, financial resources, planning, and a skilled staff in an active alumni association? An institution can begin to identify and know who its alumni are. This can be most beneficial as alumni begin to develop within their careers and in the community. The institution then will have an opportunity to call upon alumni to serve in leadership positions. The volunteer support provided by alumni can be tremendous. This allows alumni to gain satisfaction by their involvement and the institution to receive invaluable assistance.

A good image and positive public relations can be created for an institution if an army of alumni speak highly of their experiences while they were students. This public relations is difficult to measure, but more tangible signs are apparent when brothers, sisters, mothers, fathers, and other relatives of alumni enroll in classes. Recruitment of students is an important job of all institutions, and nontraditional institutions, especially, should look to their alumni for support.

Nontraditional institutions should ask their alumni for financial support. This can occur through the establishment of an annual fund, which may include direct mail and phonathon solicitation. As proven by four-year institutions, the phonathon is a most effective means to raise funds, second only to personal solicitation.

Experience has shown that two-year and community college alumni do contribute when they are asked. For example, the College of DuPage Alumni Association (Glen Ellyn, Illinois) conducted its first phonathon in November 1981. The results indicated that 65.2 percent of the alumni called responded affirmatively by making a contribution; the average gift was $20.33. Alumni donors represented class years from 1971 through 1983. The important factors to note through this example are (1) community college alumni will give if asked, (2) a tradition of giving to two-year institutions can be developed among alumni, and (3) alumni giving records can be established. This giving record will provide a basis for analysis when the staff develops plans to request upgraded gifts in the future. Phonathons are also an excellent method of involving and utilizing alumni and student volunteers. During a phonathon, students are exposed to the financial needs of an institution's fund-raising program. Before long, when they become alumni, those students will themselves be asked to give.

Two-year and other nontraditional institutions should also look to their alumni as valuable legislative resources. Alumni, as voting citizens, should be cultivated and informed so they can help the college gain legislative support.

Alumni receive the benefits of a quality education at nontraditional institutions, and it seems logical that they should have an opportunity to show their loyalty through their service and support. This can be accomplished through an active alumni relations program that, although structured much like that of traditional four-year institutions, is specifically tailored to the needs of the particular two-year or nontraditional institution.

38

John S. Bartolomeo

Using Survey Research to Improve Alumni Relations

 Surveys provide the most reliable means available for learning what the public thinks, why they think it, and thus, whether and how to persuade the public to change its mind on some issue. This chapter includes an overview of social trends and other factors that have created a need for alumni surveys, a discussion of the principal functions of surveys, and a guide to some of the decisions that must be made by the alumni relations director upon undertaking a survey.

Is There a Need for Alumni Surveys?

The need for alumni surveys will vary across colleges and universities, with some having no need at all, and others a great need. Yet general shifts in the nature of things—the overall environment in which alumni relations programs operate—would suggest that there has been an increase in the aggregate need for alumni surveys.

First, the competition for an individual's philanthropic dollar is much greater than it has ever been. Charitable institutions and other nonprofit organizations are seeking funds from the public with unprecedented vigor and acumen. Second, a consequence of the large increase in households with two wage earners (a phenomenon especially prevalent among college graduates) is that time is more precious than it has ever been before. Many alumni today simply lack the time to become involved in programs and activities.

Finally, the college generation of the sixties and early seventies, the celebrated Yuppies, has now matured. Many of their generation had attenuated loyalties to their university during their student days. How will this affect their loyalty today—and tomorrow, when the affluence that comes with career success enables them to become key volunteers and generous donors?

But even if alumni relations has become more difficult to manage than it once was, one could argue that the alumni relations function has always faced challenges that survey research could help address. These challenges relate to the effectiveness of communications efforts, the effectiveness of various alumni relations programs, and ways in which alumni attitudes toward their school can be improved and behaviors supportive of the university can be encouraged.

The Functions of Survey Research

In what specific ways might survey research help alumni relations managers? What questions can it answer that will improve the relationship between alumni and their alma mater?

Evaluating the Effectiveness of Communications Efforts. Most alumni relations offices make sizable investments in such publications as magazines, newsletters, and direct-mail pieces. To what degree are these publications read? And if they are read, do alumni see them as dull or interesting? Do alumni find them informative about things they wish to know, or do they find them far removed from their interest? Survey research, often employed to answer questions similar to these for major commercial publications, such as newspapers and magazines, is increasingly being used by alumni relations managers to assess their publications. Indeed, alumni relations managers have found it necessary to significantly alter the space allocated to certain topics in their publications and even to create new and different feature sections in their magazine, tabloid, or newsletter as a result of a survey of their readers.

Then, too, communication flows in two directions—not just from the institution to alumni but also from alumni to the university, in which case it takes the form of suggestions, criticisms, or information. How effective do alumni feel their alma mater is in receiving their opinions and comments? Often, assessment of these upward channels of communication is as important to the promotion of good will as satisfaction with publications. And again, survey research can help determine evaluations of upward communications and suggest mechanisms for improving its functioning.

Evaluating Alumni Programs. Each year, most alumni relations offices devote considerable effort to such activities as class reunions, local and regional alumni chapter activities, and special events. In addition, alumni are regularly exhorted to participate in activities, such as travel programs, that require cash outlays and to contribute their time and energy as volunteers. Have these programs achieved their full potential? If they have not, how can that potential be realized? This is a classic marketing problem and one that survey research is ideally suited to address. Such a survey would indicate whether a shortfall in participation is due to the program itself, to lack of knowledge about the program, to unsuccessful promotion and advertising, or to other causes.

An example helps illustrate the point. Suppose that an alumni relations office sponsors ten different programs and that three of these (say, class reunions, ticket sales to special campus events, and special luncheons for alumni) have been quite successful, while the other seven programs have been somewhat disappointing. What is the best course of action? Should resources be diverted from the less successful programs (and, if so, which ones?) to pull still more alumni to the successful ones? Or have the more successful programs already achieved saturation? Are there potential winners among the current losers? A survey would help resolve these issues in the following ways:

1. By determining the level of awareness of various programs. There is a world of difference between an unsuccessful program that has a 5 percent awareness level and one with 85 percent awareness. If nearly everyone knows about the program and almost no one participates, it will generally be difficult to increase participation.

2.   By determining the amount of interest in the program and the perceptions that either boost or deflate interest. For example, low interest in a travel program may be a function of low interest in travel itself, or it may be a function of misperception about its cost. If alumni are uninterested in travel, the program has little potential for growth. If, however, low interest is due to misperceptions, the program could have considerable potential once they have been corrected.

Of course, this logic can also be applied to the more successful programs. Suppose participation in a program is already high, but that nonparticipants express little interest in it even when they fully understand the nature of the program. This would suggest that the program has reached its saturation point and that use of additional resources to promote the program will yield only a slight return.

These examples could be multiplied, but the point should by now be clear. A survey of attitudes toward alumni programs is an invaluable planning tool. It helps the alumni relations manager both to make decisions about which programs to emphasize and to provide guidance about the promotional tactic—the message strategy, if you will—that will maximize program participation.

Attitudes and Supportive Behavior. Alumni relations efforts do not live by publications and programs alone. Publications and programs are designed to produce two effects: (1) favorable attitudes toward the institution and (2) behaviors supportive of the college or university, including contributions, promoting it to prospective students, offering career assistance to new graduates, attending school-sponsored activities, and speaking well of the institution to friends and associates.

Again, survey research is ideally suited to indicate whether and how these goals are being achieved. A survey can measure both general assessments of the university and specific perceptions that might account for those general assessments. These specific perceptions might include appraisals of top administrators, alumni's sense of the institution's reputation among their professional colleagues, evaluation of its academic standing, evaluation of its sports teams, and how much they feel the college or university has improved (or declined) since their student days.

Why should one care about alumni attitudes such as these, over and above the obvious reason that alumni good will is desirable? There are two principal reasons. First, analysis of how these specific attitudes are interrelated will provide insights about how to overcome the negative attitudes. For example, systematic survey research might reveal that a certain segment of an institution's alumni are disaffected because of unhappy memories of their years on the campus. It is nearly impossible to attack this feeling head-on. Nevertheless, the survey might also uncover some positive attitudes that even this disaffected segment holds. These positives become the starting point for broader attitude change. Communications, through publications or other means, can give added focus to these themes and slowly convert the disaffected, or at least a sizable number of them.

Second, attitudes affect behavior and, particularly, willingness to make financial contributions to the college or university. It becomes crucial to know which attitudes impinge on behavior if one wishes to change the behavior. For example, one might discover that unwillingness to give is related to a belief that the institution is so affluent it does not need funds from the rank-and-file of alumni. Or one might discover that unwillingness to give is related to a feeling that a college or university has been standing still and not making any improvements. Indeed, a whole range of attitudes could be correlated with one's disposition to contribute. These attitudes should become major themes of alumni publications and other communication efforts.

To sum up: A survey is not just a method for finding things out. It is, rather, a decision tool. It is invaluable for creating strategy, for establishing realistic goals, and for providing guidance on how best to achieve these goals. This is exactly how surveys are used by marketing managers of corporations and campaign managers for political candidates. And increasingly, it is the way they are being employed by alumni relations managers.

Choices About Survey Methods

It is impossible to provide a guide to the particular survey methodology that should be applied in any given instance. This is partly due to the wide set of options available, but it is also due to the fact that the purpose of a study has a strong bearing on the methods to be employed. What follows is a kind of all-purpose list of decisions that will have to be made when conducting a survey.

Decision 1: What Must Be Learned? This point is so elementary that it is almost embarrassing to stress it. Nevertheless, a clear statement of the decisions that one hopes to make as a result of the survey is the essential starting point, followed by the information goals that will enable those decisions. A survey designed to address the question What should be done to increase financial contributions? will take on a shape quite different from one designed to answer such questions as Should the content of publications be altered? or Why have so few alumni volunteered their time to the university?

Decision 2: What Type of Interview Method Should Be Used? There are several alternatives for gathering data. One is a qualitative technique known as focus groups. These semistructured group discussions, usually with eight to ten participants, are best for generating hypotheses, but they are inadequate for proving or disproving them. If a quantitative method is preferred, three options are available: self-administered questionnaires, telephone interviews, and in-person interviews. Self-administered questionnaires can be distributed through the mails or on-site at an alumni gathering. Their great advantage is that they represent the least costly data collection method. Their great disadvantage is possible bias in who chooses to respond. (And a response rate of 50 percent or more is needed to ensure that the opinions reflect those of the audience.) Unless, through several mailings, incentives, or other methods, one can secure an adequate response, it is better to use telephone or in-person interviews.

The choice between telephone and in-person interviews usually revolves around (1) cost—telephone interviews are less costly; (2) length of interview—if the interview is quite lengthy, it may be necessary to conduct it in person; (3) sensitivity of subject matter—the more sensitive the subject matter, the greater the need to conduct the interview in person. But it must be added that there are no hard and fast rules about interview methodology.

Decision 3: What Type of Sample Is Best? Sampling is often regarded as an arcane science. Laypeople, it is thought, have little to contribute to the process. This stereotype is both true and untrue. On the one hand, establishing sample size and developing random sampling procedures can be complex areas into which the layperson should venture with caution. But sample design also involves a conceptual issue and one in which the user of the survey should, and must, participate. For example, should the survey include both graduate and undergraduate alumni? Must alumni of each school or department be represented in adequate numbers to enable comparisons of results across schools and departments? Do we need to have enough contributors in the sample to facilitate an analysis of the factors that account for making cash contributions?

Decision 4: What Is the Study Worth? Decisions about sample size and interview method, questionnaire content, and length are often affected by budget. Although any study design can be endlessly elaborated and expanded, the cost implications of these extensions must be well understood at the beginning of the research project. This makes it all the more important to know just what the study must accomplish versus what one would like it to accomplish in the best of all possible worlds. The survey user must attach a value to the study based on what the study will ultimately help achieve.

This is a partial list of decisions that will have to be made. Decisions about analytical procedures have been omitted. Survey users must also be attentive to the time frame within which to obtain data and when the data will need to be applied to the institution's decision making. And not the least important of these omissions is a decision about who should conduct the study—a professional research firm or a group assembled from within the institution. Again, considerations of time, money, and know-how provide the basis for a decision.

For more information on research, see Chapter Fifty-nine, "Marketing Research: The Starting Point for Advancement Success" (p. 757).

Part Five

Improving Government Relations

Richard L. Kennedy, Editor

39   *Richard L. Kennedy*

Imperatives and Strategies for Effective Government Relations

❧ "Religion, morality and knowledge being necessary to good government and the happiness of mankind, schools and the means of education shall forever be encouraged" (from the Northwest Ordinance, 1787).

This early declaration of federal policy with respect to education provides an excellent setting in which to discuss how a present-day educational institution undertakes to foster the encouragement of education by government at all levels.

Government has been inextricably involved in education since the very beginnings of this country. Indeed, that involvement has become so pervasive that institutions now need to incorporate within their administrative structures a mechanism for the management of this interface with government. That mechanism is now commonly referred to as government relations.

Unfortunately, the need for such a mechanism is not universally held. Hundreds of our 3,000 institutions of higher education still shun any involvement in those government affairs that affect them. In reviewing many of the previous writings on this subject, one is struck by the repeated entreaties of the authors for institutions to take government relations seriously. It is hard to imagine such institutional insensitivity in the face of the overwhelming evidence that supports a contrary position.

A review of some relevant statistics compiled by the National Center for Education Statistics (1985, pp. 114, 116; 1984, p. 179) indicates that in 1982

- Federal government spending for higher education institutions exceeded $9.6 billion, with an additional $6.8 billion provided for student assistance programs.
- State governments were providing more than $21.8 billion to support colleges and universities.
- Local governments similarly spent $1.9 billion.
- Research and development expenditures by the federal government at colleges and universities totaled $4.6 billion.

And what about laws and ordinances that govern an institution's life as an employer, a toxic waste generator, a charitable organization, and the myriad other things a college and university must be to function in society? It is in these areas of support and regulation that we are subject to the action of some governmental entity, and our relative fate can be positive or catastrophic, depending on how well or poorly we are able to interact with that entity.

In 1967, John Gardner, secretary of Health, Education, and Welfare under President Lyndon Johnson, said this about the importance of government-university interaction: "I believe that those parts of the university which are already involved in extensive interaction with the larger community are going to have to take that relationship more seriously than ever before. Some academic people—including close friends of mine—are advocating precisely the opposite position: less rather than more involvement. I respect their motives; I see the point of their arguments; and it grieves me that they should be so wrong" (Gardner, 1968, pp. 116-117).

One last point on the importance of government relations to colleges and universities. Have you ever noticed what a high priority institutions place on raising private funds—how they will spend thousands of dollars to hire sizable staffs to generate gift support? The Council for Financial Aid to Education (1983, p. 72) reported that such voluntary support totaled $5.16 billion in the fiscal year 1982-83, a worthy accomplishment. Yet, as we have already shown, government support now approaches eight times that figure. This in no way diminishes the necessity for energetic private fund-raising activities on the part of colleges and universities. It simply places in some perspective the need for institutions to be similarly forthright in their approach to governmental relations.

Government Relations and Its Place in Institutional Management

We have already suggested some of the ways government can impact on institutions. It is my contention that that impact is so pervasive that an institution must account for it in determining policy and in its decision-making processes. This, in turn, means that responsibility for government relations must be at the highest levels of institutional administration. In some cases, that will mean the responsibility is shouldered by the president personally. More typically, it is one of the portfolios carried by some other institutional officer, and increasingly, it is the primary responsibility of that officer. It is no longer at all unusual to have a vice-president for government relations, or some similarly situated individual, listed among an institution's officers. The specific placement of this responsibility within an institution's hierarchy is, of course, dependent on such characteristics as size, type, or programmatic emphasis. Many larger private institutions have such specifically assigned officers, as do a much larger set of public institutions. Smaller liberal arts colleges would not typically need such an officer to spend full time on government relations. The important thing to note, however, is that government relations must be a part of an institution's thought process and of its decision-making machinery.

The organization of the government relations function is largely dependent on the size and type of institution as well as its programmatic structure.

A small, independent liberal arts college will be concerned about such issues as student financial aid, tax law, research funding, and employer/employee legislation at the federal level. State and local concerns will center on such things as state aid to independent schools, state grants and aid to students, coordination and program certification requirements, local zoning ordinances, utility charges, tax-exemption status, and local expectations about the role the institution should play in the life of the community.

In such an institution, the government relations function will typically be a responsibility shared among the chief administrative officers. In addition, the college faculty, the focal point of an institution's research effort, will play a particularly pivotal role in the attraction of governmental support for this activity. This will be true of any institution, regardless of its size or type.

In this shared-responsibility arrangement, as well as in more sophisticated organizational forms to be described later, it is important that the responsibility be clearly assigned and widely understood throughout the organization. Everyone should know who is responsible for direct contacts on institutional issues with local congressional representatives, local legislators, the mayor, and the governor. In the smaller institution, this may be the president's role. Similarly, it should be clear that the chief financial officer works with city officials on zoning matters, utility connections, and parade permits. In the small liberal arts setting, such assignments will vary. The important thing is that someone be made responsible and that everyone understands who that someone is.

In the midsize public college or university, government relations responsibilities assume a much more prominent position. In addition to the issues cited as important for the independent liberal arts college, one must now add state operating and capital appropriations. Indeed, state government now becomes the primary source of funding for the institution. Because much more of the institution's viability is at stake, the responsibility now needs more focus. A single institutional officer is appropriately assigned government relations as a specific institutional responsibility. This may not need to be a sole responsibility, but it will likely be a primary one.

Interestingly, the shared-responsibility concept does not go away. The president and other officers may, indeed, continue to carry out government relations functions, but they will do so as part of a coordinated effort that is specifically orchestrated by the officer in charge. Strategies are now more complex. There has to be one person with primary responsibility who has thought through every institutional action and reaction. This person knows the territory, and the territory knows this person.

Next comes the major independent doctoral research university. Again, the stakes escalate, especially at the federal level, and a new role emerges. Such institutions, by virtue of their importance, stature, and visibility, become major participants in the formulation of national policy with respect to higher education. The government relations responsibility now requires significant staff and other resources. Indeed, we are now speaking about national universities, about research programs that affect national capacity to compete with the rest of the world in science, technology, and the humanities. Federal funding is critical to these institutions both for research and for education. These institutions, which stand at the frontiers of discovery and knowledge dissemination, form with their sister institutions in the public sector a significant part of the cultural foundation of the nation.

So, too, the great flagship state universities and their land-grant partners. In many cases they are one and the same. Through them, the states become partners with the federal government in making possible great centers of learning and research upon which the nation's future itself is dependent.

Government relations at such institutions is not an option. It is a highly sophisticated enterprise that requires talented staffs who are well schooled in the world of political processes and strategies. On the one hand, their voices must shape institutional policy, and on the other, they must be respected as defenders against inappropriate governmental encroachment. Indeed, they operate in one of the most critical external interfaces in higher education today.

This organizational evolution has many variations. We have not covered its community college manifestation, where local government relations includes some of the same fiscal connotations as those state government relations has for the four-year public institution. Nor have we discussed the specialized institution whose programs may be specifically limited to such areas as engineering, the health sciences, or technical education. Variations of the themes I have described, however, are rather easily derived. A sensible appraisal of what is at stake at what level of government will usually dictate the amount and direction of the government relations effort. There are no perfect models to follow because each institution's organization for this function will be unique and dependent on specific answers to questions to be posed in the next section of this chapter.

Government Relations—The Function and Responsibilities Defined

The primary government relations responsibility that must be addressed by an institution and the staff assigned to this area is the determination of those governmental actions, or possible actions, that have, or can have, an impact, positive or negative, on the institution and its ability to achieve its objectives.

The second area of responsibility is to assess the extent of the impact that any particular governmental action can, or does, have on the institution. This assessment process is probably the most important single factor in determining how much of an institution's resources ought to be committed to support its government relations effort. It also determines the direction and timing of that effort.

For example, a state college or university will ordinarily depend on state government for a major share of its general-fund operating support. It is clear that, with that much at stake, a major commitment of time and effort must be made to ensure that such support will be continued and, when appropriate, increased. Determining the specific amount of time and effort, and its timing and direction, is the responsibility of the institution's government relations officer.

This leads, then, to the final area of responsibility in government relations. Having determined the relevant governmental issues and having assessed their relative importance to the institution, the government relations officer must organize and deploy the necessary institutional resources to maximize the positive impact and/or minimize the negative.

This last responsibility is probably the most difficult to accomplish. Here the government relations officer is involved with strategy development and execution in the political arena. Success or failure is most often the result of experience with the process, knowledge of the participants in the process, and skill in orchestrating the proper interaction of the participants at the right time in the process.

Operating Principles

The heart of an effective government relations program is the staff that carries out this responsibility. As a rule, that staff will not be large. Instead, it will range in size from a single person to a group of perhaps half a dozen individuals, depending on the size and type of institution. The one-person operation may be the president or, more typically, an individual on the president's staff. Larger institutions will have the function organized in a vice-presidential office. In either case, the staffing pattern needs to reflect the importance of the function and its role in the development of institutional policy.

There are certain characteristics, or operating principles, that will guide the activities of the government relations staff in carrying out these responsibilities. Interestingly, these principles will be applicable to government relations operations at all levels—federal, state, and local. A review of these characteristics should provide a helpful checklist for gauging the effectiveness of a government relations program.

Understand the Role of Communication. Government relations is, more than anything else, a communications process, a process that is highly specialized and that emphasizes personal interaction. The successful practitioners will invariably be people who can evoke the trust of public officials and their staffs by communicating convincingly with them personally. They will also be receptive listeners who can hear and respond to messages and the sometimes subtle signals that are a unique characteristic in the political process. Edwin Crawford described the importance of this personal communication in his chapter "Government Relations— An Overview," in the 1977 edition of this handbook, in which he quoted the late Edward R. Murrow, who said, "It is no miracle of communication to send a message by Telstar. It is the last three feet between one man and another that matters in getting a message across" (Crawford, 1977, p. 348).

Institutions will likely use several different communicators in government relations activities, all coordinated by the person responsible for this area of advancement. Presidents are always the principal spokespersons because they are the most visible representatives. Differing circumstances, however, will dictate a wide variety of communicators, including faculty members, trustees, other administrators, alumni, and yes, even students. It is the job of the government relations professional to know when to use a particular messenger. It is also that professional's responsibility to be sure that the message is properly framed and the communicator is properly briefed and instructed.

A variety of communication mediums will be employed in this process. There will be written documents conveying official budget requests or responding to official requests for research proposals. Traditional institutional publications, such as newsletters, alumni magazines, and other formal publications, may be helpful in providing general background information. (Care must be used with these latter vehicles, however, because they can easily be ignored or, worse, regarded as wasteful.)

The most effective communication devices are those involving personal contact. There is usually a wide variety of campus activities to which public officials can be invited that will enable such individuals to feel a part of the life of the institution. Athletic events, campus visits, building dedications, and cultural events are all occasions at which personal communication can occur. Just seeing an old, decaying chemistry building that can no longer house an adequate instructional program conveys a message that written words can never capture.

Finally, there is no substitute for the personal conversation that grows from a valued personal relationship built on trust and mutual respect. In the last analysis, this is what government relations is all about.

Know the Institution. A thorough understanding of the role of an institution and its programs, and their relationship to government, is the sine qua non of a government relations program. Put another way, knowing what there is about a given institution that can be positively or negatively affected by governmental action—or in some cases governmental inaction—is one of the essential beginning points in developing an effective government relations effort.

For some institutions, this may seem like a tall order because so many activities and programs can be affected by government. The large state university, for example, has at stake its operating and capital budgets, research programs, governance, hospital operations, personnel functions, utility systems, security responsibilities, and a plethora of other activities. Thankfully, this morass of issues is mitigated by two very important factors: time and institutional priorities.

Not all programs are equally at risk all the time or at the same time. For instance, there is usually a predictable time frame for the consideration of appropriations affecting operations and capital. Other programs are variously affected, depending on the relative prominence or obscurity of specific kinds of issues. As a result, government relations becomes manageable through planning and careful deployment of resources.

So, too, will institutional priorities affect the amount and type of government activity in which an institution will engage. Facility requirements at public colleges and universities rise and fall with the relative adequacy and condition of the physical plant. Not everyone needs a new building every year.

The important element inherent in this principle, then, is knowing what programs can be affected by governmental action; when and how they can be impacted; and how important they are to the institution at a given point in time.

Know the Process. This second operating principle is one of two that are particularly sensitive to the experience level of the government relations professional. It takes time and experience to know how government actually works and how institutional objectives can be achieved through the governmental process.

Yet this knowledge is absolutely essential. Observing a piece of legislation course its way to passage or defeat, watching the impact of subcommittees and committees, of lobbying and special interest influences is an intriguing experience. The give and take, the trade-offs, the compromises, all play a part. Success is determined by how well one plays this game. It is not a place for the amateur.

A desired governmental outcome is almost always the result of a thoughtful, strategic plan. The complexity of that plan is determined by the level of decision making required. Shepherding a bill through a legislative body is infinitely more complex than getting a decision from a single public official who has the authority to make such a decision. Even in this latter instance, however, it may require a careful assessment of such things as who asks the question, and at what point in time.

For the government relations professional, then, it becomes a matter of determining what governmental action constitutes an acceptable institutional outcome, developing a strategy for achieving that outcome, and having sufficient knowledge of, and experience with, the governmental process involved to successfully implement that strategy.

Know the Participants. As I have pointed out, the thing that makes government relations almost unique among advancement programs is the extraordinary dependence on personal interaction to achieve results. It is largely a one-on-one game that is highly influenced by personal contact, integrity, and credibility. A thorough knowledge and understanding of, as well as the ability to interact with, the people who make governmental decisions is one of the most important elements in a government relations program.

This is another operating principle where the experience of the government relations professional becomes critical. It takes time to get to know public officials and those who influence them. It takes longer to have them trust you. A friend is not necessarily someone who votes for you. It is more often one who thinks enough of you and your institution to tell you when, or why, a particular vote or decision is possible or not.

And the participants are not limited to people who cast the votes or write the decisions. There are legislative and congressional staffs, department and agency people, the city planner's office, lobbyists, and representatives from other institutions and associations of institutions—literally hundreds of individuals who can affect or influence a governmental decision that affects your institution. It is the confidence and trust of these people that the government relations professional must constantly nurture and develop.

Develop a Thorough Monitoring and Evaluation System. There is nothing quite like knowing what is going on in the world of government. For the government relations office, this is at least half the battle. Most governmental decisions that affect higher education are not initiated by institutions. Each year, hundreds of bills and proposed regulations that surface from the fertile minds of the bureaucracy or individual legislators can have an institutional impact, even though that may not have been originally intended. Finding a systematic way of discovering and following such proposals is an important responsibility.

Fortunately, there are a number of professional governmental activity watchers that are extremely helpful in providing early warnings and continuing analyses of issues as they ebb and flow in government circles. Government publications, such as the *Federal Register,* provide some very helpful information in this regard. Many of the Washington, D.C.-based educational associations produce a variety of periodicals that keep track of federal activity and, to some extent, state government developments. James L. Sankovitz (1981) provides an excellent listing of these kinds of publications. Similar journals and services that report and keep track of state governmental activity are usually available.

Other information of this sort will flow from the regular course of contacts with government and legislative offices. Legislative service bureaus, staff members in key government offices, and even careful reading of local newspapers can all be part of an institution's intelligence system for this purpose.

Equally important in this process is an institutional capacity to measure the impact of a proposal and evaluate its chances for adoption or implementation. Measuring impact often requires the ability to call on knowledgeable people within the institution. A network of such people, who can analyze a proposal's impact on a specific institutional activity or program, is vital. Similarly, a staff capacity to evaluate the political chances of a particular measure becoming a law or an operative regulation can be an invaluable timesaver.

Fit Use of Institutional Resources to the Task. Even where government relations is a one-person responsibility, it is seldom a one-person show. Higher education institutions are fortunate to have a wide range of talented individuals who are usually knowledgeable and articulate in their special fields. They also have capable administrators who are equally competent within their own areas of responsibility. For the government relations professional, each should be seen as an available resource to be called on as circumstances may warrant. The trick is to know when and how to use such an array of talent.

Of particular importance in this regard is the judicious use of the institution's president. In general, the president should be used sparingly, only when someone else simply cannot represent the institution appropriately.

Contacts with the governor on issues critical to the institution, high-visibility hearings with legislators on similar issues, and congressional committee hearings are examples of situations in which presidential involvement is usually critical. Being perceived as just one of the gang is usually not the expected image for the head of the institution, but being aloof or unnecessarily distant is equally bad. Helping the president strike the appropriate balance is the task of the government relations professional.

Develop Cooperative Lobbying Techniques with Other Institutions and Organizations with Common Objectives. This principle is particularly important for the smaller public and independent institutions at the state level and for all institutions at the federal level. In many states, independent institutions have formed strong state associations that carry the primary responsibility for representing the interests of those institutions in state government. The same is true for public community colleges. The value of such common representation can be seen from the rapid rise in state funding that has occurred for these institutions during the past two decades. In addition, cooperative efforts on the part of four-year public colleges have been credited with dramatic improvements in state funding in recent years in several states, including Florida and Tennessee.

At the federal level, such cooperation and association activity are the order of the day. Seldom, if ever, is a specific institution advantaged over all others as a result of a federal action or decision, except in the award of research grants. Even here, the processes and regulations for such awards are established by a commonly derived set of ground rules.

The incorporation of this principle of cooperation into an effective government relations program is not a call to "let George do it." Cooperative effort and association activity do not substitute for individual institutional responsibility. Indeed, without institutional involvement with their local legislators and congressional representatives, little would be accomplished by associations. Nor should institutional interests become secondary to those of their associations. Institutions must be active participants in associations to see that realistic compromises are worked out to achieve common objectives that are not inconsistent with institutional goals.

Finally, it is important to understand when, and to what degree, cooperation with representatives and lobbyists from other interest areas can be used to further institutional objectives. As employers, institutions share some of the same concerns as business firms. For example, as users of toxic or hazardous substances, there may be a commonality of interests with companies that manufacture, sell, or are otherwise involved with such substances. Cooperative lobbying efforts may be perfectly appropriate in such instances and should be pursued. However, it is important that institutional integrity be preserved in such efforts and that the amount of such involvement be commensurate with the level of the institution's interest.

Never Abandon the Truth or Compromise the Institution's Integrity. One of the maxims often used to describe the world of politics is "quid pro quo," or "you scratch my back and I'll scratch yours." In this world of trade-offs and compromise, the government relations professional must know what can be traded and where compromise is appropriate. It is equally important that others know and understand the limits you have set for yourself, and for your institution, when operating in the political arena. It will not be unusual to be pushed to those limits by individuals who expect a favor or two. Admission for unqualified applicants, grading changes, and preferential employment are all examples of the kinds of favors that some will expect for support of an issue or a favorable decision. They have no place in government relations for an institution.

There will be costs associated with adhering to those principles designed to protect the integrity of an institution. This is, unfortunately, harsh reality that is thankfully an exception rather than being commonplace or usual. However, the institutional consequences of compromised integrity are infinitely greater and usually unending.

Equally important is the credibility of the government relations professional. Unkept promises, misinformation, misleading statements, and feigned intelligence, where ignorance is fact, serve only to undermine the individual and, eventually, the institution represented.

One final note. Edwin Crawford (1975), when serving as vice-president for public affairs at Ohio State University, probably put it best when he wrote, "The time is past, if it ever really existed, when a college or university could register true and lasting gains at the expense of other institutions." There is probably no weaker institutional position than that which is dependent for its accomplishment upon disadvantaging another institution.

There is an old saying in politics. "What goes around, comes around." Put another way, it is sometimes called the Golden Rule.

Maintain an Adequate, Prompt Response Capacity. One of the most appreciated things an institution can do for people in government is to provide prompt answers to questions and a helpful response to a variety of requests. This kind of capacity is basic to any government relations program.

Lawmakers and government staff people appreciate more than anything else a single point of contact with an institution that they can depend on for a straightforward response, no matter what the request. An inquiry about the admission status of a constituent's son or daughter or a request for football tickets, a picture of Old Main, or an institutional position on an issue are all examples of requests that may be made. The government relations professional builds credibility by being the point of contact for such requests and enhances that credibility with the quality of the response.

Express Appreciation to Those Who Help. Although this notion may seem obvious and be considered common courtesy, it is amazing how often it is overlooked or forgotten. A favorable vote, a supportive floor statement, or just some procedural advice can be very helpful. A word of thanks is always in order. A similar posture with institutional colleagues is equally important.

Having described the operating principles that characterize the government relations function in general, I want to relate them now to the three levels of governmental activity—federal, state, and local. This will describe the context in which these principles guide the activities of institutions and the government relations professional that represents them.

Federal Relations

When operating at the federal level, it is important to know the role the federal government plays with respect to higher education. This section describes some of the more important current areas of federal interaction with higher education. The intent here is to illustrate how government relations programs are organized to operate at the federal level.

The federal government role in higher education can be described as both supportive and regulatory in nature. Federal programs provide a wide variety of funds to higher education. For the most part, these funds are not institution-specific. Rather, they are organized in a broad array of authorization and appropriation legislation that attempts to accomplish federal policy objectives. Those objectives fall into categories such as:

Providing Access to Higher Education. One of the basic roles of the federal government is to provide funds to

individuals whose financial capacity is insufficient to
make a college education possible.

Accomplishing Specific Manpower Objectives. Through the
use of training grants, vocational education funds,
capitation funding mechanisms, and research funding,
the federal government attempts to provide the higher
education opportunity necessary to maintain the work
force the nation needs. These funds are directed to a
changing set of occupational areas depending on
changing patterns of need.

Providing for the Discovery and Application of Knowledge.
The federal government has vested the principal responsibility for basic research in its institutions of higher
education. It has therefore provided, through a broad
variety of federal agencies, the funding capacity to support
that objective.

*Providing for the Facility and Equipment Needs of Higher
Education Institutions.* Closely related to the issues of
access and research are the facilities and equipment needed
to accomplish those objectives. Although these funds have
been greatly curtailed in recent times, the federal
government has played an important role in helping
institutions provide the necessary funds to meet their
needs for equipment and buildings.

In its regulatory role, the federal government seeks to achieve
societal objectives through the enactment and enforcement of
legislation and related rules. Such legislation is seldom specific to
higher education but is inclusive of such institutions in their roles
as employers, charitable organizations, users of the mails,
borrowers, lenders, governmental contractors, health care providers,
or educators. The impact of such legislation, and their related rules
and regulations, can be positive or negative depending on the
ability of higher education institutions, both individually and
collectively, to influence the language of such governmental action
so that it accommodates institutional goals and objectives, on the
one hand, and accomplishes legitimate societal purposes, on the
other.

As I have indicated, it is the responsibility of the government relations officer to monitor these federal issues as they arise and progress through the enactment and implementation phases. The amount of institutional involvement on any given issue will be dictated, in large measure, by assessing the impact on the institution and its capacity to affect the outcome.

For instance, take an issue such as the reauthorization process for the Higher Education Act. Almost every institution is vitally interested in this process. Most smaller institutions, however, will likely decide that the impact on them specifically will not be sufficient for them to hire or retain an institutional representative for a direct Washington-based lobbying effort. Rather, they will take steps to ensure that their interests are represented by higher education associations whose members have similar interests. Such institutions should concentrate their efforts on monitoring the progress of the issue and maintaining contact with local congressional representatives to ensure that their institutions' positions are clear.

On this issue, and a host of others, the larger institutions, both public and independent, maintain a staff presence in Washington, D.C., to monitor federal legislation; lobby for enactment; defeat or, more likely, change to optimize impact; and otherwise participate directly in developing and implementing strategies to effect favorable political outcomes. These institutions also work cooperatively with appropriate educational associations.

Because federal action is seldom institution-specific, such efforts by all institutions are aimed at achieving outcomes that are applicable to the general higher education community. This community approach at the federal level is one of the principal characteristics that differentiate federal relations programming from that at the state or local level.

Interestingly, there has evolved of late a rather unsettling alteration in this pattern. A series of institution-specific, facility-funding measures have developed; these bypassed the traditional peer review process that usually determines institutional grants for both research and facilities. A major joint effort, working largely through the educational associations, is attempting to eliminate this "end-run" approach, lest it split the higher education community and touch off a flurry of such activity that will surely work to everyone's disadvantage.

A word about the national associations. Fortunately for higher education, there are a number of distinguished associations based in Washington, D.C. Collectively, they have had an enormously significant, and largely beneficial, impact on the relationship between the federal government and higher education. Each association includes as members colleges, universities, and educationally related organizations that are allied by virtue of institutional type or programmatic similarity or professionally related administrative category. Some, such as the Association of American Universities, are invitational. Others, such as the American Council on Education, seek to represent the entire community. And still others have as members institutions of one specific type—such as state and land-grant institutions, community colleges, and independent institutions.

These associations are playing an increasingly important role in affecting federal policy with respect to higher education. They are an immensely important resource for their member institutions not only in monitoring federal activity but also in marshaling institutional efforts at the grass roots when necessary. For most, they are, or can be, the eyes, ears, and voice of the institution on federal issues. It is rare for an institution not to hold membership in at least one such organization.

It is vitally important for every institution to use these organizations as a vital component of any federal relations effort. It is equally important that institutions be active in these associations, especially in the formulation of positions on specific issues.

Charles Saunders (1981) has written an especially helpful description of this important subject, in which he describes in detail the value of associations to institutions, what they can and cannot do, and why associations cannot be effective without institutional involvement.

State Relations

The major thrust of government relations programs at most colleges and universities is targeted at state government. The reason for this is obvious. It is state government that shoulders the principal responsibility for supporting public higher education and, to an increasing degree, independent colleges and universities. And it is state law that has the most direct regulatory effect on higher education. Thus it is not surprising that the real impetus for government relations programming by institutions begins with the recognition that relationships with state government cannot be left to chance. It is simply too important to ignore.

The role of government in relation to higher education at the state level, as at the federal level, is both supportive and regulatory.

Usually by constitutional mandate, it is the states that provide a major share of the funding necessary to operate the public higher education institutions in the country. Furthermore, states are increasingly recognizing the role of independent colleges and universities as a legitimate part of the higher education system that warrants public support. Funding from the state falls into the following categories:

Institution-specific operating and capital appropriations. States appropriate funds directly to public colleges and universities to maintain the institution's capacity to carry out their basic mission of education, research, and public service. Funding for facilities is provided both by direct appropriations and through state bonding programs.

Student and enrollment-based appropriations. Increasingly, states are providing funds for need- and merit-based financial aid for students at both public and independent colleges and universities. To these programs have been added others, such as degree reimbursement, which provides direct grants to independent schools for each degree granted, and tuition differential grants, which provide independent institutions with funding for each enrolled in-state student regardless of need.

Program-specific grants. Program-specific grants to independent institutions are operational subsidies for maintaining specific programs, particularly in the health sciences.

In its regulatory capacity, state government is considerably more direct than the federal government in its impact on colleges and universities. In addition to the generalized applicability of all state legislation, there is a significant array of both constitutional and statutory enactments that affect institutional governance, coordination, program and enrollment parameters, and fiscal and accounting flexibility as well as audit and reporting requirements. The list is extensive.

It is in this context that most institutions will find government relations activities most needed and productive. The stakes for most public colleges and universities are so high that specific representation in the state capital is essential. Independent institutions will find it equally productive to sharpen their government relations focus. Monitoring activity, rapport with local legislators, and active participation in associations that may carry out direct governmental representation all mandate clear delineation and assignment for government relations.

For both public and independent institutions, state government interaction begins with the governor's office and hinges on the development of a personal rapport between the institutional president and the governor. The cultivation of this relationship should be regarded as one of the principal tasks of a president. The quality of that association is one of the single most important determinants of how an institution will fare in the unpredictable seas of state government. Once that relationship has been established, other institutional representatives can function effectively with the governor's staff or, for that matter, directly with the governor. That means access to the budget office and the principal departments and agencies, all of which can have dramatic impact on an institution.

In many states, the amount and degree of legislative interaction are determined by the constitutional or statutory mechanism that is established to coordinate higher education. All states have established some body charged with the responsibility for coordination. The degree of coordination, and the resulting institutional constraints, varies widely. In Michigan, for instance, coordination has been constitutionally vested with the State Board of Education. But the state constitution is even more outspoken in its language mandating the principle of institutional autonomy for its four-year public colleges and universities. Periodic court tests of these seemingly conflicting doctrines have tended to favor institutional autonomy.

Most states, however, vest a much greater degree of control of public institutions in coordinating bodies. Such controls, which may include budgets, programs, enrollment, and admission standards, preclude, to varying degrees, any formal involvement by an individual institution with the state legislature. In some states, these principles of coordination extend to the independent sector. Interestingly, I have rarely found an institution that ever felt completely constrained by such coordinating bodies from undertaking direct legislative relations efforts. Whatever the specific coordinating board circumstances in a given state, government relations programs must include the development and execution of constructive activities that respect the specific prerogatives and authority of the state coordinating body and the legislature and that accomplish effective interaction with both.

Councils established to coordinate higher education are not the enemy. Indeed, some have served an advocacy role that few, if any, individual institutions could match. They perform a very legitimate public purpose in determining, or advising on, resource allocation, program efficiency, institutional role and mission, and conservation of public resources. Institutional relationships with such bodies should be guided by the same operational principles reviewed earlier in this chapter.

Interaction with state legislators is probably the most interesting aspect of government relations. It is surely the most challenging. Here one meets the demanding tests of understanding individual personalities, adjusting to widely varying political philosophies and biases, competing with a maddening array of issues for time and attention, and attempting to keep everyone happy with the institution.

It is in this arena that adherence to our operating principles becomes critical. Knowing individual legislators, their likes and dislikes, the people they listen to, the interests of their constituents, their attitudes, and their relationships to the institution all become aspects of the strategic plan for the government relations effort.

Two-year colleges and independent institutions generally work within a state association framework in pursuing legislative objectives. Individual institutions need to maintain close contact with local legislators in order for an association to be effective. Thus, although such an institution may not need to maintain staffing at the state capital or a broad set of contacts among many legislators, it certainly does need to maintain close liaison with its association and a sufficient rapport with local legislators to deliver votes when necessary.

A midsize state college or university will likely need to maintain at least a modest staff presence in the state capital and an acquaintance with legislators beyond the local delegation. Because the stakes are much higher, direct contact with executive and legislative processes is considerably more important. Coordination with other public institutions needs to be maintained and can be effective in accomplishing mutually beneficial objectives. This direct legislative activity must also be consistent with, and respect the prerogatives of, any duly established coordinating body. Any short-run advantage that might be gained from "end runs" around such an agency can have disastrous longer-term consequences.

The comprehensive state university must be fully staffed at the state level, not only during formal legislative sessions but also in the off season. In addition to appropriations bills, many of the hundreds of other measures moving through the legislative process will have institutional implications. In one recent session of the Michigan legislature, more than 4,000 bills were introduced. Some 300 of them had potential impact on the University of Michigan and on many of the other colleges and universities in that state. Each of these measures had to be assessed for impact and evaluated for survivability. Each required a strategy. The price of inaction or inattention in such a setting can be staggering and at times crucial to an institution's objectives.

Community Relations

At the community level, government relations efforts become much more diffused into a general program that involves other areas of institutional advancement. To be sure, many of the governmental elements remain, especially for the public two-year colleges. Because, in many cases, operating and capital support for these institutions are at least partially dependent on a local tax base, their demeanor takes on many of the same characteristics as a local public school system. The task of a government relations professional in this context is to relate the institution directly to the voters within the district served by the institution. This requires both a much higher utilization of public media forms and staff who are expert in their use. Even so, our operating principles persist, although they are now applied to activities that would be more precisely defined as public relations rather than government relations.

This same change of emphasis is true for all institutions. There continues to be a set of governmental activities that must be addressed. The actions of a city council or a county board of supervisors can be vitally important to an institution. Local zoning ordinances, municipal utility systems, public transportation, police and fire protection, and exemptions from local property tax are all examples of the types of local governmental issues that require the attention of institutions, regardless of size or type.

There is, however, a larger set of issues that are much more relevant in the context of a community than at the state and federal government level. I would describe them as citizenship issues. The way an institution conducts itself as a member of the community can have a telling impact on the way that institution is treated in the local governmental decision-making process.

Does the institution participate in community efforts, such as United Way drives, historic-building preservation projects, and other community betterment activities? Does the institution encourage community participation in its cultural events, social activities, and celebrations? Are the educational and research programs of the institution sensitive to the needs and problems of the community? These are the kinds of questions that government relations professionals and other institutional advancement staff must be attentive to if they would deal effectively with the community.

I want to spend a moment on what is probably the most sensitive aspect of community relations for an institution. Most institutions enjoy tax-exempt status in their communities. That means that they do not pay for community services in the way citizens pay for such services. This becomes one of the most difficult points of contention in what would otherwise be a constructive relationship between town and gown.

The community usually provides police and fire protection, maintains local streets and public transportation, supplies sewer and water, manages trash disposal systems, regulates land use and construction, and provides a host of other services critical to the operation of the higher education institutions within its borders. In most cases, the provision of these services is a significant fiscal drain on communities, and institutions must be sensitive to these costs. In some cases, this may mean provision for actual payments to be made to the local government for such services.

All of these issues suggest that colleges and universities need effective community relations programming every bit as much as they need coordinated activity at the state and federal level. It is important to maintain regular contact with local officials to discuss areas of mutual concern. Where is the next college building going to go, and what will its impact be on the surrounding neighborhood? How many police officers are going to be needed for traffic control at the next football game, and who is going to pay for them? These are the kinds of questions that need to be raised and discussed so that mutually satisfactory answers, rather than anger-producing surprises, are the outcome.

On the citizenship front, colleges and universities need to assume and assign responsibility for making conscious efforts to be constructive forces in their communities. Faculty and staff should be active in service clubs, the chamber of commerce, and local planning groups. Periodic reports should be made to the community on the impact the college has on the local economy. Attention should be given to institutional purchasing and contracting arrangements so that local businesses can be advantaged whenever possible.

In short, neglect and inattention at the community level can be just as costly as at the state and federal level. A good government relations effort incorporates community relations as a vital part of its responsibility.

Some Special Considerations

Several recent developments in government relations programs deserve attention. They provide additional tools, although some are controversial at this point.

Use of Professional Lobbyists. At the state and federal levels, in particular, there is an increasing incidence of colleges and universities retaining professional lobbying firms to manage, or at least assist in, government relations efforts. If used properly, this practice can enhance an institution's effectiveness in its dealings with government. There are certain tests that can be used to determine when, and how, the use of professional lobbyists is appropriate.

In highly specialized areas of governmental activity, where an institution lacks sufficient internal expertise, a professional firm can provide excellent guidance. Examples of such specialized activity are the role of the Federal Communications Commission in regulating public radio and television and the role of the Department of Health and Human Services and its Health Care and Financing Administration in regulating health care reimbursement policies. Higher education institutions that own and operate public radio or television stations, or aspire to do so, might be well advised to retain counsel to assist them in maintaining competent representation in this area. Similarly, institutions with medical schools, particularly those that also operate teaching hospitals, may be well advised to seek professional assistance in dealing with this enormously complex area of government regulation.

Even at the state level, there are some very complex, specific issues that can warrant retaining professional assistance. State Medicaid programs, for instance, can have the same implications for university teaching hospitals as Medicare has at the federal level. The key determinant, again, is the level of expertise available internally.

In my view, the use of professional lobbyists as a general substitute for an institutionally managed and directed government relations program is a serious mistake. Such firms cannot be expected to speak with true credibility for an institution, and lawmakers are rightly offended by institutions that let "hired guns" maintain liaisons that should be the responsibility of someone in authority at, and directly responsible to, the institution.

Great care must be exercised in selecting such firms when an institution decides their use is appropriate. The two most important criteria are the firm's reputation and its client list. It is vital that a firm be respected and enjoy a high degree of credibility in those areas of government where representation is sought. It is equally important that such a firm not represent other clients whose interests are, or could be, contrary to those of the college or university seeking assistance.

Political Contributions. Among the realities of the political world are the inevitable invitations to fund-raising events to raise money for the campaigns of political candidates. The more robust manifestation of this reality is the political action committee (PAC), which is also a fund-raising device to support candidates for political office or to support or defeat ballot proposals.

For a very long time, many institutions, including those most active in the political arena, have been hesitant about involvement in such activities. Contributing to candidates and joining—or forming—PACs was seen as a blatant retreat from academic institutions' posture of a high degree of political neutrality, if not complete autonomy. That attitude has largely changed now, although many institutions still hold fast to the principle of nonparticipation.

In my judgment, institutions, or their representatives, are not compromised by a limited participation in fund-raisers for incumbent candidates or for critical ballot proposals. A good deal of care should be exercised in accomplishing this participation because of the Internal Revenue Service (IRS) constraints placed on the use of institutional funds for political activities. The relevant regulations applicable to the funds of 501(c)(3) organizations, which include most colleges and universities, describe a tax-exempt organization as a "corporation, and any community chest, fund, or foundation, organized and operated exclusively for religious, charitable, scientific, testing for public safety, literary, or educational purposes, or to foster national or international amateur sports competition (but only if no part of its activities involve the provision of athletic facilities or equipment), or for the prevention of cruelty to children or animals, no part of the net earnings of which inures to the benefit of any private shareholder or individual, *no substantial part of the activities of which is carrying on propaganda, or otherwise attempting, to influence legislation (except as otherwise provided in subsection (h)), and which does not participate in, or intervene in (including the publishing or distributing of statements), any political campaign on behalf of any candidate for public office"* (U.S. Internal Revenue Code, sec. 501(c)(3); emphasis added).

Given these restrictions, most institutions must depend on outside funds to make such political contributions possible.

Political action committees are quite another story. These are funds derived from private contributions, dues assessments, or other devices and used for political campaign contributions. They can be very large (in the multi-million-dollar category) or quite modest. Institutions themselves cannot organize a PAC internally but can encourage alumni or staff members to organize one independently for the benefit of the institution. Involvement of institutional funds would again be constrained by IRS regulations. PACs are developed by institutions interested in getting into political campaign contributions in a much more ambitious way. Robert Waldo (1981) contends that higher education should get into PACs or face the prospect of becoming ignored in a political and electoral process that seems to depend more and more on such funding.

I confess to somewhat mixed emotions on the subject of PACs. Their value in getting people's attention is unquestioned. My concern stems from not knowing where such a path would lead, and whether it starts a competitive cycle with other organizations or institutions in a never-ending effort to build larger and larger PAC funds. The debate on how far institutions should go in this area is far from over.

Candidate Campaigns and Ballot Proposals. When, if ever, should an institution take a public position, or otherwise support the campaign efforts of a political candidate, or actively engage in efforts to pass or defeat a ballot proposal? In my view, institutions should not take public positions for or against any candidate for public office. Ballot issues, however, are a somewhat different matter. There are rare occasions when the impact of a particular ballot proposal would be so serious for an institution that inaction would be almost irresponsible. In the fall of 1984, Michigan voters were asked to adopt a constitutional amendment that would have reduced state tax revenue by 20 percent. It was clear that higher education appropriations would have faced a reduction of that amount, or more, if the amendment had passed. Michigan institutions undertook an aggressive effort to educate their constituents, alumni, students, staff, parents, and others on what such a reduction would mean in terms of tuition increases, program eliminations, and erosion of quality. The measure was defeated. In such instances, I believe institutions are completely justified, if not duty bound, to educate voters about the possible consequences of their vote. Voters need not be told which way to vote, but they should know what their vote will mean.

Use of Constituent Groups. Constituent groups, such as alumni, students, staff, parents, and community leaders, can and should be an important element in an institution's government relations program. The key to the use of such groups lies in organization, education, and mobilization. This requires effort and coordination with other advancement professionals.

The alumni office is essential to the identification, training, and activation of alumni who can be helpful in effecting governmental action that advances institutional objectives. It is one of the responsibilities of the government relations professional to see that such coordination with the alumni office occurs and that government relations support becomes a part of the ongoing alumni program.

Similar efforts are·needed with the student affairs officer and the institutional relations officer and the constituent groups with which they work. Although lawmakers can often ignore the impassioned entreaties of campus-based government relations professionals, they cannot ignore the folks back home who vote and can influence the vote of others.

Assessing Your Program. One of the things that should result from reading this chapter is some soul searching on the part of those responsible for government relations to see how well their programs are meeting the objectives of their institutions. In this connection, here is the draft of a self-evaluation questionnaire developed by the Council for the Advancement and Support of Education (CASE) (Heemann, 1985, pp. 8–10). This helpful device has been designed to enable institutions to assess their programs.

Government Relations Program Evaluation Questionnaire

Objectives

1. Are those responsible for the government relations programs at the federal, state, and local levels thoroughly familiar with the school's philosophy, mission and goals, and any long-range plans?

2. Has the head of the program and his/her staff developed written short-term and long-term objectives which support the philosophy, mission, and goals of the school?

3. Has the head of the program developed procedures for determining priorities for the program; are such priorities committed to writing?

Management

4. Does the head of the program have the respect of those who report to him/her?

5. Does each member of the staff know what is expected of him/her and how it relates to the work of others; does a team spirit prevail?

6. Do the head of the program and the other members of the staff have the respect of the president, other key members of the administration and staff, and the board members and other volunteers with whom they work?

Organizational Structure

7. Is there a table of organization?

8. Are there adequate personnel, and are there job descriptions for each?

9. Are there programs for improving the performance of staff and preparing them for greater responsibility; is the staff able to capitalize upon them?

10. Have clearcut channels of authority and communications been developed for conducting government relations, and does the head of the program have ready access to the president and other key members of the administration?

Activities

11. Does the program have adequate sources of data, news, and political intelligence to monitor issues of concern, including personal contracts and subscriptions to newspapers, magazines, newsletters, government publications, and special monitoring services?

12. Does the program have adequate resources—such as researchers and computer equipment—for quickly and accurately assessing the impact of existing and proposed legislation?

13. Are there clearly understood procedures for decision making regarding legislative positions and strategies and the drafting of testimony and other statements; do the procedures help assure that the school will respond swiftly and decisively to crises?

14. Does the office use established procedures for communicating with lawmakers and other public officials, including systems for swift dispatch of form letters, mailgrams, or other special messages; maintain current directories of names, titles, addresses, and telephone numbers for all officials who may be contacted; maintain current files of correspondence and other communications with all such officials; and have procedures for prompt acknowledgments and responses to incoming correspondence?

15. Does the office maintain current files, in cooperation with the alumni office, of all public officials who are alumni of the institution; do these files include notes on the receptivity of each to contact and cultivation by the institution for government relations purposes?

16. Is there a current list of all professionals within the institution who play assigned or self-initiated roles in government relations, and are they kept informed in a systematic way?

17. Have procedures been developed for involving trustees, alumni, faculty, parents, students, and other constituents as appropriate in support of government relations strategies; are current lists of individuals with expertise, contacts, influence, or other qualifications who can be enlisted for particular purposes kept?

18. Are the active interest and involvement of any advisory committees or legislative networks maintained; are lists of members keep current, with telephone numbers and addresses; are new members oriented to their roles and responsibilities; are regular communications maintained?

19. Are the institution's memberships in local, state, and national organizations used to best advantage in pursuing government relations objectives (this includes receiving newsletters and other relevant publications for use in monitoring issues and participating as appropriate in the activities of each, with particular emphasis on assuring that the organization represents the institution's best interests in governments' arenas)?

20. Does the office play an active part in forming coalitions with other institutions and organizations to advance common interests on particular major issues?

21. Does the school have programs for actively cultivating key public officials through invitations for campus visits, speaking engagements, ceremonies, etc.?

22. Does the office have a strategy, actively pursued in close cooperation with the office of institutional relations, for using the media in support of government relations objectives?

Budget

23. Is the budget provided for government relations sufficient to support an effective program?

24. Does the head of government relations conduct a systematic and documented evaluation of the program each year?

25. Is there a formal procedure for evaluating all staff and a system of compensation based upon such evaluations?

The time has passed when colleges and universities can take government relations for granted, any more than they can now take fund-raising for granted. The stakes—both positive benefits and negative consequences—are too high.

References

Council for Financial Aid to Education. *1982–83 Voluntary Support of Education.* New York: Council for Financial Aid to Education, 1983.

Crawford, E. M. "Improving Your Public Appropriations." *AGB Reports,* Jan.–Feb. 1975, pp. 28–33.

Crawford, E. M. "Government Relations: An Overview." In A. W. Rowland (gen. ed.), *Handbook of Institutional Advancement: A Practical Guide to College and University Relations, Fund Raising, Alumni Relations, Government Relations, Publications, and Executive Management for Continued Advancement.* San Francisco: Jossey-Bass, 1977.

Gardner, J. W. "The University and Government." In *The University and the Body Politic: Proceedings from a Major Conference Commemorating the Sesquicentennial of the University of Michigan, July 12–14, 1967.* Ann Arbor: University of Michigan Press, 1968.

Heemann, W. (ed.). *Criteria for Evaluating Advancement Programs.* Washington, D.C.: Council for Advancement and Support of Education, 1985.

National Center for Education Statistics. *Digest of Educational Statistics, 1983–84.* Washington, D.C.: National Center for Education Statistics, 1984.

National Center for Education Statistics. *The Condition of Education—1985 Edition.* Washington, D.C.: National Center for Education Statistics, 1985.

Sankovitz, J. L. "Fine Tuning for Government Relations Libraries." In M. D. Johnson (ed.), *Successful Governmental Relations.* New Directions for Institutional Advancement, no. 12. San Francisco: Jossey-Bass, 1981.

Saunders, C. B., Jr. "The Role of the National Associations." In M. D. Johnson (ed.), *Successful Governmental Relations.* New Directions for Institutional Advancement, no. 12. San Francisco: Jossey-Bass, 1981.

Waldo, R. G. "New Trends in Lobbying and Higher Education." In M. D. Johnson (ed.), *Successful Governmental Relations.* New Directions for Institutional Advancement, no. 12. San Francisco: Jossey-Bass, 1981.

Part Six

Publications:
The Vital Link
to Constituencies

Ann Granning Bennett, Editor

The Publications Office: Perspectives on Quality and Professionalism

Every independent school, college, and university needs a publications office. This group is vital to the area of institutional advancement.

"We tend to forget that our publications reach our constituency in greater numbers and with more frequency than do we in all our personal visits and with all our public events," says Robert Reichley, vice-president for university relations at Brown University. "Because of this, our publications can be no less interestingly written, well designed, and professional appearing than the commercially produced publications that reach this same audience from organizations that are better funded and better able to produce high quality material. We must support our publications with the best staff and the best financial support that we are able to give."*

Nothing is more important to an institution than what it says about itself in its publications. "This is not only a matter of saying it in a way that relates to the readership's concerns and values," says Mary Ruth Snyder, university director of alumni relations and executive vice-president of the Rutgers University

---

*Unless otherwise indicated, the quoted material in this chapter was obtained through personal conversations or other communication between the author and the party being cited.

531

Alumni Federation. "It is important," she continues, "to deliver this message in concise statements and in a form that is graphically attractive and full of meaning."

David Roberts, associate vice-president of alumni affairs and annual giving at the University of Tennessee, echoes Reichley's and Snyder's statements. "If absolute power corrupts absolutely, then poorly written, designed, and printed publications absolutely destroy a positive institutional image. Good publications, folks, are vital to the advancement process. The publications function in education must be perpetuated, and we must staff this area with capable people."

This, then, is the reason that the publications office exists: To communicate persuasively to the institution's various publics through printed pieces that convey a cohesive, coherent image in words, design, and photography.

In addition to the president's office and the institution's many academic schools, departments, and administrative offices, the publications office serves all areas of institutional advancement—alumni, fund-raising, government relations, and institutional relations.

Take fund-raising, for example. "We consider it a matter of the greatest importance that our communications carry the right verbal tone and state issues correctly and accurately," says Connie Kravas, director of development at Washington State University. "We also want our publications to be visually interesting, exciting, and just plain beautiful." At the same time, she says, the publications should not look "as though we are spending huge sums to produce them."

Richard P. Hafner, Jr., public affairs officer at the University of California at Berkeley, looks at publications offices from another viewpoint: "In an institution as complex as Berkeley, an internal publications staff tuned to those complexities and nuances is a necessity. The information momentum of a veteran staff of solid skills (with proper supervision) cannot be matched by using off-campus services to produce 250 publications a year."

To accomplish the multitude of tasks required by an average institution, what kind of staff does it need? Writers, writers, and more writers.

Writers who can take institutional and academic information and translate it into copy that communicates effectively with all constituencies. Writers who know how to edit—brutally, but tempered by kindness and tact. Writers who know the elements of design—and when to call for professional design aid. Writers who know how to read a contact sheet—and circle the exact photo to do the job. Writers who know printing production, including how to run a recruitment poster and a catalogue cover on the same sheet to save stripping, plating, and press time. Writers who compose with taste, imagination, and economy.

At Council for Advancement and Support of Education (CASE) meetings, I see on bulletin boards job advertisements for "Publications Managers." This individual, says the search committee, should have professional writing, editing, design, and photography experience. Should be willing to advise the student newspaper and teach Photography 101. Should be well acquainted with trade shop typesetting and printing. (Actual experience in either of these areas preferred.) Willing to live 500 miles away from a major urban center. Should hold at least a master's degree in English, have published at least one book of poetry, and possess a working background in marketing. Salary: $17,000.

Perhaps this wonderperson exists, but I have yet to locate him or her. Instead of expecting everything, what are the most important qualities to look for in a publications manager? Ability to write clear, understandable copy stands out as the most important quality. We then would hope that person has adequate design skills to lay out essential printed pieces and the good sense to call for a professional designer or photographer when that need occurs. These qualities should be accompanied by a passion for accuracy; the ability to get, and stay, organized; an understanding of the need to meet deadlines; the experience to manage an internal staff and external vendors; and a talent for maintaining good relations with a campus-wide clientele.

Now that we have discussed what to look for in a publications manager, perhaps this is the time to discuss how these professionals look at their craft.

Bob Topor, author of *Marketing Higher Education* (1983), is the former assistant director of media services at Cornell University. He now directs marketing promotion at San Diego's Sharp Hospitals. "What we [publications managers] do," Topor says, "matters a lot. Unfortunately many of the people to whom we report—maybe some of us, as well—do not understand and/or believe in what we do. Part of this lack of understanding," he says, "is our problem. Have we spent time and effort describing how our skills and efforts can help to market, to position our institution's programs in the competitive educational marketplace? to create recognition? to describe how critical higher education is to our society, to our children? Have we described how writing, design, and production can be used to market our institutions? Have we done it well?" Topor doubts that we have.

Marie Avona, director of public relations at Pratt Institute, offers a compelling argument for the publications office. "Are our offices worth the cost? Honestly," she says, "the question ought to be, Why are we paid so little for our invaluable services? I truly think that courses wouldn't be described and departmental philosophies articulated if it weren't for copy deadlines and publications. And, even at that, no one would think twice about what they've described or articulated if it weren't that galleys have to be proofread.

"At Pratt," she continues, "publications have created an image . . . based on the original philosophy of the school's founder and embellished with current goals. Becoming part of Pratt means being part of this image, this philosophical stance. More than anything, this is our contribution to the school we serve. And this is an important one—for student recruitment, mostly, but also for how the students, faculty, and administrative staff feel about the school.

"No," she concludes, "we didn't create this feeling, this impression, out of nothing. It was there all along. But we built upon it, enhanced it, and Pratt's all the better for it.

"How much is it worth? Well, how much is higher education worth?"

But publications offices are not perfect. Flaws exist, and they are noted by our colleagues.

Robert Forman, executive director of the Alumni Association of the University of Michigan, observes: "Centralization and coordination do not, in the main, increase productivity or efficiency. Centralized publications offices frequently cause extreme difficulties in scheduling, lack of personal attention to specific problems, and a prioritization which is often placed upon the publications office by a higher authority, such as the vice-president for development. The result," he says, "is that individual clients seldom get the treatment or attention that one can obtain either by in-house staffing or professional services from the private sector."

This, he comments, "is not meant to be critical about the professionalism of institutional publications offices. I have observed that, given proper support, the quality emanating from such offices is extraordinary. The professionals are usually people who have a high sense of commitment to institutional goals, are knowledgeable about campus happenings, and are able to provide insights based on such understandings.

"My view," he concludes, "is that institutions that have a minimal in-house publications staff comprised of extraordinarily bright and competent people who make proper use of outside services will, in general, outperform those large, campuswide organizations that try to serve everyone and suffer from having 100 masters."

Ray Willemain, director of alumni relations for Northwestern University, expresses another concern. "Writers should keep in mind that the needs of their clients vary. Copy for recruitment material must be written in a tone appealing both to prospective students—the seventeen- or eighteen-year-old—and their parents. On the other hand, fund-raising material, such as we send to alumni, must be directed to the graduate, who often is interested in specific academic areas of the university. As the audience differs, so must the copy."

Robert Freelen, vice-president of public affairs at Stanford University, offers an additional caution. "During serious budget limitations, design costs should be related to proven or highly predictable results. Designers should not forget that their lay clients often do not understand the difference between good design and junk, nor do these clients understand how to measure or judge professional design." Designers, he says, should be aware of the need to educate their colleagues.

These criticisms have been heard, listened to, and acted on by most sensitive publications managers. We are sharpening our marketing skills. We are studying how to conduct a successful survey, how—and when—to hire a competent research firm, how to formulate a simple, but effective, questionnaire in-house. We are reorganizing our staffs to serve our campus clients better. We are learning about computers and word processing and how these technical advancements can be applied to our work. And we want to educate our campus publics, for how can we communicate to our off-campus constituencies if we cannot be understood by our campus colleagues?

Robert Armbruster, director of university relations and development at the University of Maryland–Baltimore County, points out a problem shared by most publications offices, that of attaching a real value to a product: "If you want documentation that good writing, good design, good photography, and good printing matter, you probably can't find it. But just based on the experience of a lot of us who've been doing this for a long time, I know that people of all ages respond positively to efforts they perceive to have been made on their behalf.

"They don't know," he reminds, "what makes the publication special—that a cutline has been rewritten six times or that sixty photos were considered before the strongest one was selected or that someone spent three hours (from midnight to 3 A.M.) doing a press check. But they do know that someone has taken the care to produce something nice for them. That's the value of our efforts," he concludes, "and that's why we should continue to do our best work."

Finally, a word or two about one of the publications office's most precious commodities: the truth.

Cynthia Moran, director of university relations at Drew University, sums up the philosophy of publications professionals. "It's not only that we put out a good product," she says, "but that we put out a good, accurate product. A big part of the measure is truthfulness—not just that I can make a campus look good, but that I can make it look as it really is in the eyes of its constituents. When

I receive compliments—'That viewbook, annual report, tabloid article, or set of photos really told it like it is'—that's when I know we're really worth it, and more, to our institutions."

Reference

Topor, R. *Marketing Higher Education: A Practical Guide.* Washington, D.C.: Council for Advancement and Support of Education, 1983.

41

David R. Hoover

Planning and Developing Publications for Diverse Audiences

The advancement efforts of any college or university require communication to large and varied audiences. Printed publications may support interpersonal communications—such as person-to-person contacts, presentations, or personal letters—or they may be the only communication an audience receives. Whether the ultimate goal of the institution's communication is to recruit 5 students into a specialized graduate program or solicit donations from 100,000 alumni, it must be produced in a time- and cost-effective method, accurately reflect the institutional mission, and convey an appropriate image. Regardless of the audience, the anticipated results, or the format of the communication, publications professionals have a responsibility to pose questions, provide answers, and produce results—through clear writing, tight editing, and quality design.

The process of planning and producing a publication involves the expertise of the publications professionals as well as the client. Each has specific roles and responsibilities. Whether the client is a development officer or a dean, a faculty member or an admissions director, that client requires professionally planned and executed communications. The staff of an institution's publications office, or other publications professionals, can maximize the effectiveness of publications. To do this, the publications director must initially ask the client several questions, including the following.

What is the purpose of the communication? The client must have a clear idea of the action the recipient is expected to take—drop a check in the mail, return a request for more information, attend an event. Based on this information, the publications professionals can provide ideas for format, message, and colors of ink and paper. But beyond that, they also can ensure that the particular piece is written and designed to complement other communications from the client and the institution. A clear understanding of the purpose and anticipated results of the communication also allows the publications office to consider the total program and to ask other questions. How will the client follow up the reply card? How will the client acknowledge receipt of a gift? Will more specific information be provided about the event? The ultimate purpose may dictate the need for a series of publications to ensure results. In recruitment, for example, a poster with a reply card will require a follow-up publication to continue the cultivation process.

The publications director has a responsibility to question the validity of a publication without a clear purpose or one with too many purposes. It is not uncommon for a client to want, or expect, one piece to meet many needs, usually for the sake of the budget. A clear understanding of the specific purpose will result in the most appropriate and effective product. Perhaps the best form of communication may be a personal letter or a slide show rather than a printed publication. It is the responsibility of the publications director to make such a recommendation and not automatically to respond affirmatively to a request for a specific printed piece. The publication director should also, then, be able to provide resources for developing alternative forms of communication.

Who is the audience? The demographics of the intended audience has a major impact on the consideration of the format and appearance of a publication. If the message is directed to an elderly audience, perhaps the type should be larger. If the audience is high school students, colors and words should appeal to that age group. Publications professionals consider other visual communications the audience is exposed to and keep abreast of the trends in successful communication. This is not to suggest that all publications should necessarily follow trends, but certain influences—video games, for example—should be considered in the planning process.

How would the publication be distributed? A publication that will be mailed requires considerations that another would not. The client's budget may have to include an envelope. And postal regulations may affect the size, shape, and weight of the piece.

What is the budget? This information may influence many decisions the publications director must make. The director should know printing capabilities and limitations, reasonable expectations for a budget, and how that budget may best be spent. Rather than spend an entire budget on a four-color poster, for example, the publications director may recommend using the same money more effectively on a less expensive two-color poster and a one-color follow-up flyer.

Recommendations regarding the format of a publication, its content, its design, or even its necessity may meet with resistance from the client. Publications professionals should be prepared to counter that resistance with facts, figures, alternatives, and friendly persuasion. Figures on impressive results of past publications; an explanation of the psychological impact of certain colors; examples of crisp, clear writing; or samples of what the competition is doing are difficult to argue with. However, a publications director who wants to win and keep the trust and confidence of a client may often have to make professional compromises. A happy client is more apt to return to the publications office next year, thus offering the publications office another opportunity for maximizing the quality of that client's publications. There is little hope for maintaining any quality control over publications that are produced elsewhere.

The majority of an institution's publications can be categorized as promotional, development, recruitment, or a combination of these. And the audiences range from high school students to alumni to legislators.

Promotional publications develop an awareness and build an image of an institution that is attractive to the general public or to specific target publics. In doing so, they create the groundwork for its recruitment and development efforts. Letting people know about the academic offerings, attractive campus, or economic impact of a college or university is the first step in raising money or recruiting quality students. The direct results of a strictly promotional piece are hard to measure but nonetheless critical to institutional advancement.

There is not always a clear distinction between promotional, recruitment, and development publications. When a viewbook contains an admissions application, it becomes recruitment. When an alumni magazine contains a pledge card for a scholarship fund, it becomes a development piece.

When supporting an institution's development efforts, it is useful to contact a broad variety of constituencies with varying degrees of interest in the institution. Public and private institutions alike are becoming keenly aware of the significance of this private support from alumni, corporations, foundations, and friends.

Relatively small gifts are usually generated through a direct-mail program. The publications office depends on the development office to maintain current giving records of donors in order to effectively target that audience. To personalize the message and maximize the success of direct-mail campaigns, the appeal must be based on the known interest of the donor. Usually, the alumni are more likely to give when approached on behalf of the academic area from which they graduated. The gift-level request should be based on past giving records—always encouraging a larger gift than in the past.

The content of the direct-mail package should reflect awareness of the interest of the donor—whether it be the alumni's area of major or an expressed desire to support a particular program at the institution. And it is important that the appeal be as personal as possible.

To raise more money, institutions should be good stewards of the gifts they receive. Whether the development office is perpetuating annual giving or soliciting one-time gifts, the donor has a right to know how past gifts have been used and how potential gifts will be used.

A letter from a dean or program director could outline the specific needs of a particular area that has been recorded as being of interest to the donor. (The more specific that information can be, the more convincing—and effective—the request.) A brochure in the package may discuss the general importance of private gifts to the institution or support a particular theme of the mailing.

The appeal should be as direct as possible and should encourage an immediate response. And that response should be easy to make. A postage-paid pledge card and reply envelope should be provided in the package. (A note on the flap of the reply envelope, however, may suggest the use of a stamp by the donor to save the institution postage costs.)

Because its message and graphics compete with a barrage of bills and letters received by the donor, the direct-mail package has to attract and maintain interest. The envelope must attract attention if it is to be opened. The use of color and graphics should be introduced on the envelope and carried throughout the package—even to the pledge card. An odd size and interesting graphics will assist in getting the package opened.

Although reflecting the excellence and quality of the institution, the direct-mail appeals should not appear extravagant or ostentatious. Overuse of color, expensive paper stock, or use of special printing techniques suggests that gifts may not be needed—particularly small gifts.

Although soliciting major gifts should be done person-to-person, the process requires printed support pieces. As in all print media, the audience determines the format and message of that piece. And the audience may be as specific as one potential major donor. The unit cost of the publication may become significant, but it should be considered an investment.

A case statement to support a major capital campaign directly reflects the institutional mission while specifically outlining the campaign's needs and goals. In every aspect, the publication must convey the level of a quality and excellence with which the donor would want to be associated. The gift request is most critical but is less blatantly presented in such pieces than in direct-mail appeals.

Recruitment publications should support a well-planned marketing strategy. The audiences range from the very general to quite specific, with a broad age range. Therefore, it is important to be keenly aware of audience demographics. Recruiting undergrad-

uate, graduate, or continuing education students should be a logical
process that provides progressively more specific information as it
is needed without providing more information than is needed by the
audience.

Visual continuity is important. The identity of an institution
or a particular program, established through the careful use of
colors, words, visuals, and paper, should be maintained throughout
the recruitment process. A brochure sent in response to a reply card
from a poster should carry out the identity established by that
poster. And as the subsequent stage in the recruitment process, the
brochure should provide more specific information than could be
provided by a poster and will lead to the next level of decision
making.

Recruitment publications may be directed to audiences other
than those being recruited. Particularly with undergraduates,
parents and guidance counselors influence the choice of a college
or university. Many institutions' admissions offices consult an
advisory board of guidance counselors. They offer an invaluable
resource for evaluating recruitment materials.

A prospectus (also called a viewbook or general information
book) used in institutional recruitment should offer a highly visual
introduction to its campus, people, and academic offerings.
Prospective students (and their parents) want to see where they may
be living, know that other students enjoy being there, and see that
they can study an area of interest. The prospectus should give,
through carefully chosen photographs and prose, a general,
promotional overview of the institution. A delicate balance of
landscapes, architecture, faculty, and students presents an
intentional image of the campus. If the campus is large, do not try
to suggest visually that it is small. Instead, highlight the positive
aspects of size. If the campus is urban, promote it as such. And be
sensitive to how you visually represent the affirmative action efforts
of the institution. An accurate balance—by race, age, sex, and
physical handicap—should be apparent.

There is a limit to the amount of specific information a
prospectus can communicate. Other formats are more appropriate
for outlining details of the curriculum, financial aid opportunities,
and career possibilities within particular academic areas. Fact sheets

for each college or area can provide more information to the interested audience. These inexpensive fact sheets can be directed to a more specifically targeted audience than the viewbook or bulletin. They should be visually compatible with the viewbook, however, and should not duplicate its content. The fact sheets, when provided as a unified package, also provide easily accessible information for guidance counselors.

As recruitment and development efforts escalate at most colleges and universities, alumni are being recognized as a more significant and influential audience. In decentralized recruiting and fund-raising programs, newsletters, tabloids, and magazines can reach, on a regular basis, a constituency with a common interest. Alumni who are kept informed of events and changes occurring at their alma mater are most apt to take a financial interest in its future. They are also most likely to join actively in its public relations efforts, both by promoting its excellence and by helping to recruit students.

A key audience in institutional communications, and one that has historically been overlooked, is the internal one. Faculty, staff, and the students themselves are institutional communicators and play significant roles in its public relations efforts. Newsletters, handbooks, and fact sheets for the internal audience can provide information that will build interest and boost morale.

Formal marketing tests, readership surveys, and interviews can establish the relative success or failure of a publication. What is more, such research done in advance can greatly enhance the effectiveness of the piece. In many cases, however, time, budget, and staff constraints eliminate those possibilities. Therefore, publications professionals often have to rely on the following types of informal means of documenting the success of a publication or a program.

Attend college fairs. Observe which recruitment pieces the audience responds to most immediately. Look at what the competition is doing. And watch the wastebaskets outside. Many college bulletins—expensive publications often misused as recruitment tools—may rarely make it to the home of the prospective student.

Talk to your admissions counselors. A major part of their job is to respond to the questions of prospective students. They will readily offer advice for improving the effectiveness of recruitment publications.

Keep in touch with clients. Has the development office increased annual giving over last year's mark? Have any reply cards been received from a poster that has been distributed? Was the concert a sellout? The publications office can certainly claim some influence on the answer to such questions.

Try some testing in direct-mail packages. Print a portion of the packages in different ink colors. Ask the donor to pay return postage in half the copies of a particular mailing. The development office does, or can, document the returns and can produce test results relatively easily and inexpensively.

Test the publication program yourself. Send in a reply card or pledge card from your home address. A publication can only be as successful as the organization behind it. Document response time—whether the response be acknowledgment of receipt of a gift or a publication supplying further information.

Enter your publication in editing and design competitions. Even though an award does not ensure the success of a piece, at the very least it boosts staff morale and builds additional trust and support of the client.

Create networks. Formal or informal exchanges with other publications professionals offer an invaluable resource of ideas and experiences. A telephone call or letter can save much time, money, and frustration by avoiding the mistakes or capitalizing on the successes of colleagues.

The expertise and experiences of the publications professionals and their clients are essential to the planning and production of effective publications. The appropriate information, communicated to a target audience and presented in a quality manner, is a key factor in successful institutional advancement. Whatever the purpose of a communication, the publications professionals are a valuable resource to ensure that success.

42

Norman A. Darais

Writing Effectively for Advancement Publications

Establishing Needs and Objectives

⌘ Before you begin work on a publication, ask and answer some key questions: Why is the piece being written? Who will be reading it? What will you say here that is not said somewhere else? Do you actually need this publication? (Ironically, sometimes the best—and clearly the most profitable—conclusion is not to generate a new publication at all. Perhaps an existing piece serves adequately, or maybe some other method of communication would be far more effective.)

Once you have established the need for a publication, you must make sure basic preliminary details have been adequately addressed. Administrators too often expect a writer to magically produce effective communication without clear-cut directions and objectives. But experienced writers have learned how seldom they can hit the mark without knowing the target.

The Objective. Be certain you have a clear understanding of the publication's objective. What is the piece trying to accomplish? Are you raising money or recruiting new students? (Usually the more focused the objective, the more successful the piece. A publication that is trying to accomplish too many things will do none effectively.)

Subject Matter. You need to know—or come to know—your subject matter intimately. What is more, you need to feel comfortable with what you are writing about. (For an administrator, this may mean that the best writer for the institution is someone who has been around long enough to understand what it is all about.) In any case, you must show genuine enthusiasm for the subject matter. You must be willing to immerse yourself in the environment of your subject. You need to get a first-hand feel for the people, facts, places, and details that become the basic ingredients of captivating copy.

The Readers. Publications that succeed are always addressed to specific people. People enjoy talking to real people, and effective publications always convey that human contact into print: "Just because people work for an institution they don't have to write like one. Institutions can be warmed up. Administrators and executives can be turned into human beings. Information can be imparted clearly and without pompous verbosity. It's a question of remembering that readers identify with people, not with abstractions like 'profitability,' or with Latinate nouns like 'utilization' and 'implementation,' or with passive-verb constructions in which nobody can be visualized doing something ('pre-feasibility studies are in the paperwork stage')" (Zinsser, 1980, pp. 125–126).

As with subject matter, the more clearly you identify and address the readers, the more successful the piece will be. You must also determine what your readers want to hear, as opposed to what they already know, what you think they need to know, or perhaps what they have ceased to be interested in. Likes, dislikes, biases, and preferences—all of these the writer must carefully consider.

The Package. After obtaining an appropriate feel for the readers, the subject matter, and the objective, you can determine an effective way to package and present the copy. Appropriate handling of the message and the style in which you present it are critical. You also must be sensitive to the graphic design, including photography and illustration, that will enhance and reinforce the written word.

Gathering and Organizing Material

Choosing the right material and organizing it well is a supreme challenge for any writer. Aristotle said: "You must state your thesis, and you must prove it" (Crosby and Estey, 1968, p. 26). Freshman English students are often admonished to tell them what you're going to tell them, tell them, and tell them what you told them. This sort of conscious planning along with an explicit statement of thesis—however basic—is not bad advice for any writer.

Organization. The type of organization you use is not nearly as important as having a plan before you begin to write. "Many writers think, not before, but as they write. The pen originates the thought" (Maugham, in Archer and Schwartz, 1962, p. 560). Failure to plan ahead often gives rise to fuzziness and obscurity.

When organizing copy, you should carefully consider the designer's plans for the publication. The best publications typically result when the designer and copywriter work as a team. "They need to complement and reinforce each other. The design should respond to the copy. The copy should amplify the design. The two should work in tandem. If the designer can be flexible and have respect for the copywriter, and if the copywriter can also have respect for the designer—can make accommodations to help the designer—they can accomplish their communication goals. They both have to be bright enough to have substance and loose enough to make shifts in order to make something work" (Bennett, 1982, p. 20).

Research and Source Material—Facts and Details. Good publications captivate readers with judicious use of specific details. They clarify, by adding life and interest, in a way that nothing else can. "Look at the work of any professional writer and notice how constantly he is moving from the generality, the abstract statement, to the concrete example, the facts, and figures, the illustrations" (McCuen and Winkler, 1980, p. 7).

Common subjects can become extremely engaging, even thought provoking, in the hands of a good writer. Notice, for example, what happens to water when Loren Eiseley describes it: "If there is magic on this planet, it is contained in water. . . . Its substance reaches everywhere; it touches the past and prepares the future; it moves under the poles and wanders thinly in the heights of air. It can assume forms of exquisite perfection in a snowflake, or strip the living to a single shining bone cast up by the sea" (Eiseley, 1957, pp. 15-16).

Although detail is a must for good writing, be careful to sift through all the possible details for that which is most cogent. Too much can be just as bad as too little. Use interesting statistics, and mention specific place names and people, along with opinions, wherever possible. But make sure that you have all your facts and quotations straight. Verify names and numbers for accuracy. Inaccuracies devastate the credibility, and hence the effectiveness, of a publication. If you are borrowing from copyrighted material, make sure you do so within the law. If permissions are needed, be sure you have them in writing prior to publication.

Effective Copy Writing: Using Good Style

Nothing is more challenging—or more rewarding for an author—than writing with style. Even more difficult is the attempt to describe what constitutes a writer's style.

Good style has been defined as "good choice of words, good choice of sentence structure; from this choice of good 'brushstrokes' comes the unique and forceful vision of things that we see in good writing. Therefore you need a professional's sense for detail in diction and syntax, so that you can make the *principled* choice among *known* alternatives which marks the finest craft of any sort" (Eastman, 1970, p. 6).

F. L. Lucas, after teaching writing at Cambridge for forty years, concluded that it was next to impossible to teach style. "To write really well is a gift inborn; those who have it teach themselves; one can only try to help and hasten the process" (McCuen and Winkler, 1980, p. 430).

Critical reading, however, was of key importance to Lucas: "One learns to write by reading good books, as one learns to talk by hearing good talkers" (p. 429). He goes on to say that "the writer should respect truth and himself; therefore honesty. He should respect his readers; therefore courtesy. These are two of the cornerstones of style" (p. 431).

In an excellent chapter on style, E. B. White offers this advice: "To achieve style, begin by affecting none—that is, place yourself in the background. A careful and honest writer does not need to worry about style. As he becomes proficient in the use of the language, his style will emerge, because he himself will emerge, and when this happens he will find it increasingly easy to break through the barriers that separate him from other minds, other hearts— which is, of course, the purpose of writing, as well as its principal reward" (Strunk and White, 1979, p. 70).

Even though it may be next to impossible to teach style, there are a few elements that are basic to any discussion of the subject. These include point of view, tone, tense; word choice; sentence structure; and beginnings and endings.

Point of View, Tone, Tense. Before setting ink to paper (or cathode ray to screen), consciously determine what point of view you will use to present your material (first, second, or third person; singular or plural). Also decide what slant or tone to give the message. (Are you going to be humorous, factual, obviously biased or unbiased, didactic, lofty, chatty, or warm and cozy?) Will your writing be basically past or present tense? Correct decisions in these categories are not a matter of right or wrong; the keys are appropriateness and consistency. Careful consideration of the purpose of the message and of its intended audience should determine the best choices. And mark this well: Honesty and sincerity must always be clearly apparent in your copy—if you do not, or cannot, believe what you write, discerning readers will doubt your message.

Word Choice. Because few, if any, words have exactly the same meanings, especially when considering connotations, make sure you have chosen the best possible words to clearly and precisely define your message. And as numerous stylists have suggested, make sure you are working with strong nouns and strong verbs. Use adjectives and adverbs sparingly. Use short words whenever possible. Favor Anglo-Saxon rather than Latin words, and avoid foreign words. Make sure each word is vital to your sentence; as the saying goes, When in doubt, strike it out.

Sentence Structure. Word order is vital to the meaning of each sentence. It is also a key element of readability. Most stylists recommend active voice rather than passive. Active voice is more forceful, more direct. Notice how prevalent the passive voice is in dull, deadly bureaucratic writing. (For example—*Dull:* Such a book costs so little, and so much is learned from it. *Better:* Such a book costs so little and teaches so much.)

Good writers vary sentence length and word order. Because most sentences tend to be long, a short sentence now and then can garner a lot of attention. No kidding. And because most sentences unfold with a subject-verb-object pattern, try changing the pattern once in a while. For instance, consider beginning with a modifying participial phrase: After rotting in the cellar for six months, the carrots were thrown away. (Just make sure not to have a dangler on your hands: After rotting in the cellar for six months, my brother threw the carrots away!)

Read your sentences out loud. This will give you a better feel for how smoothly they read; it will also alert you to any monotonous or repetitious cadence in your sentence structure. Again, variety is of prime importance.

Beginnings and Endings. Capturing reader interest is the name of the game. Otherwise, why bother? But getting a busy reader to begin and then read through to the end is not easy. Unless readers are captivated in a hurry, you are out of luck. "Readers are shy birds that have to be coaxed to come nearer. Nothing, then, is more desirable than a good opening if you want to lure rather than rebuff your potential reader. . . . The opening sentence . . . should catch the eye, hold attention, evoke interest" (Barzun, 1975, p. 167).

There are an infinite number of ways to begin, far too many to describe in detail here. Engaging dialogue, compelling narration, mind-boggling statistics, related anecdotes and humor, poetic quotations, and the time-honored who-what-when-where-why-how all have their virtues.

Once you have grabbed the readers' attention, state your thesis clearly; make sure your readers understand your message and know just what you want of them.

After you have presented the nitty-gritty details that make up the body of your text, your conclusion gives you one last chance to restate your thesis—one last opportunity to drive home your main premise. Of course it is also the time to summarize, to tie together any loose ends, perhaps to recall a particularly forceful introductory element, and to end on a poignant note. Conclusions should be consistent with the established tone of your text; they should not introduce new material.

Achieving Readability and Clarity: Rewriting and Editing

Revision. Once you have finished the first draft, you still have much more to do. You need to polish and refine the manuscript. As E. B. White reminds us, "Revising is part of writing. Few writers are so expert that they can produce what they are after on the first try. Quite often the writer will discover, on examining the completed work, that there are serious flaws in the arrangement of the material, calling for transpositions. . . . Do not be afraid to seize whatever you have written and cut it to ribbons. . . . Remember, it is no sign of weakness or defeat that your manuscript ends up in need of major surgery. This is a common occurrence in all writing, and among the best writers" (Strunk and White, 1979, p. 72).

Ernest Hemingway's rewriting the ending to *Farewell to Arms* thirty-nine times and James Thurber's reworking "The Train on Track Six" fifteen times are two noteworthy examples. As Thurber said, "For me [writing is] mostly a question of rewriting. It's part of a constant attempt on my part to make the finished version smooth, to make it seem effortless" (Memering and O'Hare, 1980, p. 19).

When reviewing the final copy, you need to determine that each sentence, each word, is essential. As Kurt Vonnegut (1980) recommends, "Have the guts to cut. . . . If a sentence, no matter how excellent, does not illuminate your subject in some new and useful way, scratch it out" (p. 1).

Some writers find it useful to analyze their readability level to help see how readily their manuscript can be understood by their readers. *The Technique of Clear Writing* by Robert Gunning (1968) and *The Art of Readable Writing* by Rudolph Flesch (1962) are two good sources for readership analysis. Using Gunning's formula, you can calculate the "Fog Index" (the number of years of education a reader must typically have to understand a given piece of writing). If you are writing to high school seniors, it is well worth your time to make sure your material is presented on the appropriate reading level.

Editing. Under ideal circumstances, you should not have to do final editing of your own work. There are simply too many niggling items to consider, and by the time you have labored through a manuscript, you are much too close to the work to be dispassionately objective, much less downright brutal. Most good writers I have known welcome a careful editorial review, however painful.

Editors have sharp eyes for detail. Using a good style manual, they review spelling, punctuation, capitalization, grammar, and usage for accuracy and consistency. Two of the most highly regarded style guides are the *Chicago Manual of Style* (1982) and the *Associated Press Stylebook and Libel Manual* (1977).

Again, the key words are *accuracy* and *consistency.* If you know the style the editor or publisher will be using before you begin writing (especially regarding the handling of such things as numbers, capitalization, and general manuscript format), you will save time and money. Experienced editors can also do a great deal to enhance and ensure readability. They are trained to look for tight, logical organization; clear, well-supported ideas; and smooth, cohesive transitions.

The Final Words. If you have been successful with the written word, you should feel good about responding to George Orwell's challenge: "A scrupulous writer, in every sentence that he writes, will ask himself at least four questions, thus: What am I trying to say? What words will express it? What image or idiom will make it clearer? Is this image fresh enough to have an effect? And he will probably ask himself two more: Could I put it more shortly? Have I said anything that is avoidably ugly?" (McCuen and Winkler, 1980, p. 339).

Or to follow the advice of a more contemporary stylist, Peter Jacobi, our writing should measure up to his ten essential C's of being "clear, concise, complete, constructive, credible, correct, coherent, conversational, captivating, and considerate" (Jacobi, 1982, p. 6).

To compete successfully with the crush of written matter that vies for our attention each day, you must work toward the paragon suggested by the brilliant stylist W. Somerset Maugham: "If you could write lucidly, simply, euphoniously, and yet with liveliness, you would write perfectly" (Archer and Schwartz, 1962, p. 556).

References

Archer, J. W., and Schwartz, J. *A Reader for Writers: A Critical Anthology of Prose Readings.* New York: McGraw-Hill, 1962.

Associated Press Stylebook and Libel Manual. New York: Associated Press, 1977.

Barzun, J. *Simple and Direct: A Rhetoric for Writers.* New York: Harper & Row, 1975.

Bennett, A. G. "Designing Minds: How Designers Heidi and Robin Rickabaugh Think." *CASE Currents,* Feb. 1982, p. 20.

The Chicago Manual of Style. (13th ed.) Chicago: University of Chicago Press, 1982.

Crosby, H. H., and Estey, G. F. *College Writing: The Rhetorical Imperative.* New York: Harper & Row, 1968.

Eastman, R. M. *Style: Writing as the Discovery of Outlook.* New York: Oxford University Press, 1970.

Eiseley, L. *The Immense Journey.* New York: Random House, 1957.

Flesch, R. *The Art of Readable Writing.* New York: Macmillan, 1962.

Gunning, R. *The Technique of Clear Writing.* New York: McGraw-Hill, 1968.

Jacobi, P. *Writing with Style: The News Story and the Feature.* Chicago: Lawrence Ragan Communications, 1982.

McCuen, J. R., and Winkler, A. C. *Readings for Writers.* (3rd ed.) San Diego, Calif.: Harcourt Brace Jovanovich, 1980.

Memering, D., and O'Hare, F. *The Writer's Work: Guide to Effective Composition.* Englewood Cliffs, N.J.: Prentice-Hall, 1980.

Strunk, W., Jr., and White, E. B. *Elements of Style.* (3rd ed.) New York: Macmillan, 1979.

Vonnegut, K. *How to Write with Style.* Elmsford, N.Y.: International Paper Company, 1980.

Zinsser, W. *On Writing Well: An Informal Guide to Writing Nonfiction.* New York: Harper & Row, 1980.

43

McRay Magleby

Designing Publications: Principles, Techniques, and Pitfalls

୬ Should you hire a designer or should you attempt to tackle the layout task yourself? To answer that question, let me describe what design is and what a designer does.

Design encompasses much more than just the arrangement of elements on a page. Good design enhances communication, affects people in a positive way, and saves money. The absence of professional design direction is a dangerous omission, usually leading to a hodgepodge look, lack of focus, and unclear communication.

Graphic designers are familiar with all the techniques of visual creation. Although designers are not necessarily artists, they are problem solvers who have an intuitive esthetic sense. They know how to art-direct a photo session, choose the best print or transparency, purchase effective illustration, prepare mechanicals, spec type, select appropriate paper and inks, and work with printing shops and binderies.

If your institution has a design staff, you will probably want to take advantage of its skills. If not, you may want to hire a local freelance designer.

Choosing a Designer

When choosing the best designer for your project, first review portfolios. Look for a designer whose samples reflect the mood and feeling you would like to see in your publications. Find a designer whose talents match your needs. While looking at the portfolio, ask questions about why certain design decisions were made; for example, Why did you choose this typeface? this paper stock? ink color? page format? photograph? illustration? Determine what the designer actually did on the projects and what was the role of the art director, photographer, or illustrator.

Find out about fees. How much will you be charged for your project? Some designers charge by the hour; others charge by the job. It is safer to get an estimate for the completed project than to agree to an hourly rate. A designer never knows for sure how long a job will take, and most designers tend to underestimate the number of hours needed to complete a project.

Always set a cost ceiling. Not having a firm budget in mind can be an expensive mistake because, in effect, you are saying, "Cost isn't a big concern." Designers sometimes use this opportunity to do a portfolio piece at your expense!

Next, ask for references. Call the references for answers to in-depth questions about the designer's dependability in meeting deadlines, staying within budgets, ability to work under pressure, and overall track record of producing successful work. Find out whether the designer is truly interested in solving the client's problems or just in producing work to win awards.

Many institutions will commission a designer on a one-time basis to establish a format for a periodical. After the first or second publication, the original designer can turn subsequent issues over to a production artist or to the editor, who follows the established grid and type specifications. Even though there is often a slow depreciation of design quality when this approach is used, the original designer's professional impact is often retained for years.

Once you have established a good working relationship with your designers, stick with them. Much time can be saved if you do not have to keep going over background and orientation material. Your publications will start to show a unified look, and a recognizable style will become synonymous with your institution.

Let your designers know that you like their work. Be generous with printed samples and heap on the praise! Do everything you can to cement a relationship with your designer, including gestures of complimentary lunches, special gifts, or bonuses.

Defining the Purpose

Many clients make the mistake of defining the physical piece before its purpose has been defined. They decide on an eight-and-a-half- by eleven-inch, sixteen-page, two-color brochure before a clear focus on purpose has been determined. Maybe a poster format would be better. The printed piece should grow out of an understanding of the desired results.

Start by defining the audience—high school seniors, alumni over fifty, business people. Decide what style or mood the piece should convey and what approaches are most likely to influence that audience—jazzy and upbeat, classical and dignified, or contemporary and stylish. Clarify the intended message—recruit students, enhance the university image, announce events, or whatever. Know what response you want to achieve—increased enrollment, larger donation pledges, capacity attendance at events.

Determine your budget limitations, time schedule, and methods of distribution. These will influence your choice of reproduction methods, format, size, paper stock, kind of art and type, and number of pages or folds.

Understand the relationship of the piece to the total university campaign. How does it tie in with what has been done before and what will be done in the future? Must the piece do the job alone, or will it be one of a series? All such questions should be completely answered before the designer and writer ever start on the first tissue rough or introductory paragraph.

Marriage of Word and Image

Now that you have chosen your designer and defined the purpose of the piece, it is time to come up with the concept.

Often, as a matter of expediency, writers will first write copy and then hope that the art director can work out the design solution to fit. The result can be a lack of unity between copy and layout.

A better idea is for the writer to team up with a designer and conceptualize through combined effort. The designer and writer should both understand the product, the sales objective, and the market or audience. Allow some time for brainstorming together, defining the problems, bouncing ideas back and forth, building idea upon idea, taking chances, and trying new directions. Several alternate solutions will usually surface, and the best one will start to take form.

The writer and designer can then go to work individually, refining and working the bugs out of their own halves of the total concept, while always keeping in close communication. If all goes well, the end result will come together in a fresh, innovative approach that will affect people with such impact that the response will be exactly what the client intended.

Getting Good Design

What first attracts a reader to an ad or brochure? Almost always, it is the way it looks. If a design is not appealing, readership falls off drastically. Ideally, the message of a piece should be conveyed visually without a word having to be read. The majority of your recipients will only glance at a brochure cover and skim the insides, pausing on the heads, photographs, and captions. If your message is buried somewhere in the type and is not supported by the design, it will be lost.

In order to judge a good design solution, we must refer back to the original problem. Does the design express the meaning of the message? For example, printing a cover in blue and white simply because they are your school colors is not necessarily good design; but a fund-raising piece for a new building printed in blue and white to simulate a blueprint could be good design.

Good design is not easy; it has to be fought for. Concepts need to be pushed all the way. A designer has to take chances, explore uncharted ground, and see beyond the obvious.

The best places to find examples of good design are in the published design annuals and at shows. The annuals of Communication Arts, the New York Art Directors Club, Graphis, the American Institute of Graphic Arts (AIGA), and Creativity and

Print Casebooks are among the most respected volumes available. All designers and copywriters should study the pieces reproduced in these annuals to build up their ability to recognize successful problem solving through design. It is even a good idea to let your clients peruse the annuals to expand their range of acceptable solutions and align their thinking more closely with yours.

I know a design is good when I say to myself, "I wish I'd thought of that!"

Some Design Problems

When judging design competitions, I have seen similar design flaws crop up again and again. Some of the most common are camouflaging the message by overdesign, thus weakening the real purpose; one or two elements that are out of place and fight with the general design theme; covers not relating to the interiors; lack of emphasis (one element should dominate all others on a page or spread); too many dominant elements fighting for attention; type that is difficult to read because of gimmicky and/or unreadable typefaces, poor leading, or poor letter spacing; trendy design solutions not appropriate to the problem; unnecessary use of color, which adds to expense but not to effectiveness; improper choice of paper stock for best reproduction; difficult-to-follow type arrangements; too many photos reproduced too small, rather than a single, striking photograph; trying to do too much in one piece; lack of unity from page to page; grids that seem to fall apart; color-loaded duotones, tint blocks, mezzotints; ornate rules; and amateurish spot art and clip art.

Good design is definitely in the minority among publications. That is why it is so refreshing to see a piece that really works.

Selling Design

One of the major pitfalls of good design is getting it past committee approvals. More often than not, a well-meaning, but esthetically insensitive, individual will ruin a design by insisting on rearranging or resizing the design elements. The designer's answer to this should be to educate, not to condemn, and that is not an easy task. It requires patience, psychology, and tact, but it is the only answer. Making too many compromises or submitting to unreasonable demands is bound to adversely affect the quality of work. As a result, the client is often ultimately dissatisfied without understanding why.

In my experience, the two main ingredients in selling design are working with the right person and logically documenting design decisions.

First, the sponsoring organization should appoint one individual who understands both the requirements of the publication and the sentiments of the group (and of the person who has final-approval authority). If your client likes your design but still has to run it by the dean for approval, you are flirting with disaster. You should be meeting directly with the dean or whoever gives the final go-ahead.

Second, you should make a list of reasons for your choice of format, color, paper, photography, illustrations, typeface, and any other unique features of the layout. Give clients the feeling that your decisions have sound logical backing; then they will be less likely to make arbitrary changes in your layouts.

The real secret to selling design is understanding not what the client wants but what the client needs—and then building a convincing case for your design solution.

Hints for Typography

Typography is usually the single most important element on a printed page. All too often, designers regard type as a necessary evil, an imposition on their beautiful design. Type should work with the layout instead of as a neutral element or, worst of all, as a detraction. In fact, the other design elements should direct the reader's eye into the typography. The designer must understand and enjoy the subtle differences in typefaces, spacing, and placement on the page before good typography can be achieved.

A good typographer who has a design sense for traditional letter forms and an understanding of the phototypesetting process is a valuable member of the communications team.

When trying out a new typesetter, it is wise to do some tests on sample pages. Take time to clearly explain your typographic requirements regarding letter spacing, word spacing, minimum and maximum line lengths, hyphenation, hanging punctuation, indents, size, and leading. Make sure the type on the typesetter's system is working esthetically before the whole job is played out.

Here are some basic guidelines to good typography that you should keep in mind when designing with type. With good reason, each of these rules can be broken, but such reasons had better be good!

- Limit the number of faces to one or two. Often a single typeface is enough to solve most design problems. Stick with the classic faces (Baskerville, Caslon, Times Roman, Garamond, Bodoni, and Helvetica).
- Choose nine- to twelve-point type for body copy. Use eleven- or twelve-point when the typeface (such as Garamond) has a small x height. (The x height is the height of the lowercase x in a particular typeface.)
- Do not set type solid, especially if line length is long. All typefaces are more legible with one or two points of leading, more for longer lines and type with a larger x height.
- Do not justify narrow columns. The combination of long words and short lines leads to rivers of white space running between words. It is better to set narrow columns flush left, ragged right. This also reduces production costs when cutting in corrections.
- Use a medium-weight typeface for text. Very bold or very light is difficult to read in any quantity.
- Avoid reversing or overprinting type in any but the smallest areas, such as captions or kickers.
- Eliminate one-word widows by rewriting. Indent paragraphs one or two em spaces—use less than an em space, and margins will curve; more, and short widows will fit into the indents below, creating the feeling of extra space between paragraphs.
- Use capitals and lowercase in headlines and body copy. This is easier to read than all caps. In addition, serif type is slightly more legible than sans serif.

- Do not stack letters. Because of their necessarily inconsistent widths, letters are not designed to spell words vertically.
- Make sure that the letter spacing is optically, not just mechanically, even. There should be an overall grayness to a column of type, rather than the dark or light areas often created by poor letter spacing.
- Finally, use a typesetter who has a background in the traditional hot-metal typography and who uses the original type fonts on the phototypesetter rather than the commonly available, but visually second-rate, rip-offs. Finding the right typesetter and establishing a good working relationship will, over a period of time, prevent many typography frustrations.

Using Photography

Good photography can work wonders in improving readability and communication of a piece. The right photograph will attract the viewer's eye in a way nothing else can. Finding the right photograph, heightening the impact with proper cropping, and getting a good reproduction are design skills that take years of experience to perfect.

How do you find the right photograph? Start with the photographer. Your photographer needs to be in tune with the design problem in the same way as the designer and writer. The photographs must fulfill a design need rather than merely fill space. Photographs should not be superficial, decorative elements; they should be treated as an equal, integral part of the total communications solution.

To ensure a collaborative effort, the photographer should be included in the initial planning of a project. A good photographer can offer suggestions about subject matter, props, composition, lighting, viewpoint, mood, and camera angle that may never occur to the designer or writer.

When choosing a photographer, many of the same principles apply as in choosing a designer. Review portfolios, ask questions, call some of the applicant's former clients, and get a feel for that photographer's compatibility with your project. Most photographers specialize. Some are better with people, some with objects.

Some photographers need art direction, some do not. Find your photographer's strengths and weaknesses.

Good photographers are not inexpensive, but you can do much to minimize costs by organizing the shooting. Arrange for models, props, and locations ahead of time. Have everything ready when the photographer arrives.

It is best to have an entire brochure shot by the same photographer so the pictures will have a uniform look that helps tie the piece together. If you are using photos from different sources, make sure the lighting, lenses, and film grain are similar.

Also establish who owns the photographs after they have been used in your publication. You can buy one-time rights or full rights (the price will be higher for full rights). Make sure that your photographer is careful about getting signed releases from subjects who appear in the pictures, especially if they are shown in a less-than-attractive way.

Be sure to specify whether it is black-and-white or color photography (or some of each) you need. Converting an existing color photo to black-and-white is not advisable.

Most photographers like to crop their pictures in the camera's viewfinder. If, at the time of shooting, you have not yet established the exact publication format you will be using, make sure there is enough background space in the photo to allow for your cropping needs. Remind the photographer that you must have full-frame prints from the negatives.

Sometimes designing with photographs will involve selecting one or two final prints from hundreds of exposures. Look for spontaneous, naturally lighted, believable photographs that tell a story and are uncluttered by irrelevant background or foreground detail. Make sure that the focus is sharp on the primary subject and that the color is temperature-balanced for the lighting conditions, or if the photos are black-and-white, that the contrast is good, with deep, detailed shadows and brilliant highlights. Do not resort to visual cliches; look for new ways to view the world through photography.

Retouching and cropping can be used to improve many photographs. Some laser scanners can remove anything, from unwanted light poles to cars, people, and buildings, during the separation process. Air-brush retouchers can work wonders on color or black-and-white prints. You should eliminate all extraneous clutter through cropping or retouching so that the full impact of the message comes shining through.

After the piece has been printed, save the photography in your photo file for future use in publications directed to different audiences.

It is a good idea to keep several photographers working on speculation in their spare time to shoot general campus scenes that might be of use in your next low-budget publication. This is a good way to build up a photo file and pay only for the prints or slides you order.

Working with Printers

There is so much to learn about printing that it could (and does) fill volumes. For starters, I suggest reading *Graphics Master* (Lem, 1984) or *Production for the Graphic Designer* (Craig, 1974). Just hanging around printers and asking questions helps, too.

The best designers are successful because they understand the strengths and limitations of the printing process. It is fine to have creative, high ideas, but to achieve the desired impact, you have to be able to pull them off in the printed version. It is sad to see a publication that has potential fall flat because the design could not be reproduced.

The best advice I can give to designers or publications directors is to get to know your printers. Show them your layouts and comps. Get their help on technical aspects of the design. Ask for suggestions on paper stock, inks, trim size, and binding. Do this at the planning stage of the job rather than when the art is camera-ready. You will be surprised at how much money you can save by making very minor changes to accommodate your printer's equipment limitations. You may even be able to add four more pages or some extra color at no extra cost.

After meeting with a printer or two, firm up your specs and go out on bid—but still be open to printers' suggestions for improving the final product.

Select your printer not only for low bid but also on the firm's reputation for quality and how well its equipment suits your particular job. You need to know enough about printing to make those determinations.

Insist on checking all proofs from blueline to color key to press proof to bindery proof. The fact that you are concerned about your publication will impress the printer enough to ensure a high quality level.

Make sure that you (or a qualified representative) are available to check proofs when the printer is ready. (It is not nice to keep the press waiting, and such inconsideration will likely be reflected in your printing bill.) Be particular about what you want. Insist on good registration. Check it with a printer's magnifying glass (loupe), and look at the ink color to ensure an even coverage and proper density. When all looks right, sign two proofs and take one back to your office to check against the finished copies.

Printers will usually reprint a job or reduce costs if the quality level drops below the signed press proof.

And finally, it is a good idea to keep a log of your publications. Information such as job name, job number, client, inks, paper, quantity, date, and cost becomes valuable when it is time to reprint. It is also nice to have documentation of dates and costs for your client in case questions come up later, and such information can help you plan next year's publication budget.

In many ways, producing a publication is like having a baby. There is that first exciting spark of an idea, the anticipation and wonder of creation, a long period of shaping and forming, and the traumatic experience of the last stages of intensive labor culminating in the delivery. Then, finally, the satisfaction of seeing the beautiful finished product makes all the pain and struggle well worth it!

References

AIGA Graphic Design U.S.A. New York: Watson-Guptill. The annual of the American Institute of Graphic Arts.

Art Directors Annual of Advertising, Editorial & Television Art & Design. New York: ADC Publications. Annual volume of the Art

Directors Club of New York, showing the top work of art directors, designers, and copywriters in several media.

Communication Arts. Palo Alto, Calif.: Coyne and Blanchard, Inc. Annual compendium of winners of show juried by panel of experts selected by *Communication Arts* magazine.

Craig, J. *Production for the Graphic Designer.* New York: Watson-Guptill, 1974.

Creativity. New York: Art Direction Book Company. A photographic review of Creativity annual shows.

Herdeg, W. *Graphis Annual.* New York: Hastings House. Annual compilation of the best in international advertising and editorial design.

Herdeg, W. *Photographis.* New York: Hastings House. Annual compilation of the best in international advertising and editorial photography.

Lem, D. F. *Graphics Master, No. 3.* (3rd ed.) Los Angeles: Dean Lem Associates, 1984.

Pocket Pal: A Graphic Arts Production Handbook. (50th annual issue.) New York: International Paper Co., 1983.

Print Casebooks. Bethesda, Md.: Print Magazine. Now in its seventh edition, this is a set of six volumes covering the best current design in advertising, annual reports, covers and posters, environmental graphics, and exhibition design and packaging.

44

David May

Understanding and Managing the Production Process

To rephrase Will Rogers's famous remark about the weather, everybody does something about production, but nobody talks about it. In spite of the amount of time they spend on discussion of writing and design, too many publications clients and producers seem to ignore production in the expectation that it will take care of itself.

Nothing could be further from the truth. From the outside, production seems to amount to nothing more than a collection of relatively mundane tasks, but publications professionals recognize that production is actually a series of closely related steps that, together, play a crucial role in both the creation of each publication and the effective operation of the publications office itself.

The purpose of this chapter is to offer a general definition of production, describe the major activities it involves, explain how these activities can be handled effectively by college and university publications offices, and suggest how the supervisor can contribute to that process.

What Is Production?

In the broadest sense, production consists of organizing and supervising all the steps that turn a manuscript and design concept into a finished publication—the steps that, taken together, might be called the *manufacture* of the publication. Understanding production, therefore, requires at least a general familiarity with the process of manufacture.

As recently as twenty years ago, manufacturing a publication was simply a matter of turning it over to a printer—and, in fact, some publications offices still proceed on that basis. Most publications professionals, however, recognize that the new technologies of computerized phototypesetting and offset printing have divided the process of manufacture into three rather distinct steps: (1) typesetting—converting the manuscript into the desired typeface, type size, and line length; (2) paste-up or mechanical art—arranging the type and illustrations into page layouts; and (3) printing and binding—making multiple copies of the pages and arranging them in the proper order.

Increasingly, these three aspects of manufacture are being handled as separate operations. Because they require special equipment and expertise, printing and binding are usually handled outside the publications office itself, either by the internal printing plant or by outside suppliers. Paste-up and typesetting, however, are more and more becoming internal operations handled by the publications office staff.

Despite the advances of technology, manufacturing a publication remains a lengthy and complicated process. Even the simplest publication may require a week or more, and the manufacture of more elaborate pieces often takes months to complete.

Major Aspects of Production

If manufacturing a publication were as simple and automatic as it seems to the layperson, there would be no need to supervise it so closely. But printing is an unruly art, and the job of making it behave is the responsibility of the production manager.

In general, the responsibilities of the production manager may be grouped into five major areas of activity: preparing specifications, purchasing, scheduling, proofing, and delivery.

Preparing Specifications. The essential first step in producing any publication is preparing a thorough and accurate list of specifications, commonly called *specs*. Basically, this list is a translation of the design concept into the technical terms understood by typesetters and printers, and it describes every physical detail of the publication: size; number of pages; typography; weight, color, and even brand name of paper; ink colors; size, number, and treatment of photographs and illustrations; style of folding and binding; number of copies; and delivery arrangements.

In order to ensure that specifications are complete, most publications offices use a standard preprinted form (spec sheet) for this purpose.

Purchasing. Deciding what services to purchase, from which suppliers, and at what cost is, without a doubt, the production manager's most complex and critical responsibility. No other production activity has such an impact on the eventual success or failure of the project.

As with any purchasing process, it is important to establish clear procedures and follow them consistently, to get competitive bids in writing on large expenditures, to make sure that all bids are based on identical written specifications, and to make decisions based on the critical factors of quality, schedule, and cost.

Purchasing printing is further complicated by the fact that no two jobs are alike, and changes in specifications occur frequently during production. In addition, the number of available suppliers in some areas is extremely limited, and because of variations in equipment, bids may vary by as much as 100 percent. And finally, the decisive factor in choosing a supplier may vary from job to job: some must be produced at the lowest possible cost, others on the shortest possible schedule, and still others at the highest possible quality.

Because of all these variables, effective purchasing of typesetting and printing is not a simple matter of following standard procedures. Good production managers get to know their suppliers personally, keep up-to-date on changes in performance and reputation, and learn to rely on their personal judgment as an important factor in making decisions.

Scheduling. Although purchasing is clearly the most crucial production activity, scheduling is easily the most frustrating. Setting up a realistic production schedule is a simple matter of allocating an appropriate number of working days to each step and arriving at a delivery date. Meeting that schedule is another matter entirely. Changes in specifications, delays in approval, mechanical breakdowns, illness, fires, floods, and snowstorms all lie in wait. And because of the sequential nature of the production process, a delay of a single day early in the schedule can multiply into a delay of weeks in terms of delivery.

The most important elements in controlling scheduling are setting realistic dates at the outset, reacting promptly to delays, and maintaining frequent communication with both suppliers and clients.

Proofing. Proofs offer the production manager and/or the client an opportunity to prove the accuracy of a project at several crucial stages in its production.

The most common proof stages are type proofs (commonly called *galley proofs*), page proofs, and blueprints (also called bluelines, brown prints, salt prints, and vandykes). Proofs of four-color photos or illustrations are usually submitted separately, at the same time as page proofs or blueprints.

At each stage, the production manager's responsibility is to make sure all proofs are checked by the appropriate people, to return them on schedule, and to review all changes and corrections with the supplier.

On particularly complicated or important jobs, the production manager may also decide to visit the printing plant while the job is on the press. Although this is time-consuming and expensive, it is often a wise investment because it both prevents last-minute errors and demonstrates the production manager's concern for quality printing.

Delivery. Arrangements for delivery are neither complicated nor difficult, but they are the most commonly overlooked area of production activity. Delivery instructions should be included on the spec sheet and should be confirmed in writing to the printer a few days before completion of the project. They should include the date of delivery, the exact address, the method of packing, and the method of shipping. As a final precaution, the production manager should verify that the proper quantity has been received, inspect copies at random for quality, and notify the printer immediately about any problems.

Handling Production Effectively

Understanding production is only the beginning. The goal is to control production, so that completed publications match the original concept, meet the specifications, are free of faults and errors, remain within budget, arrive on time, and are delivered to the right place.

Although gaining that kind of control over production is the goal of every college and university publications office, the means of achieving it display an almost infinite variety. They depend, among other things, on the size of the publications office, the scope of the program, and the individual abilities of staff members. Nevertheless, it is possible to identify some procedures and policies that will help almost any publications office handle production more effectively.

Establish a separate file for each project. Usually called *job jackets* or *job tickets,* such files are often kept in pocket folders or large envelopes. Each file should provide a complete record of the project, including copies of the spec sheet, schedule, invoices, delivery slips, and all related notes and correspondence. It should also contain two copies of the completed publication.

Put everything in writing. Whenever possible, communicate with clients and suppliers in writing. Make written records of all meetings and telephone conversations and add them to the job file immediately. Be sure to date every note; nothing is more confusing than coming across an undated note about a change in specifications.

Set realistic schedules. Given enough resources, almost any publication can be produced overnight; but under normal circumstances, even the simplest project takes weeks—a fact that many clients and bosses choose to ignore. Agreeing to an unrealistic schedule without the resources to meet it leads only to frustration and disappointment.

Remake schedules after major delays. Never assume that a two- or three-day delay early in production can be made up later; it may only get worse. Instead, wait until the job is once again ready to proceed, then consult with suppliers and remake the entire schedule.

Understand the implications of changes. Changes in copy, design, and specifications are an inevitable hazard during production, but making them at the right time may lessen their impact. For instance, an increase in quantity three days before press time may present a major problem if the printer does not have enough paper on hand; but the same increase made a week earlier could easily be accommodated. The effective production manager learns to anticipate (or even encourage) changes when they can be made easily and to resist them when they cannot.

Keep ahead of events. The production manager should run the project; the project should not run the production manager. The manager must learn to anticipate events and deal with them before they become problems. For instance, if a particular photograph is of questionable quality, have the printer make a trial halftone in advance; the few extra dollars that costs may prevent a last-minute change that will cost far more and delay delivery. In like manner, if delivery is scheduled for Friday afternoon, call the printer Thursday morning to make sure all is on schedule.

Demand advance copies. For every project, insist that the first five or ten copies be delivered to the publications office immediately, in advance of the regular delivery. In case of a problem, there may still be time to salvage part of the job. And if all is well, the advance copies can be rushed proudly to the client with the good news that the balance of the order will arrive within hours.

Learn how to solve problems. Because no amount of anticipation can prevent every problem, the production manager must learn how to solve problems quickly and effectively. Styles of problem solving are highly individual, but most good managers follow two basic principles: first, they concentrate on solving the problem rather than worrying about whose fault it was; second, they never report a problem to a client or supervisor until they have a solution in hand. For instance, they do not say, "Your job is going to be late because the printer made a mistake." Instead they wait until they can say, "I have arranged to have your job reprinted to correct an error. It will be here tomorrow."

Supervising Production

The final ingredient in effective printing production is intelligent and enlightened supervision. This is particularly the case in colleges and universities, where publications operations are often supervised by individuals whose primary experience is in other areas of institutional advancement.

Again, individual styles of supervision vary, but at least three basic principles mark the most successful operations.

Assign production to a single individual. Allowing different staff members to handle production for different projects leads only to chaos; consolidating production responsibility under a single individual is an important step toward consistency. If possible, production should be that staff member's only responsibility.

Choose the right person. The best person to handle production may not be the head of the publications office. The right qualifications might be found, instead, in a designer, an editor, or a secretary. Familiarity with typesetting and printing is an important qualification, but it is not the only one; personality and attitude are at least as important. Good production managers thrive on pressure and enjoy the challenge of deadlines, they are compulsively attentive to detail but tolerant of human error, and they are wary when things seem to be going well and optimistic when things go badly.

Mind your own business. The good supervisor learns to have confidence in the production manager, to interfere rarely, and never to second-guess specific decisions. In a sense, the production manager is like an umpire in a baseball game: calling balls, strikes, and outs; enforcing the rules; always keeping the game moving; and always, always remaining in control. In the long run, the supervisor who interrupts that process to question an individual decision accomplishes nothing more than stopping the game, undermining authority, and creating confusion about who is in control.

45

M. Fredric Volkmann

Effective Cost-Cutting
in Publications Management

❧ According to a national survey of the one hundred leading university and college publications directors conducted by this writer, the single best way to lower the cost of publications is to "edit, cut, and pare." Reducing the length of copy in everything from alumni magazine features to catalogues and student recruitment brochures may be the most difficult task an editor faces in the publish-or-perish atmosphere of higher education. Yet alternative cost-cutting methods abound. In this chapter, we review these alternatives, all of which are suggestions by our colleagues in higher education.

Effective Management

The most important single step you can take is to develop a thorough understanding of, and familiarity with, all aspects of printing and production. Putting ink on paper is a complex process, and at each step, there are opportunities for something to go awry. Know the typesetters and printers in your area. Examine their samples. Check not only their best four-color work but also samples of work comparable to what you expect to do—particularly examples for institutions similar to yours. Discuss your expectations for service and learn the plants' capabilities. Find out what they expect from you. Meet your deadlines and give your typesetter and printer enough time to do the job well.

A visit to various typesetters' and printers' plants can help you make intelligent selections of suppliers. You can see firsthand how each organization is run and how jobs are handled. Also, a visit indicates that you are a professional interested in working with your supplier to obtain quality printed materials.

The next, and possibly single most important, step is the preparation of thorough typesetting and printing specifications. Communicate your requirements on a detailed specification sheet. If you do so, there can be no question about how the finished product will look because the specification sheet shows all the details the typesetter and printer need to produce the brochure as designed. A sample specification form from Ohio State University is shown in Figure 45-1.

Among the many details the typesetter and printer need to know before planning the job are the following.

Dates. Provide both the date copy will be ready and date of expected delivery. Together, they define the time period the supplier will have for working on the job and will help determine scheduling. If it is a short period, or if there are several other jobs in the shop, the supplier may have to work overtime. On the other hand, if the plant is in a slow period, the vendor may be able to quote a lower price. Of course, if the copy deadline is not met, the printer is not bound to meet the delivery deadline and can legitimately bill for overtime.

Quantity. Because your printer uses some of the paper to set up the presses and because some is wasted at the trimming stage, more paper will be ordered than is needed to print the desired quantity. According to trade customs, the printer can deliver up to 10 percent overrun or underrun and adjust the bill accordingly. If such surprises cannot be accommodated, state that in the printing specifications.

Printing Processes. Offset lithography has almost totally replaced letterpress and gravure printing. The offset process creates a clearer impression on a wide variety of paper surfaces and allows extensive and economical use of illustrations and photographs with minimal press makeready.

Size of Publication. The printer needs to know both flat and folded sizes of the publication. This determines the press to be used

Figure 45-1. Sample Specifications Form.

OSU Printing Specifications

Description of job:_____

☐ Request for cost estimate   ☐ Final printing specifications   Printer job no. _____User job no. _____

Quantity_____   Folded size _____   Flat size_____   ☐ Special items _____

No. of pages_____   ☐ Self cover ☐ Separate cover ☐ Other _____

Paper stock
☐ Inside, or ☐ Self cover: Brand _____ Weight _____ Color _____ Finish _____
☐ Cover, or ☐ Cards: Brand _____ Weight _____ Color _____ Finish _____

Other: (Describe) _____

Ink ☐ Inside pages, or ☐ self cover, or ☐ _____	Ink ☐ Separate cover, or ☐ cards, or ☐ _____
1st color ink _____ Prints on: ☐ Two sides ☐ One side	1st color ink _____ Prints on: ☐ Two sides ☐ One side
2nd color ink _____ Prints on: ☐ Two sides ☐ One side	2nd color ink _____ Prints on: ☐ Two sides ☐ One side
3rd color ink _____ Prints on: ☐ Two sides ☐ One side	3rd color ink _____ Prints on: ☐ Two sides ☐ One side
4-color process _____ Prints on: ☐ Two sides ☐ One side	4-color process _____ Prints on: ☐ Two sides ☐ One side
☐ Varnish on: ☐ Two sides ☐ One side ☐ Spot	☐ Varnish on: ☐ Two sides ☐ One side ☐ Spot
☐ Bleeds (explain) _____	☐ Bleeds (explain) _____

Typesetting
Preferred typeface(s): Body _____Headlines_____

Body type size(s)_____ Headline size(s)_____ Column width(s)_____ Estimated total column inches _____

Galley proofs, no._____ Waxed galley proofs, no._____ Page proofs, no._____Repro proofs, no. _____

Photos and other art work
No. of photos (halftones) _____Original size(s)_____ Printed size(s) _____

No. of line art pieces_____ Original size(s)_____ Printed size(s) _____

No. of color separation(s)_____ from: ☐ 35 mm slides ☐ Photo or art ☐ Other_____ Printed size(s) _____

Special effects: ☐ Reverses ☐ Solids ☐ Screen tints ☐ Duotones ☐ Other (explain) _____

Keyline (pasteup)
☐ Camera ready from customer, or furnished by: ☐ Printer ☐ Other_____

Special printing items
☐ Die cutting ☐ Scoring ☐ Perforating ☐ Numbering ☐ Flysheet ☐ Blind embossing ☐ Other _____

Folding (job does not bind)
Describe fold _____

Binding
☐ None ☐ Saddle stitch ☐ Side stitch ☐ Perfect ☐ Plastic ☐ Drill ☐ Pad ☐ Other _____

Proofs
☐ Brown print ☐ Color key ☐ Press proof ☐ Other _____

Deliver to _____Date wanted by_____

Packaging: ☐ Box ☐ Shrink wrap _____ per package ☐ Other _____

Finished samples to _____Number of samples wanted_____

Estimated Cost $_____Costs for additional or fewer ☐ 100's $_____ ☐ 1,000's $_____

Costs for additional or fewer pages in multiples of_____are $_____

These specifications prepared by _____Phone_____Date_____

or _____

Note: Institutions using word processing may want to add the following—
*Source of material: ☐ Manuscript ☐ Word Processor
☐ Computer (explain)

and the size sheet to be ordered to allow for minimum waste and for folding with the grain of the paper. (Grain is the direction in which wood or cotton fibers are laid down in making paper.)

Stock. A wide range of fine papers is available in a variety of colors and textures. Certainly you know better than the printer what the publication should "feel" like. Once you have made this decision, accept no substitutes without seeing the alternative. A switch without prior agreement is grounds to request reprinting at the printer's expense. And make sure that the size of the publication cuts economically out of the press sheet. As the customer, you usually pay for any trimmed waste, so use standard sizes.

Inks. Number of colors, specific colors, and placement on the paper are all important factors. The printer needs to know how many inks will be used and whether they will be mixed to a formula or are four-color process (magenta, cyan, yellow, and black). To prevent misunderstandings about ink color, use an ink guide (the Pantone Matching System) so the printer knows the exact formula to use. Remember that many inks are transparent. Blue ink on yellow paper looks green unless the mixture is adjusted accordingly. If the design bleeds on any or all sides, you must note this so the printer can properly adjust the paper, plates, and press. If the design requires a large solid area of ink coverage, or if a light color is to be printed on a dark color, the publication may require two passes through the press to achieve the effect you seek. If you neglect to mention these requirements in the quotation, there may be poor ink coverage because the printer went strictly by your specifications, or you may have to pay for extra work that was not in the original quoted price.

Photographs and Other Art. Photographs and other art, which add to the impact of the overall publication, also add work for the printer and represent additional costs to the buyer. The printer may shoot solid black-and-white art or line drawings as line copy for printing. A halftone screen renders shaded illustrations and photographs as halftones. Many screens are available, from coarse to fine, and your printer should help you select the one most appropriate to the paper stock and press being used.

Four-color, or process, printing costs more than black-and-white or two-color. Four-color process is rapidly gaining in popularity for student recruitment materials. Take special care to get good quality separations from color slides (transparencies) and art of equally excellent quality. Laser separation technology is currently the best method.

Special Processes. Special techniques, such as die-cutting and embossing, require additional press work and additional time. Reversing type or art out of a solid ink also means extra steps for the printer, as do flysheets, scoring, and perforating.

Typesetting. You must specify precisely which typefaces you want for the text and headlines, including weight, size, line length, leading (spacing between lines), kerning (spacing between letters); number of galley proofs needed; and the source of material to be typeset. (Usually the designer supplies both a layout and detailed specifications.) It is often cheaper to take information electronically from your word processor or computer and have it set. This saves the cost of setting from a typewritten manuscript. Also consider using a separate typesetting house, rather than your printer, because printers often charge a higher rate for this service.

Folding and Binding. The printer needs to know the final form in which you expect your publication to be assembled. Work with the printer on this. If different stocks will alternate on the inside of the publication, this presents a collating problem. Even if the publication is just folded, the sequence of folds may require handwork if the equipment cannot handle it. You must also describe binding. Is the publication to be saddle-stitched, side-stitched, or perfect-bound? Is scoring necessary? Scoring reduces cracking in coated stocks and makes heavier-weight papers fold more easily.

Proofs. Always ask the printer for a final proof, complete with folds, binding, and samples of the stock and ink colors. This provides you an opportunity to see that last-minute typos and other alterations are corrected, that halftones are cropped correctly, and that the pages are in the correct order and lined up properly. It also allows you to show the client the publication in the form, although not the color, of the final printed piece. Although it costs more money to make corrections at this stage than in the galley or pasteup stage, it is definitely cheaper than reprinting the publication or distributing it with mistakes.

A brown print, silver print, or blueline will do for single- or two-color printing. Xerox copies of keylines or mechanicals are not sufficient because they do not indicate how the printer plans to assemble the publication. Press proofs, made on the press just prior to the run, are generally prohibitive in cost. You should ask for 3-M Color Keys or Chromaline Proofs in production of high-quality, four-color work—but this work must be figured into the original estimate.

Production Time and Schedules. When you take on a rush job, the margin for error increases. Always issue to your clients a production schedule based on the typesetter's and printer's schedule. Remind clients in writing that their delays will result in similar delays in your office and with the printer. Then meet agreed-upon deadlines. Clients always remember a late job, no matter how well it was done.

Destination of Printed Materials. Printers usually deliver publications to the destination you indicate in your specifications; this means the publications office does not have to serve as central receiving. Shipping can be expensive if there is a large volume of publications or they are being sent a great distance. Ask for an estimated delivery cost or simply state that shipment is F.O.B. (free on board) to your institution, in which case the cost of delivery is figured into the quotation. Of course, you should take the precaution of checking several samples before the job is delivered to your client.

Bidding and Purchasing Printing. Because quality control of printing and contracting for printing are usually the publications office's responsibility, that office should write the specifications and purchase the printing. Unless the campus is located many miles from any printers, it is usually not a good idea to buy all printing from one source. Few printers are equipped to produce all types of jobs equally well. In addition, a printer who serves the campus exclusively may not have the incentive to figure printing jobs as economically as possible.

It is also difficult to get consistently good printing when bidding is open to any printer. Some institutions must use this potluck method, in which jobs are awarded solely on the basis of price with no attention given to a printer's capabilities. As a result, jobs are sometimes released to printers whose equipment and expertise are not equal to the task or whose work is unacceptable. A printer may also quote a low price just to get the job and then cut corners on production to make a profit. To overcome this problem, some publications officers draw up such detailed specifications that only a few printers will qualify.

Selective bidding offers a better solution. Send requests for quotations to only three printers. Then there can be no hesitation in giving it to the printer with the lowest bid. For this method to be effective, you must be familiar with the capabilities of a variety of printers. Those who turn out small brochures and pamphlets in accordance with specifications quote on those types of jobs; those who specialize in magazines and catalogues print those publications. There is a bonus in this system: Printers who realize they have an equal chance at a job tend to compete more in their pricing and are more professional in their output.

Cost-Cutting Techniques

You can decrease expenditures in editing, typesetting, paper, printing, ink, binding, and advertising in hundreds of ways. Here are some of the most commonly suggested methods, gleaned from a survey of publications directors conducted by the author.

Eliminate Unnecessary Publications. One of the best money-savers is not to publish in the first place. Combine items that overlap to a significant degree. Explore alternatives to printing and direct mail, such as person-to-person contact, personal letters, and telephone calls.

Edit for Economy. Massive editing can mean a more significant cost saving than printing economies. Cut course descriptions by using only descriptive titles. If information is duplicated in several publications, eliminate the repetition.

Avoid Alterations. Clients rarely appreciate the costs involved in resetting type, repasting keylines, restripping negatives, and replating. The publications manager must refuse changes unless they are absolutely necessary. To save time and money, ask the client to initial galleys and prepress proofs.

Save on Typesetting. The savings realized from new computerized typesetting methods are staggering. For example, when Ohio State University reset its 512-page catalogue on a computer, margins were reduced to a minimum, lines were set solid with a typeface adaptable to this technique, and indentations were eliminated whenever practical. Even with the addition of more copy and a reduction in size from seven-by-ten inches to six by nine, the book was 100 pages shorter than its predecessor and about $10,000 cheaper during the first year alone. More savings were realized in succeeding years when changes were made only in the computer's core memory.

Make Use of Kerning. Most new photocomposition equipment is capable of kerning alphabets, that is, removing a specified amount of white space between letters. Kerning saves 3 to 5 percent on the total length of a large manuscript. Consider setting copy flush left, ragged right. It takes no more space than justified lines and is more legible for slower readers.

Computerize. If information for a class schedule, catalogue, or similar publication is being stored on a mainframe, you can transcribe this information into typeset material at a low cost. The typesetter maintains a special set of programs to convert the information into both upper- and lower-case typography. This technique is often used for campus telephone directories. If you don't have material stored on your mainframe or a word processor, optical character recognition can cut costs by eliminating the person in the middle—the keyboard operator at the typesetting plant.

Avoid Typesetting. When quality is less important than economy, computer printouts and typewriters are two ways to avoid typesetting altogether. Computer printouts are reduced to as small as 50 percent of their original size and printed with the addition of cut-in or pressed-down headlines (presstype). But if you use this technique, insist that the printout that goes to the printer be run with a new ribbon on the heaviest possible white stock, preferably unlined; this will provide the best reproduction. Some typewriters, particularly the IBM Selectric with a 12-pitch Letter Gothic typing head, provide clean, inexpensive copy that can be reduced or used full-size for reports and small flyers.

Use Presstype. For many jobs, there is no reason to spend the money to set display heads when good quality presstype is satisfactory. In recent years, prices have climbed rapidly on Geotype, Letraset, Chartpak, and similar brands, but they are usually cheaper than high-quality phototype.

Save on Paper Stock. Even though paper prices have more than doubled in the last few years and mills seem to be discontinuing their good, cheap offset sheets, you can still print a job inexpensively with quality paper. First, get to know paper merchants well and ask them to show you closeout lists. Second, familiarize yourself with standard sizes of cut papers and the ways you can fold and bind them to produce waste-free publications. Third, be flexible and redesign a publication's dimensions to fit an available, reduced-price sheet if necessary. Fourth, ask your printers which papers they stock "on the floor" because they often purchase these by the carload at reduced prices. Then design the job to use this paper. Fifth, if you are preparing a related series of brochures or posters, specify or estimate the entire job so the ultimate supplier can order all the stock at one time, thus saving you money.

Use newsprint when you need to cut costs drastically on such publications as catalogues, telephone directories, class schedules, and alumni tabloids. It is cheaper than offset, and the lighter weight makes these publications cheaper to mail. This technique, however, is economical only when web presses are used. Sheet-fed newsprint usually is not available.

Economize on stationery by switching from rag content stock to a number one sulfite bond. It is difficult to tell the difference between the two, and the shelf life and typing characteristics of most nonrag papers now rival those of papers containing cotton fibers. Use a lower-grade white offset sheet where halftones and ink solids are not a major concern. It is cheaper, and the publications can be just as effective.

Pare Prices with the Printer. Perhaps no one knows cost-cutting better than the printer, because cost-cutting on production is how profits are made. Always ask whether there are ways to reduce costs on a job by changing specifications for size, ink colors, paper, and so forth. Design publications to fit the production equipment of your printer, including presses, folders, stitchers, and camera equipment.

Cut Costs with Color. Printing one color on a colored stock can produce a range of colors by using tints and screens. Additionally, two-color presses have made two-color printing relatively inexpensive, especially on long runs. Generally, printers charge only for an extra set of negatives, a plate, setup charges on the press, and a minor additional charge for running time. A second color can greatly improve most printing jobs, but printing a third color has drawbacks. A three-color job must either be run twice through a two-color press or be run once on the more expensive four-color press.

Where color separations are a major expense, four-color printing is still impractical. However, new processes have been developed to make separations that bring four-color printing within the range of all but the most restricted budgets. Where four-color presses are available, and long press runs are planned, this type of printing does not cost appreciably more than two-color. Likewise, clever designers can avoid separations altogether on regular artwork by using trapping techniques to create colors without the need for expensive camera techniques.

Lower Prices Through Design. Avoid graphic devices that cause registration problems, two-color rules that run parallel or too close to the edges of the page, bleeds, large blocks of ink solids, and tricky stock and ink combinations, such as silver ink on black stock or white ink on a colored paper. Do not design jobs that require hand operations for binding, assembly, or insertion into envelopes. Where appropriate, replace expensive halftones and duotones with line art collected from student sources, the college archives, or various clip services.

Change Format and Save. A change of format can result in significant savings. For example, the University of Michigan took a twenty-four-page booklet with a cover and converted it to a twenty- by twenty-five-inch poster. You can publish class schedules in a tabloid format on newsprint, which will save binding and trimming costs. Publishing multiple-year catalogues provides significant savings for some institutions. Bowling Green State University saved $10,000 over a two-year period by publishing a biennial catalogue that includes general university information. A course descriptions supplement, printed on newsprint and in smaller quantities, is published annually. Also, bindery costs can be reduced by switching from magazines to tabloid formats and by avoiding saddle-stitching for booklets when a simple foldout format will do.

If a client proposes a series of smaller brochures, plan to use the same stock and ink colors so the printer can gang run them on the same press sheet for substantial savings. Preparing keylines or mechanicals in-house provides quality control and is probably cheaper than having a free-lance designer or the printer do it. This method also saves author's alterations charges because those corrections are made in-house.

Cut Mailing and Postage Costs. Because of the costs of first- and third-class mail, distribution should be taken into account when planning publications. If possible, figure out a way to avoid using the mails altogether. Distribute class schedules through campus mail instead of sending them second class. Larger cities have nonpostal, competitive door-to-door delivery systems, which can be ideal for community colleges and continuing education promotions. Institutions with extensive international distribution can save on airmail postage by using so-called "Bible" papers that reduce the weight of flyers and application forms to less than one-half ounce. Annually review your mailing lists and eliminate the names of those who are no longer members of the target audience.

You may mail specific publications that resemble periodicals or newsletters within the same county as your institution at a much cheaper second-class rate if they are published at least four times a year. (Second-class mail sent outside your county may cost the same as, or more than, third-class, however.) Postal permit application procedures are relatively simple, and handling costs are no higher than those for the more expensive third-class bulk rate. However, if you have a second-class permit, you must meet deadlines and follow regulations to the letter. Second-class items face scrutiny from the U.S. Postal Service, and those publications that do not meet requirements may be fined or the permit may be changed to a higher-rate class.

Finally, when preparing publications to be mailed, consider the capability of the mailing equipment before proceeding with design and printing. This prevents wasting time and money on printed materials that for one reason or another do not fit the equipment.

These are only a few cost-saving ideas that experienced publications directors use. Given the specific circumstances, they are worth a try.

Part Seven

Periodicals: Formats, Uses, and Editorial Strategies

Maralyn Orbison Gillespie, Editor

46   *Maralyn Orbison Gillespie*

Open Letter to New Editors on Producing Quality Periodicals

This is a personal essay. It is also defensive.

Periodicals cost big bucks. Chances are that that line item in your institutional advancement budget towers above others. Whether you are producing a magazine, a newspaper, or a magapaper—a hybrid of magazine and newspaper—the total cost can sometimes make top administrators nervous (Is this money really well spent?) or hopeful (Can we chop a bit off the budget in these times of economizing?).

Then you, the editor, point out the alternatives: Produce a second-rate periodical, and give the reader the chance to deduce a second-rate institution behind it? Reduce the frequency with which you publish the periodical just when it is more important than ever before to keep in close touch with your constituencies because you are depending on them more and more? Put all your eggs in the computer basket and gear up for communicating electronically with all your constituencies in the next decade?

The sophisticated administrator recognizes that these alternatives are either far behind or way ahead of the times. The periodical remains the most powerful tool for telling a story to the largest number of people at the most reasonable cost per person. It arrives in the home of each constituent, a tangible reminder of the institution that sent it. It is tacit evidence that the institution considers each reader an important part of its vitality, or as some people have put it, a continuing partner in its life—somebody who wants to keep up-to-date with the institution and who has the right to be kept up-to-date. As long ago as 1959, the president of a state-supported institution, the University of Illinois, said: "In the long run the alumni are responsible for what the institution becomes. They hold the ultimate destiny of the institution in their hands."

You can boast of an elaborate and active alumni club system, you can whisk your president and a faculty member or two around the country to alumni and parent gatherings, and you can attract alumni back to the campus for class reunions, but statistics tell you that you will never reach more than some 10 to 15 percent of your alumni this way.

Periodicals offer the institution a unique opportunity to tell its stories. The catch is that, if the periodicals are not well thought out and professionally executed, much of that opportunity is lost. This is where the editor comes in. For it is the editor who must set the standards, define the purpose, set the goals, and produce the periodical. Of course, the editor does not do this alone; it is a cooperative venture with the publisher, which may be the institution, one or more departments of the institution, or an independent alumni association. Responsibility for the final product rests with the editor.

I warned you at the beginning that this would be both a personal and a defensive essay. It is personal in the sense that it is based on almost thirty years' experience in editing a periodical; it is defensive in the sense that for almost twenty-five years (it took me about five years to develop an awareness of my responsibility as editor, beyond counting picas, and of the dangers, beyond misspelling names of alumni) I have seen myself the defender of my periodical against an impressive array of enemies. I do not suffer unduly from paranoia; the dangers have been, and are, real. Let me share them with you. Many of them you will doubtless recognize; perhaps one or two may not have occurred to you. I have by no means won every battle (and probably should not have!), but most of the time I have been in the fray.

In a real sense, the whole world—that part of it that touches you—is out to destroy the quality of your magazine. These well-meaning colleagues and constituents do not see it that way; they say they want to help you do a better job. For instance, engineering faculty lean on you for a major article about changes in the undergraduate curriculum; the development office would appreciate your running a profile on a rich alumnus who clips coupons to make his life interesting; your designer pushes you to choose for the cover one of several photographs because of its striking composition, with no thought as to its editorial relevance; alumni pressure you for more class notes; an alumnus writes that she would like features about emeritus faculty members; for the third straight year, the career office wants you to run a half-page copy block and return form about the need of students for summer jobs. Some requests are worthy, others not; they all are part of your constituencies clamoring to use the periodical to further their own goals. These may or may not fit in with the goals of the periodical; it is up to you, the editor, to decide when they do and do not mesh and to withstand the attack when you have identified the enemy.

The editor, and only the editor, has in mind solely the welfare of the periodical. If you believe in it and love it (you should not be its editor unless you feel passionately about it), you must defend it as convincingly as any mother tiger defends a cub.

One former editor-turned-journalism-professor exhorts editors to focus on the world "we readers live in. To serve your own purpose you must then demonstrate, as vividly as you can, how our world is related to your own cloistered world. . . . A good editor thinks of his readers. He must . . . crawl inside his readers' mind to discover what they want from his magazine that they don't get from others. . . . With your journalist's perception, you surely must recognize the folly of presuming my intense interest in everything pertaining to the old school. That's a brand of naïveté reserved for fund-raisers, alumni directors, public relations officers, and college presidents. If you want my response, then you will please behave as an editor, not as one of *them*" (Metzler, 1967).

You must fight vigorously against any temptation to bore your readers. Dullness is indefensible. Absolute defeat is producing a periodical that no one reads. A skillful editor translates the goals of a periodical into articles that address the needs and interests of its readers.

The enemy may also be the experts in editing outside your institution. When I was growing up as an editor, Randy Fort of Emory University, one of the best, and best-loved, editors in the fifties and sixties, woke me up to this danger at a conference of the American Alumni Council (AAC; a forerunner of the Council for Advancement and Support of Education [CASE]) in a talk he titled "The Things I Wish They'd Told Me." "I wish they'd warned me," he said, "not to accept as gospel every suggestion of the first expert I ever consulted and not, for that matter, to accept unquestioningly the advice of any one expert. I spent some hapless years endeavoring to follow every suggestion of every expert, with my magazine deteriorating all the time" (Fort, 1966).

I did, too. I knew I was in trouble when I had heard so many experts giving conflicting advice:

> "Use two-column pages for your front-of-the-book features; three-column pages for class notes."
> "Mix up your two- and three-column text features in the front of the book for variety."
> "Two columns are harder for the eye to grasp; forget them."

And "expert" opinion on the width of the margins of your pages is as varied as your experts.

Experts' advice can be helpful. Some of their wisdom from AAC/CASE conferences I still remember and use. From the editors of *Look:* "Never use pictures without captions. People are the key to each story. 'Sell' lines on continued pages of articles (lines picked up from photo ideas and copy on that page that are related to the main theme) are important. The major problem of a picture story is the lead picture. We are always asking ourselves, 'Do we have the lead picture yet?'"

From a *McCall's* editor: "A magazine should have enthusiasm. It is like a letter from home. Don't overlook the little things."

From a public relations officer at Inland Steel: "Most alumni magazines are too grim."

From a former editor at New York University: "When you find yourself with a story to write that you can't get a handle on for a lead, he said, 'Forget you are going to write about it. Make believe you've gone home. Your spouse asks, "What happened?" Your simple, brief conversational reply will always be the key to your lead'" (Saplin, 1958, p. 22).

From the editor of *Intellectual Digest* in answer to the question of how to recognize a good manuscript: "By what delights you."

To pile expert on top of expert, DeWitt Wallace, a founder of the *Reader's Digest,* said that when he chose articles, "I simply hunt for things that interest me."

In the last analysis, you, the editor, must become the expert for your own periodical. You are not a ninety-day-wonder expert either. You have worked hard to attain this editorial judgment.

You have gotten to know thoroughly your institution and the people who compose it. You know what is going on in the world, and particularly in the world of education. You exchange periodicals with your colleagues at other institutions, and you have studied newsstand periodicals as well. You have analyzed what you do, and do not, like about them.

You attend professional conferences for periodical editors, such as those sponsored by CASE, and after formal sessions, you have talked shop over a drink session with senior editors, picking their brains for ideas and perhaps sweet-talking them into critiquing your publication.

You have entered your publication in the CASE annual competition to find out how it stacks up against others; and when the winners are announced, you have written for copies of them.

Now you are equipped to rely on yourself and to accept your own judgment. Your homework has developed your instinct, which John Fischer, formerly of *Harper's,* called the primary piece of equipment for an editor. Fischer (1965, p. 16) identified four other characteristics of a successful editor: "curiosity in abnormal quantity; a certain ordinariness that will make him react in his bones and belly the same way as most of the people in his audience; the enthusiasm of an adolescent in the spasms of first love; and ruthlessness in rejecting manuscripts, for the kindly editor soon finds his columns filled with junk."

At times, you yourself may be your periodical's worst enemy, and you must be alert to attack from within. You threaten the welfare of your periodical when you get lazy and careless, when you fail to make the effort to look up a hyphenation you are in doubt about, when you let slide by in page proofs the column that is one line short, when you fail to take the time to justify your captions to the width of the photographs, when you do not notice (or, worse still, do not care) that *maneuver* is spelled two ways in the same article, and when you do not go back to your typewriter one more time to make sure your cover blurb is the best you can make it. As Mies van der Rohe used to say, "God is in the details."

You are most dangerous to the health of your periodical when you tilt back in your chair, flip through your latest issue, and say to yourself, "Hey, I've got a spanking good publication that's meeting the needs of my alumni and the institution." That's the time to get your defenses up. That fearsome enemy, stagnation, may have its eye on you.

References

Fischer, J. "Editor's Easy Chair: Editor's Trade." *Harper's,* July 1965, p. 16.

Fort, R. L. "The Things I Wish They'd Told Me." Address to American Alumni Council, Washington, D.C., 1966.

Metzler, K. "Letter to an Alumni Editor." *Alma Mater,* Jan. 1967, pp. 25–29.

Saplin, S. *The News Is Where You Find It.* Washington, D.C.: American Alumni Council News, 1958.

47

Elise Hancock

Shaping the Content and Character of Alumni Periodicals

ॐ I would like to start with the obvious because it is so easy to overlook: An alumni magazine is not a general interest magazine. It has a special subject: your institution. And it should have a special atmosphere: that of your institution. There should be something about it—rather like the perfume your mother always wore—that says, "This could have come from no other place." The magazine has to be rooted in the institution, or why bother?

Therefore the first thing to do, when starting or revamping a magazine, is to think about the institution. Design and format are issues for another day. For starters, you need to establish a foundation.

What is your campus like? What are its history, its basic character, and its short-term goals and broader mission? How do the older people say it has changed—and not changed? Find out why students choose your institution, not some other. What are your unique offerings, in subject and in atmosphere? The magazine must reflect them.

Our alumni are busy people with lots to do besides read about our institution. Campus magazines go into the home and compete head-to-head with *Time, Newsweek, TV Guide,* and television itself—not to mention hobbies and families. Therefore, to get alumni to read more than class notes, you will have to work from strength. What special resources can your campus muster? Are you rich in fascinating people? That would suggest a peoply magazine. Do you have an extraordinary campus photographer? Do you have some notable art collections? Do you have a notable wit who would perhaps do a column? Do you have the sort of faculty that writes well for laypeople?

Of course you want the magazine to assist the fund-raisers, but must the assistance be direct? Should there be profiles of big givers or people you hope might be big givers? stories about particular needs? Or should the magazine handle general cultivation, arousing interest and keeping the alumni in touch but leaving fund-raising to the fund-raisers?

Is the magazine intended to be a status piece, something that will win awards, or do you only care what your alumni think? (For instance, alumni like class notes, half a magazine of class notes. Award juries seldom do.)

Do you wish it to be honest, reporting unpleasant events on the campus right along with wonderful news? Candor is becoming to institutions founded to pursue truth, and it will lend the magazine a credibility that we house organs must struggle for and seldom gain. Perhaps you will want to go for moderate candor, reporting only major unpleasant events, the kind alumni can read in the newspaper anyway. Or do you want to go all-out for good news? These decisions must be made clearly and consciously, so they can be carried out consistently.

Who are your alumni? I mean the alumni as a whole, not just the rather special alumni who are active. Do they cluster in certain occupations? What is their median age? What is their general character? They all chose your institution, and they were all shaped by it. Cornellians are robust and self-assured; Swarthmore alumni, idealistic; Johns Hopkins alumni, earnest; and the editor of *Notre Dame Magazine* once remarked tersely that his alumni like to win. What traits do your alumni share? What clusters of intellectual, personal, and sportive interest do you find in them? The magazine must address those interests.

Do you have other audiences?—What about parents? Is the magazine also intended to reach your internal audience: the faculty and staff, trustees, and students? Imagine you are writing a letter to these people. What will interest them? What kind of thing will they want to hear? Break them into groups and think about each group. What kind of thing might interest that 40 percent of your alumni who are physicians? Or what about the Old Blues? the young careerists? Think carefully, because the answers born of habit may, or may not, be right.

For one thing, the internal audience and the alumni audience are radically different. You spend your working life with the internal audience, and it is easy to assume that what interests people you talk to every day must surely fascinate the alumni. But that is not necessarily so. Take three perennial stories—the new dean, the new dorm, and the retiring professor. To people on campus, these three events will affect their daily life or the lives of people they know and therefore are of intense interest. They will want to know all about them.

But will the alumni? Think about some institution you once attended but do not work for. Do you really want to know much about the new dean, someone you will never even meet? The new dorm? You will never use it. A lively paragraph or so, enough to satisfy idle curiosity about generally how things are changing, will be plenty for the alumni magazine.

I am not saying, by the way, that your alumni magazine should not cover the institution and its events. It must. But it should often cover them by means of what I call the flipflop. Readers are suspicious of public relations. They know our magazines are house organs, and they accept the idea: Any alumnus who actually reads the magazine is, like us, on the side of the institution. Nevertheless, alumni will take our good news with large dollops of salt. For example, they will be bored and skeptical about the gleaming technological wonders of your new Infant Intensive Care Unit. If an article looks like public relations, it is not likely to be read. So flipflop the emphasis and slant the article toward general interest. You'll find readers are very interested in premature babies and the wonderful things that can now be done for them. Do heartwarming news fresh from the experts at your new Infant Intensive Care Unit, not PR on the new unit.

You can see how a magazine is starting to shape up out of these questions. A magazine for alumni only will be one kind of thing; a magazine for an internal audience, another. If you have to work with both groups, the magazine has to be structured in such a way that faculty and staff can easily find their news and alumni can easily find their features.

Similarly, every alumnus should be able to find something of interest in every issue, so spotting the major clumps of alumni interest virtually defines the content of your magazine.

Statement of Purpose

Having thought about all these things, the editor should write a candid statement of purpose. (The editor writes it because the editor must execute it, but the vice-president should agree.) This statement is not for publication, so be honest. If good news is part of your purpose, put it in the statement. If covering every part of the institution equally is part of your goal, say so. If there must, must, must be some sort of institutional connection with every story, say so.

The statement should be short, twenty-five words or less, a requirement that forces you to focus your ideas. Also, if the statement is short, you will remember it, and it can function as a touchstone.

A statement might read, "to keep the alumni involved with each other and with the institution"—a reasonable goal for the warm peoply magazine of the small college that specializes in developing character. Or it might be something like "Ideas are important fun. The magazine should inform, educate, and entertain—preferably at the same time—and keep alumni in touch." This would be more appropriate for a big research university.

You might infer from these statements that the research university would never have a story on, say, reunion, and that the college always would. However, a statement of purpose need not restrict you. The fact is, there is always a way to handle any subject, however clichéd.

For instance, take the standard, old-fashioned reunion story and apply the touchstones: Does a picture of four alumni smiling over drinks do much to keep alumni involved with each other? No. Does it inform or entertain? No. How about the class group shots, which cannot be run large enough to be plain? You would do better to send the participants a good glossy print of their own class.

Where to Get Story Ideas

Now that you have a statement of purpose, you are ready to go out hunting story ideas—and the operative word is *hunt.* "How do you think up your ideas?" people always ask. A good story idea is not thought up; it is found—found, for example, over lunch, where a statistician is being comical about the logic of sports announcers. "He's due for a homer," the announcer will say, because he hasn't had one in ten weeks. By the same logic, the statistician announces, Princeton has lost the football game to Dartmouth every year for the past fourteen years. So by God, we're due to win. "In fact, so badly have we played in recent years that we're a sure thing for the Rose Bowl this year!" And so forth. Now *there* is a story idea, and Princeton ran the story some years ago. It was one of the funniest articles I've ever read. And you would never get that idea by sitting in the office thinking up ideas. The best ideas—serious, comical, visual, important, or human—are invariably found outside the office.

There are editors who systematically call on one department head after another, rotating around the institution all year. That approach is ideal, and those with a less systematic temperament should try to approximate it, eating lunch with various faculty members several times a week.

You will know a good story because your own interest level will leap. It makes me sick to remember the day a staff member came back to the office, some years ago. She had been to an internal lecture in psychiatry, about this new disease, called bulimia, in which patients make themselves throw up. It was fascinating stuff, and utterly new. We sat enthralled by every detail of the lecture, mouths hanging open. Yet I passed up the scoop. I failed to get past my immediate disgust to notice my fascination and the importance of the story (especially because many bulimia patients are college-age). It was about throwing up and so, in my mind, it wasn't an article. That was dumb. When your mouth hangs open, you have a story.

You will find lots of ideas in your exchange copies, especially the best magazines of institutions rather like your own. Even the best editors shamelessly rip off ideas—and by the time you are through with the scheme, it will have changed so much it will be fresh anyway. (It is, however, good practice to thank your colleague for reminding you how fascinating a vet school can be, for instance.)

And remember your alumni. You may have someone else handling the class notes, but you ought to read them alertly. The people who started Outward Bound and Federal Express were somebody's alumni, and those somebodies could probably have scooped the world about these fascinating new ideas.

Think hard about the people you meet, the alumni you hear about. Ask the fund-raisers for suggestions—they meet many alumni, including alumni who do not show up at reunions for you to meet. Do any of these people rouse your curiosity?

Or there may be a figure, utterly familiar to you, who would pique the curiosity of your readers. Whom do you go home and tell stories about to your spouse? Do not overlook that person as a story just because she is right under your nose. What professors do the students love?

Look in your archives. You are bound to have trouble sometime, and find yourself needing a story to throw into a sudden hole. The archives should offer you several good stories, of varying lengths. Get them written ahead of time—even laid out. Emergency supplies are useless if they are not actually in hand.

One place not to look is the national press. The fact is, if the *New York Times* magazine has done a subject, it has been beaten to death. We have too few pages to waste them on articles that will make readers say, "Oh, no! Not another story about the nuclear holocaust!" You can jump on these bandwagons only if you genuinely have something to add, something the national press has missed—and then you have to handle it very artfully to make its freshness plain.

On the whole, we do better to stick to our own campus beat, which is a fantastically rich one. In fact, so far from copying the national press, we should be able to beat them now and then. If we are alert, we can find on our campuses the stories the *New York Times* will have several years later: microprocessors, monoclonal antibodies, networking, and changes in youthful ideas of honor are some we all could have had.

In spotting the scoops, the key questions are these: Is this event or idea central to the life of our institution? of other institutions of higher education? of society? of the world? Will it change anything? What will it make possible? Many of today's important stories look boringly technical to begin with. But if the academicians are excited, look hard. And if some subject rouses a lot of debate on campus, you may have a hot one; the alumni, too, may be intrigued.

If you find intelligent humor, leap on it. Our alumni are a varied lot. Intelligent humor is scarce, yet is one of the few common traits of educated persons. (Keep it short, though. Make sure you leave them wanting more. If you do not believe humor can sour, try reading more than two Russell Baker essays at a sitting—and they come no better than Baker.)

Ask yourself, does this story have some element of surprise? Magazines are dead if they become predictable. Think of someone who has visited your home, someone whose every word could be anticipated. Do you rush to invite that person back? No. Likewise, people do not open magazines if they feel they know what will be in them. They need to feel there just may be something wonderful, something they cannot get elsewhere, something they must not miss. The fact that you are the only source of news about old Siwash is not good enough. Old Siwash doesn't change enough to generate electrifying news every other month.

Ask yourself, Could I have run this same story last year? If so, you can probably consider it dead. Attitudes shift, verbal habits shift, and timeliness is subtle, but definite.

Beware topics: A topic is not a story idea. Rather, a topic is apt to be one word, such as *rainbow,* and it can be powerfully seductive. Rainbows are beautiful objects, and there must be a dynamite story there, right? True, because there is a story in anything. But you have to find the angle. *Rainbow* is too diffuse. If you start with a topic, you get a thin, ill-focused story.

You can tell the difference between a topic and a story idea because a topic is one or two words, whereas a story idea can be written into a head and subhead. For example, a crude story idea might read something like this: "Bow of Light—A rainbow is sunlight, reflected and refracted through millions of raindrops. Here's how it happens." That is not a great idea (although pictures would help), but it is a workable story idea. It is specific.

You should also look hard at feasibility, remembering that alumni editors work in a closed community. The lady has a terrific idea? Go to the library and quietly read her publications before you ask her to write something. Ask faculty members to write only if they can translate their ideas for a lay audience because you do not want to rewrite faculty articles: They don't expect or like it, they will tell their colleagues you are stupid and uncooperative, it is a great deal of work, and the result is often stilted.

If such a problem looks likely, but the material is fascinating, perhaps an interview or profile would be a better approach. I lean toward interviews for people who are lively talkers.

As to paying faculty writers, policies vary. Most of the Top Ten magazines pay all writers, including faculty, a practice that promotes good morale. Furthermore, if faculty write for free, they are doing you and the institution a favor; you must accept a first draft, if that is what they choose to give you. But if you are paying, you can ask for a new draft. Anyway, why should faculty write for nothing? They are busy people, and writing for us is not in their contracts. At the least, it is courteous to buy lunch for your writer, or give your writer an honorarium or an appropriate gift.

Your Working Notes

As you prowl for stories, imagine you are working on a gigantic issue and make up a gigantic table of contents. To make sure you have genuine ideas, always write heads and subheads. If you have a computer to make it easy, you might produce a double version. One version would contain only heads and subheads, for quick reference. The other would also estimate how long each story might run, who might write it, and who should be featured in it. It would include notes on possible art ideas and questions that you want to look into further, and any other possibly useful information. Old-fashioned note cards also work well; the critical point is that you have room to add items as they come up, weeks or months or years from now. Some stories take years to ripen, as you wait for the right author or the perfect news peg.

Jot down good illustration and art and photography you find as stories by themselves, even if the art lacks matching thought. You will need some picture stories—for one thing, they have a handy way of shrinking or expanding by a page or so, as desired; for another, this list is a long-range project. The thought to go with those pictures may come along several years from now, and this way you will remember the pictures.

Make lists of things you learn that would be good in the news section, too. Is your news going to be strictly news, or will you include such items as things seen on bulletin boards if they are interesting? For the moment, jot it all down. The more the better.

Think about regular features that might suit your alumni. A sports column? Not for Saint John's in Annapolis. Definitely for the Big Ten. Math puzzles? Yes for M.I.T. Faculty book reviews? Maybe. Word puzzles? Do you find a tremendously good writer on your faculty or in your alumni body? Is that individual's favorite subject something you can use?

This table of contents should go on for pages, and it may take you several weeks (or even months) to create, working at it off and on. If in doubt, put the item in. If there are several good aspects of one subject, write it up each way and put them all in. Similarly, many items could be treated as news or as feature, and it is fine to list them both ways. Remember, you are not making decisions now; you are exploring possibilities. When you come back to it, it may be more clear which you would prefer. Things will crystallize as you work.

When the table of contents contains at least three times as many ideas as you would ever need, go back to that statement of purpose. Are the statement and the table congruent? Perhaps the statement of purpose was too limited, and you have found wonderful things you cannot pass up. Enlarge the statement. Or perhaps the statement was too grandiose, planning lots of continuing education and visual richness. But the list shows that your campus simply does not offer that stuff; what you have is a lot of nice people stories. Think again, and refine your statement if necessary.

You will publish a far better magazine and serve your institution far better if you are working in a mode that is natural to you. Let the next editor publish alumni poems; if you dislike poems and feel ill qualified to judge them, leave them out. Of course, you will have to run features about subjects that do not personally interest you, if they are important to the institution and to a large chunk of alumni, but do it in your natural mode. If you are a newsy person, take a news focus; if a people person, take a people focus. That way, your magazine will acquire a certain integrity of approach, a distinctive character.

Planning Issues

The last step here should be fun: You are going to plan some issues—and incidentally, discover your format. It is already there, implicit in your long-version table of contents.

How many pages do you think you can afford each issue? Out of this, how many pages do you expect to use for news, class notes, house ads, editorial, columns (if any), and other regular features? Write this out. A plan is not a plan until you get it on paper.

Now, how much room do you have left for features? At least half an issue, I hope. If not, think again. Does the news section need to be eight pages, for instance, or would four do? To give an impression of rich variety and to have a reasonable shot at reaching each alumnus, you should try to have at least four features in each issue.

Are you going to have enough room, given the story lengths you are tending toward? Should you be out there beating the bushes for more short stories?

Divide your massive table of contents into sensible issues. Try to arrange feature groups that set each other off nicely, providing variety without jarring on each other. Maybe you will have one faculty profile, a sport story, a two-page story about the

Edwin S. Jones Memorial Collection of Mummified Cats, and a political essay.

Length should also vary, some short stories and some long—in comparison with one another. For the Hopkins magazine, a two-page story is short; seven or eight, quite usual; twelve, long. I know several good alumni magazines for whom a twelve-page story is impossible, four pages long, one or two pages standard. Either extreme will work, so long as the variety is there. Variety looks better, reads more easily, and gives you a way to flag the reader that some items are more important or interesting than others.

For maximum printing economy, is your total page count a multiple of eight? Have you built into each issue one or two articles that can run a little shorter or a little longer to make the length work?

Have you planned one story too many? In real life, you should, and you might as well start now. Nothing is more certain, in doing a periodical, than that something will fall through. The photographer will be late with prints or a text will arrive in bad shape or the president's speech will be withdrawn, but you can chuckle at catastrophe if you had too much material anyway.

Now try to organize your magazine along some definite principle. News always first. News always last. Or news always just before the class notes. News always somewhere. People need to be able to find their way around. *Time* does not make you search for movie reviews up toward the news from the Middle East, and you should not make the reader search for news and letters and class notes. Give each permanent section a home, a place where it can be found in each issue. Here are a few general principles:

Think about the power of first impressions. The reader who opens the magazine and finds news leading off will expect a newsy magazine with newsy features. If news is not the focus, the news section might better be in the back.

It often works to group opinions—your editorial (if any), the president's column and other columns (if any), letters from the readers, and so on.

About one-third of readers start magazines from the back. Therefore, whatever is at the very back should be lively and easy. The old *Life* always put a comic animal picture on the last page as a lively first or last contact with readers. News does well there, but if you lead the issue with it, you will have to think of some other short and easy material for the back. Class notes are a classic for the spot, and they will work especially well if you sprinkle some lively short articles through them. Little alumni profiles make sense.

Order the features. Most people read roughly in the order you offer, so be careful to give them a more or less continuous reading experience. Do not put your best story cheek-by-jowl with your worst. The contrast will make the bad one look even more horrid. Likewise, do not put comedy after a heart-wrencher; it will look trivial.

It is often good to lead with the most appealing feature, usually the human story. The important story often had the cover anyway; if so, it needs no more billing. Or sometimes you will want to lead with your biggest graphic splash.

The center spread of a magazine is the only place where you can be positive it is okay to spread a single picture across two pages. In this one spot, the printer cannot possibly mess up the union of left- and right-hand pages.

Even more powerful than first impressions are last impressions. Your weakest story should be carefully buried in the middle of the issue, and your strongest should often fall last.

Design Fever

Everybody loves design. It is so concrete, so easy to think about, so agreeably alien to most bureaucratic tasks. But design is only a servant to the words and content, which is why the subject had to wait until now, when you have a clear conception of what your magazine should do, and generally how, and several good story lists. Only now are you ready to talk with designers.

You do need a designer, if only—this is the low-budget alternative—to establish a distinctive, but simple, format that the editor can execute. Remember, if no one reads your wonderful words and ideas, they are useless. On the other hand, display without content will boomerang because it will make the reader feel cheated. If I were a vice-president and had to choose, I would put my money into the word person, not the designer. But I would try not to have to choose. Appropriate display can make all the difference.

The medium-budget alternative is to establish a format for the news and other routine sections. The editor lays those out, and you only buy expensive design time for the features. Or you can go the grand route and have the designer lay out and produce everything for you.

Whichever you plan to do, try to talk to a number of people who specialize in periodical design. A few designers successfully do periodicals and advertisements and annual reports, but they are rare as hen's teeth. The trouble is, ads and annual reports are not intended to be seriously read, and working with them trains a designer to go for immediate graphic socko. An advertising designer may often think of a block of words as gray matter to be compensated for. Do you want your magazine designed by someone who tries to apologize for your words? The result might be beautiful to look at, but few would read it.

With the exception of picture magazines, good magazine design is unobtrusive. It causes the reader to say, "Oh! I can't wait to read that!" Something is wrong if the reader says only, "Oh, how gorgeous!" Ideally, no one but another professional will even notice the design of your magazine. It is like clothing. You want people to say, "How wonderful you look!"—not "I really like your suit."

A designer is like any other member of your staff: You have to feel comfortable with the individual. Do not hire anyone who intimidates you.

If you are talking with a firm, try to meet the person who would regularly do your work, and if that is somehow not possible, be wary: Many smaller companies farm jobs out. A series of freelancers will not give you good graphic continuity, and you could probably hire the best of those young people yourself for half to one-third the price. Do talk to freelancers.

Prices vary immensely, so ask what you will be charged for a composite ("comp"). Ideally, you want comps from several good designers. The money is not wasted because even comps that are not right will offer some good ideas.

The designers should all receive the same material, so you can truly compare their work. Give them a head-and-subhead list of several stories, one of each of the basic types you anticipate (profile, think piece, interview, and so forth), plus photographs or art for some of the sample stories (any plausible material will do), plus a memo explaining the functions of the magazine, its organization, its general tone, about how much you expect to spend on art and photographs, and anything else you think important. Even though your stories are still imaginary, it helps to offer some imaginary quotations from several; you want to see how the designer expects to handle these essential display elements.

The comp you get back (with a bill and an estimate for refining the design and for work thereafter) will show sketchy, but clear, alternatives for several covers, one or more options for the table of contents, a suggested format for each format section (news and class notes), and sample layouts for the features from your list. Do not hesitate to ask questions. You paid for this comp; you ought to understand the reasoning behind it, and you do not want to work with someone who does not respect your views or does not think clearly enough to explain the comp well.

You will probably know which comp you like at a glance. It will have an indefinable atmosphere of your institution, and my guess is it will come from the designer you found easiest to talk with.

Now All You Have to Do Is Do It

The world offers many good hands-on courses in production, and your printer will be happy to help you. So I will not discuss the details of production here. But I do have a few fruits to offer from my own sour experience.

Think about illustration from the very beginning. There is nothing more frustrating than seeing how wonderful X would have been, had you only thought of it in time. Besides, things go wrong. Perhaps the only possible time to take photographs will be early on. Perhaps the first shooting will be poor and you will have to go back. Or perhaps you are going to scout around for available art or photographs. It is mostly free from the government, not free but great from *Newsweek* and other national magazines. (Remember to ask for a nonprofit educational discount.) Scouting takes time. And even if you have a good slide, the owner of the slide may only own the slide, not the image on it. Getting permission from the photographer or artist can take weeks.

Never get so engrossed in this issue that you stop developing stories for the future. Stay out there scouting for stories, and keep soliciting when you find something good—because not all of it will be possible, at least not right away. Keep track of your hit rate (or your batting average, or however you want to think of it), and you will find it to be consistent: You have to approach three people to get one article—or four, or five. Whatever the rate, it will tell you how hard to keep working.

Never tell anyone you will think about it. When you do, people hear it as yes. Say yes or no. However disgusted Professor X is when you perversely fail to recognize the story potential in Etruscan shards, she will be a lot more disgusted if she thinks you are going to do the story—and you fail to do so. If you say no and change your mind, you will be forgiven.

Count your type before you send it to the typesetter. Our type column averages out at thirty-nine characters per line. Knowing that, we type stories to that width and can estimate how long each story will actually run. That way, we know we will have four columns of type, give or take a few lines, early enough to scout up another photograph to fill out the spread. Or early enough to free up another page, if we did not allocate enough space. Or early enough to cut the story. Do not rely on luck. Ask your typesetters to show you how their particular typebook can help you estimate length, and then do it.

Always make a map of the issue. Such a map (called a mock-up) might look rather like Figure 47-1. If you do this, you will never come to the deadline and discover you have laid out an issue with nothing for pages 20 and 21.

Writing anything substantial takes two to three times as long as you think it will. That is because writing does not start, as one is inclined to think, at the moment when that first well-crafted opening taps onto the keyboard. Agonizing and wall-gazing and

Figure 47-1. Sample Mock-up.

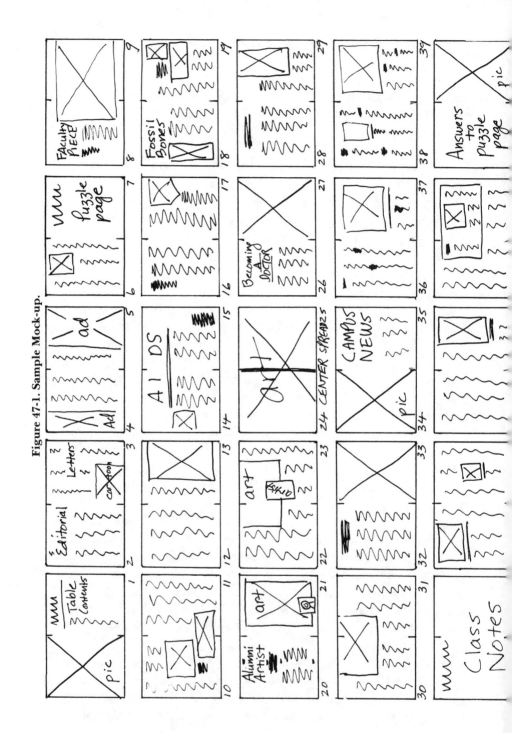

pacing and writing in your head are part of the process, not proof of inefficiency—allow time for them.

Do not send your type in dribs and drabs. Ideally, type would go in two big chunks—features first, because they are least timely and because you need longer to lay them out. At the least, send each story complete. When you have a story ready to go to the typesetter, also send the head, subhead, display blurbs, author's byline, author's blurb ("John Jones is an authority . . ."), and picture credits, if you can. If any of the captions will be complicated, send those too. If you are not sure how you want the captions, head, and display blurbs set, have them set several ways. It costs you almost nothing, and the layout sessions will go much better.

Do not edit on galleys. All you should need to do on galleys is proofread and make an occasional one-line cut so columns come out even. Otherwise, it will cost you enormous sums of money, your typesetter will get dispirited and lax, and your layouts will be fouled up. Send stories the way you want them.

If You Have to Lay It Out Yourself

No matter what your budget, do buy the best basic design you can afford. And then get it tailored—pay to have the designer critique your efforts for your first three or four issues, and periodically thereafter. That way, you will learn where you can and cannot bend the format.

When you put the job out for comps, be sure the designers understand that the design is for you to execute. It makes an enormous difference. You do not want a format that relies on picture collages, or four-column pages, or type artfully sculpted around irregular art. You will be unable to handle it; you need something straightforward.

Here are a few rules of thumb that will not win you design awards but will prevent disaster.

Do not just plunge in, tempting as that is. Measure your elements before you start the layout, and think. It will save you lots of redoing. Cut up one set of galleys for each story, tape the pieces together in order, and measure: eight and a half columns, say. If you have three columns per page, that will make nearly three pages of type. The head will finish filling the third page, and because you have good pictures, you allowed six pages for the story. Good. Now you know the spreads will average out at half art, half type. If the opening spread uses one picture for one page, that thought holds. But perhaps the best opening picture is distinctly horizontal, and its best use splashes the photo across five columns. Then you have only used half a column of type and the head. And now you know you have eight columns of type for four pages—about four columns per spread, or maybe one spread will be mostly type. The photographs will dictate which. It is not necessary to cut and recut your neat columns of type to do this. You do it in your head, with help from thumbnail sketches.

Think in spreads. A single page is never seen alone, but always with its opposite page. Therefore, lay out each two-page unit together, to make sure they work together. If a new story opens on the right, you should keep the left page rather plain, so it does not detract from the opener.

Let the art dictate the layout. Do not make a layout by sticking down the type, leaving a hole, and shoving a picture in the hole—chopping off your president at the knees to make the picture fit. Rather, pick the best picture or pictures, crop them so they look good, and arrange the type around them.

You make things fit by:

1. Sizing pictures bigger and smaller; some pictures can crop in several ways, which is useful
2. Using the head bigger or smaller
3. Using more or fewer display blurbs (that should make you glad you had those blurbs set)

Most magazine formats also allow two major options: type all the way to the top of the type space, or type all the way to a so-called *drop,* a consistent spot maybe one-fifth of the way down from the top. Often the opening spread uses the drop to get a nice spacious look. If you do so, you can use it in succeeding pages of the same feature.

The problem with layouts is that you are manipulating quite a few variables at once. (You can see why I said to stay away from four-column formats.) For the first issues, it will probably take you days to do the layouts. For the time being, just allow the time.

You may find it helpful, until you are more experienced, to cut out pieces of yellow paper, each one representing a different way to use a given photograph. For example:

One vertical president, one column wide
One vertical president, two columns wide
One horizontal new building, one column wide
One horizontal new building, two columns wide
One horizontal new building, three columns wide

Sketch each picture roughly onto its yellow paper, to avoid inadvertently planning to lay the building on its side or to set in your president gazing off the page. You already have the blurbs and the head in several sizes. Now play with the combinations until it looks good.

Whatever you do, it should look as if you did it on purpose. Therefore avoid things that nearly align—a picture half an inch higher than its neighbor on the page, for instance.

Use pictures large rather than small, and use only the good ones. Do not try to fit them all in. If you use several, vary the sizes.

Use mugshots the same size. If you must use mugshots, which I trust you do sparingly, crop them so the heads are the same size. Otherwise one of your distinguished persons is going to look grossly giantesque.

Order both horizontal and vertical photographs. Preferably, order a horizontal and vertical version of each picture. Really. Just consciously think about that as you look at every contact sheet. In doing layouts, maybe the horizontal version will look far better than the vertical. If you failed to order it, you will not have it.

Remember that a magazine does not open flat. You see the layouts flat, so headlines and faces that fall in that space between two pages (the *gutter*) look fine to you. But the reader sees a magazine that has been stapled together and does not open all the way. Therefore, faces and type that fall in the gutter are lost: Do not put them there. If you take a headline all the way across, manipulate the type so a space between words falls in the gutter.

Do not let your driving need to make it fit cause you to leave out display type. Subheads, captions, and nice swatches of quotation from the piece—blurbs, I call them—are essential. If you sit in a train station and watch people read magazines, you will find they take only one to five seconds to decide whether they want to read an article. They glance at the head and the pictures. If they like the topic, they read the captions and blurbs. Then they flip on— or they read the article. The captions and blurbs are your opportunity to sell that piece. So take the time to write them carefully, then keep them in your layouts at all costs. Drop paragraphs from the text before you drop blurbs.

No line should be more than sixty characters long. Study after study shows that the reading eye gulps several words at once— about as many as in a newspaper column, by no coincidence at all. In a longer typeline, the eye gulps several times and has to return for the next line. If lines are longer than 60 characters, the eye loses track of where it is supposed to come back to. The reader feels, vaguely but definitely, that he or she does not wish to read further.

Remember, Americans do not like to read italic type. That is another result of study after study. Just believe it, and do not use italics on anything you want read.

Nothing smaller than heads and subheads should be reversed out of black. It can look great, but if you want something to be read, refrain from doing this.

Be consistent in your use of spaces. Decide on some amount of space between text and art—one or two lines of type is conventional—then stick to it throughout the issue. Skip a consistent amount of space between the letters to the editor. Skip the same amount of space before headlines in the news. Your designer's finished format—not the comp—should include these details.

If you use rules or bars in your layouts, decide what you mean by them. Black lines, whatever you call them, should not be used just to dress up a layout. Do they mean you are about to start something new—a new news item or whatever? Or do they mean you are ending something? Place them accordingly, and stick to your plan.

Ideally, turn the page in the middle of a sentence—never at the end of a paragraph. This will keep the reader from thinking the article is over and mentally signing off.

Look at each column of type to determine whether the reader will know what to read next. For example, is it obvious that the story continues under the picture in the next column? If not, try putting the picture below the type. That short profile on the right-hand page—does it look like part of the main story? A tint block might help. And so on. To see the problem is often to see the solution.

Look at layouts upside down, squinting through your eyelashes until everything is slightly blurred. By doing so, you are looking only at the graphic elements, unconfused by their meaning or their familiarity. Are the spaces pleasing? Is there a sense of progression from spread to spread? Are the horizons of the oceans and the earth and the rooms horizontal? Does everything align that is supposed to align? What catches your eye?—and then what happens? If the spread is an opener, even upside down, your eye should travel immediately to the first words of the story.

Editorial Quick Fixes

In an ideal world, the editor would have a staff, and manuscripts would move around amongst these intelligent persons. In reality, the alumni editor is often a solo practitioner, with other responsibilities to boot. So here are some thoughts I hope may save you time.

You read it freshly only once. Do not waste your first reading of a piece by stopping to edit; just read it as a reader would. Make quick notes in the margin—like *ugh, haha, wow, ?,* and *awk*—to remind you where your attention wandered; where you felt amused, confused, delighted, or enlightened; where you thought this was getting smarmy or awkward. But do not stop to fix anything. This is your only chance to get an overview.

The first three pages are often throat-clearing. The nonprofessional writer—our usual writer—quite often starts with several manuscript pages explaining what will not be covered in the article, setting atmosphere, or something of that sort. Really, this is just warming up. If in doubt, look for the beginning of the article on page 4 or so.

The last few pages are often trickle-down. Many people do not know quite how to stop, so they grope on for several pages after the end, looking for something dramatic and conclusive to say. Or sometimes they conclude with a summary, unnecessary because our readers are intelligent and educated people. Either way, an ideal conclusion is often found several pages before the end.

Self-conscious transitions can be a mark of poor organization. Ideally, as each paragraph and section ends, the thought is exactly where it needs to be to start the next section, so that no transition is necessary. If a piece needs reorganization, it helps to take out any self-conscious transitions and see what train of thought suddenly stares out at you.

Assign each paragraph a topic. If what stares out at you is a mishmash, try writing a summary word or so beside each paragraph, to indicate its subject. Then it will be comparatively easy to find the pieces that go together.

The author's original conclusion often makes a great opening. By the end, the author finally knew just what he or she wanted to say and how to say it. Move it to the front.

Take out the garbage words. There are a number of small qualifiers that never would be missed: *very, really, somewhat, pretty, a little, sort of, kind of, quite,* and their many puny cousins. If you go through any piece and systematically substitute a single strong word for every such weak combination, you will improve the article greatly. And remember to watch for excessive use of the verb *to be.*

Show them, rather than telling them. Go through and take out the overt judgments, positive as well as negative. For example, the sentence "He is a warm and tactful man" sounds PRish and unconvincing. The piece should show the man being warm and tactful.

Put in the tact afterward. Tell your writers not to worry about being tactful. Many people assume, without asking, that alumni magazines can only run the most positive of positive bumph. So tell them to just write the way they would for any magazine, and if there is a problem you will take care of it. You will get a less stilted piece that way.

When in doubt, throw it out. Sometimes you just cannot figure out where to put a sentence or paragraph. The idea is nice, it is well phrased, and it nearly works here, and here, and here— nearly. If it does not click anywhere, it is probably a charming irrelevancy. Throw it out.

The last sentence in a paragraph is a strong position. William Strunk, Jr., and E. B. White point this out clearly. In many cases, stories improve amazingly if they are reparagraphed so that the topic sentences now end the paragraphs.

If you need to cut, keep the examples. The meaning is obvious to you without the example, of course—but only because you already know it. The poor reader needs that example. In fact, if you must cut, omit the general principle: The example can often stand for the point, never vice versa. But two examples are seldom necessary. In profiles, it helps to go through and decide what point each anecdote is making. If you have several devoted to proving the man is a kindly soul, maybe only the strongest one or two tales need remain.

And Good Luck to You!

You will need it: Short-handed, short of budget, we alumni editors have to compete for our readers with the national magazines. It is frustrating.

On the other hand, we have an exciting and important beat, we have intelligent, educated readers, and we have the enviable opportunity to play with every aspect of the magazine. Not for us being stuck in production or only writing or only editing.

Best of all, what we are doing is worth doing. Any honest editor of any magazine will admit that, in fact, we are all shilling for something—makeup or life-style or a patriotic view or a liberal view. Wouldn't you rather be shilling for higher education?

Reference

Strunk, W. S., Jr., and White, E. B. *Elements of Style.* (3rd ed.) New York: Macmillan, 1979.

48

Terry D. Newfarmer

Using Periodicals to Foster Internal Communication

❧ College, university, and independent school employees today expect to be kept in the know about what is happening in their institution, and they expect to have a say in guiding its future. The internal periodical provides the primary means for the institution to keep its employees informed, but concern for effective communication within institutions must be part of the very fiber of the administration and not a concern simply of the editor of the periodical. *In Search of Excellence,* a popular book among executives in business, contains a lesson equally applicable to administrators in education about the need for interpersonal communication. "The nature and uses of communication in the excellent companies are remarkably different from those of their nonexcellent peers. The excellent companies are a vast network of informal, open communications" (Peters and Waterman, 1982, p. 121).

In a survey of support staff employees conducted in 1980 at my own University of Utah by the International Association of Business Communicators, employees rated a "regular organization-wide employee publication" as the most preferred form of internal mass media communication. However, as sources of information about the university, they gave still higher preference ratings to four forms of face-to-face communication: immediate supervisor, small group meetings, top executives, and an orientation program. In the same survey, employees of ninety-nine non-higher-education employers ranked their top five preferred sources of information in exactly the same order. Thus the internal periodical should operate as part of an overall communication effort, and the first step in doing so is to negotiate a written set of goals for the publication.

Many internal periodicals are provided year after year with no clear statement of goals, yet it is the goals that should be the guide in selecting content and even format. If the editor and administration have agreed on the goals, then the editor can stand on firm ground in seeking need-to-know stories from reluctant sources or in turning down requests to include irrelevant fluff. One way to obtain approval for the goals is to place them as a formal proposal at the appropriate place in the institution's administrative channels, such as the president's cabinet. Colleges and universities are used to studying and acting on proposals in a structured way. The approval process will serve to educate administrators on the purpose of the periodical and at the same time provide the editor with general guidelines developed without distortion from debate on the merits of any particular story.

The list of goals might include:

To reinforce the overall goals of the institution, making them clear to the campus community and encouraging departmental efforts in keeping to these goals

To provide interpretation of seemingly isolated events and to place them in an overall context of understanding by the work force

To report the accomplishments of the institution and its contributions to the community and humankind

To improve faculty and staff productivity, morale, and sense of participation in the institution

To help employees do their jobs better and advance personally

To make employees positive spokespersons for the institution in the community

To inform faculty and staff of outside events and trends in higher education that affect the institution

To act as a forum for exchange on campus policies and issues

To foster the intellectual and cultural climate of the school

To discourage unionization

To provide recognition of departments and individuals
To act as a record of campus events and procedures

Few internal periodicals would adopt this entire list. Often a function is performed by some other medium or is not seen as a need.

A basic question that must be faced by internal periodicals at colleges, universities or secondary schools is whether a single newspaper or magazine can meet the needs of both faculty and support staff. Most attempt to do so, and many are available to students as well. Faculty have their own concerns, but they are employees too, with interests in university policies; fringe benefits, such as health insurance; legislative appropriations; recreation opportunities; parking policy and more. Support staff share the faculty's interest in the major research and other accomplishments of the institution, and according to an informal survey conducted by the University of Utah for the Council for Advancement and Support of Education (CASE) in 1982, about half of the 100 colleges and universities surveyed include their internal audiences on the mailing list for alumni periodicals (Bonus, 1984).

In theory, at least, it appears there is sufficient overlap to serve all audiences in a single periodical, but in practice, there is a danger that editors of such publications will become preoccupied with faculty concerns, thus reinforcing the destructive notion that staff members are second-class citizens. One faculty-staff newspaper is a case in point. In a sample issue used to sell advertising, its major topics are effects of funding on planning, dean's reviews of academic programs, faculty survey on unionization attitudes, competition for minority students, default rate on student loans, academic job titles, faculty senate election, endowed lectures, military research, legislative lobbying, fringe benefit reports, and coming events. Where is the staff in all this list?

The University of Utah survey provided some insight into the content that support staff would like to see in internal communication. Given a list of possibilities, the employees ranked items in this order:

The institution's plans for the future

Opportunities for job advancement

How external events, such as government regulations and economic factors, affect my job

Personnel policies and practices

How-to information related to my job

How the institution can improve productivity

The institution's involvement in the community where we are located

How my job fits into the overall operation of the institution

Where the institution stands on current issues such as energy, product safety, legislation, and environment

How we are doing versus the competition

Financial results

How the institution uses its profits

Products and operations of divisions and departments other than my own

Plans for promoting and advertising our products or services

News of personnel changes or promotions

It was possible to check "very interested" for every topic on the list without having to set priorities as editors must do because of time and space constraints. Even so, fewer than 25 percent were "very interested" in human interest stories on other employees and in personal news, such as employee birthdays, anniversaries, and retirements.

If you simply talk to individuals, you might get a different picture. I will never forget the comments of a grounds supervisor who attended one of a series of brown-bag lunches I held to gather story ideas for the Utah internal magazine. He said, "When I get the magazine, I flip through it looking for stories about the grounds department, and then I throw it away." Clearly, there was nothing new the magazine could tell him about his own department. He wanted only one thing from it: recognition. It is no accident that the survey asked individuals to state their degree of interest in stories about *other* employees. To some degree, the written survey probably draws responses of what employees think they ought to be interested in, but the results at the University of Utah were remarkably similar to the average of the 100 organizations, and they have been corroborated at some firms by consultants working with focus groups.

There is still another consideration in determining content. Internal publications have traditionally been reactive in nature: They report events piecemeal and, like the mass media, in the same random fashion as that in which the events occur. This leaves their readers to speculate for themselves about the causes and significance of events; in the absence of information, human nature fills the void with the most negative possible interpretation.

If you are summoned from a meeting for an urgent telephone call, do you assume it's *Reader's Digest* calling to give you $100,000? No, you are more likely to wonder who just died. Rather than report raw data, there is growing sentiment that internal periodicals should show the connection between events, analyze their significance, and anticipate change—this is called *proactive communication*. In *Communicating for Productivity*, Roger D'Aprix (1982, p. 56) says, "Because of a particular issue, an organization may have to take actions that look extraordinary or poorly conceived when viewed in isolation. But when the actions can be explained in light of certain issues or needs, they can begin to make very good sense."

With your goals and content plans in mind, it is time to take a long look at your format. Look at the one you are using now. Is it the best one to meet your goals? Each of the possible formats has its pros and cons in terms of frequency, lead time, space, graphics, and cost. Which of the following formats is best for your institution?

Newsletters are low-budget pieces that can be produced cheaply with short lead time. If your campus is like mine, there are probably dozens being produced by institutes, colleges, and departments to meet the needs of at least as many constituencies. Newsletters often enjoy high readership because they go to a close-knit audience with high interest in the organization or a high need to know. An important characteristic of newsletters (in the pure form) is that the usually intimate audience is expected to read every item. Like the newspapers of a hundred years ago, they have little need for fancy graphics.

The format does not lend itself to more interpretive pieces or to the graphic presentation likely to be needed to reach a more distant and diverse audience. A common practice in employee communications in industry is to combine a weekly or biweekly newsletter with a monthly or quarterly magazine so each type of story can be matched to the format that suits it best. If you frequently have news to get out quickly to your internal audience, a newsletter is a possibility as part of your overall program—if you do not have some other medium through which current information is disseminated, such as a centrally coordinated bulletin board or a telephone hotline.

Newspapers are an excellent way to present a large quantity of relatively short items from which the reader can pick and choose. Lead time can be kept fairly short, and unit cost low. Although an occasional long story can be included as a change of pace, the newspaper format demands a steady diet of short news items, some of which can be accompanied by a single photograph. A newspaper works best on campuses where you use the internal periodical to promote campus events and to cover policy proposals every step of the way through study committees, faculty senate discussions, and so forth. A large quantity of individual stories is the factor most likely to push you in the newspaper direction.

Some institutions lean too heavily on their student newspaper for internal communication. Although the quality tends to vary from year to year, the student press can be effective in communicating coming events and identifying campus issues of interest to faculty and staff as well as students. As a means of proactive faculty and staff communication, however, it seems unlikely that the student press would provide a consistent way of meeting your goals.

Magazines lend themselves to use as the flagships of an institution's internal communications program. Internal media must compete with commercial publications, and even television, for reader attention. Magazines, often with eye-catching graphics in full color on slick paper, are common in industry as effective competitors to television, and yet they are essentially nonexistent as internal media at colleges and universities. They lend themselves to more interpretive pieces and are most adaptable to extensive use of artwork and photography. They are also the slowest and most expensive to produce. A magazine can accommodate sections of short news capsules, but if many of your stories are about a half-page in length, you will experience frustration with the magazine format.

Magapapers and tabloids are a mixture of the newspaper and magazine formats, and there are numerous possibilities. According to the survey reported by Bonus (1984), tabloids are the most frequently used format for internal media in higher education. Some are simply newspapers folded to provide a magazine-style front page. Others are a blend of magazine-style graphics with a newspaper's cost-effectiveness in production. They allow versatility in content, but they are less likely than a magazine to be kept around as a coffee table item.

An important principle often cited in employee communication is that major stories, positive or negative, should be shared with employees before they hear them on the six o'clock news. Open communication of these items is important to your credibility because people tend to remember the first version they hear. This is a difficult principle to live by in higher education, especially at a large public university. It is difficult to call meetings to spread the word through a complex system of divisions and departments. News reporters are likely to attend meetings of the governing council of the institution; how many corporations have news reporters at their board of directors meetings? Sometimes it is possible to print and distribute internal information at the same time a public announcement is made, but this is a difficult procedure to use routinely. Even a high-frequency periodical is usually not fast enough, and some other immediate medium, such as a telephone hotline, is called for. A great many items will be news on campus but not in the public eye. You have to decide how often you will have items that need to go out quickly and use your answer as a criterion in selecting a periodical format or other medium.

Authorities agree that candor is the key to maintaining credibility, but this principle is acted on in different ways. Usually the issue of candor revolves around stories that administrators see as negative or unnecessary. "Why raise the issue?" they ask. And yet these are the very stories that place you in the position of a proactive, rather than reactive, communicator. At some institutions the internal periodical is based on the philosophy that credibility depends on complete editorial independence, even from the publications or public relations departments. The selection and writing of stories for such staff-produced periodicals is not usually subject to review by the administration. Mary Ann Aug, director of news and publications at the University of Pittsburgh, says independence is the only way to attain credibility. "The reasons for a free press cannot be repeated too often," she says. "First, without the assurance of such freedoms, the campus newspaper has no credibility, and thus no effectiveness as a means of communication. Second, the publication exists to serve an institution that by its nature is devoted to free and open inquiry into all aspects of human endeavor" (Bonus, 1984, p. 85).

The internal periodical is typically seen as a creature of the administration, timid about airing dirty laundry. In the IABC University of Utah survey, 21.2 percent of the support staff respondents said they agreed strongly with the statement "In this organization, official communications don't tell the full story." Another 42.5 percent said they agreed somewhat, but the Utah responses to the question were all within one percentage point of the average of responses to the same question by employees of 100 large employers all over the country. Elsewhere in the survey, 43.7 percent said they agreed somewhat that communications as a whole within the university are candid and accurate, and 10.9 percent said they agreed strongly.

Checking stories with their sources is another matter. Former newspaper journalists are nervous about such a procedure because it smacks of censorship. In my experience, showing a story to the source results in clarification and amplification of facts and in added interpretation of facts far more often than it results in a watering-down of the material. The discussion that surrounds checking a story with an administrator who is also a source is an excellent opportunity to educate that individual about the need for candor and the possible consequences of a perceived cover-up. Such individuals will be more open with you if they know they will be able to read the draft, and you, in turn, can be bolder in adding interpretation when you know the story will have the endorsement of the source before it appears in print.

The internal periodical, whatever its format, is the mainstay of virtually every college and university's ability to inform its on-campus constituencies of events and policies that affect them. For maximum effectiveness, however, it must be integrated into an overall institutional communications program.

References

Bonus, T. (ed.). *Improving Internal Communication*. Washington, D.C.: Council for Advancement and Support of Higher Education, 1984.

D'Aprix, R. *Communicating for Productivity*. New York: Harper & Row, 1982.

Peters, T. J., and Waterman, R. H., Jr. *In Search of Excellence*. New York: Harper & Row, 1982.

49
Gladys McConkey

Special-Purpose Periodicals

❧ The richness of research as a resource for university or college periodicals is a recent discovery for many institutions. A growing number of magazines and newsletters specialize in research, and their success is creating new interest in special-purpose periodicals as components of the publications program.

Every publication has particular purposes and is intended for particular audiences, so what do we mean when we speak of a special-purpose periodical published by an educational institution? Let us say it is one intended for readers who have an interest—or potential interest—in a certain aspect of a university, college, or secondary school program. The all-university alumni magazine would not qualify. We could, however, include the glossy newsletter published by the development office for the purpose of raising money and the periodical produced by the admissions office to attract applicants. Certainly we would include magazines in particular fields, such as ornithology or human ecology or veterinary medicine. And of course, we would include the research periodicals, both those with coverage across the range of academic disciplines and those restricted to a particular area of study.

Although most of my remarks pertain to research magazines because they are the kind of special-purpose periodical I have had most experience with, this focus should not obscure the usefulness of other types. A development newsletter or tabloid can be extremely effective in keeping volunteers and potential donors informed and enthusiastic about the progress of a major campaign. A periodical, even a modest one, can be valuable for maintaining contact with prospective freshmen and may effectively supplement the prospectus, catalogue, and special interest brochures. Of course, many observations about research magazines are applicable to these and other kinds of periodicals that have a particular focus.

Making Basic Decisions

Planning a special-purpose periodical involves the same kinds of decisions needed for any publication but may involve special considerations. If you are thinking of starting such a periodical, you need to address basic questions such as those discussed here.

Who are the readers? Will they all be specialists in a certain discipline? Or will they include laypersons who may or may not have a background that gives them some familiarity with the subject matter? The manner of treatment and, to some extent, the choice of topics depend on the audience.

What is your purpose in reaching these readers? You probably want to generate enthusiasm, and possibly support, for programs and projects. You may hope to provide informative, readable material of educational value. You may want to promote good will among alumni and help them take pride in their institution. You may wish to inform or impress granting agencies, your state legislature, industrial organizations, the media, and the general public. You may want to bolster the reputations of your researchers on- and off-campus and promote among them better knowledge and understanding of each other's work. Defining your objectives will help provide a focus and determine a level of writing, an attitude, a style, even a format.

How will the periodical be distributed and used? Compiling a basic mailing list is almost as important as producing a good publication: It is useful only if it is read (or at least scanned) by the people you wish to reach. University officials (including development and public relations officers) and faculty members can be helpful in suggesting recipients. Groups of alumni, such as members of a society who receive the periodical as part of their membership benefits, can constitute a good core of readers. You will have to decide whether your publication is to be distributed free (most of the current ones are) or whether there will be a subscription charge (at least one magazine, M.I.T.'s *Technology Review*, has paid national circulation), or whether a combination is feasible (*Engineering: Cornell Quarterly*, for example, is partially supported by dues-paying members of the alumni association and by a relatively small number of paid subscribers who do not qualify for free subscriptions). Regardless of how you assemble the mailing list, provisions should be made for maintaining it. This includes not only making address changes on a continual basis but also periodically updating the complimentary file.

The use of the publication for special distributions can be a valuable bonus. Delegates to a conference can be given copies as handouts. Special mailing lists can be compiled for certain issues. Departments may find particular issues useful for distribution to visitors or prospective graduate students. Thinking ahead to special uses will help in forming an overall plan for the periodical and in putting together individual issues.

You must establish how the periodical will be mailed. Possibilities include second class, or third class bulk rate, or even first class. Because so many factors—frequency of publication, size and format, possible advertising, postage costs—are involved, you should consult your mail expert on campus or your local post office.

Who will the writers be? Basically, the choice is between the people who are doing the work being written about—in the case of a research periodical, the researchers themselves—or staff or professional writers. Sometimes a combination can be effective.

There are advantages and disadvantages to every choice: Articles written by experts may be more authentic but less interest-arousing (although some scientists have a real knack for writing); articles by professional writers, however polished, may be inaccurate, misleading, or wrong in emphasis. Another factor may be the availability of good professional writers or, alternatively, the probability of success in inducing professors to prepare articles.

The reputation of the magazine, once it has become established, goes a long way in making people interested in writing for it. Also, people in key positions, such as the university president, the dean, or a department chair, can help by lending support. A dean, for example, can publicly recognize the significance of the publication by contributing an article once in a while; a department chair may be more effective in rounding up articles from members of the department than the editor, alone, could be. Budgetary constraints may be a consideration when deciding on authorship: Professional writers want to be paid, but faculty members do not make their living by writing. And then there is the question of how well the editorial staff will be able to work with one group of writers or another to achieve successful articles.

How frequently should the periodical be published? This depends on the size and other duties of the staff, as well as on the amount of potential material and the uses to which the periodical will be put. A further consideration is the effect frequency of publication may have on reader response: A sense of continuity and familiarity is enhanced when the periodical arrives regularly and fairly often. Also, a monthly or quarterly publication has more flexibility than, say, an annual report that must be comprehensive and is less able to feature particular activities.

How shall the periodical be organized? A basic decision is whether to have issues devoted to special topics or themes or whether each issue should cover a variety of subjects. Some compromise is possible: A university research quarterly, for example, could focus each of the four issues on a different area— arts and sciences in the fall, engineering in the spring, and so forth.

Each choice has its strong and weak points. A theme approach may make each issue more versatile in the ways it can be used. One year at the Cornell College of Engineering, for example, we used the fall issue on geology as a handout at the dedication ceremony for the department's new building and for fund-raising purposes; and the winter issue, celebrating the centennial of electrical engineering, was circulated at alumni gatherings around the country. The articles in two recent issues on submicron research were reprinted in book form for national distribution.

On the other hand, late manuscripts can wreak havoc with the schedule for a theme issue, and having no backlog of smorgasbord articles to fall back on can be an editor's nightmare. As with every decision, constraints are imposed by the budget and other resources (including staffing), the complexity of the institution, and the scope of the magazine. A third alternative to consider involves devoting the cover and two or three articles to one topic and the other articles to other topics.

How will the content be characterized? Is the magazine to be devoted exclusively to research or will it also cover educational matters, news items, and features of more general interest? How broad a definition of research will be applied; for instance, will the magazine treat scholarly work on literature as well as scientific inquiry? Also, you must establish guidelines concerning the nature of the articles. Especially important is the desired balance between a popular and a scholarly or professional approach.

What will be the staff requirements? Often this depends on who is already on deck. Magazine editors who also produce brochures and newsletters are probably more the rule than the exception, and one never meets an editor who does not feel overworked. How much of the work is done in-house is an important consideration, especially these days when the use of telecommunications technology is becoming so widespread. A general idea of staff size is given by the results of a recent poll of university research periodicals, which showed that the average magazine is a thirty-two-page quarterly produced by a staff that is the equivalent of two full-time people with the help of two freelance professionals (photographers, writers, artists, designers, or typesetters).

Another consideration is whether there should be an advisory board. Will such a board lend authority to the publication, or would it be extraneous? Would the members actually make decisions and helpful suggestions or might the workings of the board inhibit flexibility and originality?

What about format and design? The choices seem almost infinite. Shall the periodical be a magazine or a newsletter? If it is a magazine, how elaborate should it be? Shall it have a four-color cover? Will it use photographs and art work liberally? The overall design will have a huge effect on the success of the publication; thought should be given to how the cover can be designed to attract attention and interest, yet be consistent with the nature of the contents, and how the inside design can help sustain interest and work well in presenting the material. The help of a professional designer is valuable, but the designer should be guided in making appropriate selections. Will the design complement the contents? Will it allow for enough flexibility in fitting type and placing photographs, provide an easily discerned organization of articles and departments, and look good? Will the paper be suitable for good photographic reproduction?

To be successful, the format must augment the text; it must correspond to its tone and substance and be easy to work with. It must be appropriate.

What publishing techniques will be used? Decisions about how to produce a special-purpose periodical are the same as for any other periodical. For example, will the copy be typeset, prepared camera-ready on a typewriter or word processor, or telecommunicated? Who will do the layout and prepare mechanicals? Will printing be done commercially, or can you make use of the new laser printer in the computer science department?

A point that may be especially worth thinking about is that the great amount of rewriting and editing necessary for a research periodical makes the typesetting-via-word-processor mode particularly useful and efficient.

Editing the Periodical

Perhaps the most crucial element in publishing a research periodical is the editing. The editor is most responsible for setting the tone, infusing vitality, maintaining high quality and readability, seeing that photography and layout are well executed, and even making sure that the periodical is well circulated. The heart of the publication is the writing, of course, but behind—and sometimes ahead of—the authors, whether they are the people doing the research, professional science writers, or staff members, is the editor.

Establishing a general level of scientific or professional depth is an initial task. This depends on the expected readership— how uniform it is educationally or professionally—and the relative importance of the various purposes of the periodical. If the chief objective is to arouse interest or admiration by people who have only a vague familiarity with the subject matter, the level of content and the style would be quite different from that of a magazine intended for professionals in the field. In most cases, a university research periodical needs fairly broad appeal, so the ideal article would fall somewhere between one written for a popular magazine and a paper for a professional journal. This sounds simpler than it often is. A comment by Albert Einstein summarizes the difficulty. Written in 1948, it is even more pertinent today in the context of a heightened and rising public interest in science and technology. Einstein wrote:

> Anyone who has ever tried to present a rather abstract scientific subject in a popular manner knows the great difficulties of such an attempt. Either he succeeds in being intelligible by concealing the core of the problem and by offering to the reader only superficial aspects or vague allusions, thus deceiving the reader by arousing in him the deceptive illusion of comprehension; or else he gives an expert account of the problem, but in such a fashion that the untrained reader is unable to follow the exposition and becomes discouraged from reading any further.
>
> If these two categories are omitted from today's popular scientific literature, surprisingly little remains. But the little that is left is very valuable indeed. It is of great importance that the general public be given an opportunity to experience—consciously and intelligently—the efforts and results of scientific research. It is not sufficient that each result be taken up, elaborated, and applied by a few specialists in the field. Restricting the body of knowledge to a small group deadens the philosophical spirit of a people and leads to spiritual poverty.

Although editors of research publications for general circulation may not lay claim to such a lofty goal as quickening the spirit of a people, they must be concerned with the promotion of an understanding of research efforts, goals, and accomplishments.

Strategies and Techniques

On a practical level, how can an editor try to deal with this inherent difficulty of communication?

When lining up an article for the magazine I edit, I often suggest that an author write for a colleague in a different department of the college, or for a bright undergraduate majoring in a related subject. Our magazine does not list references (although a list of suggested reading is an interesting feature that is successfully used in similar periodicals), and we avoid highly technical details and explanations. The emphasis, we suggest to our authors, should be on the significance of the research—significance to the discipline, to science, to industry or the economy, to the university, to the environment, to people's lives. This does not mean that every piece of research should be presented as a breakthrough or as having fundamental scientific impact or the potential to change the social structure. Almost any worthwhile research can be made to sound as interesting to others as it is to those who are working on it, but it should be presented honestly.

These criteria will be understood by professional writers. Finding good science writers is difficult, however. Some editors have hired people who are knowledgeable about science but have not done much writing. Others have hired writers who know little about science. Rarely is anyone satisfied. The ideal—accomplished writers who understand the basics of the research they are writing about—will become more available in time. At Cornell, for instance, a special curriculum was recently approved for a student who wished to combine courses in writing with courses in a wide range of sciences, a combination that is not well served by the conventional major-and-minor program. Some universities have or are instituting programs in science writing.

If all or most of the manuscripts carry the byline of a researcher, the editor can use many strategies to avoid or minimize the potential problems and enhance the effectiveness of the articles. Suppose a researcher would like to contribute an article but is apprehensive about writing in a style suitable for a nontechnical publication. Sometimes, over a cup of coffee or at lunch, such a person can say what the significance of the work is, make analogies, and give examples. These elements can then be incorporated into the article.

Another technique the editor can use is to sit down with a researcher who is reluctant to write or is pressed for time and use a tape recorder to record that individual's explanation of the work being done. With someone to talk to, a scientist may find ways of explaining ideas and results that are natural and appropriate. Questions posed by the editor-writer may bring out salient points or reveal pitfalls for readers. Ideas for illustrative material may emerge. The researcher may produce a reprint that could help fill out the article or elucidate a difficult point. All of this may seem very much like what goes on in a conventional interview, and it is, except that the researcher ends up as the author. Generally the researcher is pleased with the result, has a real feeling of authorship, and may even be surprised to have been able to write so well. This approach, or a variation of it, can make possible an article that otherwise would never get written.

We have found that most authors prefer to submit a draft. Because we are almost sure to work it over extensively, we have no objection to receiving it in rough form and do not bother with instructions to authors about double-spacing, paragraphing, and the like. (We do send them a letter confirming the agreement to prepare and publish an article, confirming the agreed-on subject, indicating an approximate length, stipulating a deadline, and suggesting procedures about details, such as how graphic material can be handled.) My own experience has been that researchers rarely feel the kind of pride of authorship that makes them resentful of editorial changes and suggestions. Of course, the suggested changes must be correct, appropriate, and in keeping with the style of the author. Sometimes this involves compromise. The intriguing title or lead you think up may make the author uncomfortable, and something in between must be worked out.

Often the most needed revision is a reordering of the material. One of the professors writing for our magazine turned in a manuscript that started off with a long discussion of his school and its many fine people who were doing interesting things in mechanical engineering research and then proceeded to a graceful description of the contributions being made by everyone in his group. Then he outlined the experimental procedure used in his own research project and detailed the results. On page eighteen, he made the startling statement that with the relatively simple engine modification he had described, an automobile could meet the most stringent clean-air requirements without loss of efficiency and without the necessity for retooling in the manufacturing plant. It was a simple matter to extract the natural lead, winnow out the verbiage, and wind up with a strong closing.

Drastic editing or rewriting is not always necessary or advisable. During ten years of editing an engineering magazine, I have encountered three articles that I could print almost verbatim. Many authors turn in drafts that already have flair and essentially just need copyediting. But more often than not, an author will remark that this paper was more difficult than any he or she had ever before attempted and that the cooperation of the editor was helpful. A researcher who is also a professor is often enthusiastic about having in hand an article that can be given to students, colleagues, relatives, or funding agencies to explain the essence of his or her work.

The main responsibility of the writer-editor is to be sure that revisions do not introduce error or distortion. It is also important to retain the author's style as much as possible. (I feel most successful when an issue carries articles that sound different from one another; there is no need, for example, to chop an author's long sentences into short ones if they flow well and are readily understood.) For both these reasons, approval by the author is essential, and generally several drafts are needed to arrive at a mutually pleasing one. Flexibility is an asset and has long-term as well as immediate rewards, for authors are more inclined to attempt an article if the magazine's staff has the reputation of being reliable, cooperative, and helpful.

Certain techniques come to mind as helpful in dealing with manuscripts that are difficult because of the technical content. As I mentioned, our magazine avoids highly technical discussions. I recall the advice of a Nobel laureate I once worked for. "If you can't say it in English, you don't really understand it," he would say to graduate students who wanted to settle for a string of equations. Ordinary words can often be substituted for technical ones, but when technical terms are used, they should be defined, casually if possible. Sometimes technical detail that would greatly interest some readers but impede the flow of the article can be incorporated into a figure caption or presented in a box.

This brings up the subject of figures. Often they require almost as much attention as the manuscript, but they can be very valuable, both for the visual appearance of the publication and for making the article more appealing, accessible, and understandable. A graphic artist, perhaps a freelancer, is an important member of the staff of a research periodical because figures frequently need to be redrawn or revised in some way. Usually a figure submitted by a researcher to a general-interest magazine can be improved by simplification, more careful execution, more imaginative treatment, and the use of color if this is available. Often a technical figure can be made more understandable by spelling out abbreviations familiar only to specialists. The editor should work with the artist to achieve some consistency in treatment (in typefaces and sizes, for instance) throughout the magazine. Of course, revisions should be planned in consultation with the author, who should also review and approve the final work.

Captions are also important; good captions can help point up the main ideas of the article and lead the reader into the text. They should convey information, not just be labels, and should complement the text and provide emphasis and perhaps amplification. Some of the same principles of writing that pertain to the text apply also to captions: They need interesting short titles and effective leads. A caption must be accurate and correspond to any alterations made in the figure.

The editor is responsible for seeing that the magazine's style is consistent. It is the editor's prerogative to eliminate professional jargon and (a favorite practice with engineers, it seems) the pile-up of nouns made to serve as adjectives. Some gems collected from our bulletin board are

> High volume, repetitive operation, discrete parts manufacturing environments
> Municipal Wastewater Sludge Health Effects Research Planning Workshop

Three dimensional finite element stress intensity factor calibration

Large mid-ocean ridge spreading center magma chambers

Self-aligned ion implanted GaAs ballistic MESFET super high speed integrated circuits

Assessing the Effectiveness of the Periodical

To be successful, a university research periodical should achieve the objectives that have been established for it or those that emerge. The original intent may have been somewhat vague—to produce something that will let the world know that exciting, worthwhile research is going on—but it may be discovered that a good periodical can help raise money or garner grants. (We once rushed through some advance copies of a magazine issue that carried an article by a professor whose grant was in jeopardy; he distributed copies to committee members at a crucial meeting and the grant was restored.) The soft sell of a periodical can be very effective.

In most cases, it is difficult to find ways of quantitatively assessing the value to the university of a publication. I believe that assessments are usually made informally and subjectively. Your president visits another institution and sees your university's research magazine in an office there. A professor hears from a colleague that her article—and, in fact, the whole magazine—is very interesting; can she have three more copies? A request for twenty-five copies for class use comes in from a university across the country. Nonacademic professionals remark that they not only admire the cover when an issue arrives on their desks but also actually read the articles. The development officer finds the magazine useful in soliciting funds for renovating a laboratory. Occasionally an unsolicited gift comes in. The general impression forms that this periodical is an asset.

Another measure of success is the response of those who are asked to be contributors and of those who are on the mailing list. If researchers agree to work on articles, probably without compensation, that is an indication that the periodical has a solid reputation. If members of a department come to the magazine to ask whether there can be an issue devoted to their line of research, that is a good sign. If subscribers save their copies, that is an encouragement. If the alumni organization wants a subscription to be included in membership privileges and is willing to pay for it, that is an endorsement.

What was sufficient last year may not be next year, however. Competition for the attention of readers is bound to increase, along with the number and quantity of commercial and university research periodicals. The best course for a university special-purpose periodical is to achieve professional standards and reflect the quality and character of the institution it represents.

Reference

Einstein, A. Foreword to L. Barnett, *The Universe and Dr. Einstein.* New York: New American Library, 1948.

Part Eight

Advancing Institutional Goals Through Enrollment Management

John Maguire, Editor

50

John Maguire

Enrollment Management: Goals, Methods, and Issues

ᚳᚹᛟ Large-scale forces will have a major impact on enrollments in higher education during the 1980s and 1990s. A drastic decline in the number of eighteen-year-olds, uncertainty in enrollment rates brought on by prospects of reduced federal aid to students and of a diminishing financial return on a college degree, the differential impact of these factors on separate sectors in higher education, the search for new markets, the great sorting process and its relationship to student choice—all of these momentous and uncertain factors will profoundly influence the fortunes, and possibly the ultimate survival, of American colleges and universities throughout the next two decades. But for each of the approximately 3,000 institutions of higher education in the United States, the weighting of these forces will be different. And so the challenges and the opportunities confronting individual institutions will be unique.

Strong leadership at the institutional level can prevail; in only a relatively small number of cases is the die already cast against survival. Leaders in higher education need not view their institutions as being at the mercy of runaway economic and cultural forces that doom any optimistic vision of their future. Through conscientious planning and measured decision making, they can exert significant influences over their destiny. Indispensable keys are competence, courage, and creativity. Uncommon leadership will certainly be essential to manage dynamic equilibrium or decline in higher education. And it is precisely because these traits are so rare that it can be said with confidence that colleges possessing outstanding leadership will invariably continue to confound those who forecast their demise. It will be far easier to make aggregate statements on the future of college enrollments than it will be to predict with accuracy the fate of a single institution independent of its leadership profile.

Strategic planning must be a top priority of institutional leaders concerned with optimizing their institution's futures. Long-range fiscal and academic planning must be done in tandem to ensure that goals for the future are consistent with the needs and perceptions of the community (including trustees, the president, faculty, alumni, students, and the public) and with budgetary reality. And planning must not be a one-time event; rather, it must be ongoing, with a built-in mechanism for periodic review. This will ensure that the original goals, and their translation into academic programs, remain consistent with student and community needs and that sources of money are identified to pay for those programs.

Need for Enrollment Management

Comprehensive, long-range fiscal and academic planning will, of necessity, focus on enrollments, in both the independent and the public sectors. The following enrollment-related questions will inevitably be raised: What number of students are likely to be interested in the programs our institution now offers? To what extent do we wish to alter our mix of programs to attract a broader student clientele? Why do students choose to come to our college? What will future demand be for our programs—particularly those of a professional nature, which are so dependent on the job market? How are we doing in comparison with our competition? Is our pricing structure (tuition and financial aid) appropriate? Why do students leave our institution and what, if anything, should we be doing to decrease the dropout rate? These and a myriad of enrollment-related questions continually arise in conjunction with long-range planning.

In the past, when enrollments were expanding rapidly in all

sectors, few colleges or universities needed to be concerned about managing enrollments. Practically all of them received more applications than they could handle, and the battle for resources invariably centered on which departments or schools had first claim to expansion. The idea of contraction or elimination of programs or colleges was of little concern to institutional planners during those halcyon growth years. If the above questions were asked at all, their answers were rarely the focus of sophisticated research. Rarer still was the institution that took an integrated systems attitude and recognized that piecemeal solutions to these questions in isolation could not yield optimal results.

In the 1980s and 1990s, when enrollments will very likely decline (or at best achieve dynamic equilibrium), the approach a college or university takes to answering these questions could ultimately determine its survival. And so strategic planning at some institutions has led to the emergence of the concept of enrollment management. Simply stated, *enrollment management* is an institutionally based process that brings together often disparate functions having to do with recruiting, funding, tracking, retaining, and replacing students as they move toward, within, and away from an institution of higher education. Although most institutions use these various strategies in isolation, a few, such as Boston College, Cornell University, and the University of Massachusetts at Amherst, have been systematizing and integrating these fields into one grand design.

Various administrative structures have been devised to facilitate this holistic approach, but in the middle of the 1980s, there was no single table of organization agreed on by leaders in the field of enrollment management. One pattern that has received attention is the integration of the offices of institutional research, admissions, the registrar, and financial aid.

For some, the phrase *enrollment management* will simply be seen as a euphemism for *marketing,* although the author views marketing as a significant subcategory of the total concept. In the business field, marketing is perhaps the most multidisciplinary area; likewise enrollment management cuts across and links several areas in higher education. Educational marketing, rightly or mistakenly, focuses on admissions and institutional research, with only secondary emphasis on financial aid and virtually no concerted effort to include the registrar's operation and retention in the total concept. Enrollment management encompasses the complexities of the student accounting function and demand analysis, resource allocation, and overall systems strategies. It is not confined to larger institutions, although for universities, it becomes conceptually more differentiated from marketing than it is for small colleges. It stresses interaction among departments rather than the activities of the separate departments themselves.

At a semantic level, the phrase *enrollment management* has two advantages over the term *marketing*. First, *marketing* still has residual connotations that distress many academics. Second, *enrollment* refers directly to their own domain, and more importantly, *management* implies a proactive approach to organizational decisions on allocating resources and strategic use of personnel to achieve objectives. This emphasis is missing from such words as *marketing* or *planning*.

Goals of Enrollment Management

There is no unique way to differentiate a set of goals for an enrollment management program. The fact that we are attempting to integrate separate functions means that the whole will be greater than the sum of its constituent parts and that the interplay among the parts will have primary importance. Nevertheless, here is a set of fluid and overlapping goals or principles that can be used as the basis for development of a coherent program.

Goal 1: Organization for Enrollment Management—To organize appropriate departments in a way that facilitates coordination of staff, flow of information, and integration of decisions. An example of achieving this goal would be the systematic exchange of data between the registrar's office and the admissions office. This will make it possible to calculate accurate student quotas in all schools and classes and to realize a bottom-line enrollment for the institution. It is this goal that is clearly the most all-encompassing. Any table of organization for enrollment management will have all components actively involved in pursuing this end. This subject is treated in depth in a later section of this chapter.

Goal 2: Student Information Systems and Research—To create an integrated student data base and a capacity to use student information systems for coordinated research and planning. This goal is applicable not only to medium- and large-sized universities but also to small colleges. In recent years, with the advent of on-line computer systems, much attention has been paid to the elimination of redundancy in student data bases. Yet, in the mid-1980s, colleges and universities of all sizes suffer severely from this problem.

Individual departments, eager to retain control over their data, are fighting the efforts of centralized offices of institutional research and management information systems to standardize data collection and reporting. Some of the strongest institutions fall prey to this predicament. This problem often arises because their admissions and registrar's offices are highly competent, have produced requisite classes in the past, and see little need to cede control of their operations to outsiders who will, in their minds, deliberately or inadvertently dehumanize the process.

Ironically, it is this expanded need for using more powerful integrated student data bases that has simultaneously generated the most problems and the most opportunities in enrollment management. Both the technical difficulties associated with computerized information systems and the attendant political problems can lead to loss of confidence, internecine warfare, and sometimes eventual scuttling of the entire system—unless the perceived need is overwhelming or the leadership from the systems people and from the top administration is continuously vigorous, competent, and worthy of trust.

It is now no longer possible to maintain the offices responsible for enrollments as separate, independent entities with only tenuous administrative linkages among them. Perhaps more than any other part of the system, the research and student information component of enrollment management shows the need for synergy in administrative structure. The best way to eliminate jurisdictional squabbling and to get people working toward common purposes is to employ a coherent table of organization that addresses these problems.

Goal 3: Admissions Marketing—To develop admissions and marketing programs in order to attract outstanding students in sufficient numbers during a period of possible national enrollment declines. Until very recently, the mere mention of the word *marketing* in the context of recruiting students would probably have induced dyspepsia in most faculty members or administrators. Now, due to a more sophisticated understanding of the marketing concept (and also because, at many institutions, livelihoods are threatened), colleges and universities are becoming more comfortable with this term. The word, it must be emphasized, is not to be confused with hucksterism and slick sales techniques. Marketing is a systematic effort to merge institutional strengths with consumer (in this case, students and parents) interests. The starting point for a successful marketing strategy is the development of a long-range plan. Such a plan brings into sharper focus institutional goals and objectives, as well as the specific programs that can best meet those goals. The next step becomes the identification of potential students whose interests and abilities coincide with these offerings.

Although the admissions office is the most visible marketing agent at the institution, a successful marketing effort has its foundation in outstanding faculty and programs. The task of a good admissions operation is to communicate these strengths to the student marketplace in a forthright and persuasive fashion. In this last quarter of the twentieth century, a technological explosion is occurring in the marketing of higher education. Fueled simultaneously by growth in computer technology and escalating competition, this megatrend is transforming the way admissions offices are communicating with their markets. Text processing capabilities make it possible for individualized messages to be sent to large numbers of prospective students. Although the print media (through the use of sophisticated four-color brochures and viewbooks) are flourishing, the electronic media—radio, television, video home systems (VHS disks and tapes), computer-to-computer correspondence, and even satellite teleconferencing—are assuming growing importance in the way messages are transmitted to markets.

Goal 4: Pricing and Financial Aid Strategies—To implement pricing and financial aid strategies that will optimize the institution's ability to attract and retain the desired academic and socioeconomic mix of students. With the soaring cost of higher education, how does an institution set its tuition and package its institutional, federal, state, and private financial aid monies in a fair, efficient way to meet obligations to equity, governmental requirements, and institutional goals? Among these goals are, most pragmatically, meeting overall enrollment objectives with the most qualified student body possible and obtaining an appropriate distribution of minorities, women, commuters, low-middle-income applicants, and so forth.

This is an enormously complex problem, and there are, in the last half of the 1980s, no ready answers, either in the literature or in existing institutional models. A few heavily endowed high-prestige schools are able to meet the full financial aid needs of all accepted applicants. Meanwhile, those colleges unable to achieve full enrollments often unabashedly lure students with no-need scholarships, tuition discounts, and other even more questionable practices.

The institutions that fall between these two extremes are faced with the most difficult decision of all. These colleges and universities have very little endowment and sufficient applicants to enroll in their classes. They must carefully calculate the costs and the benefits of difficult choices involving appropriate level of tuition, total available institutional aid, percent of student body to receive financial aid, packaging approach, and so forth—all set against a backdrop of the overarching goals previously mentioned.

The administration of admissions and financial aid must be carefully coordinated so that extremely delicate balances are not upset. This is a persuasive example of the need for a systems approach to tuition-setting, packaging for incoming students, and fulfilling obligations to returning students. In this approach, the registrar's office can be a valuable stabilizing agent because the retention process will determine whether, on the one hand, incoming students have been overfunded at the expense of returning students, whose disillusionment then leads to increased dropout rates, or whether, on the other hand, overgenerous aid to upperclassmen increases retention beyond predicted levels, while the quality of the incoming class suffers measurably.

Goal 5: Demand Analysis and Institutional Response—To develop a capability to anticipate immediate and long-term student interests and methods for improving the institution's ability to provide for these interests. This is probably the most difficult, and most misunderstood, of the objectives of the enrollment management program. For one thing, very little definitive work has been done at national and state levels on manpower planning and projected student demand. For another, it is not clear to what extent a college or university strongly committed to the enduring values of a liberal arts education can, and should, adapt its curriculum to the marketplace.

Because jobs in many fields have become more scarce, students in the mid 1980s are more interested in career-oriented education than their peers of ten years earlier. Professional schools are still being deluged with applications, even though areas such as nursing and law were rapidly reaching saturation by the mid 1980s. The business school boom continues, especially among women motivated by changing attitudes and by increasing opportunities through affirmative action programs.

How can colleges and universities, particularly in a declining market, cope with this unstable situation, remain true to ideals, and meet obligations to students seeking direction in a depressed job market? First of all, we should counsel applicants at the entry point, and beyond, about the realistic odds for achieving educational objectives in such fields as medicine and law. Second, we should explore alternatives that will allow them to keep options flexible for as long as possible in case midcourse corrections are called for. Finally, and perhaps most important, we must be articulate and steadfast in defending those traditions rooted in a liberal arts, value-oriented education that contribute to making life and not merely a living.

We can do all this while conducting demand studies through external agencies, such as the College Board, and through internal processes, such as registration and periodic student surveys. At the same time, we can use this information to adjust school and departmental quotas and to reallocate resources in response to a changing market. We can use these enrollment management techniques while resisting the idea of reacting to momentary fads by making in the curriculum wholesale changes that depart from a commitment to traditional academic values. In summary, there is no necessary contradiction between using sophisticated information systems to respond to shifting student needs and maintaining a humanistic vision of what constitutes a good education.

Goal 6: Retention and Transfer Students—To formalize an institutional retention program in order to identify reasons for attrition, to minimize it to whatever extent desirable, and to enroll qualified transfer students as replacements. Every year, for a variety of complex reasons, a large fraction of the student body at a typical college or university will leave before graduation. Many of these students leave for compelling, positive reasons over which colleges can and should exert little control. The national transfer movement is growing as a more mobile population of college students seeks educational and geographical diversity. Some students redefine their career objectives and find that their curricular needs can be better served at another institution. In these instances, colleges and universities have an obligation not only to eliminate roadblocks to their departure but also to provide counseling and other positive assistance.

It must also be acknowledged that there are students who depart, confused and unhappy, for all the wrong reasons. And there are some who never should have come in the first place. In these cases, the institution must respond by adjusting aid packages, solving housing problems, increasing the availability of courses, improving the admissions selection process, and in a variety of other ways. Through surveys and exit interviews, colleges must continuously monitor reasonable criticisms by present students and those who are leaving. When appropriate, this information should be used to refine admissions policy and other services.

Retention is, of necessity, an institutional concern that involves everyone from the president to the kitchen staff. But it finds a special kinship with the registrar's office, which contains all records for present and departing students and is, therefore, the primary source of student academic and demographic information. Students wishing to withdraw will normally interact with this office to formalize their departure and perhaps to indicate an intention of returning or transferring elsewhere.

Because the registrar's office is usually neutral in any dispute between a student and areas (such as an academic department, the housing office, or the financial aid office) that may have led to the withdrawal, it may be the best place in which to facilitate reconciliation or to streamline dropping out with minimal added anxiety. A one-step, hassle-free withdrawal process, beginning and terminating in the registrar's office, will sometimes be a positive force in retention and enrollment management. Valuable information can be collected for later use in identifying problem areas. Beyond that, the message will be transmitted to all students that the institution really wants to learn from its mistakes and to assist students in locating more favorable circumstances.

The interaction between the registrar's and admissions offices deserves special comment. For colleges and universities crucially dependent on students for large fractions of their incomes (in the private sector) or for meeting budgetary targets (in the public sector), the smooth interplay between the offices of the registrar and admissions is critical. Indeed, the simplest objective of enrollment management might be to maintain overall institutional enrollments at a specified level consistent with a balanced budget. The accounting function for money is then replaced by an analogous accounting function in which the number of students becomes the final measure of income. The registrar must carefully monitor graduates, exchange students, leaves of absence, dropouts, stopouts, academic dismissals, and other assorted outmigrations of students. Then the registrar must make projections of enrollment levels in all classes and schools and transmit this to the admissions office with a recommendation for new freshman and transfer student targets that total to the bottom-line objective.

The problems created by large transfer student programs also require enrollment management solutions. In such areas as course registration, priorities must be established between returning students and potential transfers. Returning students must be treated equitably with entering students and transfers. Difficult decisions must be made about whether to make financial aid allocations to transfers when there are competing claims from present students who may say they are departing specifically for financial reasons.

There is the inherent risk in matters as complex as these that some institutions will sacrifice humaneness for mechanistic approaches. An enrollment management program is not an either/ or proposition. It is possible to use a modern systems approach while simultaneously recognizing the primacy of the counseling function in admissions, registrar, and financial aid offices. Properly developed, such a program will actually have the advantage of freeing professionals for one-to-one interactions with students.

The Table of Organization

So far, this chapter has summarized the rationale for, and the goals of, enrollment management. It was suggested that the offices central to enrollment management enterprise are admissions, financial aid, institutional research, and the registrar. Certainly, this is not the only conceivable table of organization. Each college or university—depending on fundamental goals enunciated by the president and the trustees, the number of freshman applications, administrative styles, and even political exigencies—will add or subtract functions in varying combinations. For those institutions whose primary stress might be on marketing rather than enrollments, liaisons among such offices as admissions, public relations, and development could be appropriate. Many institutions have placed recruitment functions under institutional advancement because it is perceived that they have so much in common. At smaller institutions where enrollment management is essential but computerized information systems are unnecessary, the emphasis on individual counseling could link retention with such offices as academic advisement and career planning and placement.

At every institution interested in maintaining, or even enhancing, its enrollment picture during the uncertain decade of the 1980s and beyond, there will be a need for close coordination with the academic deans and department chairs. In pursuing the analogy with the business world to its ultimate, some theorists have even suggested that institutions of higher education appoint vice-presidents for marketing, whose major roles will be to maintain a diversified and up-to-date product portfolio by working with faculty on the creation of new programs, even as others with finite life cycles and reduced demand are being phased out. Most faculties view such a proposal with skepticism and envision themselves as having sole jurisdiction over curriculum.

It may be that the job description of some future academic vice-presidencies will include aspects of marketing and portfolio management, but at most institutions, academic planning will be done by individual faculty members, by departmental committees, and on rare occasions, by long-range academic planning commissions. Such division of responsibilities adds challenge to communicate and to be well informed in several areas before making these decisions. Because it will generate the information on market demand, student flow, and retention that will assist with decisions on resource allocation for existing programs, enrollment management will have a primary role in academic planning and marketing. Only on the rarest of occasions will enrollment management become directly involved in program creation or elimination. If enrollment management is headed by a vice-president in an institution where there are strong academic ties to admissions, it could have the advantage of creating a second advocate for academic positions at the highest levels.

One program is now (with slight modification from the traditional) in operation at several institutions. Each of four distinct and autonomous areas—admissions, financial aid, registrar, and student information systems research—is situated at the same level under a vice-president or a dean for enrollment management. The title and level of placement of this latter position in the overall organizational chart will depend on the size of the institution and possibly the academic selectivity as well. In the relatively small numbers of institutions that turn down large numbers and therefore fall into the highly selective range, it may be desirable to make this an academic deanship or vice provost's position because academic selection criteria involve faculty and deans most directly in the admissions process. Even in this situation, the vice-presidential titles could apply, but the person selected for the position would often be required to have an academic background—preferably as a faculty member. In most institutions, it is essential to place this office in direct contact with the president, and so the vice-presidential title is most appropriate.

Each office can be organized along traditional lines, although creative opportunities for improvement exist. The directors are given control over their own operations, so that the vice-president for enrollment management is in no sense a substitute for these professional managers. Because they must be the acknowledged institutional experts in their own fields, they are paid at least at the level of compensation they would receive if the vice-presidency did not exist.

The primary function of the vice-president for enrollment management is to forge the links among these separate offices in order to facilitate achievement of the objectives of the enrollment management program. This vice-presidency is responsible for integrative functions that relate to the separate areas but also cut across them in the numerous ways discussed in the previous section. Marketing may originate in admissions, but it encompasses the pricing and financial aid strategies that emerge from the financial aid office as well as the demand analysis done by the registrar. Retention may have its primary focus in the registrar's office, but it relates directly to marketing and financial aid strategies as well. Research and student information systems have an identity of their own, but in a larger sense, they become the mortar that binds the other operations together.

Enrollment Management Checklist

The emerging field of enrollment management is at a stage of raising many more questions than answers. Eventually, through trial and error, and perhaps ultimately through a comprehensive theory, the formulation will be seen as the bridge between a systems theory of admissions and a systems theory of higher education. But for now, our aims must be considerably more modest, and so it is in this spirit that we begin to pose some of the questions all institutions, public and private, large and small, must ask and eventually answer.

1. Has your college or university prepared long-range (five- to ten-year) academic and fiscal plans that identify institutional goals and include enrollment objectives? Do you have a long-range enrollment plan?

2. Is your college or university preparing a contingency plan for possible enrollment declines? What is the likelihood that your institution will experience a significant decline? Is it possible that you will be forced to close or merge during the 1980s or 1990s? If so, how can this be done with minimum disadvantage to faculty and students?

3. Do you display admissions applications and deposits in tabular and graphical form on a daily, weekly, monthly, and yearly basis? Do you know precisely how many applications you are up against for this coming Monday, for this coming week, for the entire admissions cycle? Are last year's data absolutely accurate and comparable? Can you use present and past data to extrapolate trends?

4. Do you undertake more than straightforward demographic analysis of your applicant pool? Do you understand your own strengths and weaknesses as perceived by the accepted applicant pool? Cite four or five specific examples of major policy changes that have resulted from market research at your institution.

5. Do you investigate your competition to understand (a) why students make choices, (b) which institutions are perceived as most similar to yours in image, and (c) where there is the greatest application overlap?

6. Do you know how your college rates among its competition on factors that influence student decision? On what factors should you most want to rank favorably? Is it realistic to set your sights on first place for each factor?

7. Do you attempt to position yourself within the student marketplace as well as among your competitor colleges and universities? In other words, do you have a realistic understanding of the type of student who would be the best match with your institution? How do you define *quality* as it relates to a realistic positioning strategy?

8. Does your admissions system include a careful tracking of inquiries and their yield in applications? Do you understand, through research, why inquiries do or do not apply to your college or university? Do you attempt to understand the perceptions (awareness and comprehension) of your institution among students who never inquire or apply but who have characteristics compatible with the students you seek?

9. Do you encourage graduate students (and in some cases undergraduate honors students), as well as faculty members, in such departments as sociology, economics, and marketing to do research relating to enrollments? Do you have staff members who can write or supervise doctoral theses or research papers that will improve the management of enrollments?

10. Does your institution periodically seek the opinion of its own students and alumni in order to determine, among other things, how fully their original expectations have been met, how valuable their overall educations have proved to be, and how well specific programs have served them?

11. How do you involve faculty, alumni, and students in admissions? How many are active from each group? Do you have an adequate budget, staff, and orientation program to ensure success? Can you determine an acceptable level of risk for utilizing volunteer resources?

12. How many high schools does your admissions staff visit in a given year? How many major feeder schools provide you with 50 percent of your applications? Is this figure closer to. 30 percent or 10 percent of the total number of schools sending at least one application? Could you be using staff travel time more productively?

13. What percent of your applicants actually visit your campus? Is their overall impression favorable? Do you allocate adequate resources for programs that will attract students and their parents to your campus? Can they attend classes, stay overnight, and so forth?

14. To what extent are parents important in the overall decision-making process? What special programs have been devised to give parents the opportunity to assist their sons and daughters in considering your college?

15. Do you employ the Student Search Service of the College Board or other direct-mail services? How do you target mailings to achieve the best results? Do you know the yield on inquiries for different categories?

16. Who prepares your admissions literature? Are students involved? Does your admissions staff have confidence in its impact? What tests do you apply to determine how it is being received? What graphics approach does your market prefer?

17. Do you periodically employ innovative marketing techniques that can then be analyzed for cost and benefit? Taking everything into consideration, which approaches to the market work best and under which circumstances?

18. Do you actually use your admissions application and the process itself as positive marketing tools? Do you require applicants to respond to offers of admission, housing, and financial aid before they have had the opportunity to weigh offers from all institutions to which they apply?

19. Do you use College Board Validity Studies in an effort to understand which predictors best correlate with your most important criterion variables (college, grade point average, value added, law boards, and so forth)? Do you have at least a layperson's appreciation for research terminology, such as *correlation* and *multiple regression analysis*? Have you taken advantage of other College Board and American College Testing Program services, such as the Admissions Testing Program, the Summary Report Service, computerized graphs, and retention reports?

20. How well do students from your most important feeder high schools achieve at your institution? Do you weigh ranks from various high schools in order to adjust for differences in performance at your institution?

21. Does your admissions office have immediate access to the decision-making apparatus at your institution—by reporting either directly to the president or to someone else who can make important decisions quickly? Where are the financial aid and the registrar's offices placed in your table of organization? What about the office of institutional research? Who should be primarily responsible for your office's research?

22. Are you generally satisfied with the coordination among marketing, recruiting, financial aid, and retention functions at your institution? Are you, as an admissions officer, responsible only for bringing students to your institution? Who has responsibility for maintaining overall enrollments?

23. Can you obtain an accurate snapshot of student enrollments at all levels at all times of the year? Is student flow at your institution such that you must think in terms of semesters rather than academic years?

24. If you have master's or doctoral programs, does your institution apply enrollment management techniques to recruitment, retention, and funding of graduate students?

25. Is a designated official at your institution responsible for relating academic planning to long- and short-range student demand?

26. To what extent are you involved in resource allocation decisions at your institution? Can you project demand by studying the Student Descriptive Questionnaire, American Council on Education data, applications, the Indexed Course Load Matrix, internal transfers, and the job market? Have you prepared an institutional study on this subject recently?

27. Does your institution use the formal registration process as a means to assess student demand with respect to optimal course selection and distribution (time and place)?

28. Do you have a comprehensive financial aid policy at your institution? Are your goals consistent with the College Scholarship Service "Principles of Student Financial Aid Administration"? Can you operationally define *equality of educational opportunity*?

29. In addition to supporting national goals with your policy, do you pursue well-defined institutional goals? Do you offer no-need scholarships? athletic scholarships? minority scholarships?

30. Are you able to meet the full need of every accepted financial aid applicant? If not, how do you establish priorities for deciding who is eligible for your limited funds? By equity packaging (new College Board Service): either meeting equal percentages of need or underfunding by a fixed dollar amount? By

fully funding the neediest first and denying aid to others? Or by fully funding the best first and denying aid to others?

31. How do students who come to your institution with less than full need survive? Do you know what their alternative sources of funds are? Do you set aside a pool of money for upper-class students who have distinguished themselves academically or who have taken on excessive self-help burdens through loans and employment?

32. Do you know how much financial aid is forfeited by students who withdraw from your institution? How do you redistribute this money among freshmen, transfers, and upper-class students?

33. How are institutional and federal funds apportioned among schools and classes at your institution? Do you have special policies concerning work-study and loans for freshmen?

34. Do you continually analyze financial aid yield data in an effort to optimize certain quantifiable goals, such as minorities, overall enrollment, quality, net tuition, and yield?

35. Do you have a centralized office of student employment to assist all students in identifying sources of income for potential use in defraying college expenses? Do you attempt to link students to jobs by areas of interest and location? Are alumni integrated into the job locator network?

36. Who prepares research on tuition, fees, room and board (that is, pricing) at your competitor schools before your trustees set final figures? Are you satisfied that you are positioned properly in the marketplace with respect to pricing? Do you include financial aid in your pricing strategy?

37. Have you taken steps to provide accurate, complete consumer information to all potential and enrolled students and their families? Do you offer all students and their families, even those not eligible for financial aid, specific financial counseling?

38. Do you know exactly how many students leave your institution in a given year, semester, month, week, or day? What percent of all students in a typical class graduate in eight to ten semesters?

39. If you understand why students come to your college or university, do you understand why they leave and where they go? Do their reasons vary from freshman to junior year? Do transfers enter your institution making the same erroneous assumptions that prompted your dropouts to leave in the first place (the revolving-door syndrome)?

40. Do you have a centralized, adequately staffed transfer admissions program to expand your applicant pool and to maintain enrollment stability in all classes? Once transfer students have been admitted to your institution, do they have the same opportunities for financial aid, housing, and course selection as their peers who started as freshmen?

41. Are all departments within your institution involved in both admissions and retention?

42. Do you have an advisement program (faculty, staff, peers, graduate students) that relates to the enrollment management function—that is, attempts to improve retention and relate curriculum and student life to overall personal and career goals?

43. Do you have a mechanism for helping students leave your institution in cases where they would obviously be better served elsewhere (new career objectives, need to find themselves, and so forth)? Is your exit interview process an integral part of the retention function?

44. Are your student information systems integrated, so reports prepared and research generated in the area of enrollment will easily cut across the boundaries of departments and functions?

Just as the six goals of an enrollment management program must be thought of as fluid and integrated, so must the forty-four sets of questions that constitute the enrollment management checklist. Individual institutions should amend and recombine this list to best suit their own purposes. Academic areas, such as program planning and academic and career advisement, can receive greater stress. Marketing functions, such as alumni, development, and public relations (sometimes organized under a vice-president for external affairs), may also be included.

What must be underscored is the fact that this checklist is mainly a catalyst to encourage institutions to begin to ask the right questions as a necessary prelude to arriving at definitive answers. It should also be reemphasized that no two institutions will prepare identical enrollment management checklists and that a single institution's shifting priorities will call for periodic updates of the list.

Clearly, it will not be possible in the remainder of Part Eight to address all the issues raised in the enrollment management checklist. There are, as we move through the mid 1980s, many more questions than answers. This list constitutes an unfinished agenda for the 1980s and 1990s.

51

John Maguire

Student Information Systems and Research in Enrollment Planning

❧ The goals of enrollment management include a commitment to the development of integrated student information systems that can be used in research and planning for enrollments. Perhaps no other goal of the six outlined in Chapter Fifty has been the subject of so much controversy. On the one hand, institutions with strong enrollment pictures often encounter insuperable political problems, as strong-minded, successful, and creatively independent directors fight standardization and increased centralization of information control. At least part of this uneasiness may stem from their fear that someone may discover that the college has succeeded despite, rather than because of, them. On the other hand, many small colleges suffering from enrollment problems are hopelessly befuddled by the complexity of systems solutions. They are often so preoccupied with flailing out in all directions to uncover new students that they can hardly afford the luxury to think about research and planning, let alone to disengage scarce resources to attract or train the people who could actually do it.

During one of its most threatening times, therefore, we have the tragic irony of the academy—the protector, disseminator, and extender of knowledge and truth down through the ages—as an enterprise hopelessly incapable of seizing the opportunity to embrace methods of research and analysis that can lead to the very self-knowledge necessary for salvation! This contradiction prevails throughout much of the history of higher education. The institution most responsible for advancements in knowledge and reasoned decision making has itself been notoriously inefficient in applying these lessons to the painful task of self-discovery. As a result, colleges and universities lumber along with organizational structures that have deviated little from the guild model of the early European universities. And attempts to tamper with this structure, or to introduce advances in computer technology and systems analysis, are often greeted with cynicism and mistrust.

Role of Director of Student Information Systems and Research

Some of this hesitation is well founded, particularly in institutions that operate with decentralized, smoothly functioning offices and few enrollment problems. Management information systems are in one sense a great but unwelcome equalizer— removing, as they do, previous advantages held by administrators with facilities for accurate data collection and creative, albeit rudimentary, research. Moreover, such systems tend to place inordinate power in the hands of a small number of technocrats, who sometimes function more as inquisitors than as facilitators and colleagues.

For these reasons, it is important to structure research for enrollment management in such a way as to capitalize on the strengths of both centralized and decentralized research.

The table of organization proposed in Chapter Fifty recognizes the necessity for a central research and systems office within the area of the vice-president for enrollment management. This director's main responsibility will be to develop systems and coordinate research that bears directly on student enrollments. Although at times, this individual will work with the central offices of management information systems and institutional research or other areas engaged in studies of faculties, facilities, or finances, this director's functional allegiance is indisputably to the area of enrollment management.

It is also imperative that this centralization not lead to

elimination of systems and research capabilities within the separate offices of admissions, registrar, and financial aid. These area directors must each designate at least one individual within their own offices to be primarily responsible for research and computer-related issues arising within that office. This assistant, or associate director, should be a member of a committee chaired by the director of student information systems and research and should play a proactive role in initiating projects within his or her own office. The director of student information systems and research should play the role of teacher, facilitator, or catalyst for projects that relate to a single office; only with the approval of the specific director and the vice-president for enrollment management should that individual initiate research within the domain of a single area. This last proviso may sound cumbersome, but it is absolutely essential in order to ensure that individual departments will neither allow initiative to atrophy nor feel threatened by an unsympathetic, outside investigator.

The director of student information systems and research has as a primary responsibility the organization of coordinated systems and creative research in enrollment management that cut across the functions of admissions, records, and financial aid. This individual will be the project manager for all studies proposed by the vice-president for enrollment management (in market research, retention analysis, surveys of present students, questionnaire design, validity studies, graduate student or faculty research, financial aid strategies, and student flow and program demand, to cite but a few areas), will work in conjunction with systems analysts in the office of management information systems to design and document computer programs for use in enrollment management, and will serve as liaison with external agencies, such as the College Board, that provide the institution with valuable student data.

A cursory perusal of the enrollment management checklist in Chapter Fifty underscores the generalist nature of the research and student systems function. This area is identified with more separate questions on the checklist than any of the other three. In a sense, this directorship is the catalyst that facilitates the interactions among admissions, records, and financial aid.

What has been said so far applies mainly to colleges and universities whose economies of scale are such that large offices with adequate staffs exist, computerized information systems are commonplace, and the sophistication to address enrollment management questions is present. But it would be an egregious error to infer that small schools cannot benefit substantially from a strong research orientation toward enrollment management. Every college, large or small, must establish standardized procedures for collecting and communicating data, whether it be through a formal organizational structure linking enrollment management offices through a vice-president or through a small, standing committee composed of the directors of the various areas and chaired by the president or chief academic officer. There are crucial times of the year when the largest and smallest institutions should operate in the same fashion, carefully hand-counting and cross-checking to ensure accuracy.

Elements of Successful Research in Enrollment Management

Parkinson's Law applies particularly well to the field of higher educational administration. Some college officials in areas impinging on admissions and enrollment management work evenings and weekends just trying to keep pace. And the treadmill is beginning to turn more rapidly as the 1990s get closer. With all that needs to be done in recruitment, registration, and financial aid counseling, the common lament, not without justification, is: We just don't have the time for research, to say nothing of the expertise. The response to this is straightforward: The time must, and can, be found; the capability must, and can, be developed.

The ability to manage time is one of the chief attributes of a successful administrator. A second important trait is the willingness to set priorities in order to be sure to tackle the really important tasks. So it is with research—there is never enough time, because the leadership of the institution has not identified research as a high enough priority. The first step, therefore, is a firm commitment to research, which moves it to a higher rank on the list of essential things to be accomplished.

It is perhaps best at the outset of this restructuring of priorities to play a zero-sum game with time and resources. At a later date, once research and planning are entrenched, it might be desirable to have a reassessment of priorities that will lead to the hiring of additional staff. An inventory of all activities in an office should be taken, and research should displace items considered of lesser importance. For example, a four-member admissions staff visits 800 high schools for recruitment purposes during a three-month period. In such a small operation, it would be impossible to assign one person to full-time research. However, the director of admissions, in consultation with the staff, could eliminate the 100 least productive visits, thereby freeing up one staff member, and the related travel money, for about six weeks, which could be devoted solely to research and planning. At the outset, it may be necessary to invest some money in training that person to adapt to unfamiliar responsibilities, but it will earn dividends in the long term. And once the position has been established, continuity can be assured by giving others the chance to be involved and by identifying research, systems, and planning as basic parts of the position description.

In every office involved with enrollment management, a specified fraction of a slot should be assigned to research (in large institutions, this would be an entire slot). The director of student information systems and research will then be the coordinator of integrated research activities and chair of the research committee and will also play an active role in training colleagues to assume their new roles.

Research should be both centralized and decentralized, so it can simultaneously be top-down and bottom-up. Whenever feasible, the director should involve as many qualified members of the college community as possible in the research effort. Graduate students should be encouraged to write master's and doctoral theses on subjects relating to enrollment management, with the vice-president, director of student information systems and research, and individual staff members assigned on occasion to thesis committees. This is an exciting, and indeed revolutionary, notion: The office of the vice-president for enrollment management can become a focus for high-level academic activities centered on both teaching and research. This lends more credence to the notion that enrollment management is an academic function and belongs organizationally under a vice-president or a dean who has strong academic credentials and faculty ties.

An indispensable factor in a successful research program in enrollment management is the forging of bonds between research and policy-making. An often-stated complaint is that voluminous data, generated both by computer printouts and through painstaking research, ends up gathering dust on shelves. Reports and recommendations rarely filter up to the top-level administrators who actually could use this information for making decisions, and as a result they muddle their way through a complex problem using only intuition and political savvy. If this scenario is replicated too often, a damper is quickly put on the staff's enthusiasm for a research orientation.

The key to breaking this vicious cycle is leadership at the highest levels. Certainly the very existence of a vice-president for enrollment management who has a strong commitment to systems and research and a direct line to the highest decision-making levels of the institution is an important ingredient in the solution. If decisions are predicated on solid research, and if creative research can lead to major policy decisions, then unquestionably a research mechanism will be woven quickly into the fabric of the institution. So, in a larger sense, research becomes the mortar that bonds the entire institution, and not just the enrollment management function, together.

Successful policy research in enrollment management can be simple or sophisticated, but it should never be simplistic or sophistic. Administrators should develop a healthy respect for quantitative methods so they can use modeling and rough-estimation techniques as preludes to possible decisions to pursue more complex lines of inquiry. Thumbnail and back-of-the-envelope approximations will sometimes lead to counterintuitive results, and the resolution of these contradictions can yield profound and valuable insights.

But the novice researcher should be forewarned that human systems are not the same as physical systems, and as a result, research into the former must always be approached with caution. Even in a statistical sense, people do not behave with the predictability of thermodynamic systems—and behavioral research has many pitfalls.

Counterintuitive research results can often be erroneous rather than profound and insightful. Witness the example of the Catholic college that downplayed its religious heritage because a survey had shown that applicants did not rate this important at the conscious level. Subliminally, religion turned out to be of overriding significance—and the college went out of business, at least partly as a result of this move.

A good rule of thumb is that the researcher in enrollment management, and the policy maker who uses the researcher's information, should be stimulated by research but never led blindly by it. Other factors must also be considered before final policy can be forged.

There is an equal risk that research will be unnecessarily obscure. The practitioners of such techniques as multivariate analysis (who have years of background in statistical methods and computer science) sometimes seem incapable of communicating their findings in terms translatable into policy analysis. There are several reasons for this.

First, statistical analysis is difficult to comprehend and reduce to lay terms without at least a passing acquaintance with such terminology as *regression equation* or *correlation coefficient*. Second, persons skilled in those techniques can make themselves indispensable, if their track records for sound policy recommendations are good and if no one is prepared to understand their mathematics, let alone challenge them. Third, regrettably, much of this research is both highly sophisticated and trivial. Some researchers make a comfortable living saturating the journals with arguments about technique rather than substance and with correlation studies that really say nothing relevant to decision making in higher education. To overcome these deficiencies, all institutional decision makers should cultivate a healthy respect for both the power and the limitations of research results in educational decision making.

In the field of enrollment management, there is a built-in mechanism to interrelate the researchers with the decision makers. At its simplest level, they could be the same people—with the vice-president and all directors holding academic doctorates and being actively involved in multidisciplinary research related to enrollments. More realistically, one of the most important responsibilities, even obligations, of the director of student information systems and research will be to communicate techniques, as well as research results, to colleagues. Informal minicourses in statistical methods and computer science should be offered periodically to interested staff members. An attempt should be made both to translate technical jargon into lay terms and to communicate the power and beauty of these disciplines as well as a basic understanding of their languages. Simplicity should be sought wherever possible, and all should have a basic comprehension of when, exactly, such simplicity is possible. Finally, all research should ultimately be translated into policy analysis and recommendations, and it is therefore imperative that those decision makers outside the enrollment management area be involved as much as possible.

All available national and regional data—from the Census Bureau, the National Center for Higher Education Management Systems (NCHEMS), the College Board, the American College Testing Program, the National Center for Education Statistics (NCES) and regional and state boards of education—should be drawn upon in doing policy analysis at the institutional level. Research and professional journals should be scanned for topics of interest and relevance. Indeed, they should be required reading for all who do research, and all of them should be familiar with areas outside their own disciplines.

One of the best methods for developing a capability to engage in creative research is to analyze critically the works of others in one's field. When it all begins to fall into place, when some of it appears incomplete or inconsequential, then the incentive and confidence to produce one's own research grow. Another possibility for acquiring information, which of course can also be extracted from many of the previously cited sources, is to inquire directly of another college, especially one that is similarly affiliated or one that can be viewed as a competitor.

Given this plethora of information from a number of different sources, it is easy to overlook a cardinal principle of successful research in enrollment management: Each institution of higher education is unique and must therefore do individualized research. National and regional data that combine information from many institutions can be helpful in assessing trends. However, policy problems draw on such a complex array of data that opportunities can be lost by colleges that fail to recognize they may deviate considerably from the norm on important parameters.

So in summary, guidelines for successful enrollment management research include: (1) At the highest levels, commit the institution to research in enrollment management, free up the time, and train staff to do it as a top priority. (2) Each school must do its own research, using all available resources. (3) Keep research simple and sophisticated, and know when it must be one or the other. (4) Keep it centralized and decentralized, so there is strength, challenge, and creativity at all levels. (5) Relate research to policy and decision making, so the institutional commitment will be ongoing.

Research Techniques in Enrollment Management

For some, the title of director of student information systems and research is redundant—that is, the computer becomes both researcher and decision maker. At its extreme, this viewpoint replaces people with machines as the ultimate policy makers in all fields, including higher education. With the progress that has been made in computer technology, this may someday prove to be possible. But for the foreseeable future, people will be the primary decision makers, and research will continue to serve as the tool that connects the report from the computer with the policy judgments of men. For research, at its best, is really an intuitive, creative, divergent process in which data are used as an essential component.

High-speed computers have led to the development of management information systems that can revolutionize decision making in higher education. In the past, laborious collection of data and subsequent analysis could only be done in the form of frequency distribution, which oftentimes led to erroneous interpretations and, therefore, limited utility for decision making. Now software packages, such as the Statistical Package for the Social Sciences (SPSS), allow researchers to apply high-powered statistical techniques, such as factor analysis and multiple regression analysis, to the ordering of a welter of complex data. More than ever before, demographic data can be analyzed, compared, and intercorrelated in order to suggest further lines of inquiry and also facilitate decisions on resource allocation and enrollment management strategies.

Institutions of higher education have begun to use market analysis techniques, heretofore almost the exclusive province of the profit-making sector. Telephone surveys and elaborate questionnaires now routinely probe consumer attitudes. Detailed segmentation analyses are being performed based on consumer opinion and behavior. Probing telephone surveys of small select samples of different markets can be approached with a view toward using computer analysis and the above-mentioned, sophisticated statistical techniques.

This kind of sociological research, even with the aid of the computer, is subject to considerable error; therefore those venturing into this field for the first time must be forewarned that a professional approach is absolutely essential. For example, in questionnaire research, the sequence of questions, the covering letter, and the timing of the first mailing and follow-up requests must be such that a reasonable response rate will be guaranteed and that longitudinal tracking of data will be feasible. Telephone surveys with small sample sizes have the advantages of open-endedness and 100 percent response rates as well as the disadvantages of not guaranteeing anonymity and of making it difficult to generate large volumes of responses in order to apply statistical techniques to the analysis.

It must be understood that different approaches will lead, at least at first appearance, to different results. Researchers have been dealing essentially with social science techniques that have large capacity for error even beyond inappropriate methodology. The value of using multiple approaches is that paradoxes will emerge, and these paradoxes, once resolved, invariably will lead to higher orders of understanding that will result in even greater confidence in the quantitative aspects of decision making. But beyond all of this, it must be reemphasized that analytical research must be used with sensitivity, intuition, and creative thinking when coming to overall policy decisions concerning enrollment management. Just as the hunch and guess techniques of the past are no longer adequate in a complex, fast-moving decision-making environment, so the skills of the human decision maker cannot be replaced by impersonal analysis initiated by computers.

For more information on research, see Chapter Fifty-nine, "Market Research: The Starting Point for Advancement Success" (p. 757).

52

James J. Scannell

How Financial Aid Affects Recruitment and Admissions

৵৵ Perhaps never more in the public eye, opportunities and access to colleges and universities have drawn increasing attention from prospective students, parents, public officials, corporate and foundation leaders, faculty, trustees, and administrators, to name but a few. The relationship between admissions and student financial aid has come under particularly close scrutiny.

American higher education has evolved, over the last century, from an institution serving society's elite to one founded on meritocratic ideals to, most recently, one committed to egalitarianism. As the goals and objectives of postsecondary education expanded, and society's demand for college graduates grew, student financial aid began to play an increasingly important role at American colleges and universities.

Education has always been a state function. The federal government played a very minor, almost nonexistent, role in the financing of higher education until after World War II. Most state involvement in higher education was directed toward the land-grant, publicly subsidized institutions, and there was little, or no, involvement in the independent sector. Private institutions granted occasional tuition waivers for outstanding merit, mostly based on academic scholarship but periodically for distinguished achievement on the athletic field and even less frequently in the music chamber. For the most part, members of society who wanted to participate in the world of academia paid their own way or, more likely, had their parents pay. If they could not afford to attend a specific institution, they found another at lower cost or worked and saved until they had accumulated enough of a reserve to go or— most probably—did not go at all.

The GI Bill, which to date still holds title to the federal government's largest categorical contribution to higher education, changed the way people began to look at the responsibility for meeting higher education costs.

The ideal of meritocracy was replaced by the goal of universal higher education. Sputnik, John Kennedy's Eastern intellectual elite, and the civil rights movement all contributed to speeding up this process. *Access* and *choice* became the watchwords of the day. Congressional representatives, state legislators, and governors found themselves with strange bedfellows—college and university presidents, business officers, and educational lobbyists.

To guarantee equal access and choice, there had to be a redistribution of resources. Student financial assistance, first given to institutions to use at their discretion but more recently given as direct aid to students, became the instrument to accomplish this.

A private, nonprofit, government-approved agency became the vehicle for determining the degree and course this redistribution would take. Taxation schedules for discretionary income were developed by pragmatic procedural decisions of the subcommittee on computations of the College Scholarship Service. At first, no one saw a need for the system to be scientifically or empirically constructed. And small wonder, with the tuitions and enrollments only a fraction of what they are in the 1980s. Pragmatic procedures based on fairly gross assumptions worked because costs were low and income ranges narrow. However, the enrollment explosion of the 1960s and early 1970s left many institutions encumbered with a large debt service and increasingly significant fixed costs. As a labor-intensive industry, higher education fell victim to the spiraling inflation of the 1970s. When matched with tripling energy costs and, at best, a stabilizing college-bound population, tuitions continued to climb to what many believed were prohibitive levels. As state governments continue to subsidize the public sector (a commendable policy driven by the goal of access), the tuition gap between public and private higher education has widened. Private higher education, in particular, has had to turn to student aid as a resource for enabling enrollment goals to be met rather than as an instrument for implementing the worthy ideals of access and choice. Consequently, with finite funds available, and aggregate financial need far in excess of these monies, the strategy of distribution of student financial aid has become critical not only for the aspiring scholar-consumer of the goods and services but also for institutions of higher learning, which see it as a key in their struggle for survival.

The Ten Greatest Myths of Admissions, Financial Aid, and Enrollment Management

Myth 1. From the student consumer: If I apply to your institution, you ought to be able to tell me how much it will cost me to attend and how much aid I will receive. Or put another way, How can you expect me to buy your product without a final price tag?

This widely expressed perception of higher education unfortunately has received support from some fairly well-known educators and authors in the field of college choice and the influence of aid. In fact, many at high-cost institutions are concerned that applicants and their families are selecting themselves out of the system because they are unable to distinguish between the initial sticker price and the ultimate net price after financial aid has been taken into consideration. This phenomenon is further exacerbated by the gap between public and private tuitions, which as mentioned earlier, has been growing to the point where, in the state of New York, the average private independent tuition is five times greater than the tuition charged by the state system. Often the independent institutions that charge the most are the wealthiest and can discount their product at a greater rate with institutional aid. However, many families who have an urge to know up front (that is, at the point of inquiry and application, as opposed to admission) what this education is going to cost them and choose what is perceived to be the most cost-efficient road (lower sticker price) could well end up paying more.

Myth 2. Again from the marketplace: If I apply for financial aid, my chances for admissions are drastically reduced. or All selection committees read admissions applications with Financial Aid Forms, Family Financial Statements, and 1040s in their laps.

The only misperception here is the word *all,* for unfortunately, some colleges do exactly this. As a matter of fact, some very prestigious institutions apply an aid-conscious admissions policy to some in their applicant pools who sit on the margin.

This policy effectively controls the amount of need in the student body by controlling the number of needy students you allow to join that body. At some point in pursuing this policy, in even the most selective admissions processes, an institution will have to deny admission to more qualified needy students in favor of slightly less qualified wealthy ones. One could conjure up a caricature—take the rich dumb kid over the poor bright kid. So what is wrong with that policy? It is unfair to students and their families. Coupling wealth to the decision to admit is certainly a bad precedent in a country that clings tenaciously to the aristocracy of talent over the aristocracy of wealth. The aid-conscious approach eliminates financial counseling and self-help advisement. It embodies all the bad images of financial aid and more than counterbalances the satisfaction of helping when it is possible to do so. Finally, the strategic effect of aid-conscious admissions could have two overriding negative results. First would be the disastrous consequence of the domino effect if all schools pursued the policy. And second, such a policy could prevent people from applying for aid and thus send the opposite of the intended signal to the federal government. Suffice it to say, it is just bad public and institutional policy.

Myth 3. The final myth from the marketplace: If you accept me, you will give me a total financial aid package. or If I accept your offer of admission, I am entitled to as much financial aid as I think I need.

Some from a generation of the past (although not necessarily the distant past) recall the meritocratic approach to financial aid, when higher education was a privilege to be earned—either in the classroom or through hard work outside. They recall that manual labor, for instance, was not to be looked down on. With the best of intentions, it is possible that we have created an entitlement generation—a generation that feels as though it is owed an education.

Now this brings a certain amount of criticism to our profession. It necessitates such things as developing guidelines for maintaining the status of good standing in order to receive aid. Some would even go so far as to say it is, in part, responsible for the decline in standardized test scores and for the lack of incentive in our secondary school classrooms. Certainly, it draws attention to a concern, and perhaps even to a conflict. This is that the cost of educating our nation's youth is an expense we can ill afford to neglect, and yet those responsible for the distribution of resources are expected by both the public and those benefactors who support our institutions to be certain that those who receive aid will appreciate it, that they will develop a sense of commitment, not necessarily to the institution per se but to future generations who will need to depend on public and private generosity in order to realize their educational and career goals.

To change gears now, let us leave the marketplace and enter the administrative worlds of admissions and financial aid for myths also found in these arenas. And they in fact are present within the professions themselves.

Myth 4. Admissions professionals don't need to understand financial aid. or It isn't my job to talk about that!

At a typical College Night, or at a College Fair, when many admissions officers are present, observe what often happens when a parent or guidance counselor digresses from the area of admissions qualifications and enters the world of financial aid. Responses to questions about financial aid often take the form I'm sorry, but you'll have to ask our aid officer about that. And yet we are at a point in time in enrollment management when a responsible recruiter must be able to address the issue of cost and financial aid knowingly, citing well-thought-out case studies— perhaps not speaking with ultimate authority but certainly directing people to the proper sources for answers to their questions. The responsibility for developing this expertise among admissions officers rests in both camps.

Myth 5. Financial aid professionals are only technocrats. Financial aid types are green-eyeshaded, sharpened-penciled, overly regulated, uncreative accountants.

The fact is that the financial aid officer—at a time when both funds and student needs were limited, when programs were few and eligibility criteria simple—could manage the task equipped only with those somewhat caricatured characteristics. That day, however, is long gone, and today, a financial aid officer needs a keen, analytical mind and must be technically competent and patient enough to wade through, comprehend, and then implement federal and state regulations with both the student's and the institution's best interests in mind. But these are now boilerplate characteristics and do not really distinguish the good financial aid officer, the sound financial aid officer, from the person today who is at the forefront of the profession.

Today, qualities rightfully focus on effective leadership and creative management techniques. The computer will smash the hierarchical, pyramidal, managerial system built to keep track of people and the things people do. With the computer to keep track, operations and institutions can be restructured horizontally. But the definition of *leadership,* like those of other overused words, needs careful examination. The art of the creative leader in the area of financial aid is the art of the creative financial aid manager, the art of reworking human and technological materials to fashion and infuse value into the system well beyond the technical requirements of the job. That is, the leader will primarily be an expert in the promotion and protection of institutional values. What are some of the typical, major leadership tasks that will be required of the financial aid manager? The litany will include amplifying understanding, building awareness, changing symbols, legitimizing new viewpoints, making tactical shifts and testing partial solutions, broadening political support, overcoming opposition, inducing and structuring flexibility, launching trial balloons and engaging in systematic waiting, creating pockets of commitment, crystalizing focus, managing coalitions, and formalizing commitment. The role of the financial aid officer, then, is one of orchestrator and labeler—taking what can be gotten by way of action and shaping it, sometimes after the fact, into lasting commitment in a new strategic direction.

The successful financial aid manager is also one who can referee the pull and tug of head versus heart, a person of integrity who is more value driven than market driven, a person who seeks excellence in people, not in systems, who hires good people, who is not afraid of diversity or divergent thinking, who is willing to give responsibility in such a way as to encourage risk-taking and creativity. Enough of the professions, let us move on to Myth 6 and institutional perceptions.

Myth 6. Strategic packaging of institutional aid has little, if any, impact on the decision to enroll. or When in doubt just give it out on a first-come, first-served basis.

What is the value of having a strategy for the distribution of institutional aid? Does strategy have a considerable impact on the make-up of the class? Will it help those institutions at excess capacity come closer to reaching their enrollment targets? The answer is a resounding Yes! to all of these. The continuum of possible strategies ranges from providing no-need merit awards and tying admissions decisions to the family's ability to pay to meeting the full need of all students who enroll. There are no simple answers; most vary by the nature, strength, and purpose of the institution.

The development of a pricing and financial aid strategy that will most enable an institution to attract and retain students in the proper quantity, quality, and desired socioeconomic, racial, and ethnic mix is not only a commendable but also an absolutely necessary goal of enrollment management today. Long-term policy questions include pricing: Should we raise tuition and aid simultaneously? Should we position ourselves differently in the market? Should the wealthy subsidize the poor? Should we practice equity packaging, or are we tempted to pursue a bait-and-switch tactic? Broader enrollment management questions include: To what extent should values control the process? Should the more committed subsidize the less committed? How can you distinguish those who say they will not attend but do? Should aid do more than just neutralize the college decision-making process? Are heavy loans and jobs related to dropping out, or do we just think that is likely to be the case? What experiences are other institutions having? And what then should public policy be? Should we abandon the middle class in an attempt to meet the needs of the very, very poor?

Let me end discussion of this myth by highlighting the need for research. For the answer, at least from an institutional point of view, lies in our own ability to conduct research and analyze our institutional experiences. It is, of course, easier to be a critic than an author. There is no easy way out. If yields on aided students slip below those for unaided, we have to reassess. Should we lower the price? Should we increase institutional aid? Should we admit/deny with financial aid counseling? Should we develop better self-help plans, make more work opportunities available, or subsidize jobs in addition to work-study?

Myth 7. Needs analysis is a science. or The College Scholarship Service really can determine a family's ability to pay.

Although we resist a lengthy examination of the difference between ability, willingness, and necessity to pay, we recommend that those differences be clearly kept in mind. But let us focus on a key question that needs analysis cannot, and never was meant to, address: the question of value. Regardless of the commitment, energy, and intellectual and analytical power mustered in the Committee on Needs Analysis Procedures and Committee on Standards of Ability to Pay and whether or not the report to filer exists, is amended, or is terminated, no standardized examination of a family's finances can quantify the value placed by that family on higher education in general or on an individual institution in particular. That is to say that sacrifices on discretionary income will not show up in any national process. Attention to this myth is not meant to focus on the inadequacies of uniform methodology, but rather to highlight that such analysis—even in its most perfect state—will not, and cannot, capture what a family is really willing to pay. Everything is relative. Families will stretch or shrink their financial commitment on the basis of their perception of an institution's relative worth.

Myth 8. There's no discretion in financial aid. or There's an answer to every question in the Federal Regs.

This is a sequel to Myth 5 concerning the qualities and characteristics of financial aid officers. Yet the purpose of citing it has more to do with the role of the federal government than it does with the profession itself. How can one quarrel with the same government that has brought us the origination fee, the needs test, 100 percent validation, and last but not least, the Solomon Amendment? It is not that there is no chance or need for discretion in financial aid decisions; rather, it is that the typical financial aid officer is hard-pressed to find any time to use it. It is difficult to be a successful financial aid officer. The federal government, known for its partiality to the written word (but not necessarily to the literary word), strives for consistency, which Ralph Waldo Emerson tells us is the hobgoblin of little minds. In fact, there is opportunity for discretion and decision making in financial aid, despite federal regulations.

Myth 9. For those who are programmers or systems analysts, and involved in the data processing side: In developing a financial aid system, it is always advisable to use an outside vendor. or What you see is what you get.

Systems have certainly become a large part of our lives. We are told, for instance, by John Naisbitt, author of *Megatrends* (1982), that we are living between the parentheses, between the old and the new, the North and the South, the batch and the on-line, the manufacturing and the service. Can higher education administration, and in particular financial aid, be any different? Of course not. Naisbitt contends that we are moving from the industrial society to an information society. We are moving from green eyeshades to green CRT screens. In response to our new societal and administrative needs, a herd of software vendors has risen to the occasion prepared to solve our many needs with their unique approaches. But we should not be too hard on them; much of the blame belongs to us, the institutional users and the technicians. For we must adequately define our environment. We must accurately paint the picture of our needs and know under what conditions we will be operating. Our communications must be crisp; we must know unambiguously what we seek.

Myth 10. Again for those on the data processing side: Data processing administrators don't need to understand financial aid or admissions in order to build a system. (This one could be subtitled The team approach just takes too much time.)

If there is any single action that will give the hemlock to a new system, a developing system, a conceptual design, or a detail design, it is lack of communication between the data processing staff and the user (in this case the financial aid administrator). Of course, the team approach takes more time, but that investment of time is in fact a downpayment on the future success of a system that will serve the institution and the students well. It is a downpayment we can ill afford not to make.

Conclusion

Although this business of slaying myths is difficult and time-consuming, hopefully it has been a worthwhile exercise because the area of financial aid and its impact on enrollments has become a critical issue for all institutions. The field will need energetic and committed people who are placed in positions where they can use their talents and skills and make the necessary decisions. Institutions are going to have to be willing to put significant resources at the disposal of the financial aid administrator and to work with that administrator in finding solutions to institutional problems. Strategies will have to be developed, challenged, adjusted, researched, analyzed, amended, implemented, and always, always evaluated. There will be questions regarding how to market a new institutional aid policy. What populations have traditionally been served? Will we serve new populations? What will the transition be like? It presents to the weak of heart a mountain of problems; it presents to those who have a predominance of courage over timidity a tremendous reservoir of challenges and opportunities.

Reference

Naisbitt, J. *Megatrends: Ten New Directions Transforming Our Lives.* New York: Warner Books, 1982.

53

Deirdre A. Ling

Using Volunteers
in Student Recruitment

✎ Extending resources by using faculty, enrolled students, and alumni in the recruitment of students is not only a cost-effective strategy; it makes good sense in other ways—good sense because volunteers possess a credibility that paid, professional staff do not have. As goodwill ambassadors, all three groups possess the first-hand experience of the institution as they live or have lived it. Their satisfaction with the academic enterprise and the quality of life at their institution, and their articulateness in conveying their perceptions and judgments to others, greatly enhances the information an admissions candidate has to consider when deciding whether to enroll. No viewbook, catalogue, or even slide show is as effective as the testimony of such reliable primary sources.

With this in mind, it is essential, when designing programs that tap into these valuable constituencies, not to squander their time by having fuzzy goals and making inappropriate assignments. Having clear-cut tasks and objectives for volunteers—before enlisting their participation—is vital.

Every well-designed program entails carefully prepared information and training materials, a well-planned schedule of contacts that provide truly two-way communications between the admissions staff and the volunteer constituency involved, and some tasteful and sincere form of recognition of their contributions at the end of each admissions cycle. Everyone appreciates being thanked, and a certain amount of ceremony is indigenous to every culture. Whether it be a certificate or a plaque, a letter from the president

684

or a dinner in their honor, it is essential to show volunteers that their time has been well spent and to provide a sense of completion.

Volunteers are best used in response to a specific problem or objective. A scattergun approach (Wouldn't it be nice to involve some of our science faculty in high school visits?) is doomed to failure. Rather, involving outstanding science faculty in meeting accepted students who have declared an interest in majoring in a science subject may positively influence the decision of those students to enroll. Faculty enjoy meeting bright, interested students who have an interest in their own discipline. They will be speaking from strength about the subject they know best. One should not expect them necessarily to be familiar with the four hundred extra-curricular activities on their campus, however, or with the football team's record last season.

It is important to start out modestly, with numbers the staff can handle. If thirty alumni volunteers are all one staff member can manage along with a host of other assignments, it is far better to start out small and get the basic components in place during one or two admission cycles.

If the travel budget only covers out-of-state recruitment to feeder states—those states with the highest concentration of currently enrolled students—utilizing student volunteers to visit their home high schools during the Thanksgiving and Christmas breaks might be a viable strategy. On the other hand, using alumni to distribute basic information at college fairs in distant states might also be a sound decision. If applications begin to come in from a high school from which the institution has rarely or never received them, using a well-informed and enthusiastic alumni representative may have paid off.

This leads to the last key component of a volunteer program—evaluation. As one says thank you and closes the circle of the year's activities, it is crucial for continuing institutional support and credibility to evaluate the effectiveness of every program. For example, is there a correlation between personal contact—admissions, faculty, alumni, or student representatives—and students' decisions to enroll? Most institutions have developed, and distribute annually, an enrolling-student questionnaire. The institutional research office or a social science faculty member can help the admissions office design studies that will control for institutional reputation, age, size, and location when evaluating the effectiveness of a given program.

If a college or university has recently established an alumni-admissions program, a study should be designed to compare the percentage of accepted applicants who enroll after alumni contact with the percentage of a comparable group of accepted applicants who enroll without having alumni contact. The study should attempt both to get at the overall effectiveness of the program and to measure the effectiveness of specific kinds of contact: telephone, letter, reception, and so forth. Refinements can then be made during the next cycle.

Other interesting questions for follow-up research provide data useful not only to the admissions office but also to the development and alumni affairs offices: Are those students who are recruited by alumni more likely to be retained? Are relatives of alumni more likely to be retained? Do alumni volunteers become more generous contributors?

At the University of Massachusetts at Amherst, for example, a "Second-Generation Program" has been created. Although the mean age of the 105,000 alumni of the institution is only thirty-three years, there is an increasing pool of college-age students who were born to the graduating classes of the 1960s, the time when the university began to realize its greatest growth. There are currently 1,000 second-generation children enrolled, and at an opening-of-school reception under billowy tents, just as New England's Indian summer peaks, proud fathers and mothers reminisce together with their children about what the campus looked like twenty years ago. The University of Massachusetts at Amherst has found that satisfied and enthusiastic alumni are decidedly disposed toward encouraging their children to replicate their own experiences.

Adelphi University prepared a questionnaire that was administered to the entire alumni body. On the basis of responses to three questions, Adelphi identified both those alumni and their families who might be potential applicants to the university. "Alumni were asked for the names and ages of their children and, if the children were of high school age, their expected date of graduation. Alumni were also queried about their plans for further study in both degree programs and continuing education courses. Children of alumni will receive a brochure on university programs accompanied by a personal letter from the Administrative Office. Alumni who express an interest in graduate programs and continuing education courses offered by the university also receive appropriate information" (Habben and Stewart, 1980, p. 7).

Many alumni are not only parents of college-age students but have also joined the ranks of secondary education as teachers and guidance counselors. The University of Redlands has recognized what a valuable asset such strategically placed alumni can be for their alma maters. As Redlands began its program, it ordered a printout of alumni who were secondary school teachers and community college educators. These alumni formed the core of their alumni-admissions program.

Adelphi's Adult Baccalaureate Learning Experience (ABLE) program uses same-age-group alumni to recruit its nontraditional students. ABLE is directed to adult learners whose average age is thirty-nine. "Alumni of the program refer prospective applicants to the Admissions Office, attend open houses, and supplement the professional counseling staff in providing informational interviews for applicants to the program. The alumni's success is attributed, in large measure, to the fact that they are contemporaries of applicants and veterans of the same anxieties about a return to the classroom" (Habben and Stewart, 1980, p. 7). The common theme of all these successful programs is deciding carefully what the institution hopes to accomplish and then setting about identifying the segment of the constituency that can best help realize the stated objective. Cultivating interest randomly and failing to follow up are the two cardinal sins in volunteer programming.

Having described the components of successful volunteer programs, it is perhaps helpful to list some specifics of how to establish a volunteer program. Establishment of an alumni-admissions council will serve as an example.

An Alumni-Admissions Council

Identifying Prospective Members. One likely source of alumni representatives—graduating students—is so obvious it might be overlooked. There is usually a good chance that graduating student representatives might be interested in serving on the Alumni-Admissions Council. Alumni affairs and admissions may report to two different vice-presidents, and the obvious serendipitous benefits of cooperative programming are just beginning to be explored.

The alumni newspaper or magazine is a prime vehicle for advertising for volunteers. A well-written feature by a current member of the alumni-admissions program describing to peers the rewards of participation can be a highly effective means of recruiting others. Just as donors are often best at getting their peers to give, so volunteers often make the best approach in recruiting other volunteers.

It has become something of a truism that younger alumni, who may not be in their peak earning years but who have strong institutional loyalty, are a highly receptive group for volunteer participation. Joining an alumni-admissions council gives them a way of making a tangible and important contribution to their alma maters.

Older alumni, more established in their careers, are walking success stories for the college or university they attended. Many institutions target their more successful alumni to give career information and even summer employment opportunities to currently enrolled students. As alumni-admissions representatives, they are living testimony to the results of majoring in a given discipline for those prospective students considering similar careers. Whatever the source of volunteers, aim for diversity in age, sex, geographical location, and professional background in creating the council or group. Then segment the admissions pool and match volunteers to the tasks at hand.

Training. Most institutions host alumni-admissions representatives on their campuses once a year. Programs range from a day to a weekend workshop, often piggybacking other on-campus events, such as homecoming. Some institutions provide transportation scholarships for those who live farthest away. Many have developed kits, manuals, and training modules that can be mailed to those who are unable to attend and distributed at the on-campus workshop. Ideally, those who cannot return to campus attend workshops at off-campus training sites, perhaps in strategic locations where the institution has its highest concentrations of alumni.

The training manuals for their "ambassadors with portfolio," as Stevenson and McElvania (1983, p. 42) call them, generally cover the following kinds of basic information:

1. Letter(s) from the college or university president and/or director of admissions
2. A statement of purpose or mission for the alumni-admissions council and a description of the role of a representative
3. Description of contacts—programs such as college nights, high school visits and receptions, in which the representative will participate
4. Answers to frequently asked questions about admissions, financial aid, and student life
5. Description of the admissions process—including admissions requirements and key dates in the admissions cycle
6. A statistical profile of the previous year's entering class
7. A list of distinguished faculty, prominent alumni, and distinctive programs
8. Sample letters or scripts for personalized contact with applicants and accepted students
9. What to say to a student denied admission—possibilities for later transfer, for instance
10. A directory of other alumni-admissions council members
11. A set of sample key publications—a fact sheet, viewbook, sample application, and financial aid brochure
12. A who's who in the admissions office—particularly important if staff members are assigned specific geographical areas of the country or state; a list of whom to contact for timely information should be readily at hand

A looseleaf notebook is an economical way to allow for updated information, particularly if it is subject-keyed for easy reference.

The opportunity to accompany an admissions staff member on a typical high school visit or to listen to the kinds of questions most frequently asked at a college fair will familiarize the alumni representative with what to expect. It will also build confidence for the first solo assignment. Trained alumni representatives can then train others as the program matures over time.

Communications. The importance of frequent contact has already been stated. Some specific ways range from regular telephone calls from the alumni-admissions coordinator to monthly newsletters that update the representatives on developments, aberrations, and other items of interest during the admissions cycle. If applications are running 10 percent ahead of last year at the same time or if the academic profile is stronger, it is nice to let the representative share in that evolving feeling of success. Conversely, if applications are down, it gives the representative a shared sense of motivation to help the admissions staff achieve its enrollment target.

Recognition. The most successful alumni-admissions programs recognize the importance of their alumni representatives' contributions by listing their names and addresses in the catalogue and viewbook. They provide a useful means of contact for prospective students as well as honoring the alumni representatives for their service to the institution. Some offices of public information send press releases to the hometown newspapers of alumni representatives, and many institutions provide them with business cards.

Often, an end-of-year dinner presided over by the president and attended by faculty, students, and staff provides a personal thank-you and makes the alumni representatives feel like a part of the college or university community.

Use of Faculty

Now that I have stressed the importance of matching faculty strengths to the recruitment activities best suited to capitalize on those strengths, a few examples are in order.

At the University of Massachusetts at Amherst, a series of regional "Meet U. Mass Nights" are held each year throughout the state to increase yield among accepted students. Faculty and staff travel by bus to a central location, such as a high school situated in an area of the greatest number of feeder schools. Access to major roads to provide for convenient traveling from the greatest distances is one consideration. Availability of a high school gymnasium or cafeteria is another. The goal is to bring the university to prospective students and their families and to provide them with the kinds of information that will hopefully make for informed decisions. The faculty are the prime draws of the evening, although residence hall staff and financial aid advisers are close contenders. As an esprit de corps is established on the bus trip, another significant spinoff is the positive public relations the admissions office earns on campus as organizers of the event. Faculty benefit from learning how those fresh faces arrive on campus each fall, and they feel good about their contribution in attracting able students. In tenure decisions, public service may rank the lowest in the research, teaching, service triumvirate, but tenured and nontenured faculty have a stake in drawing academically qualified, culturally diverse, and interesting young men and women to their campuses.

Another cost-effective way of involving faculty in admissions is to find out where the annual meetings of the various professional associations are being held each year. These organizations often schedule locations as much as five years in advance. Often, faculty are willing to meet with a few students with whom it would otherwise be difficult for admissions staff to have person-to-person contact. By adding on an extra day to their annual meetings, faculty members can often make the contact and serve as effective ambassadors. The admissions office foots the bill for an extra night at the hotel.

Many offices of public affairs have set up speakers' bureaus, and faculty experts can be scheduled for appearances in key locations. Inviting a faculty expert to be a guest speaker at a reception for accepted students and their families is an effective way to demonstrate the quality of teaching available to the student at that college or university.

Whatever the program, faculty should not be expected to become surrogate admissions representatives. Explaining what is expected of them ahead of time will ensure their goodwill and willingness to participate again. A thank-you letter to their department head, the dean of faculty, or the provost is just as important as thanking an alumni representative.

Student Representatives

It has been said that peer solicitation is the most effective form of fund-raising. Student involvement in the recruitment of other students is equally effective if the students involved take their responsibilities seriously. Needless to say, the primary responsibility for enrolled students is to study and graduate. Thus, a well-designed program will take into consideration that their time is at a premium and that many of them are also working paid jobs in addition to pursuing their studies.

One institution employs a cadre of forty student volunteers to cover the work week. Each student is expected to do no more than one hour of service and is available to meet with both scheduled appointments and drop-ins during that time. An office is set aside as a lounge where the student representative can meet with prospective students and their families and answer questions about student life. (Many potential students, naturally, feel more comfortable asking some questions of a student than of an admissions professional.) If no one is scheduled or drops in, the student has a quiet place to study for an hour before the next class.

All forty students are selected after personal interviews by the student representative program coordinator, and a training session is provided for those selected for participation. Training often entails sitting in on an interview with a trained admissions staff member to get a flavor of what students visiting the campus most frequently want to know.

The return visit to one's high school has already been mentioned. A letter from the president thanking the students before they graduate and a reception or dinner for them is one form of recognition. The intensely vocationally oriented students of the 1980s appreciate letters from the admissions director or program coordinator for their placement files.

Some studies of the effect of various constituencies on the admissions decision place admission counselors and guidance counselors somewhat low on the totem pole. Parents and other students place a good deal higher. A well-coordinated and sophisticated approach to recruitment capitalizes on the many constituencies who are opinion leaders and image makers for the institution. Alumni, faculty, and currently enrolled students, well trained and well recognized for their distinctive contributions, go a long way toward ensuring the success of the admissions program. They provide a network of informed, positive references for the students who will be in their college or university's next entering class.

References

Habben, D. E., and Stewart, C. T. "A Model for Alumni Participation in Student Recruitment." Paper presented at the Association for Institutional Research 1980 Forum, April 1980, p. 7.

Stevenson, S. C., and McElvania, S. "Ambassadors with Portfolio." *CASE Currents*, Nov.-Dec. 1983, pp. 42-44.

Part Nine

Special Topics

A. Westley Rowland, Editor

54

G. T. Smith

The Chief Executive and Advancement

Success in institutional advancement depends ultimately on the chief executive and that officer's willingness and capacity for leadership in the advancement effort. In this role, the chief executive must provide both initiative and inspiration and attend to four essential tasks:

1. Articulate clearly and convincingly the mission and values of the institution.
2. Secure the sponsorship of the governing board.
3. Recruit and relate closely to the chief advancement officer.
4. Serve the advancement program actively and enthusiastically, with primary attention to securing major gift support.

Setting the Mission and Clarifying Values

As an institution's primary planner, the chief executive needs to clarify the broad range of priorities and areas toward which public awareness and financial resources are to be focused. This includes final responsibility for setting the mission of the institution; it also requires a hand in helping determine the relative emphasis to be given to specific advancement goals, such as improving ties with the local community, strengthening legislative relations, and determining whether funds shall be sought for current operations, endowment, buildings, and the like. Once these priorities have been set, the chief executive should require that detailed objectives be established for each program element.

In determining the mission, it is important to have wide input and counsel from within the campus community as well as from representatives of important and appropriate constituencies. Even so, it is the chief executive who must sharpen the focus of the mission statement, making certain it is stated clearly, concisely, and convincingly.

All too often, the statement of what an institution is about goes on for several paragraphs—even pages. Extensive wording may have its place, but the attention span of even the most interested observer is limited. One institution was able to limit its mission statement to a single sentence: "To provide liberal and professional learning of distinction within a caring and value centered community." Those fifteen words are reviewed periodically by faculty, administrative, and trustee planners. Even after several years, they still serve as the fundamental guide to institution decision making.

Of no less importance is the chief executive's essential role in clarifying the values that shape and guide the institution. It is increasingly acknowledged in the corporate world that the single most important role of the chief executive is to manage the values of the organization. Unfortunately, in academia, we tend to so democratize the management process that such issues are often consigned to a committee. And the outcome ends up being partly, if not wholly, inadequate.

In contrast, highly successful organizations often have a cultural dimension that reflects the values and principles of their leaders. In the statement of corporate philosophy at IBM, Chairman Thomas J. Watson summarized the company's view when he emphasized what he believed to be IBM's most important value: respect for the individual. Similarly, the college president who insists on only the highest standards of performance, or who believes fervently that most people most of the time are trying to do the right thing, will have a profound effect on the spirit of that institution. The essential element in setting a college or university's values is that the chief executive must care passionately about certain things and then see to it that they are made real.

An institution's mission and values must be not only felt but also continuously stated and restated in public appearances, in private conversation, and in writing. In this, the short-term chief executive is at a clear disadvantage, for it normally takes years before those external to the campus community can fully grasp this dimension of an institution or of its leader. Such awareness is essential if they are to care deeply about the institution and make serious commitments to it.

Board Involvement and Recruitment of Trustees

Inasmuch as a college or university rises or falls on the strength of its governing board, the recruitment of trustees is a chief executive's single most important task. The challenge, then, is to build trustee strength and make it productive. To accomplish this requires attention to the board as a whole and to the members as individuals.

Building a governing board with overall advancement strength requires the chief executive to give attention to three fundamental tasks:

1. Identifying specific advancement needs and purposes to be served
2. Recruiting trustees who have compatible credentials and capabilities
3. Developing necessary leadership within the board

Within the context of the overall mission and vision of the institution, the first step in securing board involvement is to make sure there is consistency between the nature of the institution and those responsible for its future direction, namely, the trustees. For example, an institution with a governing board largely comprising ministers and lay leaders from the church might attempt to establish a School of Business Management with little or no trustee leadership from the business community. Such an effort would almost surely meet with marginal results. Advancement success requires that program goals and objectives be both matched by potential sources of support and achievable by those responsible for securing it.

When recruiting trustees, we must follow the principles that are necessary for staffing any soundly organized enterprise. To assure that the board will have the diversity and strength required, specific criteria and expectations should be determined for every trustee position.

The following criteria should be used when recruiting trustees for successful institutional advancement:

1. *Financial independence.* Ideally, at least two-thirds of the board membership should be financially independent and capable of significant gift support.
2. *Time.* All trustees should expect, and be expected, to be actively involved in the advancement effort. At least one-fourth of the board should be eager, and able, to devote almost unlimited time to advancement affairs.
3. *Influence.* Every trustee should be part of important and complementing spheres of influence within the institution's primary constituencies. Each trustee should have the stature to ask others for important support.

Although it is reasonable to expect all members of the governing board to be engaged in the advancement program, there still must be a leadership core who want, more than anything else, to see the college or university achieve its financial and programmatic objectives. Although busy in their own corporate or professional lives, they must be willing eagerly to devote almost unlimited attention to both the large and small issues within the advancement effort. It falls to the chief executive to encourage and secure this essential involvement and commitment.

Important as the corporate roles of the governing board may be, we must remember that boards of trustees do not give to colleges and universities; individual trustees give to people and ideas and causes in which they believe and about which they care deeply. It is the chief executive's special responsibility always to regard trustees as very special human beings, each with his or her own needs, concerns, hopes, feelings, and aspirations.

Toward this end, it is essential that we avoid ever taking trustees or their relationship with the institution for granted. To reduce this risk, the chief executive should develop a clear plan for continually keeping trustees and their spouses informed, sustaining their interest, and involving them in the life of the institution. If we do this thoughtfully and systematically, investment will surely follow.

Chief Advancement Officer

We are only as good as the people we work with. Get the best, and they make us better too. This is probably nowhere more evident than when attracting a chief advancement officer and staff.

It is appropriate that there are different patterns of advancement staff organization and varying degrees of responsibility delegation among colleges and universities. These clearly must be designed to meet the specific needs of a given institution. What is universal, however, is the need for a chief advancement officer who, as colleague of the chief executive and a senior officer of the institution, is part of the executive management team.

Appointment is by the chief executive, but it is important that key trustees be involved in selecting the chief advancement officer. It is primarily they—not faculty or students or even other administrators—who must respect and be comfortable with the person who will hold this position if the advancement effort is to be effective and productive.

It is imperative that the chief advancement officer be not only permitted but also encouraged to develop close working relationships with members of the governing board as well as other key leaders. Ideally, this officer will enjoy a certain autonomy in these relationships, being free to arrange appointments, plan major strategies, and seek advice and counsel.

The chief executive must be sensitive to the unusual pressures and contrasting expectations that confront advancement officers. Often they are regarded internally as peripheral to the main business of the institution, yet they are expected to represent it with a full sense of belonging. At times, especially when traveling extensively, a staff member may be torn between almost unlimited professional demands and the need for personal time alone or with family. On a more subtle level, one often is expected to relate genuinely and enthusiastically to persons with whom one has little in common, to be an interesting conversationalist when there is little time to read or be stretched intellectually. Among the heaviest demands is the necessity to care deeply for persons and ideas and "things eternal," while at the same time meeting ever-increasing dollar goals and tight time schedules.

As the acknowledged leader of the advancement team, the chief executive has a special responsibility to give encouragement to the chief advancement officer as well as to the entire advancement staff. This can probably be best accomplished by regarding oneself not so much as the ultimate and final authority but as a major resource to the success of even the most junior staff member. If the staff is successful, then the institution—and the chief executive—will be also.

Major Gift Support

The purpose of nearly every advancement program is to help create an understanding of the special mission and values of a particular college or university and then to secure the necessary support in the form of goodwill and dollars to sustain and advance the institution. We have acknowledged that the chief executive must play an important role at certain strategic points in the process. This individual's active involvement is essential in the cultivation and solicitation of major gift support.

There are, no doubt, those occasional situations in which the chief executive can be a passive participant even in the major gift process. But generally it is the chief executive who must set this as the primary priority of the advancement effort and insist that, because 90 percent or more of total gift results can be expected in the form of special and major gifts, a proportionate share of resources (staff, time, and budget) be allocated accordingly. Unfortunately, only a very few institutions have made this level of commitment. But for those that have, the results have been extraordinary.

To cause such a turnaround requires the force of the chief executive's example, followed by consistent redirection of the advancement program. Of the steps required, the most important is the allocation of the chief executive's time. It is probably not an overstatement to suggest that no college or university can afford to have less than 60 percent of the chief executive's time devoted to meaningful development of the institution's major constituencies. (For a public institution, these include legislators and government officials.) Those who spend less are likely to do so at their institution's peril; those who spend more will likely prevail.

A Look to the Future

In nearly every human endeavor, significant achievement seems to rest ultimately on the issue of leadership. And it seems clearly evident that the future of our colleges and universities will also depend, in large part, on the nature and extent of their chief executives' effectiveness as leaders in institutional advancement.

A strong leader must have both the willingness and capacity to develop an overall institutional strategy as well as enforce the discipline needed to assure that plans, policies, organization structures, and procedures are effectively implemented on a day-to-day basis.

The chief executive who would be an effective advancement leader of tomorrow must also require and inspire people to work together in the pursuit of specific, as well as overall, purposes. The manner in which this is accomplished has an important bearing on productivity, and the chief executive must clearly understand that people perform best when they share actively in the decision-making process and when they are stretched by continually expanded responsibility and authority. Participatory management, if focused sharply on predetermined objectives and geared to a plan for success, can lead to extraordinary performance.

In developing a distinctive management and leadership style for institutional advancement, one could do worse than follow the example of Lao-tse, some twenty-five centuries ago: "A leader is best when people barely know he exists. Not so good when people obey and acclaim him. Worse when they despise him. But of a good leader who talks little when his work is done, his aim fulfilled, they will say: 'We did it ourselves' " (1948, p. 114).

The freedom won by our nation's earliest patriots is not something we can or should take for granted. Freedom is not, after all, the work of a century or two. It is the goal and the reward of an unending process of breaking down human limitations and unleashing our God-given capacities within each new generation. The political and religious liberty won by our forebears is but the essential foundation for further moral and spiritual progress. We in higher education and the advancement profession are caught up in a competition for that greater freedom—freedom from enslavement to narrow, selfish pursuits in an affluent society.

The chief executives of our nation's colleges and universities must come to see their roles in institutional advancement in a deeper context than is usually the case. We must see our tasks in the higher dimension of helping those with whom we deal to find new meaning in their lives by caring for causes of significance beyond their own self-interests.

Underlying all our efforts must be a central conception, even commitment, about human nature and the human potential. There are, of course, valid apprehensions, not only about the future of our colleges and universities but even the world's position and the direction we may be going. But it does seem there is room for at least a cautious optimism about man and higher education. For we must believe—and certainly the experience of most of us bears this out—that the good in the world far outruns the bad, that most men and women most of the time want to do the right thing.

To hold this faith and to act upon it is the real public relation. And to do so is to serve even the practical ends of fund-raising. Through the years, men and women have endowed medicine and hospitals because someone dear to them suffered or died as the result of some disease. So will they support whatever has brought a new sense of life in their own time—whatever they have come to cherish and admire.

We must, of course, organize and manage. But more than that, we have the rare and high privilege of helping those with whom we deal to know firsthand what Phillips Brooks had in mind when he wrote many years ago: "No man comes to true greatness who does not see that what God has given him He gives him for mankind" (1950, p. 89).

It seems abundantly clear that the future can be one of unbounded hope and possibility. And with the effective leadership of today's chief executives, that future will not likely escape us.

References

Brooks, P. K. *Thoughts on the Business of Life.* New York: B. C. Forbes, 1950.

Lao-tse. *The Wisdom of Lao-tse.* New York: Random House, 1948.

55

Jane A. Johnson

Advancement Strategies for Two-Year Colleges

꙳ The success of American two-year colleges during past decades has been the ability to sense, serve, and satisfy growing numbers of our diverse population with a comprehensive community-based curriculum.

Community colleges provide low-cost, near-home, open-door education—not just for the brightest and the best but also for the generations of disadvantaged but determined Americans. Most two-year schools respond sensitively to their students' varied experiences or oft-hidden potential, teaching the skills and knowledge that allow individuals to grow, to change, and to adapt. People and their needs come first.

In community colleges, the faculty and curriculum are linked with the real world, and the partnerships created help build resources and recognition for these institutions. Higher priority must be given to this teamwork within and outside our institutions—among faculty, administrators, and trustees; with external publics, business and industry, labor, high schools, and other institutions of higher education.

Contributors to this chapter include: Brice W. Harris, assistant to the chancellor, The Metropolitan Community Colleges; Bud Weidenthal, vice-president for public affairs, Cuyahoga Community College; Bill Freeland, director of communications, LaGuardia Community College; Mary Ellen Myrene, information specialist III, Community Colleges of Spokane; Robert G. Wark, administration assistant, State Board for Community College Education; Carole Rolnick Shlipak executive director, Dallas County Community College District; Richard J. Pokrass, director of public information and public affairs, Burlington County College.

This chapter brings together ideas of experienced two-year advancement professionals on how to cope in a changing environment with fiscal constraints, altered public attitudes, dramatic shifts in demographics, and the technology explosion. It also discusses communication programs and techniques uniquely geared to building public support for the comprehensive community college.

Student Recruitment

Recruiting students for two-year colleges requires a thorough knowledge of the educational products. These products frequently differ in certain ways from the programs and services of traditional four-year institutions. Generally, the market strengths of two-year institutions are low cost, variety of programming, and proximity to students. These strengths attract a greater percentage of older, more nontraditional students.

The best method for developing a good knowledge of the educational product is to develop a marketing and recruitment plan. This plan should be based on solid market research of constituents in the service area, of the college employees, and of current students. It should also include a review of the college mission statement and any long- and short-range planning documents.

Basic marketing theory suggests that an effective marketing effort includes decisions on product, price, location, and promotion. A good marketing/recruitment plan should address all these elements. Effective student recruitment is more than just running an ad in the local newspaper or calling a prospective student on the telephone.

Knowledge about educational programs and services constitutes the product element of a marketing effort. If they are to communicate educational offerings to the community, college marketers must be in constant contact with the academic decision makers. This does not mean that the marketing expert will begin to make the educational decisions for the college, but it does mean that the marketing expert must be involved in the decision-making process. All too often, consideration of informing students about new or altered programs is an afterthought.

Most leaders of public two-year colleges feel they have little flexibility in terms of price of the educational program. But standard tuition rates, the price of textbooks, and other fees often vary for individual courses. Community service courses, customized training for business and industry, and special college services also provide an opportunity for some variety in pricing. There are a number of colleges currently charging several hundred dollars for a single seminar or workshop, and some of those same institutions offer free tuition for other classes.

The location of courses is generally less of a consideration than the other marketing elements, but many colleges have successful off-campus programs. Communicating the advantageous location of a two-year college should be part of the marketing effort.

After decisions on price, place, and program have been made, the promotion strategy must be developed. The proper mix of media—direct mail, television, radio, print, and billboards—depends on the type of product and the service. Elements such as personal selling and public relations are important parts of any promotional effort. Student recruitment in the two-year college is more than traditional admissions activities, but there is still no substitute for face-to-face communication by current students and employees. The other types of media should attempt to get the student to the institution for one-on-one discussion with faculty, counselors, and admissions people who can effectively answer questions.

These activities do not take place in a vacuum. The climate within the institution (the internal image) and within the community (the external image) is extremely important. The internal climate must be positive in order for the college to project a good external image. An effective marketing/recruitment program and the projection of a positive image cannot be accomplished by one or two members of the college staff. It is the responsibility of all college staff to get involved in a team approach to marketing and image building. There must be commitment by all groups constantly to consider their colleagues and encourage them to promote the college's programs and services. Much of the responsibility for leadership in these efforts rests on the shoulders of the admissions and counseling staff, the educational department heads, and the marketing and public relations people.

Effective marketing of the programs and services of two-year colleges is a vital part of their long-term health. The strength of community colleges in the marketplace is their ability to adapt price, product, promotion, and place to the needs of the community. This requires aggressive professionals who understand that marketing can be the method to help achieve quality educational programming that is responsive to community needs.

Institutional Relations

Serving the institutional relations needs of a community college is something like running for political office. In one way or another, the college must reach out and touch its constituents almost every day of the week, every week of the year. And that constituency includes a broad segment of the community, from the pre-teen attending a "college for kids" program to the septuagenarians flocking to popular senior citizen courses. The enormous challenge of institutional relations is successfully serving this wide-ranging audience and influencing community decision makers.

It is critical to effective marketing efforts to understand the nature of the potential market as well as the changing conditions of the community. Good solid research becomes the almost daily tool of the institutional relations specialist. Such research includes measuring the job market, testing public attitude toward community college education, and gauging population shifts.

The college must link itself closely with its local political and civic leadership, as well as with state and national political power structures. Although funding sources differ from state to state, it is clear that community colleges, more than any other segment of higher education, draw on a broad variety of public sources for their operating and capital support.

Community college external relations officers must serve in a liaison capacity between the college and the community and be sensitive to public opinion. They should be involved in the chamber of commerce, public and private social agencies, local school districts, and business and professional groups.

Here are other successful institutional relations ideas:

A speakers bureau composed of the liveliest, most exciting members of your faculty and staff helps reflect quality and excellence in the community.

The college can be represented as often as possible where large numbers of people gather, such as county fairs, shopping malls, high school college nights, and major entertainment events. In some cases, colleges have effectively become partners in theatrical and musical productions that bring community leadership to the campus.

The college should take advantage of major milestones, such as anniversaries or groundbreakings. They attract local and state civic and political leaders and a large segment of the population that would not ordinarily visit a college campus.

Advisory committees for technical and career-oriented degree programs can effectively stimulate community involvement. This device not only involves business and industry in college programming but also serves as a valuable student recruitment tool. Each year, many colleges bring the advisory groups together with campus leadership for a breakfast, luncheon, or dinner at which a major speaker is featured. Such an event provides a setting for making awards to community leaders for services to the college.

Partnerships with business and industry can be created through customized training programs. It is a good idea to set up a public relations citizens committee composed of representatives of the leading businesses in the area.

Of greatest significance is the ability of a community college to link the college to the economic and civic well-being of the community. A combination of a good institutional relations program with the support of the college president can make this possible. Building the team with support from the top can assure success.

Publications

The unique challenge of a community college publications program is the need to address diverse audiences. We address the same groups as any four-year college—educated faculty, successful alumni, and influential community leaders. Yet our most important constituencies are not found within this comfortable circle. Instead, they are drawn from groups for whom college study and even basic literacy are still unfamiliar concepts. We are dealing here with higher education's newest constituencies. The challenge they pose for a publications program has never existed before.

To meet this challenge, communications professionals frequently begin by adapting the methods of the large four-year schools—approaches that are themselves an outgrowth of the corporate identity programs that began to develop during the 1950s. Under these programs, an effort is made to give everything, from business cards to annual reports, a unified family resemblance, which is often elaborately spelled out in a graphic design stylebook.

What a publications designer at a community college finds, however, is that the corporate/university model is often not effective for the two-year college because the audiences a community college must address are so extraordinarily diverse. The solution for these colleges is to adopt an alternative model, one that views audiences as discrete groups requiring individually designed publication packages created to accommodate differing reading levels, design preferences, and cultural values. Design consistency is still important, but only among those publications going to a particular group.

Only in this way is it possible to create traditional-style publications suitable for faculty and alumni, for example, without excluding the more flamboyant formats that appeal to high school students with poor reading skills or the entirely different formats suitable for older adults, who might be intimidated by materials prepared for younger audiences. The result is an admittedly eclectic program, one that can be as varied as the people it must serve.

The chief benefit for a program director is the variety of options that become available as the demands of the audience, not the stylebook, begin to dictate the solutions. Building this kind of program requires a somewhat altered process from that often followed at senior institutions. The views of the people directly involved in the use of the publications begin to take on more significance. More creative, individual solutions can be considered—solutions that meet more specific needs more effectively. This approach, however, has its complications. More aggressively designed admissions publications, for example, can prove unsettling to faculty who prefer the more elegant look of an internal newsletter that has been prepared for them.

The more we recognize the distinctive challenge of a community college publications program, the more we will be required to seek experimental solutions if we are to successfully address these new audiences. Yet it is just this requirement that can make two-year college publications the most exciting assignment in higher education.

Periodicals

A good writer turned loose at a community college will never lack for interesting stories, both from campus and most particularly from the community, where two-year institutions not only mirror the real world but often help to shape it.

The first requisite, of course, is finding a way to finance the magazine. Magazines are relatively expensive to produce. And unless the college has sufficient resources to create a good one—with strong writing, photography, and graphic design—it probably should not attempt a magazine at all.

By the same token, it could be argued that one well-produced magazine is worth a fistful of other printed pieces that may sap the budget without ever communicating the story of the institution in a way that will get people's attention and ultimately persuade them to act on the college's behalf. A single magazine not only can do that but also can reach all of the college's constituencies—from potential students to foundation donors, community volunteers, and supporters in industry. Properly executed and properly used, a magazine could be the most cost-effective tool in a community college's publications program.

The strength of a magazine, especially for two-year institutions, lies in its versatility. With careful planning, the same magazine can be used for fund-raising as well as student recruitment. It can also be a report to the community, a calling card of sorts with which to build knowledge about the institution among several different constituencies on a regular basis. Internally, it can contribute to a sense of pride among students and staff.

One of the most obvious uses of a college magazine is in the area of fund-raising and alumni development. This is especially true at community colleges where emerging development programs are just beginning to tap the enormous private resources long courted by four-year universities. For all institutions, the scenario is usually the same. When the college asks people to do something for it, they are likely to wonder what the institution has done for them. A well-balanced magazine not only can help answer that question but also can deliver much more in the way of good public relations.

An effective tool for soliciting private support, it can also document the impact of gifts to your institution and recognize the work of volunteers.

This rippling effect is even more pronounced in the area of alumni relations. One interesting story about a successful graduate will send a positive message not only to other alumni but also to potential students, faculty, employers in industry, and others involved with the institution. In each case, the message is slightly different, but the theme is the same: We are part of a winning team.

To be effective, a college magazine must successfully compete with other magazines and other media for the reader's attention. Ideally, it should be printed on good magazine stock, with strong photos, compelling graphic design, and highly readable articles. The editor can compromise on some of these things, but remember that the public has come to expect a high level of quality in magazines. If the college cannot deliver a high-quality magazine, it should attempt something more modest—a tabloid or newsletter, for example—that it can do well. Quality, not format, is what counts.

How the college markets its periodical can have a direct bearing on how well it will serve the institution. Send it to alumni before a phonathon. Distribute it to high school students, legislators, industry leaders, private donors, and volunteers. Place it in doctors' offices, and make it available to community groups on request. The truth is that nearly everybody has a need to know about the community college.

The same thing that makes these colleges interesting to write about—their diversity and involvement in the daily life of the community—also increases the need to communicate their full story. With a quality magazine, and even with an outstanding tabloid or newsletter, the odds are greatly improved.

Government Relations

In some states, state legislatures provide as much as four-fifths of the financial support of public community colleges. Some community colleges receive substantial financial support through local government. The federal government provides funds for student financial aid, vocational education, and other purposes. Thus the function of communicating with the various levels of government ranges from important in some states to critical in others, such as Washington, in which nearly all community college financial support comes from the state.

In the legislative area, community colleges have some advantages over four-year institutions. In many states, community colleges exist in every major population center and serve more citizens than the four-year institutions. The willingness of community colleges to respond to local needs is a plus. In states in which they must go to the voters for tax support, community colleges can demonstrate public acceptance in a way legislators respect. It is the function of the government relations program to convert these advantages into legislative clout.

Local support for one community college may not have much impact in the state capital. But when all community colleges present a united front, they become a force with which to be reckoned. A two-level effort is needed to achieve this. First, statewide coordination is essential. It can be performed by the state community college agency, if there is one. Or it can be done by a state association of trustees and/or administrators. Where there is a state agency and a strong state association, care must be taken to avoid conflict. A favorite legislative ploy is "Don't look to us for help until you have your own house in order."

State-level functions include (1) contacts with administrative and legislative leaders and their staffs, (2) analysis of bills, (3) arranging for pertinent testimony at appropriate hearings, (4) arranging for legislators to be contacted by their local community college people when necessary, (5) providing timely and accurate data in response to legislative requests, and (6) keeping the colleges informed about what is going on. Modern legislatures rely on professional staff work and data, and community college representatives must be prepared to deal with these realities.

The essential second level of communication is the local level. Each community college should carry on a well-organized program of legislative communication. Some legislators may view community colleges in terms of a system, but most base their decisions on how they will affect their local community college.

Local legislative contact programs may be coordinated by steering committees of trustees, administrators, faculty, and students. Trustees play a key role because, whether elected or appointed, they are viewed by legislators as having greater credibility than either students or persons hired by the institution.

At least once before every legislative session, local legislators should be invited to the campus—preferably one at a time. They should be given the opportunity to speak with groups of students and faculty. They should be briefed by the trustees and administrators. Briefings should be accurate, concise, and in English (legislators hate "educationese"). Presentations should stress the services the college provides to citizens. Appeals for more money should be kept to a minimum.

Nobody has better access to legislators than those who contribute to their campaigns, with money or with time—time for doorbelling, telephoning, or licking stamps. Most community college staffs have enough size and diversity to ensure that people can be found to work on the campaigns of every local candidate.

The government relations program needs the support of the public information program with appropriate news stories, editorials, and community leader contacts on important issues. If legislators perceive that community colleges have broad public support, they are likely to support reasonable community college legislative objectives. And when they do, they should always be thanked—in public if possible.

The government relations program must be continuous and it must have the strong commitment of the board and administration of each community college. Community colleges have too much at stake with government—national, state, and local—for it to be any other way.

Educational Fund-Raising

Those in charge of building private sector support for the two-year college should be thoroughly familiar with the major areas of fund-raising: special events, direct mail, foundations and corporations, annual giving, and capital campaigns. Evaluation and planning should follow—determining which areas will work best in the service areas, and with the constituencies, of your college. Allocation of staff and funds will then be directed to the specific areas that are most promising. As the college succeeds in these areas, it can move on to explore others, such as phonathons, gift clubs, and other techniques used by four-year institutions.

Separate but related foundations are particularly important to the success of the fund-raising strategies selected. The establishment of an institutionally related foundation permits the assembling of influential business and civic leaders as members of the foundation's board of directors. These leaders will then develop an official association and commitment to the two-year college. With proper cultivation, this should lead to increased financial support from those already contributing and to new financial commitment from those who were not previous donors. Because two-year colleges usually do not have prominent chief executive officers as graduates, membership on the foundation board of directors is an ideal means for gaining their involvement. The foundation, and in turn the college, also gains credibility as such prominent individuals assume a leadership role in the institution.

Some subjects of particular relevance to fund-raising strategies for the two-year college are worth discussing here.

Corporations as Donors. Corporations are often a major source of contributions. Certainly, corporations are in a position to appreciate the comprehensive career training offered by two-year institutions. The contributions committees of corporations regularly evaluate what organizations most benefit the community and its own employees—and allocate contributions accordingly. Particularly well received are requests for funds for programs that are related to a corporation's business operations. Corporations also are sometimes responsive to requests for in-kind contributions of equipment, staff assistance, or services.

Special Events. From auctions to walkathons, there are various events that can raise both friends and funds for the two-year institution. Essential to the selection of a special event is the analysis as to how much money it will cost and how much staff and volunteer time it will require. Then a realistic estimate must be made as to how much money will likely be raised. Should the evaluation indicate that the event will be both effective to produce and profitable for the institution, official planning can begin. Detailed plans and checklists are mandatory to produce a well-executed special event.

Direct Mail. For those colleges located in large population centers, direct mail is an effective vehicle for uncovering contributors and friends not previously known. The institution can acquire new donors by renting mailing lists of known contributors to other nonprofit organizations. These large mailings communicate the college story to a group that has already displayed civic concern. Occasionally, marvelous surprises result, as when one foundation received a $5,000 check from such a direct-mail piece.

Overcoming Objections. In sales, one is prepared to overcome objections regarding the product. Fund-raisers for the publicly funded two-year college must be prepared repeatedly to overcome objections against these institutions receiving tax support and requesting private dollars. This requires knowledge of the sources of revenue for the college and an effective explanation as to why the private dollars are needed. Certainly four-year colleges and universities that are publicly funded receive generous gifts from the private sector. But there are often influential graduates advocating these gifts. The two-year college fund-raiser must assemble compelling information that convinces the prospect of the excellent service the college is providing while pointing out important needs that are not being met with the public funds.

Although two-year institutions are unique in mission and structure, the fundamental skills of sound management principles and excellent communication with donors and prospects should result in significant and continuing private sector support.

Alumni Administration

Alumni associations have long been an integral part of life at four-year colleges and universities, where they have provided numerous services for graduates, played an important role in constituent relations, and served a vital function in fund-raising and development. With the exception of some private junior colleges that have been around for many years and a handful of community colleges, most two-year colleges have only begun to consider establishing a formal alumni association within the past several years.

A common error in setting up new alumni organizations occurs when well-meaning administrators, eyeing the success of other colleges' alumni development efforts, ask potential members for financial contributions in their first contacts—usually without offering the alumni anything of value in return.

Alumni should not be viewed as an instant money tree but rather should be cultivated and treated with care. A new alumni organization at the typical two-year college can establish its credibility through meaningful services and programs that can be offered without significant upfront costs. Job placement services, discounts to campus cultural activities, library privileges, and an alumni newsletter are just a few of the simple ways to provide something of value to graduates. Through the campus placement office, the alumni organization might cosponsor workshops on job search strategies, résumé writing, and interview techniques and skills that can be of immense value to two-year college graduates. The important thing is to offer such services before asking for financial contributions. Give alumni a reason to want to be members of the alumni association.

The backbone of any nonprofit organization, including alumni associations, is a well-organized program of voluntarism. Long-established alumni organizations at four-year colleges and universities usually have comprehensive procedures for recruiting, screening, and training their volunteers, especially those who will fill key leadership roles. The problems so many volunteer organizations face when their members do not perform their duties as expected can be significantly alleviated by paying more attention to recruiting the right people and training them properly. Too often, a new alumni organization or program is established with volunteers recommended by faculty, fellow administrators, or other alumni for volunteers. If these volunteers are not carefully screened, trained, and later motivated properly, it may be difficult to meet organizational goals.

There are a few commonsense steps to follow when establishing a new alumni organization at the two-year college, revamping an existing association, or developing a new alumni program or service. First, try to learn as much as possible about your alumni. What types of degrees did they earn? What is their average age? Do most of them still live in the college's general area? Do any of them have specialized skills that could be of benefit to the association? Second, what can your organization realistically do to meet the needs and desires of your alumni? Consider restraints due to limited financial and human resources. Third, what are other colleges doing? It is rare to find an alumni professional who will not share ideas with a colleague from another institution. Last, but not least, what should be the organizational structure for the association? Should the organization be incorporated? Should it be independent from the college and have its own governing body? If so, how many people should be in the governing body, and in what capacity should they serve?

Establishing and maintaining an alumni association at the two-year college, especially when many two-year college administrators wear multiple hats, is no easy task. It is a task well worth pursuing, however, because most two-year college graduates, especially those who have attended community colleges, have strong allegiance to the two-year school. They are willing to extend themselves to help the college, which they view as having given them an educational opportunity that otherwise might not have been available. Because of this loyalty, it is also helpful for the alumni association and public information office at the two-year college to have a close working relationship. The alumni organization can provide significant background for human interest stories about successful alumni, and the public information staff will have increased access to alumni who might be willing to participate in testimonials on behalf of the college.

There are some additional ways to utilize the services of two-year college alumni without asking them to dip into their pocketbooks. For example, an alumnus with the appropriate background might be asked to serve on an advisory committee for an academic or vocational program or special event. This person would not only be helping alma mater but also might experience increased prestige in the workplace for being directly involved in an advisory capacity for a college. Alumni also could be utilized as the initial contacts within the companies in efforts to obtain internships or jobs for other students or alumni. Similarly, under the right circumstances, the employers could be tapped for donations of money or equipment for academic programs related to the companies' fields of interest. Such methods are used frequently by four-year college fund-raisers.

Not to be overlooked is the potential impact of the political muscle two-year college graduates can muster. Because typical community colleges serve a broad cross-section of society (young and old, male and female, and diverse ethnic groups), a coordinated lobbying effort by the alumni of a two-year college could be a major influence on a particular issue—provided the issue is related to higher education in general or, even more significant, if it involves alumni of more than one college. Unlike most four-year colleges, two-year colleges do not typically compete with each other for students and therefore are more likely to have some common ground for mutual lobbying.

It should be noted that, although two- and four-year colleges are often quite different, there are many similarities in alumni programming at both types of schools. An idea that may work for a university alumni group could possibly work even better in a scaled-down way at a two-year college. There should be ongoing communication among alumni officers from all sizes and types of schools so that graduates can be served with innovative and meaningful programs and services.

56

Edes P. Gilbert

Fostering Support
for Independent Schools

Independent education is committed to and concerned with excellence of education for children and young people, preparing them for responsible participation in the adult world. To achieve this end, independent schools strive, as do public schools, to teach, guide, and support not only academics but also a wide range of personal and social values that take as many forms as there are schools. The independent sector and the public sector both aspire to educate the children of this country to the best of their abilities. Good public education enhances the private schools, as good independent schools enhance the public ones. Although the broad goals are the same, the manner of arriving at the desired end varies, which is appropriate for a country that believes in individual freedom. Whereas public schools wrestle with school boards and public funding through taxes, private schools wrestle with much-needed fund-raising that will provide the resources necessary to attract first-rate students and teachers and maintain their educational programs.

Philosophically, the independent school stands for one of our nation's most precious commitments—the right to choose. In this country where universal education is a value we hold dear, we have developed a wide variety of educational opportunities for our children and young people. There is no one school or system that is required of all—the requirement is to attend school until age sixteen. The choice of school is up to each family. The vast majority of the population attends public school. About 2 percent select non-church-related private schools, and about 9 percent choose church-related private schools. Despite a common perception that independent schools are in competition with the public sector, it is clear from the numbers that they are not. However, these schools have had a profound influence on education, both public and private. Parents choose to send their children to independent schools because they share common values or expectations with the institution. If a family believes in a strong social service component as a part of education, they will select a school that provides that opportunity. If they believe that their child is a strong classics student, they may select a school that fills that academic need. If they believe in a comprehensive college preparatory curriculum, they will select a college preparatory school. The following are some frequently cited examples of shared values: "We like the structure of the school, the small classes, and the faculty-student ratio." "My children receive individual attention, which they need; everyone knows everyone else and we like that for our children." "I want my child taught spiritual values and this school does that." It is for all these reasons, and more, that people support independent education.

Another perspective on the need for support is that many independent schools offer truly heterogeneous communities in contrast to the public system, which is often homogeneous. Families choose private schools so their children can meet a wider variety of people than they would in the public schools. This is particularly true in the suburbs and the inner city, where schools tend to stratify along fairly predictable lines. Independent schools can broaden their bases by actively recruiting diverse student bodies because of a basic precept that anyone, regardless of race, color, religion, or national or ethnic origin, is welcome. The National Association of Independent Schools (NAIS) maintains the precise and strict position that access to independent schools should be available to all. This means that any school that intends to be a member of NAIS, and an increasing number do, must support and advocate this position. In fact, the independent sector is one aspect of society that has been able to monitor itself and establish—in a group of more than 900 schools across this country, in Europe, and in Asia—a base of diversity within its separate institutions. There seems little doubt that, in the years ahead, the level of global interaction is going to continue to increase as it has over the past two decades. Independent schools offer the opportunity for young people and faculty from varied backgrounds to live and learn together in common purpose. This principle demonstrates an energetic leadership that represents the best instincts of our country and national heritage and is worthy of support.

On a related, but different, subject, the education of boys and girls, young men and women, in coed and single-sex situations is one the independent sector can address. This is a topic fraught with questions and concerns because there are some strong feelings about single-sex schools being anachronistic and, in the eyes of some, unconstitutional. Looking at the issue from the point of view of what is in the students' best interest, should this not be another choice that the independent sector offers? If there are no more children with families who choose single-sex schools, then those institutions will go out of existence. Until such an unlikely event occurs, single-sex schools are an opportunity for learning in a particular environment, as is a church-related private school or a coeducational school.

Given the real need for, and appreciation of, independent schools at the secondary and elementary levels, why has it been so difficult for them to raise the necessary money to ensure security in the future, pay teachers competitively, and release themselves from the tuition-faculty compensation treadmill? On this treadmill, tuitions can go up only a certain amount, depending on the rate of inflation and the constituencies' ability to pay. This, in turn, keeps teachers in bondage so far as realistic salary levels are concerned. Most independent schools spend from 70 to 80 percent of their income on faculty compensation, leaving a modest amount for all other expenses. Such an allocation of funds is both appropriate and understandable, but it also leaves very little room for flexibility, and there is the constant threat of raising tuition to the point where only the affluent and the poor (subsidized by scholarships) will be able to attend. The middle class, the largest group from which qualified candidates come, would be excluded.

The only way to release the schools from this potentially destructive cycle is to build endowments. This is why there has been such an increase over the past decade in fund-raising activities in schools and in the money spent on development. The schools are joining the race for dollars in which colleges and universities have been engaged for years. Over the years, patterns of support have shown that larger gifts have gone first to colleges and then to secondary schools, single-sex schools, and elementary schools, in that order.

The case for independent school advancement is both similar to and different from that for colleges and universities. On the one hand, the need may seem smaller because, in most cases, schools are not attempting to maintain the breadth of facilities or to serve as many students. On the other hand, students could not qualify for our leading private institutions of higher learning without the fine preparation provided in elementary and secondary schools. For those schools to continue this quality of preparation, there must be money (mainly for teachers but also for updating programs) for growth in such fields as women's athletics and for the security to plan for the future. It seems clear to those of us who are committed to elementary and secondary education that the beginnings for students can, in large measure, dictate the outcomes.

The commitment to diversity in faculty and students is one of the most compelling reasons for schools to raise money. Tuitions cannot support the rising deficits in schools that have attempted to address issues of financial aid and equitable faculty compensation. Cultivation of the middle class, who are often reluctant to apply for financial aid, means that money must be available for low-interest loans as well as for outright grants. To this argument the uninformed will respond, "Charge what it costs—that's the economic truth of a capitalistic society." The other truths of our society are that, in addition to economic precepts, we have profound beliefs in equal opportunity and self-improvement. If a student is qualified for a school and the family is prepared to make a commitment that reflects the most they can pay, do we not have an obligation to offer opportunities insofar as our resources permit? And is it not in the best interests of the institutions to enroll the most able students? Without this supplemental resource of financial aid, the applicant pool will shrink, and the selectivity, which is one of the critical aspects of a private school, will be diminished.

Much is being written about the teaching profession at all levels. Secondary and elementary teachers continue to be at the low end of the pay scale for professionals. The traditional pool of candidates for teachers at these levels was that of the second-income woman for whom the vacation schedule meshed with her children's and the single woman for whom the teaching profession offered a respectable way to earn a livelihood, however modest. These people have many opportunities now, and their options will increase in the future.

Women and men can earn much more money by entering other professions, and money is a crucial issue, although not the only one for teachers. The quality of life within a school, the opportunities for professional growth, and the respect in which the person is held matter a great deal in making career decisions. However, all of these features of teaching require financial support. It costs money to create a professional environment that will attract the people who have not only the abilities but also the interest in teaching our students and growing themselves.

The case for advancement in independent schools rests on the statement of mission for independent education. Before the case can be presented, however, there has to be a general definition of *independent school*. Those schools that are considered independent make up a loose collection of institutions that do not receive either public funding or financial support from a religious group of any denomination. Under this definition, church-related private schools, schools born of the fundamentalist Protestant movement, and segregation academies do not fit.

There are as many different kinds of schools in the independent community as there are schools. However, they do share some common values and, in some cases, similar characteristics. They also share with the public sector the principle that the children engaged in education in any school, public or private, should receive through the educational process the best possible opportunity to become responsible, adult citizens, participating fully in the life of this country. Within the independent sector, there is shared commitment to individuals, students, and faculty who learn and teach in environments that stress the worth of each person in relatively small classroom settings. According to NAIS statistics, the average student-teacher ratio in 1983 was 9.7:1. At all grade levels, the schools tend to be small; in 1983, the average enrollment was 389.

Another common commitment is to the quality of life for students and teachers. High academic standards, with emphasis on values, ethics, or morality and based on the complexities of life rather than simplistic answers, prevail. To this end, most schools provide a range of activities, including physical education and athletics, outside the classroom. These schools offer as varied a program as possible so that students not only are introduced to many areas where they may find new interests but also have the reward of succeeding in various areas of school life.

A third area of common concern and effort is that of social responsibility. Because of the commitment to diversity and personal freedom of choice, these schools teach that the most effective learning takes place in an environment where individual differences are accepted. Different perspectives bring insight, and the broad base of open inquiry leads to the ability to think with purpose and creativity. Through the years, independent schools have been proud of the roster of distinguished graduates who have contributed to our country's health and growth in areas such as politics, medicine, law, and the arts. In addition, a number of schools require some form of public service as a routine part of the high school curriculum, an attitude that may permeate the elementary and middle grades as well. For independent schools, concern for, and participation in, the public sectors of society is a basic tenet of their philosophies.

None of these characteristics are revolutionary. In fact, these are among the characteristics of effective education and, as such, are the special province of no school but rather are ideals to which we can all aspire. Independent schools have stated them in as many ways as there are school catalogues and have, as a group, maintained this perspective through the trends and fads that have affected our educational system as a whole. For this reason, they are an important force in American education. Institutionally, these schools have the capacity to remain firm in their stated goals while having great capacity for change as they choose. In a world of ever-growing bureaucracy, the independent school remains a corner of freedom of choice and, as such, deserves our support.

If one believes in a pluralistic society, freedom of choice, and excellence maintained through individualization and cooperation, then one supports the premises for independent education at all levels. Although the elementary and secondary levels have not in the past been as compelling in their statements of need, that posture is changing. Schools will become even more aggressive in the years ahead. The simple arithmetic of paying salaries and maintaining plants demands continual financial support in order that tuitions can remain reasonable. Many schools are reviewing faculty work load and student-faculty ratios with an eye toward cutting numbers gradually and offering larger compensation packages to fewer teachers. In addition, schools are "running lean" in administration wherever possible—again, conserving resources and paying as large salaries as possible to fewer people. Fund-raising is one side of the coin, with effective management the other. Donors want to know that schools manage their funds well, that there are confident, comprehensive policies for management of capital as well as operating funds.

One of the realities of the 1980s is that there are countless institutions, causes, and efforts worthy of support. Independent schools will have to try harder to get their fair share. They will have to become increasingly sophisticated about their management and their public relations. They will have to spend more money on development and talk more openly about fund-raising. Many of the same people who are solicited for colleges, symphonies, museums, and hospitals are those who support our schools. They must be educated to the central role that independent elementary and secondary schools play in the lives of their children and of the nation in general. When asked to give, they must be asked in appropriate ways by people who know the business of raising money. As in all specialties, there are ways to do this effectively. Skilled, well-trained, well-compensated development officers who play a central role in the life of the schools for which they raise funds are the key to future success. School heads, although essential to fund-raising, cannot be both educational leaders and development directors without diminishing their effectiveness in either or both areas. Patterns of giving have begun to change within the past several years as shown by the rising levels of fund-raising success in a number of independent schools around the nation. It is through further change that success in development for independent schools will become the norm, as it has for institutions of higher learning.

57

Wesley K. Willmer

Advancing Small and Developing Institutions

෯ Magazine and newspaper articles about small colleges often report their plight and suggest they are on the verge of closing, but little attention is given to the adaptability of these smaller institutions. Small, and often developing, colleges are more fragile and vulnerable to change (particularly to shifts in public policy) than are large institutions, but such institutions tend to be more responsive, creative, and resilient (Peck, 1984a). Within this dichotomy lies the challenge facing advancement officers at these institutions.

The small-college advancement officer's focus is cultivating friends, raising adequate funds, and attracting quality freshmen. To accomplish these difficult tasks takes a special personal commitment to the values and mission of the institution. The advancement officer at these institutions faces a never-ending challenge that, although offering little public recognition, can be rich with personal satisfaction.

Drawing from current research, the professional literature, and this author's personal experience, this short analysis provides a set of guidelines that, when applied to institutions of 2,500 full-time equivalent students or fewer, should assist in the quest to advance these colleges.

Building on Strengths

Leaders of the small or developing institution should not apologize for its size or for the fact that the college may be relatively young. Rather, they should capitalize on size as one of the college's strengths and build on that opportunity. This principle holds true in pursuing friends, funds, and freshmen. To succeed, leaders of the small college need a strong commitment to its mission, an understanding of its environment, and a commitment to manage through people.

Clarity of Institutional Mission. This is a fundamental starting point for small-college advancement. As Hobbs has said, "Unless the institution's advancement officer is able to convey the college's vision of its purpose and character to others, in terms they can understand, advancement is an empty exercise, for there is really nothing to advance" (Willmer, 1980, p. 21). The essence of an institution's mission is its values—that is, the priorities, commitments, and major themes in the college's purpose. Establishing a clear idea of the institution's mission must be a priority for, as Panas (1984) observes, the highest concern of major donors is that they like the mission of an institution. Peck (1984a) suggests that a primary strength of small and developing institutions is their unique mission. A mandate for their success is that this mission be clearly defined and appropriately implemented.

Understanding the Environment. Many forces external to a small college can have a radical impact on its future. These forces include its demographic, economic, political, organizational, technological, and social environments. Jonsen (1984) emphasizes that these forces may play a more important role in institutional fate in the future than they have in the recent past. In the 1980s and beyond, advancement administrators at small and developing colleges will be involved in strategic planning that may necessitate major adjustments in institutional courses to assure a viable institution in the twenty-first century.

It is the responsibility of the advancement officer to be keenly aware of these factors and to incorporate them into the total advancement plan. The results of this understanding are strategic management decisions for the small college based on data collected from this external environment. An analysis by Chaffee (1984) shows that, among the small colleges studied, the adaptive model of strategic management, based on the need for the college to be

responsive to the individuals and groups who supply its most
critical resources, fosters the best turnaround in a declining market.

Management Through People. An institution embodies a set
of values. These values are held and disseminated by the people who
make up their institutions. The values and commitment of these
people are critical to the future of these institutions; thus the
successful small or developing college is the one where top leaders
realize this influence. To be most successful, the top administrators
should emphasize people rather than formal structures (Peck,
1984b). Working through people allows the college to build on
strengths, achieve flexibility, and emphasize its uniqueness. This
management approach will generally enhance the institutional
advancement efforts of small colleges.

Budget Allocations

"It takes money to raise money" is a saying that is trite but
true. Similarly, in advancement it takes people and program
resources to cultivate friends, raise money, and attract freshmen.
Two measures of institutional commitment are the percentage of
the institution's budget allocated to advancement and the allocation
of dollars by advancement function.

Institutional Budget Allocation. This author's 1985 study of
the 275 member institutions of the Council for Independent
Colleges, which is composed of small and developing colleges
across the United States, shows that the mean percent of educational
and general expenditures allocated to advancement for the total
sample was 7.9 percent, with a range in the means from 4.7 to 13.4
percent (Willmer, 1985, and Table 57-1). This reflects a 1.4 percent
increase in total educational and general expenditures when
compared with the mean percent shown by this author's 1977 study
of the same group (Willmer, 1980).

As you can see from Table 57-1, the smaller the institution,
the larger the percentage of the institution's budget that is used for
advancement. Obviously, this means that these funds used for
advancement are not available for use elsewhere in the institution.
A comparison of these figures with those of the previous study

Table 57-1. Percentage of Educational and General Expenditures
Allocated to Advancement.

Enrollment	Mean Percentage	Range	
		Low	High
Up to 500	13.4	3.7	18.5
501–750	10.3	2.9	22.0
751–1,000	8.9	1.0	18.0
1,001–1,250	6.3	2.0	12.9
1,251–1,500	6.2	2.7	12.6
1,501–2,000	6.0	2.2	10.2
2,001–2,500	4.7	1.7	6.9

Source: Willmer, 1985.

(Willmer, 1980) shows that all the groups of institutions have increased this percentage slightly (from .2 percent for the larger institutions to 4.8 percent for the smaller), reflecting a higher percentage priority for advancement set by the institutions. The smaller the institution, the greater the percentage of resource commitment needed, yet the results (gift dollars) are generally proportionately less. This is part of the small-college dilemma that Astin and Lee (1972) identified.

Advancement Expenditures by Function. In addition to the comparisons made of total advancement expenditures as a percentage of institutional educational and general expenditures, it is helpful to compare the mean expenditures according to the functional advancement areas: fund-raising, public relations, admissions, and alumni affairs.

Table 57-2 shows that the mean expenditures for fund-raising activities range from $114,186 to $196,865. The mean expenditures for public relations are between $49,445 and $145,233. The alumni affairs range is $28,907 to $61,615, and the mean expenditures for admissions activities (including travel, media, and promotional expenses) are between $128,795 and $295,761. Keep in mind that these figures are means and within each enrollment size grouping the range is often diverse.

Table 57-2. Mean Expenditures for Institutional Advancement Functions.

Enrollment	Fund-Raising	Public Relations	Admissions	Alumni Affairs
Up to 500	$114,186	$ 49,445	$128,795	$28,907
501–750	129,687	67,422	202,191	38,305
751–1,000	139,839	74,954	244,650	48,868
1,001–1,250	137,611	89,598	247,841	49,732
1,251–1,500	179,891	102,737	269,904	52,679
1,501–2,000	188,336	110,837	295,761	56,629
2,001 +	196,865	145,233	261,617	61,615

Source: Willmer, 1985.

As would be expected, the larger institutions spend more money for advancement activities, but the percentage of the total institutional educational and general advancement expenditures that this represents is less than for the smaller institutions.

Staffing Needs

Adequate quality and quantity of advancement professionals are essential to small and developing institutions. In addition to the necessary skills and experience appropriate for advancement officers (Gonser Gerber Tinker Stuhr, 1984), sufficient numbers of people are necessary to carry out the required tasks.

Professional Staff. Research shows that the mean professional staff for advancement officers at small colleges ranges from six to thirteen full-time equivalent (FTE) professionals (Willmer, 1985). The range is diverse—from one to twenty FTE professional staff members. When the mean professional advancement staff is broken down into the four functional areas of alumni, public relations, fund-raising, and admissions (Table 57-3), the staffing patterns indicate that the mean range of alumni staffing is 1 to 1.4 FTE, fund-raising ranges from 2.3 to 4 FTE, public relations from 0.9 to 2.2 FTE, and admissions from 3.0 to 6.3 FTE.

Table 57-3. Number of Full-Time Equivalent (FTE) Institutional
Advancement Professionals.

	Range of Total Mean		Breakdown of Mean by Function			
Enrollment	Low	High	Alumni	Fund-Raising	Public Relations	Admissions
Up to 500	1	12	1.0	2.3	0.9	3.0
501-750	2	14	1.0	2.3	1.6	4.6
751-1,000	2	19	1.3	2.8	1.8	4.7
1,001-1,250	2	20	1.4	2.7	2.0	4.8
1,251-1,500	3	18	1.1	3.1	2.1	4.9
1,501-2,000	4	19	1.2	3.9	2.2	6.3
2,001-2,500	3	19	1.4	4.0	2.0	5.7

Source: Willmer, 1985.

Secretarial and Clerical Staff. Advancement is a communication process. Because of the volume and importance of correspondence and clerical records to the effective communication of the advancement office, adequate and capable clerical and secretarial assistance is critical. For many small and developing institutions, in fact, these people are the lifeblood of the operation.

Table 57-4 shows the average numbers of clerical and secretarial staff broken down by enrollment and function. The numerical range is diverse—from 1 to 16 FTE. There is a slight increase in support staff size as the institutional size increases.

The range of secretarial and clerical staff for alumni is 1.2 to 1.5 FTE. For fund-raising, it is 1.7 to 3.7 FTE; for public relations, 0.5 to 1.4 FTE; and for admissions, 1.8 to 4.0 FTE. These staffing-size statistics confirm that it generally takes just as much effort to run the same program at the smaller institutions as it does at the larger.

Cost to Matriculate Students

Probably the most critical management consideration in the student recruitment process is what it costs in salaries, travel, media, and promotion to matriculate one student. For most institutions, student tuition accounts for 75 to 95 percent of the revenue dollars,

Table 57-4. Number of Full-Time Equivalent (FTE) Institutional
Advancement Clerical and Secretarial Staff.

	Range of Totals		Breakdown of Mean by Function			
Enrollment	Low	High	Alumni	Fund-Raising	Public Relations	Admissions
Up to 500	2	8	1.2	1.7	0.5	1.8
501–750	1	12	1.1	2.0	0.7	2.2
751–1,000	1	12	1.2	2.1	0.9	2.3
1,001–1,250	1	16	1.1	2.4	1.0	2.3
1,251–1,500	2	11	1.2	2.2	1.2	2.6
1,501–2,000	2	15	1.3	3.1	1.2	3.5
2,001–2,500	3	13	1.5	3.7	1.4	4.0

Source: Willmer, 1985.

and so these colleges depend heavily on reaching student recruitment quotas.

Table 57-5 gives a breakdown of admissions costs by enrollment size. The mean for the study sample is $797 to matriculate one student. The range is extremely diverse—from $60 to $2,886. In each enrollment size, three or four institutions had very large expenditures, which skewed the total from $100 to $200 higher in cost per student grouping.

Fund-Raising Revenues and Costs to Raise a Dollar

The bottom line for fund-raisers is money raised. In addition, a key management tool to assess fund-raising efficiency is the cost it takes to raise a dollar. Table 57-6 displays, by enrollment size, mean gift income according to unrestricted and capital gifts.

Revenues. The mean revenues as displayed in Table 57-6 are very diverse. Enrollment size does not serve as a clear indication of gift income. The average of the mean is $689,064 in unrestricted income and $780,115 in capital income.

Fund-Raising Costs. This author's study shows that the mean costs to raise unrestricted dollars (which include fund-raising costs only, not other advancement expenses) range from $.20 to $.36 spent per dollar raised, and the mean for all colleges surveyed is $.26

Table 57-5. Admissions Costs (Salaries, Travel, Media, and Promotion) to Matriculate One Student.

Enrollment	Cost per Student	Range	
		Low	High
Up to 500	$934	$203	$2,668
501–750	939	69	2,886
751–1,000	933	60	2,065
1,001–1,250	635	134	1,023
1,251–1,500	586	140	1,238
1,501–2,000	903	235	2,243
2,001–2,500	647	134	1,361

Source: Willmer, 1985.

Table 57-6. Gift Income by Enrollment.

Enrollment	Mean Unrestricted Gift Income	Mean Capital Gift Income	Mean Total Gifts
Up to 500	$570,488	$845,933	$1,416,421
501–750	661,536	571,939	1,233,475
751–1,000	884,140	766,712	1,650,852
1,001–1,250	676,737	922,246	1,598,983
1,251–1,500	725,008	833,127	1,558,135
1,501–2,000	784,695	966,316	1,751,011
2,001–2,500	520,846	554,534	1,075,380

Source: Willmer, 1985.

per dollar raised (Willmer, 1985). When comparing the mean total (unrestricted and capital) income by the mean fund-raising costs, the range is $.10 to $.16 per dollar raised. The mean for total income per fund-raising costs is $.11. Keep in mind that these are means, and the diversity is great among individual institutions. In general, the smaller institutions are just as—or more—efficient in the money they raise compared with the money they spend.

Developing Institutions

The preceding data and analysis deal with comparisons by enrollment size. Another way to assess an institutional advancement office's process is by institutional age. In this author's study, cross tabulations were run on mean total gift income, cost to matriculate a student, and percent of educational and general expenditures to advancement (Willmer, 1985). As would be expected, the younger, or developing, institutions are usually the smaller ones.

The mean total (unrestricted and capital) gift income according to this author's study for the institutions by age is: eleven to twenty-five years—$1,055,458, twenty-six to fifty years—$1,207,987, fifty-one to seventy-five years—$1,397,795, and seventy-six years and older—$1,622,721 (Willmer, 1985). As would be expected, the older the institution, the more gift income it generates. This is consistent with the study Pickett (1984) did on factors affecting fund-raising efficiency.

The mean percentage of the educational and general budget allocated to institutional advancement activities decreases as institutions get older. Research shows these allocations by institutional age are eleven to twenty-five years, 13.6 percent; twenty-six to fifty years, 9.2 percent; fifty-one to seventy-five years, 8.0 percent; and seventy-six years and older, 7.4 percent (Willmer, 1985). Considering the high correlation between age and size, these figures are consistent with the enrollment analysis in Table 57-1, which indicates a decrease in the percentage of institutional funds committed to advancement as the institution increases in enrollment.

Doing a Few Things Well

Probably the advice most often given small- and developing-college advancement officers is to build on the college's strengths and do a few things well. Four critical areas in which it is important to do well are setting priorities, involving your president, using trustees effectively, and focusing on major donors.

Setting Priorities. This sounds simple, but it is a difficult task. As Hess (Pray, 1981, p. 323) reminds us, "You can't be a mini, many-faceted advancement program." To build your program around the components of a successful large university program will probably be a mistake. Part of setting priorities is knowing yourself. Why do your donors give to you? What do your readers think about your publications? And why do students attend your institution? This author's study shows that only 26 percent had conducted a market analysis of the donor constituency and only 23 percent had conducted a leadership survey of primary publications within the past three years (Willmer, 1985). You cannot communicate effectively if you do not know your audience. Poor priority-setting is often the result of being ingrown and not being able to see the forest for the trees. Outside advice, says Hess (Pray, 1981), can be especially helpful, whether it is professional counsel or someone from a neighboring institution. One particularly helpful source is the National Consulting Network of the Council for Independent Colleges in Washington, D.C. Good counsel is available at low cost.

Involving Your President. There is no way around the fact that the president of the small or developing college is its chief advancement officer (Fisher, 1980). The image, vitality, and vision for an institution are represented by the president and depend heavily on how he or she projects that institution. The president must evoke confidence from parents of prospective students, cultivate long-term relationships, and be able to close gifts from major donors. Particularly at small and developing institutions, the president must (1) establish and support an aggressive advancement program for the college, (2) serve as a catalyst to solve internal problems that get in the way of advancement, (3) build a management team that supports advancement, and (4) have a clear idea of how to get trustees working on behalf of advancement.

Using Trustees Effectively. Trustees can provide valuable experience for counsel and serve as ambassadors for the small college. Conversely, they can be ineffective and place low priority on advancement concerns. Advancement officers need to continually educate trustees, the owners of the institution, about their responsibility to advancement activities. One of the most effective

tools is to have a development committee of the board that takes
personal interest in, and responsibility for, the advancement affairs
of the college. Frantzreb (1981) strongly develops this concern that
trustees should be effectively involved, particularly in influencing
gifts to a college, or they should resign from the board. As Simic
(1984, p. 8) points out, "If trustees don't set an example of
generosity, giving doesn't happen."

Focusing on Major Donors. Do not major in the minors. It
usually takes just as much effort to get a $500 gift as to get a $5,000
or $500,000 gift. Special attention must be given to carefully
researching donors with gift potential, interest in your institution,
and philanthropic minds. Too often, small-college advancement
officers spend time in areas that do not produce results. "A
successful development program focuses human resources on where
major gifts are found" (Simic, 1984, p. 9). Good stewards of small-
college resources will do the necessary research and concentrate on
the donors who can produce results.

These guidelines, even though brief, provide direction for
success in the small shop. With a keen sense of priorities, a
disposition to action, and a healthy tolerance for ambiguity,
advancement officers should be able to hold a steady hand to the
tiller in the storms due to strike small and developing institutions
in the decade ahead. Keep in mind that with each challenge comes
an opportunity, and herein lie the reasons that small and
developing colleges have been resilient and have continued to
advance.

References

Astin, A. W., and Lee, C. *The Invisible Colleges: A Profile of Small,
Private Colleges with Limited Resources.* New York: McGraw-
Hill, 1972.

Chaffee, E. E. "Successful Strategic Management in Small Private
Colleges." *Journal of Higher Education,* 1984, 55 (2), 234.

Fisher, J. L. (ed.). *Presidential Leadership in Advancement
Activities.* New Directions for Institutional Advancement, no. 8.
San Francisco: Jossey-Bass, 1980.

Frantzreb, A. C. *Trustee's Role in Advancement.* New Directions for Institutional Advancement, no. 14. San Francisco: Jossey-Bass, 1981.

Gonser Gerber Tinker Stuhr. *Bulletin on Public Relations and Development for Colleges and Universities.* Chicago: Gonser Gerber Tinker Stuhr, 1984.

Jonsen, R. W. "Small Colleges Cope with the Eighties: Sharp Eye on the Horizon, Strong Hand on the Tiller." *Journal of Higher Education,* 1984, *55* (2), 171-183.

Panas, J. *Mega Gifts.* Chicago: Pluribus Press, 1984.

Peck, R. D. "Entrepreneurship as a Significant Factor in Successful Adaptation." *Journal of Higher Education,* 1984a, *55* (2), 269-285.

Peck, R. D. "Small Independent Colleges in 1984." Washington, D.C.: Council of Independent Colleges, 1984b.

Pickett, W. L. "What Determines Fund-Raising Effectiveness?" *CASE Currents,* 1984, *10* (8), 45.

Pray, F. C. (ed.). *Handbook for Educational Fund Raising: A Guide to Successful Principles and Practices for Colleges, Universities, and Schools.* San Francisco: Jossey-Bass, 1981.

Simic, C. R. "Fund Raising: Organize for Success." *AGB Reports,* July/Aug. 1984, pp. 8-10.

Willmer, W. K. (ed.). *Advancing the Small College.* New Directions for Institutional Advancement, no. 13. San Francisco: Jossey-Bass, 1980.

Willmer, W. K. "A Large View of Small Colleges: Small-College Advancement Programs." *Currents,* 1985, *11* (7), 18-21.

58

Walter C. Hobbs

Legal Issues in
Institutional Advancement

❧ The purpose of this chapter is to present and discuss several legal principles that, more than others, bear on the institutional advancement function:

1. *First Amendment guarantees* of freedom of association and expression, which may come into play when campuses permit activities that others find offensive
2. *Defamation,* which is doing injury to a person's reputation by the publication of false and damaging information
3. *Invasion of privacy,* which can include publication of information about a person, even though true, as well as a physical "intrusion upon his or her solitude."
4. *Copyright,* which governs the extent to which material produced by one party may lawfully be used—copied, abridged, circulated, displayed, performed, and the like—by another
5. *Federal tax law,* which affects, among other things, how one may best approach the task of fund-raising
6. *Criminal and civil ("tort") law,* which are called on by different parties for different purposes in response to acts of violence that (unfortunately) occur on campuses as well as elsewhere

A word of caution at the outset: In the pages that follow we shall be discussing legal principles, not applying rules of law to particular situations. The immediate, indeed the sole, objective of this chapter is to fashion a conceptual framework by which the reader might understand more clearly why the law speaks as it does to issues that permeate the professional lives of institutional advancement officers.

First-Amendment Guarantees

The First Amendment to the Constitution of the United States contains several provisions that rise to virtually sanctified status among the many values that constitute this nation's jurisprudence. They are "first" not only in the order in which they appear in that grand document but also in the esteem in which they are generally held.

Stated in full, the First Amendment provides that "Congress shall make no law respecting an establishment of religion [the "Establishment Clause"], or prohibiting the free exercise thereof [the "Free Exercise Clause"]; or abridging the freedom of speech or of the press; or the right of the people peaceably to assemble, and to petition the government for redress of grievances." The Establishment and Free Exercise Clauses need not detain us here; suffice it to say simply that church-affiliated institutions both enjoy liberties and face legal strictures that others do not (see Moots and Gaffney, 1979; Gaffney and Moots, 1982). Otherwise, we shall find it unnecessary to consult the religion clauses, except as they illuminate some recent holdings of the U.S. Supreme Court concerning freedom of expression.

The reader will notice that the First Amendment prohibits *Congress* from making any law regarding the several topics enumerated therein. Nothing is said concerning states, and clearly nothing is directed to private parties, whether persons or corporations. Does this mean that only the federal government, no one else, is prohibited by the Constitution from infringing the rights of free expression and association? Almost—and, in fact, for many years that is precisely what was meant.

The function of the U.S. Constitution as amended from time to time has always been, and is today, to establish the limits of the reach of the federal government. Some such limits have since been imposed on the states as well, but even those are applicable solely to government, not to individuals (we are considering here only constitutional provisions, not legislative enactments). It frequently comes as a surprise to persons untutored in the law to learn that there are no constitutional impediments to actions by private parties that, if undertaken by government, would be wholly invalid. A private college, for example, may constitutionally refuse permission to a given speaker to argue on behalf of elective abortion, although that same speaker would have a constitutionally protected right to make that case at a public university (within other bounds considered below). Similarly, a private institution may lawfully refuse recognition to a student gay rights organization or may likewise refuse to renew the appointment of a faculty member on grounds of that individual's sexual preference, although both actions by a public institution would be constitutionally suspect. Private colleges and universities are under no constitutional obligation to afford due process to students when disciplining misconduct, are not restricted by lack of a search warrant from entering a dormitory room, are free to censor campus publications so far as the constitution is concerned, and so on.

The reason such burdens fall only to the public sector (unless legislation or perhaps state constitutional requirements impose them in the private sector also) is the one outlined above: The Constitution of the United States addresses government, and government alone. And early in the nation's history, the Supreme Court held that unless states were expressly included in a given provision, the provision was applicable only at the federal level: A private individual whose property was "taken [by the City of Baltimore] for public use without just compensation" could find no relief in the Fifth Amendment, which, with the rest of the Bill of Rights, did not fold states and their subdivisions within its scope (*Barron* v. *Mayor and City Council of Baltimore,* 7 Pet. 243, 8 L.Ed. 672 [1833]).

Thirty-five years later, however, in the aftermath of the War Between the States, the Fourteenth Amendment to the Constitution was adopted, and it held among other things that "No state shall deprive any person of . . . liberty . . . without due process of law." Then starting in the 1930s and continuing through the 1960s, the Supreme Court began to apply most (although still today not all) the protections of the first ten amendments to actions taken against persons by state government, including its agencies and municipalities. The Court interpreted the term *liberty* in the Fourteenth Amendment to refer to many of the provisions of the Bill of Rights, such as freedom of speech and freedom from unwarranted search and seizure, thereby bridging the gap between the substance of many of those first-ten-amendment freedoms and protection against infringements of such liberties by the states found only in the fourteenth.

Nonetheless, this newer, more expansive reach of the constitutional protections still extends no farther than to actions by the states, their agencies, and municipalities. It does not encompass private parties. Hence nonpublic institutions are free to ignore the constitutional proscriptions if they so desire, unless and until other legal authority dictates to the contrary.

Consequently, all that is said herein concerning First-Amendment restrictions on institutional censorship and/or refusal to recognize campus organizations applies solely to colleges and universities in the public sector. This does not mean, however, either that public institutions are powerless to contain any person or group that wishes to "do its thing" on campus or that private institutions are free to run roughshod over anyone who speaks his or her mind in violation of institutional do's and don'ts.

The legal theory that governs most of the relations between private institutions and their various constituencies, internal and external, is the law of contract. When a private college or university adopts given policies concerning means and modes of expression on campus or procedures for the registration of recognized campus groups, it is legally bound to comply with those policies. The general rule is that no private entity is obligated to adopt a particular policy, but when it does, it legally must observe all that it has promulgated. Moreover, it cannot act arbitrarily or capriciously in its treatment of others under the policies it has adopted but must instead be evenhanded in all its decisions and actions. Therefore, although such an institution may legally preclude given speech or behavior that would be constitutionally protected in the public sector, it may not lawfully inhibit the freedoms of some people while being generous to others.

Except that no party may lawfully be arbitrary or capricious in its exercise of power, the rules concerning the regulation of expression and association on campus are substantially different in public colleges and universities, for there, the governing legal theory is First Amendment law, not contract. The courts take as given that every public institution, whether educational or otherwise, has not only the right but also the legal duty to pursue its assigned mission. Consequently, speech and association may lawfully be restricted in "time, place, and manner," lest institutional purpose be frustrated. But what is decidedly impermissible under the Constitution is restriction on the content of one's expression or of an association's ideology.

An instructive case in point arose in 1977 at the University of Missouri at Kansas City (*Widmar* v. *Vincent,* 454 U.S. 263, 102 S.Ct. 269, 70 L.Ed.2d 440 [1981]). For years, a student group called Cornerstone had been provided the use of university facilities for its meetings, which typically involved "prayer, hymns, Bible commentary, and discussion of religious views and experiences" (454 U.S. at 264). In 1977, however, the university withdrew permission for Cornerstone's use of its rooms, later arguing in court that the Establishment Clause prohibits such government advancement of religion. But the Supreme Court disagreed with the university's analysis. "The University's argument misconceives the nature of this case. The question is not whether the creation of a religious forum would violate the Establishment Clause. The University has opened its facilities for use by student groups, and the question is whether it can now exclude groups because of the content of their speech. . . . Having created a forum generally open to student groups, the University seeks to enforce a content-based exclusion of religious speech. Its exclusionary policy violates the fundamental principle that a state regulation of speech should be content-neutral. . . . Our holding in this case in no way undermines the capacity of the University to establish reasonable time, place and manner regulations. Nor do we question the right of the University to make academic judgments as to how best to allocate scarce resources or 'to determine for itself on academic grounds who may teach, what may be taught, and who may be admitted to study' [cite omitted]" (454 U.S. at 270, 272).

In short, not even the Constitution's own wall between church and state will permit the abridgment by a public university of free expression or association for reasons of content alone.

Defamation

The legal wrong called *defamation* is risked whenever comments about a third party are communicated in any form, oral or written, from one person to another. But that risk is severely increased where campus newspapers and magazines are not centrally published.

Defamation is damage to another's reputation and may be inflicted not only by words but by other means of communication as well, such as pictures, satire, or drama. One can defame a corporation or association by remarks about its financial condition or integrity, but more often it is a person who is defamed (only the living; at law the deceased cannot be). Defamation that is spoken is slander, and defamation in writing or another permanent form is libel. Each repetition of a defamatory statement is an additional defamation for which one can be held liable, but in most jurisdictions in the United States, an entire issue of a newspaper, book, or magazine is considered but one publication and therefore only one repetition.

For a plaintiff to prevail in suit for defamation, he or she must show (1) that a reasonable reader or listener or viewer would identify the individual as the subject of the defamatory material, (2) that his or her reputation was adversely affected by the statement or picture or other, and (3) if he or she is a private person, that the defendant was negligent in permitting the damaging statement to appear; if the plaintiff is a "public figure," such as a candidate for public office or an entertainment celebrity, then he or she must show that the defendant either knew the material was false or entertained serious doubts about its truth. The defendant, in response, can escape liability chiefly by showing (1) that the material was in fact true or (2) that the plaintiff consented to the publication of the material.

Institutional officials who are responsible for campus newspapers and other publications do well to ensure that everyone in a position to publish material that might reasonably be considered defamatory, especially by an aggrieved individual who is not a public figure, is clearly aware of the ingredients of this legal wrong. As in all lawsuits, even victory is expensive, certainly in time and of course in money. And defeat can be disastrous, particularly if punitive damages are awarded.

Invasion of Privacy

This legal hazard bears a striking resemblance to defamation, but it is different nonetheless. Three of the four ways in which one might wrongfully invade another's privacy include (1) appropriation of the individual's picture or name for commercial advantage, (2) publication of facts that place the person in a "false light," and (3) public disclosure of private facts about the individual. The fourth is intrusion upon the person's affairs or seclusion—either overtly, as by physically entering his or her premises, or covertly, as by eavesdropping. The likelihood of these several violations by college or university personnel is least, in my judgment, at intrusion. But the chance of their occurrence increases from appropriation to placing in a false light to disclosure of facts about the individual.

It is hard to envision institutional advancement officers prying deliberately, or even negligently, into someone's affairs and intruding either overtly or covertly on a person's living space in a manner that people would ordinarily consider objectionable. However, it takes no great stretch of imagination to envision an item in the campus newspaper advertising a service that some young entrepreneur is prepared to offer (such as moving goods from dormitories to storage at the close of a school year) and showing the smiling face of someone who is apparently vouchsafing the quality of the service in question but who, it turns out, was merely in animated conversation with a friend on campus one fine spring day. That is appropriation. Even more easily conceived is the unintentional—read *negligent*—layout of the aforementioned photograph, such that it is immediately associated in the mind of the typical reader with the exposé published on the same page concerning cheating on campus. That is placing the individual in a false light. But most easily imagined of all is the publication in publicity materials of embarrassing, though quite authentic, pictures taken in a university clinic or taken in a local welfare agency to accompany a story about an eminent alumna and her research concerning welfare clients. Those are public disclosures of private facts about individuals.

In the case of invasion of privacy, truth is no defense at all. Here, sensitivity to what the other person may experience, not one's own integrity, is the chief safeguard.

Copyright

Copyright is the property right that one may secure in the expression of his or her idea in a tangible work of literature or of art. It is not the idea per se that finds protection; rather, it is the expression of the idea in tangible form.

The Copyright Act of 1976 (17 U.S.C.) governs the legal protections available to copyrighted works. It is a federal statute, for Article I, Section 8 of the Constitution reserves to the Congress— thereby precluding to the states and to the people—"power to promote the progress of science and useful arts, by securing for limited times to authors and inventors the exclusive right to their respective writings and discoveries."

The protectable rights owned by the copyright proprietor are not merely distinguishable, they are "severable." In other words, simply selling or assigning or licensing the right to copy one's work, for example, does not mean one has sold or assigned or licensed the right to distribute those copies. Distribution (whether by sale or loan or lease or by some other means) is a separate right, and anyone who wishes to distribute the copies he or she has been granted permission to make must secure permission for the distribution as well; it does not automatically attach to the permission to copy. The same is true of all the other rights owned by a proprietor under the Copyright Act. Each right stands on its own as a right of the proprietor alone until it is conveyed to another party (or until the work slips into the public domain, in which case no one may claim any copyright therein). Those several rights include the right (1) to copy the work, (2) to distribute the work and all copies of it, (3) to prepare derivative works therefrom, such as abridgments or arrangements, (4) to display the work, and (5) to perform the work.

Possession of a physical copy of a given work does not in itself constitute copyright. The simple purchase of an audiocassette recording or a watercolor print does not convey copyright in the expression of the idea—that is, as it is found in the given medium. All that one has purchased in such an instance is the physical item: the tape with the magnetic signals or the paper with the picture. And should one infringe the proprietor's copyright by, say, reproducing the work, it will be of no concern to the law that one stands to gain nothing financial by the copying. It is still infringement, a legal wrong for which one can be held liable.

One need scarcely ponder long and hard to conceive the myriad ways in which the institutional advancement function might stumble into infringement of copyright: reprints of written and pictorial items in institutional publications, the use of protected material without express permission in publicity displays, the recording of background music in self-produced radio spots, and many more. And should the stakes be high enough to persuade the copyright proprietor that a lawsuit is in order, the entire transaction could be costly indeed—again, win or lose.

The discussion has focused on infringement because that is where the dangers lurk. One should be aware, however, that on the other side of the coin is protection for material produced in shop, whose use one would sensibly wish to restrict. The procedural niceties to be observed are somewhat detailed but not at all difficult to follow. Institutional counsel can provide instructions on how to place anything eligible under copyright.

Federal Tax Law

The legal topic that is perhaps of greatest interest to many professionals in institutional advancement, namely, tax law, is ironically one of the more arcane specialties of the field. The matter is given specific treatment in Chapter Twenty-Three, so only general considerations are discussed here.

Virtually every jurisdiction in the land levies taxes, chiefly on property (typically, real property) and on sales of goods and services. Some cities, however, as well as a few counties, plus most states, and of course the federal government also tax both personal and corporate income. The Internal Revenue Service (IRS) establishes and implements procedures for that purpose, to which most states and their subdivisions then conform their own procedures. One common such conformance by many states is the granting of exemption from liability for state income tax to organizations that the IRS has already exempted from federal income tax.

Exempt status carries two major benefits. The first, obviously, is that the exempt organization does not pay taxes. The second, however, may well be the more advantageous, at least to organizations that depend for much of their income on contributions. Such contributions are deductible by the donor from his or her taxable income, thereby providing an inducement to people to contribute funds to that organization.

Limits are imposed both by statute and by regulation on these various aspects of tax exemption and the deductibility of contributions from taxable income:

1. *The types of organizations that may qualify for exempt status.* Charitable, religious, educational, and/or scientific organizations are among those that may, but businesses operated for profit cannot.
2. *The purpose of a contribution.* The donor's gift may not "inure to the benefit of" a particular individual, nor may he or she dictate how that gift is to be used by the recipient organization.
3. *The amount in contributions that may be deducted from the donor's taxable income.* This will fluctuate with the nature of the asset that is contributed (for example, cash vis-à-vis appreciated capital gain property) and with the proportion of one's total giving to his or her adjusted gross income.

4. *Who may contribute.* Persons and corporations both may make deductible contributions, but corporations face lower limits than do individuals.

5. *The use that may be made of contributions.* If the organization accepts a gift in the role of a "fiduciary," that is, as trustee of the assets that are donated (perhaps, for example, to pay an income to someone out of the interest earned on those assets until he or she dies, at which time the organization will then own the assets outright), then in that capacity, the organization will be governed by the law of trusts.

One major caveat is in order: Exempt status is not a right that stands by itself, immune to the demands of other social policy. To the contrary, deliberate refusal to comply with duly adopted policy will jeopardize the organization's exemption, as Bob Jones University discovered.

That fundamentalist institution in Greenville, South Carolina, had denied admission to blacks from the time of its founding in 1927 until 1971, on the basis of its view that the Bible forbids interracial dating and marriage. In 1971, black applicants who were married to blacks were accepted, and following a 1975 court decision prohibiting racial exclusion from private schools (*McCrary* v. *Runyon,* 515 F.2d 1082, aff'd 427 U.S. 160, 96 S.Ct. 2586, 49 L.Ed.2d 415 [1976]), unmarried blacks were also permitted to enroll. But the university maintained its position prohibiting interracial dating and marriage and mandated expulsion of students who violated the policy and/or who "espoused, promoted, or encouraged others" to do so.

The IRS had concluded in 1970 that it could no longer justify extending exempt status to any institution that practiced racial discrimination, for such an institution is not *charitable* as that term is meant by the Internal Revenue Code (the IRS regulations). Given Bob Jones's admissions policy at the time, the IRS revoked the university's tax-exempt status. The university litigated the matter all the way to the U.S. Supreme Court and lost (*Bob Jones University* v. *United States,* 461 U.S. 574, 103 S.Ct. 2017, 76 L.Ed.2d 157 [1983]).

Said the Court (103 S.Ct. at 2026-2036):

Examination [of the framework of the Internal Revenue Code against the background of the Congressional purposes] reveals unmistakable evidence that, underlying all relevant parts of the Code, is the intent that entitlement to tax exemption depends on meeting certain common law standards of charity—namely, that an institution seeking tax-exempt status must serve a public purpose and not be contrary to established public policy. . . . When the Government grants exemptions or allows deductions all taxpayers are affected; the very fact of the exemption or deduction for the donor means that other taxpayers can be said to be indirect and vicarious "donors." Charitable exemptions are justified on the basis that the exempt entity confers a public benefit—a benefit which the society or the community may not itself choose or be able to provide, or which supplements and advances the work of public institutions already supported by tax revenues. . . . An unbroken line of cases following *Brown* v. *Board of Education* establishes beyond doubt this Court's view that racial discrimination in education violates a most fundamental national public policy, as well as rights of individuals. . . . Congress, in Titles IV and VI of the Civil Rights Act of 1964 [cites omitted] clearly expressed its agreement that racial discrimination in education violates a fundamental public policy. . . . The Executive Branch has consistently placed its support behind eradication of racial discrimination. . . .

There can thus be no question that the interpretation . . . announced by the IRS in 1970 was correct. That it may be seen as belated does not undermine its soundness. It would be wholly incompatible with the concepts underlying tax exemption to grant the benefit of tax-exempt status to racially discriminatory educational entities, . . . [w]hatever may be the rationale for such private

schools' policies, and however sincere the rationale
may be. ... We therefore find the IRS properly
applied [its ruling] to Bob Jones University.

Criminal and Civil ("Tort") Law

The violence to people and property that is so often the
subject of contemporary society's daily news is, unhappily, no
stranger to the campus. Academe also sees its share of theft, assault,
rape, and homicide, attempted and completed.

In this chapter, we are concerned not with how best to deal
with reporting such instances of campus crime, but rather with the
legal character of these matters. When one faces the task of
communicating facts to the public about criminal conduct on
campus, it is best to know the basic vocabulary and principles of
law that surround such concerns.

Imagine that someone had hidden in wait in a dormitory
room; mugged the occupant when she returned from the library late
one evening; attempted to rape her, but fled when her screams
brought others on the run; and took with him, as he went, her
wallet, which held over $300 in cash and all her credit cards. Setting
aside for our purposes the wisdom or unwisdom of disclosing all
or any part of this to the press or others, what are the legally
significant elements of the incident?

First, when the culprit is at last apprehended, not only will
that person be charged with having committed several crimes, he
will also be vulnerable to suit by the victim despite the doctrine of
"double jeopardy," that is, that a person cannot be tried twice for
the same offense. It is a settled matter at law that one can be
convicted for a crime and also held liable to pay the victim money
damages for the same offense. To be punished for the criminal
nature of one's conduct, and simultaneously to be required to
compensate the person whom one injured by that conduct, are
deemed separate legal liabilities even though they arise from a
single act. The crime is an offense against the people (that is,
against society) and is punished by them, whereas the civil wrong—
the "tort"—is against the individual, who is to be made whole (to

the extent that money can accomplish that end) by the one who has done her the injury.

Second, the terminology of criminal law is invariably distinctly different from the counterpart terminology of tort law. The crime called *assault,* for example, a physical attack on a person, is called in tort a *battery.* One must simply inquire to ascertain what words are used for what offenses.

And third, the level of proof one must reach to hold the accused liable differs between criminal and tort law, the former being the more rigorous. The standard of proof in criminal law is that the prosecution must establish the guilt of the accused beyond reasonable doubt (moreover, the accused is presumed to be innocent), but in tort law, the plaintiff seldom need show more than that a preponderance of the evidence is in his or her favor, and never need show more than "clear and convincing evidence" of his or her contentions.

On a different note altogether: The advancement officer ought to know that the campus is no sanctuary. It is not immune to entry by law enforcement officials in due course of their lawful duties. To be sure, when police come onto campus they must observe all the procedural requirements they face when entering other places to enforce the law, but the campus is no refuge from such police entry.

Similarly, the reach of the law concerning serving and consuming alcoholic beverages, and/or the possession, sale, or use of controlled substances, is not stayed at the college gate. There is no doubt that wise and effective administrators will work diligently to establish harmonious town-gown relationships with local agencies, including police departments, and that that may serve at a practical level to limit access by police to campus. But one must realize that such arrangements are a function of administrative cooperation, not the operation of law.

Conclusion

Civilized peoples live by the rule of law, and academe is a major subscriber to that long and honorable tradition as well as a major beneficiary of its pacifying influence in human affairs. It is a cause to be embraced, not shunned. But among all persons, and especially among academics, it ought to be embraced thoughtfully and knowledgeably, not resignedly.

The institutional advancement officer is no exception. Law is a boon to the realization of that officer's purpose, not a disruption to be avoided to the maximum extent feasible. But law must be approached with all the scholarly talents at one's disposal.

References

Edwards, H. T., and Nordin, V. D. *Higher Education & the Law* (with *1982/83 Supplement*). Cambridge, Mass.: Institute for Educational Management, Harvard University, 1979.

Gaffney, E. M., Jr., and Moots, P. R. *Government and Campus: Federal Regulation of Religiously Affiliated Higher Education.* Notre Dame, Ind.: University of Notre Dame Press, 1982.

Hobbs, W. C. *Academic and Legal Values: In Concert and in Tension.* Occasional Paper No. 10, Department of Higher Education. Buffalo: State University of New York at Buffalo, 1982.

Hobbs, W. C. (ed.). *Understanding Academic Law.* New Directions for Institutional Advancement, no. 16. San Francisco: Jossey-Bass, 1982 (see especially "Additional Resources," pp. 85–87).

Moots, P. R., and Gaffney, E. M., Jr. *Church and Campus: Legal Issues in Religiously Affiliated Higher Education.* Notre Dame, Ind.: University of Notre Dame Press, 1979.

Olivas, M. A. (guest ed.). Special Issue: "Higher Education Law." *Review of Higher Education,* Summer 1984, 7(4).

Cletis Pride
Joseph S. Fowler

59

Market Research: The Starting Point for Advancement Success

❧ What is market research? It is any kind of research that gives you information about the current state of your particular market and offers guidance in improving your position in that market.

In most cases, it will involve opinion research, employing scientific sampling and interviews or written questionnaires. Educational institutions most often use market research as a way to (1) increase the effectiveness of their fund-raising efforts or (2) attract more (or better) students.

Even image studies or projects that are overtly intended to solve some immediate problem usually have money or students as their final goal. State and public institutions may direct their fund-raising efforts—and related market research—at legislators rather than at private sources.

Whatever the goal, market research can help you reach it—providing you follow certain rules. The first is to define the goal very clearly at the outset. A clear definition will help you keep the project on track from beginning to end. It will assure that the appropriate groups are sampled, that the right questions are asked,

This chapter first appeared as an article titled "Market Research" in *Marketing Higher Education: A Practical Guide,* published in 1983. It is reprinted with the permission of the authors and the publisher, the Council for Advancement and Support of Education.

and finally, that results are analyzed and interpreted in the most productive way.

Careful planning on your part can also help keep costs to a minimum. Know what you want; then resist impulses to add just a little more. Add-ons lead to cost overruns—usually big ones. Almost everyone adds on in the course of a study and then is shocked by how far the final cost has soared above the original estimate.

Should You Do It Yourself?

There are two basic ways to conduct market research. You can do it yourself, or you can hire someone to do it for you.

Doing it yourself has several advantages. After all, who knows more than you about your institution's problems and needs? You can call on in-house expertise: marketing professors; statisticians; your own computer center; the graphics, copy, and printing departments in your public relations and publications offices; secretarial and clerical staff; and so on. In-house research should be significantly less expensive.

On balance, though, all of these are offset by some major disadvantages. An in-house study often lacks credibility. People, both on and off your campus, tend to be skeptical about the objectivity of a survey created and analyzed by staff members who may have a vested interest in the outcome.

The in-house team is not likely to view the institution with the detachment you could expect from outsiders. Not being able to see the forest for the trees, the insiders may write questionnaires that do not address the real issues, or even worse, that serve mainly internal political purposes. Also, inexperience may lead an in-house team to waste much time and effort debating such things as format and wording of questions.

An outside professional firm brings credibility, expertise, experience, and objectivity to the project. But it does so at a price— a high price in most cases.

A compromise arrangement, combining outside expertise and inside cost-cutting services, is possible. The outsiders can be used for such sensitive jobs as sample selection, questionnaire development, and analysis and reporting. The institution provides computer services, printing and mailing, secretarial and clerical services, and the like. This can provide professional expertise and credibility at a reduced cost.

Explore Secondary Sources

Once you have defined the problem and decided that a market research study is indicated, you must find the most effective way to go about your study. Before embarking on expensive primary survey research, however, you should explore all secondary sources for the required information. This kind of research often saves time and money. At the very least, it can help you write a more productive questionnaire.

Secondary information sources fall into two categories: external sources and sources internal to your organization. You may find valuable data that have been collected on an earlier survey, or information that was collected routinely from students or donors. You should explore all internal sources; they will be by far the least expensive.

If internal sources prove unproductive, begin checking external secondary sources. Academic, trade, and professional journals are logical starting places. The federal government is also a rich source of information: the Department of Education, the Department of Commerce *(Business Conditions Digest, Survey of Current Business)*, the Department of Labor, and the Census Bureau are four key ones.

Another useful source is the Lockheed *Dialog* data base system (Dialog Information Services, monthly), which is a computer-based reference library of scientific, trade, general interest, and governmental publications searchable by keyword. The results of many surveys conducted by or for the government are in the public domain. The *Findex* index of market research (Goldstein and Kravetz, 1983) cross-references most of this information.

Suppose, for example, that you wanted to target the most likely geographical areas for sources of new students. The Census Bureau makes available census demographic information consolidated by zip code. Your applicants for the past two or three years could be overlaid on each zip code. Your computer could then determine statistically the characteristics of the types of zip codes that were the best producers of applicants. Those and all similar zip codes should then be your most productive potential student sources.

Role of Qualitative Research

If the information you require is not available from secondary sources, then you will need some type of primary survey research. Primary research can be subdivided into two major categories: quantitative and qualitative. Quantitative research yields numerical results of some type—counts, intensity, penetration, and so on. Qualitative research yields information that is softer and is usually not numerical.

Qualitative research is employed most often as the first phase of a projectable, quantitative research project. The purpose of qualitative research is to set the agenda for the subsequent quantitative research.

The most widely employed qualitative technique is focus group research. Focus group research consists of a structured discussion led by a trained moderator in a conference room setting with five to twelve members of the target universe.

The purpose of a focus group is to elicit from the target universe members their perceptions of the issues germane to the research question. Often, the organization generating the research project has preconceptions about the issues that the research should cover. The key issues within the marketplace, however, may be entirely different.

Suppose, for example, that student applications at institution A showed a significant drop from the previous year and that, during the same period, the economy experienced a slowdown. A survey at this time would very likely tend to emphasize economic issues and price sensitivity. A few focus group sessions, however, might reveal that, although the economy was a concern, parents and students were looking for a more career-oriented curriculum than that offered at institution A. Carefully conducted focus group research will help ensure that the quantitative survey research covers all the key issues.

Another important use of the focus group environment is to pretest a questionnaire for use in subsequent quantitative survey research. Walking through a questionnaire with five to twelve members of the universe that will receive the survey can prevent expensive errors. It will ensure that everyone understands the questions, that the questions are not ambiguous, and that jumps and skips from one question to another can be followed. And because fixed-choice questions should be used as much as possible (and open-ended questions avoided), you can guarantee that all possible responses are included on the questions.

You should avoid at all cost the tendency to read more into the results of qualitative research than is really there. Because focus group results are based on the opinions of very few people, they are not projectable to the target universe. Results of such research are perfectly adequate for defining the issues and pretesting the questionnaire, but they are adequate only for these purposes. Rarely, if ever, are qualitative research findings reliable, in and of themselves, for making marketing decisions.

Quantitative Research

Qualitative research usually leads into a quantitative research phase. Quantitative research can be divided into two categories: projectable research (called *probability research* from here on) and nonprojectable research. As the name implies, probability research results can be projected to the target universe with known precision. Because nonprojectable research is conducted with a convenience sample instead of a random probability sample of the target universe, you cannot generalize from the numerical results.

One type of nonprojectable quantitative research is carried on at a central site. *Mall intercepts* are the most common type of central site research. Market research companies are now in many regional shopping centers across the United States. The companies contract to conduct surveys among shoppers in the shopping center. Trained interviewers recruit and screen potential respondents in the public mall areas—not in the stores. Short surveys may be conducted on the mall floor. For longer interviews, the respondents are taken to an interview room.

As opposed to focus group research, nonprojectable quantitative research can yield actionable marketing information. For example, suppose your admissions staff had ideas for two different brochures directed to the parents of potential students. With mall-intercept research, the most effective of the two brochures could be reliably determined with minimal expense. Of all the adults approached in the mall, only those with college-bound high school students would be interviewed. Qualified respondents would be asked to rate each brochure separately and then to pick their favorite. (To control for what is called *ordering effects*, a reaction based on the order in which people encounter things, half the respondents would be shown brochure A first, and the other half would see B first.)

These results would be sufficiently valid for selecting the most effective brochure. It may even be desirable to find the best brochure for different cities—for example, brochure A may be better in Denver, whereas B may work better in Miami.

Central site research has several advantages over other types of quantitative research: (1) it can be completed in a relatively short time, (2) it is relatively inexpensive (provided that the screening criteria are not too restrictive), (3) visual props can be easily employed, (4) large amounts of information can be collected, and (5) complex questionnaires with involved skip patterns can be used because the respondent does not have to contend with following the questionnaire.

As in qualitative research, one must avoid reading too much into nonprojectable quantitative research. Although adequate for answering many controlled experimental questions—as in the above example—results may not reflect the views of the target universe on sensitive issues.

Projectable, or probability, quantitative survey research yields results that can be projected to the target universe with a known precision. The three types of probability survey are mail, telephone, and personal (or in-home) surveys.

Each type has particular advantages and disadvantages, usually involving project cost, turnaround time, potential biases, and data volume capacity. For any given project, the constraints of the situation usually mandate one of the three techniques. Before examining each technique in detail, let us briefly examine sampling and questionnaire design.

Sampling

The device that makes projectability possible is proper sampling. The purpose of sampling is to obtain information that is representative of a universe while examining only a portion of that universe. You should carefully target the universes to be studied. Do not sample the general public if your purpose would be better served by a survey of opinion leaders or of parents of students. Some other likely targets include alumni, faculty, students, prospective students, those who applied to your institution but attended another, school counselors, legislators, donors, and media gatekeepers.

Compared with taking a census, sampling has several advantages: (1) it is significantly less expensive, (2) it is faster, (3) it is more accurate (paradoxically), and (4) it allows time to collect more in-depth information.

Sampling has two disadvantages. First, information is not collected on everyone. (Sampling could not be used to calculate electric bills.) Second, sampling error is introduced. Sampling error arises because not everyone is measured; it is the price paid for using a sample. However, the size of this sampling error, which depends on the sample size, is known; in Table 59-1, it is referred to as the *precision*.

In most cases, proper sampling means simple random sampling. That is, every member of the target universe has a known, and equal, chance of being included in the survey sample. In practice, systematic sampling is an adequate substitute for simple random sampling.

Systematic sampling is also known as nth name sampling because the total universe (that is, population) size is divided by the

Table 59-1. Choosing Adequate Sample Size.

Total Size of Group Studied (Universe)	Sample Size Required	
	Plus or minus 5% Precision	Plus or minus 10% Precision
100	79	49
500	217	81
1,000	278	88
5,000	357	94
10,000	370	95
50,000	381	96
100,000 plus	384	96

Note: See text for discussion of the tradeoffs between sample size and response rates.

desired sample size to yield the increment, or *n,* to be used. For example, if you want a sample of 400 from a universe of 4,000, you will need to sample every tenth person. But do not start automatically with one and go to ten. From a random number table (or by drawing numbers from a hat), select a random number between 1 and *n* inclusive (*n* is ten in this case). Let us assume the number you select is 6. From a list of the universe, select—or have your computer select—the person corresponding to this random number—the sixth person—as the first member of the sample. Subsequently, select sample members by taking the *n*th (tenth in this case) name from the first selected name.

The precision of the results is determined by the size of the sample and the size of the universe. Table 59-1 is a guide for determining adequate sample sizes. It is based on a 95 percent confidence level. That is, the sample size is calculated to ensure that the true universe value of a measured variable is within the range "measured value plus or minus precision" 95 percent of the time. Suppose you conduct a survey using a sample of 370 from a universe of 10,000 alumni, and find that 80 percent of your sample would recommend your institution to a college-bound student. You could be confident that, 95 times out of 100 times, from 75 to 85 percent of the entire universe holds this opinion. In doing surveys for your institution, you would probably want to hold the precision level at plus or minus 5 percent.

Note that you need the number of responses listed in the table. You must also remember that you should generally get at least a 50 percent response rate to your survey. That means you would have to double the sample size shown on the table to determine the number of questionnaires that you would send. (Both factors are vital: the sample size and the response rate. For a universe of 10,000, you would need to send out 740 questionnaires, assuming a 50 percent response rate, to get a sample of 370. You could not send out 1,480 questionnaires and be satisfied with a 25 percent response rate, even though you would receive 370 completed responses.)

If you need to make statements about subgroups of the sample with precision equal to that of the sample as a whole, the sample size for each individual subgroup must be determined from Table 59-1. In effect, a separate survey is conducted for each subgroup. This is called stratified random sampling. When the survey results are being processed by computer, care must be taken to weight each subgroup back to its proportionate size in the universe-at-large. You will need some expert help from your computer people on this.

If the response rate is too low, a significant potential for error is introduced. The error is called *nonresponse bias*. If 70 percent of the sample does not respond to the survey (a 30 percent response rate), there could be something about the 70 percent that makes it different from the 30 percent that responded. For example, suppose a survey on gun control was mailed to a random sample of the United States population. Suppose further that people opposed to gun control do not like to answer surveys. The results would indicate much stronger support for gun control than really exists in the population as a whole, because the nonrespondents as a group were more opposed to control than those who responded.

If you are familiar with the universe being surveyed, and if it is relatively homogeneous, a 40 to 45 percent response rate is adequate, provided that the demographics of the respondents match known demographics of the universe. If there is any uncertainty about the overall mix of your universe, you should aim for a response rate of 65 percent or more. You can achieve a response rate of this magnitude cost-effectively by careful application of the techniques described by Dillman (1978).

Questionnaire Design

Along with sampling, questionnaire design is a most important consideration in conducting a survey. The objective of questionnaire design is to develop a questionnaire that will reliably collect the needed information without deterring or offending respondents.

Parsimony should be a guiding rule in developing a survey. Ask no unnecessary questions; the respondent's time is valuable and by wasting it, you risk reducing your response rate. For each question suggested for a survey, you should ask, "Is there some action I can take based on the answer to this question?" If the answer is no, omit the question.

Question wording is more an art than a science. Common sense is your best guide. An excellent reference for writing questionnaires is Payne (1954). In Chapter 14, "A Concise Check List of 100 Considerations," he gives many tips, including the following:

- Use simple words.
- Do not be vague.
- Keep it short.
- Be specific.
- Do not talk down to respondents.
- Avoid bias.
- Avoid objectionable questions.
- Do not be overly specific.
- Avoid hypothetical questions.
- Do not ask two questions at once.
- Use words that will be uniformly understood.
- Do not use abbreviations or unconventional words and phrases.
- Avoid double negatives.
- Use mutually exclusive response choices.
- Do not assume too much knowledge by the respondent.
- Make sure that information in questions is technically correct.

- Provide time referents if necessary.
- Try to use questions comparable with existing data.

Use fixed-choice responses in every possible situation; avoid open-ended questions as much as possible. The response choices should be exhaustive and mutually exclusive (focus group information and pretesting are useful here). Scaled-question responses (such as 1 to 5) should be anchored on each end with a descriptive phrase (in this case, the anchors could be "very important" for 1 and "very unimportant" for 5). Intermediate scale points may or may not be anchored, but there should be a neutral center point.

On mail surveys, or in any self-administered survey, avoid complex skip patterns. They tend to confuse the respondent and can lead to lower response rates.

Order questions according to their importance in terms of the survey's goals, with the most important first. Group questions similar in content together. Order content groups along some line of logical linkage if possible. Within a content area, position more objectionable questions toward the end of that section. Place demographic questions at the end of the questionnaire.

With careful planning, you can minimize the cost of entering your survey's data onto computer cards. The choice codes the respondents mark can be the codes punched into the computer. For example, mail survey respondents could be instructed to circle the number corresponding to their response, with the responses printed as YES . . . 1 NO . . . 2, and so forth. The 1s and 2s, as marked by the respondents, would be punched into the computer.

If possible, the data card number and column position should be unobtrusively placed beside each question in small type (or beside every eighth or tenth question is adequate). Again, though, keep your focus on the respondent. If precoding is likely to confuse or deter the respondent, avoid it—hand code the completed questionnaires.

Precoding can be done with all types of questionnaires. A questionnaire administered by an interviewer can carry more detailed precoding because the respondent never sees it. But keep precoding unobtrusive on self-administered questionnaires. Be sure to seek the advice of those who will perform the data entry and computer tabulation for general coding guidelines and for answers to any specific questions.

Mail, Telephone, and Interview Surveys

Mail Surveys. Let us begin by examining mail surveying in detail. Perhaps the biggest advantage of a mail survey is cost. Despite the unrelenting increase in stamp costs, mail remains the cheapest way to administer a questionnaire. Mail surveys have other virtues, too. They are delivered into neighborhoods that interviewers may be hesitant to enter. The questionnaires may be answered by any specified member of the family at a time convenient for the respondent. Also, respondents often answer by mail questions that would otherwise be embarrassing to them.

The chief shortcoming of mail surveys is the possibility of nonresponse bias, as mentioned above, because of a low response rate. Some subgroups of the sample might not be as likely to respond as others. For example, middle-aged white women could be greatly overrepresented, and young black men might not be represented at all.

You can use follow-up mailings and incentives to avoid a low response rate. Typically, you should send a reminder about three days after the questionnaire mailing. Then send a second questionnaire mailing two weeks later.

Small monetary incentives help boost response by making the addressee feel obligated to you. Other gifts, such as calculators or books, can be equally effective. As a representative of a college, you may consider this inappropriate. If this is the case, consider a concert ticket or even a football schedule. Good cover letters, first-class outgoing postage (stamps are better than metering or indicias), and postpaid reply envelopes also result in higher response rates.

Telephone Surveys. Surprisingly enough, you can use rather complex questionnaires and collect large volumes of data by telephone. Most people will consent to interviews of half an hour and even longer, providing you catch and hold their interest.

The chief strength of telephone surveys, though, is speedy delivery of results. You can have information in hand within hours after completing calls.

Personal Interview Surveys. In theory, at least, the personal interview survey is not subject to nonresponse bias. The response rate can be 100 percent. In actuality, it is not. Interviewers do not find people at home, or they purposefully avoid unpleasant neighborhoods. Even so, true response rates in excess of 80 percent are not uncommon.

Personal interviews also permit use of long, detailed questionnaires and follow-up questioning where needed. Sessions lasting for an hour or even longer are not unusual. Visual props may be used, and the interviewer has an opportunity to explain anything that may confuse the respondent.

On the negative side, unskilled interviewers can affect the nature of the response by unintentionally cuing respondents with their own opinions. Cues can take such forms as tone of voice, inflection, facial expression, or leading probes. In addition, respondents may be reluctant to answer sensitive or embarrassing questions in the presence of a stranger.

Cost is, by far, the chief drawback in this type of survey. One can easily spend $100,000 or more on a relatively simple project.

Dickinson College greatly reduced survey costs by having a group of trained student interviewers on campus. The students, who had been trained and used by a national polling organization in connection with the Three Mile Island incident, volunteered their services. Few institutions are that fortunate.

Table 59-2 summarizes the major advantages and disadvantages of the various types of quantitative research.

Managing the Project

Good management of the survey guarantees not only timely completion of the research project but also that you will keep the price down. Early on, prepare a schedule for the major project milestones. These milestones include the problem definition or goal, draft questionnaire, final questionnaire, sample specification, mail

Table 59-2. Comparison of Four Quantitative Survey Methods.

Criteria	Mail	Tele-phone	In-home	Central Site
Handling complex questionnaires	P	G	E	E
Collecting large amounts of data	G	G	E	E
Collecting "sensitive" information	G	F	F	F
Using visual props	F	P	E	E
Controlling interviewer effects	E	F	P	P
Controlling sampling	F	G	E	n/a
Time required to complete project	P	E	F	E
Typical response rates	F	F	F	n/a
Cost	G	G	P	G

Key: E = excellent, G = good, F = fair, P = poor, n/a = not
       applicable
Adapted from: Kress, 1982.

date or date to begin field work, cut-off data, data entry completion, tabulation completion, draft report, final report, and implementation plan.

The schedule should be realistic; good research takes time. If you need fast results, use a faster research technique such as telephone; do not try to hurry a slow technique like mail. Once a schedule has been agreed to by all parties involved, stay on it.

In any type of market research, good quality control is mandatory. Even a seemingly small error, such as a typo on the questionnaire sample group key, can invalidate all of the results of a very expensive project. Check and double check each step along the way. Use the milestone schedule as a check list. If any step feels the least bit loose, revise your procedures to tighten it up. Maintain an abiding faith in Murphy's law: If anything can go wrong, it will.

Set up a system for handling and controlling completed questionnaires. Scan each one for obvious errors. When tracking individual respondents, log responses by day. Initiate additional mailing waves or telephone call-backs as necessary to control the response rate. Number all completed questionnaires, and enter that number as part of the computer data.

Prepare an explicit and complete set of coding instructions, even if you are coding the responses yourself. Code replies to open-ended questions based on a content analysis of the actual responses. (Again, avoid open-ended questions whenever possible.) The coding instructions should include several samples of coded and punched questionnaires.

The next step is getting the data keypunched onto cards or directly into the computer. This is best done by an in-house data entry department or a commercial data entry house. If at all possible, the project budget should include funds for key verification of the punched data. (Key verification is a second keyboarding of the data wherein the originally punched data are checked character by character.)

The preliminary computer runs should be "cleaning" runs looking for incorrect or illogical responses. All suspect responses should be checked against the source questionnaire. Several incorrect responses on one questionnaire probably indicate an insincere respondent; that questionnaire should be deleted from the analysis. If you used stratified sampling, responses will probably have to be weighted to represent their proper proportion within the universe.

Once the data have been cleaned, the computer tabulation can begin. The purpose of the tabulation is to tease from the collected data both the information that addresses the research questions and any unanticipated useful information. Statistics are a means to this end, not an end in themselves. Most colleges and universities have access to statistical packages such as SPSS or SAS. These or similar statistical packages are mandatory for performing the necessary tabulations, but they can be a little difficult to use. For the tabulation, you should seek the assistance of an experienced market research faculty member and your computer center.

Statistical techniques typically employed are frequencies, averages, cross-tabulation, breakdown, analysis of variance, regression analysis, and more complex segmentation techniques, such as factor, discriminate, and cluster analyses.

Always prepare a final report, and present it in clear, nontechnical language. Major findings and recommendations should be up front, on page one of the report. Be careful that personal biases do not creep into reports. Avoid bad-news-only reports, too. The research data almost always suggest remedies for problems; these should be included along with the bad news. In short, the report should be an action document, not a scholarly paper.

It must be complete, however. Include details on the sampling methods employed, response rates, mailing or interview schedules, and demographic breakdown.

Planning at the outset and implementation of results at the end are both critical to the success of market research. The more detailed the plan, the more likely you are to get usable results at an acceptable cost.

Implementation is the most important step of the entire process, but it sometimes does not happen. For one reason or another, the final report gets filed away and is never fully used. Market research is perishable; if not acted on immediately, it becomes dated.

Market research is also ongoing. You should conduct follow-up research to ascertain whether actions taken as a result of the original study did, indeed, solve the problems. Market research is an integral part of marketing; make it a way of life—not just an event.

Case Study

Pennypack University, a land-grant institution, had a threefold mission of teaching, research, and extension. As the administrative base for Cooperative Extension, it supported an extensive educational delivery network with offices and agents in every county in the state. Research by Pennypack faculty formed the basis for educational programs, and county agents delivered the programs to the public. Cooperative Extension had been active for many years. It began as agricultural education for farmers but during the last few decades had added educational programs in youth development (4-H) and home economics. Cooperative Extension has three sources of funding: federal, state and local (county).

Bob Neilson was assistant director for Cooperative Extension at Pennypack, with an office in the ag college administration building. He had been an entomology major in college but his interests were eclectic. He had recently discovered marketing and, finding himself particularly interested in market research, had begun to read about it. In fact, he became so involved that he began work on his master's degree in the college of business with a focus on market research.

Things had not been going well for Bob and his colleagues. The director was concerned because Cooperative Extension had been losing local funding. One county in particular had decided to cut back. Cooperative Extension's director told Bob that county officials were interested in funding agricultural activities but could see no reason to fund youth and home economics programs. In fact, they said their constituents were not interested in such programs, and they planned to cut two-thirds of Cooperative Extension's county funding. The director told Bob she wished she knew of some quick way to discover whether there actually was a demand for youth and home economics programs.

Could market research be used to verify to county officials that there was a need for youth and home economics programs? Maybe Bob could contact past participants in youth programs. He wasn't sure of their names and addresses. He remembered that agents in that county had been so busy with program activities that they had not developed a good record-keeping system. Besides, he wasn't sure that county officials would be influenced by past performance. How could he determine if constituent needs existed now?

Bob began by identifying a market research firm that had experience working with educational institutions. He worked with the firm to design a telephone survey instrument. The survey would measure county residents' attitudes toward Cooperative Extension.

One month after the survey had been completed, Bob reported his findings at an administrative staff meeting. He described the market research process, how the market research firm had carefully helped to gather data, how the findings had been analyzed, and how he had prepared a presentation for county officials. Bob's market research project pinpointed two things:

There were needs for youth and home economics programs, and there was outstanding recognition of past programs in all program areas. County officials were impressed. A unanimous vote guaranteed funding (and a possible increase). Bob had effectively used market research to measure client needs. He had also convinced others that market research was an important and helpful tool.

Market Research Work List

1. Think about (and discuss with others) ways that you can use market research to solve problems. Develop a list of problems and priorities.
2. Do you (and your institution) have the skills and capabilities to engage in effective market research studies? Should an outside professional firm be considered? Discuss these questions with others.
3. List secondary sources for market research information.
4. How can qualitative and quantitative market research help solve your problems?
5. What sample size should be used?
6. Think about a market research survey instrument. Who should develop it? How will it be pretested?
7. What are the advantages and disadvantages of the various forms of surveys (mail, telephone, personal interview, and central site)?
8. Who will be responsible for managing your market research project?
9. What plans can be implemented as the result of your market research findings?

For additional information on research, see Chapters Eight, Twenty-Five, Thirty-Eight, and Fifty-One.

References

Dialog Information Services, Inc. *Database Catalog*. Palo Alto, Calif.: Dialog Information Services, Inc., monthly.

Dillman, D. A. *Mail and Telephone Surveys: The Total Design Method.* New York: Wiley, 1978.

Goldstein, S., and Kravetz, E. (eds.). *Findex: The Director of Market Research Reports, Studies and Surveys.* (5th ed.) New York: Find/SVP, 1983.

Kress, G. *Marketing Research.* (2nd ed.) Reston, Va.: Reston Publishing Company, 1982.

Nie, N., and others. *SPSS^x.* (2nd ed.) New York: McGraw-Hill, 1975.

Payne, S. *The Art of Asking Questions.* Princeton, N.J.: Princeton University Press, 1954.

U.S. Department of Commerce, Bureau of Economic Analysis. *Business Conditions Digest.* Washington, D.C.: U.S. Government Printing Office, monthly.

U.S. Department of Commerce, Bureau of Economic Analysis. *Survey of Current Business.* Washington, D.C.: U.S. Government Printing Office, monthly.

Name Index

Subject Index